# THE FOUNDATIONS OF LIVING FAITHS

## *An Introduction to Comparative Religion*

Haridas Bhattacharyya

VOLUME ONE

MOTILAL BANARSIDASS PUBLISHERS
PRIVATE LIMITED • DELHI

*Second Edition : Delhi, 1994*



*First Edition : Calcutta, 1938*

ISBN: 81-208-1147-x

*Also available at:*

**MOTILAL BANARSIDASS**

41 U.A. Bungalow Road, Jawahar Nagar, Delhi 110 007
120 Royapettah High Road, Mylapore, Madras 600 004
16 St. Mark's Road, Bangalore 560 001
Ashok Rajpath, Patna 800 004
Chowk, Varanasi 221 001

PRINTED IN INDIA

BY JAINENDRA PRAKASH JAIN AT SHRI JAINENDRA PRESS, A-45 NARAINA, PHASE I, NEW DELHI 110 028 AND PUBLISHED BY NARENDRA PRAKASH JAIN FOR MOTILAL BANARSIDASS PUBLISHERS PRIVATE LIMITED, BUNGALOW ROAD, DELHI 110 007

*śrutiḥ smṛtiḥ sadācāraḥ svasya ca priyamātmanaḥ*
*samyak saṃkalpajaḥ kāmo dharmamūlamidaṃ smṛtam.*
*ijyācāradamāhiṃsādānasvādhyāyakarmaṇām*
*ayantu paramo dharmo yadyogenātmadarśanam.*

—*Yājñavalkya-Smṛti, i. 7-8.*

The scriptures, the sacred traditions, the practices of the good, the inclinations of a spiritually purified mind, and the vows proceeding from right resolve are known as the sources of *dharma* (ethical religion). Homage to God, pure conduct, self-control, non-injury, charity and scriptural study are all religious acts, but above them all stands self-knowledge through concentrated meditation.

*vedā vibhinnāḥ smṛtayo vibhinnāḥ*
*nāsau muniryasya mataṃ na bhinnam.*
*dharamsya tattvaṃ nihitaṃ guhāyāṃ*
*mahājano yena gataḥ sa panthāḥ.*

The scriptures are diverse, the sacred traditions are different, and no law-giver is worth the name unless he has a view of his own. The essence of *dharma* lies deeply hidden, and the proper path cf duty is as traversed by the spiritually great.

TO

THE SACRED MEMORY

OF

MY FATHER

PANDIT RAMPRASANNA SRUTIRATNA BHATTACHARYYA

WHOSE LIFE HAS EVER BEEN

TO ME

AN IDEAL AND AN INSPIRATION

यस्याकर्ण्य मुखात् पुरातनकथा नीतं मया शैशवं
चारित्रस्य महीयसश्च मननैस्तीर्णन्तथा यौवनम् ।
यस्यास्तिक्यधियं निधाय हृदये प्राप्ताधुना प्रौढता
स्वर्यातस्य पितुर्मुदे कृतिरियं श्रद्धाञ्जलिस्तस्य मे ॥

# PREFACE TO THE SECOND EDITION

Professor Haridas Bhattacharyya delivered Stephanos Nirmalendu Ghosh lectures in 1934. Incorporating the materials of the first six lectures, the University of Calcutta published in 1938 "The Foundations of Living Faiths—An Introduction to Comparative Religion, First Volume". In August, 1990 a committee entitled "Professor Haridas Bhattacharyya Birth Centenary Committee" was formed to celebrate Professor Bhattacharyya's birth centenary in a befitting manner. Accordingly a programme was chalked out which included:

(i) a memorial meeting held on Nov. 7, 1991,
(ii) release of a centennial volume on the same day,
(iii) two seminars in collaboration with the Ramakrishna Mission Institute of Culture, which were held on 9th and 11th Nov., 1991 respectively,
(iv) publication of a volume entitled "Essays in Honour of Professor Haridas Bhattacharyya",
(v) last but not the least, to publish the second edition of his scholarly work "The Foundations of Living Faiths, First Volume" which was originally published by the University of Calcutta in 1938 but has been out of print for quite sometime.

This monumental work on Comparative Religion contains "thoughts on a subject which is of abiding interest to all thinking minds and of profound meaning for the spiritual life of every religious community". Besides, it is immensely valuable for teachers, students and research-scholars of comparative religion. They suffer a great deal due to its non-availability. The critical analysis of each principal religion is, again, necessary for the proper understanding of each of them and also for the realisation of their underlying unity. This is all the more relevant and significant in the present-day religio-political scenario of the world.

In view of the great importance and relevance of this work of Prof. Bhattacharyya, the Centenary Celebration Committee approached the authorities of the University of Calcutta for permission to publish a second edition. They very kindly and very promptly granted this Committee permission to print a second edition subject to certain conditions which the Committee agreed to fulfil. Our grateful thanks to the authorities of Calcutta University for their kind gesture but for which the Committee could not have brought out the second edition.

The Committee would be failing in its duty if it did not express its heartfelt gratitude to the Motilal Banarsidass Publishers Pvt. Ltd., the prestigious Indological publishers and distributors of this country, for undertaking the task of bringing out the second edition.

The first edition of this book lacks an index as Prof. Bhattacharyya wished that a "fairly full index of the two volumes will be added" when the second volume is still lying in the form of manuscript. An index for the first volume is now prepared and added to the second edition of this book.

*Dol Purnima*
*March 8, 1993*

USHA R. BHATTACHARYYA
*Secretary, Professor Haridas Bhattacharyya Birth Centenary Celebration Committee*

# Preface

The invitation extended to me in 1932 by the Senate of the University of Calcutta to deliver the *Stephanos Nirmalendu Ghosh Lectures* for the year 1933 has enabled me to complete a long cherished project, namely, to write an Introduction to Comparative Religion for the benefit of my own students at the Dacca University and also students of other Universities who have to read Positive Religion as a part of their course in Philosophy of Religion. So far back as 1928-29, I contributed to the *Philosophical Quarterly* (published by the Indian Institute of Philosophy, Amalner, Bombay Presidency) three papers on *The Foundations of Living Faiths* as a part of the opening chapter of my projected work. For one reason or other I could not continue that series, and it is doubtful if this systematic work on that subject would have seen the light of day had not this timely offer come to me from my *alma mater.*

In asking me to deliver the Lectures the University made a departure from the tradition established in the past. Up till then the Lectures had been invariably delivered by distinguished foreigners, all of whom had made their mark in their particular field of work by substantial productions. Although I had published a fairly large number of psychological, philosophical and theological papers I did not have to my credit any large or systematic work; and as I had not crossed the seas, whatever reputation I possessed as a writer and a speaker was confined within the limits of India. There was, in fact, no glamour of novelty about me for I belonged to the province and had received all my education in the University itself. To appoint such a person to what might not inaptly be called the Indian

Gifford Lectureship required a good deal of confidence in my ability on the part of the Committee of Selection; I am happy to think that the founder of the Lectureship, who attended the meeting of the Selection Committee, shared the confidence which the members of that Committee reposed in me. Some of the members of the Committee had later on an opportunity of judging for themselves whether their choice was fully justified when they came to preside over my lectures; my only regret is that the founder could not be present at any of the lectures on account of an illness at the time of their delivery. It is not for me to say to what extent I have succeeded in deserving the confidence of the University of Calcutta; but I have spared neither labour nor thought in the discharge of my onerous duties as the lecturer with whom the University began the experiment of trying Indians for this work. I need not add how grateful I am to the Calcutta University for giving me this opportunity of expressing my thoughts on a subject which is of abiding interest to all thinking minds and of profound meaning for the spiritual life of every religious community.

I am much flattered to think that the distinction of a fairly orthodox Brahmin being appointed to a Christian endowment during the regime of a Muslim Vice-Chancellor should have fallen first on me. By a curious coincidence I had the unique privilege of being born in one of the greatest strongholds of Sanskrit learning and Hindu orthodoxy in Bengal, of being educated in one of the oldest Missionary Colleges of Calcutta, and of spending the greater part of my teaching career at one of the most important centres of Muslim culture in India. This accidental combination not only gave me opportunities of studying at close quarters the daily lives of the adherents of three of the most important positive religions of the world but also enabled me to understand and appreciate the springs of religious action in the communities concerned and to note the many obstacles—social, personal and dogmatic—that stand in the way of intercommunal harmony and of a calm and critical examination of different faiths, including their own, by members of these communities. Receiving my early training in practical religion under a deeply religious and learned father who combined a reverence for his ancestral creed with a toleration of all sincere faiths, of whatever stamp they might be, and my later training in theology from an equally pious Christian teacher who had the deepest regard for all genuine religions, I have realised the possibility of allying personal orthodoxy with broad sympathy for other modes of belief.

If I have occasionally criticised any religion, it is not to hurt the feelings but to quicken the thoughts of its followers; and in this I have made no distinction between Brahmanism which I personally profess and other religions followed by other people. My criticisms have proceeded from a genuine conviction that all the living religions possess good points—some more, some less—of which they may be legitimately proud but that none is perfect in spite of all that its adherents may claim on its behalf and that all are capable of development in diverse degrees and directions. This is why I have been constrained to criticise more than once the doctrine of Final Revelation, which, in spite of its value for social solidarity, is a serious obstacle to the development of individual faith and communal toleration. I have also made no secret of my belief that most, if not all, religions fight ignorance half-heartedly for fear lest a wide-spread culture should mean the disowning of all spiritual obligations and, with the extension of secular ideas and practices, a gradual loss of influence of those now in spiritual power over the uneducated masses. I have not subscribed, however, to the view that religion as a distinctive attitude towards life and reality is ultimately destined to pass away with the growth of education and the development of industry.

While I am painfully conscious of my limited readings on account of my inability to handle any foreign religious literature except in English , even of that literature in the English language I had only a narrow range in this small provincial University which was established only seventeen years ago. In fact, but for a number of happy accidents my study would have been less wide and deep for the purpose of discussing certain fundamental problems. The Dacca College, out of which the University of Dacca was developed, had a long succession of European Principals and Professors, and the present collection on Hebrew and Christian theology in the University Library is mostly due to them. The Dacca College was also in regular receipt of copies of books presented to the Department of Education, Bengal, by various bodies for distribution, and most of the books on Zoroastrianism (including some rare books) came into the possession of the University through that channel. Through the efforts of the first Professors in Sanskrit and Bengali, History, Arabic and Islamic Studies, and Philosophy a decent collection of books on Indian and Islamic religions in their different aspects and on Philosophy of Religion had also been made in the earlier years of the newly founded University. Without this nucleus of literature it would have been extremely difficult for me to make much headway in the subject chosen; still, I had to wait often for weeks and months together to get necessary books out from England, specially new publications and books out of print. A word of thanks is due to Mr. Manoranjan Roy, M.A., B.L., Librarian of the Dacca University, and to his staff for the expedition with which they collected, catalogued and issued books needed by me and for the wide latitude they gave me about the number of books taken out at a time. Among friends who helped me with the loan or gift of books which are now absolutely out of print, I record with gratitude the names of Lt.-Col. A. R. Owen Berkeley Hill, M.D., I.M.S. (Retd.), late Superintendent of the European Mental Hospital, Ranchi, and Prof. A. R. Wadia of the Mysore University.

The administrative duties of the Dean of the Faculty of Arts at the Dacca University with which I was saddled at the time made the delivery of the Lectures impossible before the closing months of 1934. Eleven lectures in all were delivered between 20th November and 17th December, 1934. The present volume incorporates the materials of the first six. In the present volume, however, I have not only broken up some single lectures into two or more chapters for convenience of treatment but also deviated slightly from the order of the lectures as delivered. Owing to the exigency of time the lecture on Zoroastrianism was not delivered at all. Following my usual practice, I delivered the entire series of lectures extempore in order to be better able to adjust my discourse to the actual audience of the day. The text of the present volume has remained unaltered since its composition in 1933-34; but I have utilised the enforced delay in publication in consulting some recent literature on the subject and adding a few footnotes here and there.

I am happy to have been able to deliver the opening lecture under the chairmanship of Mr. Syamaprasad Mookerjee, M.A., B.L., Barrister-at-Law, M.L.A., the present Vice-Chancellor of the Calcutta University. Not only do I owe to him personally a debt for encouragement and assistance in connection with the lectureship but I also owe to his illustrious father, the late Sir Asutosh Mookerjee, my migration from the staff of the Scottish Churches College (as it was then called) to the Philosophy and Experimental Psychology Departments of the Calcutta University in 1917, which ultimately facilitated the transfer of my services to Dacca in 1921. The other lectures were presided over by two High Court Judges, one ex-Vice-Chancellor of the Calcutta University, four University Professors and three Principals of affiliated Colleges.

To Professors G. H. Langley (late Vice-Chancellor of the Dacca University), J. W. Fück (late of the Department of Arabic and Islamic Studies, Dacca University, and now of the University of Frankfurt Am Main), A. R. Wadia (of the Mysore University) and S. P. Bhattacharyya (of the Presidency College, Calcutta) I am grateful for their looking over some individual lectures in manuscript and for suggesting improvements in the text here and there. None is, however, responsible for the views herein expressed. To my colleagues, Professor Dr. S. M. Hossein of the Department of Arabic and Islamic Studies, Mr. P. K. Guha of the Department of English, and Dr. B. N. Ray of the Department of Philosophy, I am indebted for occasional assistance in correcting the proof-sheets. To Mr. Guha, I am further indebted for saving me from many pitfalls in literary expression—whenever I had any doubt about the propriety of any word or the elegance of any language I invariably turned to him for advice and assistance and always with profit. Such solecisms as still remain are due entirely to me.

I would be failing in my duty if I do not close this preface with a word of praise for the staff of the Calcutta University Press. If there has been an inordinate delay in the publication of the present volume, it is due mainly to my pre-occupation with official duties and occasionally to my illness. Expert assistance in the correction of the proof-sheets has been most ungrudgingly given by the Press staff, and exasperating last-minute additions and alterations have been cheerfully incorporated to enable me to produce as perfect a book as I am capable of. I only regret that in order to prevent any further delay in publication it should be found necessary to send the present volume out without an index. Let me hope that the second volume will take less time to see the light of day: a fairly full index of the two volumes will be added there.

*Śrīpañcamī,*
*5th February, 1938* H.D. BHATTACHARYYA

# CONTENTS

| CHAPTER | | PAGE |
|---|---|---|
| I. | The Living Faiths ... ... | 1 |
| II. | The Prophets ... ... | 40 |
| III. | The Revelations ... ... | 91 |
| IV. | The Gods of Hinduism : Vedic ... | 151 |
| V. | The Gods of Hinduism : Paurāṇic ... | 202 |
| VI. | God in Judaism ... ... | 249 |
| VII. | God in Christianity ... ... | 312 |
| VIII. | God in Islām ... ... | 347 |
| IX. | God in Zoroastrianism : Gāthic ... | 413 |
| X. | God in Zoroastrianism : Post-Gāthic ... | 473 |
| INDEX | ... ... | 527 |

# THE FOUNDATIONS OF LIVING FAITHS

## CHAPTER I

### The Living Faiths

No one can take up the subject of Religion without a certain trepidation of heart. Of all the adventures which the human mind has undertaken, the adventure of faith is one of the oldest and the most formidable. In other fields of knowledge and activity the quest is likely to be attended by some degree of sure conquest, and personal conviction backed by social confirmation. In religion, on the other hand, man grapples with problems that relate primarily to his solitariness,[1] so that although in primitive forms of religion the social factor is the dominating feature of faith, in more advanced religions personal conviction plays the leading role and even social ostracism and religious oppression often fail to secure apostasy. It is a mystery and a marvel that for the impalpable entities of faith men should willingly sacrifice the concrete pleasures of the world—that for the uncertain blessings of Eternity men should cheerfully abandon the certain joys of the Temporal.

Certain it is that all through the ages man has professed to find in religion the one point of rest amidst the fluxes of worldly life—"the heart of peace" in the whirlwind of temporal existence. As Hegel says,[2] "Religion is for our consciousness that region in which all the enigmas of the world

1 See Whitehead, *Religion in the Making*, p. 6; Pratt, *The Religious Consciousness*, p. 12.

2 Hegel, *Lectures on the Philosophy of Religion* (Eng. Tr.), Vol. I, p. 1.

are solved, all the contradictions of deeper-reaching thought have their meaning unveiled, and where the voice of the heart's pain is silenced—the region of eternal truth, of eternal rest, of eternal peace.'' Or, as an Eastern sage has it,

*bhidyate hṛdayagranthiśchidyante sarvasaṃsayāḥ*
*kṣīyante cāsya karmāṇi tasmin dṛṣṭe parāvare*

—All the cords of (secular) affection (lit. the heart) are snapped, all doubts are dispelled, and all activities find their rest of him who has seen the Lord (lit. the Greatest and the Smallest). In other words, all the faculties of the soul profess to find their rest assured and their difficulties solved in religion.[3] It is not indeed contended that all religions have been equally successful in bringing about the desired consummation or that even in the most devout the religious mood or attitude may not be occasionally clouded by doubts and worldly considerations.[4] But that in spite of the many solicitations from the environment, to which his senses are constantly subjected, man is able to rise above temporal considerations even in exceptional cases is sufficient proof that in his case the spirit can be stronger than the flesh. It is interesting too that from the very time of his appearance the man of religion has ever been accorded a pre-eminence in all stages of culture and regarded as possessing something additional, to which ordinary individuals can lay no claim. The shaman, the medicine man, the priest and the prophet have always been the object of popular reverence and been treated with marked deference. Their utterances and activities have been followed with interest, awe, respect and wonder, whenever they have been regarded as acting in their religious capacity.

[3] *Cf.* C. G. Jung, *Modern Man in Search of a Soul*, p. 266 : " It seems to me, that, side by side with the decline of religious life, the neuroses grow noticeably more frequent."

[4] See, for instance, Mark 15.34; Matthew 26.36-44; also Pratt, *The Religious Consciousness*, p. 131.

That this should be so need cause no wonder, for religion has at all times been noted for releasing energies otherwise inaccessible to the individual. The consciousness of being in alliance with supernatural powers has invariably tended to elevate the individual not only in the estimation of the social group to which he belongs but also in his own estimation. In primitive forms of faith, the man of God (or of the supernatural powers) is characterised by the abundance of his energy—his frenzied dance and ceaseless movements, his weird magic and rapid and incoherent speech, his restless activity and insensitiveness to suffering, tend to cause awe and astonishment in the beholders. How else can a man commune with, appease and control the supernatural powers or use them in the interest of the social group! It is now a commonplace of psychology that an individual's isolated behaviour is different from that in a group or a crowd : a general depression of the intellectual faculties and a consequent withdrawal of mental control release the emotional and volitional energies, which thereby assume exaggerated dimensions. In the social forms of religious phenomena, whether in savage gatherings or in revival meetings, the same forces are in operation and the individual responds to the environment with an accentuated reaction. But even when alone with his gods, the individual displays peculiar reactions : is he not in the presence of powers who, though unseen, are yet not insensitive to his supplications and manipulations? He feels impelled to transcend the physical and mental limitations of finitude, which make him an unworthy or imperfect vehicle of divine expression, not always by deliberate practice but very often in a spontaneous fashion. The instincts in operation during religious exercises liberate energies and expressions which cannot otherwise be commanded, and these are of such a peculiar nature that a cold-blooded rehearsal of them in the absence of the sense of divine presence is an impossibility. Popular wisdom has embodied this experience in the adage, "Faith can remove mountains." "Verily I say unto you, if ye have faith, and doubt not, ye shall not only do what is done to the fig tree, but even if ye shall say unto this mountain, Be thou taken up and cast into the sea, it shall be done.''[5] Here, more than anywhere else, a wavering mind begets an unsteady limb. Did not Peter begin to sink the moment he doubted the words of Jesus that he would be able to walk upon the waters?[6]

The intellectual powers too are supposed to get greater insight into the mysteries of existence. Being in tune with the Infinite, the religious man sees farther into reality than ordinary mortals. Things that are disjointed and evil are made whole and good to his understanding. Most often the knowledge is of the mystical kind—ineffable, emotional and incapable of communication to others. It is certainly not scientific knowledge involving strenuous thinking and minutely articulated in its details. The world is presented to the religious man in its broad outlines, in an instantaneous exposure of its fundamental scheme or plan, in its spiritual significance. The portals of heaven open up to him the vision of things unseen; his utterances have a strange fire; his penetrating glance sees through the hollow shows and senseless formalities of everyday respectability.[7] He is the interpreter of divine wishes, the oracle of divine wisdom, the herald of divine justice. When his credentials are established, he is

5 Mat. 21. *Cf.* Lk. 17.6; Pratt, *The Religious Consciousness*, pp. 173-4.

6 Mat. 15. 28-31. On the whole subject, see ERE. viii. 246-7, 250; xii. 753.

7 The " truths " which the mystics carry away with them from the ecstasy, or hold more firmly because of the ecstasy, differ with different individuals. Their general tendency, as Professor James points out, is towards optimism and monism. Professor Ewer enumerates several of them as follows: " That reality is unitary and divine; that ordinary experience is merely phenomenal, its content only imperfectly known; that its limitations and contradictions are transcended in true knowledge; that in such knowledge the soul, which is the key to reality, rises to identity with God and infinite vision; that the Divine Presence may be found hidden in the midst of daily life; that the real is ultimately good, and sin only negative, a privation, unreal."......

We must, however, be careful to distinguish between the content of the intuition which takes place during the ecstasy, and the truths which the mystic comes to believe as a result of reflecting upon his experience......And if I am not greatly mistaken, a large number of the " mystic truths " so called—as, for instance, several of those quoted above from Dr. Ewer—are due to secondary reflection rather than to immediate intuition.—Pratt, *The Religious Consciousness*, pp. 407-8

heard with respect; his prophecies and imprecations are watched for fulfilment with interest and awe; his warnings, even when unheeded, provoke uneasy thoughts. He generally exhibits in his own life the triumph of spirit over flesh as befitting one who has risen above the worldly plane. Regardless of consequences, he dares to attack age-long prejudices, to offend social susceptibilities and to throw social decorum to the winds.

It should not be forgotten, however, that all religious temperaments are not of the same type—that between the contemplative recluse and the fighting preacher all shades of difference may be observed. Broadly speaking, to one class religion is an individual problem, if not also a personal enjoyment; while to the other class religion is a serious call to social duty. The *arhat* in Buddhism aims at his own salvation—he wants to get rid of the personal ills of this life, and that by becoming a lamp unto himself. He is too much preoccupied with his own troubles to have time and energy left to attend actively to the troubles of others. He is an introspective introvert, given to self-analysis and comparatively prone to religious selfishness. In him the dynamic functions work imperfectly, social feelings are defective or "the native hue of resolution is sicklied o'er with the pale cast of thought." He accepts the principle of minimum responsibility in life; he has an accentuated or exaggerated sense of his personal illumination; and he disowns the importance and the need of the society which gave him being and upbringing. His instinct is that of a drowning man or a man trapped in a house in flames—to him personal safety is the only immediate consideration. Religious history is replete with instances of saintly individuals who have been sought by a suffering world as ideals but who have not done anything actively to disseminate the secret of their spiritual success. If ever they condescend to remain within the access of society, wisdom can sometimes be wrung out of their reluctant mouths by the questioning multitude; but when left alone or uninterrogated, they prefer to let their wisdom and their way of peace die with them and leave no record behind.

Entirely different from the above is the ideal of life pursued by the other class. The strenuous life of a teacher and preacher is what they choose by a kind of inborn disposition. Tolerant large-heartedness towards human frailty and intolerant attitude towards unethical and irreligious life may both act as motives. Their faith in the ultimate triumph of religion is supplemented by a firm belief in the ultimate goodness of human nature and an unbounded charity towards weak souls, steeped in ignorance, sloth and wickedness. Like Zarathustra, they are fighters against lie and evil not only in their own lives but also in those of others; like Christ, they are compassionate towards sinners; like the Bodhisattva, they are willing to wait till eternity to ensure the release of every soul in bondage to suffering before seeking their own salvation. Remember the touching episode in the life of Gautama when after receiving enlightenment he was for a moment tempted to keep the saving knowledge to himself and Brahma Sahāmpati expressed great concern at this decision and implored him to disseminate the spiritual illumination for the benefit of suffering humanity. All persons do not hear the promptings of their better nature with an equal alacrity—the fatiguing prospect of a life of endless, and possibly thankless, labour acts as a deterrent to all but the most daring, dynamic and compassionate natures.

It is difficult to estimate the relative value of the quietistic and the activistic attitude towards religion and it is likely that in the long run no religious community is able to dispense with the contributions of either to its own spiritual advancement. Religious experience and insight beget in the seer a disinterested disregard of conventions, a lyrical spontaneity of self-expression in hymns, songs and acts of religious worship. The recluse dwells apart with his God—he is the only worshipper at his own inner sanctuary whose votive offerings the world may sometimes see but never share. The preacher, on the other hand, is an extravert with an inner urge to bring the tidings of religious truth to his fellowmen, to share their sorrows, to remove the bondage of their sins and their sufferings. Like Plato's philosopher, he feels that no one has a right to possess exclusively the illumination he has fortunately received. The spreading of the truth of which he is possessed is a paramount obligation with such a spirit. Possibly less intellectual than the contemplative sage and wedded more to the practical aspect of religious life, the preacher is sometimes less a revealer of new truths than a propagandist; but it would be a mistake to think that he does not intimately accept and appropriate to himself the spirit of the religion he professes and preaches. Only deep and abiding conviction can lend fire to speech, and if something constitutional makes one prone to believe and act, that does not take away from the fact that scepticism and doubt have always been fatal to the persistence of missionary zeal.

Without seers and preachers a religion can only mark time. Wherever the fountain-head of inspiration dries up, religion degenerates into conventional thinking and customary practice. Truncated of its growing point, religion loses its organic and symmetrical development, and dense collateral growths of myth, dogma and ritual overlay the spiritual character of a living faith. Except when taken over from an older creed or evolved as an integral part of the original inspiration, these invariably represent either a stagnation of religion or a concession to the weaker understanding of the ordinary laity. In them personal insight and spontaneous expression are replaced by a less spiritual mode of imagination, intellect and activity—all consciously directed towards popular edification, easy understanding, and stability and uniformity of socio-religious practices. Each of them has a tendency to become a tradition and to bring into being a special class of ministrants who gradually form a more or less rigid caste or corporation with the right and the duty of conserving the social beliefs and practices and the privilege of amending and elaborating them according to topical needs. The bard, the scholastic and the priest have each his own appointed place in the development of religion; but their achievements have always had an evanescent character, as myths, dogmas and rituals have ever changed with the times in accordance with the prevailing taste and culture of the components of the religious community.[8] The close connection between the first and the last has often been noticed—rituals instituted in accordance with myths and myths formulated to explain traditional rites. Creeds alter more slowly as they have their origin in intellectual elaboration of the elements of faith; and unless the faith itself alters materially, the creed cannot radically alter its character, for human reason is capable of far more stable formulations than human imagination and human emotion. But the ground-plan has always a preponderating influence on the superstructure and many a religious edifice has tumbled down, even when buttressed by the props of allegorical interpretation, because an undercurrent of scepticism has scoured away the foundations of faith. Dogmas have disappeared together with their religious basis in many parts of the world never to sway again the minds of men. They have, as a matter of fact, shared a worse fate than rituals which, basing themselves on inveterate habits of the body, have managed to transfer themselves from the vanquished religion to the conquering creed with a new significance adapted to the structure of the latter.[9] Think, for instance, of the many pagan rites and festivals that have survived in Christianity and Muhammadanism with an altered significance.

While the race of priests flourishes everywhere, and preachers and myth- and dogma-makers are not few, and even saints and sages appear regularly in fair numbers all over the world, the same cannot be said of prophets and founders of faith. A religious genius is like a biological freak —he is born, not made. He effects in himself an unusual combination of all those qualities that go to make a seer, a

[8] W. Robertson Smith, *The Religion of the Semites* (1914), p. 18; Hopkins, *The Origin and Evolution of Religion*, p. 226. See also Whitehead, *Religion in the Making*, p. 13f, 116, 120f, 130, esp. Ch. IV, Sec. II, Experience and Expression.

[9] Marti, *The Religion of the Old Testament*, p. 103; Pratt, *The Religious Consciousness*, pp. 82-6. For the survival of some pagan superstitions in Egypt, see W. M. Flinders Petrie, *Religious Life in Ancient Egypt*, p. 113.

preacher and a priest. He has the head to discern more profoundly than his contemporaries the ultimate principles and values of existence in their true perspective; he possesses the heart to feel the need of uplifting the moral tone and temper of his own age; and he wields the arm that is not afraid to hit hard the prejudices and superstitions of his own people. Less consciously cogitative than a philosopher and, therefore, less effective as a system-builder, the founder of a faith yet learns more from hints and suggestions that the world throws out than a philosopher does. Susceptible to the poetry of existence, his being vibrates in unison with invisible melodies; the still small voice that escapes the attention of grosser ears brings to him messages from an unseen world; Heaven beckons unto him and angels speak to him. The spirit of God bloweth where it listeth; while years of arduous preparation through intellectual and ethical culture may confer a certain amount of religious mediocrity on the plodding, the world mostly owes its profoundest moral and spiritual insights to those whose only literature was the book of the world—the stilly night, the starry heavens, the joys and sorrows of men, and an inward peace that passes all understanding. Judged by the worldly standard of acquired wisdom, they may often be called ignorant; but an innate proneness to self-analysis and contemplation, coupled with an intuitive grasp of the spiritual needs and aspirations of the age, invests them with an insight into the spiritual principles of existence, and not only produces conviction in themselves about the authenticity of their personal vision but enables them to speak the truth, as perceived by them, in a dictatorial and authoritative fashion to the world at large.[10] Just as they themselves are

[10] See *Enc. Islam*, ii, p. 486, art. ILHĀM: " Allāh reveals himself in two ways; to men individually by knowledge cast into their minds, and to men generally by messages sent through the prophets. The first, individual, revelation is *ilhām*; the second, and general, is *waḥy*. Saints, especially, are the recipients of this *ilhām*, because their hearts are purified and prepared for it. It differs from intellectual knowledge (*'ilm ' aklī '*) in that it cannot be gained by meditation and deduction; but is suddenly communicated while the recipient cannot tell how, whence or why. It is a pure gift from the generosity (*faiḍ*) of Allāh. It differs

summoned to their office by an irresistible call from within or above, so also their own injunction to others to follow them has in all ages been obeyed—at first by a small band of devoted followers and later on by a larger population of the globe.

In fact, the first missionary of every religion must necessarily be the founder himself. He does not hide the light of his spiritual insight under a bushel, nor does he bury the one talent that God has given him under the ground. He treats his revelation as a trust; he does not hoard it like a miser or use it for personal gratification or personal grandeur. He considers himself to be the mouthpiece of the divine. It is likely that just as in primitive times the discoverer of a new fetish acted as one possessed and danced and shouted in religious frenzy till he could infect the assembled crowd, so also the discoverer of a new spiritual truth is often intoxicated by the revelation received and warns and preaches because he must. He is convinced about the genuineness of his illumination and the spiritual good that it is sure to bring to the world. He has faith in the innate spiritual and moral nature of man;[11] and so the darkest degradation all around does not damp the ardour of his soul. While relentless towards the follies and foibles of his contemporaries, he is yet solicitous of their salvation. He fears their fate but seeks to save them from ruin. A cynic can never be a saviour—beneath the rind of occasional sternness there must always be a core of compassion if a prophet or a saint is to succeed in his mission.

It is a remarkable testimony to the spiritual and ethical nature of man that no appeal of higher rationality and better morality has ever gone completely unheeded. All through the ups and downs of philosophy and faith a steady march of

from *waḥy* only in that the angel messenger who brings *waḥy* may be seen by the prophet and that *waḥy* brings a message to be communicated to mankind, while *ilhām* is for the instruction of the recipient. From *waswās* or satanic whispering in the heart, it differs in respect of the causer—an angel as opposed to a devil; and in the things to which it incites—good as opposed to evil." See also Jung, *Modern Man in Search of a Soul*, p. 261.

11 J. Legge, *The Religions of China*, p. 103.

culture and conviction is clearly discernible. True, there have been occasional backslidings and stagnations, and nations and races have gone into temporary hibernations either at the suggestion of false guides, or in a spirit of tolerant accommodation and servile imitation, or under the threatening constraint or the insidious wiles of a lower culture. But the spirit of man has invariably triumphed over such temporary set-backs, and an indigenous evolution of greater consistency in thought and belief marks the history of every human race. Left unaided by the contact of higher cultures, the progress has often been woefully slow—especially in regions where the monotonous regularity of natural phenomena raised no new problems for which the customary beliefs could not provide a ready solution. But even there the venturesome mind has suggested new answers to old problems and has been respectfully heard if it could suggest any improvement upon the older solutions. *And the criterion of advance has always been the establishment of greater consistency between assumption and experience, faith and practice, personal benefit and social need.*[12]

The birth of a new faith may not inaptly be compared to an earthquake. The earth's surface is subject to ceaseless tremors which can only be revealed by a delicate seismograph. But occasionally deep rumblings are heard and then suddenly the *terra firma* begins to behave like clay in the hands of subterranean forces. The earthly frame begins to rock and heave and fall, great landslips and dislocations of levels take place, tidal waves invade the land and sweep away everything before them and huge structures and ancient monuments crumble into ruin. If the cumulative stresses in the earth's crust, produced by the ceaseless contraction of the earth, be yielded to gradually, there is no violent upheaval; but if they are resisted, they tend to increase till the rocks give way with

[12] *Cf.* Whitehead, *Religion in the Making*, p. 20: "Rational religion is religion whose beliefs and rituals have been reorganised with the aim of making it the central element in a coherent ordering of life—an ordering which shall be coherent both in respect to the elucidation of thought, and in respect to the direction of conduct towards a unified purpose commanding ethical approval."

a sudden shock and an earthquake is produced. If there happen to be lines of fracture and weakness in the earth's crust at any particular region, the succession of shocks may be quite rapid.[13] In the same fashion, the social mind is ceaselessly trying new lines of thought and action according to the eternal laws of mental development; but the changes are so small that the social equilibrium is seldom perceptibly disturbed by their operation. But let the necessary adaptation of faith to circumstances and culture be resisted for a sufficiently long time and lifeless formalities and outworn creeds usurp the place of a living and growing faith. Then a warning herald will make his appearance and be followed quickly by a new prophet whose message would explode established doctrines and inaugurate an era of new religious beliefs and social relations. Again and again in history has what I have elsewhere [14] called the triadic rhythm of devotion, hypocrisy and doubt been repeated, and faiths, that refused to listen to timely warnings, have paid the penalty of delay by being entirely engulfed or sorely battered by the rising tide of a new religious upheaval.

A few historical illustrations will put the matter in a clear light. The decay of traditional faith among the Greeks and the Romans, which the sceptical and the serious philosophers alike hastened by their exposure of the unworthy picture of the gods worshipped by the multitude, led to the spread of the Mystery religions where at least some of the demands of a genuine religious life could be satisfied. As Prof. Seeberg points out,[15] "Although the Hellenistic Mystery religions—the cults of Attis, Isis, Osiris and Mithras—began as gross and fetishistic nature religions, they developed into faiths in which the primitive elements were gradually spiritualised, and as opposed to the juristic character of

13 See W. B. Scott, *An Introduction to Geology* (1904), p. 64.

14 *Philosophical Quarterly*, VI, p. 21, art. *Reason and Religion.*

15 Carl Clemen (ed.), *Religions of the World*, p. 340. See Pringle-Pattison, *Studies in the Philosophy of Religion*, Ch. XV. Gentile Christianity and the Mystery Religions.

the religion of Rome and the aesthetic character of the religion of Greece, they attracted in a time of decadence, scepticism and mysticism large numbers by their gorgeous ritual, the magic spell of their Mysteries, their demand for an ascetic life, the blissfulness of the ecstatic state, and their promise of deliverance and immortality. . . In the centre of them all stood the incarnate God, with whom the initiate, by means of a cultus full of dramatic moments and by means of the sacraments, attained to a fellowship that was partly sensuous and partly spiritual. The myth of the God who died and rose again, and that of the saviour who was born of a virgin—these and other conceptions were distinctly present in these Oriental religions long before the appearance of Christianity." Not only did the religious need of the individual remain unsatisfied in the old religions of Greece and Rome, but, as Hopkins says,[16] "the divinities of the Mediterranean had lagged behind man in ethical progress and were in no position to act as spiritual guides:" so, as Reinach remarks,[17] "Christianity had not to triumph over official paganism; this had long been dead or effete; its rivals were the other Oriental religions." And the religions of Greece and Rome, like the religions of the Egyptians, the Assyrians, the Babylonians and the Teutons, vanished completely from the face of the earth. To-day in lands where all these religions flourished at one time the three monotheistic living religions of Semitic origin hold complete sway.

Our second illustration would be Christianity. The Jews made more than one attempt to reform their religion, but again and again there were lapses. Josiah's attempt to purify faith by concentrating all worship at Jerusalem, like a similar attempt of Amenhotep IV (Ikhnaton) in Egypt to institute a purer form of solar worship (Aton), failed to survive long his own death, and foreign gods and idolatrous practices made their appearance in the temples. In 586 B.C. the

16 Hopkins, *op. cit.*, p. 260. See G. M. Stratton, *The Psychology of the Religious Life*, p. 232.

17 S. Reinach, *Orpheus*, p. 114.

temple of Jerusalem was burned by Nebuchadnezzar who had spared it in his first campaign of 597 B.C., and the Babylonian exile of the leading Jews, begun during his first campaign, was completed. The Jews of the Dispersion could not continue their temple-service outside the holy ground of Jerusalem, and the Synagogue, the precursor of the Christian Church, came into existence and prayer replaced sacrifice.[18] But the successful Maccabaean revolt not only restored the worship in the Temple but also brought into being the puritanic Pharisees who took up the task of interpreting and observing the old laws and ceremonials as also of developing and promoting the unwritten law or tradition. The mind of the race had, however, been already infected by the virus of a less formal religion; and so, in spite of the combined efforts of the doctors of the law (the Pharisees), the priestly aristocracy (the Sadducees) and the learned scholars (the Scribes), the old religion of sacrifice, so earnestly denounced by the Prophets on account of its want of inwardness and its dissociation from high morality, tended to decline and degenerate into minute details about ceremonial purity and observance of the Sabbath, to put uncomfortable restrictions on freedom of thought and conduct, and to choke spontaneous self-expression in matters of devotion. Life tended to become a body of regulations—at least among the ordinary people, and the requirements of the temple-worship converted the sanctuary of God into a house of merchandise exactly as one can see to-day at our own Kalighat and Madura. According to an inexorable law of the human mind that a spirit of rebellion is bound to be fostered as soon as a spontaneous gift becomes a compulsory levy, especially when demanded by the religious hierophant who is personally interested in costly offerings to the gods, the advent of Jesus, closely following upon the preaching of John the Baptist, was the signal for raising the question of the

18 ERE, x. 191-5, art. PRAYER (Jewish). See also G. F. Moore, *History of Religions*, Vol. 2, p. 24. See, however, ERE, iii. 738.

utility of material offerings and the necessity of unmeaning restrictions in thought and conduct. Fortunately, in this case, the old religion possessed a sufficient surplus of ethical vitality and had, in fact, begun to develop towards a purer form of worship under the inspiration of the prophets and the exigencies of the Babylonian captivity.[19] So although a big slice was torn off its sides by Christianity it escaped total annihilation.

In a similar fashion Muhammadanism succeeded in completely suppressing the pre-Islamic polytheism of Arabia and Zoroastrianism replaced the polytheism of Persia. Reared on mythology and superstition, and making little attempt to base higher morality on the nature of the divinities worshipped, both Arabian and Persian polytheisms tumbled down before the ethical religions of Muhammad and Zarathustra respectively, after seriously minded people had begun to doubt the efficacy of effete faith and had prepared the ground for the advent of a new religion. In India, again, when the old Vedic polytheism had failed to satisfy the learned, and the abstruse nature of the Upaniṣadic Brahman had failed to grip the popular imagination, and the rank rituals of the Brāhmaṇas had tended to make worship soulless and formal, various sceptical schools, about which we read in Brahmanic, Jaina and Buddhistic literatures, arose; and soon afterwards Jainism and Buddhism appeared as organised protests against the cruel ceremonials of a creed in which the better minds had ceased to believe.[20] And when Brahmanism rehabilitated itself in popular favour by developing the Bhakti-cult and bringing religion within the comprehension of the laity by partially discarding Vedic Sanskrit, which was becoming unintelligible to the people at large, and also by concentrating on treatises like the Bhagavadgītā, which at once satisfied religious and moral needs, it managed to ward off the concerted attack of internal

[19] See Harnack, *History of Dogma* (Eng. Tr.), *Vol.* I, pp. 68-69 f.n.

[20] See B. C. Law, *Buddhistic Studies*, p. 72 f.

scepticism and alien faith.[21] But when the Paurānic literature went beyond the bounds of religious and moral ministration and began to hold up ideals and examples whose acceptance the growing moral and religious sense and acquaintance with foreign religions with a purer faith and a higher moral tone alike rendered impossible, there arose in Mediæval India a close succession of religious thinkers whose sects are still extant in different conditions of vitality. Later defections still have occurred, and the Sikhs, the Ārya Samājists and the Brāhmas claim to-day a fairly large number of adherents who have seceded from the orthodox Hindu fold. Whosoever studies impartially the history of heterodoxy in India is bound to come to the conclusion that Hinduism with its motley group of religious ideas represents a weak crust of faith and that it has had often to pay the penalty of extreme conservatism all through its history. But for the fact that through its age-long career it had made many experiments in forms of pure faith and many advances in lofty morals, which even a casual gleaner could spot with ease, it would have long been swept out of existence altogether. Even in the Mahābhārata, which is supposed to extol the achievements of the Kṣatriyas and their sacrifices, we have repeated assertions that ceremonies were multiplied through ignorance of Truth which is the main object of Vedic teaching and that Truth always prevails against customary religion (*dharma*) and is always superior to sacrifice and slaughter of animals.[22] Similar statements are plentiful among the Hebrew prophets. Judaism and Hinduism possess both the advantages and the disadvantages of not embodying the religious ideas of a single age or the ethical principles of a single man. Both possess lofty heights and abysmal depths; and while their opponents seek to pin them down to their cellars, they manage to escape through their sky-lights. This explains also why in these ethnic religions

[21] See the present writer's article on *The Vitality of Hindu Religion* in *Philosophical Quarterly*, I, p. 251f.

[22] Carpenter, *Theism in Mediaeval India*, p. 138.

protests have mostly taken the form of schismatic sects which retained the cultural tradition and even the language of the mother creed in varying degrees.

When the protests come from the rational side of man, who fails to see the significance and the utility of many of the beliefs, formalities and institutions of the religious organisation to which he belongs, they take the form of reforming movements. A reformer need not always claim divine inspiration for his self-imposed task: it is enough if he is possessed of a strong common sense and improved ethical motives. Raja Rammohan Roy and Dayananda Saraswati were reformers of Hinduism in the sense that both could see the weakness of some of the Hindu doctrines and practices and sought to eradicate them either by appealing to the purer speculations of the Hindus themselves or by pointing out the many inconsistencies of their religious lives. They did not claim anything divine for their mission, although it is not unlikely that they were fortified in their efforts by the approbation of their own conscience. Similarly, the Wahhabi movement in Muslim Arabia and the rise of the Sthānakvāsi sect among the Jains have as one of their objectives the removal of useless formalities and undue veneration of religious saints and symbols; but no divine command prompted their promulgators to undertake the task of reformation. Sects, as distinguished from reforming movements, may arise from less noble motives and are very often due to local patriotism or loyalty to a particular leader. Go through the seventy-three Muslim sects mentioned in the *Fark-bain-al-Firak* and you will wonder why some of them should have differed from each other at all. It is difficult to claim divine inspiration for the way in which religious symbols should be marked or worn on the body, and yet sometimes two Vaiṣṇava sects would probably differ in very little else. How many unseemly quarrels took place over the exact position of a word in the creed in the early years of the Christian Church! Many men have a tendency to stick to trifles for no other reason than that they have set their heart upon them, and yet they are unwilling to concede to others the same right that they claim for themselves. The same god differently named would bring different sects into being—Nārāyaṇa, Viṣṇu, Rāma, Hari and Kṛṣna, though referring to the same god, have different sets of followers in India with a fairly hostile attitude towards the votaries of the same god with a different name; and among the Spanish peasants, we are told, it is perfectly legitimate to worship Virgin Mary with one title and belonging to a particular village while reviling in unseemly language the Madonna of another village and bearing a different title.

Sects and schisms, however, have their justification and value when they imply a certain vitality of faith among the adherents of a creed and a living interest in the religion which they profess. No sect ever arises in days of general apathy and scepticism, for religion ceases then to be a matter of vital concern and, even when the routined formalities are gone through in a mechanical way, people do not bother themselves much about the niceties of detail or the proprieties of language and thought on which sects and schisms thrive and flourish. They are no longer matters of life and death to the community; and so a spirit of toleration, coupled occasionally with indolence, dictates non-interference with existing theories and practices. Like a shell bursting in its career through space, a religion breaks up into sects mostly in its initial stages when the first formulation is more or less nebulous and people have strong feelings about the necessity of an accurate creed. The greatest schisms and controversies in Muhammadanism, Christianity and Buddhism have all taken place in the effervescent phases of their opening career. When after centuries of discussion and scrutiny faiths settle down into a relatively constant body of dogmas and rituals, they are very seldom disturbed except when an evolution of a greater intellectual power or a purer ethical sense or contact with a nobler creed exposes undetected flaws or when imperceptible accretion of corrupt practices and debased thoughts stands revealed to the refined sensibility of a saint or a prophet. In religion, no less than in the region of sensation, there is such a thing as adaptation : we fail to notice the defects of our own religion just as we fail to notice the stuffy atmosphere or the stinking smell of a locality after we have been there for some time. Like the fishes of the Kentucky caves we lose the power of sight by subjection to constant darkness : our religious sense gets atrophied without regular excursion into the region of intellectual light. If the formation of a sect signifies a sally into the realm of clarity and conscience, as it certainly was in Mediæval India, it should always be hailed with delight. Even if it is reabsorbed by the original religion, it cannot fail to act as a leaven and to purify faith ; like bacteria in the nodules of the leguminosae, which fix the nitrogen of the air in the plant-body, a pure sect embedded in a torpid faith tends to increase its vitality and growth. It may not always amount to a reforming movement, which implies not only the perception of new truths but an active propagation of the same ; but when rightly formed, it acts from within in a beneficial manner and prevents that hiatus of tradition which the institution of an absolutely new creed always implies. Without any ethical or rational contribution to make to existing faith and practice, however, a sect is no better than a mere fad or fashion which is bound to disappear in course of time. What Jung speaks of the modern man is true also of the founder of a religious sect : " he must be proficient in the highest degree, for unless he can atone by creative ability for his break with tradition, he is merely disloyal to the past." [23]

But, like an ill-patched garment or a disjointed masonry, which is a cause of constant anxiety and trouble, a faith may sometimes be such a medley of contradictory beliefs or crude superstitions that it is more profitable to discard it altogether than to prolong its existence by further patch-work. It may also be without sufficient intellectual and moral foundation for the rearing of a structure suited to the growing needs of the spirit.

[23] Jung, *Modern Man in Search of a Soul* (X. The Spiritual Problem of Modern Man), p. 229.

In such cases the only remedy lies in pulling down the building and strengthening the foundations for a nobler structure, always remembering, of course, that the soil should be capable of supporting the new load. This fate, so far as empirical generalisation is permissible, is bound to overtake not only magical beliefs but also religions based on an exclusive use of the imagination to the total neglect of the intellectual and mystical operations of the mind. The spinning of an elaborate pantheon is not always a sign of religious vitality—it is very often a fatty degeneration of faith. The character of all degenerate faiths is that they forget nothing and reject nothing, with the effect that they become ultimately smothered by the accumulation of age-long traditions very often in contradiction with one another.[24] Nothing is so conducive to religious vitality as the jettisoning of dead customs and dry creeds and the reorganisation of the materials of faith with every advance in genuine philosophic, ethical or mystic insight.

The Egyptian religion perished because it was latterly dominated by a persistent theriolatry and a mass of myths about gods, rather strange in a people otherwise so advanced in civilisation. The same is the case with Assyrian, Babylonian and Teutonic religions. In Greece speculation became secular at a very early time and philosophy pursued a career independently of religion, with the effect that the popular faith was reared on Homeric tales, not always ethically palatable or philosophically sound. The best minds were obliged to evolve personal faiths; and while most of them probably conformed outwardly to the religion of the state, they were inwardly alienated from it and did not think it worth their while to waste their philosophic labours on futile popular legends. The Romans, not much noted either for their religious or for their philosophic originality, gathered gods from all corners of their far-flung empire

[24] In the language of Bernard Shaw, they can be compared only to "a store in which the very latest and most precious acquisitions are flung on top of a noisome heap of rug-and-bottle refuse and worthless antiquities from the museum lumber room." (*The Adventures of the Black Girl in her search for God*, p. 60.)

without much reference to their compatibility; and among them also the best minds sought personal solace in ethical speculations unrelated to popular religion. Buddhism could spread so rapidly in Japan because the myths of the Kojiki could not supply enough spiritual food to the thinking minds of the island race. To-day, for the same reason, in India the religion of the Purāṇas has grown shamefaced and is failing to hold the undivided attention, interest and devotion of the ethicist and the philosopher. If, however, the ship of Hindu faith is still sailing steadily on, it is because it was equipped with the double engine of myth and speculation, and wherever the one has failed the other has taken over control in thinking minds. The injection of a little speculation into religion acts like a prophylaxis when the days of rationalism and free thinking arrive: those religions that are without it are simply killed out, while those with it either escape altogether or get off with slight scars and pits.

But it all depends upon the dosing. While a moderate degree of thinking may stimulate the activity of faith, a larger dose may prove injurious or fatal. Philosophy may prove a treacherous ally to religion at any moment, and a sound instinct has in all ages prompted religious men to scent danger in excessive speculation. Religion is an affair of light and shade combined, and 'the dim religious light' always disappears in the glare of intellectual illumination. The different formulae of religion, *viz.*, that it is *according to* reason, *above* reason and *against* reason, have all been tried in different ages; the only formula, however, likely to fit is that religion is *towards* reason. What I mean is that all religions destined to survive have in them a power and a tendency to grow towards a rational understanding of the world asymptotically without however reaching the goal. A complete description is possible only of a thing finished; but in religion man is concerned with a growing point of the mind—you can describe its tendencies but not its articulations, just as you can describe in detail a detached leaf but not the growing tip of a creeper. In religion the whole personality of man is operating—his intellectual, emotional and volitional attitudes are all inextricably bound up in his reaction to the total universe of sensible and supersensible things. To understand faith you must understand its physiology and not its mere anatomy—in fact, you cannot dissociate the rational and non-rational elements without killing it. The 'numinous' element refuses to be dragged into the light of intelligibility : the roots of faith lie deeply buried within the mind and cannot be exposed to light like its foliations in philosophy and cultus. You may modify your dogmas and rituals with the help of reason and defend or destroy them with argument;[25] but the mystic core of religion eludes the reach of reason and can neither be completely justified nor be completely disproved. And so it happens that none can be made religious by arguments, nor does a religious man, unable to defend his experience by reasoning, cease to have faith.[26] Like Instinct, which has been characterised as being purposive without a conscious purpose, religious intuition or mysticism may be described as being cognitive without clear understanding. It embodies a good deal of unreason without being irrational : that is why it is so closely related to bigotry and fanaticism and can so quickly produce heat without light.[27]

25 Neander, *Lectures on the History of Christian Dogmas* (Eng. Tr.), Vol. I. p. 4 : " Dogmas are only that form of the life rooted in God which is constructed by thought and reflection."

26 See C. J. J. Webb, *Religion and Theism*, pp. 25-6 : " The attempt to deduce the reasonableness of Religion from a belief in God's existence based on other than religious grounds is bound to fail; for the non-religious arguments alleged in support of the belief can only help to establish a genuinely religious faith when they are themselves interpreted in the light of that religious experience which originally makes us aware of God at all. Apart from this they cannot reveal God to us; they can at the most remove obstacles to the reception by our minds of a revelation mediated by that capacity for communion with the divine which is a normal feature of our humanity." See also p. 111: " I do not consider that, apart from the sense, mentioned just now as natural to the human mind, of being in the presence of Something at once *ultimate* and *intimate*, the arguments for the existence of God which may be called metaphysical, and which received such drastic treatment at the hands of Kant, could establish the reality of a God who could be the object of religious worship." See also Hegel, *Lectures on the Philosophy of Religion*, I, p. 4 also p. 33 : " Religion is a product of the Divine Spirit; it is not a discovery of man, but a work of divine operation and creation in him." See Pratt, *The Religious Consciousness*, p. 14f and p. 210f, for different types of religious belief.

27 Marett, *Faith, Hope and Charity in Primitive Religion*, p. 28.

Because of this mystical element no positive religion can ever come into being by cogitation alone nor can it be fully described by any catalogue of positive dogmas.[28] No Anglican divine will admit that to him religion is summed up in the thirty-nine articles of faith, nor would any Christian agree that his belief can be completely summarised by this or that Creed as laid down by the various Oecumenical Councils. A vertebrate animal is not all spine nor is a living religion all creed: the spine no less than the creed is cast out by the process of life itself. In the process of growth rudimentary structures may very often be replaced, as when a notochord is superseded by the regular spine; so also in religious development an outworn creed is often replaced by a more adequate body of dogmas. Religion is a life and not a creed, and as it does not owe its origin to conscious fabrication, it is always regarded as an uprush from within or an invasion from without. To use Descartes' language, it is either adventitious or innate but never factitious—a message from above or an ebullition from within, but never a production of conscious art. A sect or a reform may be launched into being by conscious premeditation; it can be justified by reasons and propagated by arguments. But both presuppose a religious attitude which does not owe its existence to conscious deliberation. You cannot draw up a Memorandum of Association to inaugurate a religious community just as you can float a joint-stock company; a religion so formed will have the solidity and the chilliness of the ice which you can yourself manufacture but not the refreshing coolness of the rain, which is a gift from above, nor the spontaneity and sweetness of the gushing spring which wells up from the bowels of the earth. The older theologians called religion a possession by the Spirit of God and the modern psychologists are calling it an obsessional neurosis;[29] but none has thus far regarded it as a conscious make-believe, even though some have

28 See C. J. J. Webb, *op. cit.*, p. 110f.

29 As by Freud in *The Future of an Illusion*. For a criticism of the Freudian view, see C. J. J. Webb, *op. cit.*, p. 117.

gone to the length of describing it as a device of cunning priests to catch unwary fools.[30]

Again and again in the history of religion has it happened that a reforming movement has ended only in founding a sect. Had religion been wholly an affair of reason and the reforming movement based on absolutely unassailable arguments, the transformation of a creed would have simply been a question of time. But while every religion is benefited spiritually by ethical and rational thinking among its adherents, it is seldom, if ever, totally changed in its character by concerted action. A religious community is stratified by differences of culture and temperament; and while the more advanced section can wear religion like a corn which yields to painless operation, the more backward part wears it like a skin, which can of course be torn off by compulsory conversion or sloughed off by the growth of the mind but otherwise sticks to the constitution under all conditions. Innate conservatism—a habit to follow beaten tracks and to trust to the genius of the past worthies of the race, and an inborn fear of the unknown—a natural shrinking from adventures and experiments in a field of tremendous spiritual risk, may keep back all but the boldest from drifting away from ancestral moorings; and the number of bold spirits being naturally small, the bulk of the community affects to ignore their existence or raises protective prohibitions against their entry and influence. So, unless the *zeit geist* is favourable and the unconscious attitude of the majority is definitely hostile to an existing creed, a reforming party is bound to find itself an outcasted sect, if it has a respectable following, or a band of faddists, if the number of adherents is small. Surrounded on all sides by the major community, it very often degenerates into an esoteric society or secret cult, and, while undoubtedly ennobled by its own doctrines, it fails to achieve its purpose either on account of a lack of drive or because the soil is uncongenial to its principles.

30 See Nyāyakusumāñjali, i. 9; Carlyle, *On Heroes and Hero-Worship*, p. 9 (Blackie and Sons).

Reforms, too much in advance of their times, have seldom succeeded in converting the world: when imposed by force by a ruling minority on a cowering majority, they have very often brought about a reactionary movement of the worst type as soon as the strong hand has been withdrawn.[31] This is why reforms have succeeded most where a general advance of intellectual culture has rendered the maintenance of existing beliefs and practices difficult, if not impossible, even to the ordinary understanding; as a matter of fact, they have very often been heralded by a general decay of faith, as at the time of Socrates in Greece and of Buddha in India. Ignorance has ever been the home of obscurantism: viewed from this standpoint, the Vedic invocation to the Sun, the brightest symbol of illumination, to increase excellent understanding has a deep significance. This explains also why religious bodies have so often been faced with the task of educating the people at large to ensure an intimate and vital acceptance of their own principles. A religion, unable or unwilling to face the consequenecs of a general diffusion of culture, has practically no future before it. In proportion as the general body of believers is educated, is a religion put on its mettle and obliged to eradicate inconsistent and ignoble elements from its principles and practices. An intelligent laity cannot be always bullied or bluffed and can draw their own conclusions about and from religious injunctions: they very often bring a fresh outlook to bear upon ancient texts and make short work of the monopoly of interpretation claimed by the privileged in spiritual power. They must be met on their own grounds if ancestral faith is to retain its hold on them.[32]

31 "I am firmly convinced that a vast number of people belong to the fold of the Catholic Church and nowhere else, because they are most suitably housed there. I am as much persuaded of this as of the fact, which I have myself observed, that a primitive religion is better suited to primitive people than Christianity, which is so incomprehensible to them, and so foreign to their blood that they can only ape it in a disgusting way."—C. G. Jung, *Modern Man in Search of a Soul*, p. 282.

32 See, for instance, a trenchant criticism of Hindu beliefs by a Hindu thinker in Farquhar, *The Crown of Hinduism*, p. 110; also Govinda Das, *Hinduism*, Introduction.

A reformer, however, seldom claims divine inspiration for his work. He very often professes to rid his ancestral faith of undesirable accretions and interpretations, because to his ethical and intellectual sensitivity its doctrines do not breathe the true spirit of a pure faith. Now, this profession of veneration for a golden past may be either a genuine belief or a mere tactful move. Christianity has very often pointed to the early Church Fathers as the repositories of the pure faith, and that in spite of the fact that even St. Paul and Jesus did not teach exactly the same thing and within four centuries of the establishment of Christianity most of the important issues regarding the nature and function of Christ had been raised, not only as between the canonical and the apocryphal or gnostic literature but also as between different leaders of the Orthodox Church itself. Similarly, Islam bestowed meticulous care on the collection of genuine traditions and within three hundred years of the death of its founder his reputed sayings and acts were incorporated in six collections which now form the *Sunnah*. Here also contradictions are to be found, whether because the Prophet did not follow any uniform rule of theory or practice or because he was incorrectly reported;[33] but the idea that for supplementing the contents of the Qur'an only the testimony of the contemporaries of Muhammad is admissible indicates that in Islam too corruption was supposed to infect the source less than later traditions and customs, and the practices of the first Khalifs were regarded as setting the pattern of purity. Similarly, again, in Hinduism, it is laid down that the immemorial customs of Brahmāvarta, created by the gods, and the principles of life followed by the Brahmins of the Brahmarṣideśa, lying next to Brahmāvarta, should be the ideals of conduct and character of all mankind.[34] We have no means of ascertaining what those customs and principles were, but the implication is clear, namely, that the land of ancient traditions should control the religious belief

[33] See Guillaume, *The Traditions of Islam*, p. 127.

[34] Manu, ii. 17-20.

of the community. Till about the end of the 18th century the Indian Parsis too referred to their co-religionists in Persia on matters of doubt and dispute for authoritative decision (Rivāyat)[35] as these were supposed to be nearer the original form of their common faith. The Semitic mind turns unconsciously to Jerusalem or Mecca for the genuine traditions for the very good reason that heterodoxy becomes ashamed to parade its innovations openly in the home of the prophet where every particle of dust is likely to rebel against the profanation of the creed.

But harking back to the past has its dangers as well as its avdantages. The Protestant insistence upon going back to the life and teachings of Jesus himself is founded upon the belief that the spiritual life of the Founder of Faith is always more inspiring and ethically more worthy than the ideals of conduct and conviction established by the Church during its history. Recent researches have shown that it is not easy to fix with certainty the genuine teachings of Christ; but even when allowances have been made for conflicting testimony, desire to extol and exaggerate, anxiety to filiate Christ's mission and activity to Old Testament, traditions and Greek Philosophy, and want of critical and scientific insight among the writers of the Gospels, enough still remains to reveal a striking moral personality whose life was an inspiration and whose message was a blessing to the sinner and the down-trodden. The Protestant attitude towards later development has been well expressed by Harnack in the following lines:[36] "Dogmatic Christianity stands between Christianity as the religion of the Gospel, presupposing a personal experience and dealing with disposition and conduct, and Christianity as a religion of cultus, sacraments, ceremonial and obedience, in short of superstition, and it can be united with either the one or the other." Roman Catholicism is regarded as having developed Dogmatic Christianity towards the latter of the two and it is the aim of the Protestants

[35] Moulton, *The Treasure of the Magi*, p. 123.
[36] Harnack, *op. cit.*, p. 16.

to lead it back to the former, although, as Harnack remarks,[37] in spite of "its secret note of interrogation" against dogmas, Protestantism, "because of its tendency to look back and to seek for authorities in the past and partly in the original unmodified form" of the old dogmas, has placed more reliance upon dogmas of the 4th and 5th centuries than upon doctrines connected with justification by faith. Similar attempts to lead men back to the scripture from the Talmudic tradition (Ananite or Karaite movement),[38] or to the austere faith of the Qur'an to the total abolition of the veneration of saints and holy places and symbols, or to the non-idolatrous Vedic religion or the mystic monism of the Upaniṣads from Paurāṇic mythology and idolatrous practices are not unknown. The pure fountain of spirituality, as it bubbles up from the life of the apostles and seers, is supposed to be contaminated in its flow through time as impure hands begin to train its channels for doctrinal purposes without the gift of a perfect life. So reformers have often no other ambition than to purify faith of later additions, very frequently made by an indulgent generation in a spirit of accommodation to existing conditions as it begins to spread, or by an ethically fallen generation unable to keep up lofty heights or resist the downward pull of lower cultures. In the case of religions that have a long history and do not owe their origin to single prophets, a choice of a period or a book has necessarily to be made to fix the standard of purity.

But reference to the past may not all be genuinely inspired: it may often be a matter of tact. Being brought up in a particular tradition, we are so very prone to love it with all its faults that any suggestion to leave a sinking bark of faith may produce an opposite effect. The greatest number of converts to Muhammadanism and Christianity, the two most active missionary religions of the world, comes from savage and semi-civilised tribes not much hampered by the

37 *Ibid*, p. 19.

38 G. F. Moore, *History of Religions*, Vol. 2, p. 82.

organised traditions of an ancestral faith and from socially oppressed classes or classes ignorant of their own religious traditions. The educated persons in any community are undoubtedly the first to detect flaws in their own religion, and yet they do not make easy converts. The reason is that the unconscious attachment to one's own ancestral faith, which sends out invisible tentacles of language, tradition, custom and ceremony through one's entire being, is so strong that even when its defects loom painfully large before one's consciousness one is still unable to forsake it or see it vilified. Like a quarrelsome old wife whom one has ceased to love and yet whom one defends against outside attack, a moribund faith is an interesting psychological study. This is why if a reformer is able to revitalise the old bones of a dying creed and prevent the wholesale adoption of a more vigorous religion, totally alien to tribal, national or racial traditions and customs, he is readily heard and obeyed. Thus Sikhism partially, and Ārya Samājism wholly, returned to a purified conception of Hindu religion and stemmed the tide of Islam in the Punjab, while the Brāhma Samāj did the same thing in Bengal against the serious onslaught of Christianity. These three religious movements of mediæval and modern India gave the necessary breathing space to orthodox Hinduism for moulting and re-orienting itself to the changed social conditions of the country; and to-day signs are not wanting that Hinduism, through its missions and meetings, is beginning to adopt the policy of the vigorous proselytising religions of the world that aggression is always the best defence as it not only mobilises social forces but also compels a rational and practical re-organisation of the creed.

But appeal to social sentiment and loyalty to ancestral faith have their difficulties, disadvantages and dangers. The requirements of adjustment to advanced culture are rational coherence of doctrines and ethical motives of action; but undiluted philosophy and didactic discourse, divorced from all religious association, have no chance of success with the ordinary mind. Nor is allegorical interpretation of dubious doctrines and shady practices always a safe procedure,[39] especially when religious matters are taught through unbecoming symbols. Debasing thoughts and practices have a tendency to be taken in their utter literalness in total disregard of their esoteric philosophy and ethics; the licentious rites that grew round vegetation myths and divine amours practically in every religion of antiquity should caution us against adhering to a debased creed with allegorical interpretation, solely for the sake of continuing ancestral beliefs. A religion that is inherently incapable of sufficient rationalisation and moralisation for the advancing spiritual needs of humanity may be given artificial respiration for some time, but it will never completely revive. Even devotionalism has its peculiar language for each stage of culture: the *sankīrtana* that made Navadvīpa mad in the 16th century, and is still a potent force for religious excitement in suitable temperaments, can hardly be revived under modern conditions as a method of mass conversion—it has a limited appeal to modern minds, grown sceptical about the religious value of ecstatic trance and emotional frenzy. Similarly, socio-economic changes and man's altered conception about the nature of God have sounded for ever the death-knell of the spectacular but costly sacrificial method of worship all over the world, at least among the educated.

There is the further difficulty that unless the elements of a religion admit of picking and choosing, without committing the reformer to its undesirable aspects also for retaining its distinctiveness, no attempt to lead religion back to its original form is likely to succeed with a later generation. We may suppose such a wise selection of ancestral beliefs to have been made by Confucius[40] and Zarathustra,[41] although the latter is also regarded as having been divinely commanded to strike a death-blow at idolatry in his native soil.[42] But

39 Carlyle, *On Heroes and Hero-Worship*, p. 11.

40 J. Legge, *The Religions of China*, p. 4.

41 M. Haug, *Essays on the Religion of the Parsis*, p. 294, 301; Tiele, *The Religion of the Iranian People*, Part I, p. 68; Ch. VIII.

42 Haug, *op. cit.*, p. 295.

where the desirable and the undesirable elements form a single texture and cannot be separated without evaporating the distinctiveness of the religion sought to be reformed, all attempts at reconstruction are futile. Similar difficulties are bound to arise where there is no unanimity about the essentials of the creed itself. But where these difficulties do not exist and it is possible to dissociate the worthy elements from the ignoble ones and to interpret them in the light of existing spiritual needs, not philosophically or ethically only but in such a way that the common man may get religious inspiration from them, it is not impossible to resuscitate an ancient faith. It is true that each age introduces its own ideas into the old faith and possibly smuggles in foreign matter from alien faiths; but the phraseology and the framework being indigenous, the reformed religion proves readily acceptable to those who are unwilling to break away from ancient traditions and yet are unable to accept them wholesale as principles of a spiritual life.[43] Such reformed religions, however, do not always spread easily among ordinary people; very often a long time and a powerful patronage are required to make them popular and even then sometimes not before they have clothed themselves with new superstitions or absorbed old ones in a transformed garb. But, even when limited to a small minority, they react powerfully upon the contiguous religions of the time which, while ignoring or oppressing them, quietly drop many of their own obnoxious features.

We shall close this lecture by bringing out the implications of this backward glance. If religion is to develop by renovating old creeds, this can only mean that the spirit of man had once been in complete possession of truth and that history is the record of man's fall from a pristine purity to be recovered in part fitfully with the help of reformers. The picture of a golden age, when men talked with God or gods, or souls dwelt in stars and beheld from there the undimmed lustre of truth, beauty and good-

43 **Hegel**, ***Philosophy of Religion***, **I, p. 28.**

ness, is such a fascinating speculation that men have been powerfully tempted in many lands to advance it. If nothing more is meant than this that the laws of spiritual life are eternal and that as soon as men remove the veil of ignorance and superstition and sin from their mind and life they get an unclouded vision of those eternal laws, there is abundant justification for a backward, rather an inward, glance. In this sense it may be truly held with Plato that man learns nothing but only remembers. The prophet of any age may then be said to help men to realise the eternal laws of their spiritual life—like a true *guru*, he opens the spiritual vision by applying the collyrium of insight to eyes blinded by ignorance.

But it is not in this sense that the matter is generally understood. What is meant to be signified sometimes is that there really was a time when an actual positive religion flourished which contained nothing but the highest wisdom, the purest morality and the devoutest feeling, and that we must reinstate that time on earth by clearing the debris of unspiritual matters that the sophistication of centuries has accumulated. Now, there is not an iota of historical evidence to justify this belief in respect of any country. In the epitaphs of ancestral tablets nations have chosen to express their filial piety by following the rule, "Nothing but good of the dead." The belief that our ancestors were more religious is all of a piece with the other beliefs that they lived inconceivably longer and that they possessed infinitely larger stature than ourselves. The fact is that the only literature that nations have cared to preserve from the remotest antiquity is religious literature. Compared with the hoary antiquity of this literature, secular literature is a mere stripling: as a matter of fact, we are obliged in most cases to reconstruct their earliest secular lives from their religious documents. Why people clung so tenaciously to religious traditions in preference to secular ones is a large enquiry: this is certain, however, that this partiality has served to raise them unduly in the estimation of posterity which ascribes this phenomenon to their unusual devotion to religion.

Perhaps in one sense this is true, for religion to the ancients meant more than it does to us, as it comprehended rules of hygiene and medicine, cosmogonic and sociological speculations, magic and philosophy, in addition to modes of devotion and worship; but there is nothing to show that religion was more spiritual or more universally followed except as a blind custom of the tribe or the race. The only pragmatic justification for such a belief is that men are likely to attempt with more confidence a programme of spiritual life if they know that the highest ideal had once been actual in the lives of an earlier generation and that in trying to attain a high level of spirituality they are not working off the beast in them but recovering the angel.

The other sense in which this return-movement is understood is that no religion can rise higher than its source and that, therefore, whenever any deviation from the religious life of the founder or from the message preached by him takes place we are falling away from the pure faith. Hindu philosophers are fond of classifying things into four classes, namely, those that have neither beginning nor end, those that have both beginning and end, those that have no beginning but have an end, and those that have a beginning but no end. The belief about a last revelation that occurred in the past falls within this fourth class. The Romans used to consult the Sibylline books in times of danger and difficulty and the Protestants go back to the New Testament to combat debased faith; the mentality is the same, namely, that the wisdom displayed therein can never be excelled. Later on we shall have occasion to discuss at length this question of a last revelation: here we simply indicate the possibility of advocating this in a reforming movement. We are invited to believe that although in every realm of human activity there are manifest signs of progress, in religion alone the last thing has already been said and that, therefore, it is incumbent upon succeeding ages to cease experimenting with faith and to return to the original doctrines of the Last Prophet. Apart from the question of authenticity and consistency, we have to believe in the spiritual validity and the ethical sufficiency of his teachings for all ages and climes; and it is here that difficulties are likely to arise. The acceptance of this belief commits us not only to the doctrine of a prophet's omniscience of all the contingencies of spiritual and moral life over the whole of space and time but also to the theory of a perfect revelation of God's nature and will and of His wishes regarding the relation that should hold between Himself and man and among His creatures themselves.

The question is bound to arise: How far can a prophet see? Can we believe that a finite being can prove a perfect receptacle of divine revelation and a perfect vehicle of divine expression? Can we believe that God chose this receptacle and vehicle not at the beginning of things nor at their end but at an uncertain middle point when, barring a few gleaming hill-tops of civilisation, the world was mostly steeped in dark ignorance and superstition? Certain it is that no founder of a faith ever believed that he was a mere reformer of old creeds nor does the world believe him to be nothing else. Herein lies the distinction between him and those who only tinkered with faith and formed sects or started reforming movements. As Rabbi Leo Baeck observes:[44] "The mere reformer confines his efforts to the sphere with which he is immediately concerned. He creates new social or ecclesiastical or political structures, but these, however important they may be, are limited to their own range. But religious revolution aims at permeating the world with a new religious principle, and it is into the whole world that the new ferment is poured. It aims at a new world. This imperative comes from the Beyond; this great contradiction of the world as it is, is one that seeks the ear of the whole world." What the prophets thought about themselves and with what justification we shall discuss in later lectures. In the meantime we may refer to those who have faith in the inexhaustible inscrutabilities of the divine nature, in the reality of the temporal process and the concomitant evolution of all the spiritual sides of man, in the perfect possibility of a never-ending series of

[44] Clemen, *op. cit.*, p. 267.

more and more adequate revelation of the nature and will of God, and in a better and better understanding of His ways with men and the world. We cannot do better than quote the beautiful words with which Jung closes his paper on *Psychotherapists or the Clergy?* [45]: "The living spirit grows and ever outgrows its earlier forms of expression; it freely chooses the men in whom it lives and who proclaim it. This living spirit is eternally renewed and pursues its goal in manifold and inconceivable ways throughout the history of mankind. Measured against it, the names and forms which men have given it mean little enough; they are only the changing leaves and blossoms on the stem of the eternal tree."

* * *

Of the eternal Tree of Religion the roots lie buried within the depths of the most primitive minds—perhaps some of the elements that make for the social aspect of religious life are to be traced to those animal instincts that are responsible for the formation of animal colonies, herds and families. The first stirrings of the religious life may sometimes seem so different from what is familiar to us in its higher forms that we may be tempted to disown their spiritual significance altogether. But we shall be no more justified in disbelieving in the continuity of religious growth from those beginnings than a naturalist would be in rejecting the evolution of the frog from the tadpole or the butterfly from the caterpillar. Watch a plant shooting up and sprouting—you will be surprised at the quick changes in the form of its leaves during the first few days: when they will assume their final form you will find very little that is common between it and the initial shape. An advanced religion is not only a continuation of primitive faith but it very often carries, embedded within, vestigial remains of earlier forms, generally harmless but capable of producing injury under adverse conditions of culture.

Of this Tree of Religion, Magic, Sorcery, Witchcraft and such other arts of the primitive shaman or medicine man

[45] C. G. Jung, *Modern Man in Search of a Soul*, p. 282.

would supply the invisible roots, and Animism, Fetishism, Totemism and such other primitive beliefs the visible trunk.[46] From this trunk radiate many branches but of unequal vitality. Some of these are dead to-day either because they have been hewn down or because they have spontaneously withered or because their life-giving sap has been diverted into other channels of growth. Some, again, are carrying on with a low vitality but failing to proliferate into vigorous branchlets. Others again are vigorous and strong and developing along a single axis. Others still have lost the growing point, but fairly strong collateral branches form a dense bush at the region of the truncated tip. Some of the branches, again, are being artificially nourished or invigorated by transfusion of sap from a stronger branch. Branches, that were once widely separated, have, again, by a process of expansion got interlocked with one another and are producing either friction or fusion. On each branch, again, dead materials are accumulating; and when these are not being cast out of the system by the process of organic growth, they are retarding the vitality of the whole. Minor branches crop up and disappear on many of the main branches of this tree without affecting their general growth, while countless leaves grow and fall and keep up the vitality of the entire system by their synthesis of nutrient stuff.

Of this great Tree three main branches are still living with different degrees of vitality in their subsidiary branches. These are the Semitic, the Aryan and the Mongolian religions. On each stem many subsidiary branches are now dead; similarly many independent branches have also died out. Of these dead religions the most notable are the Egyptian, the Babylonian, the Assyrian, the Teutonic, the Scandinavian, the Greek and the Roman in the Old World and the religions of Peru and Mexico in the New. We may also refer to the Sumerian and Aegean religions whose remains have been unearthed in recent years. Many extensive cults have

[46] See Susilkumar Maitra, *Religion and Magic*, in the *Journal of the Department of Letters*, Vol. XXVII (Calcutta University).

also perished, such as Mithraism, Orphic cult, etc., while countless smaller creeds have flourished and fallen in the past and are doing so even to-day. Sects and schisms have occurred in most of the great religions of the world, but only a few of them have survived and the rest have been swept out of existence altogether. It would be a mistake to think, however, that men live the great religions they profess in a homogeneous fashion. We all have our little snug corners of faith within the bigger whole of the common religion, and these form the smaller sects with which almost every religion abounds. Many of us profess one religion and live another, as when we adhere to the socio-economic aspect of an ancestral faith and develop an independent personal religion of devotion for spiritual nourishment. Some of us; again, reject either or both of these factors of an institutional religion and become freethinkers or religious nondescripts.

The above considerations apart, the living religions growing on the Semitic stem to-day are Judaism, which has ceased to grow in extent, Christianity and Islam, both of which are still growing vigorously at the expense of the other religions of the world. Of these three, Christianity has gained in spiritual intensity also, because, unlike Islam which has practically ceased to think [47] though not to grow because of the simplicity of its creed, it is still the object of intensive thinking by some of the greatest minds of the world. On the Aryan stem we have a bifurcation into Iranian and Vedic, the former of which, after contamination by Magian and other influences, is the religion of the Zoroastrians of India (the Parsis) and Persia (the Goebers). The Vedic branch has divided into the three religions of Brahmanism (Hinduism), Buddhism and Jainism with their different sects and subsects. Jainism has become an exclusive cult, but the former two are showing renewed signs of vitality after remaining dormant for centuries. Both had at one time spread beyond the confines of India:

[47] Although Islam is again showing signs of literary activity for purposes of propaganda, it cannot critically discuss the contents of the Qur'an as Christianity does of the New Testament.

possibly in a changed world their social organisation and religious practice would have to undergo some radical changes before they can aspire to expand again among the cultured nations of the world. On the Mongolian stem grew up the three religions of Confucianism, Taoism and Shintoism, which did not possess the necessary elements of universality and ever remained confined to the Mongolian races.

Where the conquering followers of a dominant religion have not extirpated a native religion or where a lower religion has not been absorbed in a higher one, a mixture of creeds has sometimes taken place. Hinduism and Buddhism, in their original career of conquest, gave rise to such mixed religions outside Indian limits—especially Buddhism when effecting a cultural conquest of the Mongolian lands of Tibet, China and Japan. Sikhism is a union of Hinduism and Islam with Hindu elements preponderating. Brāhmaism has borrowed its elements from Hinduism, Christianity and Islam alike, the Hindu element being again predominant. Eclectic beliefs like Theosophy can hardly be called religions, for they do not possess an independent and exclusive social organisation which all institutional religions are supposed to do. They can at best form religious brotherhoods on the basis of mutual toleration and respect among the adherents of different positive religions.

In what follows we shall confine our attention to such religions as are still living and ignore altogether those that are dead and those that live within the protected enclosure of savage superstition. We shall see that there are certain fundamental beliefs without which no religion can satisfy the spiritual needs of man, and of these needs a right understanding of the nature of God and His working and a right attitude towards the world of sentient beings are the most insistent. Compared with these, the rest are spiritually subsidiary, though from the standpoint of the positive religions themselves they are very necessary as aids to right devotion and proper ethicality. Ignoring the historical context, we shall take as the text of our lectures the following beautiful words of the Qur'an (Sura ii. 172): "There is no piety in turning your faces towards the east or the west, but he is pious who believeth in God and the last day and the angels and the scriptures and the prophets; who for the love of God disburseth his wealth to his kindred, and to the orphans, and the needy, and the wayfarer, and those who ask, and for ransoming; who observeth prayer, and payeth the legal alms, and who is one of those who are faithful to their engagements when they have engaged in them, and patient under ills and hardships and in time of trouble: these are they who are just and these are they who fear God."

## CHAPTER II

### The Prophets

We shall discuss now the special significance of the prophetic mission as contradistinguished from the functions of the sage, the priest, the preacher and the reformer. In a sense, the prophet is all these combined inasmuch as he is credited with spiritual vision, active worship, persuasive eloquence and purified faith. Very often he is even more than these, for he has to legislate for his following and settle their disputes, and sometimes he has also to lead them to war and administer their conquests. A mere catalogue of these multifarious activities is enough to show that an all-round prophet must be made of a superior stuff and that a part of the homage paid to him is the homage paid to any kind of greatness by the world at large. To idolise a prophet is a species of hero-worship, as Carlyle has pointed out: that in his particular case idolisation very easily passes over into apotheosis is a very common experience. He often becomes the locus of mythical qualities and supernatural powers. Strange tales are told about his mysterious movements through space, his control over the elements and forces of nature, his conquest of bodily privations and sufferings, his miraculous cures and striking conversions, his seeing into the future, and divine and angelic aid in his mission. His birth must be heralded by angelic flourishes and attended by universal joy, his infancy must indicate his future greatness, and his death must be attended by portents and deeply mourned by the living creation.[1] The forces of sin and evil are alarmed at his birth and try to tempt and thwart him in all ways: he becomes the central figure in a cosmic drama in which the forces of good and evil strive to take possession of him,[2] and the latter are ultimately repulsed to the infinite relief and ultimate benefit of the world

[1] See Jackson, *Zoroaster*, p. 27.

[2] See Jackson, *Zoroaster*, pp. 28-29, 51.

Now, a close analysis of the powers and perfections of a prophet will show that they can all be summed up in one word, namely, the triumph of the spiritual over the material. Matter and space cannot obstruct the progress of spirit; and if a prophet is possessed of a body, he is not encumbered by it to the same extent as ordinary mortals are. So Buddha crosses rivers without boats with as much ease "as a strong man closes and stretches forth his palms," Jesus walks on the Sea of Galilee, and Muhammad makes his journey to Jerusalem through the air: nay, Buddha goes up to Trayastriṃśat heaven to enlighten his dead mother about his creed, Muhammad rides his mysterious Booraq to explore the seven heavens and meet the earlier prophets in different regions,[3] and Jesus descends into hell to give relief to suffering sinners. The births of Mahāvīra, Buddha and Zarathustra are presaged by dreams and that of Jesus by an angelic announcement; the last three are born of virgin mothers, and Zarathustra laughs on the day he is born.[4] Māra, Satan and Angra Mainyu each attempts to wean a prophet from spiritual allegiance. A forty days' fast is nothing to many of these prophets and a three days' residence within the stomach of a whale is only a bit of uncomfortable experience to one of the minor prophets. The sun stops in its mid-career at the bidding of a prophet[5] and

[3] Apart from the ascensions of Enoch (Gen. 5.24) and Elijah (2 K. 2.11), who did not return to earth, there are Jewish parallels of Muhammad's achievement R. Akiba (50-130 A.D.), Ben Azzai (2nd cent. A.D.), Ben Zoma (2nd cent. A.D.) and Elisha b. Abuyah (end of 1st cent. and beginning of 2nd cent. A.D.) were regarded as having entered Paradise. This is a part of Merkabah mysticism (referring to Ezekiel's vision of the heavenly Throne-chariot).—Abelson, *Jewish Mysticism*, p. 49.

[4] Jackson, *Zoroaster*, pp. 23-25; Stevenson, *Heart of Jainism*, p. 22 f; Hopkins, *Origin and Evolution of Religion*, p. 65 (f.n.); Moulton, *Treasure of the Magi*, p. 117; Syed Ameer Ali, *Spirit of Islam*, pp. 8-9 (signs and portents are said to have attended Muhammad's birth). For parallelism between the personal histories of Buddha and Jesus, see the quotation from T. W. Doane's *Bible Myths* in Khwaja Kamal-ud-din, *The Religion of Jesus and the Traditional Christianity*, pp. 83-93.

[5] Jos. 10.13. According to the Iranian religion, Hoshedar will perform the same feat at a future time when the sun will stop for 10 days and 10 nights.—See Casartelli, *Philosophy of the Mazdayasnian Religion under the Sassanides*, p. 99.

the storms are rebuked into silence by another. Jesus transubstantiates water into wine and multiplies loaves and fishes just as Kṛṣṇa multiplied Draupadī's vegetable-shred to feed her untimely guests. Jesus not only restores Lazarus and the widow's son and Jairus's daughter to life but himself rises from his grave, as many of the pagan gods were supposed to have done,[6] and ascends to heaven as Enoch and Elijah did before him though not after death;[7] but even his achievements sink into insignificance when compared with the revival of a dead man touched by the buried bones of Elisha and the transformation of petrified Ahalyā into living flesh at the touch of Rāma.[8]

It is evident that into the delineation of a prophet much of ancient superstition about magic and miracle manages to effect an entrance. Exceptional spirituality has very seldom been conceived in terms of ethical height and religious insight alone. A prophet must possess, in addition, power to control the material world and to rise above its laws. In primitive times the possessed spirit was credited with powers over sickness and epidemic, and his incantations and magical rites were supposed to kill enemies, produce rain and even drive away the demon of eclipse. Even now in India the credulous believe in the sanctimonious charlatan's power to turn base metals into gold and double currency notes, and fairly educated men will readily swallow many of the old wives' tales about the miraculous doings of this or that petty saint. Muhammad's confession that he made a mistake in his advice to date-growers about fertilising their palms has the merit of frankness about it. According to the Freudian principle of repression and forgetfulness, unfavourable instances of prophetic activity have a tendency to be forgotten,—they are also very often consciously suppressed in sectarian literature, with the effect that posterity

[6] Pringle-Pattison, *Studies in the Philosophy of Religion*, pp. 183 f, 223 f.

[7] See art. ASSUMPTION AND ASCENSION in ERE. ii. *Cf.* the death of Zoroaster by a flame from heaven in Jackson, *Zoroaster*, p. 124.

[8] For an allegorical interpretation of the Ahalyā story, see Rabindra Nath Tagore, *A Vision of India's History* in *Viswabharati Quarterly*, Vol. I, p. 19.

learns only about the hits and is kept in entire ignorance of the prophetic misses. Orthodoxy in all faiths takes every precaution to anathematize and extirpate the apocrypha because this holds up an unworthy picture of the prophet or exposes his feet of clay.

A prophet is not only a successor of the shaman and the magician; in monotheistic religions he is very often a substitute for one or other of the tribal gods and pagan deities.[9] It is now a well-established fact that many of the Christian saints are really transformed local deities: a thin veneer of Christianity was thrown over them to win over their devotees, and their cults were perpetuated with a Christian significance. Many of the major festivals of Christianity are really pagan festivals.[10] The social instinct of man has never taken kindly to the idea of a solitary personal god and has ever tried to furnish him with associates, as in polytheism, or with subordinate companions or personified qualities, like angels and Yazatas,[11] most of whom were originally independent deities of the old polytheism or gods of other tribes now incorporated within the monotheistic religious community. In Christianity, where the Jewish angels figure as colourless as the Brahmanic gods do in Buddhism, a persistent tendency toward trinitarianism satisfies the social instinct in relation to God. Muhammadanism, which began with a denunciation of this "tritheistic" tendency of Christianity, itself retained the

9 Thus, about the Hebrew patriarchs Lods observes, "It is a plausible supposition that several of the heroes of the patriarchal narratives were originally gods and that some part of their adventures was consequently mythological in origin. Although the proofs are not very conclusive, we may admit with E. Meyer, B. Luther and Raymond Weill that Abraham, Isaac, Jacob and Joseph, before being presented as founders of certain holy places, had been their gods or "baals": Abraham at Hebron, Isaac at Beersheba, Jacob at Bethel, and perhaps Joseph at Shechem...... One thing at least is certain, namely, that *for the Israelite writers*, the actors in the patriarchal stories were exclusively historical persons, human ancestors of real peoples and tribes."—See Lods, *Israel*, pp. 161-2, 407.

10 Stubbe, *Rise and Progress of Mahometanism*, p. 21 f., Khwaja Kamal-ud-din, *The Religion of Jesus and the Traditional Christianity*, pp. 25-81.

11 Moulton, *Treasure of the Magi*, p. 9; Dhalla, *Zoroastrian Theology*, pp. 96-100.

angels as an integral part of the creed[12] and latterly developed a theory of saints much on the lines of Roman Catholicism which believed in these heavenly intercessors. All these show the innate weakness of the human mind, which is incapable of resting content with a unitary divinity and has a tendency to lapse either into polytheism or into angelolatry or into prophet-worship.

"The most significant feature in the history of an epoch," says Carlyle,[13] "is the manner it has of welcoming a Great man. Ever, to the true instincts of men, there is something godlike in him. Whether they shall take him to be a god, to be a prophet, or what they shall take him to be? that is ever a grand question; by their way of answering that, we shall see, as through a little window, into the very heart of these men's spiritual condition." So far as the major creeds are concerned, the prophet came mostly to be venerated in course of time on this side idolatry, if not actually deified. Buddha was transformed into a god in the Mahāyāna school and an elaborate pantheon of Buddhas and Bodhisattvas with their female counterparts was evolved. In Japan this transformed Buddha became the centre of genuine religious devotion under the title of Amida.[14] Zarathustra again shares with Mazda the adoration of men in at least one verse of the Yasna and was later on credited with a goddess wife and entertainment at the table of a supreme deity.[15] Confucius too, 'unreasonably neglected when alive,' was elevated to divine rank at the beginning of the Christian era by imperial authority, extolled as being equal in virtue to Heaven and Earth, and worshipped at his spirit-tablet as something like the ancestor of the whole nation twice every year.[16] Christ

[12] See *Faiths of the World* (St. Giles' Lectures—Second Series), p. 382; Lammens, *Islam—Belief and Institutions*, p. 48; Robertson Smith. *Religion of the Semites* (1914), p. 120 f (In Islam the god of heathenism are degraded into *jinn*).

[13] Carlyle, *On Heroes and Hero-worship*, The Hero as Prophet (Blackie and Sons' Ed., p. 53).

[14] Hopkins, *Origin and Evolution of Religion*, p. 330.

[15] Ys. 42.21; Moulton, *Treasure of the Magi*, p. 76.

[16] Legge, *Religions of China*, pp. 147-8; Clemen, *Religions of the World*. p. 86.

was very early regarded as the second person of the Divine Trinity; and although Docetism, which denied his human character, was vanquished, the process of deification could not be effectively stopped.[17] He is Lord, Saviour, King and Judge; and though fitful attempts were made, as by the Ebionites, to call him, in the language of Milton, "this perfect man, by merit called my Son," it cannot be denied that Christ's utterances like "I and my Father are one" and "He who has seen me has seen the Father," have been mostly taken in a literal fashion and that the picture of God who became man but did not altogether forsake his divinity looms large before the Christian mind.[18] In fact, in most of the later creeds the divinity aspect is carefully brought out even though the human aspect is not altogether ignored.[19] In India a prophet is very often identified with a divine incarnation—even the heretic Buddha duly became an incarnation of Viṣṇu, and within the memory of the present generation the sage of Dakṣiṇeśvara, Rāmakrishṇa Paramahaṃsa has been transformed into Bhagavān Śrī-Rāmakrishṇa, and now regular religious ceremonies are held in his honour and temples are being built all over India to enshrine his figure or photo. Muhammad, of all later prophets, alone seems to have escaped deification,[20] but no other prophet's personal habits and idiosyncrasies have been so faithfully recorded and followed by his followers or his decrees invested with such divine authority. Even in the last century, again, the Bab was regarded almost as an incarnate God.[21]

When excessive veneration, identical with or bordering on divine worship, is paid to a prophet it is no wonder that he

17 See Hopkins, *Or. & Ev. of Rel.*, Ch. XX. The Christian Trinity (esp. p. 337).

18 See Bethune-Baker, *Introduction to the Early History of the Christian Doctrine* (1923), p. 63 f.

19 See art. CREEDS in ERE. iv; also Pringle-Pattison, *Studies in the Ph. of Rel.*, p. 205.

20 The Qur'an iii. 73-4 condemns the deification of the prophet. The Jewish prophets were also not deified.

21 Hopkins, *Or. & Ev. of Rel.*, p. 71.

should be credited with all those superhuman acts which are possible only to a divinity. With the lapse of time the human lineaments of the prophet grow dim, and when there is a rivalry between faiths about prophetic greatness this kind of development can seldom be prevented. At one time people quarrelled about the greatness of their respective gods; now they quarrel about the greatness of their prophets. So Christ must perform most of the miracles that the Hebrew prophets of old are recorded to have done; and Muhammad too must be credited by a later generation with having made the sun stand still in the manner of Joshua and the water flow in imitation of Moses and also with multiplying food and drink like Christ for his hungry and thirsty followers,[22] although the Qur'an explicitly says, " No apostle had come with miracles except by the leave of God " and " Nothing hindered us from sending him with the power of working miracles, except that the peoples of old treated them as lies."[23] In the popular mind the idea of greatness is so inseparable from the idea of supernatural power that prophets and saints have mostly been credited with performing miracles as signs and credentials of their spiritual greatness.[24] As Streeter points out,[25] " At certain stages of culture and in certain moods the human mind demands miracle—and in all countries and in all ages the demand has produced a supply." Even to-day no saint would be canonised in Roman Catholicism unless it can be proved that at least two miracles had been performed by him or at his tomb. In India it is believed that such powers can be acquired by Yogic culture; but the general Semitic tradition is that they are the gifts of God or divine modes of bearing testimony to the prophetic character of certain chosen individuals.

22 See G. F. Moore, *History of Religions*, Vol. 2, p. 477; Stubbe, *Rise and Progress of Mahometanism*, pp. 160-62; Lammens, *Islam*, p. 75. *Cf.* Nimbāditya, who did the same feat, in Wilson, *Hindu Religion*, p. 99.

23 Sura 13.38; 17.61. See Lammens, *Islam*, p. 51.

24 See Cohen, *The Philosophy of Maimonides*, p. 101—quotation from Maimonides, *Guide to the Perplexed*, II.29.

25 Streeter, *The Buddha and the Christ*, p. 10.

It is worthy of note too that angels are frequently supposed to be in constant attendance upon the prophets—that they do not interfere more actively in the affairs of the prophets is due to the fact that these are unwilling to take angelic help for their personal benefit. But God does not always leave His chosen people or His prophet to the tender mercies of a cruel and sinful world. So in Judaism and Muhammadanism God himself (or His angelic host) lays low the enemies of God and His prophets, and obtains for the faithful followers of the Lord miraculous victory. Zarathustra had his Fravashi (guardian spirit), and something like this was also ascribed to Buddha at a later time.[26] This belief in divine solicitation for the prophet's safety secures for him comparative immunity from molestation at the hands of the ignorant who are afraid to injure him because of this Divine guardianship.[27] A mystic fluid or aura or force is also sometimes supposed to serve as an invisible protection and to overwhelm those attempting to lay their hands on the prophet.[28] His escapes from danger are mostly interpreted as miraculous, not to mention the warnings, conveyed to him through dreams and angelic agencies, about his impending dangers.

Consistently with the view that the prophet has access to supernatural planes, he is credited with another power, namely, foretelling the future. In moments of ecstasy the prophet transcends the temporal plane and views all things from the standpoint of eternity. Things remote in space and time stand revealed to his gaze. The past no less than the future Buddha could see at a glance : he remembered all his previous incarnations, human and sub-human, and he also foretold the future greatness of Pātaligāma (Pātaliputra) and the hastened decay of his Church when nuns were admitted into his Order. The Jewish prophets foretell the fall of Jerusalem and the doom of many other cities as also the fates and fortunes of many nations and individuals. Sometimes they are informed

[26] See Grünwedel, *Buddhist Art in India*, pp. 195-96.

[27] See Wilson, *Hindu Religion*, p. 180.

[28] The persons of priests are regarded as inviolable in many religions.—See I Sam., 22.17, for instance.

in dreams and sometimes in waking moments; sometimes they profess to communicate divine utterances ('Thus saith the Lord') and sometimes they transmit their vision as directed by God ('I saw' or 'Thus sheweth the Lord'). Similarly, tongues were loosened among the immediate followers of Christ who himself also foretold some of the events of his own life. Muhammad too had visions of the future, though not of equal effectiveness.

It is curious to note,. however, that while prophetic knowledge of the future is regarded as a sign of spiritual insight, the attempt made by others to know the future is condemned in most of the scriptures. Soothsaying and divination were almost universal in the ancient world. Oracles were delivered and signs of the future interpreted in Greece, Rome, Egypt, Babylon, Assyria, the Jewish States, China and India long before the rise of monotheism proper, and various methods were adopted to know the will of the gods or to ascertain the future. Buddha warned his disciples against dabbling in foretelling; Muhammad prohibited the casting of lots;[29] and in Judaism false and pagan prophets were warned against. The psychology underlying this prohibition seems to be that in the case of the true prophet foreknowledge implies special communication by God to His chosen of what is eternally known to Himself, whereas in other cases, *e.g.* astrology and divination, it implies that the course of the world is predetermined and can therefore be calculated to a nicety, leaving Divine will and providence entirely out of account. Even in the apostolic age of Christianity a check was sought to be imposed upon unrestricted prophecy among the Apostles themselves, and with the growth of Church organisation prophecy entirely ceased.

Two aspects of this prophetic vision of the future have had profound effects upon the evolution of religion. The one is apocalyptic vision and the other is the foretelling of a future prophet, of which Christianity and Muhammadanism made an effective use. The Qur'an definies a prophet as a warner, and

[29] See Stubbe, *op. cit.*, p. 178.

although Muhammad had at first more in mind the idolatrous habits of his countrymen than their ethical iniquities, his warnings covered both classes of reprehensible conduct. Now, warning must have some reference to an impending calamity; otherwise it would be ineffective as a motivation of conduct. The apocalyptic literature, which made free use of the imaginative faculty, used, as inducements to repentance and ethical action, the joys of heaven and the terrors of destruction and hell. On the one side was depicted the benefit to be derived from the acceptance of the reformed creed and from following a proper mode of life, and on the other was painted the gloomy picture of an impending world-catastrophy, from which unbelievers and sinners would have no escape, to be followed by dire torments reserved for them in hell. Glowing pictures of the ascending tiers of heaven, corresponding to the varying deserts of the virtuous, are to be found in most of the religions, and even Buddhism and Judaism, which at the beginning discarded a celestial motive for ethical conduct, were obliged later on to delineate the joys of the different grades of heaven with their different denizens.[30] Hinduism, Muhammadanism and Zoroastrianism had similar speculations; and although in later Christianity the multiplicity of heavens was rejected, the picture of enjoyment of the many mansions of heaven stayed on and provided perennial motives of ethical action. In consonance with the 'three-storeyed' scheme of the ancient world, with Heaven above and Hell below and the Earth in between, it was even possible to conceive cases of ascension and excursion into heaven in flesh and blood, and Judaism, Christianity, Muhammadanism, Hinduism and Buddhism could all point to concrete instances of such singular prophetic greatness.

But the apocalyptic instrument that the prophets generally used was not joy to be attained but doom to be avoided. They interpreted their arrival as a signal for divine judgment upon the sinful world. Of the old Jewish prophets, it has

[30] See Morfill and Charles, *Book of the Secrets of Enoch*, Introduction, p. xxx f.; B. C. Law, *Heaven and Hell in Budshist Perspective*, Part I, Sec. I and Sec. II; also Appendix, p. xxxii f.

been pointed out[31] that they were rather censors than comforters; their spirit is expressed in the words of Amos, "Can a trumpet be blown in a city, and the people not be afraid?" The kingdom of Heaven was nigh, and woe unto those whom it would find unprepared. The feast in honour of the coming heavenly bridegroom is prepared—those without a suitable garment of morality would be cast out into the outer darkness where there shall be weeping and gnashing of teeth. Some of the Jewish prophets had indeed predicted the return of past greatness to Israel and put the nation in a mood of auto-suggestion, till the belief in their words begat the will to strike and to achieve temporary freedom. But it requires greater power than a mere appeal to the unconscious wish of a down-trodden nation to make it will for self-purification. And it is this that the greater prophets achieved. While one class was declaring the imminent arrival of a Messiah who would free it from the hateful tyranny of its foreign masters, another class was preaching the nearness of the kingdom of Heaven and the necessity of repenting for personal and national sins. The function of the prophet is to interpret the divine will and to convey warning to an erring nation, and his greatness is to be measured by the success achieved by him in these matters.

Here we come upon the heart of prophetic greatness. It is not by his interference in cosmic functions—by raising the dead or making a spectacular ascent to heaven, by fore-telling the petty events of the world, or making oil, wine and bread inexhaustible—that a prophet establishes his claim to the gratitude of the world. Faith in his own mission need not necessarily include participation in the meting out of divine justice on the Judgment Day, for Divine knowledge and Divine mercy scarcely need an advocate and an intercessor. The Vedānta Sūtra wisely laid down that the creation, preservation and destruction of the world are God's own business and that even released souls have no share in them.[32] But

[31] See Cheyne, *Jewish Religious Life after the Exile*, p. 98.

[32] Brahmasūtra, IV. 4.

the healthy instinct of warning others of bodily dangers ahead, to be found even among lower animals, can be profitably extended to warning against spiritual dangers as well, and we may readily believe that the keen ethical sensitivity of a prophet scents danger far ahead of the obtuse understanding of his sinful fellow-men and that his overflowing charity prompts him to warn them of the dire calamity impending. In this sense the prophet is really an incarnation of Divine compassion; for, as the Old Testament and the Qur'an would say, God does not punish a sinful city or nation without giving it a warning through a prophet.[33] Bigotry and spiritual blindness have often stood in the way of taking hint from prophetic warnings; but Divine Mercy operates before Divine Justice, and no plea is left to nations that they were overtaken by disaster without a preliminary warning.

Now, prophetic warning has always had reference to a defective or degrading conception of the nature of God and to the adoption of an unethical conduct towards His creation, specially the world of sentient beings. We shall have occasion to treat them in some detail in succeeding lectures; here we shall content ourselves with simply referring to these two major tasks of a prophetic career. Possibly in the last analysis the two problems would be found to be one, for man's conception of Divine nature determines his conduct towards God's creation, and, conversely, man's attitude towards the world determines his conception of the nature of God. But prophets have generally treated both as independent problems, as the human mind is not so consistent that the purification of faith would automatically lead to social concord or that proneness to social charity would immediately purify personal religion. Contrary instances are too painfully numerous in history to justify the belief that a pure faith means a pure conduct--too often has religion ended with an intellectual illumination without purifying the emotions and the will.

The magnitude of a prophet's task can be seen from the fact that he has to rouse a whole social group into a conscious-

[33] Amos 3.7; Qur'an, xviii. 57-8.

ness of its religious and moral imperfections and of the necessity of abandoning its old beliefs and practices. Very often his lone figure stands out clear against a background of sordidness and social iniquity and makes the surrounding gloom all the more visible by contrast. True, he is found in Israel warning individuals in high places against their cruel and irreligious lives; but these persons really stand as symbols of the tribe in which such things are permitted and condoned. A society that tolerates corruption at the top and has not the courage to condemn its leaders badly needs the service of one who is not afraid to champion the cause of righteousness and truth even at grave personal risks, and prophecy gains immensely in prestige when power mends its ways at its bidding. Prophets have very often found themselves in opposition both to civil power and to religious aristocracy—to princes as well as to priests, the one standing generally for unethical conduct and the other for soulless religious formality. They have sometimes, indeed, served as unconscious mouthpieces of the inarticulate protests of the dissatisfied and the oppressed sections of the community, and when they have thus voiced the general sentiments of the social group their success has been immense and abiding. To use a biological analogy, then there is not a continuous, slight, insensible variation but a mutation of social thinking and social habit. But often they have had to set to work against the whole social group, and only faith in their mission and infinite patience have enabled them to persist in their preaching. Under such conditions their faith has spread very slowly indeed; just remember that it took Muhammad nearly ten years to get a following of fifty persons and that Zarathustra could get only one follower in the same period of time.[34]

What prophecy can achieve in the religious life of a nation is best seen in Jewish history.[35] As distinguished

[34] Stubbe, *op. cit.*, p. 84; *Faiths of the World*, p. 369 (gives Muhammad fifty followers in five years); art. ZOROASTRIANISM in ERE. xii. 862.

[35] Pre-Mosaic Judaism was, as Lods observes, polydaemonism tinged with polytheism. There was belief in a number of mysterious powers, ill-defined at the beginning but gradually taking on definite personal form and becoming localised in

from the class of professional seers and soothsayers, who made a livelihood out of their strange powers of foretelling the future, there arose very early among the Israelites a class of men who did not want to be consulted but "were men of diverse callings, driven by an irresistible constraint actively to declare to Israel the word of its God."[36] They revealed to their tribes the demands of higher ethicality and purer faith, made through them by God, and promised to them, as reward, divine aid in days of adversity and prosperity alike. One of them, Moses, was credited with having led the race out of Egypt, made Yahweh the national God, and promulgated the Ten Commandments which laid the foundation of their religious and ethical greatness, while another, Samuel, was instrumental in establishing a kingdom under Saul in which the direction of national policy was to be materially under prophetic guidance. Gad and Nathan, Ahijah and Shemaiah, Elijah and Elisah, all kept a vigilant eye on the policy of the state, and by their admonitions and activities sought to maintain a theocratic ideal before the nation, and to restrain the kings from private iniquities and "political and religious obliquities."

The abandonment of a nomadic-pastoral in favour of a settled agricultural life, the establishment of a monarchy and the subsequent division of the Jewish state into the two kingdoms of North Israel (Samaria) and Judah, the multiple matrimonial relations of the kings, who wanted to humour their heathen wives, and the increase of 'mixed marriages' among all, especially the

definite sacred spots as baals or lords. There was a tendency toward monolatry in so far as there was possibly a belief in an elohim, a Supreme Being or God, but the existence of other gods was not denied and thus monotheism was yet to come.—see Lods, *Israel*, pp. 252-57.

36 Enc. Br. (14th Ed.), Vol. 18, p. 586 f; ERE. x. 388; Clemen, *Religions of the World*, p. 266 f; G. F. Moore, *His. of Rel.*, Vol. 2, Ch. II. For the distinction between seer and prophet, see Lods, *Israel*, pp. 442-48; *Dic. Bib.*, Extra Vol., p 650 f. See ERE. vii. 348 : "And on the fact of their own consciousness, the belief of their contemporaries, the unanimity of their testimony, the ethical quality of their teaching, and the beneficent results of their labours a strong foundation is laid for the truth of their assumption that they were the organs or instruments of the Most High."

upper classes, the building of the temple at Jerusalem by Solomon [37] and at Bethel and Dan by Jeroboam together with the persistence of the Samaritan sanctuary on Mount Gerizim in Shechem and of other high places, where alone originally offerings used to be made, brought endless complications into the religious life of the nation. The simple sacrifice on the altar in the open on a high place was replaced by a system of complicated temple-service, minute details of which were laid down in law-books, and in priestly codes which were suitably amended from time to time to find room for revised rituals. In place of the Ark of the Covenant, which had sufficed for Solomon's Temple, were set up gilded images of Yahweh in the form of a bull (the golden calf, denounced by Hosea) in Jeroboam's temples at Bethel and Dan, and to keep up the show and pomp of worship, the gift of the king had to be replaced by a regular national levy or sacred tithe of agricultural and pastoral products.[38] Bamôth (raised altars) to Yahweh with or without images were strewn all over the country, and Jerusalem had numbers of them in its streets.[39] Images of protective and functional deities were installed in households, thus continuing the primitive polytheism of the race in spite of the Mosaic revelation. But while religious symbols and formalities increased, the ethical aspect of communal life suffered comparative neglect, with the effect that the widow and the orphan were robbed of their riches, the poor were oppressed and left uncared for;[40] the conscience of the community was blunted in numerous ways and in place of true repentance an elaborate system of formal expiation reared its head. In religion also a spirit of *laissez faire* in relation to foreign nations prevailed, and it was freely admitted that while Yahweh was the special god of the Jews, other nations had also their own gods like Chemosh, Dagon,

37 For the syncretistic character of this temple and the pagan influence upon its construction, see Lods, *Israel*, pp. 414-15.

38 Robertson Smith, *Rel. of the Semites*, p. 246 f (esp. p. 251).

39 See Kuenen, *National Religions and Universal Religions*, p. 76.

40 Robertson Smith, *op. cit.*, p. 249.

Ashtoreth, Baal, Milcom, Molech and others.[41] Nay, the multiplication of the sanctuaries of Yahweh himself revived the dying embers of a primitive belief in local deities, as in Egypt and Assyria ; and to the popular mind the Yahweh that thundered in Sinai or reposed in Shiloah, the Yahweh that ruled in Zion or Gerizim, and the Yahweh that figured in Dan or Bethel, Beersheba or Hebron, were not always identical and practically divided among themselves the allegiance of the tribes.[42] It was only after the reform of Josiah that Jerusalem acquired its importance as the sole sanctuary of God in the eyes of the nation (which it retained in spite of the temporary revival of worship at Bethel by the special permission of the Assyrian king after the destruction of its own Temple in 586 B.C.).[43] Sacred prostitution also effected its entrance, in spite of Deuteronomic prohibition, into the temples, which were also permitted to be used for secular purposes.[44] Israel fairly threatened to lapse back not only into its ancient polytheism and idolatry but also into moral corruption and religious inanity, culminating in human sacrifices to Yahweh.

Against this general decline of religious ideals the prophets waged an unceasing war till the spiritual gifts of a minority became the inheritance of the nation as a whole. Their task was indeed facilitated by the fact that the nation, even in the darkest days of spiritual degradation, did not forsake Yahweh altogether—what it did rather was to join gods with God and to offer oblations and sacrifices to Him to the neglect of the spiritual side of worship. Although from very early times there was prophetic organisation as a national institution and the Rechabites kept to the ancestral tradition of nomadic life, monotheistic religion and simple worship without sacrifice and barbarous rites, the nation had chosen to follow false and fanatical prophets who had no objection to

[41] For Canaanite gods, see Lods, *Israel*, pp. 120-42.

[42] See G. F. Moore, *His. of Rel.*. Vol. 2, p. 23; Lods, *Israel*, p. 407; for the origin of the different Yahwehs, see Lods, *Israel*, pp. 156, 160.

[43] Lods, *op. cit.*, p. 413.

[44] *Ibid*, pp. 409, 450.

render homage to pagan gods and who fanned the political ambitions of rulers and led them to evil paths by lulling their conscience with the picture of God as an indulgent being whose stern justice might be easily averted by propitiation. Higher prophecy in Israel is characterised by a middle path between the opportunism of the false prophets and the conservatism of the Rechabites—it did not abandon the ideal of national greatness but spiritualised its significance. The Jews were the chosen people of Yahweh and Yahweh was the God of Israel—the nation or its rulers could not break this covenant without dire consequences.

It appears that the earlier prophets were more concerned about the purity of faith than about purity of conduct, more about tribal solidarity than about individual fortune,[45] although protests against the misdeeds of kings, as of David by Nathan and of Ahab by Elijah, were not absolutely unknown. The reason is obvious : the Jews were still surrounded on all sides by pagan tribes, who offered worship to molten or graven images and with whom matrimonial relations and exchange of culture were rapidly taking place. So, to guard the national allegiance to Yahweh, it was necessary to resist lapses into the idolatry that was so universal all around, especially when even Levites could be found officiating in Canaanite sanctuaries of Baals.[46] Immorality was a lesser evil than idolatry as it did not threaten the covenant with Yahweh. So God is made to tolerate the seven hundred wives and three hundred concubines of Solomon but not his worship of the gods of his pagan wives, while David's murder of Uriah the Hittite to get his wife was partially pardoned solely because David scrupulously kept the covenant with God. Elijah's murder of the four hundred and fifty prophets of Baal (we are not told of the fate of the four hundred prophets of the

[45] Marti, *Religion of the Old Testament*, p. 122.

[46] For the relation of Yahweh to pagan gods, see Lods, *Israel*, p. 403 f. Elijah and Elisha do not seem to have denounced the Bull-Yahweh worship in N. Israel. - See Addis, *Hebrew Religion*, p. 95 Lods, *Israel*, p. 411.

Asherah[47] which Ahab had made) is slurred over, presumably because it glorified Yahweh, while, on the other hand, Ahab's family was cursed probably more for his idolatry than for his unlawful possession of Naboth's vineyard.[48] It does not appear that even of the system of killing infants either as foundation-sacrifices or in fulfilment of the command in the old Book of the Covenant, of which Canaanite parallels are known from archaeological remains,[49] there was any great prophetic denunciation. Ahaz who introduced this abomination[50] does not seem to have roused prophetic wrath, and his grandson Manasseh provoked the prophets, the servants of the Lord, to denounce him, primarily for his idolatry and not for his filling Jerusalem with innocent blood from one end to another.

To the lasting credit of the prophets, who left their messages in writing from the middle of the eighth century to the middle of the fifth century before Christ, be it said that they changed practically the whole character of the ancient Hebrew religion and transformed a nation into a church. In their hands Yahweh was transformed from a national God into the God of the whole earth[51] so that no room was left for the gods of other nations or countries. Of course, the idea that Israel was the elect of Yahweh did not disappear nor the idea that He had his chosen seat in Zion; but the prophets, beginning with Amos, showed that its implication was that Israel's responsibility, because of the trust reposed in her, was correspondingly greater and that her defaults could be

47 W. Robertson Smith considers this to be a later interpolation and a confusion between Ashera and Astarte, the female partner of Baal.—See *Religion of the Semites*, p. 189 f.

48 For the vindication of Ahab, see Lods, *op. cit.*, pp. 421-22. Lods thinks that the curse was for the murder of Naboth and his sons and he sees in this a sensible deepening of the conception of the righteousness of Yahweh (see *Israel*, p. 423).

49 Lods, *op. cit.*, pp. 285-86; also pp. 89, 99.

50 But see the cases of Jephthah the Gileadite and also of Hiel the Beth-elite (1 K 16.34).

51 Addis, *Hebrew Religion*, p. 152; Marti, *Rel. of the OT*, p. 131; Kuenen, *Nat. Rel. & Uni. Rel.*, p. 119.

less tolerated by God.[52] The prophets could easily point to the many sins of the nation as a whole and predict divine justice for its iniquities, the instrument of chastisement being at first Assyria and then Babylon. The old idea that it was a matter of prestige with Yahweh to fight Israel's battles and to lead her to victory was abandoned.[53] Yahweh is on the side of righteousness and He punishes not only foreign nations but also the Jews for their sins.[54] Such a God's favour could not be bought by sacrifices and rituals when the conditions of righteousness and true religion remained unfulfilled—that is, when images were worshipped, justice was sold, power was abused, and political expediency and state-craft overrode the interests of morality and faith. As a punishment for her sins, Israel was to drink the cup of humiliation to its bitterest dregs—the loss of political liberty in both the kingdoms, the fall of Jerusalem, the destruction of the Temple, the banishment of the nobles and priests to Babylon. Fitful efforts at reform had indeed been made by kings, presumably under prophetic counsel,[55] as when Hezekiah destroyed the brazen serpent which was worshipped in the Temple; but again and again had the nation gone back to its pagan rites and admitted foreign gods into the sanctuary and permitted immorality and cruelty within the temple precincts. Even Yahweh's patience could be tired out by such repeated lapses, and then the nation was bound to face His wrath.

But even in this conception of divine justice the prophets could improve upon primitive thought. It is not out of wrath that Yahweh will punish Israel, but out of love. Hosea compares Israel going after other gods with his own adulterous wife whom he must punish but not without regret and love. Yahweh wants His love to be reciprocated, and not sacrifices

52 Marti, *op. cit.*, p. 167. Amos 3.2.

53 Marti, *op. cit.*, p. 165.

54 Elijah first ventured on the strange message that Jehovah wrought by national defeat no less than by national victory.—See Addis, *Hebrew Religion*, p. 134.

55 Kuenen, *op. cit.*, p. 149.

offered to Him or sabbaths and new moons and solemn assemblies observed in His honour, which were not only futile, as Amos had said, but positively pernicious. Hosea predicts the humiliation of the kingdom of Israel as the punishment of her sins, but at the same time holds out the hope that, when she repents, she will be restored to the love of Yahweh. "The children of Israel shall abide many days without king, and without prince, and without sacrifice, and without pillar, and without ephod or teraphim; afterward shall the children of Israel return, and seek the Lord their God, and David their king; and shall come with fear unto the Lord and to his goodness in the latter days."[56] "Mine heart is turned within me, my compassions are kindled together. I will not execute the fierceness of mine anger, I will not return to destroy Ephraim: for I am God, not man."[57] "And I will betroth thee unto me for ever; yea, I will betroth thee unto me in righteousness, and in judgment, and in loving-kindness, and in mercies. I will even betroth thee unto me in faithfulness: and thou shalt know the Lord."[58] Through all the major canonical prophets, pre-exilic and post-exilic—Amos, Hosea, Isaiah, Jeremiah, Ezekiel, Deutero-Isaiah—runs the same thought, namely, that Yahweh cannot put away Israel for ever,[59] and although, in accordance with His ethical character, He must punish Israel for her iniquities and even use foreign powers as rods of His wrath,[60] yet ultimately when she realises her folly Israel will be restored to Divine favour.[61] "Then will I give the peoples other and clean lips, that they may call upon the name of Yahweh and serve him with one accord."[62] When iniquity will be put away and even the Ark of the Covenant will be forgotten, "at that time they shall call Jerusalem the throne of the Lord; and all the nations shall be

[56] Hosea 3.4-5.

[57] Hosea 11.8-9.

[58] Hosea 2.19-20.

[59] Kuenen, *op. cit.*, p. 107 f.

[60] *Ibid*, p. 116.

[61] Amos 5.18; see Addis, *Hebrew Religion*, p. 142.

[62] See Kuenen, *op. cit.*, p. 127.

gathered unto it, to the name of the Lord, to Jerusalem: neither shall they walk any more after the stubbornness of their evil heart."[63] Israel shall be the servant of Yahweh, a light of the Gentiles, the religious teacher of all nations, so that Yahweh's commandments and thorah may be proclaimed to all nations and His salvation may reach to the end of the earth.[64] Israel is to sacrifice herself for the redemption of mankind[65]—an expression that was to have such poignant significance later on in the history of Christianity. She must have trust in Yahweh—in quietness and confidence shall be her strength: "if ye will not believe, ye shall not be established."[66] We may sum up the achievements of the Hebrew prophets in the following words of Driver and Peake:[67] "The activity of the prophets was largely called for by national crises. They were moral reformers, religious teachers, political advisers. They held up before a back-sliding people the ideals of human duty, religious truth and national policy. They expanded and developed, and applied to new situations, the truths which in a germinal form they had inherited. The nature and attributes of God; His gracious purposes towards man; man's relation to God and the consequences it involves: the true nature of religious service; the call to repentance as a condition of God's favour; the ideal of character and action which each should strive to realise; the responsibilities of office and position; the claims of mercy and philanthropy, justice and integrity; indignation against the oppression of the weak and the unprotected; ideals of a blissful future, when the troubles of the present will be over, and men will bask in the enjoyment of righteousness and felicity—these, and such as these, are the themes which are ever in the prophets' mouths and on which they enlarge with unwearied eloquence and power."

[63] Jer. 3.17.

[64] Is. 49.6.

[65] Enc. Br., Vol. 18, p. 588; Addis, *Hebrew Religion*, p. 217.

[66] Is 7.9; 30.15.

[67] Enc. Br., Vol. 3, p. 503.

It was a great thing to have inwardised the religion. Yahweh is not holy in the sense that a magic fluid issues from His Ark, and overpowers and kills the bold, the inquisitive and the careless, as it is said to have done the people of Bethshemesh and also Uzzah, the driver of the sacred cart, although no moral turpitude was involved in their conduct.[68] He is holy because He hates sin and demands atonement therefor or else punishes for unrepented misdeed. By the time we reach Jeremiah we find that Yahweh's interest is as much in personal holiness as in national purity, and that it is their own sins rather than their ancestors' that individuals have to pay for in divine displeasure and personal suffering. When we remember how tribal in their conceptions nomadic races generally are and how strong the sense of collective responsibility was among the Hebrews from the earliest times, so much so that the nation was supposed to succeed and suffer as a whole—especially from the acts of its kings or leaders, the discovery of individual responsibility was no small achievement of the prophets.[69] But they achieved something more. The pious fraud or the happy accident by which Josiah was put in possession of " the book of the teaching " through the chief priest of Jerusalem[70] not only enabled him to establish the single sanctuary of Yahweh but to recast the more primitive Decalogue in which the ceremonial aspect preponderated over the ethical. This book, now known as the Deuteronomy, purified faith (forbidding graven images of all kinds, and not merely molten images, as did the older Decalogue) and taught love of God and obedience to His commandments. The last one was to have far-reaching consequences in later times as henceforth the task of the prophets lessened and that of the scribes or interpreters of the Law increased : but the Babylonian catastrophe retarded that process for some time more and Jeremiah could still improve upon the conception of faith, as preached by Isaiah, by teaching that it is only the grace of God that can enable a man to serve Him with zeal and devotion

[68] 1 Sam. 6.19; 2 Sam. 6.7.

[69] Marti, *Rel. of OT*, p. 173; Ezek. 18.1-9.

[70] Addis, *Hebrew Religion*, p 188 f.

and that Yahweh wants people to circumcise not their foreskin but their heart.[71]

It is one of those misfortunes that meet us frequently in religious history that the Hebrew religion, which won such glorious battles under prophetic leadership, should suddenly stop in its career of spiritual emancipation. The destruction of the Temple and the removal of the leaders of thought to Babylon, which were instrumental in bringing the Synagogue into being (as sacrifices were forbidden outside Jerusalem), proved at first boons in disguise. But the nation's heart refused to be reconciled to banishment from the immediate presence of Yahweh, and a change in the royal policy at Babylon enabled the nation to rebuild its Temple (516-15 B.C.) and to return to Jerusalem not only with chastened thoughts but also with borrowed materials of culture. Religion passed over into the legalistic stage, the gulf between the Jews and the Samaritans became more widely fixed, the Zadokites practically deposed the Levites from higher priestly functions, circumcision and sabbath were more strenuously insisted on, and even the annual festivals were increased and the system of sin-offering was instituted.[72] The great names of Ezekiel and Ezra, not to mention the minor names of Nehemiah, Haggai, Zechariah, " Malachi " and Third Isaiah, are intimately associated with this restoration of ancient faith; and although faint echoes of the Temple being a " house of prayer for all nations " persisted in prophetic utterances, it was clear that the main current of thought was anti-Gentilic, so much so that the Jews had to send away their foreign wives

71 It is interesting to note that Bernard Shaw in *The Adventures of the Black Girl in her search for God* distinguishes three stages in the development of the Jewish conception of God. The first stage is represented (pp. 9-10) by the ceremonious worship of a tribal God full of wrath and vengeance and demanding cruel sacrifices—the type of God that Noah is supposed to have worshipped. The second stage is represented (pp. 11-12) by an attempt to justify the ways of God to man but not very successfully, as in the Book of Job. The third stage is represented (p. 18) by the religion of the prophets, of whom Micah is the representative: " This is a third God," she said; " and I like him much better than the one who wanted sacrifices and the one who wanted me to argue with him so that he might sneer at my weakness and ignorance."

72 Marti, *op. cit.*, p. 208.

and the children born of them.[73] Ezekiel's more moderate measures and the Law of Holiness propounded in his time had to make room for the more drastic measures of Ezra who had the priestly code, brought from Babylon, enforced in Jerusalem. The new legislation pushed back all Hebrew religious customs to the beginning of things, varnished the unsavoury tales about the patriarchs and set these up as models of piety and character.[74] It crystallised the concept of Satan possibly after Zoroastrian model,[75] tended to put on the same level of importance ceremony and purity, increased the importance of the High Priest and, while diffusing higher standards of moral life, made religion more formal.[76] When, by the beginning of the first century B.C., the canonical books, now known as the Old Testament, were fixed, no scope was left for prophetic inspiration,[77] with the effect that Yahweh took on a transcendent character and between Him and man was interposed the Law (and latterly the whole system of angels, and also certain abstractions as in Zoroastrianism).[78] Even the Messianic salvation as the reward of ceremonial observances was based more on political than on religious foundations.[79] In Yahweh's realm very little room was left for the Gentiles, who could not only not offer pure oblations to Him but also had no share in His salvation : Deutero-Isaiah's teaching on the subject was totally rejected and salvation was regarded as a reward of ceremonial piety and not a gift of Yahweh.[80] As a matter of fact, the tough-minded attitude of the patriarchal age that morality is to be practised without reference to a

[73] *Ibid*, pp. 212-13.

[74] Marti, *op. cit.*, pp. 195, 201; Lods, *op. cit.*, p. 324 : "There is not a single ritual, custom or sacred object whose origin can with certainty be traced back to the Mosaic period, not even the ark." See Canon Lindsay Dewar, *Imagination and Religion*, p. 38 f.

[75] Marti, *op. cit.*, p. 194; Pringle-Pattison, *Studies in the Phil. of Rel.*, Ch. XI. Persian Influences : Jewish and Christian Apocalyptic.

[76] See Kuenen, *op. cit.*, p. 157 f.

[77] Marti, *op. cit.*, p. 186.

[78] Marti, *op. cit.*, p. 217, also 222; see Kuenen, *op. cit.*, p. 159.

[79] Marti, *op. cit.*, p. 227.

[80] Is. 42.1-6; 49.6; 52.10. See Pringle-Pattison, *Studies in Phil. of Religion*, pp. 153-54.

future reward,[81] namely, salvation, gave way before the tender-minded apocalyptic expectation of an age of reward for virtue.[82] The genuine prophetic fire was now extinguished, and "any Jewish writer who believed that he had a religious message for his nation, a message of hope and encouragement, of consolation or warning, after the manner of the prophets, had to put his words into the mouth of one of the worthies of old time, if they were to carry any weight or find acceptance with the religious public." It is not till we come to the time of Jesus that we find another prophet who could inveigh against religious formality with the same tone of authority as did the great pre-exilic prophets of Israel. No wonder that Jesus was regarded by some as Elijah or some other older prophet reborn.[83]

If we compare the Hebrew prophets with the mediæval saints of India, we shall have some idea of the secret of prophetic success in Israel. There were, first of all, certain external advantages. The field of activity was small and any prophetic achievement was quickly reported all over the country. The population was more or less homogeneous, and, in spite of the rivalry between North Israel and Judah, all prophets spoke in the name of the same national God. There was, again, a strong prophetic tradition, and more or less organised bands or schools of prophets, who lived by their peculiar aptitude for foretelling and divination, existed in close association with the ruling powers and apparently wielded great influence. There was, again, no such difficulty as caste prejudice against a prophet—a farmer, a citizen, a priest and a follower of an older prophet could all get an equal hearing if they had any message to preach. Further, the prophets were not hampered by too much literary tradition, and any suggestion towards the improvement of ancestral faith that could enable the better minds of the nation to withstand the insidious advances of surrounding paganism and to convert

81 See Pringle-Pattison, *Idea of God*, pp. 43-44.

82 For the distinction between prophecy and apocalypse, see Pringle-Pattison. *Studies in the Phil. of Rel.*, p. 151 f.

83 Mk. 6.14-6; Mat. 17.10-13.

monolatry into monotheism was readily accepted. It is indeed true that there was kingly opposition, especially when prophecy directly affected the private conduct or the political diplomacy of the ruler; but very few prophets had to feel the agony, the persecution or the loneliness of Jeremiah. Then, again, the uncertain political future of the nation, sandwiched as it was between Egypt and Assyria (and, later on, Babylon) and situated in the midst of tribes, alien in thought and disposition, was bound to invest those able to foretell the immediate or remote future of the race with a certain amount of added importance. No prophet allowed the greatness of Israel to depart from popular thought; even her chastisement was divinely ordained to bring her ultimate triumph and exaltation. To a nation, ambitious to rise but temporarily in distress, a political message, supposed to be divinely delivered, could not fail to be attractive; as a matter of fact, Jeremiah had to pay the penalty of his prophecy because of its defeatistic attitude towards national ambition and pride.

In India, for full nine hundred years, seers, mythologists and theologians were simultaneously at work. During the period from the 7th to the 16th century when the later Purāṇas were being written and the philosophical systems were being expanded there was a regular stream of devoted men in both North and South India who failed to find satisfaction in the ritualistic practices of Hindu religion and in the rigidity of its caste-distinctions. The Tamil saints, the Mahratta mystics, the Vaisnavite poets of North India and those who, like Kabir and Nanak, came under Muhammadan influence all preached against a system of worship in which birth and not religious merit was the qualification for religious ministration and in which materials and mantras usurped the rightful place of devotion and social service. That the whole reform-movement was not prompted by hostility to the Brahmanic class is evident from the fact that many of the religious leaders were themselves Brahmans and that many Brahmans enrolled themselves as disciples of non-Brahman reformers. While tolerant in many cases of the existing polytheism and even of idolatry among the masses, the religious leaders themselves were mostly imbued with a deep monotheistic spirit, even though different saints called God by different names like Rāma, Kṛṣṇa, Hari, Śiva, etc. They preached their message in songs, hymns and verses through the vernaculars of India and could therefore make a direct appeal to the hearts of the masses to whom Sanskrit mantras were an unmeaning jargon. Although the majority of the disciples of these reformers came from the lower strata of Hindu society and failed to prove able and zealous apostles of their creeds, it cannot be denied that these movements did much to expose the shortcomings of Hindu religion as then practised, and planted in the land, especially in North India, small bands of devout men alienated to a greater or less extent from the caste-system and the religious practices of orthodox Hinduism.

That they failed to leaven the entire community like the Hebrew prophets is due to a number of causes. They could not all preach in the name of one and the same God—polytheism was then as now the prevailing form of faith and although the saints intended to preach monotheism the names they used for God were bound to rouse sectarian jealousy, while a strange name for God would have made no popular appeal. We must remember that even Moses and Muhammad had to use an already familiar name for designating God in their revelations—they did not coin the words 'Yahweh' and 'Allāh' themselves.[84] It so happens therefore that while the Tamil saints poured forth their lyrics in praise of Śiva, the Alvars and the North Indian saints used Vaisnavite names, with the effect that as there was no national God like the Yahweh of the Hebrews the reformed movements made no universal appeal. When we remember that even the Brahma Sūtra of Bādarāyaṇa was twisted like a nose of wax by learned philosophers in the interests of sectarianism we can easily understand how deep was the sectarian feeling in India and

[84] Lods, *Israel*, p. 320 f. See also R. H. Charles, *Eschatology, Hebrew, Jewish and Christian*, p. 6.

what prospect there was of any reformer being able to reconcile conflicting faiths under the banner of a single God. Truly the name was greater than the God, as so often averred by religious thinkers of this period; people could be persuaded to change deep-rooted religious convictions but not the name of their God.[85]

One other fact prevented the wide diffusion of any reformed cult. The Indian saints were mostly imbued with the sense of personal weakness and what they generally sought to achieve through their devotion was not so much regeneration of the masses as personal salvation, the most notable exception being Caitanya who attempted a mass-movement through his *saṅkīrtana*. But their personal influence and their preaching to a small circle bore fruit and at least one great religion—Sikhism—owes its origin to one such teacher, *viz.*, Nānak. Here again, as in Judaism, political circumstances favoured cohesion and growth: it is not unlikely that but for imperial oppression the Sikhs would have remained in the same insignificant position of a minor sect as the followers of Rāmānanda, Kabir, Dādu, Charan Das and other mediæval reformers are at present. What gave these minor sects their lease of life is the necessity of a less costly and more direct faith than what the ritualistic and impersonal religious organisation of Hinduism afforded.[86] The attractive personality of the reformer formed the nucleus of their faith and he was, or very soon became, God incarnate to the followers, with the effect that instead of reforming the original religion each reformer became the founder of a sect with only indirect influence upon the parent social and religious organisation. The rapidity and ease with which each religious genius becomes a god in India and stories of miracles gather round his personality, prevent the spread of the reform to the community as a whole which, though often ready to admit reasonable evolution and purification in faith, is not always willing to accord that pre-eminence to the reformer which is demanded

[85] For a similar Egyptian belief, see ERE. vii. 189.

[86] Rhys Davids thinks that costly sacrifice was one of the causes of the rise of Buddhism.—See *Buddhist India*, p. 242.

by him personally or by his followers. The Hebrew prophets too had disciples and schools, but they were never accorded divine honours; the only one who claimed and was given divine distinction was Jesus, and he failed to purify Judaism itself and became instead the founder of a separate sect. We should remember in this connection that Christianity became a religion some time after Christ's death—his immediate followers had no intention of being regarded as anything but Jews with this peculiarity that they believed that the expected Messiah had come and died and that faith must be mediated through this new Messiah. The message of Christianity was regarded as being ultimately meant for humanity at large;[87] but as Judaism had ceased to admit Gentiles within its fold nothing was left but to forsake the Jewish Church and to proclaim a new religion.[88] Even within the Christian community the question of Gentile conversion was quite acute, and only the forceful personality of Paul could triumph over the opposition of Peter and other Apostles who were for enforcing all the Jewish rites in the case of the Gentiles also.[89] Some of the mediæval saints of India had the similar problem of absorbing Muhammadans within their Church, and it is these that had to recede most from orthodoxy and to found a separate sect; for Hinduism, while tolerant of religious experiments and even of atheism, had always insisted on conformity to its social organisation as a pre-condition of recognition and it is the defiance of this organisation that made rapprochement impossible. Even the intellectuals, who on philosophic grounds had at this time been preaching a purer intellectual faith, were devoid of that Semitic urge to force a reform on the masses and preferred to follow instead the divine advice, "A wise man should not shake the convictions of the ignorant who are attached to action, but, acting with devotion himself,

[87] That this intention was not always present before Christ's mind has been pointed out by Basanta Coomar Bose, *Christianity*, p. 49. See Pringle-Pattison, *Studies in the Phil. of Rel.*, p. 164.

[88] See Harnack, *History of Dogma*, Vol. I, p. 43.

[89] Reinach, *Orpheus*, p. 270.

he should make them apply themselves to all actions.''[90] What happened, on the contrary, was that to the gods of the community were added deified teachers and preachers, and new rituals were added to old; the evolution of purity in faith and conduct in local areas and small sects was counterbalanced by the extravagant and errant fancies of later Vaiṣṇava writers. A large-scale absorption within Hinduism of Buddhists, seeking shelter from Muhammadan oppression, not only introduced the questionable practices of a decaying cult but also social complications in Northern India, as the caste-system insisted on imposing disabilities on, and assigning lower social position to, the new converts. The old bottle refused to admit the new wine for fear of going to pieces.[91]

Let us return now to the secret of prophetic success. While philosophers, theologians and ethicists have been able to influence and modify religious beliefs with the help of a slow process of filtration along with the diffusion of culture and the development of general intelligence, prophets have succeeded in spreading a contagion of faith, because, while the former are regarded as talking the language of man, the latter are looked upon as speaking the voice of God. Not only are their utterances supposed to be divinely inspired but the prophets themselves are possessed with "an irresistible sense of vocation."[92] The *gopīs* (cowherdesses) of Vṛndāvana (Brindaban), according to Vaiṣṇava accounts, used to leave everything precipitously behind when Kṛṣṇa's flute sounded on the banks of the Yamunā: so did the prophets when the divine call came to

[90] Bh. G. 3.26.

[91] The same process is in operation just now although the present reform movements in Hinduism are all secularly conceived and directed. It is easy to initiate *śuddhi* (purification) movement in imitation of the absorption of the *vrātyas* mentioned in Brāhmaṇa literature. But it is more difficult to find a suitable means of making the new converts an organic part of the socio-religious system, as Hindu society has lost in the mean time much of its earlier plasticity; and it is still more difficult to create a new caste altogether unless large-scale conversion and intermixture of castes and communities facilitate the formation of such a new caste. The Purāṇas mention many inter-castes unknown to earlier writers although the Bhagavadgītā looks upon the confusion of the *varṇas* (colours and castes) as ominous for the human race (Bh. G. i. 40-2).

[92] Pringle-Pattison, *Studies in the Phil. of Rel.*, p. 165 f.

them. Buddha and Caitanya leave their young wives behind, Christ forsakes his family and Amos his herd and sycomore trees, from an inner impulse to obey the call of religion; even the child Jeremiah felt the irresistible call to prophesy in lisping numbers just as Dhruva and Prahlāda are said to have sung the praises of Hari in their infancy. "Yahweh has spoken, who will not prophesy?" And God reveals His wisdom not to the learned but to the illiterate so that there might be no doubt that the message was not forged in intelligence but received in intuition. A Jesus, a Muhammad, a Kabir, a Rāmakṛṣṇa—what frail vehicles has God chosen through the ages to send His message to mankind! The sway that the prophets have held on men's minds is due to the fact that their messages were regarded as coming from God and they spoke with an authority not their own.[93]

But how exactly this divine message is communicated to man will, from the nature of the case, remain obscure. National traditions and contemporary beliefs have coloured all theories on the subject, and even the prophets themselves are not agreed about the method of their own inspiration. Broadly speaking, prophetic inspiration can be divided into four classes. These are (1) message by a divine incarnation, (2) message communicated direct by God to a prophet, (3) message communicated to a prophet through angelic or some other agency, and (4) message found by the prophet in his own heart, the rational order of development being roughly the order of the above statement. What exactly takes place in prophetic inspiration it is impossible to assess in view of the facts that inspiration is rare, peculiar and private, that divine communication has to use a vehicle of expression very much conditioned by tradition, training and temperament, that genuine records are difficult to obtain for they very soon

[93] This theory of inspiration as ecstasy is less widely held at present. It is now believed that instead of the powers and faculties of the soul being suspended in inspiration they are infinitely exalted, "the supernatural intensifying the natural." Inspiration becomes enthusiasm or quickening of the human spirit by the Divine breath.—See ERE. vii. 847. See also I Cor. 2.15.

become overlaid with extraneous matters, and that the prophets themselves are not always fitted by their condition of mind or power of self-analysis to distinguish the uprush of unconscious wish and phantasy, the revival of forgotten memory, and the revelation of objective truth. The many glaring mistakes about the facts of nature and history to be found in every scripture have been sought to be laid at the door of prophetic incapacity to receive and express the divine message completely,[94] the necessity of communicating through him only such ideas as his contemporaries would understand and appreciate (although at a later stage of culture these would turn out to be false), the occasional lapse of inspiration (intermittent inspiration) during which time prophetic utterances have the value of personal opinions only,[95] or the incapacity of the followers to commit prophetic utterances to memory or writing and to transmit them to posterity accurately through speech or other symbols. They have also been regarded as embellishments and fabrications of a later age calculated to round off prophetic revelations with such cosmological, sociological and historical data as were known and understood by the writers themselves or in their own times or were considered by them as suitable to show off the triumph, the superiority and the importance of their own creed. They are a part of the unconscious glorification of the religion in question, when not due to downright ignorance or pious fraud.

Hinduism affords the best illustration of the first kind of prophetic inspiration, although, coupled with it, there is the widespread theological belief that God does not create the truths He is supposed to reveal. Even the divine mind has to take cognizance of eternal and immutable laws

[94] See ERE. vii. 348.

[95] See ERE. vii. 349 for the view of St. Paul on inspiration. It is claimed that " while the Divine power which seized the *OT* prophets was intermittent, and even that which worked in the Apostles was not without breaks and flaws, the inspiration of Jesus was continuous and perfect " (*Ibid, loc. cit.*). For the various theories advanced to explain its possibility, see Pringle-Pattison, *Studies in the Philosophy of Religion*, Ch. XVII. The Christ of the Creeds.

embodied in the Vedas, which are therefore uncreate (*apauruṣeya*) and are not involved in the general dissolution of the world at the end of each cycle of existence. Now, owing to human weakness or depravity, the perception of these truths becomes dimmed in course of time,[96] there is a general decline of spiritual vision and moral uprightness, and the necessity arises of God reincarnating himself to set matters right and to re-instruct the human race in those immutable laws of being and conduct. It is difficult to say that this has been the belief of Hinduism all along or that the Vedic seers were concerned very much with the theoretical basis of their own inspiration or that the divine incarnations were more bent upon promulgating practical laws of human conduct than upon righting grievous iniquities; but at a later time the belief grew up that truth and morality were preached by God Himself either by His own incarnated life or by direct instruction. Thus Manu only lays down the laws of spiritual life as heard from Vivasvān (Sūrya), who had them from God Himself, and he communicated them to Ikṣāku from whom, through a succession of royal sages, the world received its spiritual wisdom.[97] The three major gods, Brahmā, Viṣṇu (or Sūrya) and Śiva, were credited with having taught the human race, through minor gods or sages, not only the truths of religion and morality but also cosmic happenings, names of things, arts and crafts, and social and political events of bygone ages: hence God is significantly defined as the first preceptor, the teacher of teachers, in the Nyāya treatise *Kusumāñjali*.[98] This divine function of instruction is certainly an advance upon the Greek idea that gods roamed the earth in the guise of men only to take note of human conduct.

The exact prophetic function of each incarnation is difficult to establish and the number of incarnations also did not remain uniform in different accounts. The different incarnations—the Fish, the Tortoise, the Boar, the Man-Lion,

[96] See Manu Sam., i. 82.
[97] Bh.G. iv. 1-2; but see Manu Sam., i. 58-59.
[98] See ERE. vii. 103.

the Dwarf, Paraśurāma, Rāmacandra, Balarāma (or Vāsudeva), Buddha and Kalki—were associated with Viṣṇu-Nārāyaṇa at different times[99] and were also added to in different Purāṇas to make room for additional teachers like Nārada, Kapila, Vyāsa, etc.[100] In the Bhāgavata Purāṇa such incarnations are regarded as innumerable,[101] though the later religious literature has not the boldness to assert like the Śatapatha Brāhmaṇa,[102] in the theistic sense of incarnation, that " men are Viṣṇus "—a saying which is echoed only in the pantheistic sense in the later Vedānta formula " All are Brahman." That only a Divine incarnation can preach the message of truth was certainly not the belief of pre-Gīta seers and sages, for the idea of incarnation itself was of slow growth and throughout the whole range of Upaniṣadic literature the term " avatāra " occurs twice or thrice in late sectarian books of the Vaiṣṇavas, who alone defended the doctrine with any kind of system. The other gods, Brahmā, Śiva and Śakti, generally teach without incarnations the spiritual truths necessary for human knowledge and guidance.

But when the Vaiṣṇava theory triumphed in the end, most of the prominent religious teachers of later times were supposed to be gods reborn for the instruction of the world. Śaṅkara is Śiva himself and Rāmānuja is Śeṣa, the Serpent-king, reborn.[103] Caitanya is an incarnation of Kṛṣṇa and Rādhā together,[104] and many of the mediæval saints were likewise incarnations of this or that god. Even Buddhism caught the infection and Buddha was regarded as not having been born but as having voluntarily left heaven and assumed a human shape on earth to relieve suffering and teach man-

99 H. C. Roychaudhuri, *Early History of the Vaisnava Sect*, pp. 104-05. At Puri Viṣṇu in the form of Jagannātha takes the place of Buddha, and this probably reflects with accuracy the supplanting of Buddhism by Vaiṣṇavism in that locality.

100 See Agni Purāṇa, Ch. 2 f; Garuḍa Purāṇa, Ch. 1; Bhāgavata Purāṇa, i, 3. See ERE. 7.193 fn.

101 Bhāg. Pur., i. 3.26.

102 S. P. Br., v. 2.5.2-3. (quoted in H. C. Roychaudhuri, *Early His. of the Vais. Sect*, p. 64). For the anticipation of the Avatāra idea in the Brāhmaṇas, see Belvalkar and Ranade, *Creative Period*, p. 63 f.

103 Wilson, *Hindu Religion*, p. 16; Macnicol, *Indian Theism*, p. 71.

104 Kennedy, *The Chaitanya Movement*, pp. 94-96.

kind.[105] He had come again and again in the past as occasions demanded and will do so again in future.[106] Jainism did not, it is true, regard its prophets as incarnations; but it deified them when dead[107] and also believed that Mahāvīra was not the first to teach the law of life although, unlike Buddha, he was the last of the twenty-four Tīrthaṅkaras of the present age of the world.[108] Christianity too fought for long over the question of Christ's manifestation on earth as the Logos that was made flesh and the God-man who taught the way of life and suffered for the sins of the world. We need not examine critically the arguments of Saint Augustine and Saint Anselm as to why God became man and to what extent:[109] it is enough for our purpose to point out that the necessity of a divine incarnation to teach mankind was felt quite early in the Christian Church.

The psychology of this belief is clear. Nothing can be so binding on man as divine command. A human prophet shares in the fallibility of men, and so his utterances can only be advisory but not authoritative. A divine injunction, on the other hand, is not only true for all times and places but is more likely to be obeyed, as God is the ultimate determiner of destinies and he who disobeys it does so at the peril of his soul. The very fact that many of the prophets expected or taught that their teachings would be backed by divine sanctions shows that it was felt that unless prophecy could somehow be connected with God it would fail to command attention and obedience. In the idea of God incarnating himself as man there is the additional belief that the prophetic teaching was not meant to present an impossible standard of ethical life, inasmuch as the human incarnation of God showed by actual living to what perfection of conduct and wisdom human

105 Buddhistic docetism is not unknown.—See ERE. vii. 188.

106 See M. N. Dutt Sastri, *Buddha*, Ch. VII, for facts and references; also ERE. vii. 184.

107 ERE. vii. 466.

108 For the predecessors of Mahāvīra, see Stevenson, *Heart of Jainism*, Ch. IV; Nahar and Ghosh, *Epitome of Jainism*, Appendix D; ERE. vii. 466. See also Grünwedel, *Buddhist Art in India*, p. 190.

109 See Bethune-Baker, *op. cit.*, p. 349.

nature could rise here below. It is almost certain that the process of apotheosising the prophet precedes the belief that he is a divine incarnation and that the mind, unable to comprehend how so much wisdom and goodness could reside in a mere man, ends by supposing that God (or a god) has come down below in the form of a prophet. In the theory of periodical incarnation provision is sought to be made for the relativity of revelation to the needs of the time and the intelligence of the hearers, except when it is taught that it is the same law that is preached by successive prophets (as was done by Hinduism, Jainism and Buddhism).

Those who are unable to see why God should choose to assume a human form, with all the imperfections incidental thereto, in order to enlighten man about his duties have assigned to the prophet a much humbler rôle. God is well able to communicate to man His wishes and thoughts without undergoing the trouble of descending on earth and raising ticklish questions about the exact mode and character of His earthly appearance and the relation between His abiding self and His transient manifestation. Is the essence of God partible? Was Christ of the same substance or only of a similar substance with God? Did he have a single nature or will, or two natures or wills, and what exactly was the relation between the two natures or wills if the latter supposition were correct?[110] Was Kṛṣṇa a full manifestation of Viṣṇu or only a partial one like the other avatāras? Were Paraśurāma and Rāmacandra, or Kṛṣṇa and Balarāma, independent but contemporaneous manifestations? How could one avatāra fight against another? These are some of the thorny questions that are inevitable on the theory of Prophet as a Divine Incarnation and were actually raised in Christianity and Vaiṣṇavism. To steer clear of all these difficulties, let us suppose that God has not to assume any human form to teach mankind personally; all that He has to do is to reveal Himself to a Prophet and to make known through him the laws of life. Shall we go behind

[110] See Pringle-Pattison, *Studies in the Philosophy of Religion*, Ch. XVII.

the prophetic age and suppose, like the writer of the Bṛhadāraṇyaka Upaniṣad, that Prajāpati the moral law-giver is thundering audibly to all gods, men and demons alike *da, da, da*—to be interpreted as *damyata*, 'be self-restrained,' by the gods; *datta*, 'be liberal,' by men; *dayadhvam*, 'be pitiful,' by the demons,—in other words, asking each class to control its own characteristic failing of anger, avarice and cruelty respectively?[111] Or shall we, like the writer of the Indra-Virocana episode in the Chāndogya Upaniṣad,[112] believe that Prajāpati can impart His instructions only to certain gifted individuals who have been prepared by training or temperament to receive divine communications?—that it was to Indra of the gods and Virocana of the demons that He revealed the progressive scheme of self-knowledge, by which alone is everything else obtained, and that each of them could understand it only according to his own intellect and inclination?

Experience has practically decided the issue in this matter. Every religion has been obliged to admit that spiritual insight is a gift of God and that, while every one is capable of rising to some intellectual and spiritual height by years of instruction and discipline, the revelation of the mysteries of existence and the principles of ethical conduct comes like a sudden flash of insight to the prophet. Of course, there are prophets and prophets. The Muhammadans believe, for instance, that while there have been thousands of minor prophets in all times and climes, apostles or messengers of God have been very few, the greatest of them according to the Qur'an being Noah, Abraham, Lot, Ishmael, Moses and Jesus and also, of course, Muhammad, "the seal of the prophets." The Hebrews too made a distinction between those who sought by divination and sorcery to ascertain Yahweh's will and those like Elijah, Amos, Jeremiah and others whom God inspired to prophesy, sometimes even in

[111] Bṛ. Ār. Up. 5.1-3.
[112] Ch. Up. 8.7-12.

spite of their will.[113] St. Paul again speaks of the differences in equipment of persons with peculiar gifts; " Now, ye are the body of Christ, and severally members thereof. And God hath set people within the Church to be first of all apostles, secondly prophets, thirdly teachers, then workers of miracles, then healers, helpers, administrators and speakers in tongues of various kinds." [114]

Now when God singles out Moses for receiving His laws instead of Himself descending on earth in a human form, we may very well suppose that of all the prophets of the time, Jewish and non-Jewish, Moses could alone see that a God who could materialise Himself in images, trees or stones or who could assume an animal form or even a human form, as Shamash the Sun-God is represented as doing to Hammurabi, was not wholly spiritual and formless. The difficulty is that Yahweh was represented quite anthropomorphically in the oldest (?) traditions of the Bible. To quote D'Alviella: " Yahweh moulds man like a potter; he plants the garden of Eden and walks through it in the cool of the evening like a rich Mesopotamian. Adam hears his footsteps. He comes down from heaven to see the building of the Tower of Babel. He eats and drinks with Abraham, and the latter washes his feet. He struggles with Jacob and allows himself to be overcome." We must remember, however, that all such dealings of Yahweh in human form with Adam and Abraham and Jacob were only crude Semitic myths, based mostly on Babylonian model and concocted after the return from the Exile and designed to create a belief that there was a time when even

[113] The title, *Nabi*, prophet, is used of Abraham, Isaac, and Jacob, as depositories of the worship of the one true God, but with a mission restricted to their own families; whereas Houd, Saleh, Shoaib, etc., are designated as (*Resoul*) apostles and envoys, charged with a more extended mission to the tribes of Arabia. In Moses, Jesus, and Muhammad, etc., are united the office and gift of both prophet (*nabi*) and apostle (resoul).—Rodwell's *Koran* (p. 114 f.n), xix.

See also *Foundations*, p. 97 : " A call is not the same thing as conversion. The one is a summons to a new work, the other to a new ideal; the one is merely a change of activity, the other a change of heart. Doubtless the two often go together, as for instance in the case of St. Francis of Assisi, but they are separable both in thought and experience."

[114] I Cor. 12.27-28.

the Jewish God was a tangible and visible being like the gods of the heathens but that this privilege of vision was withdrawn from a sinful world of later times. As a matter of fact, the struggle between visible and invisible God persists in the Mosaic stories all through, and even where invisibility wins, Yahweh's manifestation of Himself through voice and writing is not supposed to affect his formlessness.[115] But the tradition of visibility dies hard: would people believe Moses if he does not get his laws from the immediate presence of God? So Yahweh tells Aaron and Miriam that, unlike other prophets who can see Him only in dreams, Moses shall behold His form and with him He would speak mouth to mouth, even manifestly and not in dark speeches[116]—a fact which is historically recorded in the Deuteronomy (34.10). A compromise between the two positions is effected when Yahweh appears not in His proper form, if He has any, but through visible symbols—a burning bush, a column of smoke or fire or thick darkness, a flash of fire or lightning, a thundering, a something which is vaguely defined as 'glory'—to make His presence known.[117] But howsoever Yahweh might have appeared to Moses, the latter claimed to have received two tablets of stone from Yahweh with writings actually inscribed by Him (Exod. 32.16) or to have written out the words of the covenant, the Ten Commandments, upon the tables under Divine dictation (Exod. 34.28). In a similar fashion, Zarathustra is represented in the Behistun inscription as standing face to face with Ahura Mazda[118] and questioning Him about the laws of spiritual life. Whatever might have been the oldest Zarathustrian belief, a later age delighted to represent Zarathustra as questioning Ahura Mazda face to face and receiving a reply direct from Him

[115] Deut. 4.12. *Cf.* Qur'an, 7.139.

[116] Num. 12.5-8.

[117] It is difficult to make out what is intended by saying that Moses would not be able to see God's face but he would be able to see His back when His hands would be taken away from his eyes (Ex. 33.20). But if God so ordains, He may allow His face to be seen (Gen. 32.30; Ex. 24.10-11; Judges 6.23).

[118] The identification is doubtful.—See *Dr. Modi Memorial Volume*, p. 61 f; also Dhalla, *Zoroastrian Theology*, p. 221.

about the multiple duties of his religious community.[119] Similarly is Rāmakṛṣṇa Paramahaṃsa represented as talking to Mother Kālī in her temple at Dakṣiṇeśvara, and she is supposed to have taken food at his hand.[120] So also does Manikkavasagar, while out for finding horses for his king, meet Śiva in the form of a *guru* with the *Śiva-nāma-bodham* of Meykandar in his hand, and thereafter compose his celebrated work *Tiruvāśagam*, which revived Śaivism in South India quickly and permanently.[121] We need not lengthen the list by citing instances where God appears only in a vision or a dream and commands a prophet to take up the work of evangelisation.

The belief underlying this theory of divine communication is that God is ever watchful of the morals of man and does not have to reach His human adulthood on earth to warn against and right wrongs. He takes possession of a human soul whenever He wants to make His wishes known and, according to the inscrutable ways of His operation, it is not often the learned or the chaste that is chosen for His work. The prophet is chosen for his transparency as a medium of communication, just as in hypnotism and psychical phenomena only certain individuals are suitable subjects. Who, for instance, could diagnose from the wanton youth of St. Augustine and Bilvamaṅgala that they would one day sway thousands of human hearts by their religious zeal? So we may suppose that when the inspiration comes, a man acts as one possessed, he behaves as the visible flute of an invisible musician who plays upon his tongue and gives it utterance. The prophet has no doubt that although the vocal function is his own, the thought and language are God's; he transmits what he receives and has no hand in the composition of the message. The prophetic soul communes with God in secret; there is no collective vision of God nor does the profane ear hear with the prophet the voice of Heaven except when God so pleases. But there is a ring of truth and authority in the

119 But see Dhalla, *Zor. Theo.*, p. 20. See Ys. 28.11; 31.3.

120 Max Müller, *Ramakrishna*, p. 36.

121 Macnicol, *Indian Theism*, p. 172.

prophetic message and the world is obliged to hear and to obey. While there is obvious truth in the proposition that God's ways are mysterious and that all are not equally fitted to receive divine communication, there is an obvious danger in accepting the exclusiveness of divine inspiration. The difficulty becomes greater when such inspiration is not regarded as intermittent in character,—as occasional flashes of insight into the mysteries of divine working, but as a continuous life in God. Such continuous inspiration is claimed, for instance, for Jesus Christ and for the *jīvanmuktas* in Hinduism who, it has been said, can do no wrong and acquire no merit or demerit for their actions and are, therefore, completely released on the dissolution of their body. We are to suppose that in such cases the flesh has been completely conquered and the lower impulses totally suppressed and that the soul lives continuously in the plane of the Eternal. The physiology and the psychology of such god-like men are necessarily obscure to us and any claim on their behalf must be substantiated by reference to the continuous functioning of those powers which a prophet in his intermittent inspirations claims to possess and exercise. Any lapse in insight or action is bound to rouse scepticism. Even in the case of intermittent inspiration it is difficult to see what purpose is served by supposing that God must be physically proximate to the prophet to inspire him—the whole process of verbal inspiration looks too much like earthly intercourse between finite spirits. Besides, the processes of ecstasy, possession, vision, etc., are coming increasingly within the scope of psychology, and the uprush of unconscious or subliminal thoughts and tendencies can in many cases explain satisfactorily the accession of sudden powers and peculiarities as also sudden changes in character of the prophets. While an influx of inspiration from an outside reality cannot be definitely barred out, it may also be that religious stimuli—a flash of lightning or a peal of thunder, a dazzling light or a roaring wind—are worked up by a sensitive mind in such a way that a physical presence of God is felt, notwithstanding the fact that

God may after all be entirely formless and spiritual.[122] And this physical proximity of God has sometimes been claimed by those who did not possess such an extraordinary moral life as to deserve being singled out for such signal divine favour. It is only fair to add, however, that a prophet should be judged not by the moral standard of a later enlightened age but by the standard of conduct prevalent in his own time; and, judged by this criterion, those prophets who succeeded in convincing their fellowmen that they had been sent by God would compare very favourably with their contemporaries in point of uprightness and devotion.

We pass on now to consider those prophets who had such an exalted idea of divine majesty that they could not believe that He would ever reveal directly His message to man. While the mystic seeks union with God through ecstasy and love, the prophetic mind keeps God at a respectful distance, dreading the familiarity that breeds contempt. God in his ineffable grandeur, transcendental majesty and formless spirituality is wholly inaccessible to direct human cognition of the type contemplated in the theories of incarnation and visible presence.[123] Who can look upon the face of the Lord and yet live?[124] Did not Moses fall down in a swoon when in his pre-

[122] *Cf.* Lods, *Israel*, pp. 456-57 : " Some of the features of the conception of Jahweh are derived from ancient times, prior to the age of Moses, when the God of Sinai was associated with certain natural phenomena such as lightning, storm, earthquake and fire, possibly because the sacred mountain was a volcano. The story was told that, like the volcano, Jahweh had appeared to the Israelites in the wilderness under the form of a pillar of fire by night and a pillar of cloud by day. He had revealed himself to Abraham as a blazing torch and a smoking furnace (Gen. xv. 17). The temple was filled with smoke when the ark was brought into it in the time of Solomon (I Kings viii. 10-11) and when Isaiah received the vision there which called him to the prophetic office (Isa. vi. 4) thunder was the voice of Jahweh (Amos i. 2; Ps. xxix. 3-9). Poets described the march of Jahweh shrouded in dark clouds, discharging hail-stones and coals of fire (Judges v. 4-5; Ps. lxviii. 8-10; Isa. xix. 1; Ps. xviii. 8-15; Ezek. i). The God of Sinai appeared to Moses " in a flame in the midst of a bush." " The glory of Jahweh " was a divine fire of dazzling brightness flashing out at intervals from the storm-cloud which concealed it (I Kings viii. 11; Isa, vi. 3-4; *cf.* Exod. xvi. 10; xxiv. 15-17); sometimes this fire seems to be thought of as surrounding (for example, Exod. xxxiv. 29-35), sometimes as constituting the body of the deity. The chariots and horses of the heavenly host are of fire (2 Kings ii. 11; vi. 17)."

[123] Qur'an 6.102; 75.22-3.

[124] Exod. 20.19; see Lods, *op. cit.*, p. 458.

sumptuous inquisitiveness he wanted to see God and God turned a mountain to dust before his eyes?[125] What the Upaniṣad regarded as the triumph of divine revelation, namely, that the knower of Brahman himself becomes Brahman (*Brahmavit Brahma eva bhavati*), the Semitic mind looked upon as a danger ; that is why the punishment for eating of the tree of knowledge was so dire, for the creature would begin to consider himself as equal to the Creator and the prophet would imitate the language of the Vedic Seer Vāmadeva, "I was Manu, I was the Sun." Did not Christ use similar language and claim that he who had seen him had seen the Father? Did not certain Sufis substitute themselves for God as when one of them, Hallāj, said, "I am the Truth," and another, Abū Yazīd Bistāmī said, "Praise be to me! How great is my glory!"[126]

Now if earthly rulers can carry out their intentions through officials, how much easier is it for the King of kings to manage the divine government of the world without having to look to the details of administration or to communicate His wishes to His subjects personally? God is not what Epicurus thought He was, namely, a disinterested spectator of the world : but then He is not also so much intimately associated with it as to leave no room for others to deputise for Him in its government. He may, and does, indeed govern directly if occasions so demand, as when he personally visits iniquity with punishment; but generally He prefers to work through His angelic messengers, who not only communicate His wishes to man but also help the just in their fights by His order.[127] God's direct dealings are with the denizens of Heaven and these mediate between God and man in a number of different capacities.

In Hinduism, for instance, the divine lore of Śiva (āgama) is mostly revealed to his spouse Pārvatī or Devī, and it is she who spreads the wisdom on earth presumably through

[125] Qur'an 7.139.
[126] Lammens, *Islam*, p. 123.
[127] Qur'an 3.121; 8.9.

other intermediaries. Similarly, her own lore (nigama) is revealed to heavenly denizens and through them disseminated here below. Vohu Mano and Sraosha perform an analogous function in Zoroastrianism. In Judaism again, under Neo-Platonic and Gnostic influences, the transcendental character of Yahweh was augmented and a hierarchy of heavenly beings with ill-defined functions of mediation between Him and man was postulated.[128] Both Jesus and Muhammad are represented as believing in the existence of these intermediaries;[129] but while in the Bible some minor functions are ascribed to them, *e.g.*, Annunciation to Virgin Mary of her immaculate conception, the Qur'an ascribes to one of them, Jibril (Gabriel), the glorious task of revealing to Muhammad from time to time verses from the Heavenly Book in which God's thoughts and wishes about proper living are all recorded in Arabic.[130] The Prophet does not receive his revelations from God direct as Moses is said to have done;[131] he gets them second-hand, but he has no doubt that he is faithfully reporting the authentic wishes of God as they are recorded in the Heavenly Qur'an and as they descended on his heart through Gabriel over a long period of 23 years (610-632 A.D.).

Although the angels are coming into fashion in contemporary thought,[132] there is no doubt that in Semitic religions they served the purpose of the discarded gods of polytheism whose visible symbols the people had so long worshipped and addressed face to face. They were dethroned from their individual eminence and made to serve as divine messengers and agents and to keep up the regal pomp of the Heavenly Court. They became the ' sons of God ' in Jewish religion, but some

128 Maitreya, *Universal Religion*, p. 235; see also Dhalla, *Zor. Theo.*, pp. 27-29, 102, 228-9.

129 For a similar Sabaean belief, see Stubbe, *op. cit.*, pp. 12-13.

130 Lammens, *op. cit.*, pp. 48-49.

131 For a very full discussion regarding the nature of revelation to Muhammad, see *An Introduction to the Commentary of the Holy Qoran* (Eng. Tr. of *Al Bayan*) by Maulvi Abu Muhammad Abdul Haqq Haqqani (p. 216 f). "Muhammad has occasionally seen God in his glories and spoken to Him, but in this state the revelation of the Qoran did not take place." (*Ibid*, p. 218.)

132 See Alexander, *Space, Time and Deity*, I, p. 19; II, p. 105, 346; also Ward, *The Realm of Ends*, p. 185.

of them are also represented as marrying the daughters of men and thus establishing a direct contact with humanity and also as frequenting holy places on earth without any particular message to deliver.[133] Muhammad repeatedly denounced the Arabic idea that the angels were the daughters of the God of Mercy and not His servants merely, or that their function on earth was anything but aiding the believers and chastising the infidels. How exactly Gabriel communicated the Arabic Qur'an to Muhammad must remain problematical—it is described as descending on his heart in the form of recitations out of the copy in heaven entrusted to the guardianship of the angels from all eternity.[134] By Christian writers Muhammad has been variously described as "an enthusiast, a fanatic, an impostor, a man specially inspired by the devil, or an epileptic subject to hysterical hallucinations."[135] About his book two typical opinions would suffice. "From the literary point of view, the Koran has little merit. Declamation, repetition, puerility, a lack of logic and coherence strike the unprepared reader at every turn. It is humiliating to the human intellect to think that this mediocre literature has been the subject of innumerable commentaries and that millions of men are still wasting time in absorbing it."[136] "It is not only Mohammad's person in its entirety, not only his antecedents and general culture, that are reflected in the religion thus put together and determine its special character. Beyond all this, there is something in Islam—nay, there is much—that is simply arbitrary. The unforeseen and intrinsically incalculable plays no small part in it. The changing political relations, the circumstances of the prophet's life, and, alas! his passions also, his vengeance and his sensual desires, leave their mark on the word of Allah that he preaches,—the word which, when once it is spoken, he will lay not only upon

133 Gen. 28.12; 32.2.

134 See *Al Bayan* (Eng. Tr.) by A. M. A. Haqq Haqqani, p. 218 f, for a discussion of this point.

135 *Faiths of the World*, p. 368; see also C. T. Gorham, *Ethics of the Great Religions* (R. P. A. series), pp. 63-65.

136 Reinach, *Orpheus*, p. 176.

Arabia, but upon all the world!"[137] There can be no doubt that much of Christian spite is due to the rapidity with which Muhammadanism is spreading among the people whom the Church looked upon as its prospective converts and something is also due to an unconscious resentment against Muslim domination of European countries for many centuries and of the Holy Land down to the present times. This much is certain that the Old Testament, taken as a whole and not merely in its Prophetic part, does not present a higher standard of reasonableness or compassion in its conception of God and His dealings with man than the Qur'an does, and it is the Old Testament that the Qur'an has primarily in mind when drawing up its code of religion and morals. It may be freely admitted, of course, that the method of transmitting revelations through lesser gods or angels, as adopted by the Qur'an and some of the Hindu religious sects, is rather crude in its conception, for at one stage the physical descent of a heavenly being, as in the doctrines of Divine incarnation and immediate presence, would have to be assumed. There is the obvious risk that if disbelief in divine emissaries sets in, the bond of connection between God and man would snap. The Qur'an, therefore, had to take good care to include belief in the angels as a part of the Muslim creed, for on their mediation and help rest the possibility and the truthfulness of the scriptures themselves,[138] and possibly also the theory of an Arabic Qur'an in heaven to make the communications of Gabriel intelligible to Muhammad.

Is it not possible to discard altogether all these mechanical means of revelation and to hold the last view that God has neither to sojourn on earth nor to come down from Heaven nor to send heavenly messengers to teach the right relation between Himself and the world or among His creatures? Can we not suppose, on the other hand, that He has implanted in man at his birth faculties that possess the power of a growing appreciation of His nature, attributes and functions, and

137 Kuenen, *op. cit.*, p. 32.
138 Qur'an 2.172.

enable him to move up to God? Aristotle had said that God is the unmoved mover of the world: can we not understand this pregnant utterance in the sense that by the natural development of the faculties of his soul man spontaneously moves towards perfection? Indian thinkers have almost universally taught that sin and ignorance act as veils between God and man and that with the removal of these impediments the light of truth shines clear and the road of life is illumined. This would mean that God is always within the world in some fashion but that His presence and guidance are not felt by all alike. Subject to the limitations of finitude, however, it is possible to realise progressively the divine plan of things on condition that man bends his entire personality to the task. There is a twofold difficulty to be faced: firstly, the native endowment may not be adequate, and, secondly, all the aspects of the soul may not be equally exercised in the quest of spiritual values. We may suppose that to open the chamber of divine secrets there is only one key which must be possessed, namely, a happy combination of a sensitive soul, a compassionate mind and a purified will, and that this combination is favoured by congenital circumstances and fostered by spiritual training. If prophets are born and not made, we must suppose that the exact balancing of the elements of a spiritual life can be effected only congenitally, and that as a function of a rare biological constitution, just as the musical or the mathematical ability of a genius must always be set down to a fortunate biological variation. But while the founders of religions are those fortunate few who are thus favoured by a happy constitution and to whom, therefore, the rigorous life of discipline and the optimistic life of faith come easy, it is possible for every man to attain a certain amount of success in this direction by conducting a well balanced life and by attempting to cultivate those principles of thought, emotion and conduct which are essential for putting one in right relation to the world of men and things.[139] We may, in

[139] See E. Carpenter, *Theism in Mediaeval India*, p. 390

fact, say with Emerson :[140] "We lie in the lap of immense intelligence, which makes us receivers of its truth and organs of its activity. When we discern justice, when we discern truth, we do nothing of ourselves, but allow a passage to its beams :" and we may suppose with William James that the human brain provides the place where by disciplined living the veil of nature can be pierced in a progressive fashion and spiritual truths transmitted to the mind with increasing clearness.[141]

It is quite conceivable that different prophets should fix their gaze upon different aspects of the mysteries of spiritual life, although to be founders of faiths they must all possess intellectual insight, abiding love and moral earnestness of a greater or less degree. The nature of their message is very often conditioned by the needs of their time and the comprehension of their contemporaries. We may very well believe that to Buddha the spiritual message came in the form of an *intellectual* solution of the riddles of suffering, old age and death when at the foot of the Bo-tree he attained enlightenment. Not that he was not moved by the suffering of the innocent victims of the Vedic cult of sacrifice or the hardship caused by the inflexibility of a rigid caste-organisation; but tradition ascribes to him the primary enlightenment about the causes that lead to suffering and embodiment and an insistence upon earnest contemplation as the condition of freeing the mind from evils—sensuality, individuality, delusion, and ignorance.[142] In a similar fashion, Christ, when he is humanly conceived and not regarded as God-man, may be said to have received illumination about the proper *affective* relation between God and man and among men themselves, which he taught in his great messages ' God is Love ' and ' Love thy neighbour as thyself.' He focussed his preaching on the Fatherhood of God and the Brotherhood of Man, which had indeed been preached before his time but not with so much

140 Quoted by James, *Human Immortality*, p. 107.

141 James, *Human Immortality*, pp. 32-5.

142 Mahāparinibbāna Suttānta, 1.9 f. See also Stratton, *The Psychology of Religious Life*, p. 197.

insistence and method.[143] He too had his criticisms of the sacrificial cult and the empty formalities of faith, but his sacred heart turned oftener in sympathy to the publicans and sinners than to the intellectual solution of cosmic problems. To Zarathustra, again, the message from the sacred fire came in the form of a *moral* problem as to how falsehood and evil are to be practically tackled. The moral position of Zoroastrianism has been indicated by one of the High Priests of the creed thus : " Zoroastrianism will live by its eternal verities of the belief in the personality of Ormazd, an abiding faith in the triad of good thoughts, good words, and good deeds, the inexorable law of righteousness, the reward and retribution in the life hereafter, the progress of the world towards perfection, and the ultimate triumph of the good over evil through the coming of the kingdom of Ormazd with the co-operation of man."[144] Not that Zarathustra did not have his severe indictment of the worship of gods (daeva) or his commendation of a life based on the principle of family love and social charity; but the major burden of his religious theme is that, not by ecstasy and meditation, but by struggle and suffering must one redeem the world from the grip of falsehood and wickedness, and great is the reward of those who fight the battle of Truth and Righteousness.[145]

In spite of the great prophetic achievements of the past we may still legitimately suppose that as through the mysterious laws of life the human mind reaches higher summits, the secrets of the spiritual life would be more abundantly revealed, provided, of course, the prophet does not quail before his vision or relax his effort in their pursuit. We may also believe that what the prophets of old saw as through a dark glass would shine forth in a new brilliance to their successors and the old revelations would become relatively modes of

[143] *Foundations*, p. 105 f. See, however, Dhirendra Nath Chowdhury Vedānta vāgīśa, *In Search of Jesus Christ*, pp. 46-64, for a critical examination of this claim of Christianity.

[144] Dhalla, *Zor. Theo.*, pp. 370-71.

[145] *Ibid*, p. 15.

ignorance, the Upaniṣads talking even of the transcendence of revelation altogether in absolute consciousness.[146] But there is a sense in which a later prophet may be said to come not to destroy but to fulfil the message of an earlier prophet; he tries to make it more universal in its application. It is indeed true that at present the world is divided into conflicting religious traditions—the Semitic and the Aryan and the Mongolian, and that inner growth has been mostly confined within each tradition separately, the only notable exception being Zoroastrianism which, by virtue of its geographical position, influenced the eschatology of post-exilic Judaism and probably borrowed at least one goddess from the Semites, namely, Anāhita.[147] But now that the barriers of space and culture have practically broken down and no great religion—not even Hinduism—has any geographical limit and the scriptures of all religions are freely circulating all over the world, it is inevitable that some sensitive soul would arise and effect the first synthesis of rival traditions,—would show, in the words of Kabir, that black and yellow cows give the same white milk.[148] The Sufistic experiment, again born in the favourable soil of Persia,[149] proved abortive not only because of Arab bigotry but also because it failed to develop the social side of a positive religion, whereas the much smaller experiment of Sikhism succeeded in establishing a new faith by fusing elements of both cultures and discarding that religious selfishness, that intellectual aloofness, which is the bane of all mystic speculation. The rapprochement of faiths has not proceeded beyond the intellectual and social stages thus far, and the awakening of national and communal consciousness has temporarily accentuated the exclusiveness of different religious organisations.

146 Bṛ. Ār. Up., iv. 3.22.

147 Dhalla, *Zor. Theo.*, p. 137. The resemblance between Anāhita and Saraswatī is remarkable and deserves investigation. See also *Dr. Modi Memorial Volume*, p. 162.

148 E. Carpenter, *Theism in Mediaeval India*, p. 459.

149 See Carpenter, *op. cit.*, p. 450, and the works cited by him. The influence of Indian pantheistic speculations on Sufism is now questioned.

The Parsi, the Jew and the Jain can only be born, while the Mongolian religions—Confucianism, Taoism and Shintoism—are geographically isolated, non-proselytising and national. Hinduism, which had at no time ceased to absorb foreign elements, is again assuming a militant form, while Buddhism is showing signs of a new awakening and establishing contact with the prevailing ethical, but non-devotional, temper of the present age. Christianity and Muhammadanism have always been aggressively missionary, but the cry of Pan-Islamism had never been more vociferous before and the decay of faith in the West has only added to Christian missionary zeal in the East. But although the times are not propitious for amity, there is no doubt that rivalry will bring understanding and many a scoffer at alien faiths will remain to pray in the same Church. Manners will continue to divide men as now and dispositions will determine the character of devotion; but there will be more of good will and genuine understanding in the future. But only if a religious genius should arise to separate the essentials from the non-essentials and make provision in his religion for the systematisation of the genuine inspirations of all creeds[150] and should his vision be seconded by the levelling up of intellectual culture, aesthetic appreciation and moral habits in the civilised countries of the world, then and then only will there be a Universal Church; all of us may however in the mean time work towards that ideal in faith and hope, and trust to the increasing purpose of the world to remove progressively the veil of ignorance and sin that obstructs the vision of the ever present Eternal with which the human soul, even in its deepest degradation, never loses contact.[151]

---

150 See Whitehead, *Religion in the Making*, p. 131.
151 See Hegel, *Philosophy of Religion*, Vol. I, p. 5.

# CHAPTER III

## The Revelations

We have discussed now in broad outlines the nature of prophetic inspiration. Whitaker, the Elizabethan divine, found evidence for inspiration in " (1) the majesty of the doctrine itself; (2) the simplicity, purity and divinity of the style; (3) the antiqutiy of the books themselves (the books of Moses are more ancient than the writings of any other men); (4) prophetic oracles; (5) miracles; (6) the failure of enemies to destroy them; (7) the testimony of martyrs; and (8) the character of the writers, mostly illiterate and incapable of writing without inspiration."[1] In other words, everything connected with inspiration must be extraordinary—the language, the medium, the contents. Unlike philosophy which is meant for the higher intellect, religion is meant for all grades of understanding, and so its original language can never be anything but direct and simple, whether the speaker be Buddha or Christ, Moses or Muhammad. The inspiration has primary reference to the spiritual needs of man—to a proper understanding of the character and attributes of God and the right relation between man and man. As these needs are more or less abiding, the development of religion has always taken the form of transition from spasmodic attempts to ascertain divine wishes on individual occasions to a systematic knowledge of the unalterable will of God. The more primitive the religion the more frequent are the uses of divination and dream, of signs and omens, to get a knowledge of God's mind in individual matters. At a slightly higher level, ecstasy takes the place of divination—the individual gets into a state of mind relatively detached from worldly thoughts and emptied of those personal memories and desires that thwart

[1] Enc. Br., Vol. 3, p. 500.

the influx of divinity into the minds of ordinary mortals.[2] While ordinarily this ecstatic mood would be an affair of God, men have not desisted from facilitating His work by meeting Him half-way, namely, by adopting means that predispose one to ecstatic fits. Opium, hemp and hashish; tobacco and wine; dance, march, music and song; revival meetings and exhortations; fasting, ascetic practices and retirement into solitude; cabalistic rites and sexual orgies—these have all been pressed into the service of faith to produce ecstasy. Speaking of the Israelites, for instance, Lods observes:[3] 'The manner in which the Israelites conceived of inspiration (possession by a spirit or permeation by an impersonal spiritual force), the manner in which they explained visions (the carrying away of the seer, either in or out of the body, or second sight), the practices employed to induce the spirit to enter the inspired person (sacrifices, *incubatio*, music, dancing, fasting, the use of intoxicants) all resemble those found among many "primitives."' This is substantially true of Hinduism also, where similar beliefs and practices prevail down to the present day. In this ecstatic condition prophecies and oracular disclosures of divine intentions have been made more or less under the influence of a foreign will and without the aid of the extraneous means adopted by the diviners. The necessity and the process of miracles and magical feats are more difficult to understand: they are probably intended to establish the power of the divinely inspired person to tap the fountain of divine energy, either to establish his own claim or to right manifest wrongs or to establish the truth and greatness of God. It is an open question whether such actions are always performed deliberately or also often "by a kind of irresistible compulsion,"[4] whether they operate directly on the course of events or indirectly through the supernatural spiritual powers who control them; but there is no doubt that their performance

[2] For the theories of Plato, Philo, Josephus and Athenagoras on the subject, see ERE. vii. 347.

[3] Lods, *Israel*, p. 300; see also Stratton, *The Psychology of Religious Life*, p. 108 f.

[4] See Lods, *op. cit.*, p. 299.

is intermittent and it is not intended to prove that the divine government of the world can be carried on normally by miracle and magic. Except when these are used in the interests of morality they may serve as advertisements to power; but it is only in exceptional cases that they would predispose the spectators to piety. Besides, black art has claimed, equally with prophetic performance, the power to control natural forces, and oracles have thrived in many lands without religious association of a very high type.

The merit of the founders of faiths lies essentially in this that they have generally tried in their own way and to the extent of their own illumination to wean men's minds away from the spectacular and the occasional to the abiding laws of truth and morality. They have attempted to teach that the laws of existence and conduct work without taking unnecessary help from accessory interference. " Assuredly in the heavens and the earth are signs for those who believe firmly; and in your own creation, and in the beasts which He has dispersed abroad are signs to the firm in faith : and in the succession of night and day, and in the supply which God sendeth down from the Heaven whereby after its death He giveth life to the earth, and in the change of the winds, are signs for people of discernment. Such are the signs of God : with truth have we recited them to thee."[5] To arrive at the conception of Law as governing both physical and moral happenings is to set up a prominent milestone in the path of spiritual progress, and to believe that that law operates equally in all cases is really to free the mind from all anxiety about the uncertainties of divine action. When the Vedic seers were teaching that the first fruits of Divine fervour (Tapas) were Ṛta and Satya[6]—law and truth, that this Ṛta even the gods could not transgress, that it ruled the moral as well as the physical realm, and that of this holy law Varuṇa the " all-enfolder " was the keeper, they were making an important advance upon the more primitive belief that gods could be

[5] See *The Quran*, 45. 2-5; also Suras 16, 21, 26, 30, 31, 35, 36.
[6] RV.X.190.

persuaded to be partial to the worshipper by supplications and sacrifices.[7]

Little, however, did the Vedic seers realise that the elevation of the law was destined in the long run to dethrone the lawgiver. When Buddha summarily rejected the boon-giving capacity of the Vedic gods and set up instead the principle of Dependent Origination (*pratītya-samutpāda*), according to which the inexorable law of causality ruled mental and moral realms, the real implication of a world ruled by law came into view. In the words of Mrs. Rhys Davids,[8] "Going farther than the modern scientific standpoint, they (the Piṭakas) substituted a cosmodicy for a theodicy, a natural moral order for the moral design of a creative deity"—an order which was extended by the later Buddhists to inorganic, organic, and spiritual realms. On Indian philosophic soil the fight between law and liberty, fate and fiat, destiny and deity, was decided in favour of the former, and even the philosophy that set out to lay down the rules of interpreting Vedic texts bearing upon sacrifices ended by placing Apūrva or Adṛṣṭa (fate) over God Himself. As a matter of fact, the inexorability of law was pushed to such a length that in some of the heretical systems, familiarised to us by Buddhist and Jaina literatures, the progress towards perfection was supposed to be independent even of the moral law—the orthogenetic impulse of the world needed no moral co-operation of man to perfect itself and only waited for Time to bring it to fruition. Against these *akriyāvādins* (philosophers of non-action) even the non-theistic founders of Buddhism and Jainism had to

[7] In both Veda and Avesta *ṛita-asha* is fundamentally important. In the Ṛik it covers the threefold order, cosmic, ritualistic and moral. In the Avesta it runs out into the meanings, right, truth, righteousness, holiness,—all ethical in connotation. Veda and Avesta, then, are witnesses that the conception existed before the breaking up of the Indo-Iranian unity.

A conception like *ṛita-asha* would naturally have its effect upon the idea of God. Scholars practically agree that Varuṇa equals Ahura Mazda, that is to say, the ethical God of the Ṛik is regarded as the same in origin as the ethical and supreme god of the Avesta.—Griswold, *The Religion of the Ṛigveda*, p. 24. (See also Ragozin, *Vedic India*, p. 140 f.)

[8] Mrs. Rhys Davids, *Buddhism*, pp. 118-19; see also Stcherbatsky, *The Central Conception of Buddhism*, p. 31.

warn their followers. They were fighting for regularity in the realm of moral activity against the rule of divine caprice; they never intended to hand over the destiny of the world to the domination of a metaphysical principle after dethroning the heavenly powers. That the demand for regularity may become an overruling passion is evident from the fact that in China Lao-tse too taught:[9] "The (sage) man has for his law the earth: the earth has heaven for its law; heaven has Tao for its law; and the law of Tao is its own spontaneity." This passage has been interpreted to mean that "Tao is the ultimate Reality, anterior to and higher than heaven, existing before time began, and precedent to the manifested God. It is the principle or law of nature, eternal, unchanging, and all-pervading, and as such must have existed prior to any personification, which can only be regarded as a development and corporate expression of that principle,"[10] or that "the ground of existence being a perfectly indefinite spontaneity, a dark abysmal one from which, for no reason assigned, the multiplicity of the world emanates, by the immanence of which the world is and is moved—all this agrees with the ethical doctrine of abstention from self-determination and of sinking back on the inner ground of our being that we may be as this spontaneity in us causes us to become."[11]

The problem of the law governing divine operation is really complementary to the problem of synergism or the co-operation of the free will of man and the grace of God. In the former, as in the latter, the withdrawal of provision for the operation of grace would render all religious appeal practically nugatory, as there would be no valid motive for praise and prayer when God is unable to act in contravention of law. The Vedānta of Śaṅkara only draws the logical conclusion of this position when it lays down that Īśvara and Jīva are both beings of a lower order of existence and are bound to disappear together with the rise of the knowledge

[9] Legge, *The Religions of China*, p. 214.

[10] ERE.ix. 87.

[11] ERE. xii. 198; see also *Review of Philosophy and Religion*, Vol. III, esp. p. 175 (art. *Taoism* and *Vedanta*).

that activity does not belong to the nature of any soul in its free and enlightened condition and that what abides is an impersonal Brahman—a being with nothing to legislate for or govern. Theists have not been slow to detect the dangers of an impersonalistic spiritualism and a nomistic fatalism, and, while fighting for a monistic faith, they have been obliged to keep intact the divine prerogative of freedom to intervene effectively in the governance of the physical and the spiritual world. In fact, miracle and grace are two aspects of one and the same fact, namely, that God is not fettered by the law that He has himself imposed either on nature or on man and that He is as free to suspend the regular order of the one as to condone the breach of the moral law by the other. When, in the spirit of Isaiah, whom he quotes, Jesus preached glad tidings to the poor and proclaimed release to the captives, all " wondered at the words of grace which proceeded out of his mouth;"[12] for the Jews, in spite of their claim to be the special favourite of Yahweh as a nation, were more accustomed to " the awful majesty of justice " than to "the forgiving love" of God. In a similar vein, the Kaṭha and Śvetāśvatara Upaniṣads, and more so the Bhagavadgītā,[13] taught that God could Himself bestow favour out of His abundant grace and did not need to be coerced into beneficence by the magical efficacy of Vedic rites, performed according to the rules laid down in the Brāhmaṇas and Śrauta Sūtras. Positive religions have considered it far safer to hand over everything to the inscrutable will of God than to curtail His freedom by setting an unalterable and autonomous law of moral justice over against Him. They have agreed to sacrifice intelligible order to the inscrutable fiat of God lest the law should usurp the place of the lawgiver. God's grace manifests itself not only in incarnation and revelation, in providence and redemption without merit, but also in the purification of the sinful nature of man and in the reinforcement of his struggling moral

[12] Is. 61.1-2; Luke 4.17-22; see also ERE.vi. 334.

[13] Bhagavadgītā, x. 10-1; xviii. 61-6; Kaṭha Up., 1.2.23; Bhāgavata Pur., xi. 11. 32; Śvet. Up., 3.20; 6.21.

will by timely assistance.[14] Thus, while the cult of sacrifice insisted on the fulfilment of certain formal conditions of obtaining divine favour (except when it regarded the whole process as magical), the cult of grace, as formulated by the founders of religions, emphasised the need of fulfilling certain spiritual and moral conditions of obtaining divine aid, if not in the form of external goods, at least in that of a capacity to withstand suffering. It even went so far as to assume that in certain exceptional cases divine grace could forgive and save a sinner who had done nothing to deserve divine compassion (thereby even risking the fundamental postulate of all ethical religion that vice can never hope to be treated in the same way as virtue), in order to show the greatness of God whose patience, love and solicitude for the human soul know no bounds and who sends the sun to shine as much upon the wicked as upon the good. If God had taken pleasure in visiting iniquity with suffering, would He have sent any prophetic revelation or warning? God is both able and willing to condone sinful acts, sometimes in response to penitent prayers and at other times freely with inscrutable motives of His own or out of His abundant mercy.

This message of hope we may regard as the cardinal tenet of all theistic faiths preached by the prophets. The fear of the Lord may be the beginning of wisdom, but even the primitives would require something more to worship God.[15] If the wrath of God is incapable of being turned away by penitence and prayer, and if the law of justice is to work out its relentless destiny in all cases, what motive would be left for approaching God in a worshipful attitude? Even the primitives believe that the supernatural powers can be prayed to in a spirit of hope (when, of course, they are not regarded as amenable to magical control), and no advanced theism has been able to dispense with the same belief. Only on the portals of Hell are Dante's terrible words possible:

[14] ERE.vi.365.

[15] See Marrett, *Faith, Hope and Charity in Primitive Religion*, Lect. II, esp p. 39.

" Abandon all hope, ye who enter here."[16] Man lives by hope no less than by faith; he is ever conscious too of his weaknesses and his many shortcomings in his dealings with men and things, even when these are judged by the relative standard of traditional morality or tribal custom. The prophet of a religion has, therefore, the twofold task of awakening or accentuating the sense of sin and suffering and at the same time of bringing a message of redemption or deliverance from these.[17] Whether a religion would be pessimistic or optimistic depends upon the emphasis it lays upon the first or the second aspect. James, as is well known, distinguished between the religion of healthymindedness and the religion of the sick soul—the religion of hope in spiritual progress and immortality, based on a belief in the benignity of God, and the " hell-fire theology," based on a melancholic and defeatistic attitude towards the problems of right living.[18] But mere pessimism has never been able to constitute either a religious or a philosophic message—a way out has always been suggested, though sometimes a way that is strenuous, slippery and almost unending. Even atheistic faiths have built on hope. In Buddhism and Jainism religious suicide was not at all permitted to those who wished to escape from the troubles and responsibilities of life but only sometimes to those who had attained perfection and who wanted to quicken their exit out of the world after that happy consummation.[19] What most religions have done is to picture a God who has indeed set tasks to men but who is ever willing to help them in correcting mistakes and is satisfied with their effort at improvement even though the standard of perfection attained is not very high. God lends a helping hand to souls struggling to rise ; He breaks their fall ; He lifts them up from the ground ; He assists them with easy ascents and mounting ladders. How weak and erring is man, and how great and good is God !

[16] Dante, *The Divine Comedy*—Hell, Canto III.

[17] See Mackintosh, *The Pilgrimage of Faith* (1931), pp. 196-205.

[18] James, *Varieties of Religious Experience*, Lects. IV-VII.

[19] ERE. xii. 24 f., 34.

Even the original pre-theistic Buddhism had to show how it was possible to hope for ultimate deliverance through right contemplation, even though no God ever came to the rescue of the soul in bondage to ignorance, suffering and sin. The very fact that most of the religions, which originally started with an austere philosophy of life, had to make concession to the human demand of easy salvation is a striking testimony to the necessity of a gospel of compassion. Hinduism with its Paurāṇic message of hope is far removed from Hinduism with its Upaniṣadic message of self-knowledge and self-discipline.[20] Mahāyāna Buddhism with its compassionate Bodhisattvas is essentially different from Hīnayāna Buddhism with its insistence upon self-attained Nirvāṇa. The former even proved readily acceptable to Chinese Confucianists and Japanese Shintoists whose religions lacked this type of divine help. The success of Christian and Muhammadan missions has largely depended upon their easy and attractive scheme of salvation through prophetic mediation, against the seductive influences of which the native religions of India, China and Japan, whenever they taught crude beliefs in petty gods or lofty philosophies of self-attained salvation, have mostly struggled in vain. It is only by developing a religion, comparable in its plan of salvation with these Semitic religions, or else by intensifying a culture that can dispense with God-given deliverance, that they have managed to escape total extinction; as instances in point may be cited Vaiṣṇavism and Śaivism in India and the cults of Amida, the god of boundless light, and Kwannon, the goddess of mercy, in the Shin sect of Japan,[21] all of which have developed on the lines of faith as against the cult of restraint, meditation and knowledge advocated by the Sāṃkhya and Vedānta schools in general of India and the Zen (Dhyāna) sect of Buddhism in Japan. We shall see later on that the cult of compassion

[20] E. Carpenter, *Theism in Mediaeval India*, pp. 102-03.

[21] See Streeter, *The Buddha and the Christ*, p. 82 f.; also Kimura, *A Historical Study of the terms Hīnayāna and Mahāyāna and the Origin of Mahāyāna Buddhism*, p. 42.

is not without its dangers—the Saints in Roman Catholicism, the *Walis* in Muhammadanism, the *Gurus* in Hinduism, the Yazatas and Fravashis in Zoroastrianism, the Mother Goddess in Catholicism, Vaiṣṇavism and Buddhism, not to talk of the Tīrthañkaras in Jainism and the Bodhisattvas in Buddhism, have all swelled the ranks of compassionate intermediaries and rendered salvation easier of achievement. Again, where priestly absolution has claimed to confer release from the piccadillos of daily life and to square up periodically the accounts in the Book of Life from here below, the incentives to strenuous effort are likely to be reduced to their minimal intensity.[22] Exactly for a similar reason men have sought to swell the credit side of their heavenly account by seeking the assistance of their descendants in the shape of śrāddhas, masses, worship on tablets, etc., when they are dead, and the aid of their contemporaries, when alive, by forming " brotherhoods "[23] in which each shares the merits of all the members : so uncertain is unaided salvation when men are regarded as sinful in nature, act and disposition and also as begotten in sinfulness.[24] When the craving for outside help is so great, is it any wonder that a class of people claiming to absolve people from sin should arise or that the doctrine of supererogation, according to which a surplus of merit that can be acquired by certain privileged persons and placed at the disposal of sinners for their salvation, should form a part of the creed in some of the religions of redemption?[25]

The founders of faiths were not insensible of the danger of merely purifying the conception of God. A religion that

[22] With the growth of the opinion that penace does not presuppose full contrition, but only an *attritio*, which the sacrament of penance itself perfects, an impetus was given to the less spiritual conception, and this attained its full development in the doctrine of indulgences whereby the treasures of merit stored up by the faithful for the church, and at her disposal, could be held to remit the penalties of guilt here and in purgatory for her obedient children.—Hobhouse, *Morals in Evolution*, II, p. 143.

[23] Sullivan, *The Externals of the Catholic Church*, pp. 350-51.

[24] *pāpo'ham pāpakarmāham pāpātmā pāpasambhavaḥ.*

[25] See Hobhouse, *Morals in Evolution*, II, pp. 141 f. ; also Sullivan, *The Fundamentals of Catholic Belief*, p. 232.

concerns itself only with the establishment of a right relation with God may easily take up a negative attitude towards the world. The intensive quest of God may swallow up all other interests, and life, instead of being enjoyed as a blessing, may simply be endured as a hateful necessity. The stern duties of life may be shelved altogether and devotion to God may sum up the entire function of spiritual existence. There may be an abnormal shrinkage of the ego till the interests of the world disappear altogether from view and religion becomes altogether an affair of man's solitariness. The mystic way of life, with its stages of purgation, illumination and unification, is calculated to draw the soul away from the passions of the flesh, the call of social obligation, and the demands of sense and imagination. Even the intellectual demands of revelation may be absent and the soul may sink into the blissful quiet of the Absolute Inane through stages which can be only imperfectly described in language, such as that employed by St. Theresa and the Daśabhūmiśāstra.[26] All attempts to use God practically are totally abandoned : the soul does not approach God to get anything out of Him but to give itself up wholly to Him, and not only the worldly interests of one's own self but even the spiritual interests of others may be totally abandoned. The soul begins to seek solitude, to retire from the haunts of men, to adopt ascetic and mortificatory practices, to contemplate and meditate in order to commune with God or to empty the mind of all individualistic contents in order to realise finally the nothingness of the temporal and the pervasiveness of the eternal in its own bosom.

It is evident that this type of preoccupation with God is bound to be antisocial; and hence no religious organisation can be built up on the loose sands of individual interest and spiritual selfishness. The unkind world with its incessant demands for the fulfilment of bodily needs and with its multiple emissaries of natural evil, which prowl about in the shape

[26] ERE. ii. 743f.; ix. 98. See also James, *Varieties of Religious Experience*, pp. 408-15.

of dangerous animals, noxious vermin, germs of disease and seeds of decay, torments the corporeal frame of the saint practically as much as that of the sinner and compels him to live within easy reach of the helping hand of the society he wishes to abjure. When to mitigate some of these evils the lonely hermit turns a cœnobite, a new system of duties springs up and the task of maintaining the cœnobium brings about wider contact with social groups and lesser opportunities of solitude and ecstatic trance. But the founder of a faith is impelled by something deeper than the practical necessity of living to come into contact with society. Although his inspiration is not exclusively (and sometimes even primarily) a product of social forces, he still owes much to the level of culture which his society has attained. A Jewish prophet, with centuries of ethical tradition in the community behind him, could not fail to see more deeply into the nature of God and the requirements of a moral life than a savage born into animistic and fetishistic traditions or the cult of cannibalism. Environment does not plant the prophetic seed in human nature, but it deeply influences its germination and subsequent growth. It is into a concrete social situation that a prophet is born, and the character of his spiritual progress is largely determined by the forces against which he has to contend and the materials upon which he can rely. This is why prophetic expressions are so differently garbed even when close analysis reveals a fundamental kinship of prophetic inspirations. Mysticism, which is comparatively untrammelled by the necessity of conforming to social ideas and ideals, speaks a universal language, while revelations are clogged by the conventions of the community for which they are originally intended.[27] Could there have been so much insistence by the Hebrew prophets on the greater responsibilities of Israel if Moses had not established the tradition of a special covenant between Israel and Yahweh? Could Muhammad have incorporated the pilgrimage to Mecca within

[27] See Pratt, *The Religious Consciousness*, p. 337 f. (The last five chapters provide an excellent summary of Mysticism.)

the divine revelation had he not been an Arab and had there not been an immemorial Arab custom in its favour? Could Buddha have claimed inspiration for his doctrine of Pratītya-samutpāda had he not been brought up in the tradition of the law of Karma? The message for the mass, which revelation is ultimately destined to be, must be couched in a language suited to their need and understanding, while mysticism assumes the proper language of the soul, the spiritual Esperanto which a few indeed can understand but which is not confined within narrow communal or geographical limits. As a matter of fact, the universal element of every positive religion has a kind of mystic appeal to the spiritual nature of man when it does not appeal to his reason. That is how faiths can spread by intimate acceptance to newer social groups. To one born in the tradition the universal and the particular make equal appeal through the force of sheer habit; but when the traditional and the local preponderate over the universal, a faith loses its power of appeal to the world at large.

Now, the most universal aspect of religion must have reference to those ethical needs without the fulfilment of which society cannot hold together. Mere gregariousness may bring individuals together; but in order to cohere into social groups they must develop traits and tendencies and establish principles and practices conducive to concord. It has often been pointed out that even persons congregating together for unlawful ends or predatory purposes must have a code of morals delimiting one another's freedom at least during the period of operation, although not infrequently they fall out during the division of the spoils.[28] Conformably to this principle, the rules governing the relations of the members of a family have been the most rigid and exact, and the primary prohibitions or tabus have their first reference to the family where natural affection frequently seconds the operation of the moral sense. In the patriarchal stage of society some of these ethical forces operate without express thinking: this is why people in a tribal condition have such

[28] See Plato, *The Republic*, Bk. 1.

solidarity and why they resent so strongly any injury to their fellow-members. A religious community is only an extended tribe where the basis of unity is not sameness of blood but similarity of belief—the common ancestor is not the human father but the Father in Heaven. Sympathy goes with the kinship of a common faith and not with geographical propinquity: instructive illustrations of this are furnished by the case of the Vrātyas absorbed by Hinduism, of the strangers (*gerim*) in ancient Judaism, and of converted slaves in Muhammadanism,—in fact, of converts in every religion. Conversely, apostates and infidels are the most hateful in the eyes of the faithful.

No religion that ignores the social aspect of faith has any chance of survival.[29] All religions are ultimately tested by their bearing upon ethical behaviour and social concord. Even when under a mistaken sense of the necessities of religious life men have been prompted to adopt unsocial actions (as when human sacrifices were offered to Huitzilopochtli in the old Mexican religion, to Yahweh in Judaism, to Kālī in Hinduism), they either pleaded their helplessness before an express divine revelation or gave the whole matter an esoteric colouring, of which the main purpose was to defend on higher social considerations the adoption of such apparently antisocial measures. All primitive religions are purified by culture not only in an intellectual but also in an ethical direction; they not only attain an increasing coherence of doctrines but they also establish closer bonds of active sympathy between man and man. Without an active interest in other people's welfare it is impossible to develop the ethical side of one's idea of God. Just as it is true that from our conception of the ethical nature of God follows our attitude towards our fellow-men, so also from our acceptance of certain fundamental ethical relations between man and man follows a development in our conception of the ethical nature of God. Faith and morality purify, or else degrade, each other. We may

[29] See Pratt, *The Religious Consciousness*, pp. 7-12.

suppose, for instance, that a development of ethical notions transformed the earlier religious code of the Jewish Decalogue into a code of social morality. The decay of the cult of sacrifice all over the world is intimately related by way of cause or effect or both with a purified conception of the nature of God to whom the offerings of the heart are supposed to be more acceptable than the gifts of material objects, especially when the latter involve cruelty to men or animals. As religious thought progresses, it has not only to bind man to God but also man to man; anything that has a tendency to divide men or set up one class against another can have no abiding place in a truly religious organisation. A satisfactory *modus vivendi* of the different classes and interests within the religious group must be evolved and a direct contact between individuals, and not merely between groups, must be established. In religion, no less than in politics, the famous dictum of Sir Henry Maine holds true, namely, that " the movement in the progressive societies has hitherto been the movement *from status to contract*,"[30] not only in the sense that each individual has been treated as an end in himself, and not merely as a member of a group, but also in the sense that individuals have felt that in addition to their duties as members of a class they have direct obligations in their individual capacity, or, in other words, the voice of conscience supplements, and sometimes supplants, the voice of the tribe.

But just as danger lurks in mere devotion, so also there is risk in mere morality. In its eagerness to amend the injustice of centuries religion may be tempted to reduce itself to a mere device for social unification and social good, neglecting or minimising the devotional side of man's life and abandoning the attempt to understand the operation of spirituality in nature and history. It does not unoften happen that after capitalism and aristocracy have ground down the labouring classes for centuries, there comes a deification of the proletariat in sensitive minds, painfully affected by the miseries and disabilities of the downtrodden and the depressed. A

[30] Maine, *Ancient Law* (1891), p. 114.

Voltaire or a Rousseau, a Marx or a Lenin, a Vivekānanda or a Gāndhi, may rouse a nation's conscience to the degrading conditions under which the suppressed and the submerged classes live. A religion that does not provide for adequate consideration towards the needy and the oppressed then forfeits its right to exist, judged by the test of social benefit. A cult of social service or a religion of humanity springs up, and religion becomes identified with the establishment of right relations with sentient existence, untrammelled by transcendental preoccupations. To indicate this attitude let us quote two authors. "Religion," says Rabindranath Tagore,[31] "inevitably concentrates itself on humanity, which illumines our reason, inspires our wisdom, stimulates our love, claims our intelligent service." According to Benjamin Kidd,[32] "a religion is a form of belief, providing an ultra-rational sanction for that large class of conduct in the individual where his interests and the interests of the social organism are antagonistic, and by which the former are rendered subordinate to the latter in the general interests of the evolution which the race is undergoing." We may refer to a few historical instances to test the adequacy of this moralistic standpoint of faith.[33]

The first case is furnished by Buddhism. In opposition to the sacrificial Vedic cult, which legalised cruelty and stabilised caste, Buddha minimised the importance of the Vedic gods in spiritual matters and discountenanced all speculations about the future state of the soul; and to reinforce his teachings he preached that the soul was only a transient aggregation of five factors—form, sensation, perception, predisposition and consciousness—which was dissolved at death. But he preached at the same time the inviolability of moral justice and the necessity of spiritual progress towards perfection in its intellectual and moral aspects. He resisted in his own person the insidious advances of Māra the tempter and his

[31] R. Tagore, *The Religion of Man*, p. 114. See Pringle-Pattison, *The Idea of God*, Lects. VII and VIII.

[32] B. Kidd, *Social Evolution* (1902), pp. 105-06.

[33] See the present writer's art. *Morality or Religion?* in Dacca University Journal, 1935.

three daughters, Desire, Discontent and Lust; and he showed by the failure of the severe ascetic practices of his early career that, no less than enjoyment, mortification of the flesh was not the way to illumination and salvation. In the great sermon at the Deer-park of Benares (Sarnath) he advocated the rule of the Golden Mean, now associated in the West with the name of Aristotle, and taught that the primary object of religion was to find out the means of putting a stop to the ignorance that caused embodiment and suffering, and that the true means of Nirvāṇa or salvation was not the path of worship but the path of illumination and ethical will. He called it the Noble Eightfold Path, which may be described in the words of Prof. G. F. Moore as follows:[34] "The first step in this path is right belief; that is, belief in the four fundamental principles as enunciated by Buddha; then follow right resolution, the resolve to renounce all sensual pleasures, to have malice towards none, and to harm no living creature; right speech, abstaining from backbiting, harsh language, falsehood, and frivolous talk; right conduct, not destroying life, not taking what is not given one, not being guilty of unchastity; right means of subsistence, giving up a wrong occupation and getting one's livelihood in a proper way; right effort, the strenuous endeavour to overcome all faults and evil qualities, to attain, preserve, and cultivate all good qualities. These six paths are ways of moral self-discipline, and might be comprehended under one head. The next, right reflection, might be called the intellectual discipline, a higher ascesis by which man rids himself of lust and grief. The highest stage is the mystical discipline, right absorption or concentration, a series of trances through which man rises to the bliss which is as far beyond happiness as beyond misery, reaches the intuition of higher and higher ranges of truth, and passes into ecstasies that lie beyond consciousness." The last step at any rate would refer in most other religions to the realisation of God, but Buddha meant by it nothing but the successive

[34] See G. F. Moore, *History of Religions*, I, p. 295; Yamakami Sogen, *Systems of Buddhistic Thought*, p. 169 f.; Warren, *Buddhism in Translations*, pp. 373-74.

stages through which the mind gets rid of its contents till it is able to reduce itself to that nothingness (śūnya) which is its proper nature. It appears also that, of the forty subjects of meditation which are prescribed for training the mind in its task of self-emptying, reflection on the gods (but not in the sense of reliance upon them) is only one.[35]

Mrs. Rhys Davids has drawn attention[36] to a significant passage in the Majjhima-Nikāya (i, 134) in which Buddha compares morality to a raft meant to be used "as something to escape by, but not to be clung fast to;" but she takes care to point out also that in Buddhism "there is no other certain sanction of goodness beyond the driving force of pain waiting on immoral living, and the pleasures rewarding moral living, now or in the long run,"[37] and that "for the thoughtful Buddhist, the *Kamma-niyama* will have furnished as pressing a motive for moral conduct as if he had held that an omniscient lawgiver watched and rewarded his acts."[38] The noble eightfold path, the five (or ten) *śīlas* (namely, to abstain from taking life, not to take what is not given, sexual purity, to abstain from lying, abusive, slanderous or idle speech, to abstain from intoxicating drink) and the six *pāramitās* or virtues of perfection (namely, Charity, Morality, Humility, Strenuosity, Contemplation and Spiritual Enlightenment) sum up, with some minor overlappings, the main tenets of the Buddhistic faith[39] and provide a striking contrast to the Jewish Decalogue with its primary emphasis upon a right knowledge of God. Even the Indian language of religion was used in Buddhism in a moralistic sense. Thus *Brahmavihārabhāvanā*, which would ordinarily mean thoughts conducive to or connected with enjoyment of Brahman, is used in Buddhism synonymously with the sublime moods which include love, pity, sympathising joy and equanimity (*maitrī, karuṇā, muditā, upekṣā*) and which have no religious

[35] Warren, *op. cit.*, p. 292.
[36] Mrs. Rhys Davids, *Buddhism*, p. 155.
[37] *Ibid.*, p. 121.
[38] *Ibid.*, p. 126.
[39] *Ibid.*, p. 154 (also Yamakami Sogen, *op. cit.*, p. 305).

significance but simply indicate certain attitudes of mind towards one's fellow-men.[40]

It is not our purpose just now to discuss why Northern Buddhism could not keep up the strictly ethical attitude towards the world, preached by Buddha; what we wish to emphasise here is that revelation in the case of Buddha took the form of an insight into the necessity of a strenuous moral life without reference to God and Immortality (which form two out of the three indispensable presuppositions of morality according to Kant) with a view to stopping those conditions of suffering which bring about the germination of Karmic seeds in the shape of repeated embodiments. The mystic craving was apparently satisfied by the stages of contemplation, to be found strewn all over the Piṭakas, and these could be practised only by those who had satisfied the conditions of a strict moral life; but there is no suggestion that they could bring about a union with Brahman or Īśvara or that the moral law required any lawgiver to establish its claim to recognition. Original Buddhism is therefore atheistic in a double sense—in the Indian sense of denying the authority of the Vedas and in the Western sense of refusing to discuss the necessity and the nature of God, and yet millions of lives have been ennobled by its message of morality and meditation. It laid down elaborate rules about social, personal and family obligations and yet kept intriguingly silent over those theological questions which form the major occupation of theistic creeds.

In its emphasis upon the moral aspect of religious life Buddhism stands almost unique among older creeds. Spasmodic attempts to dispense with the necessity of theological assumptions and anxious solicitation of the favour of gods are not indeed unknown in philosophy and ethics—Epicurus, for instance, preached *ataraxy* or impassiveness of the sages and the indifference of the gods, and this is also the creed of many thinkers who have in recent times attempted to combine practical morality with theoretical agnosticism and found the inspiration of their lives in some cult, patterned after Comte's

40 Mrs. Rhys Davids, *Buddhism*, p. 218; also M. N. Dutt, *Buddha*, p. 108 f.

Religion of Humanity, with ' Deed, not Creed ' as its motto. The Ethical Movement,[41] inaugurated in the wake of Secularism, is likely to gather momentum, as years roll on, if the existing positive religions insist upon the inviolability of their dogmas and their crude cosmological speculations. But as yet no purely ethical speculation has solaced so many souls, not always well educated, as Buddhism has done; and, if secularism were to spread further, no other religion is likely to make a stronger appeal to thoughtful men with an ethical disposition than the message of the Enlightened One, subject to such local modification about its speculative part (*e.g.*, the doctrine of Karma) as may be found necessary.

Two other prophets figure large in the religious field, whose primary concern was also the purification of human lives. Mahāvīra, the contemporary of Buddha, who probably reformed the religion of Pārśvanātha, did not altogether abolish the idea of gods; but, according to Jainism, these constituted one of the four forms in which finite souls (*jīvas*) could embody themselves and, in fact, the same term *devatā* served to indicate both gods and demons.[42] The attitude towards a supreme God who helps mankind is summed up in the sentence, " Man! Thou art thine own friend; why wishest thou for a friend beyond thyself?"[43] The Siddhas, the emancipated ones, take no interest in mundane affairs and receive no prayers or offerings; the Tīrthaṅkaras are adored for their piety, their perfection, and their compassionate message of salvation, but not in expectation of any boons.[44] The ideal of purity, perfection, freedom and blessedness is God—there is not any personal being, possessing these qualities, whom men must worship for salvation. Here, for instance, is a clear statement of the creed.[45] " The Jains do believe in a God after their own way of thinking—a belief which is in and through saturated with

[41] ERE. V. 412.

[42] Mrs. Sinclair Stevenson, *The Heart of Jainism*, p. 97.

[43] *Ibid.*, p. 128.

[44] *Ibid.*, p. 191; Nahar and Ghosh, *Outlines of Jainism*, p. 264.

[45] Nahar and Ghosh, *op. cit.*, p. 260.

all the vigour and strength of life. It does not make us dependent on any Almighty Ruler for our being and beatitude here or hereinafter. It does not cast us into the mould of those weaklings who love to creep with a quivering prayer on their lips to the silent doors of the Deity; nor of those who crawl, beating breast at every step before his fictitious feet or figure to adore. Rather it makes us feel that we are independent autonomous individuals who can carve out paths for ourselves here and hereinafter both for enjoyment of pleasures and emancipation of our souls by our own will and exertion." As a matter of fact, it is openly believed that only men can attain salvation by accepting the religion of Mahāvīra and that even the gods have to be reborn as men to attain self-knowledge and emancipation.[46]

These two heterodox religions of India are instructive in three respects. They are, firstly, the earliest experiments at a systematic course of personal purity and social morality without any assumption of a moral law-giver. They are, secondly, systems of morals that resisted all tendencies towards materialistic and fatalistic degenerations and actively combated all contemporary creeds that denied the moral responsibility of man or reduced him to a mere concourse of atoms. These two systems succeeded in establishing morality without religion because they practically substituted for the impersonal Upaniṣadic Brahman an eternal moral order, the authority of which was never questioned; and, while dissociating themselves from all speculations about mystic union with the Absolute, they retained and reinforced the Brahmanic ascetic organisation with its rules of discipline, its cult of self-knowledge, and its objective of individual liberation to be attained by personal endeavour. The way for this was prepared by the decline in importance of Varuṇa, the Vedic moral god, the development of the conception of Brahman, an impersonal spiritual principle, at the cost of the plurality of more or less personal gods, the decay of sacrifices all through the periods of the Āraṇyakas and the Upaniṣads, the increase

[46] Mrs. Sinclair Stevenson, *op. cit.*, p. 268.

in idealistic tendencies due to the developing practice of self-analysis, and an intensification of the ascetic ideal of life to such an extent that even atheists renounced the world and wandered about to preach their message. The third point is instructive for a different reason, namely, that ultimately both partially succumbed to theistic temptations and satisfied the religious craving by practically deifying the prophets and worshipping them on this side idolatry, thus establishing the demand made by religion that there are certain needs of the human heart which religious devotion and feeling of trust in a higher power can alone satisfy. Even tough minds have to fight hard against theistic failings; no wonder, therefore, that weaker souls should succumb to the blandishments of faith or live in high philosophy and crude superstition by turns.

This inadequacy of the merely moral can be exemplified also by reference to another religious reformer. K'ung-foo-tsze (Confucius), the Chinese sage who was ultimately accorded divine honours, was a lover of the ancients and professed to be a transmitter, and not a creator, of the religion which now goes by his name. This religion admitted the reality of a Supreme Power which was sometimes described in personal terms as Tî or Shang Tî (Supreme Ruler) and sometimes impersonally, or less personally, as T'ien (Heaven).[47] It is to Shang Tî that the Chinese Emperor offered sacrifices on behalf of the nation during the winter solstice. No one else had a right to offer sacrifices to Shang Tî, although a deputy of the Emperor could officiate at the worship of Hu-t'u (Empress Earth) at the summer solstice. The people at large could, however, worship T'ien, the impersonal form of the Supreme Power,[48] and they did not feel the need of Shang Tî on account of a variety of reasons. Firstly, all the principal qualities of Shang Tî were ascribed to T'ien also and only insignificant differences existed between the two, both standing for " a Power

[47] Soothill, *The Three Religions of China*, p. 53, 116, 119 f.; Legge, *The Religions of China*, p. 10.

[48] Soothill, *op. cit.*, p. 129.

above, great, beneficent, and just, who rewards virtue and punishes vice, and who can be approached in prayer."[49] Secondly, the stiff formality of the Imperial sacrifice tended to discourage all personal relationship with God and to lead men to imagine Him as a sovereign ruler before whom the only appropriate feeling was awful reverence; the people at large, on the other hand, invested T'ien with qualities more favourable to personal relationship[50]—in fact, the people of the North actually personified T'ien under the title of Lao T'ien Yeh (His Honour Heaven or the Honoured Progenitor Heaven) and the ancient script represented it by a human figure.[51] Lastly, the Imperial cult recognised the existence of lower deities (*shen*) and spirits of departed ancestors, and it is these, especially the latter, that the people at large generally worshipped.

It appears, therefore, that at first sight Confucius may well be reckoned as a reformer who laid equal emphasis on devotion and duty. But a closer examination shows that his support of the national religion was dictated more by prudence and patriotism than by piety. Religion was relegated mostly to the State, and the Emperor, as the son of Heaven, was the *pontifex maximus* of the nation. Confucius purified religion in two ways: firstly, he discouraged all idolatry so that the sacrifice to Shang Tî was offered under the open sky without the help of any image; and secondly, the lower spirits were mostly worshipped on tablets with the names of the gods or ancestors inscribed thereon.[52] He even forbade the indiscriminate worship of spirits with a view to gain, and limited the popular worship to sacrifice to one's own ancestors. It does not appear, however, that his cold Mongolian temper was very prone to religious rapture. In his scheme of faith sages, rulers and ancestors could vie with the deified powers of nature, local divinities and presiding spirits of

49 Soothill, *op. cit.*, p. 127.
50 *Ibid.*, p. 125.
51 *Ibid.*, p. 122.
52 *Ibid.*, p. 131.

professions, for the homage of men[53]—a prescription which later on led to his own rank being at first fixed in the second grade of worship and subsequently (in 1907) equated with that of Shang Tî himself.[54] "He himself avoided speaking on four subjects: extraordinary things; feats of strength; rebellious disorder; and spirits."[55] He was not without his doubts about the sacrifice to departed spirits. He is credited with the sayings, "While you are not able to serve men (alive), how can you serve their spirits?" and "While you do not know life, how can you know about death?" The same tendency to avoid topics not having a direct bearing upon life, as is found in Buddha, is present in Confucius also. He refused to be drawn into discussions about the nature of the soul and the laws of Heaven, even though he laid down that the perfection of human nature, bestowed by Heaven, could be achieved by proper instruction about the right way and though he accepted the continued existence of the soul by providing for the worship of ancestors.[56] The word 'prayer,' including its synonyms, occurs only about half a dozen times in his writings and only in the sense of an invocation for temporal blessings and not in the sense of 'adoration, communion with God, or entreaty for spiritual exaltation and development,'[57] and no definite meaning can be made of his cryptic saying, "My prayer has been for long." It is not improbable that his other cryptic saying, 'He who sins against Heaven has nowhere left for prayer,'[58] indicates that he had an abiding faith in the validity of the eternal laws of morality, of which Heaven was more the symbol than the

[53] Legge points out that "even though the presidency of those objects may be ignorantly and superstitiously assigned to different spiritual Beings, the prayers to them show that the worship of them is still a service of God."—*Religious Systems of the World*, p. 69.

[54] Soothill, *op. cit.*, p. 37.

[55] Analects VII, XX; see Legge, *The Religions of China*, pp. 117-18; also Soothill, *op. cit.*, p. 172.

[56] Soothill, *op. cit.*, p. 169, 170, 176; Legge, *op. cit.*, p. 112.

[57] Soothill, *op. cit.*, pp. 138-39; *Religious Systems of the World*, p. 68.

[58] Soothill, *op. cit.*, p. 139.

founder, and that, according to him, by transgressing these laws of propriety men forfeited the right and chance of temporal benefit. But for his anxiety to conform to immemorial tradition, Confucius would have enunciated more unequivocally the autonomous working of the moral law earlier than any other religious teacher whose name has come down to us. His main endeavour was not to make men devotional but to make them moral.[59] This explains why he took such particular care to enunciate the Doctrine of the Mean, according to which harmony rules not only the mind of the wise but also the world, and the Golden Rule, according to which we are enjoined not to do unto others what we would not like to be done to ourselves.

Quite in keeping with this moral tendency, we find, Confucius uses in his writings the impersonal form T'ien (Heaven) more frequently than the personal form Tî (although not in a greatly different sense)[60] and extols the knowledge that makes the mind sincere and brings about ultimately a rectified heart, a decorous conduct, a well-regulated family and a well-ordered State in succession. Not only here do we miss any hankering after transcendental speculations in the interests of rational thinking or purer faith, but also in his enunciation of the duties of men and the virtues to be practised we search in vain for any well-defined duties of devotion. Good life in Confucianism is almost synonymous with the maintenance of the five social relations of husband and wife, father and son, sovereign and subject, elder and younger brother, friend and friend—the first four between superiors and subordinates and the last one between equals.[61] In addition to these Five Human Relationships, there are also Five Constants or fundamentals of virtue, namely, kindness, justice, reverence, wisdom and good faith,

[59] Legge, however, remarks: "The idea of Heaven or God as man's Maker and Governor was fundamental to the teachings of Confucius; and on this account I contend that those who see in him a moral teacher do not understand him."—*Religious Systems of the World*, p. 71.

[60] Legge, *op. cit.*, p. 139.

[61] Soothill, *op. cit.*, p. 190.

which also are mainly secular in character. As Parker observes, "Self-control, modesty, forbearance, patience, kindliness, orderliness, absence of effusiveness and passion, studiousness, industry, mildness, dutifulness, neighbourliness, fidelity, uprightness, moderation, politeness, ceremoniousness—these were the qualities which Confucius consistently practised and taught."[62] These constituted, according to him, the way of perfection. That the message of morality succeeded so well is due to the fact that Confucius was too wise and politic to disturb the ancient religious practices of the nation even though he was himself sceptical about their efficacy: what he did positively was to teach men to have faith in themselves and in their status and, instead of pessimistically preparing for death, to get rid of the ills of life, to strive for the realisation and perfection of the innate goodness of their own nature and "to strengthen and perpetuate the things that are seen and temporal."[63] Inasmuch as there is a moral order in the world, the strenuous life of goodness is bound to have its reward just as the easy life of evil is sure to meet its doom; and this recompense is not deferred to a realm beyond, about the existence of which there may be some doubt, but is accomplished here below according to the eternal laws of righteousness. In this respect an easy comparison of Confucianism with pre-exilic Judaism is possible, with this difference, however, that the Hebrews never for a moment believed that the moral law could operate without the will of Yahweh. The easy acceptance of Buddhism and the concurrent vogue of Taoism in Confucian China are due to the fact that these two religions also accepted the validity of the moral law and the need of social harmony, self-knowledge and self-discipline. They supplied at the same time that element of mysticism and devotion to China which Confucianism lacked because of its intense preoccupation with the practical duties of social life and its apathy towards the

[62] M. Cannay, *An Encyclopædia of Religion*, art. *Confucianism* (p. 116), quoting Parker, *Studies in Chinese Religion.*

[63] *Faiths of the World*, p. 88.

unseen universe. But the Buddhism that China accepted had to shed its pessimism and its doctrine of transmigration. In place of Nirvāṇa were preached the Mahāyānic message of the Western Paradise of Amitābha as the reward of goodness and the cult of Buddhas and Bodhisattvas[64]—just those elements about which popular mind was so inquisitive and Confucius was so silent. Even when Imperial persecution dissolved the Buddhistic monasteries and nunneries, the people continued their devotion in household chapels, Taoist shrines and Buddhist temples, again bearing testimony to the inevitable doom of mere morality in a nation or a big community where large numbers cannot be expected to find in the laws of morality their own justification or a sufficient amount of emotional satisfaction.

So long as morality is a mere tribal custom men follow it blindly without questioning; but once it is made the subject of speculation, it is bound to be viewed either heteronomously as drawing its value and validity from divine dispensation, or autonomously as the law of nature which spontaneously brings reward to merit and suffering to demerit. Positive religions have never treated morality as ego-altruistic conduct, with no bearing upon the destiny of the soul, or as a convention that can be altered by general consent. There has been enough of narrowness in social outlook, and even elementary justice has been denied to men of alien faiths; but within each religious community the claims of morality have been paramount and many of the injustices to other faiths have been done under the honest belief that interests of social morality demanded them. This has happened as much in Confucianism, where no divine favour is sought to be gained by the oppression of other creeds, as in Judaism and Muhammadanism, where a motive of pleasing God has very often been present. In fact, the greater is the conviction that their own religion is the indispensable condition of salvation the

[64] Beal traces the conceptions of Kwan-yin and Amita Buddha to Persian sources (see his *Buddhism as it exists in China*).—See ***Enlightened Non-Zoroastrians on Mazdayasnism, the Excellent Religion***, p. 55.

greater is the persecution to which zealots subject aliens and apostates not only in anxious solicitude for wayward and ignorant souls but in holy zeal for destroying all seeds of corruption.

Nowhere else is the distinction between personal religion and institutional religion more clearly brought out than in the insistent emphasis on social morality which every prophet has been obliged to lay in his revelations. In societies where an adjustment of social dealings has become automatic on a fairly high moral level or where an independent ethical literature of didactic or hortatory character has developed and spread in the community, there is less need of direct moral teaching in the scriptures. It must never be supposed that man owes his morality to prophetic revelation and that but for the scriptures men would have roamed apart and killed or injured one another at sight. Gregariousness, innate sympathy, imitation and suggestion all do their work far below the religious—and even the conscious—level to bring men together and to establish a *modus vivendi* among social components. What Rev. George Matheson wrote about Christianity borrowing the Golden Rule from Confucianism is true of moral precepts in general. Says he,[65] "That Confucius is the author of this precept is undisputed, and therefore it is indisputable that Christianity has incorporated an article of Chinese morality. It has appeared to some as if this were to the disparagement of Christianity—as if the originality of its Divine Founder were impaired by consenting to borrow a precept from a heathen source. But in what sense does Christianity set up the claim to moral originality? When we speak of the religion of Christ as having introduced into the world a purer life and a surer guide to conduct, what do we mean? Do we intend to suggest that Christianity has for the first time revealed to the world the existence of a set of self-sacrificing precepts—that here for the first time man has learned that he ought to be meek, merciful, humble, forgiving, sorrowful for sin, peaceable, and pure in heart?

65 *Faiths of the World*, pp. 83-84.

The proof of such a statement would destroy Christianity itself, for an absolutely original code of precepts would be equivalent to a foreign language. The glory of Christian morality is that it is not original—that its words appeal to something which already exists within the human heart, and on that account have a meaning to the human ear: no new revelation can be made except through the medium of an old one. When we attribute originality to the ethics of the Gospel, we do so on the ground, not that it has given new precepts, but that it has given us a new impulse to obey the moral instincts of the soul." A religious reformation can only intensify, reinforce, or widen the range of, moral operation; but it does not create a morality the seeds of which are not already latent in the human heart and do not sprout forth in social dealings. That prophets, separated from one another by wide distances of time, space and culture, should inculcate practically the same moral principles, albeit with different intensities of connotation and extensities of denotation, and that, in spite of credal dissimilarities, advanced faiths should approximate one another in their moral contents show that the needs of practice are more constant than the needs of devotion and speculation—possibly because the former overflow the bounds of a single individuality and refer to those abiding factors of social existence without which not only the race of men but even animal communities would perish. This relative constancy of moral ideas led Buckle to write, "There is, unquestionably, nothing to be found in the world which has undergone so little change as those great dogmas of which moral systems are composed. . . . If we contrast this stationary aspect of moral truths with the progressive aspect of intellectual truths, the difference is indeed startling."[66]

We hasten to add, however, that, on account of the intimate connection among the faculties of the mind, morality cannot fail to be affected by limited vision or circumscribed

[66] Buckle, *History of Civilisation in England* (Vol. I, p. 180 f.), quoted in Westermarck, *Ethical Relativity*, p. 215.

sympathy. There are certain principles of social behaviour and social adjustment which no religion can ignore without ceasing to be a message to mankind. In days of warped judgment, corrupt authority and blind faith men have hearkened to many immoral and antisocial messages, adopted many uncharitable and unsocial attitudes towards their fellow-men, and have even desecrated faith by wanton cruelty and irrational hostility; but, with the growth of culture and the return of social sanity, such practices have always disappeared and thereby exposed their own transitory character True, faiths have also fallen from their pristine greatness in many lands; but the wheel of time has crushed those degenerate faiths except when it succeeded in raising them to noble heights again with the help of an ethical lever and endowing them with a fresh lease of useful longevity. Where are those religious practices and burial customs that at one time demanded human victims all over the world? Sacrificial cruelty even to lower animals is fast disappearing from the face of the earth. No more inquisition, *auto-da-fé*, putting an entire population to the sword because religion of a particular type is not acceptable to the weak and oppressed party. The conscience of the world is deeply stirred by any rare religious persecution that takes place anywhere nowadays. Even when scriptures have been disfigured by atrocious revelations, the developing conscience of man has put secular ban on the carrying out of these religious prescriptions, and this has been necessary especially in those religions where the scope for further revelation has been denied and exegesis has not been authorised to allegorise away or palliate the cruel injunctions.

Here then is an obvious advantage for those religions which have left scope for future improvements. While from one point of view the absence of finality invests their revelations with an ethical and spiritual relativity, from another point of view there is provision in them for a never-ending progression. Judaism, for instance, held fast to Moses as the original prophet but did not put down with an iron hand the presumptions of those who felt an irresistible call to preach spiritual messages of a non-Mosaic type. We shall not refer to the tampering of the Mosaic revelations themselves[67] in order to bring them into line with the developed ethical and spiritual conceptions of a later time, for that too was done more than once. But, apart from that, the genuineness of prophetic revelations of later times was never questioned by the Hebrews; and when the time came to close the canonical literature, the entire process of the development of the religion on the ethical side was embodied in the scripture. As a matter of fact, even post-canonical formulae of faith were also accepted by the community as expressing more adequately the later spiritual and ethical conceptions of the race though now their inspirational character could not be recognised.[68]

There are certain peculiarities about the Judaic revelation which are well worth noticing. That God could make His existence, character and intention known to mankind is a belief that is common to all theistic faiths. The Hebrews went further and taught that God could personally assume the direction of individual and national affairs and that in His choice of a favoured nation He was not under any extraneous obligation. If God chose to make a covenant with the Jews, it was not because they were more moral than the rest of the ancient world but because it was His will and intention to raise the Jewish nation in power and spirituality and to use it as the tool of His ethical management of the world.[69] He did not make their virtue automatic or their power irresistible; but the nation never lost faith in divine providence or in the divine dispensation that it was to be the torch-bearer of the unity and ethicality of God. The Hebrew prophets may very well be compared with the chorus in a Greek tragedy: they pass an ethical comment on national

[67] See Pringle-Pattison, *Studies in the Philosophy of Religion*, p. 123. For similar tampering with texts in the Prophets, see footnotes on p. 89 f. in R. H. Charles, *A Critical History of the Doctrine of a Future Life in Israel, in Judaism, and in Christianity* (*Eschatology, Hebrew, Jewish and Christian*).

[68] *E.g.*, the Thirteen Principles of Faith as drawn up by Moses Maimonides (see ERE. iv. 246; viii. 341).

[69] Gen. 22.18.

misfortunes and emphasise the moral insufficiency of the race for the continuance of divine favour and protection. Their running commentaries on national events and undertakings and on individual actions and iniquities provide the second form of divine revelation to Israel: God not only deals with the race but He also speaks to the prophets. Sometimes it seems as if a combination of the two revelations is necessary to understand aright the nature of God. The race knows Yahweh as the Lord of Hosts, a majestic power pleased by strict adherence to His covenant and angered by a violation either of His sanctity or of His commandments,—yet, withal, incapable of forsaking His chosen race in its calamities or allowing it to seek the asylum of other gods. The prophets, on the other hand, reveal Yahweh as a strictly ethical God who would not hesitate in the least to use foreign nations as the avenging rods of sinning Israel or to inflict banishment from native soil as a punishment for her iniquity, but who is at the same time merciful and readily forgiving. Israel must imitate Yahweh's holiness and mercy and think of Him more in terms of personal relationship than of national help and guidance, approach Him more with prayerful mind and clean hands than with costly sacrifices and frequent importunities. The major elements of the Jewish conception of the revealed God are to be found in the *Exodus* description:[70] "The Lord, the Lord, a God full of compassion and gracious, slow to anger, and plenteous in mercy and truth; keeping mercy for thousands, forgiving iniquity and transgression and sin: and that will by no means clear the guilty; visiting the iniquity of the fathers upon the children and upon the children's children, upon the third and upon the fourth generation." We have already traced the development of Hebrew thought through the Prophets and indicated in what ways it became concerned more with individual responsibility than with tribal or 'familial' solidarity in sin and suffering. Otto has shown how the Jewish idea of the Holy underwent transformation in an ethical direction in course of

[70] Exod. 34.6f.

time and the moral aspect grew at the expense of the dynamical.[71] Herein we may trace, in fact, the general evolution of man's consciousness of the supernatural, which starts with a belief in mysterious powers controlling operations that are beyond the capacity of man but capable of being enlisted in one's favour and against one's enemies by suitable incantations and propitiatory sacrifices. It is only late that men realise that these powers are on the side of the good alone and that it is goodness that is destined to survive in the long run. But even then, in times of war, men are apt to forget the lessons of civilisation and to hold intercession services in the fond belief that God could thereby be deflected from His moral purpose in dealing even-handed justice between the combatant parties,—to forget, that is, that the object of prayer is not to influence God's will but to help man to become perfect;[72] and the effect is that, as Bertrand Russell puts it, "envy, cruelty and hate sprawl at large with the blessing of nearly the whole bench of Bishops."

The peculiar character of Christian revelation cannot be properly understood without reference to the notable advance made by Judaism in the course of its history. From monolatry to monotheism, from tribal faith to personal religion, from a God of power and wrath to a God of mercy and love, from a Lord of Hosts to a Heavenly Father, from a God fond of rituals and sacrifices to a God responding to righteousness and prayer, from a God to whom the shadowy Sheol is practically no concern to a God on whom the virtuous could always rely for immortality and merited reward in heaven—these are no mean achievements in any race, circumstanced as Israel was, during a period of about a thousand years.[73] We should add that the political vicissitudes of the race were also responsible for a growing apocalyptic literature in which the advent of the Messiah was delineated with emotional fervour and the end of all creation awaited with eager and anxious ex-

71 Otto, *The Idea of the Holy*, Ch. X; see also Hobhouse, *Morals in Evolution*, II, pp. 119 f.

72 See *Convention of Religion in India*, 1909, I, p. 51.

73 See Pringle-Pattison, *Studies in the Philosophy of Religion*, p. 147.

pectation. It has been repeatedly pointed out that if the individual teachings of Jesus are taken into consideration, it would be possible to match each of them by a Rabbinical parallel: it would be strange indeed if in a race given to religious experimentation the reverse should be the case. It would be necessary also to remember that possibly at one stage of his career Jesus adapted his message to the needs of his race, which explains the institution of the twelve Apostles, each to judge one tribe of Israel, his solicitude for the lost sheep of the house of Israel but not for the Gentiles nor for the Samaritans whom his disciples were enjoined to avoid, his scrupulous adherence to the laws and customs of the race which he said he had come not to destroy but to fulfil, and his claim to be the Messiah for whom the nation had been expectantly waiting.[74] It is possible to add that what is true of the teachings *of* Jesus is also true of the teachings *about* Jesus and that the details of his life can now be matched by Judaic, Egyptian, Hellenic, Zoroastrian, Buddhistic and other parallels.[75] His birth, ministration, sayings, institutions, trial, death and resurrection have all been found to resemble this or that feature of more ancient cults, and this has led some to go to the length of supposing that Jesus was not an historic individual at all but a mere conglomeration of ideals. It is well to remember that about Buddha and Kṛṣṇa also the same doubt has been raised and that the theory of a solar myth has been propounded in their case as in that of Jesus. We shall leave the discussion of these foundational questions to more competent hands: ours is the more humble task of appraising the value of revelations that are traditionally associated with these founders of faiths.

In what then did the originality of Jesus lie? The question is best answered in the words of Montefiore,[76] a

[74] Basanta Coomar Bose, *Christianity*, Ch. 3. Similarly, Isaiah, whom Christ adopts as his model, " nowhere extends the blessings of the Kingdom (of God) to the heathen world." See R. H. Charles, *op. cit.*, p. 93.

[75] See Dhirendranath Chowdhury, Vedāntavāgīśa, *In Search of Jesus Christ*, Chs. XVIII, XIX, XX.

[76] Quoted by Pringle-Pattison, *Studies in the Philosophy of Religion*, p. 178 (foot-note); see also *The History of Christianity in Modern Knowledge*, pp. 341-42.

liberal Jew with a candid appreciation of the merits of Christianity. "It is apparently a fact," says he, "that Jesus thought of God as his (and our) Father, and used the term Father for God more habitually and constantly than is the case with any one Rabbi of whom we know." Of the Beatitudes he says, "There is a certain glow and intensity about them which seems new and distinctive. We can find Rabbinic parallels to each of them, but as a whole they seem original." "The Rabbis," he observes, "attached no less value to repentance than Jesus. . . But to seek out the sinner, and, instead of avoiding the bad companion, to choose him as your friend, in order to work his moral redemption, this was, I fancy, something new in the religious history of Israel. The rescue and deliverance of the sinner through pity and love and personal service—the work and the method seem both alike due to the teacher of Nazareth." Comparisons are always odious, but it is always possible to appreciate what the followers of a particular religion think their prophet has done for them and for the world at large. If we turn to any Christian account of the special contributions of Jesus to the stock of man's religious experience, we shall almost invariably find an emphasis on the three following messages, as enunciated by Harnack, namely, (1) the Kingdom of God and its coming, (2) God the Father and the infinite value of the human soul, and (3) the higher righteousness and the commandment of love.[77]

Regarding the first, it is possible to differentiate the traditional and the moral aspect, which are almost equally balanced in the Synoptic Gospels.[78] On the one hand, we have the more material picture of a Kingdom of God, to be established here below by Messianic effort "before the present generation have passed away," and, as a corollary thereto, an insistence upon immediate repentance and the purging of the world of demons and diseases. There was no time to wait as the end of the world was drawing nigh and

[77] Harnack, *What is Christianity?*, p. 52.

[78] See *Religious Foundations*, Ch. VI.

the Heavenly Court was waiting for Christ and His Apostles to do their earthly office of warning and help before taking up their position of heavenly assessors. In this Jesus was simply echoing contemporary Jewish beliefs, with this difference, however, that he took active steps to show the people the way to this Kingdom and to warn them against the false sense of security engendered by conformity to customary morality. But Jesus did not also miss any opportunity to emphasise the spiritual aspect of this Kingdom—it was already in their midst, it did not come with observation, it was not of this world, it was within them. Thus the Kingdom of God was not a far-off divine event which he, as the lineal descendant of David, was to rule over with the assistance of his saints. It was a spiritual kingdom which the poor in spirit and those persecuted for righteousness' sake were alone to inherit, as also those who had the lowliness of heart and the innocence necessary to match them with little children. As such, it was present wherever men lived in "righteousness and peace and joy in the Holy Spirit," irrespective of the race or nationality to which they belonged.[79]

Now, this Kingdom of God is governed by peculiar laws. The right of naturalisation is bestowed automatically by righteous living just as forfeiture of rights follows the abandonment of the moral path. The citizens form a goodly fellowship and the relation of master and servant is unknown —in fact, all distinctions of rank are abolished—in that Kingdom.[80] Unlike the preponderatingly negative injunctions of the Ten Commandments of the Old Testament, the Christian prescription is decidedly positive,—it preaches the precepts not of fear but of love. 'Hear, O Israel; the Lord our God is One Lord.' 'And thou shalt love the Lord thy God with all thy heart, and with all they soul, and with all thy mind, and with all thy strength: this is the first commandment.

[79] See C. J. J. Webb. *The Contributions of Christianity to Ethics*, p. 98 f.; also R. M. Jones, *How shall we think of Christ?* in *Religious Foundations*, p. 24 f.; A. Alexander, *Christianity and Ethics*, p. 132 f.; also Bertrand Russell, *Why I am not a Christian*, pp. 22-23.

[80] John 15.14 f.

The second is like, namely, this : Thou shalt love thy neighbour as thyself. There is none other commandment greater than these.'[81] Paul's commentary on the prophetic message will put the matter in a clearer light : "Owe no man anything, but to love one another ; for he that loveth another hath fulfilled the law. For this, Thou shalt not commit adultery, Thou shalt not kill, Thou shalt not steal, Thou shalt not bear false witness, Thou shalt not covet ; and if there be any other commandment, it is briefly comprehended in this saying, Thou shalt love thy neighbour as thyself. Love worketh no ill to his neighbour : therefore love is the fulfilling of the law."[82] It is evident that although in a sense the laws of this kingdom are simple and positive, their fulfilment is no easy task. Love that gives away everything goes fundamentally against the egoistic instinct, and in that sense neither is the Christian task easy nor its yoke light. Hence, as Alexander points out,[83] although the kingdom preached by Christ is in one sense a present reality it is at the same time a thing of gradual growth—it is " a great social ideal to be realised by the personal activities and mutual services of its citizens." " When the same love which He Himself manifested in His life becomes the feature of His disciples; when His spirit of service and sacrifice pervades the world, and the brotherhood of man and the federation of nations everywhere prevail; then, indeed, shall the sign of the Son of Man appear in the heavens, and then shall the tribes of the earth see Him coming in the clouds with power and glory."[84]

Although there was a singular appropriateness in preaching the message of a Kingdom of God among the Jews, to whom the idea of a Heavenly Lawgiver was no novel idea, Christ brought a new significance into the matter by thinking of God not merely as King but also as Father. The divine voice had announced Christ's ministration by calling him His beloved Son : Christ held fast to this revelation and taught

81 Mark 12.29f.

82 Rom. 13.8f. See Streeter, *The Buddha and the Christ*, p. 183 (love = creative will-to-God); p. 247 f.

83 A. Alexander, *Christianity and Ethics*, pp. 136-37.

84 *Ibid.*, pp. 139-40.

that even a sinner was only a prodigal son whom a merciful Father would be ever willing to welcome back. Grace replaces Law and rays of Hope lighten up even the darkest gloom of Sin. It seems incredible that "though our sins as scarlet be they shall be bleached as white as snow;" but we are asked to believe in this miracle, to have faith in the message of salvation brought by Christ, to forgive others as we hope to be forgiven ourselves.[85]

This sonship of man depended, however, on two conditions. To know God as Father men must accept the revelation as preached by Christ. "He presented Himself as the indispensable organ and mediator of this knowledge. He, and He alone, had it; He, and He alone, had the power to communicate it; and it lay with him to determine to whom the revelation should be made."[86] His claim that he who had seen Him had seen the Father was meant to be taken in an exclusive sense as implying that in no other way was the Father knowable and in no other way except through Him was atonement with God possible. As Scott remarks,[87] "Jesus is conceived as summing up in His person the essential qualities of the Kingdom (of God), faith, obedience, love toward God, superiority to the forces of evil, life that is beyond the reach of death. And it follows that men's relation to the Kingdom is conditioned by their relation to Him. Upon that relation depends a man's attainment of the *summum bonum*, his true happiness in this life and the life to

[85] *The History of Christianity in Modern Knowledge*, p. 344.

[86] *Ibid.*, p. 341. See also Rom. 15.8-12.

It should be added that this monopoly of revelation and salvation by Christianity was not preached uniformly by the Apostles. Thus Peter is represented as saying, "Of a truth I perceive that God is no respecter of persons: but in every nation he that feareth him, and worketh righteousness, is acceptable to him." (Acts 10.34, 35). It appears also that Christ's message was primarily meant for the Jews, for Peter proceeds to add: "The word which God sent unto the children of Israel, preaching peace by Jesus Christ: (he is lord of all:) that word, I say, ye know etc." It is only fair to add, however, that the command of the resurrected Christ to "teach all nations, baptising them in the name of the Father, and of the Son, and of the Holy Ghost" (Mat. 28.19-20; Mark 16.15-16; Luke 24.47) is what the Church has preferred to follow.

[87] See *The Theology of the New Testament* in *History of Christianity, etc.*, p. 345.

come." The second condition is that men must take active steps to realise the potentialities of their sonship to God. As Jones observes,[88] " It does not follow, because God is Father, that all men are by nature sons. Sonship is not a birth-relationship. It is an attitude of heart, a spirit, a way of life. Nobody is a son until he wants to be one, until he discovers his opportunity, wakes up to his possibilities and chooses to enter his heritage. God *is* Father; we *become* sons." Or, as Scott puts it, " Jesus assumes that God is the Father of all men; He does not assume that all men are His sons. The relationship is for men potential. It requires to be realised in thought and practice, recovered, it may be, through penitence."[89]

We are not concerned just now with the development of the original revelation of Christ except in so far as it explains the rise of a new prophet. To Paul the expiatory death of Christ became the central concept of the new religion and the crucified Christ not only abrogated the Law but also abolished sin.[90] The Pharisees had insisted on the existence of a righteous people as the condition of the advent of the Messiah; Paul preached Messianic righteousness as a gift of God, and sinful men could, according to him, participate in Messianic salvation by believing in the message and the mission of the crucified Prophet.[91] " Whilst the direction of the primitive Christian consciousness was predominantly, one may say exclusively, eschatological, and the life of a Christian on earth appeared for this reason to be still an expectation, not yet a completion,.........Paul makes the " newness of life " to begin not with that completion on the other side of the grave but with the life of faith on earth of the Messiah's community."[92] He preached at the same time the heavenly origin of the person of Christ and " the part of Mediator was ascribed to the pre-existing Christ, not only in the historical revealing of salvation, but also in the creation of the world

[88] *Religious Foundations*, p. 24.
[89] *History of Christianity*, p. 341.
[90] Pfleiderer, *Paulinism*, I, p. 7.
[91] *Ibid.*, p. 12.
[92] *Ibid.*, p. 19 (see also *History of Christianity etc.*, p. 374).

itself."[93] We shall not enter here into the Christological speculations of the Apostolic and the sub-Apostolic age; suffice it to say that within a short time of Christ's death the deification of Christ was complete, and he became the second person of the Trinity, the eternal Logos, who, to redeem mankind from its sins, incarnated Himself and, offering Himself as a sinless sacrifice, effected once for all the reconciliation of God and man—the restoration or establishment of "a relation of amity, love, and sonship between man and God."[94] No wonder that the superhuman achievements of Christ should lead to his being called Lord—an epithet which in popular Christianity tended to assimilate Christ to God and, by subordinating the human aspect to the divine, to lead to a kind of deification and idolatry in some of the Christian Churches.[95] To trace the evolution of this idea would be to write a history of the early Christian Church, but we would then be in the realm of philosophy and dogma and not of revelation.

It is remarkable that while much of the theological implication of their message and the squabble over its interpretation has been forgotten, two of the religious leaders of mankind should shine with undimmed lustre all through the centuries, namely, Jesus and Buddha. Each received remarkable personal homage from a small band of devoted followers, who took infinite pains to commit to memory the sayings of their spiritual leader and arranged for their oral transmission till they were recorded in writing. Principles took flesh and blood in their own lives and each embodied in his personal character the ideals which he preached. This actuality of the ideal invested their messages with a tremendous moral force, against which bare principles could hardly hold their ground. The dignity and equality of individuals which both taught tended to break down the distinctions of class and race in Judæa and India respectively, and laid the foundations of

[93] Pfleiderer, *Paulinism*, I, p. 143.

[94] About the sinlessness of Christ, see Streeter, *Reality*, p. 189 f.; see also *Ibid.*, p. 231 f.; also *Foundations*, Sixth Essay (The Atonemtnt), by Moberly.

[95] See *Foundations*, Fifth Essay, p. 213 f. (for a discussion about the Divinity of Christianity by William Temple).

a universalism in religion to which the ancient world of either place was not accustomed. Both discarded the sacrificial religion and preached instead a message of morality and compassion, which had the effect of withdrawing the mind from formalities and concentrating it on the essentials of ethical and amicable living. It may be added, as a further point of resemblance, that veneration to each ultimately led to apotheosis with its attendant theological speculations about the nature and necessity of incarnation. But this apart, each proclaimed a way of life which subsequent ages were forced either to incorporate in their creed or to rebut but could never ignore. Buddhism marched in its victorious conquest towards the East and Christianity towards the West; but wherever either went it forced the local religions to a close self-analysis and these either succumbed completely or brought out the best in them to match its moral and spiritual grandeur. To-day the world is more Christian and Buddhist than it imagines, suspects or confesses; for all creeds, reformed since the advent of Christ or Buddha, have been quickened into ethical life by the contact of one or other of the two and Christianity, being a fuller revelation in the sense that it enunciated the laws of duty and devotion alike, has made wider appeal than Buddhism with its message of negation and its subtle philosophy.[96]

Soon, however, a new prophet arose in Arabia with a new message. It does not appear that the monotheism of the Jews, whose scriptural literature was possibly known among the Arabs, had any considerable influence on the religious beliefs of the people of Arabia. These made their annual pilgrimage to the shrine at Mecca where idols of male and female deities were deposited.[97] 'Here were ranged the three hundred and sixty idols, one for each day, round the great god

[96] See Streeter, *The Buddha and the Christ*, pp. 61-71; also Ameer Ali, *The Spirit of Islam*, p. xlv.

[97] Lammens points out that "Arab paganism knew no idols properly so called, no formal representations of divine beings. Its divinities were stones which took the most varied forms: oddly shaped blocks, monoliths, erected or strangely sculptured by atmospheric erosion, assuming sometimes the appearance of men, of columns or pylons. Some remained attached to the rock where they had been

Hobal, carved of red agate, the two ghazâlas, gazelles of gold and silver, and the image of Abraham and his son. Here the tribes came, year after year, " to kiss the black stone which had fallen from heaven in the primeval days of Adam, and to make the seven circuits of the temple naked."[98] Drinking, gambling and music were widely indulged in, polygamy and incest were rampant, and infanticide was practised.[99] The tribes were disunited and internecine quarrels marked their history. The Jews had a considerable following in South Arabia but proselytism was ceasing among them. The Christians too had a fair following in the North and also in the South but they mostly belonged to the heretical sects of the Nestorians and the Jacobites, which were constantly at strife with each other.[100] Nor was there any love lost between the Jews and the Christians. That Muhammad's restless mind, dissatisfied with the religious practices of his people, should seek enlightenment from the Jews and the Christians is *a priori* probable; but it is almost certain that in the early days of his career he, like the contemporary Hanifs, failed to distinguish them clearly and made occasional confusions between the traditions of the two.[101] His personal regard for the earlier prophets was undoubted, even though at times it seems that his main purpose was to utilise their sayings and deeds in furtherance of his own position and creed. Other traditions had also filtered down to Mecca; and it is not unlikely

discovered. Others, like the Black Stone, were preciously enclosed in a small building where the worshippers were not content to surround them with a circle of stones. Usually there was a well in the neighbourhood which served for ablutions, and often also a sacred tree, itself a god or the habitation of a divine being......All round stretched the haran, sacred territory affording the right of sanctuary to all living things, men and animals. Even the trees of the haran must be religiously respected and no branch must be plucked from them.—*Islam : Beliefs and Institutions*, p. 18.

98 Ameer Ali, *op. cit.*, p. lxiv.

99 Lammens points out that " there is nothing to prove that infanticide was prevalent in Arabia except in the Tamim tribe which appears to have practised it during a severe famine." He thinks that the imputation is based upon the disregard of the Beduins for their female children.—*Islam : Beliefs and Institutions*, p. 21.

100 Ameer Ali, *op. cit.*, p. li.

101 Lammens, *op. cit.*, p. 22.

that, as Stubbe remarks,[102] " the state of Arabia being divided into Jews, Judaising Christians, Judaising Arabs, Jacobites, Nestorians, Arians, Trinitarians, Manichees, Montanists, Sabaeans and Idolaters, gave him occasion and opportunity to examine and try all sects and sorts of religions."

The revelation that came to Muhammad was primarily directed against the polytheism and the idolatry of his own people and secondarily against the Jewish and Christian conceptions of God.[103] God is one without a second, entirely formless and immeasurably greater than the puny gods that the idolaters worshipped. Eternal hell-fire awaits those who do not forsake their idols or who place gods beside God. The world is created and governed by God not in sport but in all seriousness, and angels and other spirits act as His messengers and carry out His behests. The will of God is revealed through angelic agency to prophets, and God in His infinite mercy always warns people through their own prophets against sinful life before visiting their iniquities with dire punishment. Nothing can be hidden from His sight, but He is ever ready to forgive those who stray from the path of virtue provided they repent and leave off their sinful life and call upon the name of God and perform the practices of Islam as preached by Muhammad. A blissful state in heaven is reserved for those who believe in God and the angels and the prophets, in resurrection on the Judgment Day, when each will have to give an account of his own life, and also in separate treatments to be meted out to the virtuous and the sinful. God's power is subject to no restriction and He can enable even an illiterate man like Muhammad to reveal a book of such literary excellence that men and *jinn* together can never aspire to produce its like. To Muhammad God has sent down through Gabriel an Arabic Qur'ān from heaven, sura by sura, as occasions demanded. All salvation must be mediated through him and after him no other prophet would be vouchsafed unto nations. God is omnipotent and

[102] Stubbe, *op. cit.*, p. 143.

[103] See Ameer Ali, *op. cit.*, Part II, Ch. I, The Ideal of Islam.

good, and submission to His will is the paramount virtue. God can abrogate a previous revelation, but He does so only to give a better one in its place. He has determined all things from eternity, and none can even believe in Him without His will. All men are equal before His eyes and the duty of man is to live in peace with others. But there must be no compromise with idolatry or apostasy, and while leniency is permissible to monotheists (followers of a revealed book) like the Jews, the Christians and the Zoroastrians, polytheism and idolatry must be given no quarters.[104] The believers must be sufficiently powerful to carry out their reforms, and thus it is essential that they should be in possession of the holy places of the nation, and their power and prowess command respect elsewhere. But power must be used to succour the distressed and to help the needy. Widows, orphans and the poor of the community must be supported by the compulsory tithes of the wealthy,[105] and believing slaves should be manumitted. Usury should be abjured for it works hard on the poor. Women should be respected and provided for.

Certain broad differences between Islam and Judaism can at once be noticed, although there is no doubt that Muhammad drew largely upon Jewish sources, Biblical and Talmudic, for much of his social legislation and his cosmological and historical speculation. Direct revelation of God's will, as on Mount Sinai to Moses, is denied: God is too far above the world and too majestic to be directly accessible to man. Besides, He has no form and to that extent all stories about God's visible appearance to man must be discredited.[106] Secondly, the entire sacrificial cult of ancient Judaism is abandoned. No representation of God was to be permitted—not even symbolic ones—inside the place of

[104] Sura 2.186. Muslim, Imān, Tradition 32 (quoted by Wensinck, *The Muslim Creed*, p. 13): "The Apostle of Allah has said: I am ordered to make war upon people till they say: There is no God but Allah."

[105] Abu Bakr is represented as holding the view that between those who followed a false prophet or gave up religion altogether and those who professed Islam but paid no *zakāt* there was no difference and war was justifiable against both. Umar held a separate view. See Wensinck, *op. cit.*, pp. 13-14.

[106] On the question of seeing Allāh, see Wensinck, *op. cit.*, p. 69 f.

worship. After his breach with the Jews the *kebla* was changed from Jerusalem to Mecca, and this, combined with the retention of some of the heathen Arabic practices, *e.g.*, pilgrimage to Mecca, and the claim to reveal an Arabic Qur'ān for the Arabs,[107] must have appealed to the national pride of his countrymen and ultimately secured their conversion. Muhammad was unwilling to countenance the excessive veneration for the Law which the Jews exhibited, and close religious corporations, like the Rabbis and the Scribes, were also not to his liking. Besides, while respectful towards earlier prophets, he disfavoured the bestowal of almost divine honours upon Moses and the excessive veneration for Ezra who, because of his restoration of the national life and law, had been declared by the Jews to be the son of God. He had, of course, nothing but undisguised hatred for such Jews as continued the practice of worshipping the Teraphim—'false gods and idols,' as they are called in the Qur'ān. Islam was represented as the true religion of Abraham which the Jews had corrupted or forsaken.[108]

Towards Christianity Muhammad entertained mixed feelings. He believed in the virgin birth of Christ and also in his investiture with the Holy Spirit, his mission, his miracles and his second coming. He regarded him as belonging to the same prophetic succession as that to which he himself belonged and as confirming the revelations of earlier prophets beginning with Abraham. He disbelieved, however, in the crucifixion of Jesus and thought that another in the likeness of him had been killed by the Jews. He, however, reserved his severest condemnation for those who had wilfully removed all New Testament passages referring to his own oncoming, who preached Jesus not as the servant but as the only begotten son

107 When Muhammad called himself *ummī*, he meant thereby that he was the Arabian Prophet of the gentiles, speaking to the gentiles to whom no Apostle had ever been sent before. His feelings are the same as those of St. Paul, when he writes to the Romans: "I speak to you, Gentiles, inasmuch as I am the Apostle of the Gentiles." In the same sense Muhammad emphasises that the Kuran is an "Arabian book" or an "Arabian verdict."—Wensinck, *op. cit.*, p. 6.

108 *Ibid.*, p. 7.

of God (for God neither begets nor is begotten) and bestowed on him divine honours, and who abandoned the Jewish ideal of a householder's life in favour of celibacy and monasticism (later on accepted by the Sufis).[109] There is no doubt that Jesus is reverentially treated in the Qur'ān; how far this exceptional treatment was dictated by a hope that the Christians would readily accept his claim to be "the seal of the prophets" must remain an open question.

It must be admitted that Muhammadanism is a unique miracle of religious history. To have taught undiluted monotheism to a nation of idolaters, not far above the primitive stage in its social dealings, and to have used it as the army of Allāh to conquer a stretch of land from Spain to India within a short time of Muhammad's death are achievements to which few parallels can be found in history. Islam has ever been the champion of uncompromising monotheism; and although honest differences of opinion must always exist about the methods adopted to conquer countries and convert their citizens, there can be no doubt that lust of power and persecution was strongly reinforced by religious motives and by a genuine conviction that no souls should be left in danger of their salvation if Islam could help it. While preaching the message of peace that there should be no compulsion in religion, Islam believes at the same time that after the final revelation has come through Muhammad every soul that hangs back from it is doomed. Conversely, it is the duty of each believer to disseminate the New Dispensation: Muhammad himself set the example by inviting some of the potentates of his own time to accept his message.[110] As he had to fight

[109] See Lammens, *op. cit.*, p. 117.

[110] The view that Muhammad conceived of his mission as a universal one is naturally derived from Muslim tradition. Here it reaches its most characteristic expression in the story of how Muhammad sent letters to the Great Powers of his time, the Emperor at Byzantium (Kaisar), the King of Persia (Kisrā), the Negus of Abyssinia (al-Nadjāshī), the Governor of Egypt (al-Mukawkis), inviting them to embrace Islam. These letters are, however, of a doubtful authority, if indeed they are not wholly legendary. Signora Dr. Vacca is probably right in supposing that these and similar tales were invented to furnish the Prophet's *exequatur* for the conquerors who conducted the Muhammadan armies to the four quarters of the world.—Wensinck, *op. cit.*, pp. 7-8.

against false faith and cruel custom simultaneously, his book contains both elements of genuine theism and principles of social government—the second becoming more and more frequent and elaborate as he began to administer larger states and govern a wider population. What he did for his countrymen is best described in the language of one of the exiles to the court of the Negus of Abyssinia: "O King, we were plunged in the depth of ignorance and barbarism; we adored idols, we lived in unchastity; we ate dead bodies, and we spoke abominations; we disregarded every feeling of humanity, and the duties of hospitality and neighbourhood; we knew no law but that of the strong, when God raised among us a man, of whose birth, truthfulness, honesty and purity we were aware; and he called us to the unity of God, and taught us not to associate anything with Him; he forbade us the worship of idols; and enjoined us to speak the truth, to be faithful to our trusts, to be merciful, and to regard the rights of neighbours; he forbade us to speak evil of women, or to eat the substance of orphans; he ordered us to fly from vices, and to abstain from evil; to offer prayers, to render alms, to observe the fast."[111]

In order to indicate the historical evolution of Semitic revelation we have thus far ignored the great prophet whose eschatological teachings the Semitic creeds probably absorbed without open acknowledgment, namely, Zarathustra.[112] Carelessness, contamination and persecution all combined to hide and mutilate the true message of the Prophet of Iran, and it is only in recent times that we have been put in possession of such of the original revelation as is extant. Although his fame stood high in the ancient world his age was unknown, and even to-day we are still wrestling with the problem of his date. At a time when men were engaged in worshipping a multiplicity of spirits, good and bad, and propitiated them with

111 Ameer Ali, *The Spirit of Islam*, pp. 29-30.

112 See Söderblom, *The Living God*, Ch. VI, Religion as Fight against Evil. Zarathustra.

bloody sacrifices—perhaps by killing the animals seized unlawfully in raids upon a settled pastoral population, he claimed to have seen God and received from Him a commission to preach a new message of spiritual life. The message was at once ethical, social and religious. Man was enjoined to regard himself as a creature of two worlds,—but not in such a fashion as to imply that the abnegation of the temporal ensured the attainment of the eternal. The House of Song or Praise, as Heaven is felicitiously described, is a continuation of the earthly life, and not only the soul but also the body would wake up in heaven after falling finally asleep on earth. Legitimate pleasures of the body are not only permitted but enjoined. Asceticism is condemned while a householder's life is always praised, exactly as in Judaism and Islam: as a matter of fact, the Prophet himself was a married man and had a family. Men are asked to cultivate social virtues and to lend a helping hand to the needy and the distressed. The Ox-soul is represented as crying out for succour and help from the oppression of the nobles and the depredations of the wild nomads who carried away flocks of animals and killed them for food or at nocturnal orgiastic sacrifices.[113] The faithful are enjoined to embrace a settled life and to labour hard for the foundation of permanent homestead. "He who sows the fields that lie fallow, who tills his farms, prunes his vineyards, ploughs the furrows, pastures his flocks, extirpates the noxious creatures that infest the earth, and turns barren deserts into fertile fields, is the one that furthers the cause of Righteousness."[114]

Life under these conditions is fairly strenuous; so it is to a life of struggle against evil and imperfection that the prophet invites his followers. The responsibilities and rewards

[113] Moulton thinks that originally flesh on grass was used by the Iranians for sacrifice. Söderblom thinks that Zarathustra banned this Mithraic sacrifice from the worship of Ahura Mazda. See Moulton, *Early Zoroastrianism*, p. 68; Söderblom, *The Living God*, p. 180; Haug, *Essays, etc.*, p. 139.

[114] Dhalla, *Zoroastrian Theology*, p. 16. Söderblom thinks that agriculture was unknown to Zarathustra and that he really advocated the life of a pasture-keeper and a cattle-tender (*op. cit.*, p. 179, 226).

of a fighting life are great; hence the necessity of constant wakefulness. But the result of the fight is sure victory for goodness; hence there is ample scope for optimism. The triumph of goodness at the end is, however, not to be viewed as predestined in the sense that without the active co-operation of man the world will work out its appointed destiny. Man is a fellow-worker with God in the eradication of evil and the result of his labour is not only the defeat of evil but also the attainment of the blissful realm of Heaven, while his non-coöperation means prolonging the miseries of existence and bringing about his own suffering in hell. The greatest enemy of the human soul is Druj, *i.e.*, Lie in all its forms. Purity of thought, speech and action is the essential condition of a moral life : Zarathustra succeeded so well in inculcating this principle that at the time of Herodotus the Persians enjoyed a reputation for truthfulness which the great historian considered to be sufficiently important to deserve notice in his book.

This ethical preaching was based upon a monotheism which was a novelty in Iran. This Aryan "Puritan of the ancient world" preached monotheism with a Semitic zeal and, in the fashion of the Hebrew prophets, stigmatised the daevas as lies and abominations. He raised Ahura Mazdah,[115] the all-wise Lord, to the supreme position and, while not expressly forbidding other gods, ignored their existence.[116] He

115 The origin of this divine name is obscure. Both historical probability and analogy in the history of religion lead us to assume that Mazdah, with Ahura, as the name of the divinity, existed long before Zarathustra. Instead of the Lord, Ahura, or the All-Wise, Mazdah, Zarathustra not infrequently calls God Mazdah Ahura, in two words declined separately, the All-Wise Lord. Subsequently, in the later Avesta, the two words are otherwise juxtaposed, so as to make one double name for God, *Ahura Mazdah*, which never occurs in the Gathas as one word. The constituent parts of the double name are, however, declined separately in the Avesta. It is noteworthy that Darius I about 514-510 B.C., in his great inscription at Behishtun, employs the same firmly established divine name in one word : Auramazdah, who is there called the god of the Aryans.—Söderblom, *op. cit.*, p. 196.

Prof. Hommel's discovery of the divine name *Assara Mazās* in an Assyrian inscription of the reign of Assur-bani-pal involves an antiquity for the name of Ahura Mazdah higher than any scholar could venture to assign to Zarathustra, whose claim to the authorship of this characteristic title must, I fear, be abandoned.—Moulton, *Early Zoroastrianism*, p. 31.

116 Söderblom, *op. cit.*, p. 195; also p. 196.

does not take the credit of founding the religion to himself, for he refers to old revelations, and praises the fire-priests;[117] but there is no doubt that the world is indebted to him for preaching ethical monotheism in a region where idolatry was at one time rampant and polytheism was the prevailing creed. While it is possible to trace the germs of later dualism and the personification of abstract qualities in his own message to mankind,[118] he cannot be personally held responsible for what the Magis made out of his religion in later times. Ahura Mazdah is the sole God : his body is like the light and his soul like Truth. He is interrogated by Zarathustra as a friend by a friend on the various essentials of religion[119] and righteous living; there is nothing of the "terrific majesty" of Yahweh about Him and He does not speak in voices of thunder or from behind a veil of darkness.[120]

The message of the Prophet covers both the here and the hereafter. Whosoever in piety and devotion fights for the moral order of Ahura Mazdah and drives away the daevas and the lies from his life will pass easily over the bridge, that separates the good from the evil after their death (*Cinvato peretu*), into the House of Song or Praise (Garo demāna), the region of Best Thought (Vohu Manah),[121] being helped thither by the advocacy and guidance of Zarathustra himself, by the judgment of Obedience to religious lore (Sraosha)[122] and the merit of the virtuous soul (Daenā) that becomes fairer with

117 Haug, *op. cit.*, p. 294. Moulton and Spiegel translate the passages cited by West quite differently. See also Moulton, *Early Zor.*, pp. 30-31.

118 The six spirits who together with Ahura Mazdah later form a heptad are all mentioned in one Gatha (47 .1) :

"By his holy Spirit (Spenta Mainyu) and by Best Thought (Vahistem Manah; *Vohu Manah*, Good Thought), deed and word, in accordance with Right (Asha, *Asha Vahishta*), Mazdah Ahura with Dominion (Khshathra, *Khshathra Vairya*, the desired Dominion) and Piety (Armaiti, *Spenta Armaiti*, holy Devotion) shall give us Welfare (*Haurvatat*) and Immortality (*Ameretat*)."—Söderblom, *op. cit.*, p. 189.

119 Yasna 44 .1 ; 46 .2.

120 Söderblom, *op. cit.*, p. 202.

121 Moulton, *Ear. Zor.*, p. 162, 167, 170; Dhalla, *Zor. Theo.*, p. 57.

122 In the later periods Sraosha acts as a co-assessor with Mithra (Spirit of Illumination and Truth) and Rashnu (Spirit of Justice), who all combine to make up a heavenly tribunal for the judgment of the dead.—Dhalla, *Zor. Th.*, p. 41; also p. 106, 111.

every good thought, word and action. The opposite is the fate of those who, like the Kavis, Karapans and Usijs, indulge in non-ethical and polytheistic activities. They would be condemned to Hell which is described as "the House of the Lie (Druj) and of Worst Thought, the House of the Daevas, the Worst Existence and the like.[123] It is the realm of eternal misery, of darkness, bad food and cry of agony, of torment from one's own evil conscience. This eschatological message of Zarathustra has a special significance, for post-exilic Judaism took it over from the Persians along with their angelology and their anti-idolatrous monotheism, and made these the common property of the Semitic creeds.[124] Whatever might have been his own indebtedness to earlier religious thinkers of Persia, the message as passed on by Zarathustra to later generations acted as a powerful leaven and affected contiguous cultures in a most penetrating manner. His followers, though scattered like the Jews by persecution, have not betrayed their spiritual trust, and his faith survives as one of the beacon lights of spiritual insight, handed down from an ancient world where it had once blazed in the midst of surrounding darkness. A certain amount of degeneration and superstition has invaded Zoroastrianism in course of its progress through space and time but not to such an extent as to affect seriously its most vital elements.

We shall close our account of prophetic revelations with a reference to the other branch of the Aryan migration. In the Avesta we come across a class of people who worshipped the Daevas, perhaps with animal sacrifices, were addicted to a nomadic and pastoral life, and used to raid the settled habitations of the followers of Ahura Mazdah. References to their depredations and hostility are so frequent in the Avesta that it has not been unreasonably supposed that with these Daevayasnians the Mazdayasnians were in immediate and daily contact and that, therefore, they were not the Vedic

123 Moulton, *Early Zor.*, p. 172. See Sneath (ed.), *Religion and the Future Life*, pp. 128-29.

124 Some instructive parallels have been shown by Moulton in his *Early Zoroastrianism* (Lecture IX, Zarathustra and Israel) but with a decided bias in favour of Judaism.

Indians who have left their religious experiences, musings and doctrines in the sacred literature of the Hindus. They were probably those other Aryans of Iran who refused to accept the supremacy of Ahura Mazdah over the other gods and also other aspects of the Zoroastrian reformation and preferred to stick to the ancient Aryan tradition of nature worship, sacrificial rite and nomadic habit. We may very well suppose that the Kavis, the Karapans and the Usijs of the Avesta had their parallels in India also and that Indian religion did not at any time confine itself to mere laudation of the divinities without some formal rite. But those who profess to find in the early religious speculation of India nothing but unmeaning jargon and soulless ceremony and those who cannot credit the Indians with any religious discovery but must refer their ethical Varuṇa to Iranian Ahura Mazdah[125] and their Bhakti cult to Christianity, are blind to that intellectual vigour of the new immigrants into India which in uninterrupted succession gave to the world the Mantras, the Brāhmaṇas, the Āraṇyakas and the Upaniṣads on her native soil. In fact, so far as written records go, the Vedic religion, of all ancient religions, possessed both female and male seers[126] and thus established the equal right of women with men to receive divine inspiration. It admitted the possibility of individual seers and also families of seers,[127] the latter corresponding to the schools of prophets in Judaism with this difference probably that in India the Vedic seers were either identified or associated with priests in the majority of cases and their verses were or could easily be put to liturgical uses in connection with different ceremonies.

The contents of the Vedic revelations have been very differently assessed. The verses have been variously regarded as songs of shepherds and peasants; lyrical outbursts of pri-

125 See Griswold, *The Religion of the Ṛigveda*, p. 132 f.n.2, and p. 75. See also Keith, *The Religion and Philosophy of the Veda and Upanishads*, I, p. 33, 101.

126 Female seers are not unknown in other religions (*e.g.*, Judaism) but they are neither so prominent nor so early.

127 Griswold, *op. cit.*, p. 58.

mitive minds; laboured compositions of sophisticated poets meant for pleasing patrons and earning a living; editions of ancient materials, theistic and ritualistic, supplemented by newer materials (the language of the two parts being assimilated to each other by suitable levelling down and levelling up); divine inspirations to devout souls; eternal and uncreate truths flashed into the minds of religious geniuses at the beginning of each cycle of existence. It is indeed true that during its long religious history Hinduism made other experiments in religious experience and, in fact, leaned more and more towards the sufficiency of self-knowledge and the futility of the cult of sacrifice preached by the Vedas. But if we limit ourselves only to the religious side of Hinduism, we shall find that the Vedas set a pattern which subsequent Hinduism has more or less faithfully followed. We must not forget that even the Vedas occasionally display speculative interest and that into books, professedly religious in outlook, strange agnostic verses have found their way.

The Vedic sages were impressed most strongly by the protean variety of nature's happenings and the regularity of their order. There was Many and yet it was somehow One. The first explains their Polytheism and the second their Pantheism. Departmental deities, more diaphanous and impersonal than the Greek gods, divide the different realms of existence among themselves and are invoked as separate entities;[128] yet at the same time they are very often associated together, they are supposed to possess common attributes, and their spheres of activity tend to overlap. They very seldom quarrel and generally live in harmony and friendship.[129] As upholders of moral and cosmic order (*ṛta*), they all labour together as befits members of a single heavenly family. No wonder that the Vedic sages should raise the gods to the highest position by turns or else regard them all as at bottom one or derived out of one ultimate principle.[130]

[128] See Macdonell, *Vedic Mythology*, p. 6, 15; Griswold, *op. cit.*, p. 81, 87.

[129] See Macdonell, *op. cit.*, p. 18.

[130] Bhagavat Kumar Sastri, *The Bhakti Cult in Ancient India*, p. 10. RV.i.164; AV, ix. 5.10.

A tentative monotheism with the colourless Prajāpti as the head of the pantheon[131] was, however, soon superseded by a pantheism in which the impersonal Brahman became the sole principle of existence, and plurality came to be regarded as illusion. With decreasing respect for the category of personality the importance of the ethical Varuna, to whom prayers were originally offered for the remission of sins, diminished also; the ethical order (*ṛta*), upheld by Varuna Mitra, Agni, Sūrya and others, was dissociated from these gods and became transformed into an autonomous law of moral action (*Karma*); heaven and its denizens became transitory; and the belief that salvation was only a condition of the soul led to intense self-analysis and self-culture without reference to divine aid and worship. But the strenuous life of knowledge and discipline was at the same time recognised as being beyond the capacity of the multitude, and for them a life of sacrificial works or religious devotion was prescribed Thus, the Hindu sages recognised the temperamental and intellectual differences of men and provided for the intimate acceptance of religion by a system of graded spiritualism just as, like Plato, they practically recognised the differential capacities of men by arranging them in different castes with well-defined duties and obligations. There is thus a method in the medley of beliefs which constitute Hinduism. Basing itself on the observable diversity of natural phenomena, human constitutions and social cultures, Hinduism has ever recognised that religion in its non-rational aspects must always be diverse;[132] but recognising the fundamental identity of the rational element in man it has taught at the same time that all men are bound to agree about the unity of godhead or of the ultimate principle of existence, however it might be named and described and even if exact description be not possible. While recognising partitions, it has held at the same time that these are movable and that lower grades can

131 Viśvakarman as creator and Puruṣa as the material element of all creation are also met with.

132 See Radhakrishnan, *The Hindu View of Life*, p. 25 f.

be transcended by spiritual diligence, ethical conduct and performance of ordained rites and duties.[133] Caste disabilities have no bearing on the attainment of salvation, for this goes not with social privilege but with personal sanctity and can be secured in endless ways.[134] As Professor Radhakrishnan remarks, Hinduism does not believe in any statutory methods of salvation.[135]

Without an understanding of the fundamental basis of all existence and of the ways in which it can be approached, and assimilated to the self, it would not be possible to explain the large tolerance of the Hindu mind and the curious mixture of idolatry, polytheism, theism and pantheism effected by it. Intensely conscious of the ubiquity of the ultimate principle, Hinduism has professed to see God everywhere—in waters and stones, in plants and animals, in *gurus* and Brāhmins, in shining heavenly bodies and powers of nature, in heroes and godlings. God is everywhere just as salt is invisibly present in every part of the sea : He is most manifest where spiritual power, beauty and strength are present.[136] Reality, however, overflows its manifestations and finite beings fail to convey the immensity and immeasurability of the Infinite.[137] This has been used as a justification by some sages for transcending the category of personality in the conception of God and for holding the belief that all determination is negation. Reality is knowable only through its limitations (*upādhi*); it is then that the duality of the worshipper and the worshipped comes into existence and religion becomes possible. But it is only when the state of gnosis or absolute consciousness is reached that we realise that we are to love our neighbours as ourselves because we then know that all of us

133 The most orthodox school of Vedic theologians, the Mīmāṁsakas, go the length of maintaining that the sole aim of revelation is to teach the doctrine of sacrifice (*Karman*).—ERE. ii. 800.

134 See *The English Works of Raja Rammohun Roy* (Panini Office, 1906), pp. 129-31 (An Apology for the pursuit of Final Beatitude, independently of Brahmunical observances).

135 Radhakrishnan, *The Hindu View of Life*, p. 50.

136 Bh.G., x.41.

137 Śv. Up., 3.11-16.

are identical with the ultimate reality itself. Religious quarrels have no meaning when religion itself is bound to be superseded by absolute knowledge or when, according to another supposition, the same goal of salvation can be reached equally by all religions faithfully followed. This attitude of *laissez faire* explains why the pages of Indian history have been so little disfigured by religious wars and persecutions although there is abundant evidence that wordy battles of the sects were not unknown. Heretics, agnostics, fatalists, ceremonialists, materialists, mystics and philosophers have in their own way denied at different times this or that aspect of the theistic creed without rousing active hostility;[138] and innumerable sects have risen within the bosom of Hinduism to satisfy the religious needs of people of different climes, times and cultures without any opposition from existing creeds.

A survey of the records of revelation given above will show that while the Semitic types generally adopt a devotional attitude towards a single God and, following therefrom, an ideal of personal and social ethics, the Aryan religions of Iran and India refuse to disown the manifest multiplicity and contradictions of the experienced world and tend to be speculative and intellectual. In Iran, the Zoroastrian reformation sought to fix the unity and ethicality of godhead but later developments moved away towards duality and superstition. In India a reverse process of development took place and religious thought moved away from multiplicity to unity—to an impersonal Absolute beyond good and evil, to be realised in thought, or to a personal deity to be pleased by devotion.[139] The heterodox religions of India took over the ethical aspect of the Vedic religion, discarded the effete gods who could be constrained into beneficence by magical formulae and also the spiritual privileges that were being attached to the higher castes in course of time. They were thus primarily moralistic in temper, although they too emphasised the need of intellectual illumination and latterly made provision for satis-

[138] Sv. Up., 1.2; 6.1.

[139] ERE. ii. 789-9, art. BRAHMAN.

fying the religious need by instituting systems of worship. Still, the broad division of revelations into devotional, intellectualistic and moralistic is defensible on practical grounds, and the Hindu distinction of Bhakti, Jñāna and Karma as representing three different types of apprehending and approaching God or the Absolute is not entirely arbitrary. There is no door of the mind through which divine inspiration cannot enter; and while a religion that establishes contact with every aspect of life is certainly to be preferred, we need not sneer at those whom religious appeal can reach only through one faculty. Were not the prophets themselves differentially touched by religious fervour? Caitanya, Buddha and Zarathustra did not have the same mental make-up, nor had Muhammad and Mahāvīra. As media of revelation they had different indices of refraction; so the contents of their faith are deeply coloured by their inborn nature, social tradition and individual upbringing. It is at this point that we come nearest to an understanding of the psychology underlying the deification of prophets and belief in incarnation: unless God incarnates Himself to preach His message personally it can never represent His complete wish and wisdom. When the earthly prophet sees into the entire scheme of things, when in his goodness he desires to preach the complete truth as revealed and when he possesses the power to do so, he transcends his finitude altogether and becomes the transparent medium of divine revelation. He lays aside his limitations and becomes the veritable mouthpiece of the divine: no prophet can retain a double nature and yet become an infallible guide. The difficulty has been sought to be overcome in different religions in different fashions. Hinduism believed that God became incarnate as occasions arose to re-establish the true religion and restore the moral balance of the world; Christianity in its orthodox forms regarded Christ as the second person of the Trinity; Judaism and Zoroastrianism respectively made Moses and Zarathustra receive their messages direct from God; Muhammad is made by Islamic traditions not only to meet God but also to receive Divine revelations through an angel, who could presumably have access to divine message in a more perfect fashion than man.

But while every positive religion is anxious to show that it is the most rational of all faiths, most, if not all, are agreed that the unaided exercise of reason is not adequate for the knowledge of God. The eighteenth century deists of England sought to establish theism on rational grounds and to prove that revelation was unnecessary for those who were able and willing to draw the theistic implications of their experiences of men and the world. There was indeed disagreement about the most fruitful data, namely, whether it was the beauty and adaptation of the physical world or the demand of conscience that could unerringly disclose the existence of God; but there was agreement about the view that natural religion could claim equal right with revealed religion to make men theistic. The "proofs of the existence of God," familiar to us in the pages of philosophies of religion, are supposed to emanate from human reason and to suffice for genuine faith. Revealed religions, on the other hand, have maintained that a God that is only inferentially known can never inspire confidence and command obedience. The knowledge of God must be direct: somewhere man must come face to face with Him—if not in his visions and auditions, then in his moral and spiritual experiences. I have elsewhere called this belief "empiric faith," meaning thereby that even the most intellectual of us would like to have something more direct than a rational knowledge of God.[140]

There is a good deal of truth, however, in what Rashdall says about the relation of reason and revelation.[141] According to him, "the apprehension of religious truth does not depend upon some special kind of intuition; it is not due to some special faculty superior to and different in kind from our ordinary intellectual activities, but to an exercise of the same intellectual faculties by which we attain to truth in other matters—including, however, especially the wholly unique

140 *The Philosophical Quarterly*, II, pp. 200-31.

141 H. Rashdall, *Philosophy and Religion*, Lect. V.

faculty of immediately discerning values or pronouncing moral judgments." He adds that religious thinking is often implicit and unanalysed and the type of reasoning employed is generally probable and analogical; besides, ultimate Reality can never be adequately and completely known and the accompaniment of moral and other sentiments obscures the judgmental character of religious experience. He concludes, however, that "for purposes of life it is entirely reasonable to treat probabilities as certainties." While denying that the truth of God's existence can reasonably be accepted on the basis of an immediate judgment or intuition, because its genesis cannot be easily explained by the individual's environment and psychological antecedents, he yet admits that, in order to be true, a belief need not be arrived at by conscious logical reasoning and no prophetic revelation was ever so arrived at. Once revealed through a religious genius, the truths of theism are seen to be reasonable; but the prophet himself did not reach them by articulated thinking, and the philosopher who dissects the prophet's revelations and discovers their antecedents would never have arrived at them without the prophet's aid. While generally accepting Rashdall's view, I am of opinion that no religion can be wholly rationalised although the best ones are the most rational, and that no prophet can be an effective reformer unless he is convinced that he is doing something more than guessing divine intentions and inferring divine attributes. The soundest philosophical treatise on God lacks the power to create a religious community, which even the most defective scripture possesses. No philosopher claims to have seen God as a prophet does. Many have knocked, but to few has the door of spiritual vision been opened; many have sought, but few have found it. The immortal words of the Kaṭha Upaniṣad[142] are as much true to-day as they were thousands of years ago—

> *nāyam ātmā pravacanena labhyo na medhayā na*
> *vahunā śrutena*

[142] Kaṭha Up., I. 2.22 (also Muṇḍ. Up., III. 2.3).

*yam evaiṣa vṛṇute tena labhyastasyaiṣa ātmā vivṛṇute tanūṃ svām.*

Not by instruction is the Ātman attained
Nor by insight nor by learning of books:
Comprehended is He only by him whom He chooses.
To him does the Ātman reveal His form.

So long, therefore, as we do not know the law governing the vision of Absolute Truth, we have to admit that an element of Divine Grace operates in prophetic revelation, and that not only to the world at large but also to the prophets themselves the Divine selection of the vehicle of inspiration must remain a profound mystery.[143]

---

[143] Ranade points out that in the Upaniṣads different views of the nature of revelation are to be met with. In Bṛ. Ār. Up., II. 4.10, the Vedas and the Upaniṣads as well as other branches of knowledge, such as history, mythology, etc., are regarded as having been breathed forth by the Divine Spirit. Ranade takes this to mean " the inspirational activity of God, the philosophers to whom they are attributed having served merely as instruments for the display of this activity." In Īśa (10), Kena (I.3) and Chāndogya (VI.4.5) is to be met with " a second view which implies more or less a human participation in the transmission, if not in the composition of these revealed texts " (*i.e.* the Upaniṣads), which explains the veneration for teachers in this sacred literature. There is again a mythological account of the origin of the Vedas, and in fact of all creation, according to which the God of Death coupled himself with Speech, a creation of his own, and produced thereby these things. (Possibly, the necessity of preparation for receiving illumination is indicated in Śv. Up. VI.21, where personal penance and divine grace are regarded as co-operative causes).—See Ranade, *A Constructive Survey of Upaniṣhadic Philosophy*, pp. 8-12.

## CHAPTER IV

### THE GODS OF HINDUISM : VEDIC

A distinction can easily be drawn between beliefs that satisfy religious needs at different stages of culture and beliefs that attempt to harmonise different aspects of human experience at the same time. The distinction between a higher and a lower religion is not that the latter makes no provision for the attitude of worship but that, unlike the former, it is incapable of advancing a rational justification of its ideas and activities and of a progressive evolution. Man does not come by his religion through conscious personal thinking or deliberate choice : he is born into a religion and imbibes the acts and attitudes prevalent in the community just as he assimilates the arts, culture and traditions of the group to which he belongs. Imitativeness, suggestibility, sociality, fear of offending the social group (tempered by love and desire to please), indolence, lack of individual judgment, faith in collective wisdom, reverence of ancestors, mystic fear of novel experiments all conspire to make the primitive mind prone to self-effacement. It cannot be said that even the enlightened mind is altogether free from their influences, nor perhaps is complete freedom possible or desirable if social solidarity is to be maintained. It is always a perplexing problem as to how much of social belief, habit and organisation is to be regarded as providing the rigid and stable framework of the society concerned and what part is to be considered as plastic and admitting of growth and modification ; but there is no doubt that in primitive and conservative groups and in advanced and liberal societies the ratio of the two parts would be differently fixed. The danger of an ancient creed is the loss of pliancy: like an old tree, it accumulates dead tissues or, as in an old animal, there is a gradual sclerosis of its main arteries of thought and action. In a living body there is no doubt rhythmic action, but all repetition is attended by growth, complexity and increased vigour. The history of a living faith is similarly characterised by the evolution of complex thought, emotion, action and organisation. So long as life courses through them all, the power of adaptation to changing environment and of assimilating new materials is maintained at a steady level. The living religion reveals its plasticity not only by evolving new organisations suited to changing times and climes but also by furnishing scope for deeper appreciation in consonance with the developing intellect and the growing ethical sense of man. A living faith sloughs off useless creeds and outworn constitutions as a part of its vital growth. The accumulation of dead matter that heavily handicaps necessary reform without any appreciable benefit in return is a danger to which every faith is subject.

It is essential, therefore, that a religion should have adequate flexibility to meet new situations if it is not to degenerate into a tribal custom or a social habit. A living religion has the maximum amount of universality and the minimum amount of particularity about it. Elaborate details of social organisation, dogma and ritual are likely to prove a hindrance in the long run, whatever might be their temporary value in stabilising faith and marking off existing boundaries. The absence of a plenary authority to settle the details of dogma and ritual of the time tends to accumulate the successive faiths in the religious literature instead of retaining the most adequate forms and ejecting the antiquated ones out of the canon. The effect is that such a religion soon becomes a museum of mummified relics of ancient times—of decaying cults and dead superstitions. Such is Hinduism; such is Judaism; such is every religion that attempts to retain and justify every bit of religious thinking—good, bad or indifferent, performed by the original seer and his successors in faith. When the eternal and the evanescent jostle with each other and claim equal authority, or when contradictory and hostile traditions find equal support in the same canonical literature, doubt, perplexity and indecision are bound to assail the adherents of a faith. Before the chronology and comparative validity of divergent dogmas are settled by well-established principles of historical criticism, religious tenets can at best be subjected to canons of interpretation as elaborated and applied by professional experts ; but even these may not be universally accepted and thus the desired uniformity of faith and practice may not be secured. Besides, professional and sectarian interpretation has not always been noted for fairness or wisdom : its partiality for the traditional makes it a doubtful agent of spiritual progress and an uncertain guide in novel situations. I have already mentioned that the needs of devotion and the needs of doctrinal consistency are not identical; hence devotees of discredited gods are not small in number, specially when cultural or intellectual inadequacy renders an intimate acceptance of more advanced creeds impossible. In fact, the tendency to adjustment at a lower level is so persistent in human nature that not only is there back-sliding—an atavistic reversion to more primitive creeds and cults—but also degeneration or fall from the pristine purity of an advanced faith. When Hindus and Jews worship idols they regress to an ancient form of their own religion; but when Christians and Musalmans venerate the relics of saints they manifestly yield to the innate craving of man for tangible vehicles of supernatural power, in complete defiance of the teachings of their faith.

We shall tarry a little longer on the locus of adoration. It has been a moot question of Psychology whether there is any such thing as Religious Instinct or whether Religion is an effect of the operation of other psychical factors. Anthropologists are similarly divided into two opposite camps—some attempting to show that the idea of a supernatural power is not universal and others holding just the opposite view. Philosophers feel that the universality of belief or the consensus of opinion would show that the Creator stamped the human mind with an innate idea of His own existence to ensure that man would know his God instinctively and without social instruction or casual revelation. Similar is the belief of the Natural Religionists who think that the human reason does not stand in need of any special revelation to come to a knowledge of God. We shall not enter into any discussion of these vexed questions of Psychology, Anthropology and Philosophy of Religion. Our immediate purpose is to draw attention to the fact that the idea of the supernatural, howsoever derived, has an irresistible appeal for the human mind. Whether it was a vague sense of the numinous (Otto) or an animistic belief (Frazer) or an awe of dead ancestors (Spencer) that was at the root of religion it is difficult to say definitely. Philosophers have professed to find in the sense of religion a potential infinity in the finite mind—a capacity to transcend the infirmities of that finitude from which man suffers in his conscious moments. It is not improbable that religion has a multiple origin in the human breast and that different types of religious consciousness—theism, polytheism, pantheism—owe their existence to divergent tendencies of the human mind and to different types of human experience. But the most curious fact of human history is that man is cured of one type of religion only to fall a victim to another and that even the atheist is not seldom found to adore ideals as passionately as a savage worships idols. Freud has called Religion the obsessional neurosis of humanity and expressed the hope that this illusion, as he styles Religion, will surely disappear in the future with the growth of culture as neurotic symptoms disappear with proper treatment. But if religion be the reaction of the human mind to certain recurrent events of the physical and mental worlds and to certain persistent needs of the human heart, which no other attitude or belief is likely to meet adequately, then the disappearance of religion is a very improbable contingency. Atheism can be won only with severe mental effort and retained with constant vigilance—so persistent and imperious is the call of religious devotion to man with his developed aesthetic, intellectual and moral senses and his proneness to the pursuit of ideals.

What object has not man fastened upon for devotion in his religious quest! "Seizable, half-seizable, and non-seizable" objects have all been laid hold of for adoration and worship. As Hopkins remarks:[1] "Man has worshipped everything on earth, including himself, stones, hills, flowers, trees, streams, wells, ocean and animals. He has worshipped everything he could think of beneath the earth, metals, caves, serpents, and underworld ghosts. Finally, he has worshipped everything between earth and heaven and everything in the heavens above, mist, wind, cloud, rainbow, stars, moon, sun, the sky itself, though only in part has he worshipped the spirits of all these objects." That the list does not err on the side of exaggeration can be proved by reference to the Vedic religion[2] where not only the special gods ruling the different departments of nature (*e.g.*, *Dyaus*, sky, *Agni*, fire, *Sūrya*, Sun, *Vāta*, wind, etc.) and even the distinguishable aspects and functions of the same divinity were separately worshipped (*e.g.*, *Sūrya*, *Mitra*, *Savitṛ*, *Pūṣan*, *Viṣṇu*, *Vivasvant*, all representing different functions of the Sun),[3] but abstract agent gods (like *Dhātṛ*, *Netṛ*, *Viśvakarman*), and abstract goddesses (like *Śraddhā*, faith, *Anumati*, favour, *Aramati*, devotion, *Nirṛti*, decease) were also invoked in worship and even the fee paid to the priest (*Dakṣiṇā*) was deified. A fruitful source of multiplication of gods is sacred association: in Vedic religion things needed in rituals were themselves invoked as gods (*Grāvan*, press-stone, *Āpas*, water, *Ghṛta*, clarified butter, *Barhis*, sacrificial litter, *Yūpa*, sacrificial post, etc.), and even the implements of agriculture and war received similar divine honours (*e.g.*, Plough,

1 Max Müller, referred to by Hopkins, *Or. and Ev. of Rel.*, p. 13; see also Söderblom, *The Living God*, p. 21.

2 See Griswold, *Rel. of the Ṛig-Veda*, pp. 81-85.

3 Keith supposes that these different names of the same god might be due to local, tribal and family differences. See *Rel. and Ph. of the Veda and Up.*, I, p. 92.

Arrow, Car, etc.).[4] It seems as if man cannot help being religious: while in some cases the nature of the stimuli calls forth a religious reaction, in other cases man exercises his will to believe even in the absence of adequate stimuli. The environment determines the object on which faith fastens itself; a change in the environment would not kill faith but would simply alter the character of the object.[5] There is this much resemblance then between religion and neurosis that, being driven out of one support, each immediately clings to another. But in this respect religion also behaves like an instinct which, once being roused, persists with varied reaction to attain its object and accommodates itself within limits to the field of its operation. Although we have no means of ascertaining how in a sensitive and fertile brain the thought of taking up a religious attitude towards the world originally arose, we have sufficient knowledge of primitive minds now to assert that it arose independently at many centres of the world and that it did not owe its origin to priest-craft—it was not a deception that the first knave practised on the first fool he met. Tradition fixes the form, but something akin to inspiration or instinct determines the origin of religion and ensures its immediate extension to the social group.

Many are impatient at the laborious ways in which anthropologists and missionaries collect data of the primitive religious life. But these have exactly the same value for understanding the features of a highly developed religion as the study of the primitive forms of animal life has for the understanding of the human organism. In spite of its great difference from the lower forms of animal existence the human body betrays its origin from lowly forms through its ontogenetic stages and its vestigial organs. In a similar fashion, almost all advanced religions contain elements that have

[4] The deification of cult implements (*e.g.*, incense-burner) was not unknown in pre-Aryan India.—See Sir John Marshall, *Mahenjo Daro and the Indus Civilisation*, p. 69.

[5] See Hopkins, *Or. and Ev. of Rel.*, p. 88 f.

come down from primitive forms of faith. Like the atavistic reversion of organic forms, there is in men's minds also a tendency to slide back to lower types of belief at critical moments. As in dreams, there is also sometimes an infantile regression in men's religious attitudes and acts, and the claims of rational behaviour and individual judgment are abandoned or suspended in favour of primitive disposition to submission to authority, obscurantism and unmeaning ceremonies. A study of the primitive forms of faith is of value here in that it enables us to understand and explain the etiology of many of the crudities that are to be found in advanced religions. Hinduism and Judaism, for instance, may not inaptly be compared to palimpsests where changing conceptions have overlaid earlier creeds with fresh veneers at different periods of their history and yet not in such a way as to prevent the confusion of colours and perspectives. Similar survivals of primitive faith are to be found even in such prophetic religions as Christianity and Muhammadanism, not to speak of such reformed religions as Confucianism and Zoroastrianism.[6] Not only are there survivals, but in their process of expansion many of these religions have absorbed primitive and discordant elements from their new converts. As examples may be cited Buddhism which was contaminated by the *Bon* religion of Tibet, Judaism which was influenced by Canaanite culture, Zoroastrianism which was infected by later Magian beliefs,[7] and Vedic religion which was mixed up with the indigenous cults of India. The contact of different cultures is inevitably followed by reciprocal give-and-take in ideas and beliefs; and while the noble elements are generally taken over consciously, the primitive

[6] Even in present Christian and Mohammedan and Zoroastrian monotheism popular belief has remained impregnated with a very vital polytheism. Christian Greeks still believe in the Fates and the Nereids; the Kelts have not quite renounced the old mythology of those now called fairies, brownies, dwarfs and banshees; magic rites, implying belief in spiritual powers, the evil eye, and other remnants of an older general faith, still survive in a so-called monotheistic religion.—Hopkins, *Or. and Ev. of Rel.*, p. 281.

[7] See Moulton, *Early Zoroastrianism*, Lects. VI and VII; see also Dhalla, *Zoroastrian Theology*, p. 68 f., 76 f.

elements are unconsciously imbibed—the process of absorption possibly starting with the retention of some of the old beliefs by the new converts and ultimately ending with the general diffusion of these beliefs in the conquering creed. Much of living Christianity to-day—at least in its outer aspects—is a legacy of Mithraism, Manicheanism, Neoplatonism and Gnosticism, all of which Christianity supplanted and suppressed but not before it had incorporated some of their essential doctrines, rituals and festivals within itself.

The danger of contamination is not limited only to religions with an open canon, but it threatens also those religions which believe in a closed canon. Exegesis, esotericism and accommodativeness can always find meanings in the scriptures in accordance with personal, regional and contemporary needs: as Hegel says, the scriptures have often been twisted like a nose of wax. Besides, when the preaching of ethical monotheism is not backed by the extension of requisite culture, the illiterate and backward part of the religious community, while conforming outwardly to the purer creed, develops inferior doctrines in consonance with its own needs and spreads the contagion upward. It would be a mistake to think, for instance, that every Christian or Muhammadan of Africa is imbued with the ethical and religious ideas of the New Testament or the Qur'ān.[8] As a matter of fact, twentieth-century Christianity is still debating if the most vulnerable points of its faith are not due to the Apostle of the Gentiles whose interpretation of the life and mission of Jesus was deeply coloured by Greek learning and acquaintance with the Mystery religions of the time, and was possibly influenced also by the needs of his pagan flock.

We have remarked above that the criterion of progressive faith is harmony of experience. Prophets of advanced religions have almost invariably been noted for their deep reflection on the problems of existence. Retirement to a lonely place to meditate undisturbed is recorded not only of

8 See Westermarck, *Pagan Survivals in Mohammedan Civilisation.*

the Upaniṣadic seers and Buddha but also of Moses, Jesus and Muhammad. Such a soul in solitude, we may well believe, not only communed with God but also meditated on the problems of existence in relation to God. We have suggested already that what the prophet finds and what the philosopher establishes are not identical in their methods or contents; for the prophetic search is for a life and the philosophic quest is for an intellectual principle. The prophet seeks to ennoble by integral vision and the philosopher to enlighten by articulated thinking. It is not to be supposed that a prophet's vision of God is unnecessary to a philosopher or that a philosopher's intellectual analysis is useless to a prophet. There are problems that only prophetic insight can initiate although their implications are brought out by later philosophical analysis. Similarly, only certain types of vision are possible to a prophet after he has consciously acquired or unconsciously imbibed a certain amount of intellectual culture.[9] As Rufus M. Jones remarks,[10] "Faith of this creative sort, faith that is to be discovery, must be the product of experience, of discipline, of patience, of control, of training, of technique, of suffering, until the eye of the soul can *see* in the dark and can distinguish what is eternal from what is only the capricious wish of our feeble human desires." "It is a sign of weakness when the creative aspect drops out and faith becomes merely synonymous with *believing* some 'deposit' transmitted from the past." An harmonious adjustment to things sensible and supersensible may come to certain natures spontaneously or with ease; but

[9] Somewhat different is the view of Söderblom about the necessity of training in Mysticism: "If we ask why the great mystics of every kind despise ascetic training or have little confidence in it, the answer is easy. What they want is no perfecting of human qualities and faculties. They do not believe in any human effort. God or the Divine or the inscrutable mystery of peace in heart or that mysterious existence which they call the Infinite or Nirvana or even the Nothing, is to them much too great to be conquered by means and methods invented by men" (*The Living God*, p. 27). The great mystics believe in insight, knowledge, intuition, not in training, ascesis, just as the heroes of faith do not believe in works and exercises, but in trust.—*Ibid*, p. 28.

[10] *Pathways to the Reality of God*, pp. 16, 17.

ethical monotheism is a hard-won victory of the human mind and could only have been achieved with the help of philosophers of successive ages. By 'philosophers' we do not mean only those who construed correctly the events of the physical and the mental world but also those who interpreted aright the ethical needs of man and envisaged more adequately than before the realm of moral responsibilities and spiritual obligations. What the prophets conquer the philosophers consolidate, and this position then becomes the base of further prophetic operation.[11]

One of the most oft-quoted passages of the Hindu scriptures is, "The self is to be known (or heard), understood and meditated upon."[12] The orthodox commentary on the passage makes it to mean that the truth about the self is to be learnt first from the scriptures, then to be understood with the help of arguments favourable to the sacred literature, and then realised in one's own life. Manu lays down that those who take the help of mere reasoning—to the exclusion, neglect or condemnation of the scriptures—in any spiritual matter, should be driven out by good people. That the precaution is necessary will be evident from the fact that no positive religion, that believes in the inscrutable nature of God, has been able to dispense with all restrictions on theological reasoning. To know God fully is to be God, and no religion believes that man, limited as he is, is capable of understanding God fully.

[11] As Bergson points out in his latest book, the morality and religion of human society are static while the religion of the innovators, animators or saints is dynamic, outflowing, creative. "The inertia of mankind has never given way except to the push of genius. The only societies which have ever made any progress have been those which have been wise enough to follow in the footsteps of some innovator. Always it has been the mystics who have led, and who must continue to lead, all civilised groups. Remembrance of what these souls have been, of what they have done, is deposited in the communal memory of Humanity. Each one of these privileged souls marks a certain stage attained in the march of life; each one manifests in some original form that love of Humanity which seems to mark the very essence of creative effort. This love flows outward in a torrent of vitality, spreads its contagious fire of enthusiasm, which is never completely extinguished, and which may always be rekindled."—*Advance*, Dâk Edn. (25-9-33). quoting *Literary Digest*. See Bergson, *The Two Sources of Morality and Religion* (Eng. Tr.), pp. 23-27. 200-01. 229-31.

[12] Br. Ār. Up., II. 4.5; Ch. Up., VIII. 7.1.

In fact, lest man should, in his ignorance, presumption and folly, tear religious truths to pieces, even legitimate speculations on religious matters were forbidden at one time in many religions. Rationalists and free-thinkers have been subjected to the grossest persecution in Christianity and Islam—the two religions which believe not only in the infallibility of their scriptures but also in the impossibility of better revelations in future. The fate of the Mu'tazilites[13] comes readily to one's mind in this connection—the freethinkers of Islam who, while accepting the existence of an eternal God, denied the eternity of the Quranic revelation and opposed the concept of a God whose will makes the Good good and who preordains every event of the physical and the moral world, leaving nothing to the initiative of man. In proportion as Rationalism has been kept at bay, Mysticism has been welcomed by almost every religion as confirming the belief that human reason can never encompass the nature of God and that there is always left over an element of incomprehensibility in Reality—an intellectual gap which leaves scope for the operation of the non-rational faculties of the human mind. The Mystics use the language of the prophets themselves—they have a direct contact with Reality, their very being is flooded and enveloped by Divine Presence. As in the case of prophetic vision, so also in mystic experience, there is, as Jones remarks,[14] " an enrichment

[13] Mu'tazilite views :—

1. Man is the author of his acts and not Allāh; therefore, he is a second creator. In view of his personal responsibility man's punishment for sin would be severe. Grave sins disenfranchise a Musalman from the class of the Faithful and disentitle him from the intercession of Muhammad on the Day of Judgment, and Hell for him would be eternal.
2. Things are not good or evil because God declares them to be so, but God makes the distinction because things are in their own nature good or evil.
3. God has ordered and prohibited and promised and menaced by non-eternal speech. There are no eternal qualities or decrees; hence the Quran is not eternal. See Wensinck, *The Muslim Creed*, p. 60 f.

[14] See R. M. Jones, *Pathways to the Reality of God*, Ch. II. The God of Mystical Experience (p. 34).

of the individual mind, an increase of its range and depth, an enlarged outlook on life, an intensification of insight, a heightening of personality." No wonder, therefore, that the Mystics, in spite of their unconventional life and language, should not only be lightly let off but even treated with respect by the orthodox in all religions. For a similar reason ecstatic visions and fits of unconsciousness have been regarded as better methods of knowing God than logical thinking. The Sufis and the Yogins have always been treated with marked deference by the Muslims and the Hindus respectively as persons who have approached nearest to God. The distinctive feature of the mystic, however, is that he develops only the devotional and personal side of religion to the marked neglect of its practical and social side and is, therefore, ill suited to be the founder of a faith. Even if it be admitted that the great saints of Christendom have not always been quietistic in their attitude but have, as Bergson points out, accepted as the motto of their life 'Love, Creation, Action' (witness, for instance, the Friends of God), Eastern and Greek mystics have been generally content with passive contemplation and detachment.

It is difficult to assign an exact function to reason in any religion. Reason sets a limit to human credulity; and while it tussles with the obscure and the implicit, it rejects outright the improbable and the contradictory. Religions have always resented this arrogance of individual and inexpert judgment in matters sanctioned by collective faith and established by spiritual insight. Still, there is no gainsaying the fact that to-day the range of such matters is being definitely restricted in all religions that are aspiring after universality. It does not matter in what way uncomfortable contents are being interpreted or explained away : the truth is that the advance of knowledge in other directions has rendered many scriptural texts absolutely untenable and these are now being treated as loans or interpolations or allegories, if not actually ascribed to the limitations of the prophetic vision. Adopting the fundamental assumption that divine revelations can be neither unethical nor irrational, scriptural interpretation has sought to dissociate the eternal from the temporal factors and to reserve prophetic inspiration for the former alone. It has also, wherever necessary, sought to establish the purity of the prophet's character and purpose. Thus, Christian apologists are not wanting to justify the curse on the fig tree pronounced by Jesus and the death of the herd of two thousand swine into which Jesus had driven the devils. Similarly, the impropriety, laid at the door of Muhammad, of abrogating earlier revelations to suit changed circumstances and of contracting matrimonial alliances in excess of the number fixed by revelation has been sought to be put in a reasonable light by the followers of the Prophet. In a similar fashion, too, the portions of the religious books dealing with the amorous life of Kṛṣṇa have been sought to be explained by educated Hindus as interpolations or allegories. Rational exegesis has similarly sought to discard, twist or interpret allegorically scriptural texts that are insupportable on scientific, speculative or ethical grounds. An illustrative example is furnished by the explanation of Vedic texts by Ḍayānanda Sarasvatī, the founder of the Ārya Samāj, who sought to prove that, all through, the Vedas taught pure monotheism, correct scientific facts, and unquestionable moral action.

No religion has been entirely free from two types of dangers. The one is the danger of primitive thinking. Many of the ancient cults perished because there was no systematic attempt to develop them on rational lines. Most of them succumbed before faiths which were more in consonance with the intellectual and ethical needs of the cultured mind. Gods that are impossible to pull up by rational methods are unceremoniously rejected by a civilised race. This fate overtook the Mediterranean religions of Egypt, Greece and Rome when reason showed the futility of unethical polytheism and crude theriolatry and when at the same time Semitic monotheism offered a more satisfactory system of beliefs. Apart from the question of oppression and forced conversion, the spread of Islam in Zoroastrian Persia was partially due to its simple monotheistic creed, as opposed to the complex purificatory practices and religious rituals of the later Iranian religion.[15] A similar cause explains the rapid spread of Vaiṣṇavism in India, with its simple prescription of loving devotion and its freedom from ritualistic complications. At certain stages of culture the concrete and the spectacular have an irresistible appeal. It is only then that polytheism and idolatry, together with material offerings and gorgeous rituals, sway powerfully the minds of men. The lapses from purer forms of religion and worship are due to similar primitiveness of mentality. The lower sections of all religious communities would be found to practise a form of faith very little removed from crude superstition, primitive magic and polytheistic, if not idolatrous, beliefs. Amulets and charms still circulate, and visits to the tombs of saints are yet in vogue, in countries where ethical monotheism is the only socially recognised form of religion.

The second danger comes from extreme rationalism, which, not being satisfied with removing the primitive crudities and irrational excrescences of a religion, attacks the very vitals of the faith. Thus the pious admission of all religions that God cannot be known in His true essence by the frail intellect of man may be exploited to establish the thesis that God is unknown and unknowable and that to such a mysterious entity bordering on nothingness it is useless to offer worship (agnosticism). Or, it may be supposed that the physical and the moral world present to man such contradictory experiences that they can furnish no basis for establishing an unequivocal theism. Beauty and ugliness, adaptation and opposition, pleasure and pain, good and evil are so inextricably mixed up together that without doing violence to one's rational faculty one cannot believe that this medley is due to a single good God. The probabilities are rather that either there is no god (atheism) or that a duality of gods with opposite moral qualities rules the world (ditheism, later Zoroastrianism), or that a plurality of powers rule different departments of the world without reference to one another

[15] See ERE, vi. 151, art. GABARS.

(polytheism) or that the single power that rules the world is limited either in power or in intelligence or in goodness or in all these combined (the theory of a finite God; J. S. Mill). Any of these theories would affect man's exclusive devotion to a single ethical God. It should not be forgotten that a philosopher treats religious experience in the same manner as any other experience and subjects it to the same critical examination of reason. A philosopher does not start with the certainty of God; and even when after laborious enquiry he becomes convinced that God exists, the ultimate position he reaches is that God is an hypothesis that is not unworkable. As opposed to the direct intuition and certain faith of a religious man, a philosopher's knowledge of God is always indirect—God is at most a key that fits most satisfactorily the facts of experience, without excluding, however, the possibility of other explanations. Hence it is that philosophers have never succeeded in arguing people into devotion although they have often succeeded in adding the cogency of reasoned argument to the primary conviction of a devotional mind.

The effect of speculation on faith we shall illustrate from Indian religions as being the most instructive. Like all ancient religions, the Vedic religion also possessed a generous measure of polytheism. There were gods and goddesses ruling different departments of nature, whose personality was yet in a state of gristle[16]—vague, shadowy figures not fully personified, with physical associations too oppressively prominent to allow a thorough anthropomorphism or effective moralisation.[17] Such, for instance, were Agni (fire),

16 See Keith, *Rel. and Ph. of the Veda and Up.*, I, p. 58 f; also Winternitz, *A History of Indian Literature*, I (Eng. Tr.), p. 75 f.

17 There is Dyaush-pitā, the Sky-father with Prithivī Mātā, the Earth-mother; there are Vāyu the Wind-spirit, Parjanya the Rain-god, Sūrya the Sun-god, and other spirits of the sky such as Savitā; there is the Dawn-goddess, Ushas. All these are or were originally deified powers of nature: the people, though their imagination created them, have never felt any deep interest in them, and the priests who have taken them into their charge, though they treat them very courteously and sing to them elegant hymns full of figures of speech, have not been able to cover them with the flesh and blood of living personality.—L. D. Barnett, *Hindu Gods and Heroes*, p. 13.

Sūrya (the sun), Soma (the sacred beverage), Parjanya (the rain-cloud), Uṣas (the dawn), Sarasvatī (the sacred stream), Maruts (thunder-storm), Āpas (waters)—'transparent gods,' as Bloomfield calls them, half-humanised, mostly resisting imagery[18] and lending themselves to further speculative treatment with advancing thought.[19] Speaking of Agni, for example, Bloomfield observes:[20] "In the hieratic (in distinction from the popular) hymns of the Ṛig-Veda there will be few cases in which Agni is not more or less directly connected with the sacrifice. And it is well now to take this simple article, the sacrifice fire, and let it unfold its own story step by step. How it turns in the hands of these priestly poets into a person gifted with the thinly disguised qualities of fire; into a messenger mediating between men and gods; into an archpriest typical of holy rites; and finally into a god." The chances of personification were, however, considerably minimised by the tendency to create "mythological synonyms," as Hillebrandt calls the gods belonging to the same department of nature but possessing "special physical basis, distinguishing characteristic and theophanic moment." Let us quote Griswold in this connection:[21] "The sun has many distinguishable aspects and functions.[22] It is a bright orb (*Sūrya*), a light-giving friendly power of nature (*Mitra*), a great stimulator of life and activity (*Savitar*), a nourisher and protector of cattle, shepherding them and finding them when lost (*Pūṣan*), wide-striding from earth through mid-air to zenith, 'he of the three steps' (*Viṣṇu*), and the one who

18 Macdonell, *Vedic Mythology*, p. 17.

19 Bloomfield, *Rel. of the Veda*, pp. 85-89. See also Griswold, *op. cit.*, p. 81; ERE. xii. 605, art. VEDIC RELIGION.

20 Bloomfield, *The Religion of the Veda*, p. 157. On the different characters of Agni reference may be made to Hopkins, *Or. and Ev. of Rel.*, pp. 300-01. See also Winternitz, *op. cit.*, I, p. 98 f.

21 Griswold, *op. cit.*, pp. 83-4; also p. 277 (Savitar=the sun before rising). See also Winternitz, *op. cit.*, I, p. 76.

22 An alternative view would be that each special Sun-god was, in origin, the creation of a different Vedic tribe, all of these being finally brought together within the Rig-Vedic pantheon as parallel forms of the sun-god.—Griswold, *op. cit.*, p. 270.

at dawn shines in every direction (*Vivasvant*).[23] The functions of the god of lightning and of the god of storm are also similarly differentiated. Thus the lightning fighting to release the cows of the sky manifests itself as an impetuous warrior (*Indra*); it is the third or aerial form of fire dwelling in the clouds (*Trita Āptya*);[24] it is born of the heavenly waters (*Apām Napāt*); it grows in the mother cloud and brings fire down from heaven to earth (*Mātariśvan*); it looks like a serpent in the lower atmosphere (*Ahi Budhnya*); it leaps down from the cloud mountains in a single streak of fire like a 'one-footed goat' (*Aja Ekapād*); it strikes the earth, shatters trees and kills animals and men (*Rudra*); accompanied by thunder, wind and rain, it manifests itself in numerous lightning flashes (*Maruts*)." The process multiplied the gods of nature although it prevented their personification. Their connection with the three physical realms—earth, air (or water), heaven—was so persistent that both the Rig-Veda (I. 139.11) and the Atharva-Veda (10. 9.12) divided the gods into three groups—celestial, atmospheric and terrestrial, although gods belonging to more than one region are also mentioned in later classifications (*e.g.*, Yāska's *Nirukta*, 7. 5).[25]

But there were not only transparent deities of nature derived out of cosmic elements and local physical objects. Some of the gods had travelled down from pre-historic times—from

[23] It is interesting to note that in Egyptian religion the sun was similarly worshipped in a multiplicity of forms. Thus Rā as the sun sailing in his boat on the celestial ocean (also as Amon-Rā), Atmu or Tum as the setting sun, Khepera as the rising sun, Aten as the rays of the sun, Anher as the sceptred leader of heaven and Sopan as the cone of light before the rising sun represented different forms of the sun (ERE. v. 248, art. EGYPTIAN RELIGION). Climatic conditions did not permit a similar muitiplication of the gods of lightning and storm in Egypt as in India.

[24] Trita (AV. vi. 113.1; xix. 56.4; RV. viii. 47.13; i. 187.1; and other places) and Traitana (RV. i. 158.3) seem to have been confounded together in the Veda, whereas originally they were quite distinct from each other. Trita was the name of a celebrated physician, and Traitana that of the conqueror of a giant or tyrant; the first belonged to the family of the Sāmas, the latter to the Āptyas. In the Zend-Avesta the original form of the legend is better preserved.—Haug, *Essays on the Religion of the Parsis*, p. 278. See Bloomfield, *Hymns of the Atharva-Veda*, p. 521 f.

[25] Macdonell, *Ved. Myth.*, p. 19.

the common Aryan ancestors of the Indo-Europeans and of the Indo-Iranians.[26] There were perhaps also gods of yore whom younger gods had dethroned from the hearts of a later generation.[27] Most of these had become "translucent" in Vedic times, that is, their original physical association had grown dim in human memory. Some, shorn of their physical attributes, had dwindled into mere names; but others had undergone what Freud would call a secondary elaboration and begun to assume a personal character. Thus Bhaga, Mitra, Aryaman, Vivasvat, Trita Āptya, Apām

[26] See Griswold, *op. cit.*, Part A, Ch. I.

[27] The Veda conceives of the Ādityas as the descendants of a feminine Aditi who cuts a considerable figure as a very abstract female, suggesting the ideas of "freedom from fetters," "freedom from guilt," "boundlessness" and "universe." She is finally identified in the Hindu mind with "earth." A father who might be responsible for the offspring of this interesting lady is never mentioned. We are struck first of all by the fact that Aditi the mother, a purely Hindu product, is obviously younger than her own sons, the best of whom are at least as old as the Indo-Iranian period. I have, for my part, little doubt but that Aditi is a well-executed abstraction of some kind. In the past I have suggested that the word āditya meant originally "of yore," and that this set of antique gods whose most substantial members are pre-historic were thus fitly named "gods of yore" or "gods of old." We may perhaps contrast with this the description of Indra as "later born" (anujāvara) in a legend told in Taittirīya Brāhmaṇa (2.2.10). From the word āditya, conceived as a metronymic, the feminine Aditi might be easily abstracted. If this is well taken, we must assume that the Veda had forgotten the meaning of āditya in the sense of "of yore."—Bloomfield, *The Religion of the Veda* (1908), pp. 130-31. See Macdonell, *Vedic Mythology*, pp. 17, 120 f—Aditi; also p. 43 f—Ādityas. The number of the Ādityas is indefinite as well as their names. Mitra, Varuṇa, Aryaman, Bhaga, Dakṣa, Aṃśa are mentioned in RV. 2.27.1. Other enumerations in the Rig-Veda, Atharva-Veda and the Brāhmaṇas include the names of Dhātṛ, Indra, Vivasvat, Mārtaṇḍa, Viṣṇu, Sūrya, Savitṛ. Agni is identified with Aṃśa and Sūrya. Bloomfield has in mind Mitra, Aryaman, Bhaga, Indra and Vivasvat, which names are found in the Avesta also, though not all in the sense of a good spirit. Bhaga, in fact, belongs to the Indo-European and not only to the Indo-Iranian. Oldenberg's identification of the Ādityas with the Amesha Spentas is not generally accepted nowadays.

It has been similarly suggested that "Tvastar is the more ancient deity and that Savitar has fallen heir to some of the functions of Tvastar."—Griswold, *The Religion of the Ṛig-Veda*, p. 276.

Macdonell points out that a similar supplanting of Trita by Indra is also a possible theory—*Ved. Myth.*, pp. 66, 697. (See also Haug, *Essays, etc.*, p. 275.) But he does not accept Roth and Whitney's theory that Indra absorbed the pre-eminence originally possessed by Varuṇa (*V. M.*, p. 65). Barnett thinks that "amidst the maze of obscure legends about Indra there are three points which stand out with perfect clearness. They are, firstly, that Indra was a usurper; secondly, that the older gods fought hard but vainly to keep him from

Napāt, Puraṃdhi and some such pre-Vedic gods[28] had become more or less colourless in the Vedas; but the twin Aśvins, Indra, Varuṇa, Viṣṇu[29]—the first two certainly, and the third probably, pre-Vedic and the last Vedic—had almost shed their physical associations and acquired human qualities. Human form and equipment in keeping with their proper functions were freely ascribed to the latter class though definiteness was lacking in most cases.[30] In later Vedic literature symbols representing deities began to appear—possibly also images of Indra (RV. 4. 24.10), as Macdonell points out.[31]

But deified forces of nature in different degrees of personification were not the only gods that the Vedic Aryans worshipped. Traces of animism and fetishism[32] are to be found in the worship of deified inanimate objects like hills and rivers, forests and plants (both large and small), implements and weapons. Totemism has not been definitely established in the Vedas; but some animals, that were associated with the gods or served as fetishes or symbols, were praised and invoked, and

supreme divinity, and that in his struggle he killed his father; and thirdly, that he was identified with the warrior class, as opposed to the priestly order, or Brahmans." "Indra was originally a warrior king or chieftain who was deified, perhaps by the priestly tribe of the Aṅgirasas, who claim in some of the hymns to have aided him in his fight with Vṛitra, and that he thus rose to the first rank in the pantheon, gathering round himself a great cycle of heroic legend based upon those traditions, and only secondarily and by artificial invention becoming associated with the control of the rain and the daylight."—Barnett, *Hindu Gods and Heroes*, pp. 33-34.

28 Thus Gandharva who comes down from Indo-Iranian period is equally colourless in the Rig-Veda—Macdonell, *V. M.*, p. 136. The whole of the Fourth Lecture in Mills' *Our Own Religion in Ancient Persia* should be read in this connection, esp. pp. 75-81.

29 Macdonell, *V.M.*, p. 49 (Aśvin), p. 27 (Varuṇa), p. 39 (Viṣṇu), p. 66 (Indra). Also Griswold, *Rel. of the Ṛigveda*, p. 285 (Viṣṇu); ERE. xii. 603.

30 ERE. xii. 602-03.

31 Macdonell, *V. M.*, p. 155; ERE. xiii. 610. See however Ragozin, *Vedic India*, p. 133. The image was probably a fetish at first (*cf.* Ark of the Covenant in Israel's battles).

32 Macdonell, *V. M.*, p. 147 f. Also Griswold, *op. cit.*, p. 334, f.n. 1.

attained a semi-divine status;[33] the cow, for instance, had become *aghnyā* or inviolable (RV. 8. 9. 15-16), except for entertaining guests (Ś. Br. 3, 4. 1.2), and also a sacred animal (AV. 12. 4. 5)—nay, even the gods were supposed to be her children (gojātāḥ).[34] Similarly, the boar and the tortoise had, by the time of the later Saṃhitās and the Brāhmaṇas, become identified with the Creator Prajāpati—an identification that was to have far-reaching consequences in the history of Vaiṣṇavism at a later time when they came to be regarded as incarnations of Viṣṇu. Again, there were the tutelary deities of the household (Vāstoṣpati) and the field (Kṣetrasya pati), spirits of air (Gandharvas) and water (Apsarases), deified and immortalised men (Ṛbhus), departed ancestors (Pitaraḥ) with Yama at their head, ancient priests (Atharvan, Aṅgirases)

[33] Speaking of pre-Aryan religion, Sir John Marshall observes: "We must guard against assuming that all the animals which served as charms or talismans at Mahenjo Daro were necessarily objects of cult. Nevertheless, it is safe, I believe, to infer that the images of composite animals with human faces were intended for worship, and there is hardly room for doubt that like the Tree-faced god and Tree-goddesses on the seals, the other major animals were also deified, namely, the unicorn, tiger, elephant, rhinoceros, bison, buffalo, bull (both humped and humpless), and the ghariyal. (*Mahenjo Daro and the Indus Civilisation*, Part I, p. 71). See Keith, *op. cit.*, I, p. 61 f. Also the following from Marshall: "When we find, as we do, that most of the elements which make up this pre-historic religion—so far as we can at present analyze them—are perpetuated in later Hinduism, we are justified in inferring that much of the zoolatry which characterizes Hinduism and which is demonstrably non-Aryan, is also derived from the pre-historic age."—*Ibid*, p. 73.

For a summary of pre-Aryan religion, see the same book, pp. 76-77. "This religion of the Indus people was the lineal progenitor of Hinduism." "Many of the basic features of Hinduism are not traceable to an Indo-Aryan source at all. They come into view, not in the earliest Vedic literature, which represents the more or less Indo-Aryan tradition, but either in the later Vedas or in the still later Brahmanas, Upanishads, and Epics, when the Vedic Aryans had long since amalgamated with the older races and absorbed some measure of their culture and teachings. Chief among such features are the cults of Śiva and the mother goddess, of Krishna and of the Nāgas and Yakṣas, the worship of animals and trees and stones, phallism, yoga, śāktism, and the doctrine of *saṃsāra* (metempsychosis) and *bhakti* (devotion to a personal god)."—*Ibid*, p. 77. (*Per contra* see Keith, *The Religion and Philosophy of the Veda and Upanishads*, Vol. I, p. 54, which was written before the Mahenjo Daro excavations were widely known in their true significance.)

For a distinction between the two cultures—Aryan and pre-Aryan, see Marshall, *op. cit.*, p. 110 f.

[34] Macdonell, *V. M.*, p. 151.

and seers (Saptarṣi) and heroes (Kutsa, etc.), who dwelt in heaven—to all of these honour and worship were due. Then there were the wives of the gods—some like Indrāṇī, Varuṇānī and Agnāyī without much independent character, and others like Uṣas, Sarasvatī, Vāc, Pṛthivī, Rākā, Sinivālī, Puramdhi, etc., with some independent status of their own. Lastly, there were the demons and malevolent spirits [35]—asuras, paṇis, rakṣases, dāsas and dasyus,[36] piśācas,[37] arātis and druhs[38]—who, in tangible or intangible forms, inflict woes and injuries on men either spontaneously or at the instigation of other men, oppose the gods and, by disturbing their sacrifices or interfering with their dead bodies, prevent men from attaining their spiritual ends. These too had to be controlled or propitiated by proper incantations or offerings.

Here then is as uncompromising a medley of gods, godlings and demons as is to be found anywhere else—a rather hopeless crowd not easily reducible to any kind of system. In fact, the system of worship had a tendency to introduce new gods and fresh complications. We must remember that in the Vedas we are not at the beginning of Brahmanic religion—the primitive beliefs had already reached a certain philosophical position in the theory of gods and many myths were simply alluded to and their knowledge taken for granted. Nay, more : an elaborate system of sacrifice, which was conducted by a highly trained priesthood with scrupulous adherence to the details of the rituals and hedged in by minute prescriptions and prohibitions, had practically made the hymns liturgical in character although prayers unaccompanied by ceremonial acts were not entirely unknown.[39] Now,

35 See Macdonell, *V.M.*, p. 156 f.

36 The corresponding Avestan 'dahyus' means 'peoples,' 'tribes' and does not have the hateful sense of the Vedic word.—See Ragozin, *Vedic India*, p. 113, f.n. 1. See Mills, *Our Own Religion in Ancient Persia*, p. 92.

37 In the Tait. Saṃ. (2.4.1.1) the three hostile groups of Asuras, Rakṣases, and Piśācas are respectively opposed to the three classes of gods, men, and Pitṛs.

38 Iranian Druj. For similar distinctions among the Iranian evil spirits, see Jackson, *Zor. Stud.*, pp. 99-108.

39 ERE. xii. 610 f.

every sacrifice involved the use of certain objects and implements and also certain attitudes of mind. The association of these with the sacrifices to the gods ended in their own deification. The psychology of the transformation was perhaps this that any imperfect functioning on their part would make the entire sacrifice nugatory. In this way, the sacrificial post (*vanaspati, svaru, yūpa*) to which the victims were tied, the sacrificial grass (*barhis*) on which the gods descended to take the food-offerings, the doors leading to the sacrificial field (*devīr dvāraḥ*), the sacrificial waters mixed with Soma (*āpas*), the press-stone for crushing the soma-plant (*grāvan, adri*), the sacrificial butter (*ghṛta*) poured into Agni, " the mouth of the gods ," all received divine homage in the Rig-Veda, and in the Atharva-Veda the sacrificial ladles and even the remnants of the sacrifice (*ucchiṣṭa*) (AV. 11. 7) were assigned "divine power of the highest order."[40] Again, when the correct uttering of the mantras was regarded as essential for the successful termination of a sacrifice, a presiding genius of holy speech (*Vāc*) was inevitable and she was at the time of the Brāhmaṇas identified with the sacred stream, Sarasvatī, on whose banks sacrifices were performed and mantras supposed to have been composed.[41] A more important personification was the " Lord of Prayer " (*Bṛhaspati* or *Brahmaṇaspati*),[42] who is regarded as favouring the man who offers prayer and scourging the hater of prayer. Barnett goes so far as to suggest that even Viṣṇu was " originally nothing more or less than the embodied spirit of the sacrificial rites."[43] As is well known, these two personifications had important consequences in the later history of Hinduism—the one developing into the Absolute (Brahman) of Pantheism and through it into Brahmā, the first person of the Trinity, and the second

[40] Macdonell, *V.M.*, pp. 154-55; Griswold, *op. cit.*, pp. 84-85; Keith, *op. cit.*, II, pp. 444-45.

[41] Bloomfield, *op. cit.*, p. 243 (also p. 191); Macdonell, *V.M.*, p. 87. See the author's *Sarasvatī the Goddess of Learning* in *K. B. Pathak Commemoration Volume*, p. 32 f.

[42] Macdonell, *V.M.*, p. 103; Griswold, *op. cit.*, p. 170 f.

[43] Barnett, *op. cit.*, p. 39.

into the God of theism and later into the second person of the Trinity.[44]

But the same turn of thought that diagnosed the necessity of aid from the objects of rituals, correct speech and personified prayers and rites discovered also that there was an inner side to all external acts of the men who offered sacrifices and of the gods who received them. All worship must proceed out of faith (*Śraddhā*), piety and devotion (*Aramati*) and desire (*Kāma*).[45] The gods must similarly assume an attitude of favour (*Anumati*) and bounty (*Sūnṛtā*), and they should also be able to manifest anger (*Manyu*) and send death or destruction (*Nirṛti*). In any serious undertaking both gods and men must practise ardour (*Tapas*). All things, again, must be done in proper time (*Kāla*)[46] to bear fruit, and health (*Prāṇa*) and vigour (*Asunīti*) must be maintained. The needs of the sacrificing priests must not be forgotten by the rich patron in whose spiritual interest the Brāhmaṇa priests stirred from early dawn, and suitable sacrificial fee (*Dakṣiṇā*) should be paid at the end of a work. In this way, all the essential conditions of a successful act of sacrifice were duly deified and adored. These abstract gods were the results of reflection on the various aspects of the principal type of Vedic religion. It has been maintained not without reason that a hieratic religion, as the Rig-Vedic religion undoubtedly is, does not contain all the elements of the popular religion, and that for these we must go to the Atharva-Veda which embodies in a generous measure the popular cults, superstitions and beliefs. The contents and the traditions also make it clear that different priestly families had predilections for different deities and that the same deities were also differently conceived by them.

Rational speculation on these heterogeneous elements led to diverse results. A belief in an unredeemed plurality of gods is not favourable to a proper ap-

[44] Ragozin, *Vedic India*, p. 262; Macdonell, *V.M.*, pp. 101-02, 104.
[45] Macdonell, *V.M.*, pp. 119-20.
[46] Winternitz, *op. cit.*, I, p. 150.

preciation of the nature, functions and attributes of the super-sensible world with which man wishes to hold commerce. In fact, many polytheistic religions have been disfigured by the quarrels, jealousies and pettinesses of contending gods. The more complete the humanisation, the greater the risk of unsavoury myths recounting the passions and foibles of divine beings. It is not always an advantage to believe that the gods could come down on earth and hold social relations with men; for very often they have been pictured as being tempted by the beauties of the daughters of men and becoming the progenitors of ordinary human families—not of kingly families alone, as in China and Japan. The hieratic character of the Vedic religion[47] and the imperfect personification of most of its gods prevented many of the common pitfalls of a polytheistic faith in the early Indo-Aryan religious speculation. Compare, for instance, the Vedic and the Paurāṇic beliefs about the character and activities of the gods and you will at once be convinced that it is far better to worship imperfectly humanised forces of nature than to believe in a plurality of humanised gods with limited power, intelligence and morality.[48] A sacrificial religion which was often pragmatically interested in the gods as helpers in war and givers of plenty in peace had little incentive to look beyond the power, the grace and the bounteousness of the gods approached for favour. This will explain why most of the gods, personal or abstract, were invested with many similar attributes by the poets and worshippers.[49] Tutelary deities were few and were generally later developments—most of the gods were cosmic and nationally or tribally worshipped. This also favoured development

47 Keith draws attention to the danger of drawing too sharp a distinction between the priestly and the popular religion of Vedic times.—See *Religion and Philosophy of the Veda and Upanishads*, I, Ch. 4, § 5 (p. 55 f.)

48 Speaking of Indra, for instance, Macdonell observes, "To the more intense anthropomorphism of Indra's nature are doubtless due certain sensual and immoral traits which are at variance with the moral perfection elsewhere attributed to him and essential to the character of the Vedic gods."—Macdonell, *Vedic Mythology*, p. 65.

49 For instance, in the Atharvaveda the gods hardly differ from one another and all have become demon-killers.—See Winternitz, *op. cit.*, I, p. 124.

of speculation about their nature and a sublimation of their functions.

As in all religions, speculation was not always favourable to the Vedic gods. In a scripture primarily religious there cannot be much room for the views of sceptics and agnostics: these can at best appear as opinions that are to be abjured by the believers and the orthodox. Still, there are stray passages to show that freethinkers were not absolutely wanting even in those olden days.[50] Unfortunately, an ancient tradition considered the gods to have been originally mortal and to have acquired immortality by the grace of Savitṛ or of Agni or by drinking Soma or by practising continence and austerity[51]—a tradition which was exploited not only in the interest of later Absolutism but also for sceptical and agnostic purposes. There was also the belief that the gods had been originally few in number and that many of the gods were born later. This led some seers to ask if the ultimate principle of existence was not Nothing or Non-being[52] rather than Being and if the gods had not arisen from the non-existent—a position that we find somewhat modified in the view that chaos or primeval waters began the process of creation.[53] It is this position that the Chāndogya Upaniṣad combated in its doctrine that it is *sat* (Being or the Existent) that existed originally—*sadeva saumyedamagra āsīt*. Where creation is ascribed to a Primal Unitary Being, a doubt is expressed if it was really the work of that Being and, if so, whether that Being was conscious of its creative activity.[54] Some seers, again, express surprise at

[50] Winternitz, *op. cit.*, I, p. 98.

[51] Macdonell, *V. M.*, p. 17.

[52] RV., 10.72.6; Śat.P.Br. VI.1.1. RV. 10.129.

[53] Macdonell, *V. M.*, pp. 13-14; AV, 10.7, 15. See Muir, *Original Sanskrit Texts*, V, Sec. xxi (5).

[54] The entire Sūkta runs thus (Ragozin, *Vedic India*, pp. 427-28):

"1. Nor Aught nor Naught existed then; not the aerial space nor heaven's bright woof above. What covered all? Where rested all? Was it water, the profound abyss?

2. Death was not then, nor immortality; there was no difference of day and night. That One breathed breathless in Itself; and there was nothing other than It.

the lowly origin of Agni out of two pieces of dry wood and at the priestly or divine functions ascribed to such a being. How can a living god spring out of dry wood? How does he grow without being suckled by his mother? How horrible is it that a son should devour his parents? But, as Ragozin remarks,[55] the sense of reverence prevented open scoffing or scepticism, and so the poet who asks the third question hastens to add : 'But I, a mortal, cannot judge a god; Agni is wise and knows.' So long as the reverential attitude persisted, the position that the worshipper took up was that the questionable conduct of a god might be known but not imitated by a human being :[56] the divine standard was declared to be inapplicable to men. Fortunately, in Vedic times Indra was practically the only god who had occasional lapses from correct conduct, due primarily to his excessive drinking of Soma. No wonder, therefore, that sceptics should be found to disbelieve in the existence of a god whose moral behaviour was sometimes so much out of keeping with the general conduct of the other Vedic gods (RV. 2. 12. 5). Scepticism that made a systematic negation of the gods as helpful aids to men was a position of later development; and, curiously enough,

3. In the beginning there was darkness in darkness enfolded, all was undistinguishable water. That One, which lay in the empty space, wrapped in nothingness, was developed by the power of heat.
4. Desire first arose in It—that was the primal germ of mind, which poets, searching with their intellects, discovered in their hearts to be the bond between Being and Non-Being.
5. The ray of light which stretched across these worlds; did it come from below or from above? Then seeds were sown and mighty forces arose, Nature beneath and Power and Will above.
6. Who indeed knows? Who proclaimed it here—whence, whence this creation was produced? The gods were later than its production—who then knows whence it sprang?

He from whom this creation sprang, whether he made it or not, the All-Seer in the highest heaven, he knows it—or he does not."

For an interpretation of this alleged ignorance, see the commentary on Taittirīa Brāhmaṇa, quoted by Muir, *Original Sanskrit Texts*, V, Sec. xxi (5), p. 363.

55 Ragozin, *Vedic India*, p. 160; see RV. X. 79.4.

56 See Hopkins, *The Ethics of India*, p. 13.

it was ushered in by a theistic speculation which overreached itself. To this aspect of development we may now turn.

The line of speculation that accepted the reality of the gods but found their number and nature unsatisfactory followed the usual law of religious thinking in the human race. If anthropologists and missionaries have rightly reported the religious beliefs of the primitives, religion takes in them the form either of animistic faith in an all-pervasive consciousness, or of a fetishistic, totemistic or euhemeristic belief in the existence of a number of separate spiritual entities, or of a belief in an All-Father. These three modes of primitive religious thinking provide the germs of pantheism, polytheism and monotheism respectively. In Vedic religion also speculation developed along all these three lines, with the result that the Brāhmaṇism or Hinduism that subsequently arose out of Vedicism ended either in an impersonal Brahman or in a Trinity (or multiplicity of gods) or in a Supreme God. In the Vedas themselves the theistic current was the strongest—the spirit of reliance upon the help and mercy of the gods had not yet completely given way to the belief in the self-sufficiency of the individual soul or the inability of the gods to withstand the potency of religious rites and formulae. Later on the three factors necessary in religious worship—man, material and deity—came to receive different emphasis from different classes of thinkers. When man came to be considered as the most important element and self-knowledge came to be synonymous with salvation, the gods became superfluous for spiritual blessing. Deprived of their boon-giving capacity, the gods retained a shadowy kind of existence in the Upaniṣads, Buddhism, and Jainism, and were portrayed as being themselves in need of the saving knowledge and as approaching enlightened beings for spiritual illumination.[57] Indra was the foremost god according to the Upaniṣads because he was the first to gain self-knowledge at the feet of Prajāpati

[57] Deussen, *Philosophy of the Upanishads*, p. 173; U. C. Bhattacharyya, *The Vedic Gods in the Upanishads*, in *Phil. Quart.*, Vol. I, No. 3, p. 202. See Winternitz, *op. cit.*, I, p. 201.

(Chān. Up. 8. 7. 2) or because he was the first to know Brahman (Kena. Up. 4. 3). The mortality of the gods was reaffirmed and their heavens were declared to be transitory in character—good enough as temporary places of reward for the ritualistically virtuous but non-existent to the spiritually wise. So far as reality was concerned, there was not much to choose between god and man, heaven and earth, for ultimately all were transient manifestations of a single impersonal spiritual principle, namely, Brahman.[58]

While the increasing emphasis upon self-knowledge was a new feature, the Vedic seers had themselves sown the seed of pantheism. We have already seen that Vedic worship included practically all types of beings—gods; deified heroes, sages and ancestors; animals; plants; inanimate objects, and abstract entities. Imagination, backed by the will to believe, embraced representatives of each type; besides, the major gods themselves were intimately associated with cosmic forces and physical phenomena. This almost verged on animism, which is the forerunner of a pantheistic view of the world. In due time, one of the theories propounded was that the entire universe was derived out of a primeval Puruṣa sacrificed by the gods:[59] "Whatever is, is Puruṣa—both what has been and what shall be."[60] A similar identification of the goddess

[58] It is interesting to note that in the theistic Bhagavadgītā the Sāṃkhya Prakṛti is identified with Mahat Brahma—presumably because both were devoid of distinguishable characteristics and personal qualities (Bh. G. xiv. 3-4). But the respectful attitude towards the Upaniṣadic Brahman is to be met with in the conception of Brahma-nirvāṇa, the highest type of salvation for the wise (Bh.G. v. 24-26). (See also Bh. G. ii. 72; viii. 13; xiv. 26). The theistic attitude asserts itself in such a passage as xiv. 27.

[59] The Puruṣa Sūkta (RV. X. 90) has generally been interpreted in a pantheistic sense by Western scholars. But the verses are not unequivocal in meaning. Thus the Puruṣa is said to extend ten *aṅgulas* (fingers) beyond the earth (*bhūmi*); and though in one place the immortals are said to constitute three-fourths of him, yet in the later portion of the hymn Indra, Agni and Vāyu are said to be derived out of the one-fourth part that created the things of the earth. This permits the interpretation that even if All is God, God is not All, for He is something more. The question of the freedom of the finite spirit which in its ethical aspect is relatively independent of God does not arise in the context of the hymn, which is essentially a cosmogonic speculation.

[60] Macdonell, *Ved. Myth.*, p. 16.

Aditi " not only with all the gods, but with men, all that has been and shall be born, air and heaven " was also made (RV. 1. 89. 10). Two other divinities, both ending in *pati* (which suffix Western scholars have regarded as a sign of later speculative development), namely, Brahmaṇaspati and Prajāpati, also helped pantheistic speculation, the former in the Upaniṣads and the latter in the Brāhmaṇas. Already in the Rig-Veda Prajāpati had come to be regarded as embracing all things (RV. 10. 121. 8-10);[61] in the Śatapatha Brāhmaṇa he was regarded as all and everything (1. 3. 5. 10; 1. 6. 4. 2; 4. 5. 7. 2).[62] Brahmaṇaspati too appropriated to himself the deeds and powers of all the gods.[63] He replaced the worship of the nature-gods as the holiness and power of Prayer (*brahman*) rose in popular estimation, till at last he effected a transition from the semi-personal god of the Vedas to the impersonal Absolute of the Upaniṣads. In the Rig-Veda[64] the question had been raised about the " wood " and the " tree " out of which the heaven and the earth had been made by Viśvakarman and the Viśvedevāḥ (All-gods) and the standing place of the world-fashioner (Viśvakarman) during the process of fixing the creation. The Taittirīya Brāhmaṇa[65] gave the reply : " Brahma was the wood, Brahma was that tree out of which they fashioned the heaven and the earth. Wise ones, with my mind I declare unto you, he took his stand on Brahma when he made fast the world." The Upaniṣads took up the idea in right earnest and made Brahman the impalpable all-pervasive[66] spiritual essence of the whole world. When with this was united the other Vedic idea that the Ultimate Principle of existence possessed, like some gods (*e.g.*, Agni, Indra), the inscrutable power (Māyā) of taking diverse

61 Macdonell, *V.M.*, p. 16.

62 *Ibid*, p. 5; see Winternitz, *op. cit.*, I, p. 219 f.

63 Ragozin, *op. cit.*, p. 262; Macdonell, *V.M.*, p. 101 f.

64 ṚV. X. 81.4; see Ragozin, *op. cit.*, p. 416.

65 Taitt. Br. ii. 8. 9. 63 see ERE. i. 196.

66 The impalpable character is made out by cutting open a Nyagrodha (fig) seed which reveals no form of the future tree; and the all-pervasive character is indicated by comparison with salt which is present in every sample of the sea-water. (Ch. Up. 6.12; 6.13).

forms, the coast was cleared for the Advaita Vedānta which Śaṅkara later made familiar. Speculative and mystical interests were adequately served; but the gods disappeared as the ultimate determiners of human destiny and became reduced to a class of transient manifestations of the Absolute—in a much higher plane of existence than men, no doubt, but practically useless[67] to the latter in the matter of attaining that sense of oneness with Brahman with which alone salvation came now to be identified. In the Yoga system, which is monotheistic in its views, God was retained for cosmic functions; but so far as human salvation (*kaivalya*) was concerned He was regarded as one of the many means for the attainment of Samādhi which is essential for self-realisation by finite spirits.[68] It may, therefore, be fairly said that this line of speculation ended in an intellectualistic monism where the affective needs of the heart—love and devotion—were ignored and the entire sacrificial cult, which represented the volitional aspect of worship, was abandoned. The inscrutable nature of the Absolute, which could be only negatively described as possessing none of the attributes of worldly objects (*neti neti*), promoted mystic contemplation; religion was superseded by philosophy—and generally a mystic philosophy at that—and the gods of the Vedas fell from their pedestals of pristine glory. The emotional fervour of the Persian Sufis is lacking in the Upaniṣadic literature: the main tendency is to pander as little as possible to the sentimental aspect of human nature and to preach the message of a salvation that is beyond both good and evil, pleasure and pain. It was a great thing to have shown that a geographical heaven was a part of the transitory cosmos projected by the powers of the Absolute and to have equated salvation with the attainment of the highest plane of consciousness. But when man's self-realisation entailed a complete disappearance of the gods and even of Īśvara, leaving no provision for the gratification of those emotional cravings

[67] Maitri Up., 4. 6; Muṇḍ. Up., 2. 1. 7.

[68] Īśvarapraṇidhānāt vā (*Yoga Sūtra*, i. 23).

which a personal God can alone satisfy, the solution failed to appeal to the ordinary mind. Buddhism and Jainism dismissed the Absolute altogether but retained the new cult of stoical *ataraxia* and intellectual salvation. As against all these, the popular mind reaffirmed its faith in a personal god in the great theistic religions of Vaiṣṇavism and Śaivism that almost overtook the three earlier intellectualistic movements.

The speculative movement that emphasised the importance of the materials spelled equal disaster to the gods. A sacrifice involves the use of both material objects and *mantras*. While an insistence upon the former may lead to the belief that certain specific objects are indispensable for invoking certain deities (and even in Rig-Vedic times various favcurite objects of different gods had begun to be specified), an insistence upon the latter may engender the notion that a correct procedure and an accurate pronunciation are essential for success in any religious undertaking. The danger proceeding from the first became greater when image-worship made its appearance.[69] and material offerings and divine forms became closely associated by contiguous association. But for the fact that the extension of the Aryan settlement necessitated the use of local substitutes[70] the materials used in worship would have been still more stereotyped. In the Vedic times, however, the general absence of idols prevented the use of set material offerings; and because the fire served as the uniform 'mouth of the gods,'[71] such products of the field, the forest and the flock as could be easily consumed by fire were used as sacrificial offerings.

The case was different, however, with the *mantras*. Being linked easily with the primitive belief in the magical

69 For image-worship in Vedic times, see Muir, *Original Sanskrit Texts*, V, Sec. xxiii (3): Did the Vedic Indians make images of their gods? (3rd edn., p. 453); B. C. Bhattacharyya, *Indian Images, Part I*, p. xxiv f.; Griswold, *op. cit.*, p. 337.

70 Thus there was a break in the tradition about the Soma plant with the effect that its identity became unknown in course of time and local substitutes, nearly approximating the original plant in quality and appearance, were used. See Griswold, *op. cit.*, p. 219; also Ragozin, *op. cit.*, p. 170, f.n. 2.

71 Griswold, *op. cit.*, p. 162. Fireless sacrifice on *barhis* (sacrificial grass) was also practised as in ancient Iran.—Griswold, *op. cit.*, p. 158.

efficacy of formulae and incantations, these could soon be believed to have a power independent of the grace of the particular gods approached by prayer. The distinction between religion and magic has been well put in the pithy saying "Religion persuades the gods and magic compels them."[72] That the distinction was on the whole well observed in the Rig-Veda would be evident from a comparison with the Atharva-Veda where magic spells abound and which therefore was long kept out of the canonical list of the Vedas (known therefore as Trayī or group of three—Ṛk, Yajus and Sāman). But spells are not absolutely unknown in the Rig-Veda, as when a person uses prayer magically to oust a rival or apprehends that a god would be lured away to the sacrifice of another by the more efficacious prayer of that other (which implies that the god could not be present at even two places simultaneously).[73] Plants and waters are supposed to be able to cast out diseases and wash away sins. But, as Hopkins remarks,[74] much of the magic used was tinged with religious ideas and, in fact, the priests generally preferred to clothe their own utterances in petitions to the gods direct. For such an early religion the absence of black magic is a remarkable phenomenon and it is a striking testimony to the speculative ability of the ancient Indo-Aryans and the purity of their faith.

When, however, we reach the period of the Brāhmaṇas[75] we find that a change for the worse had taken place. The cessation of the practice of composing new hymns had invested the ancient texts with an inviolable sanctity and a mystic significance. They are now supposed to exercise a coercive force on the gods. If the formalities of a religious ceremony have been faithfully fulfilled, its attendant fruits are bound to

[72] Griswold, *op. cit.*, p. 337. See S. K. Maitra, *Religion and Magic*, in the *Journal of the Department of Letters* (Calcutta University), Vol. XXVII.

[73] Hopkins, *Ethics of India*, p. 14; Ragozin, *op. cit.*, p. 379; RV. X. 145; RV. IV. 25. 1. The Mīmāṇsā Philosophy used this as an argument against the theory of gods as boon-givers.

[74] Hopkins, *Ethics of India*, pp. 14-15.

[75] See Winternitz, *op. cit.*, I, p. 187 f.

follow—not because the gods would be pleased to bestow them but because they cannot prevent their arrival. Let us quote a typical example given by Macdonell :[76] "The notion that the kindling of Agni exercised a magical influence on the sunrise seems not to be entirely absent in the RV. Such appears to be the meaning of the poet when he explains : 'Let us light Agni, that thy wondrous brand may shine in heaven' (5. 6.4). This notion is clearly stated in a Brāhmaṇa passage :[77] 'By sacrificing before sunrise he produces him (the sun), else he would not rise' (SB. 2. 3. 1.5; TS. 4. 7. 13.3)." This looks like a bold presumption; but when we remember that not only among primitive races but even in modern times lusty sounds are produced by some Hindus to drive away the demon that is believed to be swallowing the sun or the moon during an eclipse, we can see its filiation to the magical belief that underlies such a religious act. Gradually a philosophy was propounded to show that *mantras* have an efficacy (*śakti*) of their own, and an elaborate theory of sound (*Sphoṭavāda*) was evolved to justify such a belief.[78] The Mīmāṃsā philosophy which took up the task of supplying the rules of Vedic interpretation exceeded its function when it proposed to show that the hymns were in a sense more powerful than the gods approached with their help, and that an immaculate performance of Vedic rites could produce a meritorious result (*apūrva, adṛṣṭa*) which was bound to bring in due time a favourable destiny (*bhāgya*).

What lowered the prestige of the gods still further was the increased emphasis laid on the self-suffi-

[76] Macdonell, *V. M.*, p. 98.

[77] SBE. xii. 328.

[78] The first aim of sacrifice was to present a simple thank-offering. The second aim was to nourish the gods with the essence of the offered food, and to strengthen them for their duty of maintaining the universe. The next idea was that of making these oblations the means of wresting boons from the invigorated and gratified deities, and so accomplishing some specific earthly object, such, for example, as the birth of a son. A still more ambitious object was that of employing sacrifice as an instrument for the attainment of superhuman powers and even exaltation to heaven (Monier Williams, *Brahmanism and Hinduism*, p. 22, quoted in art. HINDUISM, ERE. vi. 693); see Max Müller, *Six Systems of Indian Philosophy*, p. 402 f.

ciency of the moral law—the theory that *Karman* produced its fruits without reference to divine favour or disfavour. The heterodox systems of Buddhism and Jainism drew the logical conclusion of the *Karman* doctrine that gods were not necessary either for temporal benefits or for final blessings. Being tethered to the sacrificial system, Brāhmaṇism could not get rid of the gods altogether; but it preached the doctrine that in the act of sacrifice the *mantras* and the rites were more important than the gods.[79] It is indeed true that there was this religious development that the Mīmāṃsā did not feel the necessity of defending the independent reality of many equally powerless gods: it often thought of godhood in the singular as the locus of worship or the person sacrificed unto (*yajña-puruṣa*). But very little of the divine capacity was left to this Being when the theory was advanced that His only function was to bring about a dissolution of the world at the end of each cycle of existence in order to give a temporary respite to souls suffering from continuous rebirths, without being able to mitigate a jot or tittle of their merited doom. In fact, the relation between the law of *Karman* and God was very much like the relation between a moving train and a pointsman. Just as a train moves by the energy of its own fuel and the pointsman only shunts it on to this line or that without being able to accelerate or retard its speed, so also the condition of a soul at the beginning of a cycle or at the dissolution of its last embodiment is determined by its own actions of a previous life[80] and God can only push a soul into its appropriate material form without having any capacity to modify the desert or the doom. In extreme speculation even this little initiative of God was taken away and *Karman* was supposed

[79] A similar evolution of thought led to *Mantrayāna* in decadent Buddhism of India and Java.

[80] See Nyāya-Mañjarī (Vizianagram Series), p. 273 f; also Yoga Sūtra, ii. 13. *Vide* the author's paper on *The Vicissitudes of the Karma Doctrine* in *Pandit Madan Mohan Malaviya Commemoration Volume*, p. 491 f.

to operate directly without the co-operating activity of God. It is evident that a God to whom prayers are useless can hardly retain His title to the veneration of man. As in Greek belief, an inexorable fate (*adṛṣṭa*) above the gods took the place of a God of grace.[81] No wonder, therefore, that the Mīmāṃsakas, in spite of their faith in the sanctity of the Vedas, should come to be regarded as atheists. Unlike the followers of the path of knowledge (*jñānamārga*), these followers of the path of work (*karmamārga*) did not lose faith in a heaven to be won by the faultless performance of prescribed rites with appointed materials and *mantras*. But both classes agreed that the individual was a self-sufficient entity for purposes of salvation and that the ultimate means thereof was a true knowledge of the self and not merely a correct performance of sacrificial acts. A more radical position was taken up by the Sāṃkhya system which disbelieved in the efficacy of religious acts, in the possibility of proving the existence of God and, therefore, of concentrating attention on Him as a means to the *Samādhi* (mystic contemplation) that effects the release of the soul (*Puruṣa*) from its association with the body (*Prakṛti*), and in the final absorption of the personal finite in the impersonal Absolute (*Brahman*). The Sāṃkhya, therefore, rejected the Mīmāṃsā, the Yoga, and the Vedānta solution of the problem of God in relation to man. We need only add the views of the materialists and the sceptics (*Cārvākas*) who called the Vedas unmeaning jargon, the priestly symbols and acts mere disguises and devices to deceive fools, and sensual pleasure the highest blessing. It appears, therefore, that the majority verdict of Indian philosophers went against a belief in God as understood in the Semitic religions, namely, a unitary and ethical personality ruling the universe by moral law but capable of forgiving and willing

81 See Bhartṛhari's *Nītiśatakam*, 94-102. "Despite the handicap of an overstressed religious ritual, which nearly blinded her to the great light of ethics, India emerged with the belief that religion is a matter not of form but of mind and will, and that a good character is more essential than a good ritual."—Hopkins, *Ethics of India*, p. 236.

to forgive the penitent sinner out of His abundant grace. What prevented godlessness in the bad sense of the term was that the Indian approach to the problem was spiritual and ethical, although it was not religious as understood above. There was no attempt to equate the spirit with the body (except in the small materialistic school) or to deny the validity of the moral law; and, in the Vedānta system of Śaṅkara, the ultimate reality of Brahman, which was described as existence, consciousness and bliss (*saccidānanda-svarūpam*), was also acknowledged.

It would be idle to deny the profound influence that these philosophical speculations had on the whole trend of Indian religious thought. It is not the fool in India that said in his heart that there was no God. Although there are family books in the Rig-Veda and some families are supposed to have had a special liking for certain deities (*e.g.*, the Vaśiṣṭhas for Varuṇa),[82] there is no evidence to show that in India there was anything like the tribal monolatry of the Semitic groups of Western Asia[83] or the local monolatry of the Egyptian nomes. The speculative mind had to start with the whole assemblage of major and minor gods; and when it did not take the road to monotheism, it reached either the impersonal Absolute or the impersonal Moral Order. When, however, a renewed interest in devotional religion manifested itself and the various Purāṇas were composed, a curious intermixture of absolutistic, magico-ethical and theistic speculations took place. The Supreme God and Brahman were either identified or placed side by side, and demons were portrayed as being able to wrest from the unwilling hands of the gods any boon they desired, by dint of proper worship.[84] Sages had to be tempted with the aid of heavenly dancers (*apsaras*) lest their austerities should

[82] Griswold, *op. cit.*, p. 147; Keith, *op. cit.*, pp. 91-92.

[83] Griswold, however, thinks that "the Rigvedic pantheon probably represents the gods of different Aryan tribes" and that "political federation was doubtless followed by religious federation, according to the usual custom in ancient times."—*Religion of the Rigveda*, p. 343.

[84] See Hopkins, *Epic Mythology*, p. 195, for a list of such boons given by Brahmā.

inevitably dethrone the existing authorities of heaven who had won their posts by similar efforts in the past. No grace or aid of God was necessary to attain these heavenly positions. As a matter of fact, the gods ruled for only one cosmic age to be replaced in the succeeding age by a fresh set.[85] Thus the mortality of the gods, which was an original belief of the Rig-Veda, returned in a new form. The Vedānta thought that even the gods needed self-knowledge in order to be saved and that a finite soul attaining heaven might be regarded as being on the way to salvation (*kramamukta*), which would be attained when all things would be reduced to their causal condition (*kāraṇāvasthā*) at the end of a cosmic cycle.[86] But this intermediate stage of heavenly residence was not indispensable and finite souls of the earth could excel the gods by attaining salvation direct,[87] Jainism going so far as to suggest that only men could be saved and gods would have to be reborn as men to get their salvation after proper enlightenment. Muhammad claimed to have converted jinn as well as men and he lived nearly twelve hundred years after Mahāvīra and Buddha. No wonder that on behalf of these two teachers it should be similarly claimed that even the gods paid them homage for their spiritual wisdom.

Let us now trace the fortune of the speculation that took the gods seriously and refused to reduce them to transient manifestations of an impersonal Absolute or helpless wheels of a moral machine. Its task was much more formidable, for the Vedic gods hardly formed a pantheon with well-defined duties and relations. There was no recognised head of the groups of gods as was Zeus Pater in the Greek religion

85 Speculations on this point are neither clear nor consistent. There is very little to suggest that there have been more than one Viṣṇu or one Śiva. Possibly the rise of sectarian worship prevented the multiplication of the supreme God to rule over different cosmic ages. Viṣṇu, for instance, was supposed to get into his sleep of involution (*yoganidrā*) at the dissolution of one cosmic cycle and to wake up at the beginning of the next cycle. But Brahmā was treated as subject to dissolution (Bh.G., xv. 16). See also Carpenter, *Theism in Mediaeval India*, pp. 268-69; p. 276 (M. Bh. xii. 348).

86 Maitri Up., 4. 6.

87 See Hopkins, *Ethics of India*, p. 236, f.n. 11.

or Jupiter in the Roman religion. Father Sky (*Dyaus Pitar*) as the god of heaven had generally as his counterpart Mother Earth (*Pṛthivī Mātar*);[88] and although the gods (*devas*) were regarded as their children, Dyaus does not appear to have been at any time more than a colourless head of the divine clan in India. In addition to an imperfect personification, he and his consort are not always regarded as being 'ancient born' for they are themselves spoken of as being begotten or created.[89] Besides, the paternity of the gods does not belong to them alone, for other parents are also ascribed to the gods collectively or individually in different places.[90] Again, being too nearly related to the gods of nature, they are not usually regarded as being also the parents of men and other creatures though that relation is not entirely absent.[91] Dyaus, therefore, proved an unpromising divine unity and was unceremoniously dropped in later speculations. But the idea that the gods were related by birth lived on, and, in spite of conflicting accounts of their origin out of one another, they were conceived to form something analogous to a human tribe or clan (and even to be divided into castes) and to be actuated by a common clan-spirit or group-mind. They were often invoked together in larger or smaller groups and they were also often collectively represented.[92] The unedifying spectacle of the gods being in conflict with one another, as depicted in the Purāṇas, is almost entirely absent in the Vedas.[93] This facilitated their collection in comprehensive groups with

[88] Griswold, *op. cit.*, pp. 98-99.

[89] RV. I. 160. 4; V. 2. Griswold, *op. cit.*, p. 10; Macdonell, *V.M.*, pp. 12, 126.

[90] Macdonell, *V. M.*, p. 14.

[91] *Ibid*, p. 15; p. 126 (RV. I. 150.2; 160.2; 185.1).

[92] In RV. II. 3.4 the Vasus and the Ādityas are supposed to fall outside the All-gods group.

[93] The gods on the whole are conceived as dwelling together in harmony and friendship. The only one who ever introduces a note of discord is the warlike and overbearing Indra. He once appears to have fought against the gods in general (4. 30. 3-5); he slew his own father, and shattered the car of Dawn. He also seems to have threatened on one occasion to slay his faithful companions the Maruts.—Macdonell, *Vedic Mythology*, p. 18 (see Barnett, *Hindu Gods and Heroes*, pp. 81-2).

varying denotations. Thus in the later Vedic literature and the Brāhmaṇas the earthly gods were comprehensively called Vasus and had Agni as their leader, the atmospheric gods were called Rudras, having Indra at their head, and the heavenly gods got the name of Ādityas with Varuṇa as the chief representative.[94] The highest group comprehending all the gods received the appellation of Viśvedevāḥ (All-gods).[95]

But while the idea of a confederacy of the gods materially helped the growth of monotheism, the speculative mind could not rest with this imperfect unification. Inadequate personification and ill-defined functions obscured the boundaries of the gods. It was difficult under those circumstances to keep separate the deities whose principal functions had either a joint or an identical effect.[96] Fire and lightning, for instance, have similar illuminating functions: no wonder, therefore, if Agni and Indra should appear at first as a dual divinity and then regarded as identical, each appropriating in time the attributes of the other.[97] The loose association of functions and attributes with the gods made it possible to invest at least the major gods with all powers incidental to supreme divinity; and when in this way their distinctiveness was lost, the different deities came to be regarded as different forms of one and the same ultimate principle. If the same Agni could be simultaneously present in many houses, in the

[94] For other groupings, see Macdonell, *Vedic Mythology*, p. 130 f. The groups tend to increase. See, for instance, Chān Up. 3, 6-10 and Bhagavadgītā xi. 6 and 22.

[95] Sometimes these are distinguished from the Vasus and the Ādityas (RV. 2.3.4). Bh. G. xi. 22 follows this tradition of regarding the Viśvedevāḥ as a circumscribed group.

[96] There is the work of rain-giving, in which, to a greater or less degree, Parjanya, Varuṇa, Indra, Dyaus, Rudra and the Maruts all participate. As gods of the lightning there are Indra, Trita Āptya, and so forth; as physician gods Rudra and the Maruts, Varuṇa, Soma, Aśvins, Vāta and the Waters; as demon-slayers Agni and Indra and in general the gods of light; and as gods of song Bṛihaspati, the Maruts and the Aṅgirasas.—Griswold, *The Religion of the Ṛigveda*, p. 104.

[97] Macdonell, *V. M.*, p. 16.

lightning, and in the sun, and if Indra could multiply himself through his occult powers, why should it be impossible for a single Power to manifest itself in the different forces of nature? Both pantheistic and monotheistic speculations started from this line of thought. Passages like the following are not isolated : " The one Being sages speak of in many ways ; they call it Agni, Yama, Mātariśvan " (RV. 1.164.46). The same idea of unity was sought to be conveyed by depicting the mutual dependence of the deities. In fact, the concept of a unitary God was more easily reached than an agreed name—possibly there were champions for different deities, as is suggested by RV. 2. 1,[98] where an entire hymn is devoted to show that the different gods were in reality nothing but Agni, and by other isolated passages where similar claims are advanced for Sūrya (RV. 10. 170.4), Varuṇa (RV. 8. 41.1-7) and Indra (RV. 8. 87.2).[99] The use of terms like 'the One,' 'the One unborn,' 'the One unknown,' points to the adoption of an indefinite god as the ultimate unity; but it served the purpose of monism more than that of monotheism.[100] Hence the framing of a new name became imperative. This concrete god would correspond to the All-Father idea of primitive minds.

Now, an examination of religious speculations shows that God as Power appeals first to the human mind. A god is what one is afraid to displease. It is also a being whose aid a person seeks in order to overcome some evil or attain some good. Perhaps the second character is apprehended and appreciated earlier : we want to have the gods on our side in order to succeed in our undertakings and to defeat our enemies. Yahweh was the Lord of hosts in Israel; so also was Indra to the Vedic Aryans. But power manifests itself

[98] RV. II. 1 looks like a reply to RV. VIII. 29.2 where the hymn to the Viśvedevāḥ distinguishes the different gods; see Ragozin, *op. cit.*, p. 434.

[99] Macdonell, *V. M.*, p. 118.

[100] See in this connection Muir, *Original Sanskrit Texts*, V, Sec. xxi. (19) as to whether polytheism or monotheism was the earliest form of the Aryan religion (3rd edition, p. 412).

most strikingly in acts of creation, whether of the world or of gods and men. A world ruled by regularity and law indicates the existence of a single being who not only wields the power to bring it into being but also the will and the intelligence to regulate its working. Such a conscious fashioner of the world the Vedic Indians found in Prajāpati—a name which was coined to suit the function ascribed to it, namely, the lordship of all creatures. Prajāpati quickly replaced the pre-Vedic Tvaṣṭṛ and the colourless deities Dhātṛ (supporter), Vidhātṛ (Disposer) and Viśvakarman (All-creating), who were personifications of the architectonic and controlling activities of the Creator.[101] After being tentatively associated with Savitṛ and Soma in an adjectival form and standing for a distinct deity in a few places, the name is used in the magnificent hymn of RV. 10. 121 in the sense of the Supreme God who brought everything into being and is therefore rightly termed Hiraṇyagarbha, the germ of gold.[102] This became the established meaning of the term commonly in the later Vedic literature and regularly in the Brāhmaṇas.[103] Prajāpati was not a nature-god and so it was easy to invest him with supreme wisdom and ethical qualities: it is with this enhanced connotation that he appears in the Upaniṣads as instructing Indra and Virocana. But his principal function as "the god of offspring" and of creation in general was never forgotten, and he became latterly identified with Brahmā, the first person of the Hindu Trinity, who is supposed to be the creator of the world.[104] Brahmā, in fact, absorbed also the intellectual function of Prajāpati and became the revealer of the Vedas. In later Hinduism he also appropriated the names of Dhātṛ, Vidhātṛ, Hiraṇyagarbha and such other deities who were closely related to Prajāpati in his functional aspect. Being associated, on the

101 Macdonell, *V.M.*, p. 116; also pp. 115, 118; Barnett, *op. cit.*, p. 48 f.; Winternitz, *op. cit.*, I, p. 222 f.

102 Macdonell, *V. M.*, p. 118.

103 *Ibid*, p. 118.

104 *Ibid*, p. 119 (Āśvalāyana Gṛhya Sūtra, 3, 4, etc.).

one hand, with the sacrificial god Prajāpati of the Brāhmaṇas and, on the other, with the philosophical unity Brahman of the Upaniṣads,[105] Brahmā had a fair chance of being raised to the supremest position.[106] What went against him was the want of popular enthusiasm for a God who made no appeal to the emotional life of man and remained mostly a god of the sacrificial class. So he retained his position as the advisor of the gods in difficult situations but retired from the active government of the world after peopling it with diverse creatures, including the gods.[107] His unfitness for the supreme position was proved in popular opinion by a variety of causes. Although called *Svayambhū* (self-born), he carried with him the Vedic tradition of the waters being the source of all things and of a primeval "golden egg or germ" out of which all things arose.[108] So, in later times, he was represented as being born in the lotus issuing out of the navel of the primeval Puruṣa resting on the waters (Nārāyaṇa or Viṣṇu)[109] or as issuing out of the primeval egg grown out of the seed of the Primal Being thrown into the primeval waters.[110] Secondly, the creation of the world by him was not always non-sexually conceived and an obscure Vedic text concerning the incest of a father with his daughter and the birth of Vāstoṣpati out of that incest was foisted on him in his character as Prajāpati

[105] The Upaniṣads recognised a Saguṇa and a Nirguṇa Brahman but did not give the Saguṇa Brahman or Īśvara the name of Brahmā.

[106] Carpenter, *Theism in Mediaeval India*, pp. 10, 170; see also pp. 71, 73. Mañjuśrī was conceived to possess functions similar to those of Brahmā whose name he came to bear. And Avalokiteśvara too had some of his physical properties.

[107] Titles mean something historically, but they are no gauge of belief or of the estimation in which a god is really held......Brahman's titles......are amplified more for grandiloquence than for added meaning.—Hopkins, *Epic Mythology*, p. 192. See also p. 193 (§ 134, Brahman as Preserver) where the continuing activities of Brahmā are described.

[108] See Hopkins, *Epic Mythology*, p. 189. Similar cosmic eggs were believed in by the Phoenicians, the Babylonians, and the Iranians. See Casartelli, *The Philosophy of the Mazdayasnian Religion under the Sassanids*, p. 107.

[109] For this transformation of the independent Brahman into an agent of Viṣṇu, see Hopkins, *Epic Mythology*, p. 197. For a similar Śaivite transformation, see p. 198.

[110] For Brāhmaṇa parallels, see Winternitz, *op. cit.*, I, p. 223.

and he was represented as begetting Manu, the progenitor of the human race, on his own mind-born daughter Śatarūpā.[111] The rational and moral instincts of the race rejected a god who was neither causally first[112] nor ethically ideal. Besides, there was some incongruity between a God as Power and a God who carried the symbols of Brāhmaṇic detachment and intellectual preoccupation. His position could be maintained only so long as the old tradition of ascetic fervour (*tapas*) as the cause of creation did not completely die out.[113] When the idea of Brahmā, Viṣṇu and Śiva as a trinity was well established, possibly there disappeared also the religious motive for worshipping Brahmā. "Men worship Siva the destroyer because they fear him; Viṣṇu the Preserver because they hope from him; but who worships Brahmā the Creator? His work is done."[114] As Hopkins remarks, "Brahman comes into the group as a matter of form, because it was impossible for the sectarian worshipper to deny the old orthodox Creator, who had been chief of the pantheon, the old Father of gods and men, since the end of the Vedic age."[115] His decline from power is traceable in the Mahābhārata and the Rāmāyaṇa;[116] by the end of the sixth century of the Christian era the small sect which considered him to be the Supreme God died out, and to-day in the whole of India there are very few temples dedicated to him.[117]

111 For the offspring of Brahmā (or Prajāpati), see Hopkins, *Epic Mythology*, p. 189 f.

112 The egg-theory is repudiated in a speech ascribed to the Wind-god: "How can he who is unborn be born of an egg? The egg means space; hence only was the Great Father born. There is no (cosmic) egg; but Brahman is; he is the king, the enlivener (creator) of the world (M.Bh. XIII, 154, 19).—Hopkins, *Epic Mythology*, p. 191.

113 *Cf.* the hymn of Aghamarṣaṇa, in RV. X. 190.

114 Carpenter (quoting Hopkins), *op. cit.*, p. 182.

115 Hopkins, *Ori. and Ev. of Rel.*, p. 304; also *Epic Mythology*, p. 189 f.

116 Barnett, *op. cit.*, p. 111.

117 There are temples at Pushkar (Rajputana), Dudahi (Bundelkhand), Khed Brahmā (Mahikantha, Idar State, Gujarat), Kudakkal (Malabar), Chebrolu (Kistna district), Kālahasti (South Arcot), Mitrānandapuram (near Trivandrum).

But it is not power as such that the human mind seeks in God. A god that does not embody the ethical ideal has little chance of survival in human worship, especially when man learns to control the forces of nature himself. We are overawed by the dynamically sublime, but we require something more in God to make Him the object of our prayer and devotion. If power had been the primary qualification of godhead, Agni, who consumed everything, or Indra, whose matchless valour was so often extolled in the Vedas, or Soma, who invigorated men and inspired their muse and even made the gods immortal, would have attained the supreme position in Hindu religion. But although the Vedic seers approached these gods oftenest with their hymns, the future belonged to gods of a different type—gods that did not engage the hand or employ the head so much as attracted the heart of man. The Brāhmaṇas had extolled sacrifice and prescribed rituals. The Āraṇyakas had allegorised them. The Upaniṣads had rejected them after recording the faint protests of those who were against the mere pursuit of self-knowledge to the total abandonment of works. A time, however, soon came when the Upaniṣadic identification of Ātman (the self) with Brahman was challenged and the Vedic relation of man and God was restored with a deeper spiritual significance and ethical meaning.

The way for this consummation was being prepared in the Vedic hymns themselves. Max Müller's theory of Vedic henotheism has been discussed threadbare in subsequent literature on Vedic religion and not always in favour of that theory.[118] Speaking of the theory, Macdonell observes: "Henotheism is an appearance rather than a reality, an appearance produced by the indefiniteness due to undeveloped anthropomorphism, by the lack of any Vedic god occupying the position of a Zeus as the constant head of the pantheon, by the natural tendency of the priest or singer in extolling a particular god to exaggerate his greatness and to ignore other gods, and by the growing belief in the unity of the gods,

[118] Macdonell, *V. M.*, p. 16.

each of whom might be regarded as a type of the divine. Henotheism might, however, be justified as a term to express the tendency of the RV. towards a kind of monotheism." The gods were distinguished from other types of beings by the possession, in generous measure, of " the qualities of power, sovereignty, wisdom, beneficence and beauty."[119] They were also regarded as ' truthful ' and ' not deceitful.' They could be relied upon to keep their covenant of grace and gift, provided men, on their part, fulfilled their duties of sacrifice and prayer. Further, in relation to themselves, the gods act in unison. No invocation of groups of divinities would have been possible, had it not been prompted by the belief that they possessed perfect understanding among themselves about their proper functions and were prepared to act harmoniously together for the benefit of the worshipper.[120] In this way the gods are related to the Eternal Order (*ṛta*) which rules not only the physical but also the moral world.[121] Speaking of this aspect of divinity, Griswold remarks,[122] " All the gods are alike in either determining, or expressing or guarding some aspect or other of *ṛita*, which may be translated as ' the course of things,' ' nature,' or ' cosmic order.' Through the great conception of *Ṛita* the multiplicity of nature is reduced to a unity and the multiplicity of the gods (corresponding to the multiplicity of nature) is seen to reflect a single will, because all are ' labourers together ' in maintaining a single all-comprehensive cosmic order. Thus the

[119] Griswold, *op. cit.*, p. 109.

[120] See Keith, *op. cit.*, p. 86 f.

[121] The Vedic word *rita* (connected with Greek 'αρετη' and Latin *ratus*) means fit, orderly, good, and as a noun *ritam* is the right order of the universe, of the sacrifice, and of ethical conduct, the true way as opposed to its negative, *anṛitam*, that is, false or untrue. It connotes a certain " harmony " (which is etymologically from the same root) between ideal and practice. In a cosmic sense, it designates the harmony of the world, the regularity of nature, as evinced by the orderly procession of celestial bodies, of seasons, and of their earthly representatives in the seasonal sacrifices and the regular conduct of men, as opposed to irregular conduct. It is not, like the Chinese Tao, a cosmic power, but it is the order instituted by the Wise Spirit as regulator of the world.—Hopkins, *Ethics of India*, pp. 2-3 (see Keith, *op. cit.*, I, pp. 83-84).

[122] Griswold, *op. cit.*, p. 108; Macdonell, *V. M.*, p. 26.

tendency of Ṛigvedic religion was toward some form of unity, whether monotheistic or pantheistic."

In fact, we come in view now of the second witness to the existence of God, namely, man's moral consciousness and his yearning for a spirit that responds to the call of devotion and love. The unity that the intellect seeks and establishes is found to be also the power that makes for righteousness and social concord. The henotheistic attitude achieved three things: (*i*) it established an exclusive affection for one deity at a time; (*ii*) it raised that god to the position of the sole creator and preserver of the world; (*iii*) it invested that god with a fixed will and an ethical purpose in the government of the physical and moral worlds. It would not be true to say that the ethical character of the gods was a late achievement of Vedic speculation. What really took place was that the ethical quality, which was originally associated with one deity or group of deities, became the common property of all the gods through identification or association with the ethical divinity.[123] This could take place only when anthropomorphism had sufficiently covered up the physical origin of most of the Vedic gods and facilitated the transference of the ethical qualities of Varuṇa and the Ādityás to these deities. Western scholars have deplored the eclipse of Varuṇa, "the Indian Yahweh," in post-Vedic literature. It is true that it would have been an advantage had the selection of Varuṇa prevented the war of sects in later times. But an explanation of the supersession of Varuṇa may possibly be found in the fact that monotheism did not come by way of monolatry in India, as it did in Israel, and each of the major gods was conceived in course of time to be the guardian of the moral order (*ṛtasya gopā*).[124] This obviated the necessity of a separate ethical deity who would have assumed the position of a 'special god' of morality and affected the independence of the other gods. The ethical

[123] Hopkins, *Ethics of India*, p. 13.

[124] Aditi is several times spoken of as protecting from distress (*aṃhas*), and she is said to grant complete welfare or safety (10, 100; 1, 94.15), but she is more frequently invoked to release from guilt or sin. Thus Varuṇa (1, 24.15), Agni

Varuṇa vitalised the other gods by association and identification and disappeared from view in the process; but a realm where he could reign as a special deity of nature was found for him in the waters with which, in fact, he had Vedic associations. The other factor that contributed to the downfall of Varuṇa, as indeed of all the gods, was the development of the idea of an independent and impersonal Moral Order which had once been regarded as "the First-born" of the divine fervour (RV. 10. 190). Varuṇa, again, was the personification of the constancy and regularity that keep the physical and the moral order going. As he had not gathered round him any considerable myth of having bestowed gifts on worshippers in the past, the frankly hedonistic temper had no need of him, and later generations did not see the utility or logic of approaching him with frequent rites on the principle of reciprocal service. All these causes conspired to diminish the importance of the ethical Varuṇa; but it would be untrue to say that the moral standard of the community was materially lowered thereby. The interest of the succeeding ages was in sacrifice and self-knowledge—the one was probably accentuated by contact with indigenous belief in magic and the other as a reaction therefrom. But morality lived on even when interest in Varuṇa had waned, and an independent investigation into the conditions of moral discipline was undertaken in the different philosophies, and concrete rules of life laid down in the different codes of social and individual ethics (Gṛhya-sūtras and Dharma-śāstras).

But the Vedic Varuṇa did not really die—he rose phoenix-like out of his own ashes in more attractive divine

(4, 12.4), and Savitṛ (5, 82.6), are besought to free from guilt against Aditi. Aditi, Mitra and Varuṇa are implored to forgive sin (2, 27.14), Aditi and Aryaman, to loosen (the bonds of) sin (7, 93.7). Worshippers beseech Aditi to make them sinless (1, 162.22); praying that by fulfilling her ordinances they may be without sin towards Varuṇa (7, 87.7) and that evildoers may be cut off from Aditi (10, 87.18). Hence though other gods, Agni (3, 54.10), Savitṛ (4, 54.3), Sun, Dawn, Heaven and Earth (10,35.2-3) are petitioned to pardon sin, the notion of releasing from it is much more closely connected with Aditi and her son Varuṇa whose fetters that bind sinners are characteristic, and who unties sin like a rope and removes it.—Macdonell, *Vedic Mythology*, p. 121. (See also pp. 26 and 88.)

colours.[125] The Rig-Veda conceives of him as a noble lord, a king and a universal monarch—as a being to whom sovereignty belongs in a pre-eminent manner. He is possessed of mysterious powers; the whole world is established in him and obeys his laws. He regulates the movement of heavenly bodies and terrestrial objects alike. Nothing is secret from him—neither the hidden depths of the earth nor the hidden depths of the human soul. From his heavenly mansion of a thousand doors and his seat of a thousand columns he looks on all deeds, beholds the truth and falsehood of men and is an invisible witness of man's thoughts, intentions and acts.[126] The sun that roams over the world by day and the stars that shine by night keep a watch on the conduct of men and report it to him; and his thousand-eyed spies ferret out every wrong and are never deceived. Even the gods cannot transgress his fixed ordinances, which Varuṇa strictly guards. He hates and punishes such moral lapses as falsehood, deceit, cruelty, cheating, cursing, gambling, anger and drunkenness and afflicts with disease those that break the moral law. There is no possibility of escaping from his jurisdiction and his fetters inexorably ensnare the sinner.[127] Communion with him is broken through sin and he withdraws his friendship and favour from the impenitent sinner. But Varuṇa has a benign as well as a terrible aspect. He supports his own creation with timely rain and adequate nourishment. Being superior to the moral law, which is established in him and is an expression of his holy will, he does not insist upon strict justice being meted out to sinners. He understands their failings and is willing and able to forgive even the daily transgressions of his laws provided they are truly penitent. He is able to drive away disease and death and to release

[125] Griswold, *op. cit.*, Ch. V; Macdonell, *V.M.*, p. 24 f.; Ragozin, *op. cit.*, p. 140; Keith, *Rel. and Phil. of Veda and Upanisads*, I, p. 246f.; Winternitz, *op. cit.*, I (E.T.), p. 80 f.

[126] Whatever thing two sitting down together talk about, Varuṇa as a third knows (AV. IV. 16.2); see Griswold, *op. cit.*, p. 129.

[127] See AV. IV. 16; Winternitz, *op. cit.*, I, pp. 144-45; Griswold, *op. cit.*, p. 129.

from all sins. He is merciful and gracious and one can be restored to his favour by "moral seriousness in trying to discover one's 'hidden faults' (VII. 86, 3-4), confession of sin (VII. 86, 6; 88, 6; 89, 3), longing to be justified in the sight of Varuṇa (VII. 87, 7; 1.24. 15); prayer for the remission of penalty (VII. 86, 5; 88, 6; 89, 1, 5; I. 24, 9, 11-15; 25, 1-2; V. 85, 7-8; II. 28, 5-7, 9), purpose after new obedience (VII. 86, 7), oblations and sacrifices (1.24, 14) and hymns of praise" (VII. 86, 8 ; I. 25, 3-4).[128] So, as Macdonell points out, "There is in fact no hymn to Varuṇa (and the Ādityas)[129] in which the prayer for forgiveness of guilt does not occur, as in the hymns to other deities the prayer for worldly goods."[130] In fact, this aspect was so prominent that even when other gods (*e.g.*, Aditi) are prayed to for forgiveness of sin, the prayer often takes the form of

128 Griswold, *op. cit.*, p. 129 (with footnote).

129 The following quotation from Griswold neatly puts the relation between Varuṇa and the Ādityas :—

Varuṇa stands out clear and distinct with sharply defined characteristics. Mitra his companion and double is in most matters simply the replica of Varuṇa. What is true of Mitra is true of all the other Ādityas in their relation to Varuṇa their head. They have little or no individuality or real personality. They indeed form a system with Varuṇa, revolving about him, as it were, like planets about a central sun. But in relation to Varuṇa they are little more than expressions of his divine nature, personified aspects of the same,—in short, little more than names of the great god. Thus Mitra and Aryaman explicate the social nature and laws of Varuṇa. Mitra, 'he of the compact,' signifies that Varuṇa is a covenant-keeping god and demands that men should be like him in this respect. Aryaman 'the loyal,' 'the true' with special reference to the marriage contract means that Varuṇa desires truth and loyalty in the marriage relation. Bhaga, 'he of bounty,' and Aṃśa, 'he of the due share,' emphasize the bountiful and gracious character of Varuṇa who 'gives to all men liberally,' and to every man his due. Dakṣa 'he of strength, cleverness, insight, will' emphasizes the creative purpose, power and skill of Varuṇa. In a word, if the Ādityas are in the aggregate sense gods of celestial light, they are also, 'in the aggregate sense,' gods of truth and righteousness, the creators and directors of an eternal and inviolable world-order, both physical and moral. Being 'observers of order' '*ritavānāḥ*,' *i.e.* holy themselves, they are able to say with one voice: "Be ye holy, for I am holy"—*The Religion of the Rigveda*, p. 143 (see Keith, *op. cit.*, p. 99). For a comparison of the Ādityas with the Amesha Spentas, see Griswold, *op. cit.*, p. 145 f., and Keith, *op. cit.*, p. 102. For a comparison of the Vedic list with the Paurāṇic, see N. K. Bhattasali's *Iconography of Buddhist and Brahmanical Sculptures in the Dacca Museum*, pp. 154-55.

130 Macdonell, *V. M.*, p. 27.

seeking to be released from the fetters of Varuṇa with the help of these gods.[131]

But the future allegiance of Hinduism belonged to other gods. Simultaneously with the Aryanisation of the land, there went on an imperceptible absorption of indigenous culture and this led to a shifting of emphasis to such Vedic gods as could be easily assimilated to objects of local worship. Possibly also, the fitful monotheism of the Vedas did not satisfy those who had passed through the baptism of Upaniṣadic monism and a more systematic attempt to lead things to a primal personal unity was the crying need of the hour. The Vedic gods, again, were gods of the whole tribe, although it is not improbable that this or that god was occasionally preferred as being the best and highest. But as the area of Aryan culture extended, local considerations must have dictated the ranking of the different gods, with the effect that, after the period of the Upaniṣads, sectarianism began to rear its head and to look upon this or that god as the supreme entity and the source of all things. A change in the popular idea regarding the proper method of approaching God, howsoever caused, was also responsible for the development of theism. Not intellectual contemplation but loving devotion was looked upon as the proper way of gaining divine help and guidance, and so the impersonal Brahman was replaced in popular affection by the personal gods of later Hinduism. Two gods towered above the rest henceforth in popular esteem, namely, Viṣṇu and Śiva; but the Vedic solar worship also managed to survive in some form all through the centuries by the side of Vaiṣṇavism and Śaivism. The cult of Śakti, the Mother Goddess, also attracted some earnest minds and managed to fuse together Vedic and aboriginal beliefs. Gaṇeśa, probably the god of a local cult, also gained some following and was duly affiliated to the cults of Śiva and Śakti. Many of the Vedic gods were totally forgotten in the new pantheon of Hinduism—specially, the minor and older

131 Macdonell, *Vedic Mythology*, p. 121.

gods, and some were allied to the new divinities. A new literature grew up to discourse on these sectarian gods and hostile traditions were established among the new theists of India.

## CHAPTER V

### The Gods of Hinduism : Pauranic

We must see in the raising of Viṣṇu to the supreme position an attempt to combine the power of Indra, the sacrificial and creative aspects of Brahmanaspati and Brahmā, and the moral government of the world associated hitherto with Varuṇa.[1] An additional motive must have been supplied by the tradition that Viṣṇu had laboured in the past for the benefit of man (RV. 7. 100.4 ; 6. 69.5-6 ; 6.49.13). His famous " three strides," encompassing the whole realm of existence, had also established his omnipresence, including his home in the highest heaven, and his kinship with the rolling disc of Sūrya who was worshipped in a variety of forms in Vedic times. Barring a vague solar association,[2] however, Viṣṇu had very little of physical origin about him and he could, therefore, be easily personified and endowed with necessary intellectual and ethical qualities.

But the rise of Vaiṣṇavism cannot be wholly explained by the above considerations. We must assume that the mind of the nation was being insensibly prepared for a new theistic cult. The better minds must have had enough of sacrificial cruelty and fanciful rites meant to placate the gods, and the popular mind must have indicated in no uncertain terms its

[1] Macdonell, *Vedic Mythology*, p. 37 f.; Griswold, *op. cit.*, p. 282 f. For the ousting of Indra by Viṣṇu, see B. Sastri, *Bhakti Cult in Ancient India*, p. 99 f. (Ch. IX. Vishnu Everywhere).

[2] See Barnett, *op. cit.*, p. 38; Hopkins, *Epic Mythology*, p. 206. The modern *dhyāna* of Nārāyaṇa places him in the Sun (*savitṛmaṇḍalamadhyavartī*). See Bharatan Kumarappa, *The Hindu Conception of the Deity*, pp. 89, 111, 117 f. In the Nāt-hlaung Viṣṇu Temple at Pagan (Burma) where different Avatāras of Viṣṇu were inserted in niches, an image of Sūrya of South Indian variety probably figured as an avatāra.—Niharranjan Ray, *Brahmanical Gods in Burma*, p. 42. (But in Java an identification of Siva and Sūrya is not rare.)

dissatisfaction with the cold speculative unity of Brahman. A simplified and less costly rite and a god capable of responding to the needs of the human heart could alone bring together in common worship the wise and the ignorant, and a god that had sacrificial association and carried with him a tradition of willing helpfulness to man was just what the nation wanted at the time. The unity of godhead had been almost achieved in the Vedic age; and in the sub-Vedic age, namely, in the Upaniṣads, Monotheism had even passed over into Absolutistic monism. All that was needed was to fix up the name and attributes of the unitary God and to define the proper attitude of worship towards him.

We may very well believe that the Vedic Viṣṇu was found suitable for achieving this purpose. When Prajāpati had satisfied the cosmogonic interest but was found to be unsuitable for the government of the world, the religious temper found satisfaction in Viṣṇu who took interest in human affairs. Already in the Brāhmaṇas stories had begun to be told of a god who exerted himself on behalf of gods and men in various assumed forms. The fish that saved Manu from the deluge, the tortoise that created offspring to people the world, the boar that lifted up the submerged earth and the dwarf that outwitted the demons and helped the gods are instances in point and, as is to be expected, Prajāpati was credited with some of these achievements. But very soon all these,[3] and more besides, were ascribed to Viṣṇu in his capacity as the moral governor of the world, and of all gods he alone was supposed to have come down periodically to set matters right, whenever the world was in distress, not because of any sacrificial compulsion but out of his own free will and grace.

It is at this point probably that by a happy stroke of speculation Viṣṇu was identified with Puruṣa Nārāyaṇa who in the Satapatha Brāhmaṇa (XII, iii. 4. 1) was regarded as having pervaded the whole of nature.[4] This term waked up

[3] Winternitz, *op. cit.*, I, p. 205—the identification was probably effected through sacrifice, with which both Prajāpati and Viṣṇu were identified. See also B. Kumarappa, *op. cit.*, p. 89.

[4] Barnett, *op. cit.*, pp. 76-77.

reminiscences of the Vedic Puruṣa who had allowed himself to be sacrificed so that the universe might come into being, and it also facilitated the fancy that this primeval spirit was also Nārāyaṇa (of the family of Nara)[5] or identical with man in his spiritual qualities. For one endowed with such qualities it is not only possible to take actual human form, if necessary, but also to reciprocate at all times the love which his devotees bestow on him. The former aspect proved the basis of the theory of incarnation (*avatāra*) and the latter of the path of devotion (*bhakti*).[6] This is evident in the Nārāyaṇīya section of the *Mahābhārata* (XII, Chs. 336-343) and the *Bhagavadgītā* (VI. 35-42), in both of which we have a message of spiritual, as opposed to animal sacrifice, of a god without whose 'co-operative grace' salvation is not possible, and of a life devotional which obviates the necessity of austere practices, Vedic rites and intellectual speculations alike. The latter refers to the many descents of God, whenever virtue declines and iniquity prospers, in order to set right a disjointed world; the former specifies these different descents.[7] The ethical character of the supreme God is brought out in the usual Indian way

[5] This is Barnett's suggestion, only that he thinks that this Nārāyaṇa, "a man of the Nara family," was originally a divine or deified saint, a *ṛishi*. He refers to divine saints mentioned in the Rigveda and the Brāhmaṇas as being creators of the universe and treated in legends as being the equals of the gods, attaining divine powers by their mystic insight into the sacrificial lore. We have taken the term in a slightly different sense. It may be added that the orthodox derivation of the term which makes it to mean (as hinted at, *e.g.*, in the *Manu-Saṃhitā*, I) "one who rests on the ocean" (referring to the Paurāṇic belief that Viṣṇu rests reclined in mystic sleep on his serpent-couch in the ocean of milk) links it up with the Vedic primeval waters out of which creation originally arose.—See Barnett, *Hindu Gods and Heroes*, p. 77.

[6] Bhakti connotes chaste fondness as well as devout faith. (The Vedic Sraddhā and the Brāhmaṇic Preman are earlier terms.—Hopkins, *Ethics of India*, p. 194. See also Sir Charles Eliot, *Hinduism and Buddhism*, II, p. 180 f., for the early beginnings of Bhakti in Indian religious literature.)

[7] The list omits the names of Fish and Buddha and substitutes Kṛṣṇa for Balarāma. Another list substitutes Swan (in which form Viṣṇu is supposed to have communicated the Vedas to Brahman) for Fish (which in later mythology does not save the life of Manu but rescues the Vedas from the Deluge) (M.Bh. XII. 340. 100).—See Carpenter, *Theism in Mediaeval India*, p. 239 f. The list of incarnations is not uniform (see art. INCARNATION (Indian) by H. Jacobi in ERE. vii. 193, f.n.l), nor is incarnation understood in a uniform sense, for it

by supposing that Nārāyaṇa was born as a son of Dharma or Righteousness.

But the stream of Vaiṣṇavism was apparently fed by many rills of thought.[8] Literary and archæological remains refer to a Bhagavat or Lord—the name borne as a part by the *Bhagavadgītā;* a Vāsudeva who claimed a sect of followers (as did Arjuna); and a Kṛṣṇa, son of Devakī. What clans, tribes or peoples worshipped the supreme God in these different names can only be a matter of conjecture now; but the tradition of Kṛṣṇa's association with the Âbhīras (cowherds) and of the worship of Vāsudeva-Kṛṣṇa by the Sātvata tribe lends colour to the supposition that possibly these gods were worshipped by people who were either scripturally or intellectually incapable of, or traditionally averse to, performing Vedic rites[9] and understood the deep Upaniṣadic Philosophy, which Kṛṣṇa Devakīputtra learnt from Ghora Âṅgirasa, in a devotional sense. It is also probable that, being outside the Vedic pantheon and originally having no association with Viṣṇu, these new gods could not be worshipped in the Vedic way and consequently the simple worship practised by their original adherents passed over into the Brāhmaṇic cult. By the time of the Nārāyaṇīya section of the Mahābhārata some sort of federation of these faiths had been firmly established, for we are told that, as Dharma's son, Nārāyaṇa had three brothers—Nara (a previous incarnation of Arjuna), Hari (or Viṣṇu) and Kṛṣṇa who, being regarded

covers alike actual descent (plenary or partial) and manifestation (real or docetic). See also Sir Charles Eliot, *Hinduism and Buddhism*, Vol. II, p. 147 f.; Hopkins, *Epic Mythology*, pp. 217-18; Barth, *Religions of India*, p. 170 f.; Schrader, *Int. to the Pāñcarātra and the Ahirbudhnya Saṃhitā*, p. 42; B. Kumarappa, *op. cit.*, p. 110 f.

8 The reader is referred to the illuminating article of H. Jacobi on INCARNATION (Indian) in ERE. vii. 193 f. See also R. G. Bhandarkar, *Vaiṣṇavism, Śaivism and Minor Religious Systems*, Parts I, VI, VII, VIII, IX; also Sir Charles Eliot, *Hinduism and Buddhism*, Vol. II, p. 152 f.; p. 201. For difference between Nārāyaṇa and Kṛṣṇa, see Hopkins, *Epic Mythology*, p. 214. See Bharatan Kumarappa, *The Hindu Conception of the Deity*, Chs. II-IV. (The present writer got this excellent manual too late to be able to utilise it fully.)

9 See Sir Charles Eliot, *op. cit.*, p. 156; N. N. Ghosh, *Indo-Aryan Literature and Culture (Origins)*, p. 47.

as the son of Vasudeva (and Devakī), was also called Vāsudeva. The *Taittirīya Āraṇyaka* (X. i. 6) had referred to Nārāyaṇa, Vāsudeva and Viṣṇu as three phases of the same god. Not only was this confirmed but even a philosophy of emanation (the theory of Vyūhas) was reared upon the relationships of Vāsudeva—his brother (Balarāma or Saṅkarṣaṇa),[10] son (Pradyumna) and grandson (Aniruddha) being deified with different divine functions,[11] and sometimes the whole group being regarded as forming a hierarchy of beings emanating from Nārāyaṇa.[12] In short, a serious and systematic attempt was made to posit a self-sufficient unitary divinity, creating and controlling the physical and the moral universe and holding spiritual and moral relations with man.[13]

10 It appears from Kautilya's *Arthaśāstra* (Eng. Tr., Bk. XIII, Ch. 3) that an ascetic sect owing allegiance to Saṅkarṣaṇa existed at one time and that it used a sacrificial beverage. See Barnett, *op. cit.*, p. 91.

11 Speaking of the origins of Vaiṣṇavism Sir Charles Eliot observes (*op. cit.*, II, p. 197 f.) : "The Pāñcarātra was not Brahmanic in origin....It seems to have grown up in north-western India in the centuries when Iranian influence was strong and may owe to Zoroastrianism the doctrine of the Vyūhas which finds a parallel in the relation of Ahura Mazda to Spenta Mainyu, his Holy Spirit, and in the Fravashis. It is also remarkable that God is credited with six attributes comparable with the six Amesha Spentas." The four forms had no fixed functions. Lokācārya in his *Tattvatraya* assigns knowledge (*jñāna*) and strength (*bala*) to Saṅkarṣaṇa, lordship (*aiśvarya*) and power or virility (*vīrya*) to Pradyumna, and ability (*śakti*) and energy (*tejas*) to Aniruddha. Schrader in his *Introduction to the Pāñcarātra and the Ahirbudhnya Saṃhitā* gives an elaborate account of these guṇas and their relation to the Vyūhas (p. 29 f.) and queries if these six divine attributes were not borrowed from Zoroastrianism in which also God is ascribed six attributes (p. 176). See B. Kumarappa, *op. cit.*, p. 99 f.

12 For Vyūhas in the Caitanya school, see Bhandarkar, *op. cit.*, pp. 12, 53, 85. Elsewhere (M. Bh. VII. 29.26 f.) the four forms are differently conceived and do not refer to the four Vyūhas. See Carpenter, *Theism in Mediaeval India*, p. 242; Barnett, *op. cit.*, p. 86. For a similar conception in Śaivism and Buddhism, see Sir Charles Eliot, *Brahmanism and Buddhism*, II, p. 198. H. C. Raychaudhuri (*Early History of the Vaiṣṇava Sect*, p. 105) remarks : "The ousting of the Vyūhas by the Avatāras was one of the characteristic signs of the transformation of Bhāgavatism into Vishṇuism."

13 Speaking of the predominance of Śiva and Viṣṇu in the later religious literature, Sir Charles Eliot remarks : "The change created by their appearance is not merely the addition of two imposing figures to an already ample pantheon; it is a revolution which might be described as the introduction of a new religion, except that it does not come as the enemy or destroyer of the old."—Sir Charles Eliot, *Hinduism and Buddhism*, II, p. 186.

**We shall** quote Carpenter's admirable summary of the religious position attained by Viṣṇu-Nārāyaṇa-Kṛṣṇa in the Epics:

> "Above all gods he rises, like Brahman of old, or Śiva as Maheśvara, into sole Deity. Nature is the scene of his sovereignty; there he reigns as King of kings; foremost in the universe, there is no higher Being in the three worlds. Hymn after hymn celebrates his unceasing activity. The mighty frame of earth and heaven constitutes his body; the sky is his head, the sun and moon his eyes, the winds his breaths. Without beginning and without end, an infinite eternal energy, he pervades all worlds, the unchanging fountain of all power, so that the whole creation springs from him and disappears in him. He is the Infinite Self (*anantātman*), Teacher of the heavenly powers, the Unmanifest Spirit of all matter (*pradhāna*), Soul of the universe, with the All for his Form..............Vishnu is no mere metaphysical entity transcending the Three Strands,[14] an abstract magnitude, an intellectual identification of Cause and Effect, a ritual harmony of sacrificer, priest, offering, and deity. He is God with a character, Source of all Morality, Revealer of all Truth. Not only is he the divine Author of the Vedas, the Instructor in all the sciences, the Master in all learning, he is the supreme Providence, Ordainer of ordainers, "he who does good to everyone"...........True, he is the destroyer of sin as well as of grief and pain; but he has no personal anger against the wicked; he forgives all injuries, he is inclined to show favour to all, he purifies the sinner and protects

[14] The Sāṃkhya guṇas—Sattva, Rajas and Tamas—out of which the material world arises.

> the pious, and he has come on earth a hundred times. Such a Deity needed no slaughtered animals upon his altar.........and the path to union of spirit with him lay through lowly surrender of all desire for personal reward of right action, and that meditation on the Eternal which freed the soul from bonds of sense and time...... The universe was not a regrettable necessity whose existence was to be deplored, nor was it to be thought away as an illusion; it was real, and to be "seen in God" (to use the phrase of Malebranche), the product of divine love, the sphere of discipline for man's fellowship with the Most High."[15]

The *Bhagavadgītā*, though eclectic in character, substantially holds up the above ideal of God and attitude of worship towards Him. Again and again does it point out that God can be realised not by the study of the Vedas and other scriptures, nor by performing penances, austerities, sacrifices and rites, nor by ceremonial gifts, but by Divine grace and by lowly surrender and dedication of self to God. But it does not attack the caste-organisation—on the other hand, it insists upon the fulfilment of the duties of one's status and station in life without the hope of any benefit in return. It sanctifies all moral acts that are performed in a spirit of detachment and not with the idea of coercing God into beneficence nor in a spirit of religious beggarliness. To see God in everything and everything in God is the proper object of worship and only a life of discipline and devotion can attain this object.

It is impossible to exaggerate the influence of this new idea of God and man's relation with Him. The philosophers now got materials of a new interpretation of those Upaniṣadic texts which had taught the origin of all things out of a unitary

[15] *Theism in Mediaeval India*, pp. 242-3; see also Hopkins, *Ethics of India*, p. 213.

being. The theistic philosophers of South India, who inherited the legacy of the Epics, as augmented by the contributions of the Purāṇas and of their own Dravidian devotees—the Âlvārs, challenged the absolutistic interpretation of the Vedānta by Śaṅkara and gave the whole system a theistic turn.[16] The schools of Rāmānuja, Nimbārka, Madhva, Vallabhācārya (originally of Viṣṇuswāmin), and Caitanya had their own commentary on the *Brahma-Sūtra*, but all agreed that God and His devotee were both real and that devotion was the only sure way of knowing Him and communing with Him. True, the ascetic ideal of India continued to sway the minds of most of the founders of these Churches; but the lay householder was assured of the fruits of his devotion even though he had not recited a single Vedic hymn or performed a single sacrificial act. New scriptures depicting the exploits of Viṣṇu were composed and canonised. There were even occasional and serious attempts, more or less successful, to democratise society by abolishing caste-privileges and, by admitting people of alien faiths into the fold, to universalise the religion as in the early days of Vaiṣṇavism when a Greek ambassador Heliodora could call himself a worshipper of Bhagavat and erect a Garuḍa-column to Vāsudeva.[17] Each man was called upon individually to make peace with his Maker and to be at peace with the whole world.

We shall not tarry over the shortcomings of a creed that tended to produce a serious emotional unbalance when sensuous elements effected an entrance into the constitution of devotion. The disinterested love of God got mixed up with illegal human love that brings no return except social

16 The most surprising and historically important fact in the various lauds of Viṣṇu as All-God is that he is nowhere called by the sacrosanct formula of the Vedānta. He is wise, knowing, blest, true, joy, etc., but he is not even said to be possessed of *cit*, still less is he designated as being *saccidānanda* in the phrase of the later Upaniṣads and Vedānta.—Hopkins, *Epic Mythology*, p. 208. See B. Kumarappa, *op. cit.*, Ch. IV.

17 Barnett, *op. cit.*, p. 88; Bhandarkar, *op. cit.*, p. 3; H. C. Raychaudhuri, *Materials for the Study of the Early History of the Vaiṣṇava Sect*, p. 58.

27

obloquy, and a secondary growth of unsavoury myths round the personality of Kṛṣṇa tended to undo, in minds prone to confusing symbols with facts, the good achieved by emphasising the emotional needs of man. The classic philosophies of India had tabooed the emotions in matters spiritual; the new creed sanctified the feeling life of man—the mutual love of a father or mother and a child, of a friend and a friend, of a man and a maid. That God is Love was preached in all possible forms and the danger of corruption was not scented afar. An association with the lower Śakti cult—partly due to Vedic tradition of female deities, partly due to the identification of Śakti with the Vedāntic Māyā and partly due to the psychological necessity of postulating an eternal object of Divine love—transformed the spontaneous sportiveness of God in creating the world and the longing of the finite for the infinite into the guilty amours of a cowherd Kṛṣṇa and the wanton abandon of the youthful girls of Bṛndāvana.[18]

The danger came from an altered conception of the nature and necessity of divine incarnation. The Vedas had talked of deified men, of gods coming down to the seat of sacrificial grass (*barhis*), of the many forms of Agni and the occult powers (*māyā*) by which Indra could assume many forms. Religious speculation had regarded the early descents of God (*e.g.*, of Prajāpati) as casual and prompted by the need of

[18] For a defence of the Kṛṣṇa-Rādhā-*cum*-Gopī relation, see B. Sastri, *Bhakti Cult in Ancient India*, p. 329 f. (Ch. XXII. Suddha-Prema); G. N. Mallik, *The Philosophy of Vaiṣṇava Religion*, Book III, Ch. II. (The Principle of Rādhā). A passage like the following from the *Bhagavadgītā* may, for instance, admit both of a spiritual and of an unholy interpretation :—

sarvadharmān parityajya māmekam śaraṇam vraja
aham tvām sarvapāpebhyo mokṣayiṣyāmi mā śucaḥ.

"Leaving all dharmas take refuge in me alone; I shall release thee from all sins, do not grieve" (Bh. G. 18.66).

In the *Kulārṇava Tantra* t *sādhaka* (religious devotee) is enjoined to cut off the bonds (*pāśa*) which make him a soul in bondage (*paśu*), namely, pity (*dayā*), ignorance (*moha*), shame (*lajjā*), family (*kula*), custom or habitual conduct (*śīla*) and caste (*varṇa*). This again may have dangerous as well as spiritual implications. (See Avalon, *Tantra of the Great Liberation*, Int., p. lxxxi.)

meeting a definite situation. The later idea of a god beginning his life on earth with infancy and ending it with death like ordinary human beings necessitated the filling in of the details of temporal life with miraculous deeds and heroic exploits. As the divine objective was in all cases the rewarding of virtue and the punishment of sin the divine incarnation was naturally endowed with martial valour ; hence either Kṣatriyas or warlike Brāhmaṇas were alone thought of as possible manifestations of the Deity.[19] The effect was that divine and human irresponsibilities managed to coalesce in some of the incarnations—especially in the two forms of the Dvāpara Age, namely, Balarāma whose drunkenness and fits of violence under the influence of wine were notorious and Kṛṣṇa who took undue advantage of the passionate love of the wives of the cowherds of Bṛndāvana. How these unethical myths gathered round the greatest religious preacher of India must remain for ever obscure just as we cannot explain now how obscene figures came to adorn the exterior of temples in Orissa : the fact remains that an enlightened posterity has expressed in no uncertain terms its disbelief in and disapprobation of the kind of conduct attributed in the Purāṇas to Kṛṣṇa, and has either ascribed it to contemporary vicious taste or seen in it an allegory of the mutual yearning of the finite and the infinite soul. But as Kṛṣṇaism is not the whole of Vaiṣṇavism and Hinduism has chosen to follow the domestic ideal of Rāma and Sītā, of Lakṣmī and Nārāyaṇa, rather than the relation of Kṛṣṇa and Rādhā[20] or the sixteen thousand cowherdesses of Bṛndāvana,[21] its baneful influence on social life has been less than that of debased Śāktaism and decadent Tantric

[19] See the author's *Vitality of Hindu Religion* in *Philosophical Quarterly*, Vol. I.

[20] Rādhā does not appear by name either in the Viṣṇu Purāṇa or in the Bhāgavata Purāṇa. See, however, *Bhakti Cult in Ancient India* by Bhagavatkumar Sastri, p. 105, and also *Philosophy of Vaisnava Religion*, Book III, Chap. II (The Principle of Rādhā) by Girindra Narayana Mallik, who quites a Ṛk Pariśiṣṭa Śruti. Rādhā is a popular figure in early erotic Prakrit Literature (*e.g.*, the *Gāhāsattasai*) round whom many love romances form and grow. It was another step to take her up in the plane of religious and mystic worship.

[21] Carpenter, *op. cit.*, p. 431; Hopkins, *Epic Mythology*, p. 214.

Buddhism.[22] When not taken allegorically, the amours of Kṛṣṇa may be interpreted physically rather than ethically, that is, they may be regarded as the indication of a superhuman vigour that is possible only to an incarnate Deity—God is great in all things, not excepting the possession of sexual virility when he takes a human form. Still, it is only candid to admit that the influence of this debased conception of God on the unconscious mind might be considerable,[23] and that in certain deformed cults Kṛṣṇaism did exercise a baneful influence just as a literal imitation of the union of the two generative principles of Śiva and Śakti produced orgiastic rites in "left-handed" Śāktaism.

It is almost certain, however, that Vāsudeva-Kṛṣṇa[24] was originally conceived in noble terms. It is now conclusively established that there could have been "no Christian influence at work in originating the worship of Kṛṣṇa" (because "the Jains have built up their entire hagiology on the model of the history of Kṛṣṇa") nor is the Bhakti cult an import from the West.[25] The philosophy of the *Bhagavadgītā* generally follows the alignment of the culture and tradition of Indian religious and philosophical thought, intensifying at the same time the theistic and devotional element of religion, and, for that purpose, setting up the figure of Kṛṣṇa as a worthy object of adoration and worship. The other element that enforces attention is the direction to renounce the fruits of action. We may very well suppose that the Vaiṣṇava religion, as taught in the *Bhagavadgītā*, was extremely well-timed. It was the first[26]

[22] Hopkins, *Ethics of India*, p. 203; see Sir Charles Eliot, *Hinduism and Buddhism*, II, p. 124 f.

[23] See Hopkins, *Ethics of India*, p. 211.

[24] H. Jacobi adduces evidence to show that the two were originally treated as distinct individuals.—ERE. vii. 196, art. INCARNATION (Indian).

[25] ERE. vii. 196; ii. 548. See also H. C. Raychaudhuri, *Materials for the Study of the Early History of the Vaiṣṇava Sect*, Lecture III; and Barth, *Religions of India*, p. 167, f.n. 1; p. 219 f.

[26] Barth argues for the priority of the Śaivite religion but admits that Śaivism "early lost its hold over religious epic poetry." (*The Religions of India*, p. 196 f.)

great theistic movement, after the Absolutistic upheaval of the Upaniṣads, which claimed that all worship paid to other gods was appropriated by Lord Kṛṣṇa himself.[27] It thus continued and ennobled the Vedic religious tradition. It recognised class distinctions but gave no pre-eminence to any class in matters spiritual: it taught that a faithful performance of ordained duties without any hankering after the fruits thereof was religiously meritorious in all cases.[28] Incidentally, it set up the toiling Lord as the great exemplar of disinterested service. It attached a higher value to mental operation and attitude in worship than to its material side.[29] it admitted, however, temperamental differences in methods of approach, while holding up intelligent faith and active devotion as the ideal of a spiritual life. We may very well suppose that the great principle of *Karmasannyāsa* (renunciation of the fruits of action) was a compromise between a contemporary ideal of non-action (*akriyāvāda*), which was combated by Brāhmanism, Jainism and Buddhism alike,[30] and an ideal of interested action (*kāmātmatā*, in the language of the *Manu-Saṃhitā*), designed to bring temporal and transcendental benefits to the self. We may suppose also that the foundation of a liberal non-sacrificial theistic neo-Brāhmaṇism which was ascribed to Kṛṣṇa Devakīputtra, regarded as a Kṣatriya, and the non-theistic reform movements of Mahāvīra and Buddha, both also assigned to the Kṣatriya caste, were not wholly accidental but represented an attempt to establish the leadership of the

[27] Bh.G. 9.23. See B. Kumarappa, *op. cit.*, Ch. II. Conception of the Deity in the Bhagavadgītā.

[28] Bh.G. 18.41-9.

[29] Bh.G. 4.24-38. See in this connection Bh.G. 18.5-6; also 12.12 and 10-25.

[30] Many of the heretical teachers taught a philosophy of inactivity or of spontaneous perfection or a philosophy of chance or time bringing things to fruition. See Śvet. Up. 1.2; also B. M. Barua, *Pre-Buddhistic Philosophy*, p. 189. The doctrine of Karman (and transmigration), we may very well suppose, got its emphasis and universality at about this time in Brahmanism, Jainism and Buddhism by way of reply, although the Gītā did not fail to point out how the potency of Karma seeds could be destroyed, *viz.*, by disinterested action.

Kṣatriyas[31] in non-conventional religious thinking in imitation of earlier heroes.[32] The *Bhagavadgītā* achieved something more. At a time when the Vedic gods had become mostly mythical or symbolic owing to Upaniṣadic influence it proposed a personal god who was supposed to have walked the earth and was, therefore, not an unreal personage. Here we have the figure of a god whose exploits are described with graphic details and whose friendly instruction to a companion in doubt breathes a spirit of disinterested service in the cause of humanity and the world at large. It is doubtful if at a time when the scriptural prescriptions were being perfunctorily obeyed or viewed with scepticism any one but a living teacher, or one supposed to have lived on earth, could have caught the ears of the public.[33] The times longed for a new creed, and a new teacher was immediately forthcoming. The demand created the supply : this alone renders intelligible

[31] In the Buddhistic scriptures the order of enumeration of the castes is always Kṣatriya, Brāhmaṇa, Vaiśya and Śūdra. Mahāvīra is also supposed to have been transferred from the womb of a Brāhmaṇa woman to that of a Kṣatriya lady as he refused to be born " in a beggarly caste." Havell has suggested that Viṣṇu and his śikhara temple are modelled on an Aryan chieftain (of the Kṣatriya clan) and his royal chapel with the high-peaked crown (see Havell, *A Handbook of Indian Art*, p. 57 ; see also p. 77). Possibly the Brahmanic claim to be considered as ' gods on earth ' was partly responsible for Kṣatriya revolt.

[32] The great Kṣatriya figures of the Upaniṣads are Janaka, Aśvapati Kaikeya, Pravāhana Jaivali, Ajātaśatru. Western scholars whose jealousy and hatred of Brahmanic ascendancy in India take the form of ascribing all religious originality to the Kṣatriyas need be reminded of the Upaniṣadic text uttered by Ajātaśatru : *pratilomaṃ caitadyadbrāhmaṇaḥ kṣatriyamupeyāt* (That a Brāhmaṇa should approach a Kṣatriya is against the normal order of instruction), which makes it clear that a Brāhmaṇa seeking enlightenment at the hands of a Kṣatriya was unusual and exceptional, the normal relation being just the reverse. See Muir, *Original Sanskrit Texts*, I, Ch. IV, Secs. xiv-xv (3rd Ed., p. 426 f.). See also Keith, *Aitareya Āraṇyaka*, Introduction, p. 50.

[33] Similar conditions are prevailing in India to-day. Rāmakrishṇa Paramahaṃsa, Vijayakrishṇa Goswāmī, the Brahmacārī of Bāradi, Vāmākṣepā (the mad Vāmā) of Tārāpiṭh, Kāṭhia Bābā and many lesser luminaries have left or are leaving followings of different sizes in Bengal. Mediaeval saints of India —Rāmānanda, Kabīr, Nānak, Dādu, etc.—left similar followings in the past. For an account of the mediaeval saints, see *Sketch of the Religions of the Hindu Sects* by H. H. Wilson; *Theism in Mediaeval India* by E. Carpenter; *Indian Religious Sects* (in Bengali) by Akṣayakumāra Datta; *Saints of Mediaeval India* (in Bengali) by Kṣitimohana Sen; *The Religions of India* by A. Barth.

the ready acceptance of the three new creeds of Vaiṣṇavism, Jainism and Buddhism by a large portion of the population without much opposition and bloodshed. We may also believe that there was a popular revulsion of feeling against the cult of sacrificial cruelty and those responsible for its continuance: this alone can explain why with a singular unanimity the message of Ahiṃsā (non-injury) was preached by all these new movements and a gradual decline in the sanctity of caste-distinctions took place. A compassionate preacher, seeking out the weak and the sinner, and a gracious Lord, condescending to come down on earth to put down iniquity and to lend a helping hand to struggling souls, were just the helpers that men wanted when their faith in the magical efficacy of Vedic rites and in the possibility of attaining eternal existence and happiness through mere meditation began to wane. True, Vaiṣṇavism sometimes went to the opposite extreme and thought that the taking of the Lord's name, even once with the last dying breath, would wipe away the sins of a life-time; but the magic effect of name is an ancient inheritance of man and was also a necessary, though exaggerated, reply to those who had deprived God of all grace and power to save the sinner. The traditions of devotion, compassion, non-injury, Divine grace and equality of men Vaiṣṇavism has, except on rare occasions, followed all through its history down to the present times, and its strong hold on the popular mind is mostly due to its appeal to the sentiments of men who crave, out of their weakness and failing, for a Divine Deliverer, merciful rather than stern, anxious to save His creatures rather than solicitous of their oblations and offerings. It has also set its face all along against Absolutism and absorption of the finite in the infinite and thus satisfied the craving for individual immortality and a blessed personal existence in proximity to God as a reward of virtuous and devotional life.[34]

[34] See G. N. Mallik, *The Philosophy of Vaiṣṇava Religion*, Bk. IV, Ch. VI. The Highest Good or *Summum Bonum* in the Vaiṣṇava System. See also M. T. Kennedy, *The Chaitanya Movement*, p. 98 f.

Vaiṣṇavism contributed something more to the religious tradition of India. Although in Vedic times certain priestly families were specially associated with the adoration of certain divinities they did not form any well-defined sect with special modes of worship and organisation. Different tribes or clans did not have their own patron gods; each god was a god of the entire community. Whether due to the fact that Vāsudeva-Kṛṣṇa was originally the patron deity of a special tribe or clan or whether because he was originally the local deity of a small area or whether because the Viṣṇu-Kṛṣṇa cult was from the very beginning a proselytising religion, Vaiṣṇavism soon developed into a definite religious community with an organisation of its own and established the brotherhood of its adherents through the common fatherhood of the Lord and the common spiritual headship of the Âcārya (the spiritual preceptor). The communal spirit was probably intensified by its rivalry with Śaivism, Jainism and Buddhism; and that spirit is not dead even to-day, although conciliating souls have suggested the devices of Harihara, the composite divinity, half Viṣṇu and half Śiva,[35] and Trimūrti, the divine Trinity of Brahmā, Viṣṇu and Śiva, to indicate the complementary character of the major deities[36] and even gone to the length of identifying Śiva and Viṣṇu by making one a form of the other and ascribing the function of each to the other. But it was not without its advantages, because a common faith brought men closer together in weal and woe and established bonds of fellowship, sympathy and mutual help

[35] See Barth, *The Religions of India*, p. 185. Sir Charles Eliot, *op. cit.*, II, p. 193. For the popularity of this combined deity in the ancient Indian colonies in the Far East, see Bijan Raj Chatterji, *Indian Cultural Influence in Cambodia*, p. 51 : "The cult of Hari-hara seems to have been popular in Kambuja, as there are many images of the combined deities still existing" (see also p. 52). The same was the case in Java.

[36] Barth, *op. cit.*, p. 179 f. Hopkins points out that "the union of the three highest gods into a trinity forms no part of epic belief" (*Epic Mythology*, p. 231). Trimūrti was a favourite assemblage in Ancient Indian colonies like Cambodia (see B. R. Chatterji, *op. cit.*, p. 105). Buddha sometimes replaced Śiva in this Trinity (see *ibid.*, p. 183; also p. 261). A single image embodying the Trinity (as in the cave at Elephanta near Bombay) is not rare in Java.

among them. In the Caitanya school mutual helpfulness and collective devotion are the most outstanding features and the spirit of service and kindly feeling encompasses the whole of sentient creation. It is, therefore, pre-eminently a religion of love : its motto is the same as that of Christianity, "Peace on earth, goodwill towards men." It has not unreasonably been said that the cult of compassion and non-injury, preached by the three religions of Vaiṣṇavism,[37] Jainism and Buddhism, is responsible for the loss of martial traditions in India and its subjection to foreign conquerors. Vaiṣṇavism absorbed many martial as well as savage races within its fold during its march of conquest and thereby changed the whole tenor of subsequent civilisation in India. Killing in any form has now become abhorrent to Indian minds : in Vedic rites, in oblations to the manes, in the entertainment of guests and even in Śakti worship vegetables and cereals have entirely replaced animal offerings[38] and the fish-eating Bengali and Sārasvata Brāhmaṇas are looked down upon by the other Brāhmaṇas of India although the older scriptural traditions are entirely in favour of the former.[39] Food-taboos were not unknown in Vedic times; but thanks to Vaiṣṇavism, Jainism and Buddhism, life in all its forms became sacred throughout the length and breadth of India in later times as a logical consequence of the message of universal compassion

[37] It has been suggested that Vaiṣṇavism fell in line with Jainism and Buddhism in order to convert the Jainas and the Buddhists near about the Mathurā region.—See A. Avalon, *Principles of Tantra*, Vol. I, Introduction, p. xi.

[38] See Hopkins, *Epic Mythology*, pp. 209, 217; Sir Charles Eliot (*Hinduism and Buddhism*, II, p. 152) thus puts the Upaniṣadic origin of this cult : "The Upaniṣad does not refer to Krishṇa as if he were a deity, and merely says that he received from Ghora instruction after which he never thirsted again. The purport of it was that the sacrifice may be performed without rites, the various parts being typified by ordinary human actions, such as hunger, eating, laughter, liberality, righteousness, etc." He also thinks (pp. 159-60) that the preponderating influence of Buddhism round about Muttra (Mathura, the seat of the epic hero) might be responsible for the milder rites of Vaiṣṇavism. (See also pp. 170-1).

[39] The Vedic Aryans are a nation of meat-eaters, who appear to have had a general aversion to fish, since there is no direct mention of fishing in the Vedas.—Sir John Marshall, *Mahenjo-Daro and the Indus Civilisation*, Vol. I, p. 111.

See, however, the story of Sāraswata in MbB., Śal. Par., li. 35-48.

preached by these religions. About its influence on national health, national outlook on war and national capacity to withstand foreign aggression there may be some honest differences of opinion; but there can be no doubt that practical benevolence could go no farther and that if the nations of the world could be persuaded to beat their swords into ploughshares, to abandon all territorial ambitions and imperialistic designs, and not to injure any living being wantonly for sport or aggression, their practical religion would not be very far from the Vaiṣṇavism of India.

What the spirit of religion can achieve with an unpromising material we shall now illustrate by the history of Śaivism, the rival of Vaiṣṇavism as a popular religion.[40] In popular Hindu religious worship offerings are made to Dharma (Law or Morality), Jñāna (Knowledge), Aiśvarya (Power) and Vairāgya (Dispassion or Detachment).[41] We may very well suppose that Varuṇa, Brahmā, Viṣṇu and Śiva represent the essence or embodiment of these virtues respectively. Śiva is the ideal Yogin and, in his aspect of a meditative god, is the patron deity of Sannyāsins. He lives far away from the haunts of men. His home is in the inhospitable mountains; he holds the Ganges in his matted locks; his wife is a mountain-maid; and his son Skanda was nursed by the six Kṛttikās (Pleiades) in a bed of reeds in the Himalayas.[42] For arm-band, girdle and sacred thread he has snakes; for his loin-cloth, the skin of a tiger (or elephant); for his vehicle,

[40] See Macdonell, *Vedic Mythology*, p. 74 (Rudra); Hopkins, *Epic Mythology*, p. 219 f.; Sir R. G. Bhandarkar, *Vaiṣṇavism, Saivism and Minor Religious Systems*, p. 102 f.; Muir, *Original Sanskrit Texts*, IV, Ch. III; Keith, *Religion and Philosophy of the Veda and Upanishads*, I, p. 142 f; Sir Charles Eliot, *op. cit.*, II, p. 192.

[41] It is interesting to note that in Java a Caturaiśvarya mantra, addressed to Dharma, Jñana, Aiśvarya and Vairāgya—represented as lions with white, red, black and yellow colours respectively—was used. In fact, the Hindus invoke their opposites also, *viz.*, Adharma, Ajñāna, Anaiśvarya and Avairāgya, just as they invoke the goddess of small-pox (Śītalā) and the snake-goddess (Manasā) in order to be rid of their attacks and attentions.

[42] Hopkins, *Epic Mythology*, p. 227.

the bull;[43] and for his ear-tops the *dhatura* flower. When he is conceived as a dweller of the plains, he is pictured as living in cemeteries, wearing a garland of skulls and besmearing himself with ashes. He is reputed to have burnt the God of Love to ashes when the latter had dared to disturb his meditation. But, although noted for his anger, he is equally famous for his quick forgiveness and his ready bestowal of boons. He is directly accessible to all persons in all conditions, being in this respect the most democratic of the gods. Very simple offerings please him and a Brāhmaṇa is not always needed to officiate at the religious ceremony.[44] No complicated rituals grew up round his worship nor did extensive incarnation-myths gather round him. He does not disdain to mix with the lowest class, and when Arjuna fights with the incognito god the latter was dressed as a Kirāta. Bhūtas (ghosts) and people of the hill and the jungle are his companions. But, though unsocial in his outward behaviour, he is most benign, and demons as well as men have often got from him boons that puzzled and perturbed the gods. He is the friend of the entire creation too. When the churning of the ocean brought forth good things, the other gods appropriated them; but when poison was thrown up, only Śiva could and did swallow it and save creation—that is why he became blue-throated.[45] His terrible (*ghora, bhairava, rudra*) form is born when crime is committed or iniquity is performed, just as with his benign (*aghora, śiva, dakṣiṇa*) form he bestows blessings. He casts his terrible noose round sinners, and

[43] Probably the Tibetan yāk is meant (see Sven Hedin, *Trans-Himalaya*). But Mahenjo-Daro excavations prove that the bull was the object of an extensive cult among the pre-Aryans from whom probably Śiva has been borrowed. See Marshall, *Mahenjo-Daro and the Indus Civilisation*, p. 52 f.

[44] ERE. xi. 92, art. SAIVISM.

[45] Rāmāyaṇa, i. 45. This adjective comes down from Vedic times. See Vājasaneyi Saṃhitā 16, 7, where he is called 'blue-necked.' The mythological explanations are various. The blue throat is regarded as having been caused by the swallowing of poison, the biting of Uśanas's snaky locks, throttling by Nārāyaṇa and smiting by Indra's axe (see Hopkins, *Epic Mythology*, p. 226). Religious devotion in India has managed to forget all but the beneficent episode of swallowing the poison.

even the gods are not exempt from his moral government. Did he not tear off the fifth head of Prajāpati who cast incestuous looks at his own daughter?[46] He is the lord (*pati*) of finite spirits (*paśu*); he releases them from sin if they worship him mentally, and he grants them salvation. If he is the ordainer of disease and death, he is also the great healer,[47] being himself the conqueror of death (Mṛtyuñjaya). So, both for soul and for body, men need Śiva's help, and the gracious god never fails to help those who sincerely seek his aid and banish from their minds anger and greed.[48] The *Śvetāśvatara Upaniṣad*, in which a systematic attempt to sublimate his character was made,[49] describes him as a " god who has no parts, who does not suffer change, who is all peace, has no defects and is unpolluted, the bridge for crossing over to immortality." He is described as being concealed in all beings, as all-pervading, " the internal soul of all beings, presiding over all actions, the support of all beings, the witness of all, the life-giver, absolute and without qualities."[50] He can be known only by *bhāva* (faith, love or pure heart),[51] and to know Śiva is to be free from all nooses and to attain eternal peace. The philosophical schools that arose in Kashmir and in the South all treat him as the ultimate principle of existence, and they all lay down rules about the way of obtaining salvation through him. In the true Bhāgavata way Śiva was regarded as the origin as well as the ultimate refuge of finite souls.

Let us look for a moment now into the antecedents of a deity who divides with the different forms of Viṣṇu the

[46] In the Śatapatha Brāhmaṇa (9.1.1.1-6) the gods are depicted as being afraid of the strung bow and the arrows of Rudra, lest he should destroy them.—Macdonell, *V. M.*, p. 76.

[47] At Tārakeśwar (Dist. Hughli, Bengal) there is a regular system of fasting at the door of the deity in order to obtain medicines for hopeless cases and almost incurable diseases. The tradition of being a healer comes down from Vedic times.—See Macdonell, *Vedic Mythology*, p. 76.

[48] For the Pāśupata vow, see Bhandarkar, *Vaiṣṇavism, Saivism, etc.*, p. 112.

[49] See Bhandarkar, *op. cit.*, p. 110.

[50] *Ibid.*, p. 109.

[51] *Ibid.*, p. 109.

allegiance of the major portion of the Indian population and whose spiritual kingdom covered at one time the distant islands of the Indian archipelago and reached the shores of the Chinese Sea. The distribution of the adherents of Śiva is significant—they, in alliance with the followers of Gaṇeśa and Śakti, formed at one time a ring round the worshippers of Viṣṇu.[52] From Nepal, Tibet and Kashmir on the north we might travel down to Cape Comorin (and Rāmeśvaram) on the south along the sea coast and then travel up the Tamil land till we reach Bengal and Assam, practically without losing contact with the cult of some member of the Śaivite household. The middle of this circle is mostly occupied by Vaiṣṇavism. Although notable exceptions occur, yet it may be safely said that Śaivism is more in contact with the original non-Aryan population of India than Vaiṣṇavism which circulates in the heart of the Aryan settlement.[53] This distribution is quite in keeping with the historical origin of the creed. If the remains of the recently excavated Indus valley civilisation at Mahenjo-Daro, Harappa and other places can be trusted to reveal the truth, the cult of Śiva (both figured and phallic) is not an Aryan monopoly or even an Aryan discovery.[54] The original Aryan attitude[55] towards the phallic symbol was definitely hostile, for in the Rig-Veda Indra is invoked to keep off the *śiśnadevas*[56]

[52] See Muir, *Or. Sans. Texts*, IV, p. 241.

[53] Eliot remarks (*Hinduism and Buddhism*, I, p. xxxvi) that "many legends in the Epics and the Purāṇas indicate that there was hostility between the old-fashioned Brāhmaṇs and the worshippers of Rāma, Kṛishṇa and Śiva."

[54] For the prototype of Śiva in pre-Aryan Indus valley civilisation, see Sir John Marshall, *op. cit.*, p. 52 f. The phallus (with the yoni), the yoga attitude, the three faces, and the lordship over animals (paśupati) are all present in the archæological remains (see p. 54).

[55] Bhandarkar thinks that the Liṅga-worship had not come into vogue at the time of Patañjali who refers to an image or likeness (pratikṛti) of Śiva as an object of worship (*op. cit.*, p. 115). After the discoveries at Mahenjo-Daro and other places it would simply mean that the Aryans were slowly accepting this mode of worship.

[56] Macdonell, *op. cit.*, p. 155. There is some difference of opinion about the exact meaning of the word. Most writers agree that it means the worshippers of the phallus (Bhandarkar, Macdonell, etc.); but Ragozin thinks, perhaps wrongly,

(devotees of the phallic cult) from the sacrifice, and the conquest and carnage of Indra in the lands of the latter are recalled.

There is no doubt that in the Vedas and in sub-Vedic literature (excepting, of course, the *Śvetāśvatara Upaniṣad*), the terrible aspect of the deity was most in evidence.[57] Although prayers for blessings, healing remedies, protection against the anger of and evil from other gods, and welfare for men and beasts are not unknown and his knowledge of the doings of men and gods and the ease with which he is invoked are referred to, the frequency with which malevolence is attributed to him and his fierceness described and feared, makes it clear that the title of Śiva (benign or auspicious)[58] was only euphemistically used of him. "He is implored not to slay or injure, in his anger, his worshippers, their parents, children, cattle or horses."[59] All the most terrible substances enter into his composition[60] and he assails men with fever, cough (consumption), poison and celestial fire and is a veritable man-slayer. He leads a host (*gaṇa*)[61] of equally ferocious beings who attack men and animals, and the prayers are directed to keep him and his band away. He is prayed to in later literature "for safe conduct when traversing a path, coming to a place where four roads meet, crossing a river, getting into a ferry boat, entering a forest, ascending a mountain, passing by a cemetery or by a cow-shed or such

that it refers to serpent-worship (*op. cit.*, p. 293). Roth suggests the translation 'tailed (or priapic) demons' and Muir is not sure if phallic worship is meant (*O.S.T.*, *IV*, p. 348). Sāyana translates it as 'unchaste or lustful men' (see *O.S.T.*, IV, p. 347). Sir John Marshall remarks that "the belief in Nāgas is unknown to the Vedic age" (*Mahenjo-Daro, etc.*, Part I, p. 68. See art. *Liṅgopāsanā* by Vidhushekhar Bhattacharyya in the *Prabāsī* (Bengali Monthly), Vol. XXXIII, p. 741 f.

57 Macdonell, *V. M.*, p. 76; Bhandarkar, *Vaiṣṇavism, Śaivism, etc.*, p. 102; Muir, *O.S.T.*, IV, p. 340.

58 Vāj. Saṃ. 3. 62; 16. 41.

59 Macdonell, *V.M.*, p. 75.

60 A.V. 3. 83.1.

61 Bhandarkar, *Vaiṣṇavism, Saivism, etc.*, p. 104; See Muir, *O.S.T.*, V, p. 272 f. (quoting the Śatarudrīya).

other places." He and his followers received the omentum or the bloody entrails of the victim at a sacrifice and were thus treated on the same level as demons. He was even regarded as the patron of robbers and pilferers and as being similar to them in nature. No wonder, therefore, that in the Brāhmaṇas and the Sūtras Rudra should be isolated from the other gods who are generally beneficent in character and disposition, and that it should be stated of him that when the gods attained heaven, Rudra remained behind.[62]

That Rudra did not exactly conform to the ideal of an Aryan god can be proved by a number of concurrent testimonies.[63] The celebrated sacrifice of Dakṣa,[64] which ended so disastrously, was sought to be performed without Śiva's presence and the violence with which it was broken up by Śiva or his followers may be interpreted as a forcible entry into the Vedic pantheon by him. Apparently Śiva had originally no share in the sacrifice[65] and this is alluded to in many places of the *Mahābhārata*,[66] and references to his seizing the property of other gods are not infrequent.[67] On the other hand, human offerings to Rudra are contemplated by Jarāsandha (in the Sabhāparvan),[68] and the later literature depicts in no uncertain manner the anti-Vedic propensities of

62 Śat. Br. 1.7.3.1.

63 The precise relation between Śiva and Rudra is not yet satisfactorily traced out. The introduction of an entirely new divinity from the mountains of the north has been supposed, who was grafted in upon the ancient religion by being identified with Rudra; or again a blending of some of Agni's attributes with those of Rudra to originate a new development: perhaps neither of these may be necessary; Śiva may be a local form of Rudra, arisen under the influence of peculiar climatic relations in the districts from which he made his way into Hindostan proper; introduced among, and readily accepted by, a people which, as the Atharva shows, was strongly tending toward a terrorism in its religion.—Whitney, quoted by Muir, *O.S.T.*, *IV*, p. 338.

64 Muir, *O.S.T.*, IV, p. 313 f.

65 The Pañcaviṃśa Brāhmaṇa (VII. 9. 16) alludes to the exclusion of Rudra when domestic animals were divided among the gods and also to his character as the slayer of cattle.—Eng. Tr. by Caland, p. 157.

66 Bhandarkar, *V.S.*, p. 113; Muir, *O.S.T.*, IV, p. 314.

67 Muir, *O.S.T.*, IV, p. 241.

68 *Ibid.*, p. 246. Father H. Heras, in a lecture before the Bombay Branch of the Royal Asiatic Society on 26th July, 1936 (as reported in the *Advance* of Calcutta of 5th August, 1936—Dāk edition), mentions the fact that human sacrifices in batches of seven or multiples of seven were offered by the Mahenjo-Daro people

the followers of Śiva.[69] His followers were mostly despicable in Aryan eyes—gaṇas, bhūtas, Kirātas, Niṣādas, rogues, robbers and cheats;[70] his wife too is painted in no attractive colours nor are her attendants and associates—Śabaras, Varvaras and Pulindas—less repulsive to the Aryan people.[71] This persistent tradition of a savage association renders it extremely probable that Rudra of all the Vedic gods was thought to be similar to some savage deity and that his worship was instituted on savage models at first. That non-Brāhmaṇas could worship Śiva (and sometimes Brāhmaṇas could not worship the phallic symbol) is an additional evidence in this direction.[72] Some obscure verses of the *Pañcaviṃśa-Brāhmaṇa*[73] probably allude to the absorption of the followers of Rudra within the Aryan fold by permitting them to recite some Vedic verses. It is also permissible to think that in the interesting Brāhmaṇa stories about his successively getting from Prajāpati his present epithets[74]—Rudra, Śarva, Paśupati, Ugra, Aśani (Bhīma), Bhava, Mahān-deva (or Mahādeva), Īśāna—epithets that apply half (Rudra, Śarva, Ugra, Aśani) to the terrible and half (Bhava, Paśupati, Mahān-deva, Īśāna) to the benign aspect,[75] we have probably the story of a gradual progression of Śiva towards ultimate supremacy, after an intermediate identification with Agni, Vāyu, Parjanya, Prajāpati (or Soma-Candramas), Indra and Âditya (Sūrya) had transferred to him some of the attributes of these other gods.[76] But while, on the one hand, identification with

to the god who had the trident, the axe and the snake as his associates and who was presumably the prototype of Śiva.

69 Muir, *O.S.T.*, IV, pp. 320-21.

70 *Ibid.*, p. 273.

71 *Ibid.*, pp. 369, 370 (quoting Harivaṃśa).

72 *Ibid.*, p. 344 (f.n.), 317.

73 Pañcaviṃśa Brāhmaṇa, XVII, 1.1 (Eng. Tr. by Caland, p. 454). See Winternitz, *op. cit.*, I, p. 154.

74 Muir, *O.S.T.*, IV, p. 283 f.; 286 f.; p. 342. (The identifications are slightly different in the Śatapatha and Sāṅkhāyana Brāhmaṇas.)

75 Bhandarkar, *Vaiṣṇavism, Śaivism, etc.*, p. 105.

76 Rudra's description tallies most approximately with that of Agni. So also does that of his wife who bears names denoting fire—its flames, smoke, etc.

Father Heras, in the lecture referred to in footnote 68 above, mentions the interesting fact that the Mahenjo-Daro supreme god *An* also possessed eight forms

beneficent deities ennobled Rudra's character, his similarity to some non-Aryan divinity, on the other, led to the transference to him of some of the repulsive features of the latter, and not only was the darker Vedic side retained but it was actually accentuated by the addition of savage traits from non-Aryan sources, till Rudra came to be regarded as unfit for heavenly company, frequenting cemeteries, besmearing himself with ashes, smoking narcotics, wearing repulsive apparel and ornament, and forcing his entrance into the Vedic pantheon with the help of turbulent followers who threatened to stop the sacrifice to the other gods. The latter identification also led not only to easy unconventional worship but probably introduced the originally condemned phallic cult into the Aryan religion.

We shall close our account of Śaivism with a reference to this phallic cult in order to remove some misunderstandings. We may admit at the outset that just as the guilty love of Kṛṣṇa, when dwelt upon in excess of religious need, may lead to corrupt thoughts, so also an immoderate pre-occupation with the sexual symbol of Śiva may lead to orgiastic rites, especially when complicated by extreme Śākta tendencies. Sanskrit literature is unfortunately not altogether free from lascivious descriptions of the divine amours of Kṛṣṇa and Śiva, although it may be admitted at the same time that they might have been more considerable without the religious restraint. But sex-symbols have a less activating effect on imagination and action in a country where climatic conditions enforce a semi-nudity on its male inhabitants during the hot months and where traditions of austerity and detachment have made even the complete nudity of the ascetic followers of some religious sects not a thing of shame. In fact, the Buddhist monks alone were directed to be decently dressed in ancient times, as contrasted with Jaina monks of the Digambara sect and Hindu sannyāsins whose ideal of perfection was complete apathy to their physical environment and their social sur-

and was identified with the sun which passed each year through the constellations of the Zodiac, then regarded as only eight in number as against our present twelve.

roundings. The origin of the Liṅga (phallus) was not due in India to vegetation myths or to esoteric obscenity nor was the sexual symbol the earliest representation of Śiva.[77] The earliest references like the *Mahābhārata* and the *Vāyu-Purāṇa* ascribe its origin to Śiva discarding his organ of generation and becoming a yogin, when other gods had been found to undertake the task of creation. The shedding of the liṅga was thus symbolic of abstention from creative activity and its worship, therefore, an adoration of sexual restraint.[78] The other story that Śiva killed Kāma (Cupid) when the latter attempted to disturb his meditation confirms the tradition of his conquest over sexual passion. It is almost certain also that in the earliest Brāhmaṇic literature the liṅga (the male genital) was not associated with a yoni (the female genital) and that the liṅga became a procreation symbol later when the yoni was added.[79] This changed conception about the sexual symbol was reflected also in iconographic representation, and Ardhanārīśvara images, combining Śiva and his spouse Pārvatī in their half-figures, made their appearance.[80] The wives of the Vedic gods were shadowy figures by the side of their husbands; but the increasing association of Śakti with Śiva shows that equality of the female with the male was a trait of the people from whom the Śiva-Śakti cult was derived or, if two independent cults fused into one, their gods, male in one case and female in another, had already been developed too much on monotheistic lines into supreme deities to be subordinated to each other in the new synthetic creed.

77 Bhandarkar, *op. cit.*, p. 115. Patañjali refers to images of Śiva being sometimes made of precious metals. See p. 228 *infra*.

78 Creation was often conceived in terms of procreation even in Vedic times—See Macdonell, *Vedic Mythology*, pp. 11-12. See also p. 221, f.n. 54, *supra*.

79 Most of the Paurāṇic references to the sexual aspect of the Liṅga are to be found in Nagendranath Vasu's *Viśvakośa* (Bengali Encyclopædia). XVII, p. 256 f. (under art. LIṄGA. In the Rigveda the fire-drill in the wood (*araṇi*) rouses associations of procreation because it resembles the phallus in the yoni.

80 Even Harihara figures have been sexually explained. See the *Viśvakośa* article referred to in the last footnote.

Father Heras, in the lecture referred to in footnote 68 above, suggests that the combination of the Mahenjo-Daro god *An* with the goddess *Amma* (the mother) might have been the original of the Śaivite Hara-Pārvatī figure of the Ardhanārīśvara type.

Just as in the worship of the Trinity, when not complicated by sectarian bias, no godhead is really subordinate to the other two, so also in the composite Śiva-Śakti cult an attempt was made to recognise both the gods as complementary to each other and neither as subordinate to the other.[81] It is not unlikely that a polyandrous social organisation and an extensive Mother-cult[82] provided the soil for the equality of the female principle with the male and that both the Vedāntic Māyā and the Sāṃkhya Prakṛti were pressed unconsciously or consciously into the service of the Śiva-Śakti cult.[83]

Let us return, however, to Śiva. Liṅga, in the sense of that which is destroyed or which is ultimately dissolved, is a fairly ancient term.[84] It is permissible for us to speculate that the destructive aspect of Rudra, which ultimately made Śiva the third person of the Hindu Trinity, would receive the epithet liṅga,' and then, by the principle of symbolisation or visual representation (which Freudian psychology has now familiarised to us in the domain of dreams), the representation would take the form of the other meaning of liṅga, namely, sexual organ. It is not improbable that by a similar process of transference the epithet *sthāṇu*, which means immobile existence, was transferred to the immobile ascetic god rooted at one spot like a post or a bare tree-trunk (the other meaning of *sthāṇu*).[85] In fact,

81 This might explain why in Tantra literature Śiva and Devī (Śakti) are both revealers of spiritual truths—the former of Āgamas and the latter of Nigamas. —See A. Avalon, *Principles of Tantra*, p. lxi. This might also explain the Ardhanārīśvara figure (the androgynous Śiva).

82 Speaking, for instance, of the village gods of South India, Bishop Whitehead remarks: "Speaking generally, in the Hindu pantheon the male deities are predominant and the female deities occupy a subordinate position. This is characteristic of the geniis of the Aryan religion, but in the old Dravidian cults a leading feature was the worship of the female principle in nature." (*The Village Gods of South India*, p. 17; see also Index of the Gods, p. 167, in support of the above.)

83 See Wilson, *Sketch of the Religions of the Hindu Sects*. p. 151 f.

84 See, for instance, Iśvarakṛṣṇa's Sāṃkhya-kārikā, 10.

Just as death and the God of death are both denoted by the term *mṛtyu*, so also destruction and the God of destruction may both be called *liṅga*. The other meaning of *liṅga*, *viz.*, subtle (as in *liṅgaśarīra*), may also be implied.

85 It is not improbable that this immobility is responsible for the rule that a Śiva-liṅga, once fixed, should on no account be removed.—*Mahānirvāṇā Tantra* (Eng. Tr. by A. Avalon), Ch. XIV, 93.

the *Vāyu-Purāṇa* account, which depicts Viṣṇu as digging into the ground as a boar to discover the root and Brahmā as flying in his swan-vehicle to find the top of the Liṅga,[86] has the tree-analogy in mind (and the comparison of God with a tree is pretty old in Indian religious literature).[87] Worshipping a tree as a symbol of the five-faced god (Pañcānana or Śiva) is not yet a dead village-cult in Bengal. If the liṅga had originally a sylvan origin (and Śiva's association with forest tribes does not rule that possibility entirely out), the phallic cult in India in its original conception could be easily related to the worship of sacred stakes, trees or groves which, according to Grant Allen, is one of the origins of gods,[88] and would thus resemble the Hebrew *asherah*. But the hilly association is so persistent that possibly the cult of the liṅga could be more easily related to the worship of sacred stones, practised at one stage of culture by all nations of the world. Still, even in that case, it is possible to agree with Grant Allen that " the standing stone may have been and often was, in later stages, identified with a phallus " and that " the liṅgam, instead of lying at the root of the monolith, must necessarily be a later and derivative form of it."[89] Speculative minds could easily see that there was an obvious advantage in using a shapeless stone as the proper symbol of one whom philosophy had described as formless by nature.[90] The Śaiva *liṅga* and the Vaiṣṇava *śālagrāma* are both

86 *Vāyu Purāṇa*, Ch. 55; *Liṅga Purāṇa*, I, 17, 5-52. The episode is inscribed in stone at the Mīnākṣī Temple. Madura, as also in Hoà-Qué Stelae Inscription of Bhadravarman III (of Champā), dated 831 Śaka year. (See R. C. Majumdar, *Ancient Indian Colonies in the Far East*, Vol. I, Champā, p. 175, Bk. III, p. 116.)

87 Kaṭha Up. 6.1; Bh. G. 15.1-3.

88 See Grant Allen, *Evolution of the Idea of God*, Ch. VI (Sacred Stakes) and Ch. VII (Sacred Trees). Some have traced the origin of the liṅga to the yūpastambha, the sacrificial post.—See *The Proceedings of the Convention of Religions in India*, 1909, Vol. II, p. 124, f.n. 6.

Sir John Marshall describes tree-worship among the pre-Aryan population, from whom the phallic cult might have been taken, in *Mahenjo-Daro and the Indus Civilisation*, Part I, p. 63 f.

89 Grant Allen. *op. cit.*, pp. 73-74.

90 It is not improbable that Muhammadan iconoclasm is responsible for the *liṅga* and other shapeless forms in North India as more likely to escape notice or less likely to offend Islamic susceptibilities, while the absence of continuous Muhammadan hostility in South India made images more frequent there.

shapeless stones,[91] and it is not very unlikely that the so-called Svayambhū liṅga, or pebble rounded and shaped by the forces of nature, was the original form under which Śiva was worshipped. The fact that both in India and in the Far Eastern Hindu colonies liṅgas with one or more faces carved at the top (*mukhaliṅga* images)[92] have been discovered shows that the phallic association was not obtrusive in the popular mind. It has been almost universally admitted, moreover, that the atmosphere of a Śaiva temple is intensely religious, if not puritanic, and that the orgiastic rites, which one would expect of crude phallism, are absent in India even though the temples are frequented by men and women together in large numbers and, except in very orthodox South Indian temples, all have direct access to the divine symbol.[93] It has been admitted by all, for instance, that the Liṅgāyats, who

91 Speaking of the Smārta method of worshipping the five sectarian gods (Siva, Viṣṇu, Sakti, Sūrya and Gaṇeśa), Farquhar writes thus: "The worship of the five gods in *Pañcāyatana Pūjā* is observed at home. Images or stone and metal symbols, or diagrams, or earthenware pots, may be used to represent the divinities. The image or symbol of the god whom the worshipper prefers is placed in the centre, and the other four are so set as to form a square around the central figure." He then adds the following footnote: "The more usual symbols are: Vishṇu, the *Śālagrāma* pebble; Śiva, the *Narmadeśvara* pebble; the Devī, a piece of metal, or the *Svarṇarekhā* stone found in a river in South India; Sūrya, a round piece of *Sūryakānta*, *i.e.*, sun-stone, or of *sphaṭika*, *i.e.*, crystal; Gaṇeśa, the *Svarṇabhadra*, a red slab from a stream near Arrah."—J. N. Farquhar, *Outlines of the Religious Literature of India*, p. 293.

92 It was a regular custom with the kings of Champā to instal these mukhaliṅgas, to carve a face like their own at the top to indicate their unity and identity with the godhead as preached by the Vedānta and to name them after themselves as lord of so and so.—See R. C. Majumdar, *Champā*, p. 186. This probably follows earlier Indian models.—See *Epigraphia Indica*, XXI, p. 7 (D. R. Bhandarkar, *Mathura Pillar Inscription of Chandragupta II*: *G. E.* 61).

Even in M.Bh. four-mouthed Mahāliṅga is referred to. (See A. Avalon, *Principles of Tantra*, p. lii.) Iconographic representations of Śakti appearing from a Śiva-liṅga are not unknown (see Bhattaśāli, *op. cit.*, p. 192).

93 As Sir John Marshall puts it: "In mediæval and modern India it is only very rarely that liṅgas take at all a naturalistic form. Ninety-nine per cent. of them are so conventionalised that most people would find a difficulty in recognizing their phallic character."—*Op. cit.*, p. 60. "Nothing is more likely than that, as Saivism developed, it largely absorbed the older bactylic worship and appropriated its symbols to phallic worship. This would explain why the vast majority of mediæval and modern liṅgas are fashioned more like bactylic cones than phalli."—*Ibid.*, p. 61. The corrupt taste of Orissan sculptors, however, is reflected not only in obscene decorations of the temples at Puri and Konarak but also in naturalistic representations of the phallus in some temples at Bhuvaneśvara.

are under a religious obligation to carry a small *liṅga* in a reliquary hung round the neck,[94] are noted for the purity of their worship (and they worship no images). It is well to remember that in the *Mahābhārata* words like *ūrdhva-liṅga* and *ūrdhva-retas*, used of the god of the phallus, bring out the sense of sexual restraint even in the original conception of the symbol.[95]

It has been observed by many writers that the Śaivas form a far more compact sect than the Vaiṣṇavas. Two reasons have been suggested to account for this fact. The one is that, although there are differences in the philosophies of the various Śaivite sects, the god worshipped is one. Vaiṣṇavism worships the supreme God under many names—Nārāyaṇa, Kṛṣṇa (with or without Rādhā), Rāma—and the sects and sub-sects are not always on the best of terms, as if the gods worshipped are different and behave like rivals for the affection of the devotees. Śiva or Paśupati is a single god, and, even when different names and forms are ascribed to him, no rival sects worship these different forms. The antisocial aspect of the god has attracted some morbid minds, and the existence of at least two sects—Kāpāla and Kālamukha, noted for their practice of what society would consider to be revolting and unethical, indicates what the possibilities of the darker side of Śaiva religion are; but these two sects worship the same god as the other Śaivites do. The eight forms of the deity—Śarva, Bhava, Rudra, Ugra, Bhīma (or Aśani), Paśupati, Mahān-deva (or Mahādeva), Īśāna—have no separate biographies, and his five faces[96]—Īśāna (or Sadāśiva), Vāmadeva, Aghora, Tatpuruṣa and Sadyojāta on the top,

94 Wilson, *Sketch, etc.*, p. 139. Farquhar, *op. cit.*, p. 261. See Bhandarkar, *op. cit.*, p. 135, for the different conceptions of Liṅga in the Liṅgāyat or Vīra-śaiva school.

95 The Mahenjo-Daro three-faced (and also three-eyed, says Father Heras in his lecture referred to in footnote 68 above) God who is regarded by Marshall as a prototype of the historic Śiva is probably *ūrdhvameḍhra* although in a yoga attitude If the figure has been correctly made out (there is some doubt about it still), the erect position of the sexual organ is not priapic but symbolic of the reverse function, *i.e.*, sexual restraint. (See Marshall, *op. cit.*, p. 52.)

96 Eliot, *op. cit.*, II, p. 198. Śiva with more or less faces is also known. If the Elephanta cave figure is not of the Trimūrti but of Śiva alone, then this will correspond to the three-faced prototype of Śiva of the Mahenjo-Daro excavation.

north, south, east and west sides respectively, indicate the single deity's power of superintendence in all directions.[97] No wonder, therefore, that Advaitism should be the favourite philosophical creed of the Śaivites, and their religion monotheistic. Śiva has no avatāras as Viśṇu has; hence it is easier to think of him as eternal. The *Bhagavadgītā* refers to the many previous births of the Lord Kṛṣṇa and the different avatāras, again, have not always come with plenary power and inspiration, many of them having been obliged to seek earthly alliances to overthrow their adversaries. But, although Śiva has his band of terrible followers, he always acts direct without assuming an earthly figure.[98] We might even go so far as to assert that he has been more democratically conceived than other gods: he has been given a permanent earthly residence in Mount Kailāsa, though references to his heavenly home in Śivaloka are not absent. Brahmā and Viṣṇu, even when resting in the ocean of milk—the one on the navel-lotus of the other, are farther away from the land of mortals and they are more often thought of as residing in heaven than on earth. We may also see in Vaiṣṇavism and Śaivism two opposite types of religious appeal. Vaiṣṇavism claims allegiance on behalf of a god who periodically becomes man to share men's sorrows and bring succour to them in distress. Śaivism, on the other hand, calls upon men to worship a god who is easily accessible but who does not at any time forsake his divinity and subject himself to human infirmities.[99]

[97] Other functions are also ascribed to these faces. Thus, according to one school of thought, the four Vedas came out of the four mouths and from the central mouth the Tantra of the higher tradition (*ūrdhvāmnāya*) issued; according to another tradition, the twenty-eight Tantras of the higher tradition sprang from the upward current and issued from the five mouths while the Tantra of lower tradition has been produced by ' the downward current ' ' below the navel.'—See A. Avalon, *Principles of Tantra*, Vol. I, Introduction, p. xxx f.

[98] Brahmā has no *avatāras* either; but as he has no function of moral government, an avatāra of Brahmā is unnecessary. Puṣkara, the most noted earthly seat of Brahmā, is a place noted for Brahmā's own sacrifice rather than for people seeking his help there.

For Lakulī as incarnation of Śiva, see J.B.B.R.A.S., XXII, p. 154 f; see also *Ep. Ind.*, XXI, p. 5.

[99] We may quote Sir Charles Eliot in this connection: " Krishṇa is in the

Both agreed, however, that the old Vedic religion of sacrifice had failed to satisfy the human heart and to provide for weak and erring mortals who felt the need of forgiveness proceeding out of divine grace and who had no faith in formal expiation achieved with ritualistic ceremony. Both, therefore, set God above the law of Karma and, while emphasising the necessity of a moral life lived in devotion to God and service to man, admitted the possibility of working off the injurious results of occasional lapses by sincere repentance through the forgiving grace of God. In both systems Bhakti was laid down as the essential condition of a religious life and the authority of the Vedas was slackened by the admission of non-Vedic authority as embodied in the sectarian literature.[100] Not only was provision made for a less formal mode of worship but the Śūdras were also granted a right to use this sacred literature in lieu of the Vedas, which they could not read,[101] and to worship God without the help of the Brāhmaṇa priest. The result was immediately visible in a large extension of the Hindu community not only in India but also in the islands of the Indian Archipelago and in Kāmboja and Campā. Śaivism, being still less trammelled by orthodox traditions than Vaiṣṇavism, made more extensive conquests in these Far Eastern Hindu Colonies[102] and quickly fused with Mahāyāna Buddhism not only there but also in Nepal.[103] The ugly features of the god were forgotten to satisfy the need of an ideal, and the

main a product of hero worship, but Siva has no such historical basis. He personifies the powers of birth and death, of change, decay and rebirth—in fact all that we include in the prosaic word nature."—*Hind. and Bud.*, I, p. xvi.

100 As the *Kulārṇava Tantra* says, for each age (*yuga*) a suitable Shāstra is given—namely, in Satyayuga, Shruti; in Tretā, Smriti; in Dvāpara, the Purāṇas; and in the Kali age the Tantra.—A. Avalon, *Principles of Tantra*, Vol. I, Introduction, p. xxii. See also A. Avalon, *Tantra of the Great Liberation*, p. 1.

101 S. S. Sūryanārāyaṇa Sāstrī does not accept the view that the Śaiva Āgamas were non-Vedic and non-Aryan in origin. See *The Sivādvaita of Śrīkaṇṭha*, Note D. The Āgamas and the Mahābhārata (p. 81 f.). Also p. 4 f. for a discussion of the Dravidian origin of the Āgamas.

102 The greater hold of Śaivism may also be due to the fact that the Tamils who emigrated to these places were mostly Śaivites and Śaivism had greater popular and royal backing in South India than Vaiṣṇavism at the time of the colonisation.

103 It is still a matter of dispute as to whether Śaivism engulfed Mahāyāna Buddhism or *vice versa*.—See A. Avalon, *Principles of Tantra*, Vol. I, Int., p. lviii.

hymns offered to Śiva, as to Viṣṇu,[104] are the purest expressions of monotheistic devotion. As a personal God, he is regarded not only as Mahākāla, who destroys all creation, but also as the creator and preserver of the world ; the serene ascetic who sets an example of self-restraint ; the moral governor who punishes sin and rewards virtue ; and the gracious Lord who forgives the penitent sinner, affords him fresh opportunities of a spiritual life and grants salvation to all his devout worshippers.[105] The secret of the success of sectarianism in India lies in the fact that in India Philosophy and Religion are far more intimately associated than anywhere else and the theory of the savant becomes the common belief of the popular mind within a short time. The Upaniṣads and the Vedānta system have established once for all the sole reality of Brahman, and every supreme god is identified with the Vedāntic Absolute, with the attribute of personality added or emphasised. The other gods tolerated or recognised then become merely different forms of this supreme god, if not his creatures and attendants. Even when there is no predilection for any particular god, all the different gods are conceived to be ultimately one in essence, sharing among themselves the different aspects, attributes and functions of one supreme deity.

Extreme caution is needed in dealing with a faith like Hinduism which a writer does not live or see from within.

104 For the All-god character of Viṣṇu, see Hopkins, *Epic Mythology*, p. 207.

105 Speaking of the greater appeal of the Naṭarāja image in South India and of the Mahā-yogin image in North India, Havell makes the following fine observation (*Handbook of Indian Art*, pp. 182-83) :

" In the pellucid air of the Western Ghats, washed clean by monsoon storms, the Brahman at his evening prayers heard day by day Śiva's drum, the time-beat of the ocean, thundering along the shore, and saw the golden sun throbbing on the western horizon as it sank slowly into the jaws of the mysterious dragon of the nether world. So the Brahmanical art of Southern India is a true interpretation of Indian history and, like all true art, holds the mirror up to nature in revealing to us the beatific vision of the Universal Lord in his mystic Dance of Creation and Dissolution. And in like manner the calm serenity of those majestic peaks of the Himalayas in the still moon-lit nights, when every sound is hushed and all nature lies asleep, gave to the northern artist his inspiration for the image of the Lord upon His exalted Lotus-throne, the Great Spirit " brooding over the face of the waters " who is cause everlasting of the cosmic rhythm."

Historical treatment of a god may not reflect adequately—often it totally misunderstands and misinterprets—the spiritual evolution of man's ideas regarding that god. It is not difficult to point out in a religion, ennobled or degraded by the imagination[106] of the inhabitants of a vast continent teeming with a heterogeneous population with different grades of culture, the shady past of a god or a mixture of light and shade in his character. What is more difficult is to understand and appreciate how the tribal memory manages to forget most of the unsavoury tales about a god in the same way as the individual mind represses its own unpleasant memories. If the idea of a moral god ennobles human ideals, so do advancing moral ideals raise the standard of divinity; and this is what has actually occurred in India as elsewhere.[107] It may be freely admitted that in a weak mind a bad divine example is sometimes likely to find an imitator, just as it should also be admitted that a bad prophetic example may similarly prove equally harmful. But such cases are bound to be rare and are not likely to occur when the developing ethical sense of society eliminates the ugly features of a god. When society wills to turn the blind eye to the faults of a god and fastens upon and magnifies his good qualities, surprising results follow: every one of the major religions of India can be cited as an instance of what the will to believe can achieve in the nature of devotion and practice. Let us illustrate this point from the remaining religions of India.

The five gods (*pañcadevatā*) who are supposed to have a following in India at present are Viṣṇu, Śiva, Śakti, Gaṇeśa

[106] The degradation may sometimes be apparent. Thus it has been said that much of the opposition to Śāktaism comes from a misunderstanding of the esoteric meaning of many apparently unmeaning mantras and revolting ceremonies, of which the spiritual significance can be learned only from a *guru* after undergoing a fairly strenuous moral discipline.

[107] Keith, commenting on the decline of Varuṇa from a moral god in the Vedas to the god of waters in later literature, remarks that "in the fact of the failure of morality to develop itself as an important factor in the nature of the gods lies a deep distinction between Indian and other religions." This remark is too sweeping in view of the ethical development of the present-day sectarian gods. See Keith, *Rel. and Phil. of the Veda and Upanishads*, I, p. 247.

and Sūrya. The last two, however, have a very small following although there are references to the existence at one time of as many as six classes of devotees of each of these gods.[108] Of these Sūrya could not be personified to any very great extent; and although a few myths about him were circulated, he remained mostly a Vedic god to whom the Brāhmaṇas offered daily the twilight and mid-day oblations. A Magian immigration from Persia or Scythia (Śakadvīpa) probably popularised his cult for some time and some fine temples were built to enshrine his images. But barring a few casual verses, describing him as the soul of all movable and immovable things and as Brahman, there is nothing but Vedic tradition regarding Sūrya to justify the continuance of his worship. The longevity of the cult must be due to the fact that the solar worship comes nearest to the veneration for the glowing Agni (and Sūrya is a form of Agni) which was such a prominent feature of the Vedic religion and that it alone represents whatever has been left of the Vedic religion, the cult of all the other gods having developed non-Vedic features of worship. The Solar cult is therefore a survival of Vedic worship—probably of Indo-Iranian worship, and the Gāyatrī (familiar to scholars in its derivative appellation Sāvitrī), daily recited by the twice-born of India, is an invocation addressed to the Sun. It is probable that while Viṣṇu appropriated the personal aspect of godhead and its relation to man, its impersonal element and its function of supporting the physical world were assigned to Sūrya. He is the great source of life and health. He witnesses man's deeds from above and the powers of darkness all vanish in his presence.[109] He sets the example of regularity and beneficence to human conduct, always rising and setting at the appointed time and helping the circulation of water in the atmosphere. His benignity extends to saints and sinners alike, for on both he casts his vivifying rays. He quickens the intellect and forgives sins just as he heals the body.[110]

108 Bhandarkar, *op. cit.*, pp. 149 and 152.

109 Hopkins, *Epic Mythology*, p. 84.

110 Tradition credits Kṛṣṇa's son Sāmba, who was cured of leprosy by worshipping the Sun, with the importation of Magian priests to India for conducting

He is supposed to have revealed the Yajurveda, and Manu is regarded as having derived both his existence and his wisdom from him. Yama, "the lord of righteousness" (*dharma-rāja*), is his son in later mythology[111] and he is also the progenitor of the race in which Rāma was born. If one carefully scans the beliefs of this Solar sect, one would find that the choice has fallen on such aspects of the god as could be spiritually and ethically used. Again, the multiplicity of forms in which the Sun was worshipped in the Vedic age[112]—Mitra, Sūrya, Aryaman, Savitṛ, Pūṣan, Viṣṇu, Vivasvat, Âditya—was abandoned in later times, and, with the exception of Viṣṇu, all the other forms were rolled together to form the conception of a unitary Solar deity raised, in sectarian worship, to the position of a supreme god, pure, omnipotent, omnipresent and omniscient, upholder of regularity and righteousness, beneficent and forgiving. That the cult lacked vigour, in spite of royal support,[113] is due to the fact that a deification of the visible luminary is difficult except in primitive times and such a cult could thrive only as a survival of ancient belief, modified and allegorised to suit the monotheistic and moral needs of an advanced religious community. The solar cult in India, however, never grew to such dimensions as Mithraism in the nearer West; and in later times it was assimilated into the cult of the Trinity, the morning, the noon and the evening sun being identified with Brahmā, Viṣṇu and Śiva respectively.[114]

the worship of the Sun on account of the unwillingness of the local Brahmans to officiate at his Solar temple on the bank of the Candrabhāgā as regular priests. (Bhandarkar, *op. cit.*, p. 152; see Bhattasali, *op. cit.*, p. 166.)

111 Yama is the son of Vivasvat in RV. 10, 14.5; 17.1 just as Yima is of Vivahvant in Avêstan literature.

112 See Macdonell, *Vedic Mythology*, p. 29 f. Farquhar, *An Outline of the Religious Literature of India*, p. 151 f.; Barth, *op. cit.*, pp. 19, 20.

113 On Kaniṣka's coins a figure with the name Miiro (Mihira = Pers. Mithra = Sans. Mitra) is to be found. Harṣavardhana and his immediate ancestors styled themselves as "great devotees of the Sun."—Bhandarkar, *op. cit.*, pp. 154-55. The cult was very popular in Bengal where a large number of Sun-images has been found and where the Varman and Sena kings called themselves Sauras.—Bhattasali, *op. cit.*, p. 166.

114 See *Tantratattva* (Eng. Tr. by A. Avalon, Vol. II), Part II, Ch. XI, p. 1 f.

A more instructive example of the working of the spiritual sense is afforded by the development of the cult of the other god, *viz.*, Gaṇeśa.[115] Being originally the lord of the *gaṇas*, *i.e.*, the wild and terrible followers of Rudra, namely, the Maruts, he could not have possessed at first attractive features of character and, in fact, down to the time of the *Mahābhārata*, the malevolent demons, the Vināyakas, could be traced.[116] The Gaṇeśvaras, Gaṇapatis and Vināyakas were originally many in number, being identified with the lords of malevolent spirits who were present everywhere; but latterly their number was fixed at four (or six) and possession by them was supposed to work sure evil, which could be prevented only by exorcising them by appropriate ceremonies.[117] But the religious need of man can work wonders. These malevolent spirits were reduced to a unity and a single Gaṇapati or Vināyaka was raised to supreme godhood with all the functions appropriate to it. Whether casual identifications of Bṛhaspati, Indra and Viṣṇu with Gaṇapati, the lord of a host, helped the process of transformation it is difficult to say;[118] but certain it is that, in spite of the survival of such a wild trait as an elephant's head, Gaṇeśa became transformed into an ideal of wisdom and beneficence. It may be that the invocation of Gaṇeśa at the beginning of every non-Vedic religious worship is meant to have the same effect as the ceremony of sending away the demons, also observed as a preliminary rite;[119] but piety looks upon it with a different eye and sees in it the supremacy of Gaṇeśa over all other gods. His figure and name are to be found in most Bengali shops, as he is supposed to give success (*siddhi*)[120] in all undertakings, and his wisdom

[115] For the worship of Gaṇeśā, see Mahānirvāṇa Tantra, Ch. X, 113 f. (Tr. by A. Avalon, p. 250.)

[116] Hopkins, *Epic Mythology*, p. 207.

[117] Bhandarkar, *op. cit.*, p. 147.

[118] Macdonell, *V.M.*, p. 101. Bhandarkar, *op. cit.*, p. 147; Hopkins, *Epic Mythology*, p. 207.

[119] Even though *bhūta-śuddhi* does not always mean the sending away of demons, there is a *bhūtāpasāraṇa* (demon-removing) mantra for this purpose. (See Avalon, *Tantra of the Great Liberation*, Int., p. cvi.)

[120] In the characteristic popular way Siddhi, which means in Sanskrit 'Success,' was transformed into a pouch of *cannabis indica* (which is another meaning of the Bengali word 'Siddhi') in Gaṇeśa's hand, just as Prajāpati, the

is symbolised by the reed (*viśikhaka*) he carries in his character of the scribe of the gods, who, in fact, even condescended to take down the dictation of the *Mahābhārata* by Vyāsa on condition that if Vyāsa did not stop anywhere in the middle of his composition he (Gaṇeśa) would not write down a single verse without understanding its meaning. Though his sonship to Śiva (Rudra) betrays his origin, his later developments serve to show how the religious mind can transform almost intractable materials into lovable figures and to change a troublesome spirit into "the genial protector of households and the personification of common sense, whose aid should be first invoked in all worldly enterprises."[121]

The same process is at work in the Śakti cult, although there the original form is not so definitely anti-divine.[122] The Aryan aspect of the Śakti cult is more allied to the creative side, while the non-Aryan contribution is probably more concerned with the destructive side of the divine nature. The Aryan prototypes of Śakti are the originally colourless wives of the Vedic gods,[123] who were latterly invested with the function of energising their lethargic husbands and, in fact, of using them as the instruments of their creative activity. Then there are Aditi,[124] the great mother out of whom all creation comes; Māyā, without whose association Brahman is unable to create; and Prakṛti, which alone brings this varied world into being while Puruṣa behaves as an inactive spectator of the world-drama. It would be interesting to know if the belief in the destructive aspect of a Mother-Goddess was a satire upon the increasing disinclination to kill among the Aryans as a result of Jaina, Bauddha and Vaiṣṇava teachings and embodied a vision of days when, should men become effeminate, women

lord of creation, who is invoked in letters of invitation to marriages, takes the form of a butterfly which is another meaning of the Bengali word 'Prajāpati.' (For the more usual articles in the hands of Gaṇeśa, see Bhattasali, *op. cit.*, p. 145 f.)

121 Havell, *op. cit.*, p. 191.

122 See N. K. Bhattasali's *Iconography of Buddhist and Brahmanical Sculptures in the Dacca Museum*, p. 178 f. for Vedic references.

123 See Keith, *Rel. and Phil. of the Veda and Upanishads*, Vol. I, p. 218.

124 *Ibid.*, p. 215 f.

would become manlike and destroy all evil threatened from enemies and savages. Possibly the mother-cult came from people worshipping female spirits of dark intentions who were propitiated by suitable offerings. We still have among us such "negative" goddesses as Śītalā, the goddess of small-pox, and Manasā, the goddess of snakes, who are prayed to not so much for granting the worshipper any good as for leaving him alone in peace. The fire-association of many of the names of Śakti[125] may also be due to the fact that it is in connection with huge forest-fires, where a veritable holocaust of animals would take place, that the cult arose. Corresponding to the *gaṇas* a troop of female furies was associated with Devī, the Śakti of Śiva. The tradition that she had her home in the Vindhyas and was fond of flesh and wine and that her devotees were hilly tribes would point to an admixture of aboriginal worship in her cult.[126] In her terrible forms of Kālī, Durgā (or Mahiṣamardinī), Candī and Cāmundā she has exacted the homage of her worshippers as a proper consort of Rudra or Mahākāla. Her insatiable blood-thirst has been symbolised by the Chinnamastā image, in which she is depicted as a decapitated female figure holding the severed head in her hand and sending up a fountain of blood into her own mouth. There is no doubt that the cult is a composite one[127] and that both Vedic and non-Vedic elements have entered into its structure.

Here, again, has devotion achieved wonders. The unerring human instinct, which finds in the mother the first tender source of satisfaction of its hunger and thirst, felt the need of

125 See Muṇḍ. Up. 1. 2. 4 for the names of the seven tongues of fire (the first two are Kālī and Karālī).

126 See Bhandarkar, *op. cit.*, p. 143; see Bhattasali, *op. cit.*, p. 127.

127 Muir observes as follows : "As in Siva, first of all two gods, Agni and Rudra, are combined, so too his wife is to be regarded as a compound of several divine forms, and this becomes quite evident if we look over the mass of her epithets. While one set of these, as Umā, Ambikā, Pārvatī, Haimavatī, belong to the wife of Rudra, others as Kālī, Karālī carry us back to the wife of Agni, while Gaurī and others perhaps refer to Nirṛiti, the goddess of all evil."—*O.S.T.*, IV, Ch. III, Sec. viii. For Vaiṣṇava association, see Arjuna's hymn to Durgā in M.Bh., Bhīṣmaparvan, 796 f., and also Virāṭaparvan, 178 f., and Harivaṃśa, 3236 f. (See Muir, *ibid.*, p. 368 f. and p. 361, f.n. 337.) See Hopkins, *Epic Mythology*, p. 224.

a similar divine being who would take greater pity on human failing and suffering than a stern Heavenly Father. God as Mother could fulfil at least two of the conditions of divinity, *viz.*, creation and preservation, if the human mother is to be taken as an earthly analogue. Only there may be some doubt about her capacity to destroy. The cruel and destructive aspect of Śakti served to show that if due occasion should arise, she would not be found wanting even in that capacity either: possibly there was an element of over-compensation in the process and the terrifying colours were painted more thick than necessary.[128] But the primary interest must have been the need of a female god to whom the sinner could unburden his soul more fully than to a male deity and with surer chance of forgiveness. In Vaiṣṇavism where Lakṣmī remained to the end a devoted wife, she is prayed to for interceding[129] on behalf of the sinner and securing the relenting grace of her husband. But Devī or Śakti is a far more independent deity[130] from the beginning and she herself absolves the sinner from his guilt out of motherly affection. In popular hymns fervent prayers go up to her to forgive her foolish and erring sons as all good mothers are wont to do. We thus reach the position that Śakti is not an intercessor but the supreme divinity herself.

According to the philosophical view that Śakti (energy) and Śaktimat (the being possessing the energy) are non-distinguishable (*abhinna*) it is not possible to keep Śiva and Śakti separate—Śiva (or Brahmā or Viṣṇu) cannot act without Śakti and therefore the two are identical. Here is a quotation from a Tamil Śaiva saint, Arul Nandi, where Śakti is not absolutely independent of Śiva but is an expression of his powers. " She, who is Īśa's *kṛpāśakti* (grace), *icchāśakti* (will), *kriyāśakti* (action), *jñānaśakti* (knowledge), who is the cause of all creation, sustentation and destruction, who is

128 Cruelty associated with a mother-cult is not present in Hinduism alone. See Eliot, *Hinduism and Buddhism*, II, p. 276.

129 See B. N. Seal, *Comparative Studies in Vaiṣṇavism and Christianity;* see, however, *Tattvatraya* (Chowkhāmbā Ed.), p. 98, where Mahālakṣmī appears in an opposite role.

For the increasing importance of Lakṣmi in later Vaiṣṇavism and its causes see H. C. Raychaudhuri, *op. cit.*, p. 106.

130 Keith, *Rel. and Phil. of the Veda and Upanishads*, I, p. 218.

*rūpa* (form) and *arūpa* (formlessness) and neither, who is the consort of Īśa in these forms, who is all this world and all this wealth, who begets the whole world and sustains them: the Gracious Feet of this *our Mother,* who imparts blissful immortality to souls, and removes their bondages of birth and who remains seated with *our Father* in the hearts of the Freed, let me lift upon my head."[131] But it is possible to go beyond this stage and to think that Śakti is the support of the whole universe and Brahmā, Viṣṇu and Śiva are only forms assumed or created by Śakti to fulfil different cosmic functions. This is mythically represented by Śiva, Viṣṇu and Brahmā being made to be the children of Śakti who then chooses Śiva as her spouse,[132] presumably because destruction is a more palpable expression of energy than creation and preservation. When this conception is reached. Śakti becomes identified with Brahman, the formless Absolute from which all things proceed and in which all things are dissolved. Numerous passages can be quoted from the Tantras, the special Śākta literature, to prove this identification, and some parts of the Tantra literature, *e.g.*, the first few *Ullāsas* (chapters) of the *Mahānirvāṇa Tantra,* would read like a Vedāntic manual. Conformably to this belief, the worship of other gods and all non-Tāntric modes of worship are regarded as inferior and incapable of liberating the soul. Here is a characteristic passage from *Tantra* literature: " The human being, desirous of final emancipation, enters the path of devotion, first as a *Saura*

131 *Proceedings of the Convention of Religions in India*, 1909, Vol. II, p. 128. For the relation of Śiva and Śakti, see Arthur Avalon, *Tantra of the Great Liberation*, p. xix f.

132 A goddess with a young subordinate god is known in early times on every coast of the Mediterranean which looked towards Crete. In Punic Africa she is Tanit with her son; in Egypt, Isis with Horus; in Phoenicia, Ashtaroth with Tammuz (Adonis); in Asia Minor, Cybele with Attis; in Greece (as especially in Greek Crete itself), Rhea with the young Zeus. Everywhere she is *parthenos, i.e.*, unwed, but made the mother first of her companion by immaculate conception, and then of the gods and all life by the embrace of her own son. In memory of these original facts, her cult (especially the more esoteric mysteries of it) is marked by various practices and observances symbolic of the negation of true marriage and obliteration of sex. A part of her male votaries are castrated; and her female votaries must ignore their married state when in her personal service, and often practise ceremonial promiscuity.—ERE. i. 147 (art. AEGEAN RELIGION).

(worshipper of the Sun) and for twelve successive lives, goes to the Solar regions and comes back, finally to attain the *Sārṣṭi-mukti* after losing himself in Brahma at the end of a *kalpa*. He is then born again as a *Gāṇapatya* (worshipper of Gaṇapati) in the next *kalpa* and after eight births, attains similarly the *Sāmīpya-mukti*. In the next *kalpa*, he is born again as a *Vaiṣṇava* (worshipper of Viṣṇu), and after seven births, attains the *Sālokya-mukti*. Similarly, in the succeeding *kalpa*, he takes birth as a *Śaiva* (worshipper of Śiva), and worshipping Śiva for five births, obtains the *Sāyujya-mukti* and for the life-time of a hundred Brahmas, lives in Śiva-like form in the *Śiva-loka*. He again takes his birth and in pursuance of his ideas and customs, worships Śakti for four lives, after that he takes his rest in *Cit* (Intelligence Pure) and attains the *Kaivalya-* or *Nirvāṇa-mukti* or the Highest Salvation. Of all the worshippers of the five gods, only the devotee worshipping with the *Śakti mantra* attains *Nirvāṇa-mukti* or Salvation.''[133]

When we are talking of the evolution of the Śakti cult we are referring not so much to the addition of Absolutistic terminology as to an emphasis upon it, for even very early speculations had invested the deity with some of the highest qualities of divinity. In the Kena Upaniṣad Umā Haimavatī appears as a revealer of the nature of Brahman and she was herself frequently identified with Sarasvatī, the personified Vedic lore. A transition to the Absolutistic conception was therefore easy and natural. Duly she became the revealer of the Nigama—the body of spiritual truths which she discoursed to Śiva for the benefit of the entire creation in the Kaliyuga. The Tantras reiterated the efficacy of *mantras* and prescribed certain *yantras* or diagrams as representing the forms in which the different deities received their offerings. The mantras arranged in and about a *yantra* formed a mystic

[133] Quoted in the *Proceedings of the Convention of Religions in India*, 1909, Vol. II, p. 149. For the five types of *mukti*, see Kennedy, *The Chaitanya Movement*, p. 98 (*sālokya*-being in the same plane with God; *sāmīpya*-nearness to God; *sārūpya*-likeness to God; *sārṣṭi*-equalling the glory of God; *sāyujya*-absorption in God).

divine body and everyone had to receive Tāntric initiation (*dīkṣā*) to be entitled to spiritual comradeship and salvation. The Purāṇas had supplied the mythology of the gods; the Tantras provided the rituals. In course of time the cult overstepped its original Śaiva limits and not only acknowledged the wives of the other gods as the Śaktis of the latter, just as Durgā, Pārvatī, Umā or Gaurī was of Śiva, but also prescribed forms of ritualistic worship for all gods, male and female. While it provided for congregational worship of a questionable type in the Śrīcakra (the circle)—practically the only other congregational worship outside Vaiṣṇavism—and abolished caste-distinctions there, it definitely raised the dignity of women, remembering that these belonged to the same sex as the Supreme Goddess, supported the marriage of widows and opposed the practice of *Satī* or immolation of women on the funeral pyres of their husbands just deceased.[134] Now it is these appeals that could spread the cult from Kashmir to Cape Comorin (Kanyā-kumārī) among philosophers and devout men and not the *Pañca-makāra*, the so-called five M's, namely, *madya* (wine), *māṃsa* (meat), *matsya* (fish), *mudrā* (parched grain)[135] and *maithuna* (coition), which to ill-informed minds carry the entire significance of Śāktaism. As to the liberties permitted to the "hero" (*vīra*), it is well to remember that he has been defined as one who has controlled his senses, is truthful and ever engaged in worship and has sacrificed lust and other passions.[136] Did not the Upaniṣad speak in almost identical terms of what is permitted to the liberated, knowing full well that to such natures morally reprehensible acts are impossible? [137] In fact, the aim of the entire Tāntric discipline is to sublimate the lower instincts and to raise the soul from sex (*Mūlādhāra*) to salvation (*Sahasrāra*) after transcending the intermediate obstacles.[138] As usual, the danger has come

134 See Eliot, *op. cit.*, II, p. 285.

135 The translation is of A. Avalon.—See *Tantra of the Great Liberation*, Introd., p. cxi f.; also p. cxviii f.

136 *Ibid.*, Intr., p. cxii.

137 Chān. Up., 5. 10. 9-10.

138 The six *cakras* or centres are Mūlādhāra, Svādhiṣṭhāna, Maṇipūra, Anāhata, Viśuddha, and Ājnā from below upwards. These *cakras* (they have been

from using equivocal language in spiritual matters, for the ordinary mind, failing to make out the symbolism, has fixed upon the letter of the text and thereby excused itself into indulgences, superstitions and magical practices.

We shall now close our review of the major sects of Hinduism with some general reflections and some account of later developments. An historical study of the different forms of faith reveals the interesting fact that the Indo-Aryan mind gradually outgrew its Vedic polytheism with unaided effort only to transcend theism altogether and land in a speculative monism which, while degrading the status of the gods, increased enormously the prestige of the wise man. The popular mind, however, while it reconciled itself gradually to the loss of most of the Vedic rituals, refused to abandon the gods, with the effect that monotheism in some form or other reared its head. Even the Vedānta system, which summarised the Upaniṣadic teachings, had to provide for the satisfaction of the theistic bent of the human mind by postulating the reality of God at least for devotional purposes, and some Vedāntic commentators could also make adequate provision for the reality of the individual soul and the divine government of the world in their interpretation of the *Brahma-Sūtra*. Increased acquaintance with simpler forms of worship and contact with indigenous population led not only to increased emphasis on the element of devotion but also to the relaxation of caste rules. The acceptance of a Supreme God led to the subordination of the law of Karma to Divine grace and to the softening of the rigours of the law of transmigration. In its search after an ideal godhead the growing ethical sense moralised the character of one or other of the ancient gods and laid emphasis not only on the unitary character of God but also on His holiness, His abhorrence of sin and His ready

often identified with the plexuses) must be pierced or conquered before the union of the Jīva with Parama-Śiva (which is the *sāttvika* or spiritual meaning of *Maithuna* or coition) can take place. See Avalon, *Tantra of the Great Liberation*, Intr., p. lvii f.; p. cxxxii f. Union with Tripurāsundarī became an objective in some Sakti cults.—See Bhandarkar, *op. cit.*, p. 146.

forgiveness of sins confessed and abandoned. While the danger of lapsing into an unethical religion, owing to the persistence of early literary traditions and the equivocal language of devotion, could not be entirely overcome, a sense of propriety limited its extension to society at large in the past and has now practically overcome it altogether.

We approach now the post-Paurāṇic religious history of India where religious forces other than Hindu came into operation. Genuine indigenous development of religion took the form of syncretism and toleration. The non-difference of Hari (Viṣṇu) and Hara (Śiva) has already been referred to. The association of Brahmā, Viṣṇu and Śiva with their respective Śaktis, of which Buddhistic analogues are well known, was established. The trinity of Brahmā, Viṣṇu and Śiva with their respective cosmic functions of creation, preservation and destruction was introduced, and a combination of these functions in each god, especially in Viṣṇu and Śiva, was preached, thus recognising that the three were ultimately one in essence. When Brahmā disappeared from the field of religion and Śakti, Gaṇeśa and Sūrya were added, the same syncretism manifested itself in the worship of the five gods among the Smārtas, which thus broke down the religious isolation of the different sects, especially in South India, but re-introduced a limited polytheism, at least in appearance, among the largest majority of the Hindu population. But for the fact that Hindu polytheism is always tempered by Vedāntic monism (of which the philosophy of Rāmakṛṣṇa Paramahaṃsa is a modern example), this might have led to a recrudescence of crass polytheism : actually, however, it led to a henotheism where there is for the time being only one principal god and the other gods are subordinate to him. The preaching of Rāmakṛṣṇa Paramahaṃsa that each method of belief is equally with others a true path of religion[139] is as much a reaffirmation of the Gītā ideal of manifold approach as a reiteration of the creed of syncretistic Hinduism of this type.

139 See Farquhar, *Modern Religious Movements in India*, p. 192 f. Keshab Chandra Sen's New Dispensation was a similar eclectic belief.—*Ibid*, p. 57 f.; p. 64.

The introduction of Semitic monotheism in India through Christianity and Islam has deeply affected not only Hindu social organisation but also Hindu religious thought. A deeper appreciation of the unity of God from the latter and of the value of devotion from the former led to a number of reforming movements in mediaeval and modern India. Some like Kabir and Nānak attempted to fuse Hinduism and Islam through ethical non-ritualistic monotheism while retaining for the most part Hindu religious ideas and appella tions. Some like Rāmānanda, Caitanya, Nāmadeva and Tulasīdāsa stuck to Vaiṣṇava monotheism but flooded it with the language of piety and devotion and used the vernacular medium in their preachings to bring religion home to the minds of the people. Similar Śaivite revivals took place in South India.

Brought face to face with the monotheism of the West, three reforming movements have arisen to stem the tide of conversion. The Ārya Samāj has revived Vedicism[140] and, while abolishing caste and idolatry, has given a monotheistic interpretation to the Vedic religion. It has revived oblation (*havana*) with an altered meaning and without animal sacrifice but has abandoned most of the later Hindu beliefs. The Brāhma Samāj was conceived in a different spirit. While the Ārya Samāj was launched in opposition to Islam and Christianity, the Brāhma Ṣamāj wished to utilise the best points of both, while professing to revive the religion of the Upaniṣads. The three earliest reformers belonging to this Church—Ram Mohan Roy, Devendra Nath Tagore and Keshab Chandra Sen—were influenced most deeply by the Qur'ān, the Upaniṣads and the Bible respectively; the first adhered more to an impersonal Absolute, however, than to a personal God, which the second advocated, and the third introduced many Christian conceptions in the relation of God to man. Brāhmaism to-day, however, is, like the Prārthanā Samāj built on its model, more Hindu than anything else in its philosophy of life and religious nomenclature. The return

[140] See Farquhar, *op. cit.*, p. 120 f.

to Paurāṇic religion was inaugurated by Rāmakṛṣṇa Paramahaṃsa in the characteristic Bengali way by worshipping Kālī, as Ram Prasad Sen had done before him.[141] But Vaiṣṇavism, which has by its past history proved itself to be most capable of development in a theistic direction, is coming to its own not only in the worship of the great charioteer of Arjuna (whence Kṛṣṇa as the discourser of the Gītā is called Pārthasārathi) in Hindu Missions, which are working among outcastes, apostates, hill-tribes and people of alien faiths, but also in an increased appreciation of the message of the Gītā by eminent thinkers like Tilak, Arabinda Ghosh and Gandhi. Thus the Vedas, the Upaniṣads and the Purāṇas have all been revived in Modern India in search of an indigenous monotheism, and contemporary political events have added patriotic zeal to religious revivals. Unattractive social features which cramped missionary activities in the past are being ignored or abolished, and Hinduism is fast becoming a Church militant with fresh ambitions for a career of conquest.[142] This is indirectly helping the religion itself, for aggression to-day is possible only for those who are best protected. Hinduism in its orthodox form is linked up with idolatry : we shall study this aspect of Hinduism in a subsequent chapter. It remains to be seen how Hinduism transforms itself to resist the onslaught of alien faiths and to win fresh converts among the cultured nations of the world. To a world suffering from national rivalries, political struggles and luxurious modes of living the Hindu message of non-injury, toleration, peace and renunciation as the highest ideals of religious life may yet prove a soothing salve. On the other hand, to those in Hindu India who choose to follow the western ideals of strife the cult of Kālī or the Kṛṣṇa who incited Arjuna to violence

[141] Keshab Chandra Sen apparently got his concept of God as Mother from association with Rāmakṛṣṇa Paramahaṃsa.—See Farquhar, *op. cit.*, p. 58.

[142] See, for instance, *Hinduism invades America* by Thomas Wendell. Attempts have also been made to preach Hinduism in Europe and will possibly be made to get into touch with the still extant old Hindu colonies of the Far East (including Bali and other islands of the Indian archipelago). Indian emigration to different parts of the world is also helping to spread Hinduism abroad.

See the writer's article on *Our Changing Social Relations* in the *Dacca University Journal*, 1936.

may prove immensely attractive, to the infinite woe of humanity at large. Signs are not wanting that even latent atheism and scepticism, which are such abiding features of Hindu philosophic thought all through its history,[143] are rearing their heads in the trail of material ambition and political struggle. The future religion of Hindu India is thus shrouded in obscurity and will undoubtedly be shaped materially by world forces and inter-communal relations. In the meantime small bands of enthusiastic disciples are gathering as of old round devotional minds for inspirational talks and religious discourses and deification of these local saints is going on as usual all around. Never before was such a conscious attempt made to explain, understand and appreciate the eternal verities of Hindu religious thought or to put the social structure in a satisfactory order. The neo-Vedāntic movement with its message of equality and fraternity is rapidly pervading Hindu society and there is a definite tendency now to equate the service of God with the service of the socially depressed, the poor and the fallen. The preacher Vivekānanda, the poet Rabindranath and the political saint Gandhi have chosen as their ideal of divine service ministration to the needs of the poor and the down-trodden and sent forth a message of social sympathy which is being widely responded to and carried out in practice. To the negative prescription of non-injury has been added the positive prescription of active helpfulness as a mode of fulfilling religious obligations. What stood so long in the way of practical charity of this kind is the characteristic Hindu way of dissociating philosophy from social life. We may hope that as the messages of purified Vaiṣṇavism, Śaivism and Vedānta are more intimately followed, Hinduism will not only evolve on purer lines of speculation and worship but also usher in fuller appreciation of the brotherhood of man through the common fatherhood of God or through the ultimate identity of all finite spirits in and through Brahman.

---

143 See the writer's article on *The Polite Atheism of Indian Philosophy* in the *Dacca University Studies*, Vol. I.

## CHAPTER VI

### God in Judaism

It may be admitted without any discussion that when earlier and later beliefs jostle with one another in the scriptures of any particular religion, often to the confusion and dismay of its adherents, the reason is to be found in the almost universal disinclination to tamper with a sacred text. It is not in every religion that an ' Uthmān edits the sacred literature with the motive of enforcing uniformity of belief and preventing future dissension, or wields the authority to impose a standard version upon the entire religious community. Attempts made in India to codify socio-religious practices ended in the setting up of regional compendia (*nibandhas*) sanctioning conflicting customs and practices and adding to the vast extant basic religious literature of the country. The puerilities, errors and contradictions to be found in most, if not all, religious literatures—especially in those that have had a long and varied history—provide a happy hunting ground to students of ethnology, anthropology, psychology, ethics, social history and comparative religion. From the side of the religions concerned, however, they represent successive or separate speculations, some lofty and others lowly, to conceive or construct the essentials of faith and practice in keeping with the intellectual ability, the ethical stature or the regional or contemporary necessities of their adherents. Not unoften they are due to the influence of contiguous alien faiths with which some sort of rapprochement seems desirable either to fill up an existing lacuna, or to cultivate social concord, or to facilitate the ready acceptance of those religions by fresh social groups. It is not always that the victors have suppressed, supplanted or modified the faiths of the vanquished. History is replete with instances where the vanquished have immensely influenced the religious beliefs of the conquerors, and this is true not only in cases of cultural conquest but also in those of political domination. In state religions such absorptions have sometimes been deliberately and officially made; but where religion is only a social institution the changes are generally gradual and unconscious and must be deemed to satisfy a social need, sane or morbid, or at least a social craze for novelty. The composition of the group very often determines the direction in which the unconscious changes take place, namely, whether towards evolution or towards degeneration; and by 'composition' is to be understood not merely the strength of number but also the strength of conviction that the group possesses. The informed reader will readily remember the expansion and modification of Judaism, Islām, Hinduism, Buddhism and Christianity in different fashions in different regions in past and present times.

It is not possible to indicate a single source of religious development and all causes do not operate at the same time. By far the most potent and abiding cause, however, is the rational and ethical faculty of man which cannot rest permanently satisfied with the latent contradictions of a creed or the antisocial implications of a baneful religious practice. It is indeed true that very often in a backward race the quickening of theoretical and practical reason has to be achieved by painful and persistent effort, if not by active interference from without: but once the social quickening does come, it is impossible to stem the tide of progress, even though occasional retardations, due to the imitation of lower ideals or to momentary weakness of the social mind in times of crisis, are not unknown in religious history. Men may grow to the stature of great ideals—that is the hope and justification of missionary activity among backward races; but those who are engaged in the actual task of conversion know it only too well how comparatively easy it is to secure external conformity and how difficult it is to make the higher religion a living faith. The religion a man professes provides, in fact, the nucleus round which his whole life crystallises and the entire system of his thoughts and actions is organised. We have already remarked that intellectual culture and a deepened moral sense, howsoever acquired, deeply affect man's religious ideas just as, conversely, a developed religious consciousness has profound effects upon man's ethical ideas. In delineating the historical development of certain Indian religious systems we have indicated how man's conception of the nature and function of God is profoundly modified by subjective needs of the head and the heart and how when old practices are continued they are invested with a nobler spiritual significance. As Reinach pertinently remarks:[1] "The Deity is inaccessible to man; but at the various epochs traversed by civilisation, humanity has made God in its own likeness, and the gradual idealisation of this image is an essential part of the history of humanity itself."

It will be our task now to show that every living religion has been obliged to have recourse to some or other of these expedients to escape annihilation and that the course of development has always lain in the direction of a fuller recognition of the unity and ubiquity of God and of the brotherhood of men with its implications of social concord and social service. It is evident that unequal emphasis will be laid on these two aspects by different religions according as they were originally defective on the side of duty or on the side of devotion. The Hebrew religion with its well-developed conception of a tribal or national God required development on the aspect of social duty and intercommunal sympathy, while Buddhism with its elaborate ethical code required the complementary development on the aspect of religious devotion. Even where provision already exists for meeting both the demands, philosophical speculation and practical need may show the inadequacy of the existing concepts of deity and duty alike and lead to a more

[1] S. Reinach, *Orpheus*, p. 185.

comprehensive grasp of the nature of God and His relation to the world and of the domain of social obligations.

As Judaism furnishes a most instructive parallel to Hinduism, which we have already studied, we shall begin our exposition with that religion. There are obvious difficulties in comparing two creeds one of which has remained almost ethnic to the end among a people singularly inartistic in character while the other has developed on divergent lines of speculation and myth and did not remain an exclusive possession of a particular nation or tribe. The difficulties are increased by the fact that the Hebrew nation did not treat its scriptures consistently with the same reverence as the Hindus did, with the effect that later beliefs and traditions were more than once pushed up to the beginning of things.[2] Biblical scholars are now agreed that the Pentateuch in its present form is a synthesis of at least four different schools of thought [3]—the Yahwist, the Elohist, the Deuteronomist and the Priestly; that although manifest repetitions and contradictions and abrupt changes in matter and style serve to reveal the composite character of the collection in some places, it is not always easy to allocate to each tradition its share in the whole; and that here and there are evidences of much more ancient materials being embedded in the documents of Hebrew religious thought. But, in spite of the dovetailing of different traditions, the Old Testament contains sufficient indications, on the surface, of the tampering of earlier texts by later beliefs. Besides, the different books belonging to different ages present divergent pictures of the national God: in fact, the differences are sometimes as great as those in Hinduism between the Upaniṣads and the Purāṇas regarding the nature and function of God.

A close examination of the books of the Bible as also of the archæological remains in the Canaanite home of the

[2] See W. Robertson Smith, *Old Testament in the Jewish Church*, Lect. XIII. The Narrative of the Hexateuch (p. 388f).

[3] Lods, *Israel*, p. 10f.; Bettany, *Judaism and Christianity*, p. 2f; *Hexateuch* (Vol. 2, p. 363) calls them the Covenant Code, the Deuteronomic and the Priestly (see also p. 365).

Jews has disposed once for all of a pre-Mosaic monotheism in which Renan and the pan-Babylonist school of Winckler fondly believed.[4] Neither the Semitic tribes as a whole nor the nomadic tribes in general nor the Israelites in particular were free at all times from the taint of animism and polytheism; and among the Semites, as among other primitive races, monotheism has been won by hard thinking and unremitting zeal. As Lods remarks,[5] " There is one fact which puts out of court the theory of a pre-Jahwistic Hebrew monotheism, in whatever form it may be advanced. It is that the Israelites, when they emerge into the full light of history and up to the time of the great prophets, although Jahwists, were not monotheists. They worshipped only one national god, Jahweh; but they believed in the existence and power of other gods: they were monolaters. But monolatry is a form of polytheism. Israel only attained to monotheism in the eighth century and to a clear and conscious monotheism only in the sixth, and that by a slow process of internal development whose stages we can trace." By collecting the traces of ancient thought and practice in Israelite institutions and beliefs of the better documented periods and by comparing these with the beliefs and customs of nomadic Semites—of pre-Islamic Arabs and Bedouins of to-day, Lods has proposed the following reconstruction of pre-Mosaic Hebrew beliefs. Like all primitive peoples the Hebrews were given to magic and believed in the efficacy of certain practices and objects in controlling " invisible powers, gods, demons, spirits, the souls of things." They regarded the dead with religious awe, invested them with divine character and worshipped their dead ancestors with libations on a *maṣṣebah* or a stele set up near the tomb.[6] They also worshipped a great number of trees, springs and rivers, caves and mountains. The sun, the moon and the stars were supposed to play an impor-

[4] Lods, *op. cit.*, p. 253, Appendix. (But see Sir Charles Marston, *The New Knowledge about the Old Testament*, Ch. III, for the opposite view; also p. 142.)

[5] *Ibid*, p. 257

[6] *Ibid*, p. 228.

tant part in men's lives.[7] Demons too were believed in as also possession by them. A belief in some god being the ancestor of a particular tribe or clan was present and even a physical relationship was often conceived. Nay, even "the constituent elements of the totemic system" were also present.[8] There was at first no clear differentiation between the various supernatural powers, which were often impersonally conceived; but latterly polydemonism moved towards polytheism and different gods even came to be regarded as "fathers" of different human groups and therefore as persons. It is doubtful, however, if there was any hierarchy of the gods, but it is very likely that Yahweh, the god of Sinai, had assumed sufficient personality before Moses made him the god of the Hebrew tribes as a whole. As compared with this name, the other three names of the Hebrew God,[9] *viz.* *Elohim* (deity), *El Shaddai* (almighty god?), *El Elyon* (God Most High) are definitely less personal.[10]

[7] Lods, *op. cit.*, p. 231.

[8] *Ibid*, p. 249. (See also Sir Charles Marston, *op. cit.*, p. 37; Cheyne, *Traditions and Beliefs of Ancient Israel*, p. xv.)

[9] *Ibid*, p. 210.

[10] See D'Alviella, *Origin and Growth of the Conception of God*, p. 149 f., where a similar impersonal sense is ascribed to the gods of the Western Semites (Baal, Adon, Moloch or Melek, El, etc.).

Many of the magical practices, the beliefs relating to the contagious nature of holiness and uncleanliness, and to the way in which the influence of the dead could attach itself to clothing and hair, show how far, at a certain period, superhuman powers were conceived as a fluid, as an impersonal force.

According to certain critics, the very ancient term which is found in all Semitic languages to express the idea of "god" under the various forms of *'el* (Hebrew), *ilu* (Babylonian), *ilah* (Arab) originally denoted the vague force which is the source of all strength and life, the divine rather than a god or a divine personality: it would have had a meaning similar to that of the term *mana* among the Polynesians, the Indian *brahman*, and the Latin *numen*.—Lods, *Israel*, p. 250.

It would also seem that the simplest explanation of the very peculiar use of the *plural elohim* to denote *a* god lies in this early lack of differentiation between the various supernatural powers. In Hebrew, the word *elohim*, literally meaning *gods*, in the plural, may be used to denote either several divine beings, or in speaking of a single god or goddess. And even when it has a singular meaning it may be construed with plural adjectives and verbs. The Phœnicians used the plural *elim* in the same way, while the Babylonians also applied the plural *ilani* to a single god......Doubtless, the worshipper, uncertain whether, in any particular place, he had to do with one or several supernatural beings, used the expression *elohim*, in the indeterminate sense of "the divine powers."—*Ibid*,

Mystery hangs round the name and origin of Yahweh whom Moses revealed to the Hebrews at Mount Sinai. The derivation of the word is uncertain,[11] but the general intention was to use it in the sense of an eternal being, possibly with the additional connotation of being a chastiser. This particular *elohim* is generally supposed to have been worshipped in this name by the Kenites who lived on the slopes of Mount Sinai; but the wide distribution of the name and its derivatives even in pre-Mosaic times lends colour to the supposition that "the worship of this god in pre-Mosaic times extended far beyond the narrow circle of the Kenites to Canaan and Babylonia," possibly even to Syria.[12] The supposition of the Elohist and the Priestly Code that the name was revealed for the first time to Moses [13] is certainly wrong, although it is not improbable that the Israelites had forgotten its original significance and had to give a new mean-

p. 251. The *Dictionary of the Bible* says that the term is a plural of eminence (Vol. II, p. 199). See also Otto, *The Idea of the Holy*, p. 205.

Söderblom's supposition is that the notion of Yahweh had its point of origin in earlier 'animistic' ideas......But what distinguishes Yahweh from El-Shaddai-Elohim is not that the former is an 'anima,' but.........that, whereas in Yahweh the numinous preponderates over the familiar 'rational' character, in Elohim the rational aspect outweighs the numinous.—Otto, *The Idea of the Holy*, pp. 76-7. See Abelson, *Jewish Mysticism*, pp. 150-1, where Yahweh is taken to represent the justice and Elohim the mercy aspect of God.

[11] The various meanings attached to the word are 'He that is,' 'He that calls into being,' 'He who makes fall' (*i.e.*, strikes down his enemies with the thunder-bolt). Exodus iii. 13-14 makes it "I am that I am" where "I am he who *is*" is meant, probably to make expression intentionally vague.—Lods, *Israel*, pp. 322-3. (See *Religious Systems of the World*, p. 52 n; Cheyne, *Traditions and Beliefs of Ancient Israel*, p. 530.)

Even its pronunciation is far from certain. Of course, it was never read as Jehovah: this name arose from a gross blunder of the first Christian Hebraists who, in the thirteenth century, read the consonants of the divine name *jhwh* with the vowels of *adonai* (lord), the word which the Jews, from reverential motives, substituted for it in the reading of the sacred text. The latter indicated this substitution by writing those vowels under the consonants of the tetragrammaton (*i.e.*, the four letters of the sacred name), in accordance with their usual method of marking a variation between the written and the spoken text: thus *JeHoWaH*.—Lods, *Israel*, p. 321. See also *Dic. Bi.*, Vol. II, p. 199; Extra Vol., p. 625f; also Kuenen, *National Religions and Universal Religions*, Note IV, p. 308f; Cheyne, *op. cit.*, pp. 99-100 (relation of Yahweh to Elohim).

[12] Lods, *op. cit.*, p. 320. See, however, W. Robertson Smith, *Old Testament in the Jewish Church*, p. 245 (with foot-note).

[13] Exod. 6.2-3.

ing to the term later on in conformity with contemporaneous religious ideas. Speaking of Moses' contribution, Lods remarks, "The true origin of his work must be sought in his remarkable conviction that his God was almighty and paramount, that he would deliver the Hebrews and make them his people." We may very well suppose that on embracing the creed of Yahweh the Israelites took the Kenite "mark of Yahweh" on their hand and their forehead[14] and that circumcision replaced later on this branding of the flesh.[15] It is almost certain that this device of warding off dangers from invisible powers was replaced also by phylacteries, or leather cases containing passages of the scriptures, which pious Jews of later times fastened at those places.[16]

Certain persistent traditions in connection with the cult of Yahweh can be safely utilised to gather together the factors that went to form this particular God-idea.[17] Thus Yahweh is said to have promised to Abraham in Haran that He would make of him "a great nation;" and this promise is repeated and observed over and over again in the Old Testament, so that there can be no doubt that Yahweh is "a god of increase, of generation, of populousness, of fertility." He was prayed to, by or on behalf of barren women, for children—Sarah, Rebekah, Leah, Manoah's wife, Hannah, all

[14] Exod. 13.16. See Lods, *op. cit.*, pp. 324-5; Marti, *Religion of the Old Testament*, p. 60f. ERE. vi. 254, states that the Kenite derivation is more than dubious.

[15] Three explanations of the origin of circumcision in Israel will be found in Ex. iv. 24-6 (Yahwist); Joshua v. 2-3, 8-9 (Elohist); Gen. xxxiv (Priestly). See also Gen. 17.10-4. The practice was not confined to the Israelites alone, for the Egyptians, Arabs, Phoenicians, Edomites, Ammonites and Moabites all practised it, the only exception being the Philistines. See Cheyne, *op. cit.*, pp. 532-6.

Originally the custom was a social rite without religious significance and it was only "during the exile, when the Jews came into close contact with peoples like the Babylonians and Persians, who did not practise the rite, that circumcision took on in the eyes of the Israelites the character of a symbol of nationality and religion." "Then it was that circumcision became the sign of the covenant between Jahweh and his people (Gen. xvii—Second Priestly) and was required of all, stranger or slave, who partook of the Passover (Exod. xii. 44, 47-9)."—Lods, *Israel*, p. 198f.

[16] Lods, *op. cit.*, p. 325. These phylacteries are still used by pious Jews.

[17] See Grant Allen, *The Evolution of the Idea of God*, Chaps. IX and X. Lods, *op. cit.*, p. 456f.

conceived by Yahweh's grace. As among the Hindus, barrenness was a curse among the Hebrews and they therefore permitted not only the remarriage of widows but also levirate and adoption.[18] As the lord of fertility and population, Yahweh could very well claim the first fruits of the field and the flock and also the first-born of men as His share.[19] At least three national festivals were held in connection with the harvest[20]—the Passover which was a "harvest thanksgiving" after barley-harvest, the Pentecost or the Feast of Weeks when the wheat had been completely gathered in, and the Feast of Tabernacles or of Ingathering after the whole of the yearly crop had been collected and the vintage prepared. "Young trees were not to be cropped till three years had passed; in the fourth year the fruit was offered to Jehovah, and only afterwards did it come into use by man."[21] Firstlings were sacrificed to Yahweh. The first-born sons, "in later stages at least, were either made over as Nazirites or redeemed with an offering or a money-ransom."[22] The

[18] Lods, *op. cit.*, p. 228.

[19] It has been suggested by Grant Allen that circumcision was probably practised at first on the first-born alone and then extended to all Jews.—G. Allen, *op. cit.*, Ch. X. See *Cambridge Ancient History*, Vol. III, p. 452.

It is not unlikely that Yahweh as the god of fertility belongs to the sphere of rural life in Canaan and represents the second stage only, the first being that of a god of the desert.

[20] Lods, *op. cit.*, p. 435; Marti, *op. cit.*, p. 101.

As the connection of these festivals with country life was gradually forgotten, the agricultural feasts were transformed into memorials of historical occurrences. The Passover, which had originally an entirely different signification, and the Feast of Mazzoth, the religious celebration of the beginning of harvest, became the historical anniversaries of the Exodus. Later, the Feast of Weeks was interpreted as the memorial celebration of the giving of the law on Mount Sinai—so we learn from sources outside the O.T.—while the Feast of Tabernacles, which had likewise been at first simply a harvest festival, was brought into connection with the dwelling in booths during the journeyings in the wilderness.—Marti, *op. cit.*, pp. 203-4. See also ERE. v. 864-5; Cheyne, *op. cit.*, p. 548.

The Passover is really a combination of two different festivals, namely, (1) the old Passover of the *nomads*, a spring festival in which the new-born animals of the year were sacrificed, and (2) the festival of the *peasants* at the beginning of the barley-harvest.

[21] Bettany, *op. cit.*, p. 45. Lev. 19. 9-10, 23-5; 23.22; Deut. 24. 19-22. The practice was Canaanite and meant to palliate the spirit of the field, the vine or the tree.—Lods, *op. cit.*, p. 402.

[22] Exod. 13.12-15.

legend of Moses and Zipporah, where circumcision is regarded as having been instituted as a substitute offering for a child, shows, however, that the dangerous logical practice of the sacrifice of the first-born, as was re-instituted later on by Ahaz and Manasseh, was not merely theoretically held but, as recent excavations reveal, was actually in vogue among the Hebrews as among the Canaanites,[23] thus fulfilling to the letter the divine injunction that on the eighth day "Thou shalt give to me the first-born of thy sons" (Ex. xxii. 29-30).

Closely related to this aspect are two other facts connected with the worship of Yahweh. It is difficult to explain how and why Yahweh came to be worshipped as a bull of gold in Dan and Bethel. Theriomorphism was rampant in Egypt where the ancestors of the Hebrews had sojourned long, and in Canaan itself Adad (or Hadad), a storm-god like Yahweh himself, had the bull as his sacred animal.[24] It is not unlikely that this universal symbol of virility was felt to be most congruous with the god of fertility which Yahweh was, and it is not till we come to the age of Hosea[25] that this mode of worship was publicly denounced. Yahweh was sometimes called a young bull and his temples were also decorated with bull-images.[26] The institution of circumcision and the practice of sacred prostitution in connection with the cult of Yahweh also bring out the prominence of the fertility-idea. The other fact is the prominent association of Yahweh with sacred stones. Grant Allen premises[27] "that the worship of the Baalim (gods), within and without

[23] Lods, *op. cit.*, pp. 89, 285-6, 292-4. (On p. 294 Lods's own theory on the subject would be found.) The practice of circumcision on the eighth day (Gen. 17.12) may be a reminiscence of the injunction to sacrifice the first-born on the eighth day to Yahweh. 1 Kings 16.34 is a fulfilment of Josh. 6.26 and does not probably refer to any human sacrifice.

[24] Lods, *op. cit.*, pp. 407, 459. For Egyptian influence, see p. 264 *infra*, f.n. 51.

[25] See *Dic. Bi.*, Vol. II, p. 423 (art. HOSEA).

[26] Lods, *op. cit.*, p. 458; also Grant Allen, *op. cit.*, pp. 131-2, where it is suggested that this symbol was transferred to Yahweh from some other god like Molech or that it was due to sacrifice of bulls to Yahweh. See 1 Kings 7.25, 29, 44; in Num. 23.22 and 24.8; buffalo horns are possibly ascribed to Yahweh (Lods, *op. cit.*, p. 458).

[27] Grant Allen, *op. cit.*, p. 131.

Israel, was specially directed to upright conical stones, the most sacred objects at all sanctuaries: and that these stones are generally admitted to have possessed for their worshippers a phallic significance." He hints at the possibility of a similar stone-pillar being the original content of the ark or chest in which Yahweh was supposed to possess his earthly seat and of the slabs of Ten Words (Commandments) being a priestly invention or a later substitute.[28] The association of upright stones (*maṣṣebah*) and wooden posts (*asherah*)[29] in the worship of Yahweh may also be referred to in this connection: they may have provided not merely visible symbols of the deity but also his original phallic significance.[30]

28 As the contents of the Ark were not allowed to be looked into, there is no exact description of them. It has been suggested that it probably contained "a meteorite stone, which, as it fell from heaven, was regarded as the abode of Jehovah." For other theories, see Lods, *op. cit.*, p. 425f; Marti, *op. cit.*, p. 44, 69; *Dic. Bi.*, Extra Vol., pp. 628-9; see also Grant Allen, *The Evolution of the Idea of God* (Thinker's Library Ed.), pp. 137, 139; Cheyne, *op. cit.*, pp. 31-5. It is not improbable that the Ark itself was made in commemoration of the Ark of Noah, the first prophet whom God favoured and saved and who was the mythical progenitor of the Semitic races through one of his sons. The infant Moses also floated in an ark before being rescued (see Gen. ii. 3-5).

29 Grant Allen thinks (*op. cit.*, p. 58) that both these were originally associated with burial—the wooden stake marking the grave and the standing stone serving as the tombstone. Of their further development he writes: "The wooden stake seems to form the origin or point of departure for the carved wooden image, as well as for such ruder objects of reverence as the cones and wooden pillars so widely reverenced among the Semitic tribes; while the rough boulder, standing stone, or tombstone, seems to form the origin or point of departure for the stone or marble statue, the commonest type of idol the whole world over in all advanced and cultivated communities."

30 See J. P. Peters, *Early Hebrew Story*, p. 181f. The following quotation is instructive (pp. 182-3): "There is a survival of this sexual cult in another form in the oath which Abraham exacted of his servant, with his hand upon his genitals (Gen. xxiv. 2). The thought behind this is, after all, the same in principle as the thought which originally connected itself with those pillars (*mazzebah*) which are so frequently mentioned in Genesis, and which formed an integral part of the Yahweh cult itself, in the conception of the best minds in Israel, as late as the time of Isaiah. Both the pillars and the oath suggest the meaning which originally attached to such a cult, expressing itself by worship offered to a stone of phallic shape, the use of phallic symbols as oblations, the oath by the organs of reproduction, and finally in prostitution itself as a ritual act." Lods, however, points out (*op. cit.*, p. 262) that as the pillars set up by the Semites might equally represent *goddesses*, the phallic significance could not have been universal. (See also p. 259 for the discussion on sacred stones.)

A second stream of thought that possibly entered into the composition of the Yahweh-idea was ancestor-worship and, in a country where the dead were buried and not cremated,[31] also the cult of tomb-stones. Although the oldest Hebrew belief was vague about the future state of the departed, the cult of the *manes* was fairly universal and the *teraphim*, sometimes of human form and size,[32] could be found in all households; food was offered to them as to household gods or departed ancestors at stated intervals; and "they were consulted on all occasions of doubt or difficulty by a domestic priest clad in an ephod." [33] It would be unusual in such a community not to possess monumental stones associated with this or that tribal ancestor, and, as a matter of fact, we find that, by the side of sacred trees, there were such stones as the altar of Abraham, the altar of Jacob, the memorial of Joshua and the altar or stone-pillar of Isaac.[34] One writer [35] observes: "Since we find the graves of the ancestors of Israel situated on mountains, or connected with places where there stood either a tree or a stone, it is impossible to avoid the conclusion to which we are led by many other considerations that the pre-Jehovistic worship was that of ancestors." In fact, all the four varieties of early tombstones, namely, the standing stone (*menhir*), the stone-table (*dolmen*), the stone-heap (*cairn*) and the stone circle (*cromlech*), could be found in Jewish religion: "the *menhir* is 'the pillar' of our Authorised Version of the Old Testament; the *dolmen* is the 'altar'; the *cairn* is the 'heap'; and the stone circle appears under the names Gilgal and Hazor."[36] A shaped stone, the mark of a ghost or god, was

31 The pre-Semitic inhabitants of Canaan used to burn their dead as excavations at Gezer show.—Peters, *op. cit.*, p. 98.

32 But see *Dic. Bi.*, Vol. II, p. 200.

33 Grant Allen, *op. cit.*, p. 126. Hosea seems to have considered the *teraphim* as indispensable in worship (Hos. 3.4).

34 Grant Allen, *op. cit.*, p. 129. Tombs of ancestors and heroes often appear as places of worship, *e.g.*, the grave of Miriam at Kadesh.—Marti, *op. cit.*, p. 54.

35 Rev. A. W. Oxford in *Religious Systems of the World*, p. 56.

36 Grant Allen, *op. cit.*, p. 68; see also art. GILGAL in *Dic. Bi.*, Vol. II, pp. 176-7. It is interesting to note that trees as well as these different kinds of stones were worshipped also in the Aegean religion.—See ERE. i.143.

known among the Hebrews as a Beth-el or "abode of deity."[37] Grant Allen throws out the suggestion, which he himself calls purely hypothetical, that just as 'cones with pyramidal heads, bearing inscriptions to the deceased, were used by the Phoenicians for interments,' so also 'the original Jahweh may have been such an ancient pillar, covered with writings of some earlier character, which were interpreted later as the equivalents or symbols of the "Ten Words" or, in other words, the conical stone pillar was 'the grave stone of some deified ancestor: and of this ancestor "Jahweh" was perhaps either the proper name or a descriptive epithet.'[38] If Moses is represented as setting up twelve stone-pillars[39] and an altar to Yahweh after receiving the revelations at Sinai,[40] it may be assumed that the former were meant to represent the twelve tribes of Israel—a kind of tribal memorial round the stone seat of the deified ancestor of the tribes Obviously keeping in mind the various modes which the worship

37 Grant Allen, *op. cit.*, p. 128. "Holy stones existed at Bethel (Gen. xxviii.18; xxxv.14). Ophrah (Judges vi.20), Zion (2 Sam. xxiv.16), Shechem (Josh. xxiv.26), Gilead (Gen. xxxi.45), Gilgal (Josh.iv) and other places" (*Rel. Sys. of the World*, p. 55). "If he (the Israelite) desired to know why there were specially sacred holy places in certain localities, such as Shechem, Bethel, Hebron, Beersheba, Penuel or Mahanaim, tradition replied that it was because in this particular spot, under the shade of this tree, beside this spring, at this sacred stone, Jahweh appeared to one of the ancestors of Israel in a dream (Bethel), in bodily form (Hebron, Penuel), by a verbal communication (Lahai Roi), by a miracle (at the waters of Kadesh)."—Lods, *Israel*, p. 156. See, in this connection, J. P. Peters, *Early Hebrew Story*, Lect. IV. Survivals—Legendary and Mythical; also Lods, *op. cit.*, pp. 261, 266. It is interesting to note that "the Jewish settlers at Elephantine, who still preserved in the fifth century (B.C.) many of the ancient customs of pre-exilic times, assigned to Jahweh a female consort, whom they called indifferently Anath-Jahu or Anath-Bethel" (Lods, *Israel*, p. 124; see also p. 135). See also *Camb. Anc. His.*, Vol. III, p. 430; Cheyne, *op. cit.*, p. xvi.

38 Grant Allen, *op. cit.*, p. 140. Lods is willing to admit that the ark was possibly a sacred sarcophagus in Canaanite sanctuaries later assumed by the Hebrews, but he does not think that Yahweh was ever regarded as an Osiris or an Adonis who died and was reborn annually (*Israel*, pp. 428-9).

39 Exod. 24.4 (*cf.* Josh. 4). Hosea (3.4; 10.2) and Isaiah (19.19) considered these pillars to be as indispensable as the altars themselves. The sacred poles (*asherah*) are similarly mentioned as standing by the altar of Yahweh (see *Rel. Sys. of the World*, p. 56) but they became objects of condemnation to strict Yahwists long before the pillars (Lods, *op. cit.*, p. 425).

40 In later times altars of brass were raised in the temple at Jerusalem; but Exod. 20.24, 25 tacitly condemn them. (See also 2 Kings 16.10-1.)

of Yahweh assumed in later times, Grant Allen traces the following interesting development from ancestor worship to nature worship:[41]

"In the first place, we must recollect that while in Egypt, with its dry and peculiarly preservative climate, mummies, idols, tombs and temples might be kept unchanged and undestroyed for ages, in almost all other countries rain, wind, and time are mighty levellers of human handicraft. Thus, while in Egypt the cult of the Dead Ancestor survives as such quite confessedly and openly for many centuries, in most other countries the tendency is for the actual personal objects of worship to be more and more forgotten; vague gods and spirits usurp by degrees the place of the historic man; rites at last cling rather to sites than to particular persons. The tomb may disappear; and yet the sacred stone may be reverenced still with the accustomed veneration. The sacred stone may go; and yet the sacred tree may be watered yearly with the blood of victims. The tree itself may die; and yet the stump may continue to be draped on its anniversary with festal apparel. The very stump may decay; and yet gifts of food or offerings of rags may be cast as of old into the sacred spring that once welled beside it. The locality thus grows to be holy in itself, and gives us one clear and obvious source of later nature-worship."

We have, however, already alluded to the fact that the peculiar theophanies of Yahweh are intimately associated with certain elemental phenomena. Numerous passages can be quoted [42] to prove that Yahweh was sometimes conceived as the storm-god and that every thunder-cloud disclosed his presence. "Since the sight of Jehovah brought death, the thunder-clouds which concealed him were regarded as friendly spirits; they were called Cherubim.[43] The flashes of lightning, too, were regarded as spirits, and called Seraphim,

[41] Grant Allen, *op. cit.*, p. 145.

[42] For instance, Judges 5.4; 6.21; Ps. 29; Exod. 3.2; 19.16; 1 Kings 8.10; 18.38; Isaiah 6. (See *Religious Systems of the World*, p. 54; *Cam. Anc. His.*, III, p. 430; Cheyne, *op. cit.* p. 30f.)

[43] Ps. 18.10; 1 Kings 6.23. See ERE. vi. 254 where the storm-derivation is regarded as merely conjectural.

probably from an old idea that they were snakes."[44] Probably because clouds so frequently rested on mountains, Yahweh was supposed to have his seat on mountains,[45] and hence when the Israelites occupied Canaan, the high places where the Canaanite gods (*baals*) used to be worshipped could very easily be converted into sanctuaries of Yahweh. In fact, this mountain abode was such a persistent association among the Hebrews (who probably imitated in this respect the Babylonians whose great temples were modelled on mountain sanctuaries and had *ziggurats* or peaks at the top) that in their temples a dark chamber on the summit of an artificial mountain (in imitation of a cloud-capped peak) was reserved for God and offerings were made at the foot of this artificial mountain.[46] But as the mountain where Yahweh first manifested himself to Moses, namely, Mount Sinai, was probably a volcano, the features of that mount attached themselves to Yahweh—possibly this association was even pre-Mosaic.[47] To quote Lods:[48] "The story was told that, like the volcano, Jahweh had appeared to the Israelites in the wilderness under the form of a pillar of fire by night and a pillar of cloud by day. He had revealed himself to Abraham as a blazing torch and a smoking furnace (Gen. xv. 17). The temple was filled with smoke when the ark was brought into it in the time of Solomon (1 Kings viii. 10-11) and when Isaiah received the vision there which called him to the prophetic office (Isa. vi. 4). Thunder was the voice of Jahweh. Poets described the march of Jahweh shrouded in dark clouds, discharging hail-stones and coals of fire. The God of Sinai appeared to Moses " in a flame in the midst of a bush." " The glory of Jahweh " was a divine fire of dazzling brightness flashing at intervals from the storm-cloud which concealed it; sometimes this fire seems to have been thought of as surrounding sometimes as constituting the body of the deity. The chariots and horses of the heavenly host are of fire." When

44 Isa. 6.6 (*cf.* Ahi Budhnya of the Rigveda). See 2 Kings 18.4.

45 Gen. 22.14; Num. 23.3; Deut. 33.19; 2 Sam. 15.32; 1 Kings 20.23.

46 Peters, *op. cit.*, pp. 102-3.

47 See Exod. 19.18-9. See Cheyne, *op. cit.*, p. 563.

48 Lods, *op. cit.*, pp. 456-7.

Yahweh was invoked to consume the offering of calf on the altar, he came down as a lightning and burnt up the sacrifice and he sent down fire frcm above to consume Ahaziah's 'captain of fifty with his fifty' at Elijah's invocation.[49] When he wanted to punish sinners he sent down fire and brimstone.

But there were other natural associations too. The recent discovery of the Laws of Hammurabi and the general resemblance of the Jewish laws with these laws of Babylon raise a very strong suspicion that "Palestine was a descendant of Babylonia, not in the literal sense of descent of blood, but in the equally real sense of descent of thought, religion and civilisation."[50] Sandwiched between the two imperial powers of Egypt and Babylon, which possessed advanced civilisations of their own, and politically dominated by these and other superior powers for a long time, the Palestinian civilisation could not avoid either unconscious or deliberate absorption of other cultures. All facts connected with the history of Moses (as of Joseph) point to the infiltration of the culture of the west,[51] while the eastern culture seems to have come through a mythical ancestor, Abraham.[52] The Judaean tradition connects Abraham with Haran in Mesopotamia and Ur

[49] 1 Kings 18.38; 2 Kings 1.10; Judges 6.21; 13.20.

[50] Peters, *op. cit.*, p. 157. See Lods, *op. cit.*, pp. 165-6; also *the Laws of Hammurabi* (R.P.A. series). Prof. Clay thinks that the greater part of the Code of Hammurabi originated in Aleppo.—See Lods, *op. cit.*, p. 81. Marti thinks that there was no direct borrowing.—See *op. cit.*, p. 12.

[51] Peters shows the similarity between the exposure of Moses on the Nile and that of King Sargon of Babylonia on the Euphrates.—See *op. cit.*, p. 192 Also Marti, *op. cit.*, p. 19.

Marti thinks that the Egyptian influence came during the Canaanite period rather than at the time of the Exodus (*op. cit.*, p. 44). See Lods, *op. cit.*, p. 318 f. (Appendix). The trend of modern opinion is that the Exodus was from North Arabia and not from Egypt. See Cheyne, *op. cit.*, p. xviif.

[52] The distinction between the stories of Moses, Samuel and David and the stories of Abraham, Isaac and Jacob is that in the former the legendary elements are adornments of the tale due to the fancy of the story-teller, his desire to display his knowledge of the times and conditions in which his heroes lived and acted, and his effort to make vivid and real the tale which he tells; in the latter the legend is the essence, the kernel of the story; the character itself is legend.— J. P. Peters, *Early Hebrew Story*, pp. 194-5.

in Babylonia, both of which were famous for their worship of the moon-god Sin. Further association of Abraham with this god is indicated by certain names in the family of Abraham. The sons of Terah are Abraham, Nahor and Haran, the last of which name is the same as that of the Mesopotamian seat of the moon-god. The wives of Nahor and Abraham, again, are Milkah and Sarah, and these are also titles of the goddess associated with Sin at Haran (and possibly also at Ur).[53] Now it is at Sinai, the mountain seat of Sin,[54] that Moses received his revelation, which probably means that Yahweh replaced Sin at that sanctuary; but the fact that the Jews of later times managed to forget even the identity of this cradle of their religion [55] raises the suspicion that the place never became a stronghold of Yahwist worship at any time. Probably the movement of the population further north into lands where other high and holy places were available rendered the retention of the Sinai sanctuary unnecessary—the Bible says, the Israelites were driven away by Yahweh from the foot of Sinai where they had wished to settle (Ex. xxxii. 34; xxxiii. 15). The relation of Sin and Yahweh at Sinai was reflected in Hebrew genealogy where Moses is made a descendant of Abraham,[56] just as independent cycles of legends connected

See, however, Reinach, *Orpheus*, p. 200: "Abraham, Jacob and Joseph, often supposed to have been tribal gods, may have been real persons." See also *Dic. Bi.*, Vol. III, p. 200.

[53] Peters, *op. cit.*, pp. 158-9. See, however, Marti, *op. cit.*, p. 39f; he thinks that Arabia was originally the home of the peoples of the Semitic world (p. 41). For the identification of Haran, see Sir Charles Marston, *op. cit.*, pp. 51-3; Cheyne, *op. cit.*, pp. 211-5.

[54] See Enc. Br. (14th Ed.), Vol. 20, p. 703, art. SINAI; *Dic. Bi.*, IV, p. 536, art. SINAI MOUNT; *Century Dictionary and Encyclopaedia*, VI, p. 934. See, however, Cheyne, *op. cit.*, pp. 526-7, also p. 28. The etymology of the word is uncertain; generally it is derived from a word meaning 'thorn-bush.'

See also Sir Charles Marston, *op. cit.*, Ch. XIII. Sinai. He refers to the Temple of Serabit where Hathor was worshipped by the Semites who worked the neighbouring turquoise mines.

[55] Interesting information about the attempts to identify Sinai would be found in Lods, *Israel*, p. 176f. He thinks that the eastern coast of the Gulf of Akabah in Arabia proper (where there is a line of craters, now extinct, but one of which, Harrat al-Nar (crater of fire), near Medina, is attested to have been active during the historical period) is probably the location of Sinai.

[56] For Israelite holy places associated with Abraham—Hebron, Beersheba,

with Abraham, Isaac, Jacob and Joseph were unified through a similar genealogical succession.[57] Other associations with the cult of heavenly bodies are not locally absent. Jericho, Laban (Jacob's father-in-law) and the Lebanon mountains all carry the moon-association, while the cult of Shamash, the sun-god of Babylonia, lingers in such names as Samson, Bethshemesh, etc., and in the practice of setting up pillars to Yahweh as to Shamash. Although rarely, Yahweh is represented by the winged disk,[58] symbolising the Sun; and the monoliths which more frequently stand for Yahweh have been regarded also as representing the solar rays.[59] The sabbath and the newmoon were taken over from the Babylonian cult of the heavenly bodies and attached to Yahweh,[60] which explains the hostility of the prophets to these heathen institutions. The horned altars of Yahweh, if not derived from a bull, were probably taken from the crescent moon. There is no doubt that the temptation to find room for the solar cult within Yahwism persisted as an undercurrent and the influence of Babylonia and Assyria could not be entirely stemmed. Ahaz and Manasseh only systematised the worship of the heavenly bodies, and horses and chariots were given to the Sun at the entrance of the temple of Yahweh himself by the kings of Judah. The facility with which the cult of the various Baalim was absorbed must be due to the same reason, for a Baal represented not only the generative principle in nature (as Ashtoreth the productive principle) but also the Sun-god

Bethel and Shechem, see Peters, *op. cit.*, p. 165. Jacob was associated with the last three as also with Mahanaim, Penuel (or Peniel), Gilead and Mizpah. Isaac was associated with Beersheba and Joseph with Shechem.—*Ibid.*, p. 137.

57 Peters, *op. cit.*, Lect. III. The Patriarchs and the Shrines of Israel (esp. pp. 114 and 126). In later times there was a regular worship of the Moon (Ishtar, the queen of heaven) by the women specially (see Jer. 7.18; 44.17-9, 25).

58 Lods, *op. cit.*, p. 459. See *Dic. Bi.*, Vol. II, p. 429 f.n. (under art. THE HOST OF HEAVEN); also *Cam. Anc. His.*, III, pp. 428, 431. Josiah broke down the sun-images above the altars of the Baalim (2 Chr. 34.4-6). See ERE. vii. 488, art. MASSEBHAH (astronomical association).

59 Lods, *op. cit.*, p. 237 for association with the sun, the moon and the stars in pre-Mosaic belief.

60 Lods, *op. cit.*, p. 438f.

"In Babylonian the corresponding word 'sapathu' (sabathu) denotes not the seventh day but the full moon. The weekly festival of the Sabbath only arose, therefore, by an artificial transmutation of the festival of the full moon,

(like Adad and Rimmon).[61] The cult of the heavenly bodies could be conquered only when Yahweh came to be called the Lord of the Host, when the stars came to be regarded as "the visible image, or counterpart, of the host, or army, of angels, by which Jahweh was conceived to be surrounded," [62] and when even the prophets of Israel were considered to be able to make the sun stand still.[63] The iconoclasm of Josiah, who completed the act of religious reform initiated by Hezekiah, saved Israel from this solar cult.

It may at once be admitted, however, that by the time of the Old Testament the phallic, the euhemeristic and the naturalistic associations of Yahweh [64] had been so well dominated by the personal aspect that there was no serious danger about the Israelites forsaking that aspect in favour of the different primitive elements that must have originally entered into the composition of Yahweh. Cook well observes: [65] "Preserved here and there in the Old Testament we have, in fact, the *disjecta membra* of cults which are more reminiscent of the barbarism and mythology of the old Oriental world than of that spiritual idealism and ethical monotheism which distinguish the higher religion of Israel from other religions. How the cult of Yahweh was introduced we do not really know, and the deeper study of the Old Testament in the light of archæological and other evidence suggests the very important conclusion that an older and cruder Yahwism has disappeared, and an entire chapter is missing between the Amarna age [66] and the rise of the Old Testament." The

which was not peculiar to Israel alone.—Marti, *op. cit.*, p. 15; also p. 85. See ERE. v. 863; also Cheyne, *op. cit.*, p. 69.

61 See *Cambridge Companion to the Bible* (1893), pp. 162-3; also *Cam. Anc. His.*, III, p. 431.

62 *Dic. Bi.*, Vol. II, p. 430.

63 Jos. 10.12-3.

64 See *Cam. Anc. His.*, III, p. 426f (II. The Old Yahwism).

65 *Cam. Anc. His.*, III, pp. 431-2.

66 The reference is to the correspondence of the princes of Syria and Palestine with their overlords Amenophis (Amenhetep) III and IV (Akhenaten) discovered at Tel el-Amarna. See Sir Charles Marston, *op. cit.*, Ch. XV. Tel El-Amarna.

same writer points out [67] that in the construction, contents and ritual of the Temple of Jerusalem could be found elements borrowed from surrounding cultures, including those of South Arabia, Crete and Cyprus. Again, Egyptian, Mesopotamian, Babylonian, Hittite and other religions contributed to the evolution of the composite temple-religion of the Israelites, for when they moved into Canaan they could easily come into contact with the cult of the gods of those religions as absorbed by the native population and utilise the necessary elements to start a new temple-cult after old well-established models. In fact, it would not be inappropriate to compare the Hebrew conquest of Palestine with the Aryan invasion of North-west India—both the Hebrews and the Aryans were less advanced in material civilisation than the Canaanites and the Indus-valley people whom they respectively displaced and they could not resist the temptation of mixing or identifying this or that feature of their own religion with similar features of the native cults. One notable absorption in both Palestine and India was serpent-worship, perhaps derived ultimately from Egyptian sources in the one case and from savage tribes in the other. The brazen serpent (probably a Jebusite idol), pushed back to the Mosaic age,[68] became an integral part of the Yahweh cult in the Hebrew religion (as did a goddess Asherah) and disappeared only after Hezekiah's reform, while the serpent found its way into both Vaiṣṇavism and Śaivism as indispensable to Viṣṇu's rest on the Ocean of Milk, the churning of the ocean, and the ornamentation of Śiva's body, in addition to being the object of an independent cult (of Manasā) down to the present day.[69] But

[67] See *Cam. Anc. His.*, III, p. 427 (and Lods, *op. cit.*, p. 415) for the probable origin of the ark, the cherubim, the lion, the lions, the molten (brazen) sea, the shewbread, the horned altar, the bronze pillars, the sacred pillars, etc., in the Temple of Jerusalem. (Also Reinach, *Orpheus*, pp. 187, 197; Sir Charles Marston, *op. cit.*, p. 60 f., for an account of the Phœnician Tablets found at Ras Shamra.)

[68] Lods, *op. cit.*, p. 404; J. Yahuda, *Law and Life according to Hebrew Thought*, p. 27.

[69] See Vogel, *Indian Serpent-Lore*, p. 192 f; see p. 202: "Whereas Śesha is closely connected with Vishṇu, we find Vāsuki associated with Śiva: the Serpent-King is supposed to be slung round that god's neck." Association with Śiva

in Palestine there were other assimilations too. The Canaanites had drawn freely upon the Aegean, the Egyptian, the Babylonian, the Hittite and other surrounding cultures for secular objects and religious symbols [70] and also the Phoenician for their alphabet. Recent excavations have brought out interesting remains of many foreign gods in Palestine of the pre-Israelite age,[71] many of which were possibly used as amulets. Sacred pillars, grottos (possibly inhabited by a serpent-god), chambers, altars, censers, etc., formed part of the religious equipment,[72] and human sacrifice was practised generally as a foundation-rite. Theriomorphism was present—possibly also totemism.[73] Local divinites were worshipped " on every high hill and under every green tree " under the title of Baals,[74] and inasmuch as they were conceived as persons they often figured as relations.[75] More often these gods were regarded as overlords of their own special cities or tribes, as Milkom of the Ammonites, Chemosh of the Moabites and Baal-zebub of Ekron, although some like Hadad, Shemesh, Gad and Dagon were more widely worshipped.[76] Possibly, Yahweh himself was worshipped in Canaan before the Israelites settled there.[77] There were female deities (Baalath) too, and of these Astarte was the most prominent (and sometime the general designation). [78]

would be more natural if this God had a Sumerian prototype as is claimed by Sir John Marshall in his *Mahenjo Daro.*

70 See Lods, *op. cit.*, p. 63f (II. Foreign Relations).

71 Lods, *op. cit.*, p. 86; p. 137 (Foreign Divinities). See also Marti, *op. cit.*, p. 72f; he thinks that the images of Egyptian gods were worshipped probably by the Egyptian residents of Canaan (p. 79).

72 See *Cam. Anc. His.*, III, p. 447.

73 For similar beliefs in Judaism after settlement in Palestine, see *Cam. Anc. His.*, III, p. 444.

74 Lods, *op. cit.*, p. 120; Marti, *op. cit.*, p. 91.

75 Marti thinks that this was due to the extension of the cult of ancestor-worship.—*Op. cit.*, p. 54. See Lods, *op. cit.*, p. 241.

76 Individual deities stand out from the great mass of demons, and these were plainly imagined to be personal gods, such as Astarte and Baal by the side of Hadad and Aschirat.—Marti, *op. cit.*, p. 83.

77 Lods, *op. cit.*, p. 132. See Sir Charles Marston, *op. cit.*, p. 61.

78 Lods, *op. cit.*, p. 132f.

Astarte must have been the object of especial veneration, for many pictures have already been found of this goddess, whereas no single image of Ba'al has

So when the Israelites moved into Canaan they came into a region where polydaemonism and polytheism were the prevailing creed and religious worship centred round the local baals and astartes and was often sanguinary in character.

That the immigrants quickly adopted and then persisted in the worship of many of these baals and astartes can be made out easily from the repeated denunciations of the popular religion by the prophets of Israel.[79] They had possessed only a nomadic cult suited to the austere life of the desert and so when they moved into a region full of fertile low lands, where agriculture was the main occupation, they simply imitated the local inhabitants in the cults connected with their new occupation.[80] In fact, even when they overthrew the worship of the local deities and installed their own Yahweh in their place, the Canàanite cults lingered on and were, therefore, often attacked by the prophets at a later time. Thus the sanctuaries of Yahweh were multiplied and planted where the baals had been worshipped before, much as Christian churches were built on the foundations of pagan temples at a later time, and very often Yahweh himself was supposed to possess different attributes and powers at these different places.[81] "One temple implied one God" and "a local Jehovah was practically a local Baal."[82] It was left to Josiah (and the Deuteronomic Code) to prohibit all sacred places outside Jerusalem and to restore visibly the unity of Yahweh. Thenceforth pilgrimage to these different shrines

been discovered in the soil of Palestine. It is no doubt possible that this may be accounted for by the fact that the Astarte was the goddess of the home and of the increase of the family, whereas the images of Ba'al were not kept in the house, and had therefore disappeared.—Marti, *op. cit.*, pp. 92-3.

79 Gideon, Jephthah, Samuel, Saul, David, Solomon, Ahab and many such leaders and kings were guilty of religious lapses. (See W. R. Smith, *Old Testament in the Jewish Church*, p. 235f.)

80 Marti, *op. cit.*, p. 104. The nature of Yahweh as originally a storm-god facilitated the transference to him of the functions of the Canaanite gods of agriculture.

81 Marti, *op. cit.*, p. 105; Lods, *op. cit.*, p. 407; *Rel. Sys. of the World*, pp. 54-5. *Cf.* Deut. 6.4: "Hear, O Israel, Yahweh, our God, is one Yahweh." This is the Shema which is recited morning and evening as a confession of faith.

82 *Dic. Bi.*, Vol. III, p. 788, art. JOSIAH; W. R. Smith, *Old Test. in the Jewish Church*, p. 243.

ceased. It is in Canaan, again, that regular national festivals, generally associated with agriculture, were instituted, and, in place of the occasional sacrifices of the nomadic days on an improvised altar of earth or unhewn stone as sacramental communions, there was instituted a regular system of national and private sacrifices, on fixed altars, of first fruits and firstlings, as thanksgiving festivals,[83] and the revolting practices of human sacrifice and sacred prostitution were also introduced. Against these too the classical prophets had to wage relentless campaigns, and although they could not abolish the sacrifices altogether they could invest some of them with an enhanced spiritual meaning. That the nation as a whole did not entirely forget the good old nomad days is evident from the fact that the Rechabites bound themselves to observe all the rules of nomadic life (2 Kings x. 15-16; Jer. xxxv), that the Nazirites abjured, among others, wine, presumably because it was a product of Canaanite vineyards [84] and a favourite libation of the baals, and that the Passover of the nomad days, when probably the first-born of the flock were sacrificed, became the most important national festival.[85]

Lods has given an excellent summary of the effects of the Canaanite contact on the religion of the Israelites.[86] Some of the immigrants forgot their national god altogether and began to worship the baals and the astartes. The majority worshipped the baals and Yahweh simultaneously, for it was felt that Yahweh's seat was in Sinai or Mount Seir and he had no fixed seat in Canaan. Some worshipped Yahweh in days of trouble as the national deliverer while in the days of prosperity they paid their homage to the baals. Idols, such as the

[83] Marti, *op. cit.*, p. 102; Lods, *op. cit.*, p. 290. For the sacrifices mentioned in the Ras Shamra Tablets, see Sir Charles Marston, *op. cit.*, p. 62.

[84] Lods, *op. cit.*, pp. 101, 283, 305f, 410f and also p. 388 (the Kenites). Hosea had to preach that corn, wine and oil all came from Yahweh and not from the baals as the people seemed to think (2.8, 22), thus establishing the claim of Yahweh to be the only giver of all goods. See *Dic. Bi.*, Extra Vol., p. 657 f.

For the Nazirite vow, see Num. vi.

[85] Lods, *op. cit.*, p. 290 f.

[86] Lods, *op. cit.*, p. 403f; see *Cam. Anc. His.*, III, p. 434; *Dic. Bi.*, II, p. 446, art. IDOLATRY; also J. Huxley, *Religion without Revelation*, p. 233f.

brazen serpent and the Asherah, found their way into the temples of Yahweh and even female consorts were found for him. Gradually, however, Yahweh became the sole object of worship; but all the titles and attributes of the baals were transferred to him either because some similarity was established by the Israelites between him and these gods or because the native population gave a place to the god of the immigrants in their own sanctuaries and he later usurped all the sacred spots (high places, springs, trees, stones, etc.), associated with the baals. Readily, some mythical patriarch or other was supposed to have established those sanctuaries as seats of Yahwist worship in remote times or possibly these baals were themselves converted into some remote human ancestors of the Jewish race.[87] Finally, Yahweh became *the* god of the land and Palestine became the land of Yahweh,[88] although the multiplicity of the original Canaanite gods continued to manifest itself in the multiple rites, attributes and powers attached to Yahweh at different places. He himself was frequently called *baal* (lord) and was transformed from a god of nomads to a god of peasants with the local rites and practices transferred to his cult. But there was also some real gain during the Palestinian settlement, for the power of Yahweh was now extended over the whole of Canaan and the Israelites could now have faith in the power and providence of Yahweh wherever they might go and did not have to serve other gods, as was the nomadic custom when people moved into other lands or were outlawed or exiled (1 Sam. xxvi. 19).[89] Yahweh ceased to be conceived regionally and became a truly national god of the Israelites, more powerful than the gods of their neighbours. He confounded the calcula-

87 Abraham, Isaac, Jacob and Joseph, before being presented as founders of certain holy places, had been their gods or "baals": Abraham at Hebron, Isaac at Beersheba, Jacob at Bethel, and perhaps Joseph at Shechem.—Lods, *op. cit.*, p. 161. See D'Alviella, *The Origin and Growth of the Conception of God*, p. 136.

88 Lods, *op. cit.*, p. 451f.

89 The principle was later on extended to other gods and the wives of the Israelite princes often brought the statues of the gods of their own country and even had temples built to them (1 Kings 11. 7-8; 16.31-2).

tions of the Syrians under Ben-hadad who had thought that as a god of the hills he would be powerless on the plains (1 Kings xx. 28). In fact, he always led the Israelites in their battles and his ark was carried before the Jewish host as an emblem of his presence in their midst wherever they might go.[90] But the idea very often was that although he could be invoked anywhere, he had his special earthly seat originally in South Palestine and the desert (Deut. xxxiii. 2; Hab. iii. 3) and later on in the temple at Jerusalem (although Solomon himself had his doubts if God could be confined to any earthly seat, including the temple built by him, when "heaven and the heaven of heavens" could not contain him).[91] The compromise between the two views took later on the form of a temple-worship strictly confined to Jerusalem and a less formal worship offered at any place to Yahweh, just as an earlier compromise had permitted the retention of the sanctuaries in high places but cut down the image of the Asherah and destroyed the idols (1 Kings xv. 12-3).[92]

That the exclusive cult of Yahweh could be established only with great difficulty and retained with equal difficulty is evident through every epoch of Jewish history. The original immigrants did not question the right of the different nations and tribes to have gods of their own, and when they protested against their own people worshipping or consulting the oracles of the gods of other people it was not because these gods were " nothings," as the later prophets said, but because it implied scant respect paid to their own god Yahweh : " Is it because there is no God in Israel, that ye go to enquire of Baal-zebub the god of Ekron?" is the question that the angel of Yahweh asked Elijah to put to the mes-

90 See, for instance, Deut. 23.12-4 where the Israelites are directed to keep their tents clean because God walks in their midst there.

91 1 Kings 8.27. See *Cam. Anc. His.*, III, pp. 432-3.

92 See Lods, *op. cit.*, p. 413. Asa and Hezekiah were responsible for these reforms before Josiah (1 Kings 15.12-3; 2 Kings 18.4, 22) : if Hezekiah had also removed " the high places," they apparently grew up again. For Hezekiah's reforms, see *Dic. Bi.*, II, pp. 376, 148.

35

sengers of Ahaziah, the king of Israel.[93] They took delight in the humiliations that Yahweh inflicted on the gods of other people, *e.g.*, on Dagon, the Canaanite corn-god.[94] The large-hearted tolerance and the universalism of Yahwist worship that could prompt an Isaiah to say,[95] " In that day shall Israel be the third with Egypt and with Assyria, a blessing in the midst of the earth," or a Malachi to make Yahweh say,[96] " From the rising of the sun even unto the going down of the same my name is great among the Gentiles; and in every place incense is offered unto my name, and a pure offering," were absent at the time of the Palestinian settlement and Yahweh was veritably " a jealous god," [97] insisting upon the strict obedience of the Israelites (whom He had led out of Egypt and through the wilderness and the sea to a land of comparative plenty and peace and formed into one nation) [98] and probably also prohibiting the indigenous population from worshipping him with full rites.[99] This exclusiveness the Jews have practically retained ever since, although matrimonial and other alliances with the native population, a limited amount of proselytization and the sojourn of a large body of strangers (*gérim*) in their midst at one time must have inevitably led to the inclusion of a large number of non-Israelites within the Hebrew fold: as a matter of fact, Judah was an object of contempt to Israel exactly because a larger admixture of non-Jewish population had led

93 Lods, *op. cit.*, p. 455; also p. 313.

94 1 Sam. 5.3. See also Lods, *op. cit.*, p. 128 for note on Dagon.

95 Isa. 19.24.

96 Malachi 1.11.

97 Lods points out (*op. cit.*, p. 313) that in this the Hebrews did not stand alone, for other nations had equally jealous gods.

98 The period of the sojourn at Kadesh, culminating in the journey to " the holy mount," seems to have been the decisive moment when the Hebrew tribes formed themselves into a nation, and adopted the worship of Jahweh as their national religion.—Lods, *op. cit.*, p. 180.

99 For attitude towards different tribes and nations, see, for instance, Deut. 23.3-8.

to the debasing of the Yahwist cult there.[100] Idolatry, however, soon made its appearance all over Palestine—sometimes in a gross form and at other times in a subtle form—and images of Yahweh and the brazen serpent were plentiful in number even in Jerusalem where the Great Temple of Yahweh, housing the Ark which David had brought to Zion, should have rendered them unnecessary. Household gods (teraphim) too, a legacy of the nomadic times, continued to exist undisturbed by the side of Yahweh, of whom probably the baals were formidable rivals in men's allegiance but the teraphim were not foemen worthy of his steel.

The survival of primitive beliefs of the pre-Mosaic age,[101] which the Hebrews shared with other nomadic Semites, also hindered the spiritual development of the Yahweh-concept. There was not only a fully organised cultus of the ancestors of families and clans and of heroes as well, but also a widespread belief in " invisible powers, gods, demons, spirits, the souls of things " and in the capacity of man to control them by appropriate acts and utterances,[102] either in the interest of the individual or in that of the tribe. Blessings, cursings, oaths and mourning rites were supposed to have a magical effect;[103] divination and prophecy were regarded as methods of revealing the divine will;[104] springs and rivers could mete out punishment and expose guilt in trials by ordeal without any reference to God; and evil could be averted by charms, talismans and ornaments that had magical properties. Evil spirits in animal and hybrid forms infested the deserts and the tombs, and also caused madness, leprosy and plagues of all kinds. Trees, springs and mountains, on the other hand, were the haunts

100 Gideon's golden ephod and the graven image at Dan prove that even image worship was no innovation of Jeroboam.—W. R. Smith, *Old Testament in the Jewish Church*, p. 244. See *Dic. Bib.*, II, p. 447. For the post-exilic attitude of the Jews towards the Samaritans, see Cheyne, *Jewish Religious Life after the Exile*, p. 25 f.

101 See Lods, *op. cit.*, p. 209 f; *Dic. Bib.*, II, p. 445 f, art. IDOLATRY. See p. 253 *supra*.

102 Num. 22-24.

103 Lods, *op. cit.*, p. 479.

104 *Ibid.*, p. 299f.

and abodes of gods, and Moses is represented as putting a boundary round the foot of Mount Sinai lest the people at large should touch the mountain impregnated with divine energy and have to be stoned or shot through. The gods were often looked upon as members of the social group. The moon and the stars were regarded as divine and as capable of aiding or injuring men. There were, again, taboos of various sorts, mostly connected with sex-life, death, food and worship, which determined the nature and duration of ceremonial purity and impurity and the distinction between clean and unclean (or sacred and secular) persons and animals.[105] Blood was ceremonially spilt on sacred stones to honour or invigorate a god (just as libations were offered to departed persons on pillars near their graves); they were kissed (as the Black stone of the Ka'ba is still done by the pilgrims at Mecca) and anointed with oil; incense was burned to them; and they were very often erected in holy places and addressed as gods. Ceremonial slaughter of criminals and enemies (*herem*) took its rise most probably out of this bloody sacrifice to sacred stones, and Yahweh was often represented as directing the Israelites to put whole populations to the sword and punishing them in case of default.[106] It appears, therefore, that, as Lods observes, " the Hebrews peopled their world, in pre-Mosaic times, with powers and spirits whom they regarded in much the same way as the Canaanite countryfolk seemed to have thought of their baals. And this comparison helps us to understand why the Israelites, when they settled in Palestine, found it so easy to adopt the religious practices of the natives: it was because these practices corresponded to the ideas and the needs which had been those

[105] *Rel. Sys. of the World*, p. 58.

[106] 1 Sam. 15.3; Jos. 6.21; 7.19-25.

In the unique Moabite stone (*circa* 850 B.C.), now in the Louvre at Paris, which is " the oldest historical inscription in any dialect nearly allied to Hebrew," the Moabite Mesha describes how, after sacking the Israelite sanctuary of Nebo, he slew the whole population--" 7,000 men and male sojourners and women and female sojourners and maidens "—in honour of Chemosh (and Ashtor).—See *The Legacy of Israel*. Ed. by E. R. Bevan and Charles Singer, p. xiiif; also *Camb. Anc. Hist.*, III, pp. 372-3. Deut. 20.12-3 limited destruction to the males only in the case of distant cities.

of their ancestors." The only difference was that whereas the baals of the Canaanites were " pre-eminently local and agricultural divinities, controlling the fertility of their respective spheres of influence," the *elohim* worshipped by the Hebrews in their nomad period were protectors and patrons of human clans, tribes and confederations.[107]

Here then is as unpromising a beginning for a monotheistic spiritual religion as one might imagine; and yet out of this grew up not only the ethical monotheism of the Jews but also the daughter creeds of Christianity and Islam, the one in opposition to and the other in imitation of Judaism. Certain circumstances favoured this development of the Hebrew religion. From the very beginning Yahweh's primary relation was to the tribes of men and not to departments of nature. The nature and origin of the physical world formed a very subordinate quest and the Creation passages are all comparatively late. God's existence was taken for granted and the heavens which declared the glory of God and the firmanent which showed His handiwork were regarded even at a later time not so much as premises to prove God's existence, with the help of the cosmological and teleological arguments as used by later theologians, as conclusions following from His existence:[108] at the dawn of Hebrew religious history nature's happenings did not seem to have furnished any serious problem at all. Moses declared to them the god of their fathers, the god of Abraham, of Isaac, and of Jacob—the same disinclination to worship a novel and unknown god is manifest here as in Hinduism. Although this Mosaic message did not overthrow the gods of other tribes or the popular cults of the nomads, referred to above, it reinforced the revelation to Abraham [109] who was supposed to have discarded the many gods whom the fathers of the Jews had served " in the days of Terah, beyond the River " (Jos. xxiv. 2, 15). By laying

107 Lods, *op. cit.*, p. 241.

108 See J. R. Dummelow. *The One Volume Bible Commentary*, p. xcixf.

109 See *Dic. Bi.*, II, p. 446, art. IDOLATRY.

emphasis on the aspect of relation to man—as the god of the Israelites whose patron and protector Yahweh was declared to be—the Mosaic revelation at once invested God with a personal character. Yahweh did not exercise subtle influence on the world like an astral being nor did His major labour consist in providing a home for man out of chaos or cosmic waters. He was conceived to hold moral relations with man, although at first that morality was mostly connected with magical practices and ceremonial observances.[110]

That the magical and the miraculous formed a considerable part of the divine manifestation would be evident from the pages of the Pentateuch. God's spirituality did not include originally very much beyond the attribute of consciousness; it was very often conceived materialistically as a subtle substance, a mystic fluid or energy which could be poured out (Isa. xxix. 10) and which it was dangerous for all but the elect and the ceremonially pure to touch or handle. Not only did theophanies often take material forms—presumably because to the ignorant nomads spiritual inspiration by God would have conveyed little or no meaning—but the taboo of divine presence was so great that looking into the contents of the Ark or touching it involved, in the case of the unauthorised, instantaneous death, as if by lightning-stroke,[111] and death was the penalty for those who would touch Mount Sinai when Yahweh descended on it to reveal Himself to Moses,[112] although the act might be unintentional and no moral turpitude might be involved. It is necessary to know these primitive origins, for otherwise we shall fail to understand why the High Priest alone[113] is authorised to enter the Holy of Holies on the annual Day of Atonement and to cleanse the people that they may be clean from all their sins before Yahweh (Lev. xvi. 30), and why "the mass of the people have no direct access to their

110 See W. R. Smith, *Old Testament in the Jewish Church*, p. 228f.

111 1 Sam. 6.19; 2 Sam. 6-6, 7; Lev. 16.1.

112 Exod. 19.12, 21.

113 See W. R. Smith, *Old Test. in the J. Ch.*, p. 445.

God in the sanctuary" and "only the priests, who live under rules of intensified ceremonial purity, and have received a peculiar consecration from Jehovah Himself, are permitted to touch the holy things," [114] pretty much as in orthodox Hinduism the Brāhmaṇas alone are authorised to worship the gods and touch the sacred objects. "The prophets had no power to abrogate any part of the law, to dispense with Mosaic ordinances, or institute new means of Grace, other methods of approach to God in lieu of the hierarchical sacraments."[115] It is not inconceivable also that the institution of kingship and the building of a temple for Yahweh, which are almost synchronous in Israelite history, were both modelled on the practices of the surrounding nations and that the persistence of the temple-rituals was a relic of the Canaanite religious ceremony just as many Roman Catholic practices to-day are survivals of pagan customs. The Ark of the Covenant was in fact a sort of compromise between spirituality and idolatry:[116] it satisfied the craving for a visible symbol without providing an image and the tradition that it contained the two tables of Divine injunction must have invested it with an ethical meaning. The nearest modern analogue of this would be the worship of the Granth Sahib by the Sikhs who venerate and adore in much the same way their scripture on this side idolatry.

The conception of God as a person could lead in Judaism, as in other religions, to divergent types of development. Thus personification might lead to anthropomorphism or thinking God in terms of man. This anthropomorphism might be taken literally or figuratively, *i.e.*, God

114 W. R. Smith, *Old Testament in the Jewish Church*, p. 229. Even the Levites, who formed a second cordon of holy ministers between the people and the priests, might not touch either ark or altar, lest both they and the priests should die (Num. 18.3), not to talk of the laity (Num. 17.13); and the stranger was ordained to be put to death if he approached nigh unto the priests in the tent of meeting or the tabernacle of the congregation (Num. 18.7).

115 W. R. Smith, *Old Testament in the Jewish Church*, p. 231.

116 The common idol was an uncouth figure of clay or wood; the more pretentious was of gold or silver, or at least plated.—*Dic. Bi.*, II, p. 445. (See Isa., 44.11-9.)

might be invested with the limitations of man or He might be described in terms of human character as this is the nearest category applicable to him. When anthropomorphism extends to the attribution of human organs to God we have the basis of idolatry. Physical descriptions are not rare even in the oldest traditions. "Yahveh moulds man like a potter; he plants the garden of Eden and walks through it in the cool of the evening like a rich Mesopotamian. Adam hears his footsteps. He comes down from heaven to see the building of the Tower of Babel. He eats and drinks with Abraham, and the latter washes his feet. He struggles with Jacob and allows himself to be overcome." [117] He smells the sweet savour of Noah's sacrifice after the Deluge. He is described as having eyes, ears, a mouth, nostrils, hands, a heart and bowels, and his breath as being long or short.[118] It is difficult to say that "the language only testifies to the warmth and intensity of the religious feelings of the writers;" [119] it is far more probable that these realistic tales, like the fables in the Purāṇas, were devised to satisfy certain types of mind. In fact, there is a method in the presentation of these human characteristics, for they become rarer in God's dealings with the Hebrew race in course of time. The underlying idea probably was that there was a time when God conversed with the patriarchs of the race face to face and that, therefore, Yahweh was to them not an object of faith or speculation but a visible presence in human form.[120]

This remark may be illustrated further by the way in which Yahweh deals with Moses. Possibly the narrator wished to indicate the spiritual advance effected in the creed of Moses by representing Yahweh as manifesting Himself through signs and symbols—through a burning bush, a column of smoke or fire or what is vaguely described as His

117 D'Alviella, *op. cit.*, p. 216.

118 Lods, *op. cit.*, p. 457. See, however, the explanation in A. Cohen, *The Teachings of Maimonides*, p. 84 f (*Guide to the Perplexed*, 1.46).

119 *Dic. Bi.*, II, p. 198.

120 Attempt is made to defend invisibility by suggesting that God appears to men in dreams or at night and not in waking or normal moments. Yahweb wanted to leave Jacob as the day was breaking (Gen. 32.26).

glory. There is a hesitation about visible presence to Moses: although we are assured that with Moses Yahweh " will speak mouth to mouth, even manifestly and not in dark speeches, and the form of the Lord shall he behold " (Num. xii. 8), we find that what Moses actually saw was the back of Yahweh when He took away His hand from his eyes (Ex. xxxiii. 23). Later Jewish commentators, in order to attenuate the physical presence still further, held that it was the knot on the phylacteries of Yahweh that Moses saw;[121] and the Qur'ān, which is generally more opposed to anthropomorphism than other scriptures, lays down that Moses never saw the form of God but swooned away when a mountain was turned into dust by Him in answer to his prayer that God should show Himself to him (Sura vii. 139). That the popular belief about Yahweh with a physical frame revived in later times is undoubted, for from the 3rd century to the 10th century A.D. various speculations about God's stature, the paraphernalia of the heavenly court and even God's daily occupations were indulged in, till the Karaites began to ridicule this whole method of mystical anthropomorphism.[122] The Deuteronomy, as is to be expected, denied altogether that Moses saw Yahweh (iv. 12) and added as a reason that otherwise people would be tempted to worship idols (iv. 15-19):[123] " Take ye therefore good heed unto yourselves; for ye saw no manner of form on the day that the Lord spake unto you in Horeb out of the midst of the fire: lest ye corrupt yourselves, and make you a graven image in the form of any figure, the likeness of male or female, the likeness of any beast that is on the earth, the likeness of any winged fowl that flieth in the heaven, the likeness of anything that creepeth

[121] The Talmudists represented God not only as wearing the phylacteries but also as reading the Torah much as a pious Jew of the times used to do.—See ERE. vi. 296

[122] ERE. vi. 296.

[123] Canon Lindsay Dewar points out that this Deuteronomic legislation was responsible for diverting the nation's imagination to the Temple and, after its destruction, to the Messiah and the idealised Zion. It was also responsible for fastening the imagination on the *letter* of the law.—See *Imagination and Religion*. p. 86.

on the ground, the likeness of any fish that is in the water under the earth: and lest thou lift up thine eyes unto heaven, and when thou seest the sun and the moon and the stars, even all the host of heaven, thou be drawn away and worship them, and serve them, which the Lord thy God hath divided unto all the peoples under the whole heaven." But very often this invisibility was qualified by two ideas. The one is the belief that Yahweh is not really invisible but that no one can see His face and yet live (Ex. xxxiii. 20). The other is that Yahweh may sometimes show His form and yet choose not to kill, as when He spared the lives of Jacob (Gen. xxxii. 30), Manoah and his wife (Judges xiii. 22), Gideon (Judges vi. 23), Moses, Aaron, Nadab, Abihu and seventy of the elders of Israel (Ex. xxiv. 9-11).

But the creation of man after the image of God (Gen. i. 26-27), if taken in a physical sense, is bound to cause difficulty:[124] and this is likely to be accentuated by the possibility of "sons of God" marrying the daughters of men (Gen. vi. 2), whatever meaning we might attach to the word 'sons' here.[125] The difficulty was sought to be overcome by suggesting that all descriptions of Yahweh's form were figurative or illusory. The various organs stand for the different powers and attributes of God and have no physical meaning. In the Targums (*i.e.*, versions in the Aramaic vernacular) "all anthropomorphisms, with few exceptions, are paraphrased and spiritualised. Thus, *e.g.*, by the eyes and ears of God are understood His omniscience, by the hand His omnipotence, by the mouth of God His immediate communication with man, or inspiration (*e.g.*, Nu. 12 [8]). The finger of God in Ex. 8 [19] is rendered 'this is a plague from before Jahweh.'"[126] Or, again, all physical activities of God were

[124] For the spiritual and rabbinical interpretation of Man being made in the image of God in the Book of *Zohar*, see Abelson, *Jewish Mysticism*, p. 130 f (esp. p. 135).

[125] *Dic. Bi.*, II, p. 217.

[126] ERE. vi. 295. Maimonides in his *Guide to the Perplexed* adopts a similar device (see ERE. viii. 342).

either qualified by the use of the words ' as it were,' or described in vague general terms or entirely removed. Thus, He did not actually eat with Abraham or wrestle with Jacob—it only appeared *as though* He did.[127] The informed reader will readily remember in this connection Ezekiel's visions of God in the opening chapter of his book [128] where, speaking of the enthroned God, he writes that " upon the likeness of the throne was a likeness as the appearance of a man upon it above " and that this was " the appearance of the likeness of the glory of the Lord." But as the pure spirituality of God did not seem to have been adequately secured even by these devices, a number of intermediate beings and angels were latterly conceived to take over all physical manifestations of God. Thus in the later Jewish literature man was supposed to have been created not in the image of God but in that of the ministering angels.[129] Similarly, wherever the personal appearance of Yahweh had originally been described, one or other of the many *theologumena* took its place. The substitutes were invested with the anthropomorphic functions of Yahweh so that His own transcendental and spiritual character might not be affected in any way Of these passing appearances of Yahweh, which do not exhaust His being completely,[130] mention may be made of ' the angel of Yahweh,' which has been described as ' a temporary descent of Yahweh into visibility;' ' the face of Yahweh ' which partially manifests Him, possibly in association with the sacred Ark ; ' the glory of Yahweh ' which is His manifestation to Israel on solemn occasions in the form of fire and brightness in general ; ' the name of Yahweh ' which is His manifestation in the attitude of help.[131]

127 *Dic. Bi.*, II, p. 206. See Hughes, *Dictionary of Islam*, p. 239, art. JEWS.

128 Ezek. 1.26, 28. With this may be compared the more realistic descriptions of Daniel, 7.9 and Rev. 4.2.

129 *Dic. Bi.*, II, p. 206.

130 See *Dic. Bi.*, Extra Vol., p. 638 f, for a full description of these different forms. See Lods, *op. cit.*, p. 460; Cheyne, *Traditions and Beliefs of Ancient Israel*, pp. 277 f, 528.

131 Islam adopted the term ' Face of Allāh ' in imitation of the Jewish description and the Mystics of Islam also used the expression ' the Name of Allāh.'

There is no doubt, however, that what the Deuteronomy pictures as a possible consequence of seeing God's form was what was actually practised by the Israelites at large and that personification led to idolatry in various forms. We are told, for instance, that in the private sanctuary of Micah the Ephraimite there were an ephod, teraphim, a graven image and a molten image,[132] and also that Gideon made an ephod of gold;[133] and it may be presumed that regular religious service was held in their honour with the help of priests, as in Hindu temples to-day. The figure of God was probably human in most cases;[134] but, as in popular Hinduism to-day, other forms also were not unknown. The bull-image of Dan and Bethel, the brazen serpent, the maṣṣebah, the ark, the asherah, the teraphim and the ephod (the exact nature of the last two being still a matter of dispute) [135] were all associated with the Yahweh-cult and lowered the religion even below the anthropomorphic level and reduced it, in the eyes of the prophets to a primitive superstition. But even anthropomorphism puts obvious limitations on divine omnipresence; no wonder, therefore, that it should be necessary to allot to Yahweh an earthly seat. At a time when He was not regarded as having His seat in heaven (of which Genesis xxviii is the first intimation) the multiplication of His sanctuaries in the old Canaanite high places and in new seats was a real spiritual gain inasmuch as the partial limitation incidental to a human figure was thereby removed.[136] Still, human limitations lingered on and Yahweh had to leave either heaven or Sinai in order to inspect distant things and events and to render effective help to His chosen race.[137] From this

[132] Judges 17; 18. Lods thinks that there was only one statue (*op. cit.*, p. 430 f.n.l).

[133] Judges 8.24-7.

[134] *Dic. Bi.*, Extra Vol., p. 627. See J. Yahuda, *Law and Life according to Hebrew Thought*, p. 25 (Representation of the Deity).

[135] Lods, *op. cit.*, pp. 430-1; *Dic. Bi.*, II, p. 201; Extra Vol., p. 628 f.

[136] See *Dic. Bi.*, Extra Vol., p. 646.

[137] Though Heaven was His throne, He manifested himself over all the earth,—to Abraham in Ur and Canaan; to Jacob in Mesopotamia, to whom He also said, 'Fear not to go down into Egypt; I will go down with thee' (Gn. 46.3);

point of view, Josiah's concentration of all worship at Jerusalem was a doubtful immediate blessing, for it must have diverted a portion of the popular veneration from the public cult of a unitary Yahweh to the private worship of the many household gods (teraphim),[138] as the people could not have easily changed over from the cult of a near but limited presence to that of a distant but ubiquitous Yahweh. It is needless to add that a purely spiritual God with a centre everywhere and a circumference nowhere was established in the popular mind after prophetic denunciations of centuries, and that the disappearance of the Ark [139] and the destruction of the Temple of Jerusalem materially contributed to the final overthrow of idolatry among the Jews.[140]

The spiritual development of Judaism may be measured not only by its success in working off the imperfect representations of Yahweh through visible symbols but also by its transcendence of that anthropopathy with which early thought had invested Him.[141] It is in the prophetic writings [142] that Yahweh could say that He is God and not man, for in earlier books He is so far assimilated to man that not only human traits but also human imperfections cling to Him.[143] If, like man, He

to Moses at Sinai and in Egypt; to His people, going before them into Canaan (Ex. 33.15). There, though His presence was specially attached to the Ark, He also revealed Himself to Joshua as the captain of the Lord's Hosts (Jos. 5.14).—*Dic. Bi.*, II, p. 203.

138 See W. R. Smith, *Old Testament in the Jewish Church*, p. 248, on the loss of personal contact with God on account of the suppression of the local sanctuaries; also p. 364.

139 Five things which existed in the first Temple were lacking in the second. These were (*a*) Fire from on High, (*b*) Anointing Oil, (*c*) the Ark, (*d*) Holy Spirit (*i.e.*, canonical prophecy), (*e*) the Urim and Thummim.—Abelson, *The Immanence of God in Rabbinical Literature*, p. 261. See p. 267 n(2) for later substitutes of (*b*) and (*c*).

140 For the incorporeality of God in Maimonides, see Cohen, *op. cit.*, p. 36 f. See ERE. vii. 342.

141 See Maimonides, *Guide to the Perplexed*, 1.56, 57 (Cohen, *op. cit.*, pp. 86, 89).

142 Occasionally elsewhere also: see 1 Sam. 15.29—'The Lord is not a man that he should repent;' also Num. 23.19.

143 For an instructive list of quotations on this topic from Talmudic literature, see P. I. Hershon, *A Talmudic Miscellany*, p. 128 f.

is a conscious personality, like man also is He limited in knowledge. Being not omniscient,[144] He has to come down from heaven to see the building of the Tower of Babel [145] and to verify the reported wickedness of Sodom.[146] Possibly also the direction to Moses to ask the Israelites to mark their door-posts and lintel with the blood of a lamb, so that He might "pass over" their houses and smite the first-born in Egyptian homes only, was prompted by a sense of His limited knowledge, although the motive to test their obedience was also present.[147] He possesses most of the human emotions, good and bad. "He repents that He made man (Gn. 6 [6]), and also of the evil that He intended to do (Ex. 32 [14]); He is grieved (Gn. 6 [6]), angry (1 K. 11 [9]), jealous (Dt. 6 [15]), gracious (Ps. 111 [4]); He loves (1 K. 10 [9]), hates (Pr. 6 [16]), and much more." [148] He is afraid of the men that He had Himself made lest they should obtain too much power—that by eating of the fruit of the Tree of Knowledge Adam should be like Him and that by building the Tower of Babel men should reach heaven and gain divine power; and He behaves towards them just as Indra does towards aspirants after his heavenly throne, *i.e.*, He confounds them and crushes them.[149] A certain amount of anthropopathism is inevitable in any description of God if there is to be any distinction between His attitude towards saints and that towards sinners. It is only in philosophies like those of Śaṅkara and Bradley, where Brahman is impersonal and the Absolute super-personal, that characterisation belongs to a lower form of the Ultimate Principle—Īśvara in the one case and God in the other—and the Ultimate Ground of all being becomes indeterminate. Later Judaism did not escape this tendency altogether when, presumably under the influence of Greek Philosophy, God

[144] See Num. 5.15; 1 Kings 17.18. A meal offering of memorial, bringing iniquity to remembrance, was practised.—See Lods, *op. cit.*, p. 467.

[145] Gen., 11.5. See Cheyne, *op. cit.*, p. 201 f.

[146] Gen., 18.21.

[147] Exod., 12.13.

[148] *Dic. Bi.*, II, p. 198. See 1 Sam. 15.11 and also Num. 23.19, 1 Sam. 15.29.

[149] See L. T. Hobhouse, *Morals in Evolution*, II, p. 121.

was removed far away from the world and contact with Him was effected through intermediate beings, emanations or manifestations, possessing some sort of substantial existence of their own by the side of God Himself. The early writers, however, did not have the scruple of the philosophers or of the authors of the Septuagint version or the Targum literature, who either used paraphrases for these human thoughts and emotions, when used of God, or else removed them wholesale.[150] They not only used freely these expressions regarding God but had no scruple even in suggesting that God incited the Israelites to steal the silver and gold of their Egyptian neighbours on the eve of their flight from Egypt as a timely provision against the days of impending necessity;[151] that He agreed to put the innocent Job to trial at the suggestion of Satan;[152] and that He sent lying spirits to entice Ahab so that he might be killed.[153]

What hindered the moral development in the idea of Yahweh was the reminiscence of the needs of nomadic days. The Hebrews of those times thought in terms of their tribes as did the other Semites, and the character of Yahweh was modelled on tribal needs and tribal ideas. Their salvation lay in close unity for purposes of defence against the Egyptians and the Philistines and offence against the Canaanites whose fertile land they coveted. Naturally, therefore, the God that revealed Himself to Abraham and Moses was primarily needed for tribal expansion and tribal cohesion so that a nation might evolve out of scattered groups. This explains two features of Yahweh's character—His martial temper and His partiality towards Israel. Yahweh is the leader of the Israelites in war. He was their only King before the

150 *Dic. Bi.*, II, pp. 206-7.

151 Exod. 11.2.

152 Job. 1.12; 2.6.

153 1 Kings 22.20. See Lods, *op. cit.*, p. 469 f. Thus Abimelech would have been slain by God if he had lain with Abraham's wife, Sarah, although he did not know her to be another man's wife and would then have been innocent from a moral point of view (Gen. 20.3-7).

establishment of the monarchy;[154] He is the lord of host [155] —*Yahweh Zebā'ôth* who often leaves His dwelling place on Sinai to lead the Israelites personally to victory.[156] His angels fight the battles of Israel and even the stars in their course fight against Sisera at His command, as described in the Song of Deborah (Judges v.20), and the captain of His host comes to the help of Joshua (Jos. v. 13 f). He makes known His march by the rustling of leaves (2 Sam. v. 24), He gives out a lusty shout on arrival at the Israelite camp;[157] He lays low their enemies or pursues them with great slaughter. To quote Lods:[158] " In time of war, Jahweh aided his people in counsel as well as in action: he aided them in counsel by revealing through oracles, dreams, or omens, the fortunate or fatal result of the intended campaign, and by pointing out the necessary strategy;............in action he aided them by spreading panic among the enemy, by pouring down hail upon them, by causing the sun and moon to stand still in order to allow his people to dispatch the fugitives, by producing a storm or an earthquake.........In Hebrew poetry Jahweh is 'a man of war'; he overwhelms his enemies with his arrows and smites them with his sword." As His visible presence, the Ark was carried in front of the advancing Israelite army, and there was tumultuous joy at its arrival at the camp. " Only so much is clear that after the permanent establishment of the Ark in the mysterious darkness of the *adytum* of the temple, its former connexion with the war-god, *Jahweh Zebā'ôth*, must have vanished from the popular consciousness, and that in place of this the awe-inspiring majesty of this God must have come into the foreground." [159] It is in his capacity as the war-lord of the

[154] Monarchy was instituted with mixed feelings or rather viewed differently at different times. See Judges 8.22-3; 1 Sam. 8.10 f; 1 Sam. 9.16.

[155] See *Dic. Bi.*, Extra Vol., p. 636 f., for the various meanings of this appellation.

[156] In Num. 21.14 reference is made to a Book of the Wars of Yahweh which is now lost.

[157] Num. 23.21.

[158] Lods, *op. cit.*, p. 462; see also p. 294.

[159] *Dic. Bi.*, Extra Vol., p. 637. This change is reflected in the change in the meaning of the term *nebi'im* which originally signified probably those who

Israelites that Yahweh insists on the wholesale slaughter of conquered enemies and the destruction of their properties—a direction that was softened at a later time and also originally in the case of distant cities.[160] His treatment of offending Israel or else of its enemies often looks like a punitive measure more allied to military discipline than to justice tempered by mercy, and very often the offence is merely technical. He is frequently represented as quick to take offence, subject to " unaccountable humours " [161] and revengeful to a degree—whether the picture is a survival of ancient belief or a warning against moral and spiritual lapses it is difficult to say.[162]

These unattractive features of Yahweh disappeared as Israel succeeded in its wars with the Canaanites; but still no quarter was shown to those who forsook Yahweh [163] and went after the local baals. Israel was the people of Yahweh and had special responsibilities in the matter of worshipping Him and Him only. Yahweh ceased to fight Israel's battles, and even used Assyria and Babylon as avenging rods, when Israel forgot its covenant with Him. The Prophets were responsible, however, for bringing about a change even in

were seized in holy frenzy and produced ecstatic cries in connection with the battles of Yahweh, the war-god, but at a later time those who revealed the spiritual aspect of religion (although they too were always imbued with a national spirit). In early times the prophets were called 'the chariots and horsemen of Israel' (2 Kings 2.12; 13.14). See *Dic. Bi.*, Extra Vol., p. 653, 655, 656. They originally corresponded to Dervishes.—See Huxley, *Religion without Revelation*, p. 235.

160 The spirit of fanaticism becomes dangerous and homicidal when it eggs on the worshippers to aggressive wars against people of alien cults and when it justifies as pleasing to its god the cruelties inflicted on the conquered. This is the spirit of old Israel and of Islam.—L. R. Farnell, *The Attributes of God*, p. 76.

Deut. 20.19 forbids the destruction of fruit trees which 2 Kings 3.19 enjoins.

161 See Exod. 33.19.

162 The great prophets and their post-exilic disciples explained the anger of Yahweh by the injustice of man (the people, the generation or the individual) which required to be punished; but the ancient Israelites, while not unmindful of the relation between guilt and punishment, thought of many more causes why God should take offence or regarded Divine anger as inscrutable.—See Lods, *op. cit.*, p. 467.

163 Another great offence in ancient times was offence against Yahweh's own person or sinning against the Lord (1 Sam. 2.25) as when Eli's sons took their portion of the sacrifices before Yahweh had received His own or before the other guests had theirs (1 Sam. 2.13-6).

this conception of Yahweh. It is not out of anger but out of His love that He chastises sinning Israel so that she might return in penitence to her rightful Lord.[164] In a well-known passage of Exodus (xxxiv. 6) God is described as "full of compassion and gracious, slow to anger and plenteous in mercy and truth, keeping mercy for thousands, forgiving iniquity and transgression and sin;" but the passage ends with the threat that God "will by no means clear the guilty, visiting the iniquity of the fathers upon the children; and upon the children's children, upon the third and upon the fourth generation." It was left to the Prophets to inculcate the first part of this description and to modify the last part in so far as it related to punishing the guiltless posterity of sinners. St. Paul may be said to have partially undone the work of the Prophets regarding the second part in so far as he made the whole human race the inheritors of the sin of Adam and found in the unmerited suffering of Jesus the Divine scheme of human redemption: the Doctrine of Original Sin is fortunately not necessary for a proper appreciation of the life and death of Jesus or the message of salvation preached by him.[165] The whole burden of the

164 *Cf.* The Proverbs 3.11-2: My son, despise not the chastening of the Lord; Neither be weary of his reproof: For whom the Lord loveth he reproveth; Even as a father the son in whom he delighteth.

165 See L. R. Farnell, *The Attributes of God*, p. 125; also O. Pfleiderer, *Paulinism*, Vol. I, Chaps. I and II.; *Dic. Bi.*, Ext. Vol., p. 666; also Gen. 8.21; Ps. 51.7-15; Job 14.4; 15.14; 25.4 f.

"The *first* signification (both in origin and importance) of the redeeming death of Christ is connected with the sentence of guilt, by which man, as the object of the wrath of God, was placed under *the curse of the law*, subjected to death as the punishment of sin. Man is ransomed from this disastrous state of punishment in that the demand for his punishment is satisfied by the death of Christ as a vicarious *expiatory sacrifice*. Through this ransom the death of Christ is the cause of the appeasing of the wrath of God, or of the manifestation of his love, and thus it is a purely *objective* act of God or Christ *in our behalf*, for the purpose of our rescue. But, *at the same time*, the death of Christ frees us from the *power of sin* which dwells in the flesh, for this principle of sin is destroyed, first in Christ himself, and then in us through our mystical communion with him. From this point of view the death of Christ as a *mortification of the flesh* is the commencement of a *subjective* ethical process, which goes on and completes itself *in us*."—Pfleiderer, *Paulinism*, I, p. 92.

It is interesting to note that Rai Bahadur G. C. Ghosh, the founder of the present Lectureship, although a devout Christian, does not think that Christ came

later Prophetic teaching, on the other hand, is that individuals are punished for their own sins by Yahweh and not for the iniquities of their ancestors, kings or leaders, as was preached in olden times when, for instance, the Pharaoh's personal guilt entailed the death of all the first-born of Egypt [166] and David's blunder in taking a census in spite of Joab's warning sent seventy thousand innocent people to death while he himself escaped.[167]

That, in spite of a change in the concept of Yahweh, the Temple-service should be marked by extensive ceremonial slaughter of animals of different kinds and this should be acquiesced in by the Prophets [168] must be due to the fact that Yahweh absorbed the magical sacrifices of blood, which were originally made to fetishes in the pre-Mosaic days of the Semitic tribes (and confirmed by Moses in his code of religion), and also retained the character of the war-lord. The Law was to the Jews the only means of Divine grace [169] and the law laid down in minute details the quantity and quality of each object of gift to Yahweh. All that the Prophets could do, therefore, was

as the Second Adam to undo the sin of the First. In an article entitled 'Lamentations of Christ' in the *Amrita Bazar Patrika* (Calcutta) of 26th Dec., 1933 (Dâk edition), he writes : "In my Father's kingdom the offering of a ransom for one's sin or the pleading by another on behalf of the sinner does not avail : every unrepentant sinner shall suffer for his sin, but none in his stead; heaven will not be filled by unregenerate beings." See also his article on *The Theory of a special divinity of Christ* in the *Proceedings of the Eleventh Indian Philosophical Congress*, p. 187 f.

166 Exod. 11.5.

167 2 Sam. 24.15; see, however, 1 Chr. 21.1. See R. M. Jones, *Religious Foundations*, p. 92.

168 See Dummelow, *The One Volume Bible Commentary*, p. lxxiii, for later references than O.T.; also W. R. Smith, *Old Test in J. Ch.*, p. 238 f.

169 See *Dic. Bi.*, II, p. 208 : "Thus God Himself was regarded as devoted to the study of His own Law, and not only of the Law but even of the rabbinical developments of the Law. By day He 'is engaged upon the 24 Books of the Torah, the Prophets, and the Hagiographs, and by night He is engaged upon the 6 divisions of the Mishnah. God is even represented as having companions in the study of the Torah. At least we have, according to *Baba Mezia*, 85*b*, even in heaven an assembly, like the high schools on earth, devoted to the investigations of the Torah. Here the great Rabbis sit in the order of their merit and of their knowledge of the Law, studying *Halacha*, and God studies with them. They dispute with one another and lay down Halacha'."

to point out that a just and merciful god wanted something more than offerings of animals and cereals and liquids in order to be pleased.[170] In their zeal for multiplying religious services and for collecting the sacred tithes [171] the priests forgot the oppression and hardship likely to be caused to the poor. The centralisation of all worship at Jerusalem had, again, an adverse effect on those Levites who were scattered through the provinces; they lost their priestly occupations and were thrown upon the charity of the landed classes along with the strangers, the widows and the orphans.[172] The earlier Prophets could not condemn the sacrifices altogether, as, before the return from Babylon, gifts to the sanctuary were spontaneous and private, and not, as after Ezekiel's and Ezra's reforms, an official business conducted with the help of " a fixed tribute in kind upon all agricultural produce and flocks." [173] But they and their successors had hard words for those in power who were buying out the poor proprietors of land and who thought that justice could be sold, unlawful pleasures of all kinds indulged in, and the poor neglected or oppressed with impunity, provided the sacrifices sent to the Temple were regular and ample.[174] " Hear the word of the Lord, ye rulers of Sodom; give ear unto the law of our God, ye people of Gomorrah. To what purpose is the multitude of your sacrifices unto me? saith the Lord: I am full of the burnt offerings of rams, and the fat of fed beasts; and I delight not in the blood of bullocks, or of lambs, or of he-goats. When ye come to appear before me, who hath required this at your hand, to trample my courts? Bring no more vain oblations; incense is abomination unto me; new moon and sabbath, the calling of assemblies,—I

170 W. R. Smith, *Old Test. in J. Ch.*, p. 240.

171 *Ibid.*, p. 442 f.

172 Deut. 12.12, 18; 14.27, 29; 16.11, 14; 26.11 f.

173 W. R. Smith, *Old Test. in J. Ch.*, p. 375. During pre-exilic days the Temple was the king's sanctuary and the regular offerings were his gift. The people, however, agreed to pay a regular voluntary poll-tax for the regular offerings of the Second Temple.

174 Micah 6.7, 8; Jer., 7. See W. R. Smith, *Old Test. in J. Ch.*, p. 372.

cannot away with iniquity and the solemn meeting. Your new moons and your appointed feasts my soul hateth: they are a trouble unto me; I am weary to bear them. And when ye spread forth your hands, I will hide my eyes from you; yea, when ye make many prayers, I will not hear: your hands are full of blood. Wash you, make you clean; put away the evil of your doings from before mine eyes; cease to do evil; learn to do well; seek judgment, relieve the oppressed, judge the fatherless, plead for the widow." [175] Deutero-Isaiah is more outspoken against the whole Temple-cult: "Thus saith the Lord, The heaven is my throne, and the earth is my footstool: what manner of house will ye build unto me and what place shall be my rest? For all these things hath mine hand made, and so all these things came to be, saith the Lord: but to this man will I look, even to him that is poor and of a contrite spirit, and that trembleth at my word. He that killeth an ox is as he that slayeth a man; he that sacrificeth a lamb, as he that breaketh a dog's neck; he that offereth an oblation, as he that offereth swine's blood; he that burneth frankincense, as he that blesseth an idol." [176] In the same strain speaks Micah: "Wherewith shall I come before the Lord, and bow myself before the high God? shall I come before him with burnt offerings, with calves of a year old? Will the Lord be pleased with thousands of rams, or with ten thousands of rivers of oil? shall I give my first-born for my transgression, the fruit of my body for the sin of my soul? He hath showed thee, O man, what is good; and what doth the Lord require of thee, but to do justly, and to love mercy, and to walk humbly with thy God?" [177] In spite of these denunciations, so long as the Temple lasted there could be no question of abolishing the rituals. But during the Babylonian exile the nation had learnt to worship Yahweh in a different manner, for outside Jerusalem no sacrifice could be offered and people had to eat

175 Isa. 1.10-17; also 59.1 f. See Amos 5.21; 1 Sam. 15.22.
176 Isa. 66.1 f.
177 Micah 6.6-8.

'unclean food.'' Hence after the return of the remnant from captivity, in addition to some improvement in the temple-worship, which was resumed with some enthusiasm by the returned exiles as a public cult with a new code of rules, the exilic custom of "the devotional study of the scriptures, the synagogue, the practice of prayer elsewhere than before the altar," which were "all independent of the old idea of worship," was continued as a daily religion and made up for "the narrowing of the privilege of access to God at the altar."[178] A growing sense of abiding sin and the necessity of Divine forgiveness required a different God from the one whose wrath was not turned away except after inflicting injury, and who insisted on his quota of vengeance for a transgression of his ordinances.[179] The Prophets taught that Yahweh was ever ready to extend His loving forgiveness to the penitent "without the intervention of any ritual sacrament" for He is 'God and not man" (Hos. xi. 9). "God is with Israel in his sin, only because He has implanted within him this virtue of repentance."[180] This penitence, however, must show itself not in outward observances but in active charity and by undoing the wrong done: "Is it to bow down his head as a rush, and to spread sackcloth and ashes under him? wilt thou call this a fast, and an acceptable day to the Lord? Is not this the fast that I have chosen? to loose the bonds of wickedness, to undo the bands of the yoke, and to let the oppressed go free, and that ye break every yoke? Is it not to deal thy bread to the hungry, and that thou bring the poor that are cast out to thy house? when thou seest the naked, that thou cover him; and that thou hide not thyself from thine own flesh? Then shall thy light break forth as the morning, and thy healing shall spring forth speedily: and thy righteousness shall go before thee; the glory of the Lord shall be thy rearward." (Is. lviii. 5-8.)

In the conviction, therefore, that God's punishment is not wanton or vindictive but prompted by a desire to reconcile

178 W. R. Smith, *Old Test. in J. Ch.*, p. 379.
179 *Ibid.*, p. 372.
180 Abelson, *The Immanence of God in Rabbinical Literature*, p. 140.

man to Himself through the purification of suffering and repentance Israel could not but look upon Yahweh as the well-meaning Father who chastises him out of love.[181] Long before the Lord's Prayer was uttered or penned the Jews had learnt to look upon Israel as God's son and Yahweh as the Heavenly Father (Is. lxiii. 16, lxiv. 8) towards whom trustful resignation was the only proper attitude.[182] He became the Holy One of Israel [183] who looked to men's motives and not to their acts. Israel is to circumcise his heart and not his foreskin to find favour with Yahweh. God is to be worshipped in spirit and in truth if His redeeming mercy is to be sought. Nor did the prophets nor even the legalists leave the people in any doubt about what they meant by a spiritual religion. Here, for instance, is an illustrative quotation from Ezekiel (xviii. 1-9, 23) which may be compared with the Quranic injunction quoted at the end of the first chapter : " The word of the Lord came unto me again, saying, What mean ye, that ye use this proverb concerning the land of Israel, saying, The fathers have eaten sour grapes, and the children's teeth are set on edge? As I live, saith the Lord God, ye shall not have occasion any more to use this proverb in Israel. Behold, all souls are mine ; as the soul of the father, so also the soul of the son is mine : the soul that sinneth, it shall die. But if a man be just, and do that which is lawful and right, and hath not eaten upon the mountains, neither hath lifted up his eyes to the idols of the house of Israel, neither hath defiled his neighbour's wife, neither hath come near to a woman in her separation ; and hath not wronged any, but hath restored to the debtor his pledge, hath spoiled none by violence, hath given his bread to the hungry, and hath covered the naked with a garment ; he that hath not given forth upon usury,

181 Proverbs 3.12.

182 Wendt, in his *System der Christlichen Lehre*, counts no less than 23 passages in the Old Testament in which God is conceived as father exactly in the same way as we find in the gospels.—Dhirendra Nath Chowdhury, *In Search of Jesus Christ*, p. 20. (See other references there.) See also Abelson, *Jewish Mysticism*, p. 79 f; *The Immanence of God in Rabbinical Literature*, p. 51. See art. GOD in *Dic. Bi.*, II, p. 208 for references.

183 For the evolution of the meaning of ' Holy,' see *Dic. Bi.*, Extra Vol., p. 681 f.

neither hath taken any increase, that hath withdrawn his hand from iniquity, hath executed true judgment between man and man, hath walked in my statutes, and hath kept my judgments, to deal truly; he is just, he shall surely live, saith the Lord God." "Have I any pleasure in the death of the wicked? saith the Lord God; and not rather that he should return from his way, and live?" [184]

The failure of Judaism to become a world-religion in spite of these spiritual developments must be laid at the door of that Jewish exclusiveness which is at once the wonder and the despair of all nations who have come into contact with the world's most despised and persecuted race. From the very dawn of his history Israel has suffered from a tribal paranoia with its characteristic symptoms of megalomania and persecution delusion. Israel is God's chosen race, Yahweh's own anointed seed, His first-born: to Israel of all nations has He chosen to reveal Himself and His name.[185] It is not to individuals in their private capacity that God has chosen to speak nor did He wait for them to approach Him with a spotless and spiritual life before making His wishes and graces known.[186] The glorification of Israel was a part of Divine policy—through him had Yahweh decided to spread the message of true devotion and upright conduct. When He promised to Abraham that He would make a great nation out of his seed or called Moses to preach His name, He was dealing with them as representatives of the future race. He established a covenant between Himself and Israel as is done between two nations so that no scope might be left for prevarication and no chance given to the race to plead its inability or unwillingness to ratify the transaction. He wrote down the conditions of Israel's guidance in two tables of stone and sealed the covenant with Moses by summoning to His presence, in addition to Moses and Aaron,

[184] See *Dic. Bi.*, Extra Vol., p. 675.

[185] *Dic. Bi.*, Extra Vol., p. 684 (the relation of Yahweh to Israel). This appears specially in the Deuteronomy.

[186] See W. R. Smith, *Old Test. in J. Ch.*, pp. 235-6.

seventy-two representative Israelites who all celebrated the event by a friendly feast.[187] But God did something more. He gave them Canaan as an inheritance after leading them out of Egypt, saving them from the pursuing Egyptians and also providing for them in the wilderness. The nation was to remember that Yahweh was its special god and that the worship of any other god before or beside Him was forbidden nor were matrimonial alliance with the pagan Canaanites,[188] worshipping at their sanctuaries and consulting their oracles permitted. The sin of a single leader was regarded as a default of the nation, for in those nomadic and patriarchal days the tribe had a collective responsibility and the iniquities of the fathers were visited on their sons.

In its original form this exclusive alliance of Yahweh with Israel did not always prove morally satisfactory. Moses could insinuate that foreign nations would not think highly of Yahweh if after extending His protection to the Israelites He should refuse to help them in their distress—it was more or less a point of honour with Him to help Israel against the foreigners who were backed by their own gods.[189] "Thus," as Kuenen observes,[190] "in the conception of the people, Yahweh's might, or, if you prefer to put it so, Yahweh's obligation to display his might, must often have overbalanced both his wrath against Israel's trespasses and the demands of his righteousness." But as soon as Yahweh was invested not only with moral *attributes* but with an ethical *character* by the Prophets, this partiality for Israel had to disappear from His nature, just as with it disappeared also the reality and necessity of the gods of other nations.[191] Yahweh's scheme of the government of the world now included not only Israel but also Assyria and Babylon, the rods

187 Exod. 24.9-11; also Num. 11.16 f. It is curious that the Septuagint version should be ascribed to seventy or seventy-two translators—the two being additional numbers like those in the above places of the O.T.

188 Exod. 34.15-6; Deut. 7.2; Judges 2.2. See Lods, *op. cit.*, p. 403.

189 Whence the inflictions on Pharaoh (Gen. 12.17) and Abimelech (Gen. 20.4 f).

190 Kuenen, *op. cit.*, p. 116.

191 For the solity of Yahweh, see *Dic. Bi.*, Extra Vol., p. 680.

with which Yahweh had scourged Israel because of the latter's faithlessness to the covenants with Him : He could also punish the non-Israelites or use them as aids to Israel's revival if He so pleased.[192] Yahweh is no longer the 'God of gods' and 'Lord of lords' (Deut. x. 17) but is God (Deut. vii. 9) and 'beside Him there is none.'[193]

The only logical conclusion of this position is that Yahweh is the God of the Jews and the Gentiles alike and that not only for Israel but for the whole human race Yahweh alone is God. This would have entailed the bestowal of the full rights of Judaism on all who acknowledged Yahweh as God and also an active enrolment of Gentiles within the fold of the Jewish Church. It appears, however, that just as the non-Aryan tribes of the hills and the plains were slowly absorbed within Hinduism in India without much missionary activity and could generally obtain only an inferior social status, so also the non-Israelites of later times were permitted to follow Jewish religious customs but did not obtain the full rights of spiritual citizenship. The contempt for the Gentiles was quite open and dining with them or entering their houses brought about ceremonial uncleanliness. Even the Hellenizing Jews were not free from this anti-Gentilic feeling,[194] and it appears that this contempt was carried over to Christianity itself where the quarrel between the Jewish Christians and the Gentile Christians was fairly acute and the work of St. Paul among the Gentiles was bitterly opposed.[195] No wonder, therefore, that in spite of some proselytism in their midst these did not acquire even the rights of the strangers (*gerim*) or sojourners who lived in close association with the Jews. Thus, though it was permitted to the non-proselyte Gentiles to bring offerings to Yahweh, they had admission only to the outer court of the Temple, much as to a Hindu village god some Indian Musalman might

[192] Isa. 8.9, 10, 12 f; 10. See specially Kuenen, *op. cit.*, p. 124 f.; also Isa. 44.28.

[193] Deut. 4.35, 39; 1 Kings 8.60; 2 Kings 19.15; Isa. 37.16.

[194] *Legacy of Israel*, p. 32.

[195] *Dic. Bi.*, III, p. 149.

bring gifts in fulfilment of vows without being allowed entrance into the sanctuary. During the early days of settlement in Canaan Israel took it for granted that other nations had other gods, and Israelite kings contracting mixed marriages took it as a matter of course that their foreign wives should have temples raised to their own gods—a belief which was subsequently worked up into the theory that Yahweh had assigned to the other nations the sun, the moon and the different constellations for their gods. But the concession granted to the heathen neighbours could not be extended, without serious risk, to the sojourners in their own midst,[196] for these would spread their contaminating cult to their Jewish masters, patrons, protectors and friends. Hence the practical necessities of the case demanded that these foreigners in their own midst should be differentially treated. Being originally permitted to act only in menial capacities in the Temple, they were gradually invested with the same rights and duties as the Israelites themselves and subjected to the same laws of cleanliness and purity in the later Priests' Code (as contrasted with the Deuteronomic legislation). Thus no difference existed latterly between Israelites and *gérim* in the following matters :—" The *gér* is to participate in the Feast of Weeks (Dt. 16 [10f]), of Tabernacles (16 [13f]), in the offering of first-fruits (26 [11]), the Sabbath rest (5 [14]), the tithes (14 [28f]), the gleanings of the field, etc. (24 [19f]), and he is to have equal justice done to him (24 [14])".[197] In the Priestly Code, established after the drastic reforms of Ezra and Nehemiah, " the *gér* is placed practically on the same footing as the native Israelite ; he enjoys the same rights (Nu. 35 [15]; *cf*. Ezk. 47 [22]), and is bound by the same laws, whether civil (Lv. 24 [22]), moral and religious (18 [26] 20 [2] 24 [16]; *cf*. Ezk. 14 [7]), or ceremonial (Ex. 12 [19], Lv. 16 [29] 17 [8 10 12 13 15] 22 [18], Nu 15 [14 26 30] 19 [10]); the principle

[196] For the attitude of the Israelites towards foreigners, see *Dic. Bi.*, III, esp. p. 51, art. FOREIGNER.

[197] *Dic. Bi.*, III, pp. 156-7, art. GER. See J. Yahuda, *Law and Life according to Hebrew Thought*, VII. The Status of Strangers.

"One law there shall be for the home-born and the stranger," is repeatedly affirmed (Ex. 12 $^{49}$, Lv. 24 $^{22}$, Nu. 9 $^{14}$ 15 $^{15\ 16\ 29}$), the only specified distinctions being that the *gér*, if he would keep the passover (which under no circumstances is the foreigner permitted to do), must be circumcised (Ex. 12 $^{48}$), and that an Israelite in servitude with him may be redeemed before the jubilee (Lv. 25 $^{48f}$), a privilege not granted in the case of the master's being an Israelite" (Lv. 25 $^{40f}$.) Having lived as exiles twice, namely, in Egypt and in Babylon, the Israelites had a soft corner for the strangers in their midst and conceded to them the right to adopt the Jewish faith; but in relation to foreigners they were almost absolutely exclusive and it is only a prophet like Isaiah that could promise to the heathen a share in the glorious future of the Israelite faith (Is. lvi. 6-8; *cf*. Zeph. iii. 9). When Israel will have acted as a light to the Gentiles and the servant of the Lord would bring to them His message, Jerusalem shall turn into a house of prayer for all nations and unto Yahweh shall all knees ultimately bow (Is. xlv. 23). 'There is no God but Yahweh and Israel is His prophet.'[198]

That these noble sentiments should be more preached than practised is a fact of history that cannot be ignored or explained away. Whatever tendencies towards universalism might have been present in the Prophets, the Rabbis who succeeded them gradually limited the applicability of 'the Fatherhood of God and he sonship of Man' to the Jews alone.[199] Judaism thus deliberately excluded the heathens from the salvation of Yahweh which some of the prophets had preached as being destined for all alike. The reason of this is to be sought in the post-exilic emphasis on legalism, which the destruction of the second Temple and the development of mysticism failed to counteract completely. Hinduism affords an instructive parallel in this matter. There too speculative philosophy affirmed the equality of all souls before, or rather their identity in and through, Brahman;

198 *Dic. Bi.*, III, p. 157.
199 Abelson, *Jewish Mysticism*, p. 80; p. 96.

but practical religion limited the blessings of salvation to the Hindus alone and latterly resisted the inclusion of non-Hindus within the fold of Hinduism. The domain of Yahweh similarly remained limited to the Jews and the original proselytes.[200] Although the whole development of Judaism from Moses to Malachi was directed towards establishing the authority of Yahweh over the Jews and the Gentiles alike and the equality of all moral individuals before Yahweh,[201] the only solid advance made was that the reality of other gods by the side of Yahweh was denied and idolatry in all forms was banished altogether from the Jewish religion. The Gentiles remained outside the Jewish fold in spite of the fact that Hellenizing Jews were innumerable and Greek philosophy was largely utilised in building up a conception of the operation of God in the world.

In other directions also the original limitation of Yahweh was sought to be removed but sometimes with equally dubious final results. The original Judaism had no otherwordly gaze [202] and Yahweh's covenant did not at first extend beyond death. Yahweh was originally the god of the living and not of the dead and His punishments and rewards had reference to this life alone. Much of Yahweh's hard dealing with individuals, tribes and races can be explained if we remember that the Jews did not originally believe that Yahweh could pursue the prosperous sinner beyond the grave or reward struggling virtue with post-mortem happiness. The horror of death to a pious Jew consisted in banishment from Yahweh's jurisdiction and realm and in incapacity to praise Him; that is why Hezekiah prays for an extension of his life on earth.[203] The dead became *elohim* in their graves or in Sheol and they were worshipped, appeased and approached by the living for deriving benefit and guidance. It is only gradually that Yahwism replaced this cult of the dead by representing them as being devoid of knowledge and strength, and, about the

200 *Legacy of Israel*, p. 29.
201 See Marti, *op. cit.*, pp. 173, 235f.
202 *Legacy of Israel*, pp. 24, 39.
203 Isa 38.18-19. *Cf.* Ps. 30.9; 88.1-6, 11.2; 115.17.

second century B.C., it asserted the jurisdiction of Yahweh over the dead also in the shape of a judgment after death, a resurrection and an immortality.[204] 'To the moral attributes of Deity, to His supreme pity and justice, there are endless references in the Psalter and the Prophets; to the divine omnipresence there are but few.'[205] It was a kingdom won for Yahweh when it began to be believed that He was present not only in the highest heaven but also in the lowest pit.[206] Everywhere Yahweh reigns supreme. This extension of Yahweh's jurisdiction was a direct effect of exile in a land where similar beliefs about the destiny of the departed held sway. But, conversely, a contraction of His realm occurred when, in imitation of the Zoroastrian model, Judaism began to exonerate Yahweh from the creation of evil and ascribed it to Satan, the Semitic counterpart of the Zoroastrian Angro Mainyu.[207] The motive was undoubtedly good, for it was felt that a good and merciful Yahweh could not, consistently with His character, create evil.[208] Eve was tempted by Satan in the garden of Eden, and through him did Sin and Death invade mankind—a conception which has been so graphically described by Milton in his *Paradise Lost*. The peculiar Christian view of redemption through the Logos that took flesh and brought Messianic salvation to mankind was based upon this later Jewish belief of the responsibility of Satan for the fall of Adam.

The idea of the holiness of Yahweh and the sinfulness of man became almost an obsession in

[204] Lods, *op. cit.*, pp. 218 f; also p. 455. This was closely connected with the doctrine of the Messiah whose advent was believed to be imminent in the book of Daniel where the doctrine of individual resurrection is first found.—See Marti, *op. cit.*, p. 229; also p. 235. James Orr in *The Christian View of God and the World* (Appendix to Lecture V. The Old Testament Doctrine of Immortality), p. 200 f., states that the doctrine of resurrection is "one of the very oldest doctrines in the Bible."

[205] *Dic. Bi.*, II, p. 207, art. GOD.

[206] Ps. 139.8.

[207] Lods, *op. cit.*, p. 470.

[208] Ps. 5.4, "Evil shall not sojourn with thee," was used as a text by the Midrash to dissociate God from evil and to interpret such passages as Gen. 1.5, and 3.16-17 where the pronominal form "he" is substituted for Yahweh.

later Rabbinical literature. He was considered to be so holy that pious Jews were afraid of uttering His name and used a substitute, like *Adonai* or *Elohim*, or a paraphrasis, when reading His name aloud.[209] Even the Rabbis pronounced the name with bated breath and quickly slurred over it.[210] The mystery surrounding the Divine name, which is so often repeated in the Old Testament,[211] was deepened in Rabbinical literature, which began to dabble in the occult lore of its formation out of the letters of the Hebrew alphabet [212] and it became a symbol of Yahweh's transcendental purity. Blessings were invoked on the Divine name whenever it was mentioned just as peace is invoked on Muhammad by the Musalmans whenever his name is uttered. Now, this excessive reverence could have but one effect, namely, to remove God as far as possible from this world of sin and suffering. Hosea had spoken of Yahweh returning to His place till offence was acknowledged [213] and the Song of Songs Rabba had described the successive withdrawals of the Shekinah of God to the ascending tiers of heaven with the increasing sins of men ;[214] but, as Abelson points out,[215] "to the old Rabbinic mind there was always a very real glimmering that however all-pervading and all-embracing God may be in an immanental sense, He is yet marked off from the world by some not easily discernible line of separation."

209 Abelson, *The Immanence of God in Rabbinical Literature*, p. 207. See *Dic. Bi.*, II, p. 206.

210 Abelson, *Jewish Mysticism*, p. 27.

211 See, for instance, Exod. 3.14 and Judges 13.18.

212 Abelson, *Jewish Mysticism*, p. 25; also Ch. V. The Book 'Yetsirah' (p. 98 f).

213 Hosea 5.15.

214 The most striking passage in this connection is Song of Songs Rabba vi: "The original abode of the Shechinah was......among men. When Adam sinned it ascended away to the first heaven. With Cain's sin it ascended to the second. With Enoch to the third. With the generation of the Flood to the fourth. With the generation of the Tower of Babel to the fifth. With the Sodomites to the sixth. With the sin of the Egyptians in the days of Abraham, it ascended to the seventh. Corresponding to these, there arose seven righteous men who brought the Shechinah down, back again to earth. These were Abraham, Isaac, Jacob, Levi, Kehath, Amram and Moses."—Abelson. *The Immanence of God in Rabbinical Literature*, p. 136 (see also *Jewish Mysticism*, p. 93).

215 Abelson, *The Immanence of God in Rabbinical Literature*, p. 38.

Christian writers, who are often unconsciously biased in their estimate of Judaism, like to dwell upon the distinction between the transcendental deity of the Old Testament and the outward observances necessary to please Him, on the one hand, and the pervasive presence of the Christian God and the inwardness necessary to worship Him, on the other. They think that after removing God to transcendental heights Rabbinical Judaism invented a few mechanical devices to bridge the gulf between God and the world. Thus Dummelow observes,[216] " What is called the transcendent view of God became predominant; that is to say, He was so far exalted above the world as to be out of touch or communication with men. He who had formerly tabernacled with His people and spoken familiarly to the prophets, seemed now to dwell in a far-off heaven where no personal intercourse could be had with Him." Now let us hear what a Jew has to say to this charge, for, as I have maintained in connection with Hinduism, it is always good to refer to the followers of a faith for a more correct estimate of the vital significance of dogmas and rituals. Says Dr. Abelson,[217] " A theology which posits a far-off God, separated from man by an unfathomable distance, could never give that large scope to the doctrine of repentance which we find in the pages of the Rabbins. This doctrine is of itself sufficient to stamp Judaism as a religion of the heart. And if mysticism is "religion in its most acute intense, and living stage," then must Rabbinic Judaism hold a foremost place in the category of mystical religions. For few could have realised the Presence of God more acutely, more intensely than the Rabbinic Jew, who aimed at sanctifying even the smallest details of the physical life, because he regarded nothing as being too humble to come within the purview of Him, whose glory fills the universe, and whose word is the mainstay of all."

We may well believe that in later Judaism the problem was to reconcile a Holy God with a sinful world, a God who

[216] J. R. Dummelow, *A Commentary on the Holy Bible*, p. lxvii. See also Harnack, *What is Christianity?*, p. 52.

[217] Abelson, *The Immanence of God in Rabbinical Literature*, pp. 15-6

was far removed and a God who was yet accessible, a God whose form was unknown and a God whose manifestations were yet not infrequent in Israel's history. Yahweh was regarded as having a manifestation in the physical world, and also a manifestation in human minds, in the tribal life of Israel, and even in human history and cosmic happenings. The most notable of these mediating conceptions is the Holy Spirit which later on played such an important part in the Christian doctrine of the Trinity.[218] Although there are numerous references to Spirit and the Spirit of God in the Old Testament and the Apocrypha, it is only in two places (Ps. li. 11 and Is. lxiii. 10, 11) of the Old Testament that the term Holy Spirit occurs; it is only in the Talmud and the Midrash that it is most frequently used. These terms were intended to convey the idea of Divine presence in the world of men and things. When an act of heroism or good government is performed on behalf of Israel, or when the nation receives a physical or spiritual quickening, it is the Spirit of God that is operating. When an individual is possessed with a sudden fit of inspiration or when he acquires a permanent insight into the will of God and a moral inclination, he is drawing his strength and impulse from the Divine Spirit. It is the Spirit of God, again, that brings the world into being, fills it with living and sentient beings, and preserves it in existence and guides its destiny:[219] in this aspect it is called the Wisdom of God which is "a cosmic power, the all-encompassing intelligent will of God manifesting itself in the creation and preservation of the world, and as an eternal and unerring

218 See Abelson, *The Immanence of God in Rabbinical Literature*, Chs. XIV-XXI, for an exhaustive treatment of this subject (esp. p. 198).

Mills remarks (in *Our Own Religion in Ancient Persia*, p. 11): "Ahura Mazda, the Living Lord, the Great Creator (or possibly the 'Wise One'), has a most Bountiful, or most Holy Spirit, who is sometimes identical with him, and there is precisely the same difficulty in distinguishing between Ahura and His Holy (?) Spirit, which meets us in the Semitic when we endeavour to decide positively in the analogous obscurity. (Often we cannot tell whether Yahveh's attribute or His creature is meant)."

219 In *Zohar* mysticism the *En-Sof* (the Infinite) was regarded as having similar functions.—See Abelson, *Jewish Mysticism*, p. 142 f.

guide and ruler of mankind.'' [220] The ever-present Spirit of God began to be conceived in two different ways. In the Old Testament a sensuous presence of Yahweh to Moses, Isaiah and Ezekiel had been alluded to: '' God's Immanence, His accessibility, His nearness, His all-encompassing and all-embracing reality became so deep-rooted a conviction to the minds of individual Rabbis here and there, that the barriers separating the intellectual and emotional aspects of mind broke entirely away, and they saw with the eye, and heard with the ear, sights and sounds from an unseen world, traces of a Presence which impinged upon them, invaded them, filling them with high and divine impulses, raising them to the position of the elect whose state of life is a complete unity of being with God.'' [221] The appearance of the Spirit of God as Light or Fire or Sound or a Dove was an article of creed in Rabbinical literature before Christ's time, and Christianity took it over as a well-known method of Divine manifestation. The mystic Jehuda Ha-Levi (1085-1140) taught in the '' Kusari '' (Book iv. iii) that '' by means of a system of vigorous self-discipline it was always possible for the worthiest spirits among the Israelites to have that degree of communion with God which enabled them to see God by the medium of what is termed ' Glory ' or ' Shechinah ' or ' Kingdom,' ' Fire,' ' Cloud,' ' Image,' ' Likeness,' ' appearance of the bow'.'' [222] Although doubts were sometimes expressed as to whether the manifestation of God was possible outside the Holy Land of Palestine or the Israelite nation, a few bold thinkers conceded that any one could so sanctify his body,

[220] Abelson, *The Immanence of God in Rabbinical Literature*, p. 199.

[221] *Ibid.*, p. 213.

[222] *Ibid.*, p. 252.

' Ten times the Shechinah came down into the world :—at the garden of Eden (Gen. iii. 8); at the time of the Tower (Gen. xi. 5); at Sodom (Gen. xviii. 21); in Egypt (Exod. iii. 8); at the Red Sea (Ps. xviii. 9); on Mount Sinai (Exod. xix. 20); into the Temple (Ezek. xliv. 2); in the pillar of cloud (Num. xi. 25). It will descend in the days of Gog and Magog; for it is said (Zech. xiv. 4) '' And His feet shall stand in that day upon the Mount of Olives.''—Avoth d'Rab. Nathan, Ch. 34 (quoted in Hershon, *A Talmudic Miscellany*, p. 145; see *loc. cit.* for the gradual ascents of the Shechinah).

mind and spirit as to be capable of receiving the Holy Spirit of God.[223] The only condition of Divine inspiration was intellectual wisdom, moral richness and physical strength.[224] The stages of spiritual perfection have been thus summarised by R. Phinehas b. Jair (2nd century A.D.): "The Torah leads to carefulness, carefulness to diligence, diligence to cleanliness, cleanliness to abstemiousness, abstemiousness to purity, purity to piety, piety to humility, humility to fear of sin, fear of sin to holiness, holiness to the Holy Spirit, Holy Spirit to the Resurrection of the Dead." [225] The Jews rejected the Christian doctrine of Incarnation as in their religious literature, especially in Rabbinical literature, it was laid down that every one could reach the ideal of Holy Spirit by guiding his faculties aright. Here is a great resemblance between Hinduism and Judaism, for the former also recognises the capacity of each individual soul to realise its potential infinity. Like Hinduism, again, Judaism admitted that legalism and ceremonialism had their social and spiritual value, but that the individual soul could at all times realise its mystic union with

[223] Abelson, *The Immanence of God in Rabbinical Literature.* Ch. XXI. Holy Spirit in its relation to Non-Jews; also pp. 299 f., 370. See *Jewish Mysticism*, pp. 4 f, 96; also W. R. Smith, *Old Testament in the Jewish Church*, pp. 356-7 in this connection.

[224] Abelson, *The Immanence of God in Rabbinical Literature*, p. 247; *Jewish Mysticism*, p. 89.

Maimonides enumerates the following as the essential factors of a prophetic faculty :—" (1) Physical strength, so as to endure the strain involved in the moments of ecstatic communion. (2) A training of the intellectual faculties to the highest pitch of perfection. (3) Great imaginative power. This is closely allied with emotion; the vision, etc., that the prophet beholds is (?) the outcome of emotional imagination. (4) Exceptional moral discipline. (5) The absence of all physical, intellectual or moral disturbances. There must be no pain, no sorrow, no feeling of degradation. (6) The will of God, into which an element of the miraculous or unaccountable always enters."

Maimonides rejects the suppositions that God can choose whomsoever He pleases for infusing His spirit and that men by training their intellect to the necessary pitch of perfection by study and other methods can acquire prophetic power. He thinks that in addition to intellectual and moral perfection there must be a Divine inspiration or call to prophecy.—See Abelson, *The Immanence of God in Rabbinical Literature*, p. 246 f.

[225] Abelson, *The Immanence of God in Rabbinical Literature*, p. 271 f.

God.[226] Prayer took the place of sacrifice in this method of approaching God.[227] In fact, the Essenes seemed to have observed only the Sabbath and to have neglected most of the other prescribed practices of the Jewish religious life.[228]

But there was one thing which the Jews always dreaded and that is the identification of God and man. They had resisted the temptation of divinising their patriarchs (possibly they had humanised the pagan gods into patriarchs) and they had also refused to admit that a unitary God could be partially incarnated on earth.[229] Jewish mysticism could never rise to Upaniṣadic heights, and statements like 'I am Brahman,' 'I and my Father are one,' etc., would have sounded blasphemous to Jewish ears. As Montefiore observes,[230] "It (Jewish Theism) clings to two aspects of God, summed up in the twofold metaphor, which, though a metaphor, yet, as Judaism insists, describes a reality, 'Our Father, our King.' *Abhinu, malkenu.* So Judaism addresses its God, and it refuses to let go either term, either metaphor." Thus while, on the one hand, "Hebrew faith has left to mankind no finer witness than the readiness with which it received and the fullness in which it has transmitted, by prophet as well as by psalmist, the gospel of the Divine participation not only in human sorrow and suffering—*in all our affliction He was afflicted*—but even in shame and trouble of men's guilt, and in spiritual agony for their redemption and holiness,"[231] "the danger of a

[226] Abelson, *The Immanence of God in Rabbinical Literature,* p. 285.

[227] *Ibid.,* p. 325.

[228] Abelson, *Jewish Mysticism,* p. 30; *Dic. Bi.,* Extra. Vol., p. 53; ERE. v. 396 f.

God in His transcendent holiness seemed to have vanished from the sinstained land......The sense of fellowship with Jahweh was broken. Yet His Law and promise were there in written form. In three directions relief was sought: first, by filling up the interspace between God and man with heavenly hierarchies; second, by the formation of quietist circles like the Essenes, who sought, away from the clash of the world's warfare, the lost secret of the ancient fellowship with Jahweh; and third, by the cherishing of apocalyptic dreams, in which the Day of the Lord was seen as the sheer and sudden act of God breaking in upon the course of history.—ERE. vii. 508.

[229] *Legacy of Israel,* p. 108.

[230] *Ibid.,* Epilogue, p. 519.

[231] *Ibid.,* p. 25.

degeneration into Pantheism through an identification of the Deity with the world," on the other hand, "is avoided by making the Shechinah or Holy Spirit a possession, a kind of emanation of God."[232] God is a Person and cannot, therefore, be dissipated into an impersonal essence of the world even though His presence is ubiquitous. To solve this difficulty Judaism not only evolved certain phenomenal appearances of Yahweh but even personified them. Although Jewish writers think that the Jewish-Hellenistic 'Wisdom,' the 'Word' of the Fourth Gospel, the 'Memra' of Targumic literature and the 'Shechinah' of the Talmud and Midrashim all point more or less to "the immanent manifestation of Divine Wisdom, Divine Power, Divine Love, Divine Justice,"[233] they are themselves obliged to admit that these were often anthropomorphically viewed as dealing directly with the world so that the holiness and inscrutability of Yahweh might not be compromised by contact with a sinful world.[234] In consonance with this oscillation of thought we find that, on the one hand, God is supposed to create the world through ten agencies which are really His attributes, namely, wisdom, insight, cognition, strength, power, inexorableness, justice, right, love and mercy (and which supplied the basis

232 Abelson, *The Immanence of God in Rabbinical Literature*, p. 368.

233 Abelson, *Jewish Mysticism*, p. 78; *Immanence of God in Rab. Lit.*, p. 153.

The other personifications are Metatron of the Gaonic-mystical literature, the 'active intelligence' of Gabirol and Maimonides, the 'Ten Sepiroth' of the Kabbalists.—See Abelson, *Immanence of God in Rab. Lit.*, p. 167.

The *Memra* is a personification, almost a hypostatising, not of the Divine Reason, but of the executive Divine Word......All bodily appearance or bodily action is ascribed, not to God, but to His *Memra*......The *Shechinah* differs from the *Memra* as being [originally] impersonal. Prayer and trust are predicated of the one, but not of the other......The 'Spirit of God' is repeatedly spoken of as the source of inspiration and of revelation......Besides these intermediate agencies there is the *Messiah* ('Son of Man' in similitudes of Bk. of Enoch), whose function is esp. that of judgment and of the restoration of the chosen people. And there is also the whole celestial hierarchy of *angels*.—*Dic. Bi.*, II, p. 207, art. GOD.

234 Abelson, *Jewish Mysticism*, p. 71; *Immanence of God in Rab. Lit.*, pp. 231 (the Torah is personified as also the Holy Spirit), 204, 199, 173 n (31) (emanation doctrine to avoid change in the nature of God), pp. 159-60. See esp. Ch. VIII of Book of Proverbs. See Dummelow, *op. cit.*, p. lxviii and p. 382 about Wisdom; also Cheyne, *op. cit.*, p. 38 f.

of the Ten Sefirot of the Kabbalists),[235] and, on the other, He is withdrawn from the world to such an extent that it became necessary to associate with Him certain pre-existent entities to take charge of the creation and guidance of the world.[236] The Babylonian exile familiarised the Jews with the Zoroastrian system of angels and personified abstractions, and it is likely that the tendency to return to the regal conception of Yahweh was accentuated thereby and the Apocalyptic visions and Messianic pictures were modelled on Zoroastrian ideas. It would not be unfair to say that Judaism was so far influenced by Platonism, Gnosticism, Mithraism and Zoroastrianism during the centuries just preceding the birth of Jesus that the immanence of God in the world and His nearness to the Israelites as individuals and as a nation were in some danger of being lost sight of and that the reformation of Jesus originally consisted in emphasising the aspect of the Fatherhood of God as against the aspect of the Kingship which involved the necessity of intermediaries in God's government of the world. It is indeed true that in the Gospel of St. John and in the Epistle to the Hebrews much of this latter-day Jewish belief invaded Christianity also; but Christianity in its original conception must have been directed against the mystical philosophy about a transcendent God and the formalities, associated with the worship of a Heavenly King, as laid down in the books of Law. It must also have taken more earnestly the injunction to bring the nations of the

235 Abelson, *Jewish Mysticism*, pp. 109, 137 f. The ten Sefirot are the Crown (the dynamic force of En-Sof or Infinite), Wisdom, Intellect (or Intelligence), Compassion (or Greatness), Justice (or Force), Beauty, Victory, Glory, Royalty and Foundation.—*Ibid.*, pp. 140-1; also ERE. ix. 112.

236 See art. MYSTICISM (Hebrew and Jewish) in ERE. ix. 108 f.

Before the world came into existence the following were created :—(*i*) the Torah (Prov. viii. 22); (2) the Divine Throne (Ps. xciii. 2); (3) the Temple (Jer. xvii. 12); (4) Paradise (Gen. ii.8); (5) Hell (Is.xxx.33); (6) Repentance (Ps. xc. 2-3); (7) the Name of the Messiah (Ps. lxxii. 17); and sometimes also (8) the Patriarchs and (9) Israel (Ps. lxxiv.2) and (10) the Holy Land (Proverbs viii. 26).—Abelson, *Jewish Mysticism*, p. 70; *Immanence of God in Rab. Lit.*, p. 162, 171 n(25).

world to Yahweh's sanctuary [237] and to bring home to them the message of the Psalter: [238]

> " Who shall ascend into the hill of the Lord?
> And who shall stand in his holy place?
> He that hath clean hands, and a pure heart."

It certainly did one thing: it proclaimed that the expected Messiah had come not only with a message to mankind but also with a way of life, lived in the constant presence of God, for others to accept and follow.

237 Ps. 22.27-8.
238 Ps. 24.3-4.

# CHAPTER VII

## God in Christianity

A variety of reasons makes the study of the original form of Christianity an extremely difficult task. We do not possess an accurate record of Christ's sayings nor was any of the Gospels composed before 60 or 70 A.D. Older abstracts were utilised and expanded,[1] and in the process many of the contemporary religious beliefs managed to effect an entrance. The present Gospels were either selected because they supported these contemporary beliefs or edited with a view to the propagation of certain contemporary ideas. To quote Reinach:[2] "There were a great many writings called Gospels. The Church finally adopted four, guaranteeing their inspiration and absolute veracity, no doubt because they were in favour in four very influential Churches, Matthew at Jerusalem, Mark at Rome or at Alexandria, Luke at Antioch, John at Ephesus." What enabled St. Paul, again, to put his own interpretation on the life and mission of Christ was the fact that the beliefs were even in his time in a state of gristle and each interpreter could put his own ideas into the message of Christ.[3] The result has been that to-day it is difficult to

[1] Reinach, *Orpheus*, p. 229 f., 235 f; *The History of Christianity in Modern Knowledge*, p. 338 f; *Dic. Bi.*, Ext. Vol., p. 5 f; James Moffatt, *The Approach to the New Testament*, p. 19, 41 f.

[2] Reinach, *op. cit.*, p. 232. For the revelationary or inspirational character of the New Testament, see Moffatt, *op. cit.*, pp. 44, 78. There were Churches in the second century which read only one gospel, or perhaps two, and these not always any of the gospels which afterwards became canonical. Marcion's churches were content with one gospel, an edition of Luke. There were even churches of a more central type, like the Syrian Church, which for a time preferred a harmony like the Diatessaron to the four canonical gospels.—Moffatt, *op. cit.*, p. 50.

For the *Apocryphal Acts*, see B. H. Streeter, *The Primitive Church*, Lect. I (see also p. 52).

[3] It is highly probable that no one of the Synoptic Gospels was in existence, in the form in which we have it, prior to the death of Paul. And were the docu-

distinguish the religion of Christ and the Christian religion—the *history* of Jesus and the *myth* of Christ, as Reinach puts it.[4] To understand aright the genesis of the complicated literature, now known as the New Testament, it is necessary to remember that it originally aimed at reaching the Jews and latterly the Gentiles also. It had to take note of the leading philosophies and ethical ideas of the time—Greek (Platonic), Gnostic, Judaic (Philonic and Rabbinic) and Roman (Stoic), in formulating its final speculative doctrines and moral ideals. It could not also ignore the Mystery religions[5] which satisfied the spiritual needs of those who had lost faith in the creeds and formalities of their decaying ancestral religions and found in the cult of Dionysos-Zagreus, Attis, Osiris, Adonis or Persephone (based on the conception of a god who could dispense his or her salvation to those who would join mystic rites and communal feasts) an emotional satisfaction of religious needs and the craving for immortality.[6] The latest addition to these cults was Mithraism in which the worshipper was not, as in the worship of Attis and Osiris, identified with the god but Mithras (the Vedic Mitra and the Zoroastrian Mithra) acted as a mediator,[7] saviour and

ments to be taken in strict order of chronology the Pauline Epistles would come before the Synoptic Gospels.—*Christianity etc.*, p. 338. The inclusion of the Pauline epistles in the Christian collction was due to the fact that for the second century Paul was pre-eminently "the apostle."—Moffatt, *op. cit.*, p. 51. See Royce, *The Problem of Christianity*, I, p. xxi.

4 Reinach, *op. cit.*, p. 229.

5 Whatever elements Christianity may have assimilated from the contemporary cults, it never followed the mystery-religions by making any secret of its sacred books.—Moffatt, *op. cit.*, pp. 104-5. See pp. 121 and 162 in this connection.

6 See Franz Cumont, *The Mysteries of Mithra*, pp. 143-8. Mystery associations were founded for the worship of many other deities beside Attis and Dionysos and Osiris and Persephone; we hear of associations which worship as their special deity Zeus, Athena, Apollo, Artemis, Aphrodite, Hermes, Poseidon, Herakles, the Muses, Asklepios, Serapis. For all we know, the great majority of mystery associations had no reference at all to a death of the deity, and represented the god or goddess worshipped to be simply present as invisible guest at the communal feasts.—*Christianity etc.*, p. 100.

7 For the mediating function of Mithra in Zoroastrianism, see E. Benveniste, *The Persian Religion according to the Chief Greek Texts*, p. 87 f. See also Franz Cumont, *op. cit.*, pp. 127-8.

guide and was worshipped without those orgiastic rites which degraded the Dionysiac, the Phrygian (Attis) and the Egyptian cults. " Mithras-worship had its sacraments with a sufficient resemblance to the Christian sacraments for Christian fathers to regard them as deliberate counterfeits produced by devils. There were lustrations connected with initiation and a communal partaking of bread and a chalice of water; a sign was imprinted upon the forehead of the man admitted to the grade of soldier;[8] the first day of the week was sacred, as the day of the sun."[9] It is not unlikely that when the first few years of missionary activity among the Hebrews alone did not lead to any tangible result, the Apostles turned increasingly to the Gentiles for converts, and the absorption of elements from the beliefs and practices of surrounding paganism, not radically in opposition to the central tenet of Christ's religion, was permitted, practised and possibly encouraged. Thus Rev. C. A. Scott observes,[10] " It was once thought possible to deduce from the various documents of which the New Testament is composed a uniform and homogeneous theology, to which all the various writers, so to say, have subscribed. Closer study has revealed a very different situation. Instead of one type of religious thought common to all the documents we have to begin by recognizing many types, almost as many indeed as are the writers involved.

[8] Unlike Zoroastrianism, Mithras-worship was a definite mystery religion. Its rites and doctrines were disclosed only piecemeal to initiates under vows of secrecy, as they passed upwards through a succession of grades or orders. The highest grade was that of a Father (*pater*); then came the sun-runner (*heliodromus*), the Persian, the Lion, the Soldier, the Concealed (*cryphius*), the Raven. —*Christianity etc.*, p. 103. (See Franz Cumont, *op. cit.*, p. 152 f.)

[9] *Ibid.*, pp. 103-4. In one point there seems no doubt that the Church did borrow from Mithraism—the fixing of Christmas on 25th December, the birthday of the " Unconquerable Sun " (p. 104). In some Western inscriptions the ' unconquered Mithras ' is identified with the ' unconquered Sun (*Sol invictus*) '; in others Mithras and the Sun appear portrayed as two different personages (p. 101). Mithras-worship did not get its extension westward till the field had already been occupied by Christianity and seems then never to have penetrated far outside the army (p. 114). (See Franz Cumont, *op. cit.*, p. 121 : " In reality there were two solar divinities in the Mysteries, one Iranian and the heir of the Persian Hvare, the other Semitic, the substitute of the Babylonian Shamash, identified with Mithra " (see also p. 158 f.)

[10] *Ibid.*, pp. 337-8.

And in particular there are three major types, the Synoptic, the Pauline, and the Johannine, along with certain others which may be called minor, as less fully elaborated and less influential upon later thinking. Of these the Epistle of James, the Epistle to the Hebrews, and the first Epistle of Peter are representatives.........The Johannine documents may show little internal variety; but the Pauline are marked by certain indications of change or development, and the Synoptic Gospels when compared with one another show even more clearly the successive effects of reflection, experience, and possibly assimilation from other sources.'' It is not improbable that when the sayings and doings of Jesus were no more than a floating mass of popular traditions they should be modified unconsciously or deliberately to suit local and contemporary needs in order to win the allegiance of Jews and Gentiles alike, and be reared on the popular philosophies and expectations about a Messianic intermediary among the Jews and a saviour-god among the Gentiles.[11] Divine Trinities also were not unknown in neighbouring religions nor even the Mother and the Child.[12] In due time these ideas too found room in the New Testament—the former first inserted probably in 2 Cor. xiii. 14 and then interpolated in Mat. xxviii. 19.[13]

The great advantage that the New Testament possesses over all other scriptures is that its canon was fixed after contact with contemporary religious and philosophical speculations had enabled it to incorporate the elements necessary to satisfy not only local conditions but also thinking minds of a certain type. We may perhaps go further and assert that a change in the conception of Jesus Christ took place as the appeal of his life and teachings was extended from the Jews to the Gentiles. Although most of the anti-Gentilic passages have disappeared from the New Testament now, a few unhappy expressions serve as rude reminders that

11 Even the Sermon on the Mount is supposed to have been edited by Luke (as contrasted with Matthew) to attract the Gentiles.—See *Dic. Bi.*, Ext. Vol., p. 8.

12 Jameson, *The Legend of the Madonna*, p. xxii.

13 *Dic. Bi.*, II, p. 213, art. GOD; but see Ext. Vol., p. 308, art. TRINITY.

possibly the original message was primarily, if not exclusively, designed to suit the ears of a Jewish audience.[14] There is evidence to show that originally conversion was limited to the Jews and their proselytes, and that circumcision and keeping of the Law of Moses were demanded of all converts. To St. Paul must belong the credit not only of admitting into the fold Gentiles, like the Roman Cornelius, who had not passed through the Synagogue, but also of dispensing with the necessity of circumcision, as in the case of the Greek Titus. The Judaizers, however, opposed him all along and put him on his mettle to defend his actions in spirited epistles;[15] but even Paul believed that " only Christians who were Jews by birth were the good olive tree, while the Gentile Christians were only grafts from the wild olive tree," and he taught that the Jewish Christians should continue to observe the Law of Moses even though it had been abolished by the new covenant with God, established through the atoning death of Christ on the Cross.[16] The Ebionites, who denied the divinity of Christ and rejected St. Paul as an apostate, and the Nazarenes who made a distinction between Jewish and Gentile Christians in so far as the observance of the whole Mosaic Law was concerned, may be regarded as representing the Jewish view of Christ.[17] We may very well believe that the importance

Dhirendranath Chowdhury in his *In Search of Jesus Christ* (p. 4) goes so far as to assert that " the contributions of the Krishna *cum* Buddha cults to the evolution of Christianity from long before the Christian era cannot now be reasonably challenged." See in this connection Royce, *op. cit.*, p. 332 f; Streeter, *The Buddha and the Christ*, Lect. 2.

14 In John 17.9 Christ even says : " I pray not for the world, but for those whom thou hast given me." See, however, Moffatt, *op. cit.*, p. 33 f. He admits however that " the mission to the Greeks at Antioch was critical " and that " these innovators were not led by any apostle, nor, so far as we know, did they possess any explicit word of Jesus which warranted them in undertaking such a revolutionary campaign " (p. 100). See Arthur Levett, *A Martian examines Christianity*, p. 54.

15 See ERE. vii. 609 f, art. JUDAIZING ; also Streeter, *Prim. Ch.*, pp. 35-38 ; p. 44 f, p. 56.

16 For the use of the term ' covenant ' in the Last Supper instead of the usual word ' kingdom ' by Christ, see Moffatt, *op. cit.*, pp. 22-3 ; also p. 36 ; for later interpretation, p. 61 f. For the development of the term ' New Testament,' see *Ibid*, p. 54 f.

17 Bethune-Baker, *Early History of Christian Doctrine*, p. 62 f. See also B. H. Streeter, *The Primitive Church*, p. 8.

and influence of Marcion among the Gentiles, on the other hand, lay in the fact that he absolutely rejected Judaism and all historical beginnings of Christianity; accepted St. Paul as the true Apostle in so far as he opposed the Jewish Law; and preached that, as compared with the good God that Christ revealed, the just God of the Jews "was the author of evil works, bloodthirsty, changeable—far from perfect, and ignorant of the highest things, concerned with his own peculiar people only, and keeping them in subjection by means of the Law and the terror of breaking it."[18] These conflicts of views show that the nature and message of Christ were not understood in a uniform sense by the primitive Church and that, as among the followers of Socrates, there was room for genuine differences of opinion. We may presume that the Synoptic Gospels, which were supposed to give an account of Christ's life, ministry and utterances, underwent the greatest amount of retouching at the hands of the finally victorious party just as the Old Testament had undergone revision at the hands of the Deuteronomists and the authors of the Priestly Code, and that necessary omissions and interpolations were effected to present as coherent a canon as was possible in the circumstances. Thus, even if Jesus be an historical personage, it would be risky to affirm that the New Testament gives a verbatim report of all his speeches.[19] This remark applies even to the Sermon on the Mount, for scholars are not agreed as to whether Matthew or Luke gives a more accurate description of what Jesus actually said on the occasion or even whether Jesus delivered the Sermon at all.[20]

18 Bethune-Baker, *op. cit.*, p. 82.

19 See Moffatt, *op. cit.*, p. 151, in this connection.

20 See art. SERMON ON THE MOUNT in *Dic. Bi.*, Ext. Vol., p. 1 f: also Arthur Levett, *A Martian examines Christianity*, pp. 47, 74.

These (the first three) Gospels are not, it is true, historical works any more than the fourth; they were not written with the simple object of giving the facts as they were; they are books composed for the work of evangelisation. Their purpose is to awaken a belief in Jesus Christ's person and mission; and the purpose is served by the description of his deeds and discourses, as well as by the references to the Old Testament.—Harnack, *What is Christianity?*, p. 21.

The conviction that Old Testament prophecy was fulfilled in Jesus' history had a disturbing affect on tradition.—*Ibid.*, p. 241. For a defence of consulting

In fact, the New Testament teachings may very well be regarded as summaries of current ethical maxims and of moral principles originally embedded in larger discourses of Jesus or scattered among his different sermons. There is an obvious advantage in this procedure, for it reduces the size of a scripture and enables the hearer to remember more easily the broad principles of spiritual life and of ethical conduct. We may point, as an illustration, to the analogous case of the Bhagavadgītā : its popularity too depends upon the fact that it summarises the spiritual teachings of the earlier Brāhmaṇical sacred books and is, like the New Testament, put forward as the message of a single teacher.[21] It is also probable that what has been regarded as a gradual consciousness of his own mission by Jesus is really a development in the conception of his nature and mission in the minds of his followers, who expected him originally to function as a temporal saviour[22] and only after his crucifixion began to appreciate and expound the spiritual significance of the Messianic kingdom.

It is necessary to make these remarks because the Christian conception of God is inextricably bound up with a proper understanding of the nature of Christ and because the heretical systems were mostly anathematised on their Christology.[23] It is not unlikely that the first Christians realised the importance of adhering to the rabbinical speculations about divine manifestations which would simultaneously ensure the uniqueness of Christ as a prophet and a messiah in one[24] and satisfy the

the O. T. prophecies in elucidation of the facts of Christ's life and ministry, see Moffatt, *op. cit.*, pp. 85 f, 165.

[21] W. D. Mackenzie points out (ERE. vii, 508) that parallels to many of the features of Christ's teaching can be found in many quarters. "But in the teaching of Jesus they acquire unique significance for three facts : first, from their being unified in the thought of one mind, as they are nowhere else; second, from the exclusion of any alloy of formalism, worldliness, superstition or mere ceremonialism; third, from the fact that they evidently express, and find their unity and power in, His own religious experience and moral character."

[22] Mat. 20.21.

[23] The Gospel, as Jesus proclaimed it, has to do with the Father only and not with the Son.—Harnack, *What is Christianity*?, p. 147 (see also p. 150).

[24] See Harnack, *What is Christianity*?, p. 134, 135 f.

Gentile craving for a plurality in godhead and a saviour god. As a matter of fact, the Cappadocian theology commended its speculations to the thought of the time by an attempt to show that " the Christian doctrine of the Trinity was the mean between Judaism on the one hand and Hellenism on the other (Basil and Gregory of Nyssa)."[25] So the process of hypostasis was pushed farther than in Jewish writings of the pre-Christian era and in Platonic speculations, and Christ was transmuted into the central figure of a cosmic drama, the opening scene of which was laid in the Garden of Eden, where the first parents of man disobeyed the divine injunction through the machinations of Satan, and the last scene in heaven, where the risen Christ sat at the right hand of God, judging individuals by the degree of their acceptance of. the message of salvation preached by him during his incarnation as Jesus. A heavenly pre-existence[26] for him could be easily defended even on Jewish presuppositions; but there was apparently a difference of opinion as to whether that pre-existence was divine or human—even St. Paul refers to him in a solitary passage (I Cor. xv. 47) as the second man from heaven[27] although his general position is that Christ was the ' Son of God ' and truly divine. The books of Isaiah and Daniel, on which much of the original Christology was based, told respectively of the Servant of the Lord[28] and the Divine Ruler and Judge :[29] possibly these two traditions were combined to form the picture of the suffering Christ, the Son of Man, and the risen Lord, the Son of God. Christ sought out the sinner to redeem him just as God had sent down Christ to redeem the sinful human race : so far then as spontaneous grace was concerned Christ could very well say that he who had seen him had seen the Father.

[25] ERE. iii. 214.

[26] *Cf.* John 8.58 : Before Abraham was, I am. See Pringle-Pattison, *Studies in the Philosophy of Religion*, p. 191 f (Christology of the original disciples was one of apotheosis, that of St. Paul one of incarnation).

[27] The first man is Adam. For a discussion of this passage, see Orr, *The Christian View of God and the World*, p. 220 f.

[28] Is. 42. 1 f; also 9.6,7.

[29] Dan. 7.13, 14.

Possibly, there was one other motive involved in the deification of Christ. To a Jew religious law could come only from God, and by religious law a Jew understood not only rules of spiritual and moral life but also socio-religious prescriptions and ceremonial observances. Christ professed to teach the Jews the god of their own ancestors—the God of Abraham, Isaac and Jacob; but unless he were God Himself, he could not possibly abrogate or modify existing religious practices and teach a new method of worshipping Him.[30] The only logical conclusion of this position is that there could be no essential distinction between God and Christ and that the historical Jesus was in fact the incarnation of the eternal Christ who was consubstantial with God Himself. Those who preached docetic doctrines and those who regarded Christ as merely human were equally guilty of heresy,[31] for only the real God could preach a new message of salvation. It was a most vital question with the Church whether Christ was of the same substance with God or only of similar substance with Him and whether he had one nature and will or two natures and wills, human and divine, and if the latter, how the two were related and also whether the humanity was brought from heaven or assumed on earth. The final position that the primitive Church assumed is best summarised in the words of Martineau[32] who points out that the term 'Son of

30 This explains the similarities between Mosaic revelation and the message of Christ. The Sermon on the Mount was modelled on the revelation at Sinai; the forty days' fast on forty days' journey through the wilderness; the gift of tongues of his disciples on law-giving in seventy languages at Sinai (a rabbinical tradition).

31 See *Religious Foundations*, p. 16; ERE. iv. 832.

32 *The Seat of Authority in Religion*, pp. 428-9, quoted in Orr, *op. cit.*, p. 219.

Martineau summarises the views of the Unitarian Church, to which he belongs, in the following words: "As objective reality, as a faithful representation of our invisible and ideal universe, it (the Messianic theology) is gone from us, gone, therefore, from our interior religion, and become an outside mythology. From the Person of Jesus, for instance, everything official, attached to Him by evangelists or divines, has fallen away; when they put such false robes on Him, they were but leading Him to death. The pomp of royal lineage and fulfilled prediction, the prerogative of King, of Priest, of Judge, the advent with retinue of angels on the clouds of heaven, are to us mere deforming investitures, misplaced, like court dresses, on the 'spirits of the just,' and He is simply the Divine

God,' applied to the Word of the Fourth Gospel, can be understood only in one way. Says he, "The oneness with God which it means to mark is not such resembling reflex of the Divine thought and character as men or angels may attain, but identity of essence, constituting Him not God-like alone, but God. Others may be children of God in a moral sense; but by this right of elemental nature, none but He; He is, herein, the only son; so little separate, so close to the inner Divine life which He expresses, that He is in the bosom of the Father. This language undoubtedly describes a great deal more than such harmony of will and sympathy of affection as may subsist between finite obedience and its infinite Inspirer; it denotes two natures homogeneous, entirely one; and both so essential to the Godhead that neither can be omitted from any truth you speak of it......It was one and the same Logos that in the beginning was with God, who in due time appeared in human form, and showed forth the Father's pure perfections in relation to mankind, who then returned to His eternal life, with the spiritual ties unbroken which He brought from His finished work." To such a God-man the ordinary methods of birth and death are an impossibility—so Immaculate Conception[33] and Bodily Resurrection are logical corollaries of the manifestation of this Divine Being. So also "the whole apostolic conception of Jesus as

Flower of humanity, blossoming after ages of spiritual growth—the realised possibility of life in God......All that has been added to that real historical scene,—the angels that hang around His birth, and the fiend that tempts His youth; the dignities that await His future,—the throne, the trumpet, the assize, the bar of judgment; with all the apocalyptic splendours and terrors that ensue,—Hades and the Crystal Sea, Paradise and the Infernal Gulf, nay, the very boundary walls of the Kosmic panorama that contains these things, have for us utterly melted away, and left us amid the infinite space and the silent stars." (*Loss and Gain in Recent Theology*, pp. 14, 15, quoted in Orr, *op. cit.*, pp. 392-3.)

See the paper on *The Unitarians* by H. W. Crosskey in *The Religious Systems of the World*, pp. 602-19, for a summary of Unitarian beliefs.

33 The apocryphal *Protevangelium of James* gave an account of the miraculous birth and espousal of Virgin Mary which ultimately led to her adoration as the Queen of Heaven.—See *Christianity etc.*, p. 330. See also A. Levett, *op. cit.*, p. 80 f, for other virgin births.

For an historical account of the worship of Virgin Mary as the Mother of God (*Theotokos*), see Jameson, *The Legend of the Madonna*, p. xxi; G. C. Coulton, *Five Centuries of Religion*, Vol. I, Chs. IX and X (also Appendix 19).

Risen Saviour and Lord was utterly inconsistent with any thought of His own guilt and need of pardon or redemption;"[34] hence Christ was regarded as absolutely sinless.

But speculation did not stop with ascribing to Christ a heavenly pre-existence and a bodily ascension, nor did the Messianic function remain limited to providing a willing sacrifice for the atonement of man's sins and a heavenly intercessor at the bar of Divine judgment.[35] In the last two or three centuries before the Christian era a fairly big literature, mostly collected now under apocryphal and apocalyptic writings, had grown up, voicing forth Israel's faith in a heavenly 'Son of God' or 'Son of Man' and in a Messiah who would bring back its past glory and rule over the whole earth.[36] To the Son of God was assigned the right of final judgment; and with the Messiah was also to return the Holy Spirit to inspire again the prophets of Israel. The other intermediaries like the Wisdom, the Angel and the Word were identified with and ultimately set aside in favour of a supreme Mediator who is the 'first-born' of God and even 'Christ the Lord;' they were also often identified with the Holy Spirit and He is described as coming with 'Christ the Lord' who appears in wisdom of the spirit and righteousness and power.[37] There was a marked tendency towards hypostatising these beings, and thus the uncompromising monotheism of the Jews was

[34] ERE. vii. 509.

[35] Mat. 10.32-3.

Contrasting Christ with the Levitical high priest, the writer of the Epistle to the Hebrews declares that "no defilement unfitted Christ for His sacred ministry. As a Son, he was perfected for evermore, and had no need either to offer for His own sins or to repeat His sacrifice made once for all when He offered up Himself. B. F. Westcott shows that the fulfilment of the Levitical type by Christ takes three forms: (1) He intercedes for men as their present representative before God (He. 7.25 f; 9.24); (2) He brings man's prayers to God (He. 13.15); (3) He secures access for man to God (He. 4.16; 10.19 f)."—ERE. vii. 184, art. INTERCESSION.

[36] See *Dic. Bi.*, Ext. Vol., p. 308 f for references.

Wernle thinks that "the choice by Jesus of the three titles, Messiah, Son of God, and Son of Man, 'from the first turned out to be the misfortune of the new religion'." (ERE. vii. 507.) See Moffatt, *op. cit.*, p. 164.

[37] *Dic. Bi.*, Ext. Vol., p. 308; also Orr, *op. cit.*, p. 264.

moving towards " a doctrine of distinctions interior to the Divine essence;" and, in the development of the doctrine, the plural form 'Elohim' and Yahweh's consulting the angels or a heavenly family were utilised to relieve the blank monadism of the divine nature. It appears, therefore, that most of the elements that went to form the basis of the Christian doctrine of Messiah (and of Trinity) were in the air,[38] and what we get in the New Testament is a more or less organised picture of these ideas with the conception of the Messiah assuming human existence—of the Word becoming flesh—superadded. For this last the prophetic passages about a virgin (interpreted to mean not a young woman married for the first time but a woman who has known no man) being with a child and the suffering servant of the Lord[39] were found extremely useful. In due time Christ was conceived as existing from all eternity with God, as responsible for the creation of all things, as revealing the nature of God by his love, his sinless conscience and his redemptive act of sacrifice on the Cross, as acting both as intercessor and judge on the Day of Judgment and as returning in glory and establishing for ever the kingdom of God. The Nicene Creed is a fair summary of the final claims put forward on behalf of Jesus : " one Lord Jesus Christ, the Son of God, begotten of the Father, only-begotten, that is of the substance of the Father, God of God, Light of Light, very God of very God, begotten, not made, of one substance with the Father, by whom all things were made, both those in heaven and those on earth : who for us men and for our salvation came down

38 " Such terms as Redemption, Baptism, Grace, Faith, Salvation, Regeneration, Son of Man, Son of God, Kingdom of Heaven, were not, as we are apt to think, invented by Christianity, but were household words of Talmudical Judaism. No less loud and bitter in the Talmud are the protests against lip-serving, against making the law a burden to the people, against 'laws that hang on hairs,' against Priests and Pharisees. That grand dictum, 'Do unto others as thou wouldst be done by,' is quoted by Hillel, at whose death Jesus was ten years of age, not as anything new, but as an old and well-known dictum, that comprised the whole Law."—Emanuel Deutsch, quoted by Bettany in *Judaism and Christianity* (1892), pp. 101-2.

39 Bettany, *op. cit.*, pp. 82-3; also p. 61, n.1 for the Messianic foreshadowings in the Psalms. See also Moffatt, *op. cit.*, p. 24, 94. See Levett, *op. cit.*, p. 8?

and was made flesh, and lived as Man among men, suffered, and rose the third day, ascended into heaven and is coming to judge the quick and the dead." When deification had proceeded so far it was difficult to keep God and Christ entirely distinct and the monotheistic motive, which was never abandoned seriously, could only lead to the assimilation of Christ to God. So Christ claims to be one with his Father[40] and preaches that he who has seen him has seen the Father and that he is in the Father and the Father is in him; and, " while citing Old Testament Messianic sayings, He sets Himself in the place of Jahweh—*e.g.*, Mt $11^{4f}$ = Is $35^{3}$ $61^{1}$, Lk $4^{17}$ = Is $61^{1f}$, Lk $7^{27}$ = Mal $3^{1}$." We are back, in other words, to that familiar mode of thinking in which the apotheosis of the prophet plays an important part, only that the process is here covered up by the assumption that he had a heavenly pre-existence and that he only descended on earth to perform a redemptive act of grace. The position is thus intermediate between a full-fledged incarnation of the deity, such as we met with in Hinduism, and a deification of the prophet, as was done by Buddhism.

It may very well be asked if the original picture of Jesus is not that of a teacher after the manner of the old Jewish prophets and if the Synoptic Gospels do not represent a transition to the aspect of Divinity.[41] Thus Scott remarks,[42] "It is of great significance that of the two earliest attempts to collect what was remembered about Jesus, one (Q) appears to have recorded one miracle only (if that), otherwise (apart from the narrative of the Passion, if that were included), it is wholly occupied with the discourses of Jesus." The *Didache*. in its two titles 'Teaching of the Twelve Apostles' and

40 As against John 10.30 (I and my Father are one) we have John 14.28 (My Father is greater than I). In the tenth chapter we have within nine verses (30-38) three slightly different wordings : 'I and my Father are one,' 'I am the Son of God,' and 'The Father is in me and I in Him.' This last is repeated in the fourteenth chapter (10,11) although the first is implied also (7).

41 See Streeter and others, *Foundations*, III. The Historic Christ (esp. p. 80 f).

42 *Christianity etc.*, p. 346.

'Teaching of the Lord through the Twelve Apostles to the Gentiles,' also limits itself mostly to an exposition of the essentials of Christ's message and the method of government of the incipient Church, and there the itinerant prophets and teachers take precedence over the local bishops and deacons.[43] Christianity is here expressed in forms determined by Judaism;[44] but as Christianity begins to develop on Greek and Roman soil, "the ministry of the Word is thrust into the background and the Sacraments usurp the primary place,"[45] and very likely an alteration in the conception of the nature of Christ in the meantime was responsible for this change.[46] Scott remarks,[47] "The Christology of the Synoptic Gospels comprises two distinguishable elements. There is the record of what may be called the spontaneous revelation of the character and nature of Jesus, culminating in certain glimpses of His own consciousness regarding Himself;[48] and there is the evidence, partly direct and partly indirect, as to the interpretation which was put upon all they knew concerning Him by those who formed the inner circle of His disciples. What these Gospels thus provided is not a Christology so much as some of the materials for a Christology, together with certain incipient forms into which these incomplete materials provisionally crystallised." Do we owe this transformation of a prophetic Jesus into a divine Jesus to St. Peter, and were the keys of the kingdom of heaven a reward for thus elevating Jesus to the rank of God? "Now when Jesus came into the parts of Caesarea Philippi, he asked his disciples, saying, Who do men say that the Son of man is? And they said, Some say John the Baptist; some, Elijah: and others,

43 Streeter and others, *Foundations*, p. 388; Moffatt, *op. cit.*, p. 106; see Streeter, *Primitive Church*, pp. 77 f, 145, and 149 f.

44 *Dic. Bi.*, Ext. Vol., p. 448, art. DIDACHE.

45 *Foundations*, p. 388; Moffatt, *op. cit.*, pp. 45-6.

46 Harnack speaks of Jesus in the following terms: "This feeling, praying, working, struggling and suffering individual is a man who in the face of his God also associates himself with other men."—*What is Christianity?*, pp. 129-30.

47 *Christianity etc.*, p. 346.

48 For a discussion of the self-consciousness of Jesus, see Orr, *op. cit.*, Lect. VI. Appendix (p. 248 f); also ERE. vii. 508 f; Moffatt, *op. cit.*, p. 159 f.

Jeremiah, or one of the prophets. He saith unto them, But who say ye that I am? And Simon Peter answered and said, Thou art the Christ, the Son of the living God. And Jesus answered and said unto him, Blessed art thou, Simon Bar-Jonah: for flesh and blood hath not revealed it unto thee, but my Father which is in heaven. And I also say unto thee, that thou art Peter, and upon this rock[49] I will build my church; and the gates of Hades shall not prevail against it. I will give unto thee the keys of the kingdom of heaven; and whatsoever thou[50] shalt bind on earth shall be bound in heaven: and whatsoever thou shalt loose on earth shall be loosed in heaven. Then charged he the disciples that they should tell no man that he was the Christ."[51] To quote Dummelow,[52] "The other apostles had by this time attained to the conviction that Jesus was the Messiah, but only Peter had made the great venture of faith which is implied in the acknowledgment of the divinity of Christ." Thus the Christ who is made to say in the right Jewish fashion, "Why callest thou me good? none is good, save one, even God,"[53] ultimately assumes all the titles of God and receives the homage of mankind as the Saviour and the Lord.[54] And he who had said, "I came not to judge the world, but to save

[49] The Roman Catholic Launoy reckons that seventeen Fathers regard Peter as the rock; forty-four regard Peter's confession as the rock; while eight are of opinion that the Church is built on all the Apostles.—Dummelow, *op. cit.*, p. 681.

[50] But see John 20.22 23; Mat. 18.18-20. See Streeter, *Prim. Ch.*, p. 60.

[51] Mat. 16.13-20. Mark 8.27-9 and Luke 9.18-20 simply refer to Peter's confession without the promises of Jesus. For an instructive discussion of the episode, see Dummelow, *op. cit.*, p. 681.

[52] Dummelow, *op. cit.*, p. 681.

[53] Mark 10.18; Luke 18.19.

It is interesting to note that Matthew who records Peter's confession about the divinity of Christ omits (19.17) to mention God specifically in connection with the episode. See Pringle-Pattison, *Studies in Ph. of Rel.*, p. 164 f.

[54] See *Religious Foundations*, pp. 21-2.

For a list of passages embodying Jesus' claims, see Basanta Coomar Bose, *Christianity*, p. 66 f. Moffatt points out, among other things, that the rise of the term "Lord" as applied to Jesus is by no means so obvious and plain as some text-books suggest (*op. cit.*, p. 203).

the world,''[55] was raised to the position of one who would judge the quick and the dead.[56]

We reach now a point where the Jewish conception of a transcendent God is counteracted by the Christian belief in a God who walked on earth and exercised all divine functions. Miracles are performed to signalise his entry into earthly existence; water turns into wine, fishes get into nets and loaves and fishes are multiplied at his wish;[57] the diseased are healed, the blind receive their sight, the dumb speak, the paralytic walk, and even the dead are raised; the sea fails to drown him and the winds and waves are rebuked by him into silence; evil spirits leave their victims and even fig trees wither at his word of command,[58] and finally he ascends bodily to heaven after he had been in the grave for three days.[59] The assimilation to God proceeds further. The prophets of old, and even John the Baptist, had called the people to repentance; but Christ assumed the right to forgive the sinner, which the Jews had reserved for God alone. With the assumption of this Divine right all resemblance to ordinary mortals in respect of relation to God the Father naturally ceased. If the Sermon on the Mount represents

55 John 12.47; 1 John 2.1.

56 2 Tim. 4.1.

57 For rabbinical and other parallels of these feats, see Moffatt, *op. cit.*, pp. 128-33.

58 W. H. Pinnock, *An Analysis of New Testament History* (1878), pp. 320-1; *Religious Foundations*, p. 17; also Harnack, *op. cit.*, pp. 29-30.

59 For any one who reflects, there can be little doubt the appearances which convinced the original disciples of their Master's continued life and activity were, in point of fact, visions of the same nature as St. Paul records in his own case. —Pringle-Pattison, *Studies in Ph. of Rel.*, p. 182.

This series of visions lasted for some time ("forty days" is, of course, a round symbolical number), and the affairs of the divine kingdom are probably the interests and prospects of the new messianic era, as we see from the context (Acts i. 2-3). But later tradition seized upon this tale for its own purposes. The forty days were extended to eighteen months and even twelve years in order to allow time for the communication of a vast esoteric doctrine to the apostles.— Moffatt, *op. cit.*, p. 190. It is interesting to note that Mahāyāna Buddhism also claims to derive its origin from similar esoteric teachings of the Master not to be found in the Hīnayāna texts. See E. J. Thomas, *The History of Buddhistic Thought*, Ch. XIV; also Winternitz, *A History of Indian Literature*, Vol. II, p. 229.

anything like the original position of Jesus,[60] we can understand why there alone the expression 'Our Father' should find a place in the Lord's Prayer.[61] Once Christ was raised to the divine plane, his Father and the Father of the Apostles or of the people at large could not be conceived in identical terms; the unique relationship of Christ to God, on account of which God reveals Himself completely to and through him,[62] was distinguished both from the relationship of the believers and disciples to God and from the sonship of the rest of mankind, including "the unthankful and the evil," to Him. While it was not denied that the individual soul could enter into direct communion with God, it was affirmed at the same time that it could do so only "as a member of the kingdom of His Son."[63] No wonder, therefore, that St. Paul's exhortation to pray for those who were outside the Christian fold, so that they might "come to the knowledge of the truth" (I Tim. 2.1-4), should be practically ignored and that neither in Justin Martyr (*circa* 150 A.D.) nor in the *Didache* should be found any trace of liturgical intercession for any one outside the

60 The Sermon seems to have been delivered almost immediately after the appointment of the Twelve Apostles. The Gospel of Matthew agrees with that of Luke in locating the Sermon on the Mount in the first half of Jesus' ministry in Galilee, although Matthew places it somewhat nearer to the beginning of that period......But on any chronological hypothesis the discourse stands about half-way between the beginning of Jesus' public work and His crucifixion.—*Dic. Bi.*, Ext. Vol.. pp. 2-3, art. SERMON ON THE MOUNT. (But see Note 20 above.)

61 T. von Haering finds in the use of the words 'Our' and 'us' in the Lord's Prayer a justification for belief in intercession (ERE. vii. 383). But a more natural explanation is that the prayer was meant to be used in a congregation of the faithful and perhaps recited in a chorus where the plural form would be the most natural.

62 All things have been delivered unto me of my Father: and no one knoweth the Son save the Father; neither doth any know the Father, save the Son, and he to whomsoever the Son willeth to reveal him.—Mat. 11.27.

(This passage does not match very well with the one preceding where God is addressed by Jesus.) See also John 3.18: He that believeth on him is not judged: he that believeth not hath been judged already, because he hath not believed on the name of the only begotten Son of God. See *Dic. Bi.*, II, p. 209, art. GOD.

63 Orr, *op. cit.*, p. 79.

Church,[64] thus establishing once more the triumph of the spirit of Jewish exclusiveness from which primitive Christianity does not seem to have completely extricated itself.[65]

There were, however, two elements in the Christian conception of God which were bound to give it an advantage over Judaism. The Jews had indeed attempted to develop the conception of the immanence of God in a number of ways, but except in the conception of the Holy Spirit, which perennially inspired men ethically and spiritually, they had not succeeded in establishing the indwelling of the deity in the world. Christianity did not indeed abandon altogether the casual manifestation (theophany) of a transcendent God through such visible symbols as a dove[66] or a tongue of fire; but in preaching that the Divine Messiah had come down to dwell among men as Man, it definitely raised the dignity of human life and provided for men's participation in divine life through Jesus Christ the God-man.[67] It did something more The Old Testament had not speculated very much about the motive of Divine manifestation, although it had a general theory that God manifested Himself whenever the needs of righteousness demanded it and also when some good to Israel was intended by Him. That God incarnated Himself through Jesus to redeem the sinner; that what punishment He in His justice was obliged to inflict on man He wished to take away in His mercy through the sacrifice of Jesus so that men might not have to pay the wages of sin, which is death, but might enjoy eternal life;[68] that God did not wait for the disappearance of sin through human effort before ushering in His

64 ERE. vii. 385, art. INTERCESSION (Liturgical).

65 The New Testament basis for this would be John 17.9: I pray not for the world, but for them whom thou hast given me; for they are thine.

66 Canon Lindsay Dewar suggests that the true meaning of the dove-symbol is to be found in the fact that the Hebrew word for 'dove' is Jonah and that Jonah who lived for three days in the whale's belly was a sign of Christ himself who was to be in the grave for a similar period.—See *Imagination and Religion*, p. 58.

67 See J. Caird, *The Fundamental Ideas of Christianity*, II, p. 104 (also 114).

68 This statement does not exhaust the entire theory of Christian atonement. W. Adams Brown in ERE. v. 650 thus summarises the matter: "Whether we consider the Atonement from the point of view of its nature, its object, its

Kingdom on earth—the belief in these gracious acts of God marked a definite advance upon the Jewish prayer for the forgiveness of sins and the Jewish belief that the removal of sin was a pre-condition of the advent of the Divine Kingdom. The institution of the Day of Atonement,[69] when the Jewish nation as a whole confessed its sins before Yahweh through the High Priest, "ever held before the people's eyes the mysterious connection of forgiving love with awful justice;" but that Yahweh would himself condescend to provide a better atonement than goats and bulls out of His love for the world and thus hasten the advent of His own kingdom on earth the Jews did not think it possible. To the repentant sinner and to those who doubted the possibility of winning Yahweh's salvation through individual effort the call of Christ—"Come unto me, all ye that labour and are heavy laden, and I will give you rest. Take my yoke upon you, and learn of me; for I am meek and lowly in heart: and ye shall

necessity, or the means by which it is made practically effective in men's lives, we find differences of views so striking as to make any attempt at harmony seem hopeless. The atoning character of Christ's death is now found in its penal quality as suffering, now in its ethical character as obedience. It is represented now as a ransom to redeem men from Satan, now as a satisfaction due to the honour of God, now as a penalty demanded by His justice. Its necessity is grounded now in the nature of things, and, again, is explained as the result of an arrangement due to God's own good pleasure or answering His sense of fitness. The means by which its benefits are mediated to men are sometimes mystically conceived, as in the Greek theology of the Sacrament, sometimes legally, as in the Protestant formula of imputation; and still, again, morally and spiritually, as in the more personal theories of recent Protestantism." (For *Imputation*, see ERE. vii. 180).

He notices five types of interpretation of Christ's death (ERE. v. 641 f): (1) That it is a fulfilment of OT prophecy (Act 3.18); (2) that it is the establishment of a new covenant between God and his disciples through the sacrifice of his own life-blood (Mat. 26.28; Heb.9.11-28); (3) that it is a ransom paid to deliver men from sin (Mark 10.45; 1 Cor. 6.20; 7.23; I Pet. 1.18 f; Tit. 2.14; Eph. 1.14); (4) that it is the expiation demanded by Divine justice for the wilful sin of humanity with which Christ identifies himself and for which he becomes a substitute (of which the OT originals are 1 Kings 2.31; 2 Sam. 24; 1 Chr.21; Isa. 53); (5) that it is "a part of the entire process of the Divine self-identification with humanity" which enables men to partake of his life and share in his triumph over death. See in this connection Royce, *op. cit.*, p. 271 f; R. J. Campbell, *The New Theology*, Chs. viii-x; Caird, *The Fundamental Ideas of Christianity*, Vol. II, Lects.xvi-xvii.

69 Bettany, *op. cit.*, p. 31 f.

find rest unto your souls. For my yoke is easy, and my burden is light.''—must have sounded extremely inviting. And the message that he taught—'' God so loved the world, that he gave his only begotten Son, that whosoever believeth on him should not perish, but have eternal life. For God sent not the Son into the world to judge the world; but that the world should be saved through him.''—must have revealed a new aspect of God's love, namely, that He not only feels for the sinner but takes active steps to save him by sending a redeemer.[70]

The fatherhood of God now takes on a new significance. Like a loving father, ever ready to welcome back the prodigal son, God is only waiting for sinners to confess their guilt and accept His message of redemption preached through Christ in order to make them inheritors of an eternal life. Through faith, obedience, prayer and right living man can always win back the affection of God, for God is Love[71] and He ever responds to human appeal of love and overlooks the past faults of a repentant heart. There is to be no compromise, however, with unrighteousness; and no amount of formal observance of the Mosaic Law and the Temple Sacrifice or even of Synagogue Prayer would avail a man unless he purifies his heart and extends to his fellow-men the same charity as he expects of God and shows the same indulgence towards the latter's failings which he hopes God to show to his own.[72] By using the epithet ' Father ' in preference to other epithets of God, Jesus brought home to the mind of the people the aspect of His lovingkindness which Jeremiah had taught before and the relative unimportance of the ceremonial method of approach which was inseparable from the idea of Yahweh as King in Jewish minds. We may not subscribe to the

70 Rom. 5.8. See *Dic. Bi.*, II, p. 211 : The absolution of the sinner is no act of momentary indulgence, but a deliberately contemplated incident in a vast and far-reaching plan which has for its object the restoration of the human race.

71 1 John 4.8, 16.

72 If a man say, I love God, and hateth his brother, he is a liar : for he that loveth not his brother whom he hath seen, cannot love God whom he hath not seen. (1 John 4.20.) See Mat. 5.21-22, 44-7; 6.12, 14.5; 18-22.

trinitarian view that God the Father is inconceivable without an eternal God the Son towards whom possibly His eternal love is directed,[73] just as we may oppose the Vaiṣṇava idea that an eternal Rādhā is necessary for the eternal love of Kṛṣṇa. But it is no small confidence that a sinner acquires if he be convinced that justice is going to be tempered by mercy and that the Divine Judge is also the Father in heaven who would stretch forth His arms to receive him as soon as proper atonement has been made: "perfect love casteth out fear" and "he that feareth is not made perfect in love."[74] And the corollary from this belief is of great importance to society. If God is love, His entire creation must be knit together by the silken cords of mutual goodwill and affection and all disagreement and dispute are out of place in His realm: there must be peace on earth and goodwill towards men if the glory of God is to shine here below. And by goodwill is to be understood not a mere benevolent disposition but an active charity towards the poor and the oppressed, the widow and the orphan,[75] as the prophets had preached before, and also an active interest in the life of the sinners, which the prophets and the rabbis had not practised systematically. "Faith without works is dead."[76]

Although it is very likely that at one time there was a tendency to recover the lost sheep of the house of Israel alone and to eschew the Gentiles and the Samaritans[77] and it is only when the appeal to the Jews did not meet with the success expected that the command to teach all nations and preach repentance and remission of sins was put into the mouth of the

[73] Thus Martensen in his *Christian Dogmatics* writes, "When then we teach with the Church the eternal preëxistence and independence of creation not only of the Father but also of the Son and the Spirit, we thereby affirm that God, in order to be self-revealing, self-loving God, must eternally differentiate himself into I and Thou, and just as eternally unite himself with himself as the Spirit of love that proceeds from the relation of contrast."—Quoted by Ward in *The Realm of Ends*, p. 190.

[74] See 1 John 4.16-19.

[75] See Mat. 25.35-40; Luke 14.12-4.

[76] James 2.26 (see the whole chapter).

[77] Mat. 10:5-6; 15.24; 18.17; Mark 7.27; and many other passages (see Basanta Coomar Bose, *Christianity*, p. 55).

resurgent Christ,[78] still Christianity should be tested not by its beginnings but by its later developments. There can be no doubt that the message of Christ was understood and applied in a universalistic sense by the primitive Church, mostly under the influence of St. Paul perhaps, and that 'Salvation is of the Jews only' and such other passages that limited missionary activity exclusively or primarily within the Jews were practically ignored after the first few years of Jesus' death.[79] To the end of his days Jesus remained a Jew and only asked his hearers to remember the spiritual aspect of their own religion while fulfilling the Law, just as Ram Mohan Roy at a later time asked his fellow-Hindus to follow the monistic tenets of their own Upaniṣads and Vedānta philosophy: ultimately, however, both became founders of new religions. The reason in the case of Christianity was that the followers of Jesus preached him, with the effect that the Christian religion widely diverged in course of time from the religion of Christ.[80] Possibly, there was no other way of reaching the non-Jews under the conditions of the time: the Gentiles could not, and possibly would not, have taken part in the Jewish religious service, and a saviour-god was nearer their own heart and conviction at that time.[81] St. Paul "views Christ's coming and work both as giving sonship to those who were only servants, and also as giving full filial rights to those who were children under age. But not as if it were the former only to Gentiles and the latter to Jews as such; but that it was a real gift of sonship to all, whether Jews or Gentiles, who were without God; and to all who were really seeking him, in whatever nation, though they might be very immature in their spiritual life, it was the bestowal of the full privileges of sons of full age having free and direct access

[78] See Acts 28.23-8.

[79] See Moffatt, *op. cit.*, p. 26. For Paul's contribution to the doctrine of love, see Royce, *op. cit.*, p. 91 f. The passage has also been interpreted to mean that the Jews alone are privileged to preach the message of salvation to mankind.

[80] See Pringle-Pattison, *Studies in the Phil. of Rel.*, p. 177 f. On Paul's contribution to this development, see Harnack, *What is Christianity?*, p. 179 f; on its weak points, p. 186 f.

[81] See Pringle-Pattison, *Studies in the Phil. of Rel.*, p. 205 f.

to God as their Father.''[82] But this sonship has to be acquired: "every one that doeth righteousness is born of him''[83] and "Whosoever is begotten of God doeth no sin.''[84]

The fatherhood of God, therefore, has far-reaching consequences for Christian life inasmuch as it includes the practical recognition of the brotherhood of man, the necessity of righteous living as exemplified in the life of Christ, and the acceptance of Jesus as the Son of God who by his atoning death on the Cross effected a reconciliation between Divine justice and Divine mercy and brought salvation not to the Jews alone but to every one who would accept him. Incidentally, it diminished the importance of ritualistic worship—external conformity to written and unwritten law in matters of prayer, sabbath-keeping, gifts to the Temple, circumcision. observance of the national feasts, and such other matters; it also emphasised the need of purifying motives, abandoning pride and adopting humility, confessing sins, trusting to Divine providence even in matters of daily maintenance, and practising charity to the needy.[85] Jesus did not have to preach a new religion so far as the Jews were concerned, for their own religion contained most of these injunctions: what he had to do was to put them in mind of what their own prophets had taught.[86] But to the non-Jews the message of a God whose lovingkindness encourages sinners to confess their guilt and to trust to His guidance must have been a novel idea;[87] and when this was coupled with the provision for indi-

[82] *Dic. Bi.*, II, p. 218, art. GOD, CHILDREN OF.

[83] 1 John 2.29.

[84] 1 John 3.9. In the combination of these ideas—God the Father, Providence, the position of men as God's children, the infinite value of the human soul—the Gospel is expressed.—Harnack, *What is Christianity?*, p. 70.

[85] See Mat. 23 in this connection; the picture is apparently overdrawn when applied to the Scribes and the Pharisees as a class.

[86] See *Foundations*, p. 20: "He preached no new theology, but grafted his message of fulfilment into the stock of Jewish faith in God wheresoever it was alive."

[87] In the so-called Zadokite document of Jewish piety, just before the days of Jesus, the idea of a new covenant, a covenant of repentance, began to be linked to the expectation of a messiah.—Moffatt, *op. cit.*, p. 60.

vidual immortality through participation in the spirit of a saviour-god, the appeal must have been almost irresistible.

The over-emphasis on the Messianic concept had the effect of obscuring the ideas regarding the other manifestations of Yahweh, particularly the idea of the Holy Spirit. The Spirit of God as the abiding witness of the presence of God in the human mind was conceived in Judaism as producing, among other things, prophetic inspiration, moral purity and religious consecration.[88] The Apostolic Age began to conceive of the salvation of Jesus as meant for all men and for all times; and when God Himself was supposed to have spoken through Christ direct and not through the imperfect medium of a human prophet, naturally the need of further prophecy was over. So Christ was not only the author but also the finisher or perfecter of faith.[89] No new revelation of God's will could come after Christ had taught[90] and such prophecy as persisted for some time in the infant Church came from and through the Spirit of Christ.[91] It appears, therefore, that this virtual supersession of the Jewish idea of Divine manifestation through the human spirit (signified by the term 'Holy Spirit') by the ideas of a pre-existent Messiah and Wisdom or Logos rolled into one (standing for the cosmic dealings of God through Christ) was responsible for the theory of Last Revelation—only that a careless slip about sending a Paraclete after Jesus had ascended to heaven[92] was promptly seized upon by Muhammad as Jesus' prophecy regarding his (Muhammad's) own advent as

88 *Dic. Bi.*, II, p. 411.

89 Heb. 12.2.

90 Acts 4.12.

91 The original belief was that the Apostles were directly and completely inspired. In the second century came the belief that every document which claimed admission to the sacred canon must be inspired or composed by an apostle.—See Moffatt, *op. cit.*, pp. 47-8 (See Rev. 19.10).

In the Old Testament prophecy had reference to national needs; but in the New Testament the prophets speak to the Church alone.—Moffatt, *op. cit.*, p. 212.

92 John 14.16, 26. Christ says he will pray the Father and He will send the Comforter. See 20. 22 where the Holy Ghost is breathed by him into his disciples.

the Last Prophet.[93] But even in the New Testament there are evidences to show that the physical manifestation of the Holy Spirit, about which the Rabbis had spoken, was originally accepted as true, and in immaculate conception, at the baptism of Jesus, and at the meeting of the Apostles on the eve of their ministry after the death of Jesus, the Holy Spirit assumed some sort of physical appearance and it also came to Simeon and others, at the time either of Jesus' conception or of his birth, in a more intangible form. The personality of the Holy Ghost is, however, pale and shadowy by the side of that of Jesus,[94] and but for the fact that a few passages retain the more ancient tradition that the Holy Spirit comes directly to all individuals (*e.g.*, Luke xi. 13) it would have been difficult to find a place for the concept in the Christian gospels. As a matter of fact, the manifestation of " a divine spirit of Mercy and of Wisdom and of Truth,"[95] which the Holy Spirit stands for, was so diversely identified that while, on the one hand, it was equated with Christ himself, later Christianity in some of its forms felt no scruple, on the other hand, in identifying it with a Mother-God (unconsciously imitating thereby the Osiris-Isis-Horus group or resuscitating the feminine term 'Wisdom' of Jewish religion)

93 Mānī, the founder of the eclectic Manichaeism, had made the same claim before Muhammad.—See Jackson, *Researches in Manichaeism with special reference to the Turfan Fragments*, p. 7.

94 Paul's language concerning the Holy Spirit does not bear so immediately upon his doctrine of God, because the word 'Spirit' sometimes indicates a gift of God to men and sometimes God Himself working in men, as it did in the OT. A closer examination shows that the Holy Spirit is not a mere gift or influence; yet, while Divine, He is not the whole Godhead. The intensely personal language employed in such passages as 1 Co 2.10, 11, Ro 8.15, 26, and elsewhere, combined with the distinction maintained between the Spirit and Christ, the Spirit and the Father, makes the interpretation of the Holy Spirit in an OT or 'Unitarian' sense impossible. Again, apart from the phraseology of benediction in 2 Co 13.14, the general tenor of description in such passages as 1 Co 12. 4-6 and Eph. 2.18, 22 shows that St. Paul thinks easily and naturally in terms of a Tri-unity in the Godhead, when speaking of Divine operations in the salvation of men and in the worship of the Church.—ERE. vi. 258, art. GOD (Biblical and Christian). See also ERE. xii. 459-60, art. TRINITY; also xi. 793 f.

95 Hopkins, *The Origin and Evolution of Religion*, p. 339.

—and this Mother was indifferently thought of as Mary (the Mother of God)[96] or the Church (whose children the Christians are) or even as the deaconesses of the early Church.[97] If the interpolated passage in the last chapter of Matthew be kept out of account, it would be difficult to establish a trinitarian belief on the New Testament, where, in different parts, two only of the Divine Trinity are more often referred to together.[98] But the later belief that Christ sent the Holy Spirit to abide permanently in his Church had a tendency to assign to the latter a definitely inferior status, which is a complete reversal of the position that the Son of God was born of the Holy Ghost[99] and that "Whosoever shall speak a word against the Son of man, it shall be forgiven him; but whosoever shall speak against the Holy Spirit, it shall not be forgiven him, neither in this world, nor in that which is to come."[100] When God and Christ were assimilated to each other, the Holy Spirit came to be regarded as proceeding from both the Father and the Son : it is in this form that the belief appears in the *Westminster Confession* and on this is based the fiction that from the pre-existent Son of God proceeded the inspiration that gave to pre-Christian prophets their spiritual insight and their power of revelation (' Before Abraham was, I am'). As a matter of fact, the tendency of subsequent thought was to limit the gift of the Holy Spirit (in the sense of divine inspiration) to the Church as a whole[101] or at least to the assembly of pious Christians,[102] although the Apostles had no difficulty in promising the gift of the Holy Ghost to all who

[96] In the Qur'ān the Christian Trinity is taken as composed of God, Mary and Christ.

[97] Hopkins, *Or. & Ev. of Rel.*, p. 338.

[98] See 2 Cor. 13.14; 1 John 5.7-8; also Mark 12.36; Luke 2.26; Acts 1.16; 20.28. Refer in this connection specially to Bethune-Baker, *op. cit.*, Ch. XIII. The Doctrine of the Holy Spirit and the Trinity.

[99] Luke 1.35.

[100] See Mat. 12.31-2; Mk. 3.29; Lk. 12.10.

[101] 2 Pet. 1 20 (See Dummelow, *op. cit.*, p. 1050). See esp. ERE. xi. 795 where the distinction between Pauline and Johannine conceptions is to be found.

[102] Quakerism may very well quote Acts 2. 1-4 in support of the view that when people are ' with one accord in one place ' (The Revised Version has ' all together in one place'), the Holy Ghost descends on the assembly and moves the tongue.

would accept the message of Christ[103] and in preaching that the operation of the spirit of God might endow different individuals with different powers.[104]

So far as the development of the Christian life is concerned, it is immaterial, however, in what relation the Holy Spirit stands to God the Father and God the Son or whether it is sufficiently hypostatised, so long as it is acknowledged that people could draw the inspiration of their lives from the influx of divinity into themselves by initiation into the Christian religion. God as the ultimate source of all spirituality in man, the Holy Spirit as the power of God working in man in the form of striving towards moral and spiritual ideals, and Christ representing the possibility of a perfect realisation of infinite ideals in a finite life constituted a trinity which satisfied all spiritual needs;[105] and the enthusiasm and energy of the first disciples (who mastered different tongues to speak to the surrounding nations in their own languages[106] about the message of Christ) can only be compared with those displayed by the Arabs after their acceptance of the message of Muhammad. The following quotation well summarises the effects of the belief, that the spirit of God had come to dwell in the Church, as gathered from *the Acts of the Apostles*: "There was a wide-spread diffusion of the Spirit not only in Palestine, but further afield in the Roman Empire, and it was manifested, abnormally and explosively, by extraordinary elevation of human faculties, so that miracles, prophecy, glossolaly, and visions were abundant; more normally in great enthusiasm, new courage, liberty of speech, skill in debate, keen insight into and wise use of scripture, sound judgment of human character, business aptitude, and comfort in suffering. The Spirit is not presented as the principle of ethical life, as in Paul, yet ethical qualities of repentance,

[103] Acts 2.38-9 19.6. See *Foundations*, pp. 42, 69.

[104] Acts 2.4-11.

[105] See J. S. Huxley, *Religion without Revelation*, Ch. II.

[106] The gift of tongues, referred to in Acts ii. 4, is probably an echo of the Jewish traditions of the Law-giving in seventy languages at Sinai.—See ERE. xi. 792.

obedience, and faith are needed for its reception, and it belonged to every believer. In the communal life of the Ecclesia it inspired mutual service, generous self-sacrifice, joyous fellowship, thus transforming and socialising human nature. The Spirit supervised every stage of the Ecclesia's advance, but neither conferred infallibility nor superseded human judgment. It is described impersonally as a gift, which God gives or the Son outpours, more usually as power. Yet personal actions are attributed to the Spirit: it 'speaks,' 'bears witness,' 'separates' for service, 'approves' a conciliar decision, 'forbids,' 'appoints overseers,' and can be 'resisted,' 'tempted,' and 'lied against.' In these last cases the Spirit is co-ordinated with God, but there is no attempt to think out the relation of the Spirit to the Father and the Son. Once, though perhaps the passage denotes merely a vision, it is called 'the Spirit of Jesus' ($16^7$). But, as regards men, the Spirit denotes the divine, the supernatural, for it comes from God, indicates Jesus' claim to be Messiah, authenticates His exaltation, fulfils OT prophecy, and is the medium whereby He is present and operative within His Church.''[107] In Pauline literature the operation of the Holy Spirit was deepened; the possession of "all the blessings of God's kingdom—faith, righteousness, joy, and peace"—was ascribed to its operation, as also the quickening of conscience, love, holiness and immortality. In Johannine literature "the Pauline characteristic of the Spirit as power is dropped, as also that of the Spirit as source of ethical gifts like faith and peace, whilst the operation of the Spirit as life-giving is more emphasised." It will thus be seen that, on the whole, the Christian interpretation of Holy Spirit was an advance upon the Jewish conception in that although it tended to limit inspiration to the Church, it yet provided the basis of that universality and that ethical idealism which have characterised the progress of Christianity in space and time.

We may very well believe that with the lapse of time the Christian Church gained a deeper appreciation of God's rela-

107 ERE. xi. 792; also xi. 808-9.

tion to man, especially to those who would accept Christ. Human history was conceived as moving towards the ideal of a theocratic regime, the germs of which had already been laid in the minds of the pious few. The Son of Man would come in glory to rule over a purified world and unceasing preparations must go on to hasten his advent. Israel had dreamt of a day when even animals would forsake their ferocity and from all corners of the world would gather nations, or a pious remnant, to establish under a Messiah a new covenant with God and to establish His kingdom for ever at Zion. The Apostles taught that the Son of Man had already appeared, being duly announced by John the Baptist who had asked the people to prepare the way of the Lord for His kingdom was near at hand. But, that the kingdom that the Messiah would establish is not a political but a spiritual one, established through his atoning death, that those in power in that kingdom are not the rich and the proud but the poor and the meek, and that the greatest privilege there is not to rule but to serve—these ideas were novel in the Christian message and were unacceptable to the Jews, who therefore rejected him.[108]

It must be admitted that this exalted conception of the Kingdom of God was of a slow growth in the minds of the Apostles—perhaps even in the consciousness of Jesus. At this distance of time we can only make guesses on the basis of extant documents that have passed through the editing hands of a later generation who had lived to see the futility of Jewish Messianic hopes about a Deliverer who would bring back the political glory of Israel and establish the spiritual superiority of Israel over other nations. In order to win Jewish converts the idea of a political saviour

[108] The Kingdom has a triple meaning. Firstly, it is something supernatural, a gift from above, not a product of ordinary life. Secondly, it is a purely religious blessing, the inner link with the living God; thirdly, it is the most important experience that a man can have, that on which everything else depends; it permeates and dominates his whole existence, because sin is forgiven and misery banished.—Harnack, *What is Christianity?*, p. 64. See *Foundations*, p. 111 f; Caird, *The Fundamental Ideas of Christianity*, Vol. II, Lect. XIX; also Royce, *op. cit.*, p. 36 f, 49 f, 350 f.

was not totally abandoned and a number of passages can be easily quoted to show that attempts were made to identify Jesus with the Jewish Messiah. Thus he was regarded as having a Davidic descent (the immaculate conception necessitating a belief that not only Joseph but also Mary belonged to the royal house), his disciples speculated about their positions in his kingdom,[109] and his last entry into Jerusalem was pictured as a triumphal procession. There is reason to think that he was regarded as stirring up the lower classes to rebellion by preaching the evils of the capitalistic regime, promising blessings to the poor and gathering round about him a number of men who had left their families to help him in his mission of the sword as against that of peace. At his trial and on his conviction, reference to his being the King of the Jews was also made by his accusers. Those who asked him whether payment could be legitimately made to Caesar had a similar motive, namely, to ascertain whether he admitted his political mission. The belief that such a Messiah would come is still a part of the Jewish creed, and the Christians, who, even after the failure of Jesus' political mission and his ignominious death, continued to believe that the Kingdom of God had come through his sufferings, were anathematised as sectaries in the Jewish formula of faith.

In consonance with the systematic practice of the editors of the Gospels to invent sayings and situations which would confirm Old Testament prophecies in the life of Jesus we have another set of ideas regarding the Kingdom of God. The Book of Daniel had spoken of one like unto a son of Man coming with the clouds of heaven and given an everlasting dominion.[110] In Rabbinical and Apocalyptic literature a judgment of the world was a prominent belief, and John the Baptist too had taught that the Kingdom of heaven was at hand. These current eschatological beliefs could not fail to affect the conception of the kingdom that Jesus was supposed

[109] Mk: 10.37.

[110] Dan. 7.13-14, 27.

to have come to establish.[111] It was confidently expected that the end of the world was in sight; and Jesus too was made to say that the Kingdom of God was surely coming—possibly before his contemporaries had all died[112]—and in his instructions to the Apostles he asked them to preach the nearness of the Kingdom of heaven[113] in order to bring home to the people the urgent necessity of squaring up their earthly accounts by repentance and acceptance of his message. Christ could allude in this connection to the many mansions in his Father's house and it is of this kingdom of heaven that Peter was promised the keys by him. The message was taken so literally by some of the faithful that the rearing of a family was regarded by them as unnecessary in view of the impending catastrophe which would separate the wheat and the tares that were growing up together in the meantime.[114] In the kingdom to come many of the sons of Abraham would find no place but many Gentiles would.[115]

If then the first conception of the Kingdom of God to be ruled over by the Messiah was meant for the glorification of Israel, the second was reserved for the righteous irrespective of nationality. But both were concerned with certain objective events—a change in political conditions in the one case and a change in cosmic conditions in the other. A truer insight is to be found, however, in other passages where the

111 See Mat. 19.28; also Harnack, *What is Christianity?*, p. 175; *Foundations*, p. 88 f, for a summary of previous speculations on this aspect of the advent of the Messiah.

112 The statements are slightly conflicting. In Mat. 24.34-6, Mk. 9.1 and Lk. 9.27 the day and hour are not known definitely but "this generation shall not pass till all these things be fulfilled"; in Lk. 17.20 and Mk. 13.32, 35 reference is made to the fact that the kingdom of God does not come with observation or man's knowledge and that all that we can do is to watch and pray. See Harnack, *op. cit.*, p. 42 f, 53 f

113 Mat. 10.7; also 4.17; also Mk. 1.15.

114 Moffatt thinks (*op. cit.*, p. 109) that "it was not the New Testament, it was the reading of the uncanonical Acts, the Acts of Paul, of John, of Philip, of Peter, and so forth, which was responsible for the unhealthy stress on celibacy and the morbid antipathy to marriage during the second and the third centuries, and which eventually emerged in some forms of monasticism."

115 See Mat. 8.11-12; 13.40-43; 19.28-30; 25.31-46; John 14.1-2; Lk. 13.28-30.

Kingdom of God refers to certain changes in the hearts of men which tend to alter so materially the existing conceptions of social relationship that if they can be brought about, heaven would come down on earth.[116] The Kingdom of God is within us.[117] It begins without their knowledge in the small acts of love (which Christ compares to mustard-seeds) provided men abandon the sophistications of age and regain the innocence of childhood. Commenting on the passage, "Suffer the little children to come unto me, and forbid them not; for of such is the Kingdom of Heaven,"[118] Neander observes: "This single saying expressed the whole nature of the Gospel preached by Christ. It implied that he viewed the Kingdom of God as an invisible and spiritual one, to enter which a certain disposition of heart was essential, *viz.*, a child-like spirit, free from pride and self-will, receiving Divine impressions in humble submission and conscious dependence: in a word, all the qualities of the child, suffering itself to be guided by the developed reason of the adult, are to be illustrated in the relations between man and God."[119] Quite in keeping with the above is the other teaching of Jesus that it is only to the poor in spirit that the kingdom of heaven belongs[120]—a very useful corrective to the impression that might have been created in the minds of his following that heaven belonged to the poor in wealth and to those who had forsaken their relations and possessions for him[121] and that the rich would have no access, or a very difficult access, to heaven.[122] "Except a man be born again, he cannot see the Kingdom of God."[123]

116 *Cf.* The Lord's prayer: Thy kingdom come. Thy will be done, as in heaven, so on earth.

Obviously this can refer only to men choosing freely what God wishes them to do. (*Cf.* Mat. 7. 21.)

117 Lk. 17. 21. See Harnack, *op. cit.*, p. 57; also p. 63.

118 Mat. 18.1-11; Mk. 10.14-5.

119 Neander, *Life of Christ* (Bohn's ed., 1871), pp. 364-5.

120 Mat. 5. 3.

121 See Harnack, *op. cit.*, p. 81 f, p. 90 f.

122 Mat. 19.24; Mk. 10.24; Lk. 6.20; 18.29-30.

123 John 3.3; also 3.5.

There can be no question that in the Epistles taken as a whole it is this spiritual interpretation that dictates social dealings.[124] Husbands and wives, masters and servants, fathers and children, brothers and brothers, are to accommodate themselves and be just to one another to establish a peaceful and pure society,[125] and people are advised not to drag their complaints before unbelievers or a court of law but to the saints or to the wise elders of the Church. Sinning either with the body or with the mind is the surest way of excluding oneself from God's Kingdom and the mere external observance of formalities does not make a man righteous, just as its non-observance does not make a man vicious. "Know ye not that the unrighteous shall not inherit the kingdom of God? Be not deceived: neither fornicators, nor idolaters, nor adulterers, nor effeminate, nor abusers of themselves with men, nor thieves, nor covetous, nor drunkards, nor revilers, nor extortioners, shall inherit the kingdom of God."[126] Defilement does not come from food and drink but from unrighteous thoughts and acts: "for the kingdom of God is not eating and drinking, but righteousness and peace and joy in the Holy Ghost."[127] Although the beginning of this kingdom through Jesus was an act of Divine grace, yet its consummation depends upon steady faith and constant prayer even under the provocative oppression of the unbelieving and the unjust.[128] The standard of spiritual attainment necessary for entrance into this kingdom is indicated by the saying of Jesus that the righteousness must be both qualitatively and quantitatively—more qualitatively than quantitatively—better and greater than that of the Scribes and the Pharisees and that the least in this kingdom is greater than even John the Baptist,[129] who

[124] See *Dic. Bi.*, II, p. 852; also Harnack, *op. cit.*, p. 10 f.

[125] Harnack, *op. cit.*, p. 174.

[126] 1 Cor. 6.9-10.

[127] Rom. 14. 17. *Cf.* Gal. 5.22: The fruit of the Spirit is love, joy, peace, longsuffering, kindness, goodness, faithfulness, meekness, temperance.

[128] See ERE. vii. 512, art. JESUS CHRIST.

[129] Mat. 11. 11; Lk. 7.28.

was the best representative of the old morality as taught in the Law and the Prophets. But, for this spiritual attainment, confession of sin, rather than obedience to the Law, is essential, and many a publican and many a harlot will qualify for admission into this realm of everlasting life while many children of Abraham and Isaac and Jacob will be wailing and gnashing their teeth outside its walls. Moral perfection is individual and not tribal, and there is no limit to spiritual perfection attainable by man : " Be ye perfect, even as your Father which is in heaven is perfect."[130] Unto righteousness all things are added—a Divine Providence looks to the daily needs of the righteous and they need not be worried by the thought of being forgotten by a God without whose knowledge not even a sparrow falls to the ground.[131] So it is not the needs of temporal existence that should absorb the attention of men but the demands of eternal life. What shall it profit a man if he shall gain the whole world and lose his own soul? Interpreted rightly, " the Christian religion," says Harnack, " means one thing and one thing only : Eternal life in the midst of time, by the strength and under the eyes of God."[132]

It would be idle to deny the tremendous influence that Christianity wielded at one time over the hearts of men when of all religions it alone remained missionary and invited people to forsake their effete ancestral creeds in favour of its own message of salvation. Born at a time when the old Mediterranean religions were in a decadent condition, it could rouse the conscience of better minds

130 Mat. 5. 48. In Catholicism this was mellowed down into the distinction between a perfect and a sufficient morality.—See Harnack, *op. cit.*, p. 217.

131 See Basanta Coomar Bose, *Christianity*, p. 41.

132 Harnack, *op. cit.*, p. 8.

Ritschl's definition of Christianity represents an ideal : "Christianity is that monotheistic religion, wholly spiritual and ethical, which, based upon the life of its author as redeemer and as the founder of the Kingdom of God, consists in the freedom of divine sonship, involves the impulse to active conduct from the motive of love, aims at the moral organisation of mankind, and lays the basis of bliss in sonship towards God as well as in the Kingdom of God" (quoted by Moffatt, *op. cit.*, pp. 207-8).

to a sense of the degeneration of the spiritual element in religion and the necessity of a more ethical and less formal method of divine worship. Christ was a Saviour-god but was also at the same time an ethical personality, and the religion that he preached was the well-known religion of the Jews which emphasised the holy character of God. The difficulty arose when the Apostles and their followers began to invest Christ with a divine character; for it was then that speculations began about the exact nature and significance of the advent of Jesus. To make the religion acceptable, contemporary predilections for a Saviour-god, a Messiah, a Sacrifice to appease Justice, and a pre-existent Principle had all to be satisfied: the effect was Christological speculation with its hair-splitting distinctions and its gradual tendency to emphasise the divinity of Christ and a consequential plurality within the inner life of God. Sects and schisms rapidly arose mostly over the question of the nature of Christ, and by the end of the 6th century most of the theories about the nature and necessity of the mediation of Christ had been propounded and defended with zeal, if not with bitterness also. The spiritual message ran some risk of being relegated to a secondary position in order to make room for the Messiah in men's minds, and slowly but surely many pagan ideas, associations, cults and ceremonies effected an entrance into the service of the Christian Church. Time was again ripe for an organised protest against over-subtlety in faith and plurality in godhead; and the protest came from the Arabian deserts where debased and heretical schools had been preaching a Christianity far removed from the simple message of Christ to suffering and sinful humanity.

## CHAPTER VIII

### God in Islam

Muhammad's chief merit lies in his uncompromising monotheism which is perhaps partially due to the fear that any concession on that head would lead to polytheism—a form of belief which he detested. Convinced that the idols that disfigured the Ka'ba[1] were nonentities and that the Arab belief that Allāh had sons and daughters was radically false, he laid down that God was one and everlasting, that He did not beget any being nor was He Himself begotten and that there was none like unto Him.[2] And this conviction did not remain a mere intellectual formula but became an overmastering passion which drove him to proclaim his belief openly, with grave consequences to his personal safety. How he arrived at this conception of a unitary godhead is yet a matter of dispute. Judaism and Christianity were not unknown in Arabia, and Muhammad in his travels to distant regions in charge of caravans must have known of their religion and their method of worship. It is doubtful, however, if at first he knew the Bible with any intimacy at all,[3] for references to it are such as would betray simply an acquaintance with tit-bits of Jewish and Christian tales about past heroes, prophets, miracles and such other spectacular personages and

[1] It has been suggested that the cult at the Ka'ba with its 360 idols was astral in character; possibly it was syncretic.—See *Encyclopaedia of Islam*, II, p. 591.

[2] Sura cxii.

[3] Bell, *The Origin of Islam in its Christian Environment*, pp. 46, 67, 136, 140; Rodwell's Koran, Preface, pp. xviii-xix: Lammens, *Islam: Beliefs and Institutions*, p. 39; Nöldeke, *Sketches from Eastern History*, p. 30 f.; ERE. viii. 874.

events—possibly oral stories repeated with circumstantial details in the manner of the Talmudic and the Apocryphal literature.[4] Jews had settled in Yathrib (Medina) and elsewhere in the pursuit of trade; and Christians, mostly of heretical schools, driven out from the then centres of Christian culture, had taken refuge in South Arabia, Abyssinia and the fringes of the Hijaz, and the Christian hermit, it appears, was not an unknown figure even to pre-Islamic poets.[5] But even though there were Jewish and Christian converts among the Arabs, their allegiance was of the shallowest type and their knowledge of the deeper principles of their own religion was at best insignificant.

But the collective influence of the religious forces on a few pre-Islamic Arabs manifests itself in the absorption of a number of Aramaic, Ethiopic and Abyssinian words connected with religion, a knowledge of the sacred books possessed by the Jews and the Christians, possibly also a belief in a future life.[6] Again, as Bell remarks, "what was meant by a prophet, a holy book, revelation, prayer, and praise, cannot have been entirely unknown to the Arabs."[7] Some passages in the Qur'ān make it probable that the tribal polytheism was being gradually tempered by the recognition of a supreme deity[8] sometime before the birth of Muhammad, and that, while in distress, the people called upon him for safety and help although in more peaceful times they went back to their idols.[9] In fact, since the time of the Elkesaites (*c.* 100

[4] Bell, *op. cit.*, p. 110; also p. 112. See Hughes, *Dictionary of Islam*, art. JEWS (p. 235) for Muhammad's knowledge of Jewish religious literature. See also Sir William Muir, *The Mohammedan Controversy and other articles*, pp. 129-30.

[5] Bell, *op. cit.*, pp. 43 f., 143; Sir William Muir, *Life of Mohammad*, pp. xcv, 22; see Khuda Bukhsh, *Essays Indian and Islamic*, p. 5; also Archer, *Mystical Elements in Mohammed*, p. 58, p. 61 f.

[6] Bell, *op. cit.*, p. 50 f. See Nöldeke, *op. cit.*, pp. 37-38; Archer, *Mystical Elements in Mohammed*, Ch. VII (pp. 61-70).

[7] Bell, *op. cit.*, p. 52.

[8] Bell, *op. cit.*, p. 56 f. Guillaume, *Traditions of Islam*, p. 143; Macdonald, *Development of Muslim Theology*, p. 124.

[9] Sura xxxix. 11.

A.D.),[10] whose beliefs are remarkably similar to those of Islām, the conjoint influence of Judaism and Christianity was responsible for sporadic monotheistic attempts by persons who claimed prophetic designation and honour—false prophets, according to Christianity and Islām. The people who influenced Muhammad's thought most were probably the Ḥanīfs,[11] who were indigenous monotheists attached neither to Judaism nor to Christianity—a designation of uncertain derivation used in the Qur'ān specially of Abraham [12] to whom Muhammad went back in search of a monotheist who had flourished long before the founders of the Jewish and Christian faiths were born, and who, through Ishmael, was the father of the Arab race.[13] It would be strange indeed if a rest-

10 Bell, *op. cit.*, p. 59 f. ERE, art. ELKESAITES, does not admit that the Elkesaite influence on Islam is proved.

11 See footnote 1 in Rodwell's Koran, p. 216, to Sura xvi. 121. Also Bell, *op. cit.*, p. 57 f. Islam has sometimes been designated as Hanifism.—see *Enc. Isl.*, II, p. 259 (art. HANIF); also Archer, *op. cit.*, p. 58 f.

12 In the sense of one who was neiher a Jew nor a Christian and yet was no idolater. It was also used in respect of one steadfast in the Islamic faith. It originally applied to persons who had turned away from the idolatrous religion of Arabia to a monotheistic faith.—See Hughes, *Dictionary of Islam*, *sub voce* HANĪF (p. 161). It is not impossible that Muhammad borrowed this appeal from Moses to Abraham from the Christians.—*The Legacy of Israel*, p. 131 (See Gal. iii. 7-8, 15-17). See Moffatt, *op. cit.*, p. 63. Commenting on Sura xxx. 29, Bell remarks, "The term *hanīf* is associated with Abraham not, I think, because Abraham is regarded as specially a *hanīf* more than others, but rather because the recognition of the place of Abraham, and the idea of this eternally existing religion again and again renewed by the prophets, came to Muhammad about the same time. Other prophets and other true believers were *hanīfs*."—Bell, *op. cit.*, p. 182; also pp. 57, 129 f. See Sell, *Essays on Islam*, p. 242 f.

13 Ishmael was the son of Hagar, the bondwoman of Abraham's wife Sarah, while Isaac was Sarah's son. (Hence the Arabs and the Jews were brethren or cousins). Greatness was promised of the progeny of both Isaac and Ishmael (Gen. 22. 16-18; 21. 13). For an interesting allegorical use of the relation between Isaac (the Christians) and Ishmael (the Jews), see Gal. 4. 21 f. (See Moffatt, *op. cit.*, p. 134, for interpretation.) For the influence of the religion of Abraham's Harran, see ERE. viii. 875.

Snouck Hurgronje (and before him Sprenger) has pointed out that in the Meccan Suras it is often said that no prophetic admonisher had been sent to the Arabs before Muhammad and that although Abraham occupied a prominent place among the prophets there was nothing to distinguish him from the rest so far as the Arabs were concerned. In the Medinese Suras, however, after the breach with the Jews, Muhammad began to teach that Abraham had lived in Mecca and

less mind, convinced of the futility of polytheism and idolatry, should not seek the company of those who could enlighten him on points of doubt ; but at the same time one would not seek such company if one had not independently arrived at a tentative conclusion regarding the unity of godhead. It is not possible for any man to escape the influence of contemporary social movements : it is not impossible that Jewish, Christian and indigenous monotheistic ideas were unconsciously in operation in Muhammad's mind, although it is quite possible that he never consciously borrowed elements from their religion till his own faith had been firmly fixed and the necessity had arisen of showing its filiation to previous systems of belief.[14]

It is easier to show that, in spite of his uncompromising hostility to the general Arabic belief in a multiplicity of gods and disbelief in future life,[15] he was anxious to retain as many of the Arab practices and prejudices as he could, consistently with a monotheistic creed. He tacitly consented to the continuance of the heathen Arabic (and Semitic) custom of circumcision and possibly only his ignorance of the covenant with Abraham, his religious hero, prevented him from giving it a religious sanction.[16] "His teaching developed in the early period, not according to Biblical models but in the style of the pagan Arab sooth-sayers with their oracles, formulae for blessings and curses, etc.," and their rhymed prose (*sadj*).[17] After some hesitation he retained 'Allāh' as the name of God although it had polytheistic association, this

founded the sanctuary of the Black Stone with his son Ishmael.—See *Enc. Isl.*, II, p. 1075; also p. 432.

14 See *Legacy of Israel*, p. 132 f.; Sir William Muir, *Life of Mohammad*, pp. 102, 143 f.

15 Sura xxiii. 33-40.

16 " Circumcision is not once alluded to in the Qur'ān...It is held to be *Sunna*, or founded upon the customs of the Prophet, and dating its institution from the time of Abraham. . . According to several Muhammadan doctors, there were seventeen of the prophets born in a circumcised state " (Muhammad was one of them).—Hughes, *Dic. Isl.*, p. 57, art. CIRCUMCISION. See in this connection footnote to Sura ii. 132 in Rodwell's *Koran*.

17 *Enc. Isl.*, II, p. 1066; see Lammens, *op. cit.*, p. 46 : " This use of oaths grows less as the Prophet nears the Hijra, and ceases entirely at Medina." See Macdonald, *Religious Attitude and Life in Islam*.

being the name of the supreme deity among the other gods of pre-Islamic Arabia.[18] The Ka'ba was permitted by the iconoclastic reformer to retain its sanctity and its black stone, pilgrimage to Mecca continued as in the days of yore, and some of the ancient Arab customs and acts continued, albeit with a new significance, in the rules about pilgrimage, which ultimately became one of "the pillars of Islām."[19] When he failed to carry the Jews with him, Muhammad changed the *Kibla* from Jerusalem to Mecca even though the latter had no monotheistic associations before his own reforms.[20]

pp. 31 f., 64 f. For Muhammad's belief in evil eye and spells against its influence, see Sura cxiii. 1, 2, 5; Westermarck, *Pagan Survivals in Mohammedan Civilisation*, p. 55; also pp. 115 (where references to swearing by the moon would be found), 117 (where "God loves the odd" is exemplified).

18 Bell, *op. cit.*, pp. 55, 116 f. For Muhammad's attempts to accommodate Meccan beliefs, see ERE. viii. 875. See Hughes, *Dic. Islam*, p. 197, *sub voce* IDOLATRY; Gibbon, *Decline and Fall of the Roman Empire*, Ch. 1, Vol. II, p. 425 f. (ed. Ward, Lock and Co.).

Nöldeke remarks, "Among the heathen Arabs of later times Allāh is extremely common both by itself and in theophorous names" (ERE. i. 664). "In theophorous proper names the deity sometimes appears as a lord, while the human individual is his servant, his hand-maid, his obedient subject (*ṭau'*); sometimes, again, the deity is described as gracious, while the human individual is his gift, his reward, his act of favour, the aid which he supplies, his *protégé* who seeks refuge with him, etc. At other times the deity is represented as increasing the family, as sending a good-omen and good fortune.. Some of these compounds are of doubtful meaning. With the exception of a very small number of uncertain cases found in inscriptions, there are absolutely no names which designate a human being as the kinsman or descendant of a deity, like those which we find among the Hebrews and other Semites." (ERE. i. 665).

For Quranic references to pre-Islamic Allāh, see *Enc. Isl.*, I, p. 302, art. ALLĀH.

19 See, *e.g.*, Sura ii. 153. See *Enc. Isl.*, II, pp. 587 f., 444 (Id al-Aḍḥā) 199 f. For a modern interpretation of the rites of the pilgrimage, see Lammens, *op. cit.*, p. 218.

20 See Sura ii. 136-45, which abrogate ii. 109. See also Sura ix. 1-12, 28, 35 f. See Sir W. Muir, *Life of Mohammad*, pp. 189, 195; T. W. Arnold, *The Preaching of Islam* (1913), pp. 26-27. Abraham and Ishmael are claimed as the founders and builders of the Ka'ba at Mecca and the historical basis of Islam is assured.—*Legacy of Israel*, p. 132. See Sura xxii. 27, 77; iii. 60, 91, and many other places about Abraham being the founder of monotheism (and Islam). See Bell, *op. cit.*, p. 144. For legends, see *Enc. Isl.*, II, p. 589 (Adam is supposed to be its founder); also p. 543. For the antiquity of Mecca, see Sir William Muir, *Life of Mohammad*, p. cii f. Mecca is regarded by Islam as the navel of the earth. "It forms the part of the earth which was created before the rest of it and around

What is more important to consider is the light in which Muhammad took his own prophetic mission.[21] Judging by the probabilities of the case, it is likely that his soul was primarily stirred against the debased religious beliefs and the iniquitous social practices of his countrymen.[22] No doubt can be entertained about the sincerity of his convictions or his zeal in proclaiming them in no uncertain terms;[23] for he knew very well the risk he ran in touching a lucrative source of revenue of the Koreish and a deep-rooted pagan sentiment of the people at large. That he felt a call to act in the manner of earlier prophets may be admitted without any question: he was no deceiver or charlatan who wanted to gather a following or a fortune by his prophetic office, if the unanimous testimony to the beginning of his prophetic career can be relied upon. As Dr. Leitner observes, "If self-sacrifice, honesty of purpose, unswerving belief in one's mission, a marvellous insight into existing wrong or error, and the perception and use of the best means for its removal, are among the outward and visible signs of inspiration, the mission of Muhammad was inspired."[24] It is extremely likely that originally Muhammad considered himself to be a warner[25] in the fashion of John the Baptist, announcing the nearness of the Last Judgment and calling his countrymen to the worship of a unitary God [26] and the belief in a destiny beyond the

which the rest stretches. It is also the highest point, the place which provides the whole world with its nourishment; and it forms the place of communication with the upper and the under world.—*Enc. Isl.*, II, p. 590. *Cf.* Proverbs viii. 22-26. See Muhammad Ali's *Holy Quran*, p. 170 f., notes 467-69.

21 See Sir W. Muir, *Life of Mohammad*, Ch. III; also p. 71.

22 During the ten first years of his prophetic career Muhammad only attacks the heathen, and refrains from falling upon the Jews and Christians with whom he believed himself to be in agreement on the fundamentals of his preaching.—Lammens, *op. cit.*, pp. 46-47.

23 The oldest Suras are "the most animated, the most lyrical, and also the most abrupt." Another peculiarity is "the multiplicity and piling-up of oaths."—See Lammens, *op. cit.*, p. 46; also Nöldeke, *Sketches from Eastern History*, p. 35.

24 *Religious Systems of the World*, p. 293.

25 Sura xxix. 49.

26 The idea of the unity of Allāh does not occupy so large a place in the earliest parts of the Kur'ān; later, however, it occurs many times.—Wensinck, *The*

grave. At a later time when he put forward Abraham (Ibrāhīm) as 'the friend of God' (*Khalilullāh*) he represented him as doing to his father's idols what he himself intended to do to the idols at Ka'ba, namely, utter destruction.[27] With increased success and greater knowledge of the achievements of earlier prophets he could tell his people that the treatment that they were meting out to him had befallen the lot of these earlier prophets also, but that their countrymen had to pay dearly for their unbelief. Here Muhammad figures as one prophet among others and he could preach that Allāh sends to each nation its own prophet whom it should hear and obey.[28] When he began to recite the Quranic verses in his public ministry at Mecca and conceived the idea of a divine mission,[29] two ideas were combined: he was not an ordinary prophet but an Apostle and a law-giver like Moses and Christ[30] and through him the Arabs were going to get from heaven a sacred book in their own language as the Jews had theirs through Moses.[31] His sole ambition seems to have

*Muslim Creed*, p 4 (References are to Suras cxii, ii. 256, xxvii. 26, xxviii. 88; see also iv. 40, 51, 89, 116). Snouck Hurgronje called attention to the very important point that Muhammad did not from the very first proclaim strict monotheism as the principal thing but the approach of the Last Judgment, from which he was to save his countrymen. The assertion that there is no god but Allāh appears sporadically from lxiii. 9 onwards; and it must certainly have taken some time before there was a definite breach with the idolaters (Sura cix) and before he met them with the declaration of the oneness of God (Sura cxii).—*Enc. Isl.*, II, p. 1075, art KORAN.

27 The story in Sura xxi. 52 f. The story is taken from Rabbinical literature (see *Legacy of Israel*, p. 141). See *Enc. Isl.*, II, p. 431, art. IBRAHIM. See also Sir W. Muir, *The Life of Mohammad*, pp. 408-09.

28 Sura iv. 161-63, 168. See Bell, *op. cit.*, p. 127.

29 For the arrangement of the Suras according to periods, see Hughes, *Dictionary of Islam*, art. QUR'ĀN, p. 492 f. There is no unanimity about arrangement: compare, for instance, Rodwell and Hughes.

30 Bell, *op. cit.*, p. 125 f.

31 See art. PROPHET in Hughes, *Dictionary of Islam*, p. 475; also Bell, *op. cit.*, p. 93 f. Muhammad is divinely authorised to communicate the Book of God. He even communicates it in his own language, but whether the original is in Arabic is not clear; there is at least a suggestion that it is in a divine language: "We have made it an Arabic Koran that ye might understand it, but in the original with us it is sublime, wise (xliii 2)."—Margoliouth, *Early Development of Muhammadanism*, p. 9. On 'Arabic Qur'ān,' see *The Apology of Al Kindy*, pp. 79-84; T. W. Arnold, *op. cit.*, p. 27.

been originally to be recognised as a genuine vehicle of divine decrees and not to be stigmatised as an impostor, a mere poet,[32] a plagiarist or a redactor of ancient prophecies. He repudiated the suggestion that he had confederates—possibly Jewish and Christian—from whom he borrowed materials and that he was trying to pass off his own composition as divine revelation, sent down from heaven through angelic agency.[33]

But very soon Muhammad assumed a more ambitious rôle. He not only believed that an illiterate man like himself[34] could not have composed such elegant verses—and he challenged his contemporaries to produce ten verses to match

[32] For Muhammad's attitude towards poets, see Archer, *op. cit.*, p. 79 f.; Macdonald, *Religious Attitude and Life in Islam*, p. 18 f. See Sir W. Muir, *Life of Mohammad*, pp. 78, 127.

[33] At a later period of his career no one would venture to doubt the divine origin of the entire book. But at its commencement the case was different. The people of Mecca spoke openly and tauntingly of it as the work of a poet, as a collection of antiquated or fabulous legends, or a palpable sorcery. They accused him of having confederates, and even specified foreigners who had been his co adjutors. Such were Salman the Persian, to whom he may have owed the descriptions of Heaven and Hell, which are analogous to those of the Zendavesta, and the Christian monk Sergius, or as the Muhammadans term him, Boheira.—Rodwell, Preface to Koran, p. xvi. See Hughes, *Dictionary of Islam*, art. JEWS, p. 236. The whole article is worth reading.

[34] In this connection it is important to consider the term ***ummī***, one of the favourite epithets Muhammad gives himself in the Kuran. Later writers usually explained this term as meaning "illiterate" and connected it with the problem of Muhammad's ability to read and write. *Umma* conveys the meaning of "people." When the term is used in a religious sense it means community; in a profane sense it is *ethnos* and *ummī* is *ethnikos*. When Muhammad called himself *ummī* he meant thereby that he was the Arabian Prophet of the gentiles, speaking to the gentiles to whom no Apostle had ever been sent before.—Wensinck, *The Muslim Creed*, p. 6. See Rodwell's *Koran*, p. 331, footnotes 1 and 2 on Sura vii. 156. See, however, 'Ali Ṭabari, *The Book of Religion and Empire*, (Tr. by A. Mingana), p. 54 f. Muhammad Ali (*The Holy Quran*, p. 361, footnote 950) says that the *ummī* prophet conveys any one of the following three significances, *viz.*, (1) one who knows not reading or writing; (2) one from among the Arabs (among whom reading and writing were rare); and (3) one coming from Mecca (*umm-ul-Qura*, the Metropolis of Arabia). Sura xxix. 47: "And Thou didst not recite any book (of revelation) before it: with that right hand of thine thou didst not transcribe one," is taken by Musalmans as conclusive evidence that Muhammad was illiterate before he received the Quranic revelation. "There is a difference of opinion, however, as to whether he could read or write after revelation." See Muhammad Ali, *The Holy Quran*, p. 362: Enc. Br., Vol. 15, p. 646,

those of the Qur'ān [35]—and boasted that even if men and jinn were to combine they could not produce a similar book,[36] but he began to believe also that he was "all the Apostle of God," [37] "the seal of the prophets." [38] Two consequences followed from this position. The first is that his advent was not unexpected, for earlier prophets had predicted his oncoming and even his name,[39] and he haḍ come to give a fuller revelation of God's essence and attributes than the earlier prophets had done. Although in the Qur'ān the references to such prophetic Biblical passages are meagre, the hint thrown out was seized upon with avidity by Muslim theologians and the Old and the New Testament were ransacked for finding out appropriate prophecies regarding the future greatness of the progeny of Ishmael and the advent and achievements of

35 Sura xi. 16; ii. 21. See Nöldeke, *op. cit.*, p. 36.

36 Sura xvii. 91, Muhammad Ali translates jinn as evil-disposed men (*The Holy Quran*, p. 579, footnote 1466); but only some Mu'tazilites took the word in this sense. See art. GENII in Hughes, *Dic. Isl.*, p. 133 f, and *Enc. Isl.*, I, art. DJINN, p. 1045. See also Westermarck, *Pagan Survivals in Mohammedan Civilisation*, pp. 12 f., 17.

37 Sura vii. 157 f. See Wensinck, *op. cit.*, p. 6, on the interpretation of this passage.

38 Sura xxxiii. 40. The seal of prophecy was a mole of an unusual size on the Prophet's back which, according to the predictions of the scriptures, marked him as the Seal of the Prophets (see Hughes, *Dictionary of Islam*, p. 567; Sir W. Muir, *The Life of Mohammad*, p. 529). The following quotation from Mirza Ghulam Ahmad of Qadian, the founder of the Ahmadiyya Movement, who claimed to have combined in his own person the functions of the Mahdi and the Messiah, is of interest here: "The chosen ones of God even now drink deep at the fountain of His inspiration and no one ever set a seal upon the lips of God. His grace even now flows in abundance and is bestowed upon men as it was bestowed of old. It is true that the revelation of a perfect Law and necessary rules for the guidance of mankind has put an end to the need of a fresh Law to be revealed from the Almighty, and apostleship and prophecy have attained their perfection in the holy person of our Lord and Master (?), the Prophet Muhammad, may peace and the blessings of God be upon him, but still an access to the sacred fountain of inspiration is not thereby debarred.—*Teachings of Islam* (1921), p. 78.

39 Sura lxi. 6; ii. 83 (see Rodwell's notes). See Macdonald, *Aspects of Islam*, p. 225 f. It seems probable, from the traditions, that the Prophet did not adopt the name Muhammad till after the Flight, and that he was previously called Abd-Allah.—Rodwell's Koran, p. 446 (footnote to lxi. 6). See however ERE. vii. 873. Later theologians gave him 30, 300, or even 1,000 names.—ERE. viii. 872. art. MUHAMMAD. Muhammed Ali, *Muhammad the Prophet*, Ch. IV., gives the prophecies about the advent of Muhammad.

Muhammad.[40] The other is the claim put forward in the Qur'ān that although the earlier prophets had taught monotheism, their successors had allowed their true teachings to be forgotten or mixed up with undesirable ingredients and that, in conformity with later beliefs, the earlier scriptures too had been tampered with and corrupted.[41] Later Muslim theologians believed also that many passages alluding to Muhammad had been deliberately expunged or altered or perversely interpreted, when retained, to defeat his claim to be recognised as the Last Prophet.[42] Muhammad had perhaps hoped that by putting himself in the prophetic line of Moses and Christ, he would be able to win the support of the Jews and the Christians, of whose prophets he always spoke with the greatest reverence.[43] His failure to win them over altered his entire attitude towards these communities, although a superstitious veneration for a revealed book was responsible for a more tolerant attitude towards them than towards people of other faiths. Possibly the nearness of the Day of Judgment which he preached in his earlier career was in the manner of the Jewish prophets, including Jesus, and the virtual abandonment of this idea of the imminence of Divine Judgment, or at least a catastrophe, was due either to his failure to convert the Jews and the Christians wholesale or to his acquisition of temporal power.[44]

40 See, *e.g.*, *The Book of Religion and Empire*, by ' Ali Tabari (Tr. A. Mingana). See Macdonald, *Aspects of Islam*, p. 234 f., p. 240.

41 Sura ii. 70-73, 169, 254; iv. 48; v. 16-18, 45. See *Enc. Isl.*, II, p. 1066; Macdonald, *Aspects of Islam*, Lect. VII, esp. pp. 219-22.

42 History has a curious habit of repeating itself. "The Shi'as in their hatred of ' Othmān, their great aversion, assert that the original text has been gravely changed and even mutilated. The Khārijites exclude the 12th Sura, which they treat as a romantic story."—Lammens, *Islām : Beliefs and Institutions*, p. 38. See *Enc. Isl.*, II, pp. 1070-71; Sir William Muir, *The Mohammedan Controversy and other articles*, p. 150; *Life of Mohammad*, p. xxiii f.

43 The Muhammadans believe that the faults in action and knowledge of the prophets to be found in the scriptures of other religions are partly due no doubt to their human nature but they are also partly due to fabrications of the Jews and Christians.—See *Al Bayan* (Introduction to the Commentary on the Holy Qoran), p. 193, by M. A. M. Abdul Haqq.

44 Lammens, *op. cit.*, p. 47. The doctrine of the future life was preached in the early days as a warning of the approaching end of the world and the Day

Muhammad's conception of the function and power of a prophet seems to have undergone considerable modification in course of his ministry. His original intention seems to have been to go back to the later Jewish conception of a prophet who is a messenger of God, no doubt, but who has no superhuman pretensions. His greatest objection to Christianity was that it had deified Christ and Mary and reduced God to a third of three.[45] He vehemently denounced what he considered to be a tritheism and repeatedly urged that Christ was a man and an apostle of God like other prophets before him. While he was quite willing, therefore, to believe that Christ was immaculately conceived, performed many miracles and even escaped the Cross (a likeness of Jesus being really crucified), he systematically rejected the idea of the divine sonship of Jesus (as of Ezra)[46] although assigning to him a distinctive position among the prophets by calling him the Spirit of God or the Word which God conveyed into Mary.[47] Conformably to this line of thought,

of Judgment; yet he had afterwards to make the martyrs in his cause enter paradise at once, and his enemies enter hell immediately after death—a belief not easily reconciled with the former.—ERE. viii. 875. See Bell, *op. cit.*, p. 201 f.

45 Muhammad thought that the Christian Trinity was composed of God, Mary and Christ and that Gabriel was the Holy Ghost. See Sura v. 77-9, 116; iv. 169. It has been suggested that the mistake of Muhammad arose from the fact that the word *Rouah*, the Holy Ghost, is of the feminine gender in some Oriental tongues and is figuratively styled the mother of Christ in the gospel of the Nazarenes. (See in this connection Cheyne, *Traditions and Beliefs of Ancient Israel*, p. 20 f.) But, as Gibbon points out, "the Christians of the seventh century had insensibly relapsed into a semblance of paganism : the public and private vows were addressed to the relics and images that disgraced the temples of the East : the throne of the Almighty was darkened by a cloud of martyrs, and saints, and angels, the objects of popular veneration; and the Collyridian heretics, who flourished in the fruitful soil of Arabia, invested the Virgin Mary with the name and honours of a goddess."—Gibbon, *op. cit.*, Ch. l, Vol. II, p. 432 (with footnote). See ERE viii. 476.

46 Sura ix. 30. That the Jews regarded Ezra as a son of God is due to Muhammad's own invention.—Rodwell's Koran, p. 524, f.n. 9. See also Gibbon, *loc. cit.*, p. 432 (with footnote). See also Sura ii. 261 and *cf.* Neh. ii. 13.

47 See Sura iii. 48. For the Christology of the Qur'ān, see Lammens, *op. cit.*, p. 50 f. and art. JESUS CHRIST in Hughes, *Dictionary of Islam*, p. 229 f. (esp. p. 233 where a *Hadīth* has been quoted). In his celestial journey, however, Muhammad saw Jesus in one of the lower heavens. See Hughes, *op. cit.*,

Muhammad calls him a messenger and servant of Allāh and thinks that nothing prevented Allāh from endowing him (Muhammad) with the power of performing miracles except that these had been treated as lies by their contemporaries, when performed by earlier prophets.[48] The miracle on which he bases his prophetship[49] during this period is the miracle of the Qur'ān; but for this it is not necessary to suppose that he was anything more than a mere man.[50] In fact, a tradition records that his right of interceding with God accrued after God had forgiven his sins, both first and last.[51]

But another strain of thought soon crossed this line of thinking. Performance of miracles had come to be looked upon as a part of prophetic function and the Jews and Christians could score an obvious victory over the Apostle of Islām by pointing to his incapacity in this respect.[52] Then, again, Christ had been regarded as sinless and he was believed to

pp. 235, 351-52. See Wensinck, *op. cit.*, pp. 243-44 (reappearance of Jesus to slay the anti-Christ); Macdonald, *Aspects of Islam*, p. 244 f; Sir W. Muir, *Life of Mohammad*, p. 143 f.

The Ghassāniyas alone denied the apostleship of Jesus.—See Wensinck, *op. cit.*, p. 114. *Per contra* see Ghazālī who avowed that 'Christianity would be the absolute expression of truth were it not for its dogma of Trinity and its denial of the divine mission of Muhammad' (See Lammens, *op. cit.*, p. 121).

48 For the most part the old prophets only serve to introduce a little variety in point of form, for they are almost in every case facsimiles of Mohammed himself.—Nöldeke, *Sketches from Eastern History*, p. 29.

49 According to Islam miracles happen either to support Allāh's Prophets in a visible way (*mu'djiza*) or to signify Divine Grace towards the saint through whom they take place (*karāma*).—See Wensinck, *op. cit.*, pp. 224-26; also Macdonald, *Rel. Att. and Life in Isl.*, p. 49 f. (discussing Ibn Khaldūn's theory); Macdonald, *Asp. of Isl.*, p. 231. For the conception of miracles in Islām, see Muhammad Ali, *The Religion of Islām*, p. 240 f.

50 See Suras xvii. 92-7; xxix. 49; xiii. 27-30; xviii. 110. See Macdonald, *Aspects of Islam*, p. 232. See also Nicholson, *Idea of Personality in Sufism*, p. 58: Both the Sufistic *walī* and the Shi'ite Imām are claimed to be "divine men, really one with God, whereas Mohammed, as described in the Koran, is no more than a man subject to human weaknesses, who receives at intervals the Divine revelations, not from God but from an angel." For the origin of the cult of saints in Islam, see Westermarck, *Pag. Sur. in Moh. Civ.*, p. 94 f.

51 Mishhāt, Bk. XXIII. Ch. XII, quoted by Hughes, *Dictionary of Islam*, p. 233 (art. JESUS CHRIST). *Cf.* Sura xlviii. 2.

52 It is interesting to note that the Christian claim was responsible for the introduction of the miraculous into Zoroastrianism also.—See Dhalla, *Zoroastrian Theology*, p. 195.

have bodily ascended to heaven after his crucifixion.[53] The Qur'ān does not contain the full reply to these allegations of inferiority but it does contain the germs. Just as an obscure Vedic passage would often be elaborated in the Purāṇas, so also on the few stray and obscure passages of the Qur'ān were built up in the Traditional literature (*hadith*) many stories of Muhammad's achievements in the fields of prophecy and miracle. In the Qur'ān itself there is reference to the splitting of the moon (liv. 1-2),[54] angelic help at the battle of Badr (iii. 120)[55] and the night journey from Mecca to Jerusalem (xvii. 1). But the Traditionalists, obviously keeping in mind what miracles Jesus and other prophets had performed, ascribed similar works to Muhammad[56] and went one step further by supposing that, mounting on the mysterious Burāq, he had ascended in the body, while awake, to heaven and conversed with God, thus excelling in a way the feat of Jesus;[57] they also enumerated the events, predicted by him, which took place either during his life-time or after his death.[58] In a similar fashion the sinlessness of the prophets, at least after accepting their vocation, became a dogma in

53 The Talmudists mentioned nine (or thirteen) individuals who were translated to heaven.—See Rodwell's Koran, p. 115, n. 2. (Sura xix. 58).

54 See Rodwell's Koran, p. 64, n. 1; Hughes, *Dic. of Isl.*, pp. 350-51.

55 This occurs in a Medinese Sura. See also another Medinese verse, Sura viii. 17. See also xxxiii. 10.

56 For a list see Hughes, *Dic. of Isl.*, p. 351; 'Ali Tabari, *op. cit.*, p. 30 f.; ERE. vii. 878. Muhammad's own belief was that "no apostle had come with miracles unless by the leave of God" (Sura xiii. 33). See Bell, *op. cit.*, p. 198 f; Margoliouth, *Ear. Dev. Muh.*, p. 239 f; Gibbon, *op. cit.*, II, pp. 436-37; Sir William Muir, *Life of Mohammad*, pp. xlvii, lviii. For a severe criticism of the miracles ascribed to Muhammad by the Traditional Literature, see Sir William Muir, *The Apology of Al Kindy*, pp. 53-62. For the assimilation of Muhammad to Christ, see Guillaume, *op. cit.*, p. 132 f.

57 Some commentators make it a vision as indicated in Sura xvii. 62. But the orthodox creed demands a belief in the reality of the night journey and the ascension. See Macdonald, *Development of Muslim Theology*, p. 298 (Appendix 1—A Short Creed by Al-Ash'ari); also p. 313. See Muhammad Ali, *The Holy Quran*, p. 572, footnote 1441. A full treatment of the subject is to be found in J. C. Archer, *Mystical Elements in Mohammed*, pp. 44-55: he calls it "a mystic experience, a breaking through into the unseen world, a snatching away in the spirit, and withal, a conviction" (p. 49). See *Enc. Isl.*, II, p. 553, art. ISRĀ'

58 'Ali Tabari, *op. cit.*, p. 37 f.

later Muslim belief although earlier accounts were entirely different and even in canonical *hadith* "Muhammad's unpeccability is never mentioned,"[59] not to talk of his freedom from polytheism at all times.[60] The whole belief was evidently modelled on Christianity and gave rise to the tradition that the heart of Muhammad was taken out by two angels and washed clean with snow of all sinful elements in order to qualify him for his unique relationship to divine revelation.[61]

The last stage is represented by Muhammad's belief that not only was he a prophet after the manner of earlier prophets but also an Apostle destined to be the last one. He no longer believes that "to its own book shall every nation be summoned" [62] on the Day of Judgment and that salvation was not of the Muslims only but also of the Jews, the Christians, and the Sabeites.[63] No difference is made between the prophets of old so as to give any pre-eminence to the followers of Moses and Jesus, and all people are expected to receive Islām as an indispensable complement to their faith in order to be saved.[64] "This day have I perfected your religion for you and have completed my favours and blessings upon you, and I have been pleased by making Islām your religion."[65] The

59 ERE. xi. 568, art. SIN (Muslim). Wensinck, *op. cit.*, p. 218.

60 See Wensinck, *op. cit.*, p. 192. It has been pointed out that one of the sons of Muhammad bore the pagan name 'Abd Manāf. "Sprenger has conjectured that 'Abd Allah, Tāhir, al-Tayib and other epithets were later substituted for the name 'Abd Manāf."—Wensinck, *op. cit.*, pp. 240, 242.

61 Margoliouth, *Ear. Dev. Muh.*, p. 248. Gabriel is also credited with the same function. See M. Ali's *Holy Quran*, p. 1201, note 2761. Also Archer: *Mystical Elements in Mohammed*, p. 41 f, for versions and interpretations.

62 Sura xlv. 27. *Cf.* 2 Tim. 3.16: "All scripture inspired of God is profitable for teaching, for reproof, for amendment, and for moral discipline, to make the man of God proficient and equip him with good work of every kind." See Bell, *op. cit.*, p. 124.

63 See Rodwell's Koran, p. 373, n. 2 to Sura ii. 59; v. 73.

64 Sura ii. 130, 285 (thus abrogating or contradicting ii. 254 and some verses in xix and xvii. 57); iv. 151. See Wensinck, *op. cit.*, p. 113. For the development of the idea that Islām is the only true religion, see Sir William Muir, *Life of Mohammad*, pp. 150-54; also T. W. Arnold, *The Preaching of Islām*, p. 3 f.

65 Sura v. 5. See Muhammad Ali, *The Religion of Islām*, p. 208 f.

revelation 'Let there be no compulsion in religion'[66] was never intended to be applied to the idolaters of Arabia (or to apostates),[67] either in theory or in practice, for iconoclasm (and extreme punishment of infidels and apostates) was a religious duty with Islām; to the people possessing a 'scripturary' religion, toleration was conceded in theory but often administered with galling severity in practice.[68] To quote Margoliouth,[69] "The ultimate system adopted was to permit the existence of communities which professed to follow a revealed book, but to disarm them and make them tributary; this condition is identified by some purists with that of slaves. The existence of communities to which this description did not apply was forbidden."[70] Possibly the older view, 'The Qur'ān in one hand and sword in the other' as the method of Muhammadan conversion, requires a little modification to-day, but there can be no doubt that at times and in places the victorious armies of Islām did follow this fanatical procedure in times of war,[71] remembering that "only the faithful are brethren,"[72] and that, in times of

66 Sura ii. 257. See iii. 19. See *The Apology of Al Kindy*, p. 98.

67 A well-authenticated tradition ascribes to Muhammad the saying "I am ordered to make war on people till thy say: There is no God but Allāh."—See Wensinck, *op. cit.*, pp. 13, 19. See also Sura xvi. 108.

68 See *The Apology of Al Kindy*, p. 97. See Margoliouth, *Ear. Dev. Muh.*, p. 104 f. The toleration did not extend to Arab Jews or Christians (p. 105).—See pp. 118 f., 132; also Sir William Muir, *Life of Mohammad*, p. 454.

69 ERE. viii. 877. See Hughes, *Dic. Isl.*, p. 243 f., art. JIHAD (The whole article is illuminating as regards the war ethics of the Muslims). Jihād was regarded as the sixth pillar of Islam by the Kharijites.—See Lammens, *op. cit.*, p. 62. See Guillaume, *Traditions of Islam* (1924), p. 110 f., on Jihād; *Enc. Isl.*, I, p. 1041.

70 Margoliouth admits, however, that "exemption from military service and from the burdensome ceremonies of Islam aided the tolerated communities in a variety of ways, and counteracted some of the effects of humiliation and oppression."—*Early Development of Muhammadanism*, pp. 100-01. See T. W. Arnold, *op. cit.*, pp. 59-62.

71 In *The Apology of Al Kindy* (tr. Sir William Muir), p. 61, occurs, for instance, the following sentence: "Instead of miracles, the claim of thy Master was enforced simply by the sword." (See also pp. 95, 100.) See art. PERSECUTION (Muhammadan) in ERE. ix. 607; also the saying of Muhammad, quoted in Sir W. Muir, *Life of Mohammad*, p. 448: "There shall not cease from the midst of my people a party engaged in fighting for the truth, until Anti-christ appear." See T. W. Arnold, *op. cit.*, pp. 69, 75 and 57 (the ordinance of Umar).

72 Sura xlix. 10.

peace, they heaped such indignities, inconveniences and insecurities on the adherents of other faiths that the civil and moral coercion amounted almost to a forcible conversion. When Muhammad conceived Islām to be destined for the whole world—as "an admonition to all created beings,"[73] he could not obviously regard himself as no better than his predecessors nor could he concede that each nation was to have its own prophet.[74] He claimed that he had been sent as "mercy unto all creatures" and that to him belonged the unique distinction of closing the prophetic line altogether: henceforth salvation was of the Muslims only [75] and the Qur'ān was the uncreated word of God much as the Logos was in Christianity. He thereby negated in practice, in so far as it related to the future, his own revelation: "To each age its Book. What He pleaseth doth God abrogate or confirm: for with Him is the source of revelation."[76]

To this stage belongs the famous declaration of Muslim faith (*shahāda*): "There is no God but Allāh and Muhammad is the Apostle of Allāh." The Jews had preached that

[73] See Suras xxxviii, 87 f; xxxvi. 69 f; xxi. 107; xxv. 1.

The doctrine of predestination compels the Muslims to believe, however, that even in the remotest future the distinction between Muslims and non-Muslims will persist. How else would this verse be fulfilled?: 'Moreover had thy Lord pleased, He had assuredly made mankind of one religion: but those only to whom thy Lord hath granted his mercy will cease to differ. And unto this hath He created them; for the word of thy Lord shall be fulfilled, "I will assuredly fill hell with Djinn and men together"' (Sura xi. 120).

[74] See Wensinck, *op. cit.* pp. 5-6; T. W. Arnold, *op. cit.*, pp. 28-31; Muhammad Ali, *The Religion of Islām*, p. 258 f.

[75] Thus in Sura vii. 155-56, God speaks to Moses in the following way:—'I will inflict my chastisement on whom I will, and my mercy embraceth all things, and I write it down for those who fear Me, and pay the alms, and believe in our signs, who follow the Apostle, the unlettered Prophet—whom they find described with them in the Law and Evangel. What is right will he enjoin them, and forbid them what is wrong, and will allow them healthful viands, and prohibit the impure, and will ease them of their burden, and of the yokes which were upon them; and those who believe in him, and strengthen him, and help him, and follow the light which hath been sent down with him,—these are they with whom it shall be well." (*Cf.* Christ's saying: "For my yoke is easy, and my burden is light.")

[76] Sura xiii. 38-39. Md. Ali translates the verses in a different way and with a different meaning (see *Holy Quran*, p. 508).

Yahweh was one Yahweh and Israel was his prophet and the Christians had substituted for the prophetship of the tribe the individual and unique prophetship of Jesus. In the Islāmic formula of faith, while the first or negative half was directed against polytheism of all kinds, the second or positive half was directed against other monotheisms. It is not enough to believe that God is one; it is also necessary to believe in the revelation of God through Muhammad.[77] No longer does he say that he is a mere warner or that he is like one of the Apostles that had gone before or that he came to confirm their messages.[78] He now claims to have come as the special Apostle of the Meccans to preach God's message in the form of an Arabic Qur'ān, and it is not open to them to place him alongside the prophets of other people.[79] He is the last and the best of the Apostles and the Qur'ān is an infallible guide. Muslims are forbidden henceforth to scan the Qur'ān too scrutinisingly and to find out that certain statements there contradict Biblical accounts—that, for instance, Moses' (and Aaron's) sister and Jesus' mother are not identical, that Christ did not escape the Cross,[80] that Baptism was not a dyeing of the Christians' clothes, that no table was sent out of heaven that it might be a recurring festival (the

77 *Cf.* Sura lvii. 28 : "O ye who believe! fear God and believe in his Apostle : two portions of his mercy will He give you."

78 See Sura ii. 114 : "But until thou follow their religion, neither the Jews nor the Christians will ever be satisfied with thee. Say : verily, guidance of God,—that is the guidance! And if after 'the knowledge' which hath reached thee, thou follow their desires, thou shalt find from God neither helper nor protector. They to whom we have given the book, and who read it as it ought to be read,—these believe therein : but whoso believeth not therein, these are they who shall be the losers." See Lammens, *op. cit.*, p. 50.

79 See Wensinck, *op. cit.*, pp. 202-03.

80 On the Quranic view that Christ did not die on the Cross is based the following belief of Mirzā Ghulām Ahmad of Qādiān, the founder of the Ahmadīya Movement : "Jesus did not die on the cross, but was taken down by his disciples in a swoon, and healed within forty days by a miraculous ointment called, in Persian, *Marhām-i-'Isā*. He then travelled to the East on a mission to the ten lost tribes of the children of Israel, believed by Ahmad to be the peoples of Afghanistan and Kashmir, and finally died at the age of 120, and was buried in Khān Yār Street, in Srinagar, the capital of Kashmir." (H. A. Walter, *The Ahmadīya Movement*, p. 90). For similar belief in Christian sects, see Beil, *op. cit.*, p. 154.

Eucharist) to the Christians [81]—and that for certain other statements the authority is not the Bible but the Talmudic literature and certain Christian heresies.[82] The faithful are to learn their Biblical history from the Qur'ān which is the revealed word of God :[83] any discrepancy between it and the Bible is to be set down to the loss of tradition among the Jews or to parts of the Bible being composed by secular hands.[84] For the message of salvation that he brought Muhammad could claim that for all times to come peace should be invoked on him personally whenever his name is uttered and Divine mercy invoked on him and his descendants in the daily prayers of the faithful [85] in addition to the acknowledgment of his Apostleship.

How far Muhammad conceived his message to be universal is difficult to ascertain. He thought as a Semite and

[81] Hughes, *Dic. Isl.*, p. 54, art. CHRISTIANITY, and p. 110, art. EUCHARIST. A critical revision would have cut out the most glaring anachronisms : the confusion between the two Marys (19, 22), between Haman, minister of King Ahasuerus, and the minister of Moses' Pharaoh (Qoran 28. 5-7, 38; 40. 38); the fusion into one of the legends of Gideon, Saul, David and Goliath (2, 250, etc.); the story of the Samaritan (*sic*) who is alleged to have made the Jews worship the golden calf (20, 87, etc).—Lammens, *op. cit.*, p. 39. See, however, Muhammad Ali, *The Holy Quran*, p. 117, footnote 331. See Hughes, *Dic. Isl.*, art. 'IMRĀN; also *Enc. Isl.*, II, pp. 475-76.

[82] Muhammad's justification for treating the Jewish written and unwritten laws on the same level is that the Jews themselves believed that they had both been revealed to Moses on Mount Sinai. The Musalmans followed the Jews in this respect and treated the traditions of the Prophet as equally binding on the faithful with the Quranic revelations.

[83] "Whatever Allah quotes in the Kuran from Moses or other Prophets, from Pharaoh or from Satan, is the speech of Allah in relation to theirs. The speech of Allah is uncreated, but the speech of Moses and other creatures is created."—Art. 3 of The Fikh Akbar II (Wensinck, *op. cit.*, p. 189). See Sura xcviii. 2-3.

[84] See Khwaja Kamaluddin, *Islam and Zoroastrianism*, p. 170 f; Margoliouth, *Ear. Dev. Muh.*, pp. 53, 64, 232 f; Muhammad Ali, *The Religion of Islām*, p. 211 f.

The number of sacred books delivered to mankind is said to have been 104; of these ten were given to Adam, fifty to Seth (a name not mentioned in the Qur'ān), thirty to Enoch, ten to Abraham, the Taurāt to Moses, the Zabūr to David, the Injil to Jesus, and the Qur'ān to Muhammad. The one hundred scriptures given to Adam, Seth, Enoch, and Abraham are termed *Ṣahifah* (a pamphlet), and the other four *Kitāb* (a book); but all that is necessary for the Muslim to know of these inspired records is supposed to have been retained in the Qur'ān.—Hughes, *Dic. Isl.*, art. PROPHETS, p. 475.

[85] These form part of the Tahiya and the Tashahhud in the Ṣalāt (namāz or daily prayer). See Hughes, *Dic. Isl.*, art. PRAYER, p. 468. See 'Ali Tabari

regarded himself as confirming the message of Biblical prophets and a few others whose identity cannot be definitely established now.[86] He was the divinely chosen prophet of the Arabs and at one time accepted the position that other nations had their own prophets by whose revelations they would be judged on the Day of Judgment. He undertook to rid Arabia of its idolatry and polytheism, and he conceded that on the Day of Judgment other Apostles would similarly act as witnesses in respect of their own people. Tradition, however, ascribes to him a number of letters written to contemporary potentates —the Emperor at Byzantium, the King of Persia, the Negus of Abyssinia and the Governor of Egypt—and inviting them to embrace Islām. If their authenticity can be established— Wensinck thinks they are " of a doubtful authority, if indeed they are not wholly legendary,"[87]—they will prove that

(*op. cit.*, p. 40) who connects this with Sura xciv. 1-4. (For Jewish and Christian influence on Muslim prayer, see Bell, *op. cit.*, pp. 142-43.)

[86] The names of 28 prophets are said to occur in the Qur'ān, but there is doubt about two (Aesop and Alexander the Great). Muhammad is related to have said that there were 124,000 prophets and 315 (313?) apostles. Nine of the apostles or messengers—Noah, Abraham, David, Jacob, Joseph, Job, Moses, Jesus and Muhammad—are called " possessors of constancy," and six—Adam, Noah, Abraham, Moses, Jesus and Muhammad—are dignified with special titles (Muhammad being called Rasūlu'llāh, the Messenger of God).—See Hughes, *Dic. Isl.*, p. 475. See Wensinck, *op. cit.*, pp. 202-04, 267. Post-canonical Tradition shows a perpetual tendency to enlarge the number of Prophets as well as that of Apostles. The latter do not exceed the number of 315, whereas that of the Prophets varies between 1,000 and 224,000.—Wensinck, *op. cit.*, p. 204. In the Kuran a difference is made between the Apostle and the Prophet, in so far as the former is representative of a community or people (*umma*) to which God has sent him. . . The Kuranic series of Apostles comprises Nūh (Noah), Lūt (Lot), Ismāil, Mūsā, Shu'aib (Jethro), Hūd, Sālih and 'Isā (Jesus). The number of Prophets mentioned in the Kuran is larger. . . They are not sent each to a different people but they walk in the footsteps of the Apostles, their predecessors. Consequently, according to the doctrine of the Kuran, every Apostle is as such also a Prophet; but not every Prophet is at the same time an Apostle. This is also the view of early Christianity.—Wensinck, *op. cit.*, p. 204. See also Sura ii. 254 : " Some of the apostles We have endowed more highly than others." See also Suras ii. 137; vii. 5; also Wensinck, *op. cit.*, pp. 177, 203.

[87] Wensinck, *op. cit.*, pp. 7-8. But see *Ency. Bri.*, Vol. 15, art. MOHAMMED. See Sir W. Muir, *Life of Mohammad*, Ch. XX; T. W. Arnold, *op. cit.*, p. 28.

Muhammad intended to carry out in practice the Divine injunction, "We have not sent thee otherwise than to mankind at large, to announce and to warn."[88] We now see the full significance of the *shahāda*. Muhammad wished to steer clear of the weakness of Judaism which did not give to prophets a place in the creed on account of its strict monotheism, and of Christianity which elevated the prophet to such a divine height that monotheism itself was in danger. The *shahāda* preserved both Jewish monotheism and Christian emphasis on the importance of the prophet.

Matters became complicated when the Apostle was conceived to combine in himself the functions of a warner on earth and a witness and an intercessor before God, the traditional literature going as usual beyond the Quranic position. There is every reason to think that while in its theory of God Muhammadanism went back to Judaism, in its theory of Prophet it absorbed more and more Christian ideas. It is difficult to see how if God had predetermined certain souls for salvation and others for hell-fire, intercession could be of any avail;[89] but in Muhammadanism, as in other religions, the logic of the heart was allowed to overthrow theological consistency

88 Sura xxxiv. 27. See also xxi. 107; v. 5 (See M. A. Alam, *Islam and Christianity*, Ch. V; T. W. Arnold, *op. cit.*, pp. 4-6.)

89 The Wahhābis distinguish three types of intercession of which one only is applicable to Muhammad's intercession with Allāh. First, there is "the intercession from regard" (*Shafā'at-i-Wajāhah*) as when a king pardons a criminal on the intercession of the vizier whose position merits consideration of a request from him. Secondly, there is "the intercession from affection" (*Shafā'at-i-makabbah*) as when a king pardons a criminal on the intercession of the queen or the princes whom he loves. But to suppose that God would pardon a sinner out of regard or affection for any individual is a *Shirku'l-taṣarruf*, ascribing power to others than God. The true interpretation of intercession is that a king may himself wish to pardon the criminal but fears that the majesty of the law would thereby be lowered. At this point the vizier (or the queen or a prince) intercedes with the tacit consent of the king. This is "the intercession by permission" (*Shafā'at-i-ba'izn*) and Muhammad will have this power with God. The Wahhābis hold that Muhammad does not have this power now but will possess it at the Day of Judgment; but all other Musalmans believe that he has it now.—See Hughes, *Dic. Isl.*, art. SHIRK, pp. 579-80. See also *Enc. Isl.*, IV, p. 378 f. (esp. p. 380).

and the orthodox community finally accepted the intercessory power of the Prophet as a part of the creed.[90] The most intractable passage is Sūra ii. 45: "Fear a day in which a soul shall not avail for a soul at all, nor shall any intercession be accepted from them, nor shall any ransom be taken, nor any help be given them."[91] while Sūra xxxix. 45 lays down that intercession is wholly with God. But possibly here too Muhammad had to bow down to a tribal superstition. The Meccans evidently believed that lower gods could intercede with Allāh[92] and at a moment of weakness Muhammad too had conceded that of Al-Lāt, Al-Uzzā and Al-Manāt, the three exalted female deities, intercession might be expected—a statement which he later on ascribed to Satanic suggestion and withdrew.[93] Apparently he felt that a substitute was wanted but that the supreme authority of Allāh must at the same time be maintained. The Qur'ān nowhere mentions explicitly that Muhammad will act as an intercessor, but Muhammadan theologians have professed to find a justification for their belief in his advocacy in Sūra xvii. 82: "It may be that thy Lord will raise thee to a glorious station,"[94] and in Sūra xciii. 5: "And thy Lord shall assuredly be bounteous to thee and thou be satisfied." The Mu'tazilites felt justified in rejecting the doctrine of intercession as being contrary to the main teaching of the Qur'ān (and also because it seriously affected the question of Divine justice for voluntary sin) and taught that no deliverance of one who had entered Hell was possible;[95] but, possibly under Christian in-

[90] See Waṣīyat Abī Hanīfa, art. 25, and Fikh Akbar II, art. 20, in Wensinck, *op. cit.*, pp. 130, 194 (also pp. 180 f and 61 f).

[91] See also lxxiv. 49; lxxxii. 19.

[92] Suras x. 19; xliii. 86.

[93] Sura liii. 19-20. See Rodwell's Koran, p. 56, footnote 6; Sir William Muir, *Life of Mohammad*, p. 81 f.

[94] In Rodwell's Koran this is xvii. 82. The uncertainty of interpretation is brought out by the fact that this identical passage is recited during the Azān (call to public prayer) by religious Muslims as a prayer to God that He might grant the Maqām Maḥmūd to the Prophet.—See Hughes, *Dic. Isl.*, p. 313, art. MAQĀM MAḤMŪD.

See also Wensinck, *op. cit.*, p. 181.

[95] See Wensinck, *op. cit.*, p. 61.

fluence, orthodoxy veered round to the view that Muhammad was "a living intercessor at the throne of God."[96] Obviously this intercession, consistently with the general tenor of Quranic teaching on the subject, must be permitted by Allāh,[97] and this permission is granted either to pure beings like the angels (Sūras xl. 7 ; xlii. 3 ; xxi. 28-29) or to those who bear witness to the truth (Sūra xliii. 86)[98] and whose words are approved by God (Sūra xx. 108) ; and again such intercession is permissible only in respect of those who have entered into covenant with the God of Mercy (Sūra xix. 90).[99] The final opinion of Muslim orthodoxy is that Muhammad intercedes for those who have committed great sins[100] and the right of intercession extends also to angels, prophets, the learned and the martyrs.[101] To quote Wensinck : "In early Christian literature we find the angels, the patriarchs, the Prophets, the Apostles and the Martyrs as those who will intercede on behalf of sinners. The same classes of men are the holders of the privilege of intercession in Islām."[102] The superiority of Muhammad is established by the fact that when on the Day of Judgment the Faithful will approach other prophets for intercession they will all excuse themselves but Muhammad will, with the permission of Allāh, "rescue from Hell all those in whose heart a grain of faith has persisted."[103]

96 The Wahhābis state that the intercession of their prophet will only be by the permission (*Izn*) of God at the *last day*, and that there is no intercession for sins until the Day of Judgment. The teaching of the Qur'ān and the Traditions seems to be in favour of this view.—Hughes, *Dic. of Isl.*, p. 214, art. INTERCESSION.

97 Suras ii. 256; x. 3; xx. 108; xxxiv. 22; lxxviii. 38.

98 Muhammadan commentators include here Jesus and Ezra.—See Rodwell's Koran, p. 136, n.1.

99 There could be no intercession for infidels (Sura ix. 114).—See Wensinck, *op. cit.*, pp. 183, 239.

100 See Wensinck, *op. cit.*, p. 182 f. The Mu'tazilites say that Muhammad's intercession is not for the prevention of punishment but for the increase of merit.—See Hughes, *Dic. Isl.*, art. INTERCESSION, p. 215.

101 Hughes, *Dic. Isl.*, p. 215.

102 Wensinck, *op. cit.*, pp. 180, 182. Even Allāh Himself is supposed to intercede (p. 182).

103 Wensinck, *op. cit.*, p. 182. The traditions are not definite about the place where the intercession would be made—it might be either at the bridge (over

Apparently here was something to match Jesus' descent into Hell to release its inmates. The last transformation in this line of thought is the doctrine of the Light of Muhammad[104] which is supposed to have existed before all creation, being the first thing to be created by God, and to have given rise to all other things, including the heavens, the paradises and hells, the throne of God, the angels, and the mind. The assimilation with the pre-existent Messiah of the Christians is almost complete in this conception, the only distinction being that whereas Christ was regarded as co-eternal with God and was himself invested with the creative function, the light of Muhammad is a thing created from the light of God [105] and only furnishes the material of subsequent creation. Similar to this type of thought is the belief that "the Prophet's call was at least coeval with the creation of Adam," that he was appointed to the prophetic office when Adam was only half

which all souls have to pass after death) or at the balance (where merits are weighed) or at the basin (the pond of abundance) —*Ibid*, p. 169. (Another tradition substitutes the reading of the book for the pond of abundance.)

104 The following description from Hughes, *Dic. Isl.*, art. AL-HAQIQATU 'L-MUHAMMADĪYAH, p. 162, will suffice :

The Prophet said, "The first thing created was the light of your Prophet, which was created from the light of God. This light of mine roamed about wherever God willed, and when the Almighty resolved to make the world, he divided this light of Muhammad into four portions; from the first he created the Pen (*qalam*): from the second the Tablet (*lauḥ*); from the third, the highest heaven and the throne of God ('*arsh*); the fourth portion was divided into four sections: from the first were created the *Hamalatu'l-'Arsh*, or the eight angels who support the throne of God; from the second, the *kursi*, or lower throne of God; from the third, the angels; and the fourth, being divided into four subdivisions, from it were created (1) the firmaments or seven heavens, (2) the earth, (3) the seven paradises and seven hells, (4) and again from a fourth section were created (1) the light of the eyes, (2) the light of the mind, (3) the light of the love of the Unity of God, (4) the remaining portion of creation." See also *The Legacy of Islam*, p. 225; Nicholson, *Idea of Per. in Sufism*, pp. 58-60; Sir William Muir, *The Mohammedan Controversy and other articles*, pp. 77-79.

105 *Cf.* The Nicene Creed : 'Light of light.'

Jīlī considers the created Rūh or the archetypal Spirit of Mohammed as a mode of the uncreated Holy Divine Spirit and as the medium through which God becomes conscious of Himself in creation."—Nicholson, *Studies in Isl. Mys.*, p. 110 (See also *Idea of Personality in Sufism*, p 46).

created.[106] The conception of the Mahdi or the Guide[107] who, according to Muslim tradition, will appear in the last days to "fill the earth with equity and justice" and to "give strength and stability to Islām," has obvious analogy with the Christian belief about the sending of the Comforter and the second advent of Christ and was apparently prompted by the latter, only that the orthodox believe that both the Mahdi and the Messiah (Jesus)[108] would come to "fill the whole world with the knowledge of God." It is not impossible that both in Christianity and in Islām the idea of a last prophet was connected with the belief in the imminence of the Day of Judgment and that in both a change in that belief led to the idea of a return of the Prophet during the last days.

We may now return from this digression about the nature and function of Muhammad as the Prophet of God to a consideration of the nature of God as revealed in the Qur'ān. As is to be expected, the hostility of Muhammad to all sorts of polytheism made him disown not only his country's gods but also the Christian trinity and go back to the awful majesty of the Jewish unitary God.[109] The use he made of Allāh was

106 Margoliouth *Ear. Dev. Muh.*, pp. 242, 248. In a tradition Allāh is made to declare: "Had it not been for thee, I had not created the worlds."—Macdonald, *Religious Attitude and Life in Islam*, p. 10. In his *Mishkāt al-Anwār* Ghazāli introduces a being called by him *al-Mut'ā*, "the Obeyed One," which Nicholson interprets as "the archetypal Spirit of Muhammad, the Heavenly Man created in the image of God and regarded as a Cosmic Power on whom depends the order and preservation of the universe." If Nicholson's interpretation is correct, "Ghazāli believed that while God in His essence is known only to those who have realised His unity in the all-consuming mystical experience, His will and providence are manifested in the world through the idea embodied, as it were, in the person of Muhammad" (*Idea of Per. in Sufism*, pp. 46-47). See also p. 63.

107 See art. AL-MAHDI in Hughes, *Dic. Isl.*, p. 305; THE MAHDI in M. Cannay, *Enc. of Rel.*, p. 228; Wensinck, *op. cit.*, pp. 243-44. About the conflict of opinions regarding the appearance of the Mahdī, see Guillaume, *The Traditions of Islam*, pp. 91-93.

108 The founder of the Ahmadīya movement (Mirza Ghulam Ahmad) claimed to have combined in himself the functions of both.—See A. Walter, *The Ahmadīya Movement*, p. 25 f. For the ingenious way in which Muslim traditionalists reconciled Muhammad being the last Prophet and the Messiah descending on the last days and adding to the lawful, see Guillaume, *The Traditions of Islam*, pp. 72-73. For a contrary view about the advent of Jesus, *ibid*, pp. 157-58. See also Muhammad Ali, *The Religion of Islām*, p. 260 f.

109 Between God and man there is no direct and regular communication. Every effort to lessen the distance which separates them appears tainted by

similar to what the Jews made of Yahweh, for like unto Moses, God dictates to Muhammad through Gabriel (Jibril) a whole body of social laws in addition to religious prescriptions and ethical principles. As has been well said : " The Koran is the general code, social, civil, commercial, military, judicial, criminal, penal and yet religious."[110] As social regulations presuppose the existence of a community of the faithful, these came naturally as revelations in Medina; but broad principles of religion and ethics lie scattered in the Meccan *Sūras* and can be found in a convenient summary in Sūra xiii (Thunder). Two seemingly contradictory views of God appear in the Qur'ān. There is, first, the idea, familiar to us from later Rabbinical literature, that an adequate comprehension of the nature of God is beyond the capacity of man, for God is unlike everything that we have experience of in this world. The general tendency of the Qur'ān is to prevent the assimilation of God to worldly things : Muhammad knew too well the dangerous tendency of the human mind to rely upon the things of the world in religious devotion. Material objects and heavenly bodies, forces and phenomena of nature, holy persons and abstractions of thought were being worshipped all around either in pagan or in scripturary religions, and the Jews and Christians were twisting the fatherhood of God (so he thought) into a physical relationship.[111] So, to guard against lapses into idolatry and polytheism, it was necessary to make it clear that God was far

'*shirk*,' a move in the direction of polytheism. The soul, in its struggle to gain salvation, cannot rely on the aid of any intermediary. In the most idealised portraits of the Sira and the ḥadīth Muhammad is never shown except as the instrument of revelation. Even then he did not receive the trust direct, but through the ministrations of an angel.—Lammens, *op. cit.*, pp. 113-14. See Macdonald, *Rel. Att. and Life in Islam*, p. 38.

110 Khwaja Kamaluddin, *The Threshold of Truth*, p. 127 (quoting Devonport).

111 The attitude of the Muhammadans towards the idea of God as Father may be gathered from the following typical quotation : " We must realise, if we are really advanced, that our relation to God is unique. It is neither like the relation of a son to his father nor like anything in the world. . . We must fear, love and respect Him at the same time. . . Is the word " Father " indicative of this attitude of man towards God? Is it not using too familiar a word?... As a matter of fact, to apply to the Deity terms indicative of human relationship is

removed from all worldly objects in quality and that there was nothing like unto Him.[112] This could lead to only two conclusions, namely, that Allāh was absolutely indefinite and that He could be described only negatively. A third conclusion is also possible, namely, that Allāh is absolutely incomprehensible and unknowable; but that tendency was checked by the consideration that in that case doubt would be cast on the existence of Allāh—a position which the Qur'ān could never be expected to countenance. But the other two tendencies became evident in " the doctrines of *tanzīh* (removal) and *mukhālafa* (difference), *i.e.*, the removal from Allāh of all qualities of impermanence, and assertion of the essential difference of his qualities and the similarly named qualities of human beings," [113] and also in the Mu'tazilite idea of God which practically consists of a string of negations. The following quotation from al-Ash'arī describes the Mu'tazilite position :[114] " Allāh is one, without equal, hearing, seeing; He is no body, nor object, nor volume, nor form, nor flesh, nor blood, nor person, nor substance, nor *accidens*, nor provided with colour, taste, smell, touch, heat, cold, moistness, dryness, length, breadth, depth, union, distinction, movement, rest or partition. Neither is He provided with parts, divisions, limbs, members, with directions, with right or left hand, before or behind, above or beneath. No place encompasses Him, no time passes by Him. The ideas of intercourse, withdrawal and incarnation cannot be applied to Him. He

clearly obnoxious to those religiously most advanced. For this reason we cannot properly call God Father, Mother or anything indicative of human relationship. He is no relation of ours. He is unique and we must bear this in mind. To establish relationship with God is to tamper with His uniqueness."—Muhammad Amir Alam, *Islam and Christianity* (1923), pp. 153-54. See, however, Macdonald, *Rel. Att. and Life in Islam*, p. 39. The Muhammadan religion does not permit the ascription to Allāh of any name which is not *tauqifī*, that is, authorised in some revelation—Quran or tradition. " Father " is not one of the names used by Muhammad and is not included in the list of the ninety-nine names of Allāh. (See ERE. vi. 299; Hughes, *Dic. Isl.*, pp. 141-42; Lammens, *op. cit.*, p. 113; Macdonald, *Rel. Att. and Life in Islam*, p. 211).

112 Suras cxii. 4; xlii. 9; xxii. 73; xvi. 76. (*Cf.* Ex. xx. 4.)

113 *Enc. Isl.*, p. 305.

114 Quoted by Wensinck, *op. cit.*, p. 73. For the Mu'tazilite articles of belief, *ibid*, p. 58 f. The whole of Ch. IV is worth reading.

cannot be described by any description which can be applied to creatures, in so far as they are created, neither can it be said that He is finite. He cannot be described by measure, nor by movement in a direction. He is not definite; neither begetting nor begotten; measures do not encompass Him, nor do curtains veil Him. The senses do not reach Him, nor can man describe Him by any analogy. He does not resemble the creatures in any way. Neither accident nor detriment can touch Him. Nothing of what occurs to any mind or can be conceived by phantasy resembles Him. He has not ceased to be the first, the foremost, He who preceded created things and existed before the creation. He has not ceased to be knowing, deciding, living, nor does He cease to be so. Eyes do not see Him, sight does not reach Him, phantasy cannot conceive Him nor can He be heard by ears. He is a being, but is not as other beings; knowing, deciding, living, unlike those who measure living beings by their knowledge. He alone is eternal; there is none eternal besides Him, nor a God like unto Him. He has no partner in His Kingdom, nor a vizier in His government, nor any who assists Him in producing what He produces and in creating what He creates. He has not created the creation after a foregoing pattern. The creation of one thing is neither more easy nor more difficult to Him than the creation of any other thing. There is no kind of relation between Him and what gives profit; no harm can touch Him; neither joy nor pleasure can reach Him, nor is He moved by hurt or pain. There is no limit set to Him, to make Him finite. The idea of ceasing to be cannot be applied to Him, nor is He subject to weakness or diminishing. He is exalted above touching women and above taking a companion and begetting children." True, this description does not exclude positive qualities altogether; but when it is remembered that the Mu'tazilites were uncompromising opponents of the ascription of eternal qualities to God and that even when they admitted their existence they considered them to be indistinguishable from His essence, it can be seen at once that the rationalists of Islām did not think that there was any necessity for ascribing to Allāh anything more than reality or essential existence or of regarding the attributes as anything but allegorical.

It would have been strange, however, if orthodoxy had accepted the validity of the Mu'tazilite conception. The central theme of the Qur'ān is Allāh and His working in nature and human history.[115] The Quranic revelation would have had no meaning, had not God intended to reveal His nature and will to man : a revealed religion is necessary because the imperfect reason of man is incapable of arriving at a true conception of God without His own aid. It is not denied that man cannot know God unto perfection : but it is denied that God's unity and independence exclude the possession of real attributes or that it is permissible to reject them altogether because of their ambiguities and apparent contradictions. Did not the Qur'ān say,[116] " He it is who sent down to thee " the Book.' Some of its signs are of themselves perspicuous;—these are the basis of the Book—and others are figurative. But they whose hearts are given to err, follow its figures, craving discord, and craving an interpretation; yet none knoweth its interpretation but God. But the stable in knowledge say, " We believe in it : it is all from our Lord." Yet none receive the admonition (*i.e.*, bear this in mind), save men endued with understanding "? So the orthodox ultimately settled down to the view that the meaning of the ambiguous verses describing God and His attributes was known to God alone and that the duty of the faithful was to believe in them without discussion—" without enquiring how and without making comparison."[117] A typical instance would suffice. God is described in the Qur'ān as " the most merciful of those that show mercy " and yet He tortures children in a number of ways even though they have no fault of their own and they cannot be punished for

115 Khwaja Kamaluddin, *Islam and Christianity*, Ch. VI; *Threshold of Truth*, Ch. III.

116 Sura iii. 5. See ERE. vi. 300 f. See Muhammad Ali, *The Holy Quran*. pp. 141-42, f.n. 337-39.

117 See ERE. ii. 300-01, art. GOD (Muslim); also Wensinck, *op. cit.*, p. 229.

the fault of their ancestors.[118] Ibn Hazm's solution of this difficulty is thus summarised by Macdonald :[119] "Mercy, in our human sense, which is high praise applied to a man, cannot be predicated of God. What then does the Qur'ān mean by those words? Simply that they—*arhamu-r-rahi-min*—are one of God's names, applied to Him by Himself and that we have no right to take them as descriptive of a quality, mercy, and to use them to throw light on God's nature." So the attributes are neither to be rejected nor to be literally taken : in this, as in many other matters, the general Quranic prescription to adopt the middle path should be followed, namely, the mean between divesting God of all attributes and ascribing to Him qualities borrowed from this world.[120]

But the trouble does not end here. The Qur'ān makes reference to the various attributes and activities of Allāh in no uncertain terms; if there are ambiguous passages in which the faithful are expected to believe without question, there are also perspicuous passages of which the import can never be mistaken by the understanding. Then, again, appeal is made in the Qur'ān to certain obvious signs in nature from which the discerning mind can arrive at a conclusion regarding the existence of God. "The creation of the sun, the moon and the stars, the order and design witnessed in those orbs which constitute the host of heaven, the consummate laws of order that regulate the universe, the formation of man's body and mind, the marvellous power and wisdom discernible in the government of this universe,"[121] the due order in which the

118 Islam does not admit either metempsychosis or original sin. In its solicitude to safeguard the direct dealing of Allāh with each individual it went to the extreme of suggesting that diseases never spread by contagion but only by God communicating them directly to each individual. See A. Guillaume, *The Traditions of Islam*, p. 123; also p. 178.

119 Macdonald, *Development of Muslim Theology*, p. 210.

120 See Mirza Ghulam Ahmad, *The Teachings of Islam*, pp. 94-95.

121 Muslim theologians are generally of opinion that while it is permissible to use the reason to arrive at a theistic conclusion, the certainty about God's existence comes not from human reason but from Divine revelation. See, *e.g.*, Mirza Ghulam Ahmad, *The Teachings of Islam*, pp. 75-77 : "In short, unless

seasons come in their rotation and dead nature springs to life with the returning rains, the supremacy of man over land and sea and, lastly, the conscience and the faith that man finds engraved on his own heart [122]—all bespeak the existence of a unitary God and the operation of a merciful Providence. "Assuredly in the heavens and the earth are signs for those who believe firmly; and in your own creation, and in the beasts which He hath dispersed abroad are signs to the firm in faith: and in the succession of night and day, and in the supply which God sendeth down from the Heaven whereby after its death He giveth life to the earth, and in the change of the winds are signs for people of discernment. Such are the signs of God."[123] None but Almighty God could have ordained all these and yet people in their ignorance join other gods with God and even bow down before idols which are themselves the creations of man.

Muslim theologians have collected with commendable diligence the different attributes, functions and names of God mentioned or implied in the Qur'ān, and many have been the disputes over their exact significance among the different schools of thought. The final orthodox opinion may be summed up in the propositions that Allāh is the personal name of the Muslim God who, if He is to be called a thing or substance, is not to be conceived as like other things, and that of this Allāh there are ninety-nine other excellent names (*al-àsmā' al-husnā*),[124] all equally eternal and all equally im-

Almighty God reveals Himself by His word spoken to His servants as He reveals Himself by His work as witnessed in nature, a rational persuasion of His existence, which is the outcome of an observation of His works, is never satisfactory" (p. 76).

122 Suras lviii. 22; xlix. 7, 8.

123 Sura xlv. 2-5. See also Suras ii. 159; iii. 187; xxx. 18-24; xvi. 2-16; xxi. 31-35; xxxi. 28-30.

124 On 'ninety-nine,' see the author's article on *The Sense of the Incomplete* in *Calcutta Review*, January, 1928.

It is curious that the Muslim tradition of Allāh's ninety-nine names should lead Jaffur Shurreef, the author of *Qanoon-e-Islam* (tr. G. A. Herklots, 1832), to omit, on p. 358, al-Bārī (The Maker). But the number is really 100, including the name of Allāh which is to be put either at the beginning or at the end. For the list of names, see K. Kamaluddin, *The Threshold of Truth*, pp. 122-23 (also

portant in so far as they all refer to His being.[125] Whether other names deduced from these " excellent titles "[126] or the synonyms of Allāh in other languages (such as the Persian Khudā or the English God) are permissible is doubtful,[127] but, as a matter of fact, such other names have also been applied to Him. These names, however, are not all of equal loftiness[128] and there has been some speculation also about " the exalted name " (*Ism al-A'zam*), the choice being limited to those used in Sūra ii. 158 and Sūra iii. 1 (*i.e.*, the Merciful, the Compassionate, the Self-subsisting and the Living) and to the name ' Allāh.'[129] Religious exercise includes the recitation of all these names with a rosary, but a distinction is drawn, as in Śaivism, between the glorious (or auspicious) and the terrible aspects of Allāh in these ninety-nine names, and, as in Vaiṣṇavism, different names are taken for the fulfilment of different purposes.[130] They do not exhaust the list of Divine qualities but they describe only those aspects in which Allāh has disclosed Himself to the human mind:[131] to think that He possesses no more qualities is, as Rabbi Hanina remarked on the lengthy enumeration of Divine attributes in post-Biblical

*Islam and Zoroastrianism*, pp. 101-03); Hughes, *Dic. Isl.*, pp. 141-42. (There is some difference between the two lists of names and their meanings). Sir Mohammad Iqbal's attempt to understand some of these ancient names (*e.g.*, *Dahr*) in the light of Modern Philosophy, as Dayananda Saraswati's of Vedic words, is misplaced ingenuity (see Iqbal's *Six Lectures on the Reconstruction of Religious Thought in Islam*, 1930, p. 101 f). Nobody else, again, would read in Sura xv. 21 an anticipation of the Quantum theory (*ibid*, p. 93 f.). See Kamaluddin, *Threshold of Truth*, p. 27.

125 Wensinck, *op. cit.*, pp. 188, 206.

126 Suras vii. 179; xvii. 111; lix. 24 (more than a dozen names are packed together in Sura lix. 22-24).

127 ERE. ii. 299. Some names do not occur in the Qur'ān but the sense is found there (See Hughes, *Dic. Isl.*, p. 427; *Enc. Isl.*, I, art. ALLĀH, p. 302 f.) See however, art. 24 of Fikh Akbar II in Wensinck, *op. cit.*, pp. 196 and 236.

128 Wensinck, *op. cit.*, p. 239.

129 Hughes, *Dic. Isl.*, p. 142; ERE. ii. 299.

130 Some count the names with the finger. The Hindu practice also follows both methods. The rosary was borrowed from the Buddhists through the Sufis and passed on to the Christians during the Crusades.

See ERE. vi. 299. Similar is the case with the names of Viṣṇu.

131 K. Kamaluddin, *Islam and Zoroastrianism*, p. 93; *Threshold of Truth*, p. 121.

literature, like calling a millionaire the possessor of a hundred thousand.[132] An analysis of these different names shows unmistakably Muhammad's lofty conception of Allāh. Christianity inherited the Jewish idea of God and had only to deepen its significance here and there; but Muhammad had to attempt a comprehensive description to replace the many gods of the Arab religion, and so he had to concentrate in One God the different divine functions distributed among these gods of polytheism.[133]

In his emphasis upon the unity of God Muhammad went back to Judaism with its famous monotheistic creed, 'Hear, O Israel : the Lord our God is one Lord.' The short chapter on The Unity (Sūra cxii) was directed against all types of polytheism (*shirk*), *viz.* "a belief in the plurality of gods, a belief that other things may possess the perfect attributes of the Divine Being, a belief that anything may be related to him, and a belief that others may do what is ascribable only to the Divine Being."[134] The lonely majesty of God was so far emphasised that the world was regarded, though not as a sport, yet as a mere episode in His eternal life—created by Him, maintained and guided by Him, and destroyed by Him.[135] Many of the "excellent names" bring out this aspect of Allāh : He is the Creator of souls (Al-Khāliq), the Maker of bodies (Al-Bāri'), the Fashioner of the image in the womb (Al-Muṣawwir), the Guardian (Al-Wakīl), the Preserver (Al-Ḥāfiẓ), the ever Maintainer (Al-Muqīt), the Great Beginner (Al-Mubdi'), the Restorer (Al-Mu'īd), the Life-giver or Quickener (Al-Muḥyī), the Killer (Al-Mumīt), the Ender of everything (Al-Mu'akhkhir), the Gatherer (Al-Jāmi'), the Nourisher (Ar-Rabb), the Director (Ar-Rashīd), the Bestower (Al-Wahhāb), the Provider (Ar-Razzāq) and

132 ERE. vi. 297, art. GOD (Jewish).

133 On pagan gods in pre-Islamic Arabia, see ERE. i. 660-5, art. ARABS (Ancient) by Th. Nöldeke. See also Sale's Preliminary Discourse in his *Comprehensive Commentary on the Qurān* (ed. E. M. Wherry), Vol. I, pp. 34-44.

134 The Holy Qur'ān (tr. by Muhammad Ali), p. 1235, f.n. 2817. For the Wahhābi classification of *Shirk*, see Hughes, *Dic. Isl.*, p. 579; see also Muhammad Ali, *The Religion of Islām*, p. 145 f.

135 See *Enc. Isl.*, II, art. KHALK, p. 892.

the Destroyer (Al-Muzīl). Allāh is dependent for His existence on nothing and is for ever and for ever—He is He (Hoo), the Living (A-Ḥaiy), the Self-subsisting (Al-Qaiyūm), the One (Al-Wāḥid), the Eternal (Aṣ-Ṣamad, Al-Azalī), the Forerunner (Al-Muqaddim), the First (Al-Awwal), the Last (Al-Ākhir), the Alone in His attributes (Al-Aḥad), the Independent or Self-sufficient (Al-Ghanī), the Survivor or Enduring (Al-Bāqī), the Inheritor (Al-Wārith). He is the Incomparable (Al-Badi‘) and nothing can equal or approach Him in greatness and glory—He is the Mighty (Al-‘Azīz), the All-compelling (Al-Jabbār), the Great (Al-Mutakabbir), the Dominant (Al-Qahhār), the Grand (Al-‘Aẓim), the Exalted (Al-‘Alī, Al-Aāla), the Ever Great (Al-Kabīr), the Majestic (Al-Jalīl), the Glorious (Al-Majīd), the Strong (Al-Qawī), the Firm (Al-Matīn), the Powerful (Al-Qādir), the Prevailing (Al-Muqtadir), the One above all others (Al-Muta‘ālī). Now as the supreme example of earthly majesty is the King, so Allāh naturally gets epithets of dominion also—He is the Master (Al-Mālik), the King (Al-Malik), the Protector (Al-Muhaimin), the Governor (Al-Walī), the King of All Kingdoms (Māliku'l-mulk), the Lord of Majesty and Liberality (Dhu'l-jalāli wa'l-ikrām). The name of the essence of God is Allāh —a word which has been understood by Muslim theologians in the sense of a " Being who exists necessarily by Himself, comprising all the attributes of perfection."

The uncompromising monotheism of Islām is such a well-known fact that it is not necessary to dwell upon it longer. Suffice it to say that in the eyes of Islām polytheism is an unpardonable sin and no personal merit or prophetic intercession would succeed in outweighing this single guilt of denying or qualifying the unity (*tawḥīd*) of God. Conversely, an infidel could save his life from the Muslim sword by declaring his belief in the unity of God even though it was prompted by fear, and not by conviction, and even though the Apostleship of Muhammad was omitted from the *shahāda*.[136]

[136] Wensinck, *op. cit.*, pp. 29-32.

In fact, the profession of Divine Unity sometimes went to such length that it alone was considered sufficient for entry into Paradise even though theft and fornication had been committed.[137] Against this Murji'ite belief in the sufficiency of faith in Allāh without work,[138] the Khārijite view that a person committing gross immoral acts like fornication and theft ceases to be a Muslim and becomes a *munāfiq*, a possessor of sham faith, was extremely necessary. But orthodoxy has inclined more towards Murji'itism than towards the Khārijite view inasmuch as it has upheld the position " that whoever commits fornication or theft or other grave sins, except *shirk*, may not be declared an infidel for this reason; he is faithful, but his faith is incomplete. If he repents, his punishment is cancelled and when he persists in his sins, he is left to the mercy of God; if He pleaseth, He will punish him and cause him to enter Paradise afterwards.''[139] But lest people should grow neglectful, works were enjoined; still faith continued to be regarded as alone sufficient for salvation.[140] As Wensinck points out, [141] " The identification of faith and knowledge was a doctrine of the Murdjites, which was received into some forms of the orthodox creed. A consequence of this doctrine was that little importance was attached to works or to the ethical and emotional sides of religion.''

With Muslim theologians the unity of Allāh was such a fundamental article of belief that there was some danger of denying not only external distinctions but also internal distinctions in relation to Allāh, as was done by Śaṅkara in relation to Brahman. There was not only no other god either in a polytheistic or in a trinitarian sense; but doubts were

137 Wensinck, *op. cit.*, p. 46; also *Enc. Isl.*, II, p. 269, art. KHAṬṬA.

138 Macdonald, *Development of Muslim Theology*, p. 126 f; Wensinck, *op. cit.*, p. 45; ERE. v. 695, art. FAITH (Muslim): " An illustration used is that a tree may have neither leaves nor fruit and still it is a tree."

139 Wensinck, *op. cit.*, p. 47. *Enc. Isl.*, II, p. 927; also p. 474 (art. IMĀN; ERE. v. 695, art. FAITH (Muslim).

140 Wensinck, *op. cit.*, p. 49.

141 *Op. cit.*, p. 120. See ERE. v. 695, art. FAITH (Muslim).

raised as to whether the qualities of Allāh could be co-eternal with His essence, and if so, whether they could be distinguished from it.[142] The problem was acute in respect of the seven attributes (*ṣifāt*) which, by unanimous agreement, were assigned to Allāh, namely, Life (*ḥayāh*), Knowledge (*'ilm*), Power (*qudra*), Will (*irāda*), Hearing (*sam'*), Seeing (*baṣar*), and Speech (*kalām*). The orthodox Attributists (*ṣifātīyah*) could not discard either the attributes or the unity of Allāh. So they held that the attributes of God were eternally inherent in His essence without separation or change and that all the attributes were conjoined with Him, as life with knowledge, or knowledge with power,—the attributes were eternal but indistinguishable from Divine essence.[143] The Mu'tazilites, who were stricter adherents of Divine unity, not only discarded the last three attributes as " accidents peculiar to corporal existence " but denied that eternal attributes could coexist with the Divine essence without multiplying eternal existences and jeopardising the unity of Allāh.[144] In a veritable Upaniṣadic fashion Allāh was assigned contradictory qualities—only that whereas the Upaniṣads ascribed to Brahman opposite positive qualities, some of the Mu'tazilites described Allāh by a double negation,[145] and others obliterated the distinction between His essence and His attributes.[146] But, more frequently, the Mu'tazilites

142 For a thorough discussion of the relation of Divine attributes to Divine Essence, see Wensinck, *op. cit.*, pp. 70-77.

143 Hughes, *Dic. Isl.*, art. SIFATIYAH, p. 582. ERE. vi. 301, art. GOD (Muslim).

144 See Wensinck, *op. cit.*, p. 84 (quotation from al-Shahrastānī). For another view, see Hishām ibn-al-Hakām in ***Moslem Schisms and Sects*** (tr. Seelye), pp. 68-69, according to whom attributes are neither eternal nor created but are identical with the Divine Essence and not capable of predication in relation to God. See Nicholson, ***Studies in Islamic Mysticism***, pp. 128-29.

145 Thus ' Abbad ibn Sulaiman and his adherents say : It is forbidden to say God has knowledge, power, hearing, sight.' Likewise it is forbidden to say God has no knowledge, no power.' (See Wensinck, *op. cit.*, p. 77.) Similarly they say : It is forbidden to say that the Creator has not ceased creating or that He has not ceased not-creating (or, ceased sustaining or ceased not-sustaining) (*ibid*, p. 75).

146 Thus Abu'l Hudhail and his adherents say : Allah has knowledge which is Himself, and power which is Himself, and life which is Himself, and hearing which is Himself (*ibid*, p. 77). Some went so far as to deny that anything what-

regarded eternity (including, of course, unity) as the only eternal quality of Allāh and relegated the other attributes to the class of created, and therefore non-eternal, things (in which class was necessarily included the Qur'ān, the speech of Allāh).

A sounder theological instinct, however, led the orthodox to keep closer to the language of the Qur'ān and to defend against the Mu'tazilites the position that a multiplicity of eternal qualities or names does not impugn the unitary character of God. They also maintained against the Sifātites or Attributists that attributes were separate or different from essence logically, though neither in reality nor in time, even in God. Hence it is possible to affirm that Allāh possesses eternal qualities and also names indicating those qualities and the functions arising out of the single or joint operation of those qualities,—only that we must remember that "no one participates with God in His person and attributes"—"nought is there like Him,"[147] and that therefore the qualities are not to be understood as being like unto the qualities of earthly things. Thus God is living, but He does not possess a body as we do; unlike ourselves (including the apostles), He does not begin or cease to be, and He neither begets nor is begotten; slumber does not overtake Him nor sleep, nor is He ever fatigued by His creative and preservative acts.[148] It is from Him,—the eternal, the ever-living and the subsistent, that all life, nourishment, death and immortality proceed; it is unpardonable blasphemy to join with

ever could be predicated of God; others rejected only some of these qualities.—*The Legacy of Islam*, p. 263 (see also Wensinck, *op. cit.*, pp. 76-77).

147 Sura xlii. 9. The problem of the relation between these qualities and the essence "was eventually given up by orthodox Islam which took refuge in the statement 'they are not He (*i.e.*, Allāh Himself), nor are they other than He'; this was an admission that the relationship was a theological mystery, ungraspable by human thought."—See *Enc. Isl.*, II, p. 671.

148 Sura ii. 256. This is directed against the Jewish belief that on the Sabbath day God "rested from all his work which he had made" (Gen. ii. 2-3; Ex. xx. 11); but the Deuteronomy had already prescribed the keeping of the Sabbath as a remembrance for the safe exodus from Egypt (Dt. v. 15). The Sabbath may have been derived in the first instance from some form of moon-worship (ERE. v. 863).

such a living God the manufactured idols of paganism or the blind forces of nature or the heavenly bodies or even saints, prophets or messiahs.

But God is not a mere *Elan Vital* or blind power without knowledge and purpose. If God possesses life and power, He also possesses knowledge and will. God's knowledge is eternal and belongs to His essence : it is not adventitious and acquired. The past, the present and the future are all equally present to His knowledge : " He knoweth what is present with His creatures and what is yet to befall them; yet nought of His knowledge do they comprehend, save what He willeth."[149] Nothing hidden or manifest in heaven or earth falls outside His knowledge; and the inmost thoughts and the most secret deeds of all creatures as well as their words are all known to Him : " And with Him are the keys of the secret things; none knoweth them but He : and He knoweth whatever is on the land and in the sea; and no leaf falleth but He knoweth it ; neither is there a grain in the darkness of the earth, nor a thing green or sere, but it is noted in the perspicuous book. And it is He who taketh you to Himself at night, and knoweth what ye have merited in the day : then He awaketh you therein, that the set life-term may be fulfilled : then unto Him is your return; and then shall He declare to you that which ye have wrought."[150] " Three persons speak not privately together, but He is their fourth; nor five, but He is their sixth; nor fewer nor more, but wherever they be He is with them."[151] " He verily knoweth the secret whisper, and the yet more hidden "[152] " verily God knoweth whatever thing they invoke in His stead."[153] He never suffers from forgetfulness, negligence and error. " He is the Subtile, the All-informed." [154]

149 Sura ii. 256.
150 Sura vi. 59-60; see also lxvii. 13.
151 Sura lviii. 8 (*cf.* Atharva-Veda, IV. 16.2).
152 Sura xx. 6.
153 Sura xxix. 41.
154 Sura vi. 103.

But Allāh's knowledge is not a mere awareness of physical, mental and moral events; it includes His wisdom in dealing with the needs of His creation. "He causeth the dawn to break, and hath ordained the night for rest, and the sun and the moon for computing time! This is the ordinance of the Mighty, the Wise! And it is He who hath ordained the stars for you, that ye may be guided thereby in the darkness of the land and of the sea."[155] When man offers up prayer to God for help, He knows whether or not to listen to it: out of His wisdom He chooses the best for the supplicant. A number of epithets indicating the knowledge and wisdom of God are included within the excellent titles of Allāh. He is the Knower (Al-'Alīm), the Knower of Subtleties (Al-Laṭīf), the Aware (Al-Khabīr), the Reckoner (Al-Hasīb), the Recorder (Al-Muḥṣī), the All-Comprehending (Al-Wāsi'), the Wise (Al-Hakīm), the Finder (Al-Wājid), the Guide (Al-Hādī). Closely associated with the above is Allāh's pervasiveness, although orthodoxy fought shy of delineating the exact relation of Allāh to space. He is the Evident, the Without Az-Ẓāhir), the Hidden, the Within (Al-Bāṭin).

Inasmuch as God's knowledge is direct and nothing is hidden from His view, seeing is one of His attributes. He is the seer (Al-Baṣīr), the Watcher (Ar-Raqīb), the Witness (Ash-Shahīd). It is difficult to make out the exact necessity of seeing (or hearing) as a Divine attribute separate from knowledge; but it is likely that the former was reserved for an awareness of men's moral actions, especially of those actions which are hidden away from the eyes of other creatures. "No vision taketh Him in, but He taketh in all vision."[156] He is ever-watchful and He can see the motives from which actions proceed; but He does not require eyes like our own to perform the act of vision nor is His vision a temporal act.

What is true of Seeing is true of Hearing also. Allāh truly is the Hearing (As-Sāmī)[157] and He hears the smallest

155 Sura vi. 96-97.
156 Sura vi. 103; also lxxxix. 13.
157 Sura xliv. 5.

sounds. The Faithful are enjoined not to shout during their devotional exercises, for Allāh is not deaf and He does not hear with ears like ourselves. He is the Ever-Hearer of Prayers (Al-Mujīb).

The Divine attribute over which much bitter controversy was waged is Speech. In two matters the assumption of this attribute became inevitable. Allāh had spoken to Moses, who therefore came to be called *Kalīmu'llāh*, Converser with God, in Muslim Tradition.[158] Although Muslim Tradition later on elaborated Muhammad's vision of the Night Journey into the story of his conversation with Allāh, it never advocated the theory that any of the Quranic revelations came from that interview. As the Divine Speech would have been in that case a temporal event, probably it was felt that that would go against the eternity of the Qur'ān. Hence the eternal speech of Allāh was limited to the Quranic revelation, which consisted not of the meaning of the words of Allāh, which could be found in earlier revelations also, but of the actual words of God, the Muslim commentators would say ;[159] the speech was conveyed through angelic medium to the heart of Muhammad. From the very nature of the case a good deal of speculation was inevitable on the subject of Divine speech,[160] especially when matters were complicated, first, by the Quranic assumption of a preserved table (in imitation of the Mosaic tablets); secondly, by the belief in an eternal Arabic Qur'ān ;[161] and lastly, by the doctrine of abrogation

158 See art. PROPHET in Hughes, *Dic. Isl.*, p. 475.

159 See Hughes, *Dic. Isl.*, art. QUR'ĀN, p. 484 f. "Of all the divine books, the Qur'ān is the only one of which the text, words and phrases have been communicated to the Prophet by an audible voice."—Ibn Khaldun, quoted in ERE. vii. 355, art. INSPIRATION (Muslim). See *Al-Bayan* (Eng. Tr.) by Aboo Muhammad Abdul Haqq Haqqani, p. 216 f. ; Sir William Muir, *The Life of Mohammad* (1923), p. xiv, f.n. 1; see p. 47 : "So scrupulous was he (Mohammad), lest in his words there should be even the appearance of human influence, that every sentence of the Kor'ān is prefaced by the divine command 'SPEAK' or 'SAY' which, if not expressed, is always to be understood."

160 The reader is referred to *Enc. Isl.*, II, art. KALĀM (p. 670 f.) for some of the speculations on the exact nature of Divine speech and its communication to Moses and other Prophets.

161 Sura xii. 2. For the claim of Arabic to be the proper vehicle of Final Revelation, see K. Kamaluddin, *The Threshold of Truth*, Ch. VI, pp. 106-12.

(which would mean something like eternal scoring through some passages in the preserved table of heaven).[162] But inasmuch as God speaks with a tongue not like man's, the Qur'ān is not the eternal speech of God in respect of "the glorious expressions revealed to the Prophet, because these are originated," but only in so far as it "subsists in the essence of God." [163] Still, the Qur'ān is a plenary inspiration,[164] because Muhammad did not use here his own mental powers under divine guidance (*ilhām*) as other prophets did[165] but uttered the very words which God wished him to give forth as the divine message. It is an "external inspiration" (*waḥyi zāhir*), in which the passive mind of Muhammad was completely possessed by an alien power and which is superior even to the "sign of the angel" (*ishārat al-malak*) or inspiration received through Gabriel but not orally.[166] The Divine

[162] For the list of abrogated verses, see Hughes, *Dic. Isl.*, p. 520. Commenting on some cases of abrogation, Margoliouth remarks, "If we admit the theory that God's commands are dictates of prudence, *i.e.*, are temporary rules accommodated to the varying circumstances of a few days or years, the question suggests itself: did circumstances cease to change on the Prophet's death? Changing so quickly within the twenty years of his activity that the rule which suited the first year was wholly inapplicable in the last, can they in the last year have become so stereotyped that no further alteration is required?" (*Early Development of Muhammadanism*, p. 50). See *Enc. Isl.*, II, p. 1065; also Muhammad Ali, *The Religion of Islām*, pp. 35-44.

[163] ERE. vii. 356. "Even the oldest short *Sūras* which might have been heard by him in their present form very probably received their present form with rhymes, etc., in a later recasting."—*Enc. Isl.*, II, p. 1065.

[164] For the various (55) names of the Qur'ān, see Hughes, *Dic. Isl.*, p. 485; also M. Ali's *Holy Quran*, Preface, p. xxviii.

[165] Gabriel sometimes, without appearing in person, so influenced the mind of the Prophet that what he spoke was a divine message. This is *ilhām*, the inspiration of the traditions.—ERE. vii. 355.

[166] ERE. vii. 354, art. INSPIRATION (Muslim). See also Hughes, *Dic. Isl.*, art. INSPIRATION, pp. 213 and 485 (modes of Muhammad's inspiration). There is only one distinct reference to Gabriel as the medium of inspiration in the Qur'ān, *viz.*, ii. 91. The other references are to Faithful Spirit (xxvi. 193), One terrible in power (liii. 5), the Holy Spirit (xvi. 104), and illustrious messenger (lxxxi. 19). Gabriel is simply mentioned also in lxvi. 4; also as the Holy Spirit who strengthened Jesus (ii. 81, 254; v. 109). *Cf.* Dan. viii. 16; Lk. i. 19, 26. See *Encl. Isl.*, II. art. KORAN, p. 1064. See also M. Ali's *Holy Quran*, p. 1166, note 2683; also Archer, *op. cit.*, p. 79 f. (esp. p. 83 for Quranic references). For the Muslim conception of Gabriel, see *Enc. Isl.*, I, art. DJABRĀ'IL, pp. 990-91. See also Sir W. Muir, *Life of Mohammad*, pp. 72, 156; Muhammad Ali, *The Religion of Islam*, p. 206, f.n. 1 and also p. 25.

speech took the form of "command, prohibition, promises and threats." "When the revelation was one of denunciation or a prediction of woe, the angelic nature of Gabriel overcame the nature of Muhammad, who was then transported to the angelic world; when the message was one of comfort and consolation, the angel, in the form of a man, delivered his message:" [167] thus believed the Traditionalists. But in the list of excellent names nothing directly corresponding to the aspect of Speech appears as an epithet of Allāh, although there is an oft-quoted and much discussed passage in the Qur'ān, "Our word to a thing when we will it, is but to say, 'Be,' and it is."[168]

The two other attributes, Power and Will, are closely related in their operation,—power denoting the potentialities of action, and will the mental movement towards actual acts. God's power is not limited by His will, for He might have willed things in quite a different way from what He has actually done and no injustice would have attached to Him had He done so. "Verily God hath power over all things." He gave Muhammad victory at Badr but not at Uhud.[169] God is powerful enough to "raise the dead, make stones talk, trees walk, annihilate the heavens and the earth, and recreate them." [170] He has created the earth and the seven heavens, one above another; He has created the night and the day, the sun, the moon and the stars, and made them subject utterly to His command; He has created life and death; He sends the thunderbolts and strikes with them whom He pleases.

"It should be noted that five kinds of the *waḥy* (literally *revelation* or *inspiration*) of Allāh are mentioned in the Holy Qur'ān; *viz.*, first, in its relation to inanimate objects, as *earth* in 99 : 5; secondly, in relation to living creatures other than man, as the *bee* (in 16 : 70). thirdly, in relation to men and women other than prophets, as the apostles of Jesus in 5 : 111 and the mother of Moses in 28 : 7 (Rodwell's 28 : 6); fourthly, in relation to prophets and apostles; and fifthly, in relation to angels."—Muhammad Ali, *The Holy Qur'ān*, p. 547, note 1379. See also his *Religion of Islām*, p. 202 f.

167 ERE. vii. 355, art. INSPIRATION (Muslim).

168 Sura xvi 42. See Sura vii. 141 (*Enc. Isl.*, II. p. 671).

169 Sura iii. 158-59; also xli. 14.

170 ERE. vi. 300, art. GOD (Muslim).

Palgrave's description of the omnipotence of Allāh [171] will show what the Arabs intended by the credal formula, 'There is no god but God.' Says he, "The words in Arabic and among Arabs imply that this one Supreme Being is also the only one Agent, the only force, the only act existing throughout the universe, and leave to all beings also, matter or spirit, instinct or intelligence, physical or moral, nothing but pure unconditional passiveness, alike in movement or in quiescence, in action or in capacity. The sole power, the sole motor, movement, energy and deed, is God; the rest is downright inertia and mere instrumentality, from the highest archangel down to the simplest atom of creation...... Thus immeasurably and eternally exalted above, and dissimilar from, all creatures, which lie levelled before Him on one common plane of instrumentality and inertness, God is One in the totality of omnipotent and omnipresent action, which acknowledges no rule, standard, or limit, save His own sole and absolute will. He communicates nothing to His creatures, for their seeming power and act ever remain His alone, and in return He receives nothing from them; for whatever they may be, that they are in Him, by Him, and from Him only. And, secondly, no superiority, no distinction, no pre-eminence, can be lawfully claimed by one creature over its fellow, in the utter equalisation of their unexceptional servitude and abasement; all are alike tools of the one solitary Force which employs them to crush or to benefit, to truth or to error, to honour or shame, to happiness or misery, quite independently of their individual fitness, deserts or advantage, and simply because 'He wills it,' and 'as He wills it'."

Although the language of the above description is a bit strong, there can be no doubt that the logic of the Qur'ān would demand an approximation to this ideal. We have already referred to the titles of might, greatness and dominion; some more may be pointed out in this reference. Thus Allāh is the Restrainer (Al-Qābiḍ), the Abaser (Al-Khāfiḍ), the

171 Quoted in Hughes, *Dic. Isl.*, p. 147.

Exalter (Ar-Rāfi'), the Honourer (Al-Mu'izz), the Debaser (Al-Mudhil), the Enricher (Al-Mughnī), the Giver (Al-Mu'ṭī), the Withholder (Al-Māni'), the Distresser (Aḍ-Ḍārr), the Profiter (An-Nāfi'). "Say, O God, to whom belongeth dominion, Thou givest dominion to whom Thou wilt, and from whom Thou wilt Thou takest it away; Thou exaltest whom Thou wilt, and whom Thou wilt Thou humblest. In Thy hand is good. Verily Thou art all-powerful. Thou causest the night to pass into the day, and Thou causest the day to pass into the night; and Thou bringest forth the living from the dead and Thou bringest forth the dead from the living; and Thou givest sustenance to whom Thou wilt without measure."[172] So, as Wensinck remarks,[173] "the prevailing feature of Allāh in the Kur'ān is His absoluteness, His doing what He pleases without being bound by human rules. He extends His bounty, His mercy and His wisdom to whomsoever He pleaseth; He guideth in the right way and He leaveth to go astray whom He pleaseth; if He had so pleased, He would have guided all men in the right way; He createth what he pleaseth and formeth man in the womb as He pleaseth; He forgiveth unto whom He pleaseth; in short, He doeth what He pleaseth."

To such a God the only possible human attitude is abject submission. Muhammad was, therefore, logical when he called his religion Islām,[174] *i.e.*, resignation to the will of God, and regarded the relation of the living creation to Allāh as one of servitude. Allāh, to a Muhammadan, means "The Obeyed,"[175] and the Apostles, including Jesus and Muhammad, are the servants of Allāh.[176] The democratic ideal of

172 Sura iii, 25. For Al-Fudali's interpretation of the seven connections with the quality of Power, see Macdonald, *Development of Muslim Theology*, p. 329. For the relation of Will to Power, see *ibid*, p. 330 f. For al-Ash'ari's interpretation, see *ibid*, p. 295; for al-Ghazālī's, p. 302.

173 Wensinck, *op. cit.*, p. 84.

174 Sura iii. 79.

175 K. Kamaluddin, *Threshold of Truth*, p. 63.

176 The Koran starts with the notion of Allāh, the One, Eternal, and Almighty God, far above human feelings and aspirations—the Lord of His slaves

Islām proceeds from the fact that all are equally insignificant before God. McDougall has ascribed the rapid spread of Islām in Oriental countries to the fact that people there are used to the despotism of their temporal rulers and the Islamic attitude towards God is one of similar submission, servitude and resignation.[177] Similarly, Sell remarks, "God is described as Merciful and Gracious, the Guardian over all, the Provider of daily bread, the Reviver of His people and their Deliverer, and many similar terms; but all that the Qur'ān says of the loving-kindness of God is overshadowed by the teaching of Muhammad in the Qur'ān and the tradition as to His power. This is the prominent element in the conception of God as taught by the Prophet; it has ruled the Muslim world, and still rules it. The most excellent names, ninety and nine in number, do not contain any term which denotes the relation of God as a Father to His people. The idea is repugnant to the Muslim mind, and so in Islām the relation of man to God must ever be that of a slave, who lacks the freedom and dignity of a son."[178]

The last attribute belonging to Divine essence, namely, Will, raised still more formidable difficulties. The omnipotence of God is not peculiar to Muhammadanism; but most other religions use the term with a certain reservation in so far as it relates to the actions and destinies of finite spirits.[179] Creation of second creators was repugnant to Islām: did not Allāh declare that He had created all things after a fixed

not the Father of His children; a judge meting out stern justice to sinners, and extending His mercy only to those who avert His wrath by repentance, humility, and unceasing works of devotion; a God of fear rather than of love.—Nicholson, *The Mystics of Islam*, p. 21.

177 McDougall, *The Group Mind*, pp. 113-14.

178 ERE. vi. 302.

179 For very similar beliefs in Jewish literature, see ERE. v. 793, art. FATE (Jewish). Possibly the Qur'ān is indebted to it for some of its articles of belief on Predestination. Wensinck observes: "The orthodox doctrine of heavenly decrees is not specifically Islamic. It has a broad Semitic basis, as is proved by Babylonian and Israelitic religious tradition, which regards not only the ways of man, but the course of the world as the *replica* of what had been recorded long before in heavenly books or on heavenly tablets" (*op. cit.*, p. 54). For the whole subject, see Muhammad Ali, *The Religion of Islām*, Ch. VII. Gadar or Taqdir.

decree?[180] Allāh has eternally fixed the destinies of all things[181] and of all nations,[182] and nothing can befall any being but what God has destined for it.[183] Not only have the birth[184] and the span of life been fixed for all creatures[185] but even their alliances,[186] their vocations[187] and their fortunes: "No mischance chanceth either on earth or in your own persons, which, ere We brought it into being, was not in the Book;—Verily, easy is this to God—Lest ye distress yourselves if good things escape you, and be over-joyous for what falleth to your share."[188] God vouchsafes the gifts of grace to whom He wills,[189] for all sovereignty is in His hands;[190] He visits the wrong-doers with punishment in due time even though they may prosper for a while.[191]

Now, the bearing of this doctrine on the destiny of man was not left to inference, for the Qur'ān itself drew out the implications of this doctrine in relation to all the activities of the human mind—its knowledge, faith and works. Allāh knows and wills from all eternity what every man will know, believe, like and achieve. Wensinck quotes three traditions[192] to show that there was some difference of opinion about the time when the Divine decree was recorded in the case of an individual—one fixing it at the forty-second day of conception, another at fifty thousand years before the creation of the heavens and the earth, and the third accepting the second as the time at which it was written on the preserved

180 Sura liv. 49.

181 Sura lxxxvii. 2.

182 Sura vii. 92.

183 Sura ix. 51.

184 Sura liii. 33.

185 Suras iii. 139, 148, 162; viii. 17.

186 Sura xxxiii. 37 (which practically declares that Muhammad's marriage with the divorced wife of his adopted son Zaid was made in heaven by a fixed decree).

187 Sura xxxiii. 38-9.

188 Sura lvii. 22-23.

189 Sura lvii. 29.

190 Sura xiii. 30.

191 Sura xvi. 63.

192 Wensinck, *op. cit.*, pp. 54-55.

table or elsewhere[193] but holding at the same time that the decree was eternal. But in the Traditional literature and the philosophies the Divine decree was conceived in a more extreme fashion than it is set forth in the Qur'ān, with the effect that although the Jabrites, who denied all reality to human activity,[194] and the Qadarites, who rejected the eternal decree of Allāh,[195] were both stigmatised as heretical, the orthodox view leaned towards the Jabrite doctrine [196] and anathematised the Qadarite freewillists as dualists (Mazdians) and forbade the Faithful the visiting of the sick and following the biers of the dead of the latter sect.[197]

In two matters, especially, there could be serious differences of opinion regarding the interpretation of the Qur'ān. The one relates to the faith and works of men and the other to their destiny.[198] As Macdonald remarks: "Antinomies had no terrors for Muhammad. He, evidently, never thought about predestination and free-will, whatever later traditions may have put into his mouth; he expressed each side as he

[193] In the Qur'ān reference is made to three books, kept in heaven, relating to the record of actions and events :—

(1) The 'perspicuous book' in which are recorded all the happenings of the world from all eternity (though the Qur'ān does not expressly mention its eternal character).

(2) The Book of the righteous (Illiyūn) and the Book of the wicked (Sijjin), in which have been written down, Tradition says, eternally (although there is no indication in the Qur'ān about their eternal aspect) the deeds of men and which would be used on the Day of the Last Judgment.

(3) The book relating to each individual, in which are recorded (probably at the time of each occurrence) the good and bad deeds of each individual and this will be used as evidence of his career on earth on the Judgment day.—ERE. v. 794. (See Sura xvii. 14.)

[194] The extreme Jabrite view is found in the Jahmīyah sect. See Hughes, *Dic. Isl.*, art. AL-JABARĪYAH, p. 223; also Wensinck, *op. cit.*, p. 119 f.

[195] See K. C. Seelye, *Moslem Schisms and Sects*, Part I (1920), Ch. III (p. 116 f.); also p. 37 for their 20 (or 22) sub-sects

[196] Mu'tazila writers however also charge the orthodox Ash'ariya with being Djabarīya, which as Shahrastānī rightly points out, is not strictly correct as, although they deny the freedom of the will, they allow that man has some influence on action (*kasb*, appropriation).—*Enc. Isl.*, I, p. 985, art. DJABARIYA.

[197] Wensinck, *op. cit.*, p. 57; Margoliouth, *Ear. Dev. Muh.*, p. 224.

[198] See Wensinck, *op. cit.*, p. 55 f.

saw it at the moment, and the need of the moment stood.''[199] '' His predestinarian position steadily hardened towards the close of his life, and the earliest conscious Muslim attitude on the subject seems to have been of an uncompromising fatalism.''[200] Muhammadan orthodoxy could at best suggest certain mediating doctrines to reconcile predestination and free-will,[201] of which a specimen may be given from the Waṣīyat Abī Ḥanīfa :[202]

'' We confess that works are of three kinds, obligatory, supererogatory and sinful. The first category is in accordance with Allāh's will, desire, good pleasure, decision, decree, creation, judgment, knowledge, guidance and writing on the preserved table. The second category is not in accordance with Allāh's commandment, yet according to His will, desire, good pleasure, decision, decree, judgment, knowledge, guidance, creation and writing on the preserved table. The third category is not in accordance with Allāh's commandment, yet in accordance with His will; not in accordance with His desire, yet in accordance with His decision; not in accordance with His good pleasure, yet in accordance with His creation; not in accordance with His guidance; in accordance with His abandoning and His knowledge; yet not in accordance with His intimate awareness[203] or with His writing on the preserved table.''[204]

199 *Enc. Isl.*, I, p. 304, art. ALLAH. See Archer, *Mystical Elements in Mohammed*, pp. 34-35.

200 *Enc. Isl.*, II, art. KADAR, p. 605.

'' Of this doctrine Muhammad makes great use in the Koran, encouraging his followers to fight without fear, and even desperately, when the occasion might require, since caution is of no avail against the decrees of Fate and life cannot be prolonged when the destined hour arrives.—Sir A. N. Wollaston, *The Religion of the Koran*, p. 18 (Wisdom of the East Series).

201 See art. KADAR in *Enc. Isl.*, II, p. 605.

202 Wensinck, *op. cit.*, pp. 126-27.

203 *Ma'rifa*, a knowledge more intimate and sympathising than '*ilm*.—Wensinck, *op. cit.*, p. 127, footnote; see *Enc. Isl.*, II, art. 'ILM for distinction between the two (p. 469).

204 Wensinck sums up the last in the following words : '' Sins result from Allāh's decision, decree, creation, knowledge, writing down, will and abandoning; not according to His command, desire, pleasure, judgment or guidance '' (*op. cit.*, p. 143).

That all such attempts at mediation were destined to be half-hearted is due to the fact that the will of God was not unequivocally conceived in the Qur'ān in relation to the will of man. Thus a number of Quranic passages and traditional sayings can be quoted to show that Allāh's decree extended over all human motives and actions. God has created us and all that we make.[205] He has graven the faith on the hearts of the believers [206] and sealed the hearts of the unbelievers and the transgressors that they may not hearken or believe or understand.[207] God misleads whom He wills, and whom He wills He guides or puts on the right path.[208] If God had so pleased, He would have guided all aright [209] and made them all of one religion; [210] but He has guided only some of them and the others He has abandoned to themselves [211] or decreed to err.[212] " He whom God guideth is the guided and they whom He misleadeth the lost." [213] Man does not spontaneously take to the path of virtue or vice : " Whoso willeth, taketh the way to his Lord; but will it ye shall not, unless God will it."[214] Orthodox Islām did not deny that man possessed a sense of freedom; but, in order to explain it, it went to the length of suggesting that not only human acts but also the sense of freedom accompanying them had been willed and decreed by Allāh.[215] " Man accepts for himself the action of Allāh and his accepting is man's consciousness of free will." " The action of a creature is created,

205 Sura liv. 49.

206 Sura lviii. 22.

207 Suras iv. 154; vii. 98; ix. 88, 94; x. 75; xvi. 38, 110; xviii. 101; xxx. 59; xl. 37; xlvii. 18; lxiii. 3. But see Sir W. Muir, *Life of Mohammad*, p. 516 · " Mohammad held the progress of events in the divine hand to be amenable to th influence of prayer."

208 Sura xiv. 4; also vii. 39; lxxiv. 34; li. 9.

209 Sura vi. 35, 150.

210 Sura xi. 120.

211 Sura iii. 154; see art. KHADHLĀN in *Enc. Isl.*, II, p. 860; also Wensinck, *op. cit.*, p. 213.

212 Suras xvi. 38; xxi. 101.

213 Sura vii. 177.

214 Sura lxxvi. 29-30.

215 *Enc. Isl.*, II, art. KASP p. 786.

originated, produced by Allāh but it is 'acquired' (*maksūb*) by the creature, by which is meant its being brought into connection with his power and will without there resulting any effect from him in it or any introduction to its existence, only that he is a locus (*maḥall*) for it."[216] It is not necessary to enter any further into these theological discussions except to point out that the Mu'tazilites in general (following the Qadarites)[217] were obliged to combat practically every item of this orthodox predestinarian belief, namely, want of human freedom and the illusoriness of free choice, Divine grace as producing faith in believers and Divine will as prompting unbelief in infidels, arbitrary morality and eternal decree, and the positive relation of God to evil or wrong.[218] But all spirits did not possess the boldness of the Mu'tazilites; and so, as Nicholson remarks,[219] "the fatalistic spirit which brooded darkly over the childhood of Islām—the feeling that all human actions are determined by an unseen Power, and in themselves are worthless and vain—caused renunciation to become the watchword of early Moslem asceticism."

Divine will affected not only the wills of men but also their destinies—we may even say that it is because Allāh had fixed the fates of men that He determined their will. By an eternal decree the destinies of men have all been fixed and recorded in the preserved table and no one can escape the unalterable fate fixed by God. The tradition about the heartless manner in which Allāh is supposed to have elected some for salvation and the rest for damnation has often been

216 This is Al-Ash'arī's doctrine of *intisāb*. See *Enc. Isl.*, II, pp. 605 and 786; Sura viii. 17; also Wensinck, *op. cit.*, p. 213.

217 Of course, there were exceptions.—See Wensinck, *op. cit.*, pp. 78-82.

218 The prevailing conception of God as the All-Powerful is not far removed from the idea of a despot, and fear, thus separate from love, is either the incentive to all effort or leads to the repression of all energy in the Muslim. The idea of unlimited arbitrary power, unrestrained by any law of holiness, has so filled the Muslim mind that sin is regarded less as a breach of moral law than as a violation of some arbitrary decree. Certain actions of the Prophet were evil according to any law of righteousness; but no Muslim would admit that in doing them Muhammad committed a sin, for he acted under the command of God.—ERE. vi. 302. See also xi. 149, art. SALVATION (Muslim).

219 Nicholson, *The Mystics of Islam*, p. 36.

quoted: "When God resolved to create the human race, He took into His hands a mass of earth, the same whence all mankind were to be formed, and in which they after a manner pre-existed; and having then divided the clod into two equal portions, He threw the one half into hell, saying, "These to eternal fire, and I care not"; and projected the other half into heaven, adding, "and these to Paradise, I care not."[220] Moral regeneration may be the condition of salvation, but no man can bring that about except with God's permission, decree and will. On the other hand, "the process of perdition is that God abandons man by withdrawing His guidance; thereupon man abandons his faith and the *tertius gaudens*, Satan, is at hand to rob him of it."[221] A distinction was indeed drawn between God compelling belief and unbelief and His foreknowing and willing the same,[222] but the final position was summarised in the tradition:[223] "If Allāh should punish the inhabitants of His heavens and the inhabitants of His earth, He would not thereby do injustice. And if you should spend in the path of Allāh an amount larger than Mount Uḥud, He would not accept it from you unless you believe in the decree and acknowledge that what reaches you could not possibly have missed you, and what misses you could not possibly have reached you." Or, as al-Ghazālī puts it,[224] "His justice is not to be compared with the justice of men. For a man may be supposed to act unjustly by invading the possession of another; but no injustice can be conceived by God, inasmuch as there is nothing that belongs to any other besides Himself, so that wrong is not imputable to Him as meddling with things not appertaining to Him......Loving kindness, the showing favour and grace, and beneficence, belong to Him; whereas it is in His power to pour forth upon men a variety of torments, and

220 See Hughes, *Dic. Isl.*, p. 148 (art. GOD); also p. 472 (art. PREDESTINATION). But see Muhammad Ali, *The Religion of Islām*, pp. 335-37.

221 Wensinck, *op. cit.*, p. 235.

222 *Ibid*, pp. 191, 211.

223 *Ibid*, p. 108.

224 Hughes, *Dic. Isl.*, p. 146 (art. GOD).

afflict them with various kinds of sorrows and diseases, which, if He were to do, His justice could not be arraigned, nor would He be chargeable with injustice."

That the problem of adjusting Divine justice to Divine decree raised acute difficulties can be easily gathered from the Traditions. If " everyone is guided to that for which he was created,"[225] one can never be sure how one would finish one's career. A life-time of good works may be spoiled by that stubbornness of heart which refuses to acknowledge the unity of Allāh and the apostleship of Muhammad; and a life spent in evil may be redeemed at the end by the timely acceptance of the saving creed. Wensinck quotes a number of traditions[226] in support of the views that "There is no living soul for which Allāh has not appointed its place in Paradise or in Hell, and the decision of happy or unhappy has already been taken," and " Works must be judged from the concluding acts (*al-khawātīm*) only." To quote one of them:[227] "A man may perform the works of the dwellers in Paradise for a long time, yet his work may receive finally the stamp of that of the dwellers in Hell. Likewise a man may perform the works of the dwellers in Hell for a long time, yet his works may finally receive the stamp of that of the dwellers in Paradise." It appears, however, that where the criterion of faith was inapplicable, there was a good deal of difficulty in assessing the final destiny. Thus the fates of the children of infidels and believers who die in infancy were subjects of considerable discussion.[228] A strong tradition upheld the

[225] See Wensinck, *op. cit.*, p. 56.

[226] *Ibid*, pp. 55-56.

[227] *Ibid*, p. 55.

[228] For a discussion of the whole subject, see Wensinck, *op. cit.*, pp. 42-44. " Al-Ghazāli developed the doctrine of a Limbo for those who, by reason of youth, mental affliction, historical and geographical situation and environment, had not been able to become Muslims and, therefore, had no works of obedience, in the technical sense, to their credit."—*Enc. Isl.*, II, p. 1051. See the Fikh Akbar III, art. 4, in Wensinck, *op. cit.*, p. 265. *Cf.* the Fikh Akbar III, art. 21 :—

It would be absurd to suppose that Allāh should wrong anyone. He is free to impose suffering on innocent children and animals without indemnifying them.—Wensinck, *op. cit.*, p. 267.

view that every child is born in the *fiṭra*, the natural basis of the true religion, and that it is his parents that make of him a Jew or a Christian or a Parsi;[229] but another tradition laid down that when God knows that a child will become a Muslim, it is born in Islām,—otherwise it is born in unbelief.[230] We are interested in these arid discussions of dogma only in so far as they throw light on the nature and limits of Divine volition in relation to human destiny. The futility of works under those conditions was foreseen and works were enjoined not to force the hands of Allāh regarding a better future but to indicate rather that one was living under Divine guidance.[231]

The Mu'tazilites were not slow to perceive, as the Qadarites had done before them, that unless man's acts were his own, he could not be held responsible for them or their consequences, and that Divine justice would be impugned by accepting the view that God decrees Paradise or Hell before man has deserved either of them by his virtuous or vicious acts. But even al-Ghazālī, dealing with the acts of Allāh, could remark that "there does not rest on Him any obligation to give laws, to create, to give reward, to take into account what is salutary for His servants; that it is not absurd that He should command them to do what is above their power; that He is not obliged to punish sins; and that it is not absurd that He should send Prophets."[232] Fortunately, the Qur'ān contains many verses in support of the freedom of the will[233] and the justice of Divine dealings with saints and sinners alike. God not only watches and records the deeds of men but He visits the iniquitous with dire punishment on the Day of Judgment when the creatures wronged bear witness against their oppressors, the good and the evil done by each individual are carefully and justly weighed against

229 Wensinck, *op. cit.*, p. 42. See Muhammad Ali, *The Religion of Islām*. pp. 339-40.

230 *Ibid*, p. 43.

231 *Ibid*, p. 56.

232 *Ibid*, p. 95.

233 See Wensinck, *op. cit.*, p. 50 f.

each other in the Balance,[234] and the intercession of interceders do not avail.[235] He and His vigilant agents, the angels, watch over the thoughts and acts of men by day and by night:[236] every soul "shall enjoy the good which it has acquired and shall bear the evil for the acquirement of which it laboured,"[237] even though either should be only of the weight of an atom or of a mustard-seed.[238] Righteousness is serving Allāh as if He were before one's very eyes.[239] Again and again are the Faithful commanded to enjoin the right and forbid the wrong,[240] and they are even praised as being the best folk that hath been raised up for mankind" inasmuch as they enjoin the Just, forbid the Evil and believe in God.[241] A religion which insists on justice being an essential condition of the religious life cannot but invest God with the same attribute. God is not unjust towards His servants.[242] Orthodox Islām, with its predestinarian leanings, could not subscribe wholeheartedly to the Mu'tazilite view that sinning was wholly due to human volition [243] and it had therefore to combat these "partisans of unity and justice" (*ahl al-'adl wa'l-tawḥid*), in so far as they made man wholly responsible for moral evil in order to defend Divine justice.[244] But with

234 Suras xxi. 48; vii. 7.

235 Suras lxxiv. 49; lxxxii. 19; ii. 45.

236 Suras xiii. 11-12; lxxxii. 10-12.

237 Sura ii. 286.

238 Suras xcix. 7, 8; xxi. 48; iii. 111; xxxi. 15; also iv. 52.

239 See Wensinck, *op. cit.*, p. 23.

240 Sura iii. 100; ix. 72, 113; xxii. 42; *cf.* also Sura vii. 156; iii. 110; xxxi. 16.

241 Sura iii. 106.

242 Sura iv. 44.

243 The orthodox position is summed up in Fikh Akbar II (art. 22) as follows: Allāh guideth whomsoever He pleaseth, by grace, and He leadeth astray whomsoever He pleaseth, by justice. His leading astray means His abandoning, and the explanation of "abandoning" is that He does not help a man by guiding him towards deeds that please Him. This is justice on his part, and so is His punishment of those who are abandoned on account of sin. We are not allowed to say that Satan deprives the Faithful of his faith by constraint and compulsion. But we say that man gives up his faith, whereupon Satan deprives him of it (Wensinck, *op. cit.*, p. 195).

244 The Mu'tazilites did not reject the connection between Allāh and evil in the sense of accidents, sickness, and so on. At least one thinker, however, rejected even this connection.—See Wensinck, *op. cit.*, p. 145.

a happy inconsistency it looked upon Allāh as the Just (Al-'Adl), the Faithful (Al-Mu'min), the Judge (Al-Hakam), the Righteous (Al-Bārr), the Equitable (Al-Muqsiṭ), and also the Lord of the Day of Judgment,—variously described as the opener (Al-Bāsiṭ), the Great Opener (Al-Fattāḥ) and the Opener of the Tomb or the Raiser (Al-Bā'ith) and the Avenger (Al-Muntaqim). He does not forsake those who obey His commands, for He is the Great Grateful (Ash-Shakūr); in Him can all take refuge in case of injustice, for He is the Friend, the Patron (Al-Walī), of all creatures; and on those that believe and do the things that are right He bestows His love,[245] for He is the Loving (Al-Wadūd).

But if God is loving, will He not take compassion on the frailty of man and temper justice with mercy in cases of lighter faults?[246] Even in cases of grave sins, we have already seen, the Qur'ān provides for intercession with Allāh's permission, which means that God does not wish to abandon the sinner altogether and consign him to eternal hell if he has died with belief in Divine unity.[247] To suppose that the whole process is illusory in view of the predestined end of every single individual might yield consistency of thought but not satisfaction of the heart. No religion that believes in the incapacity of man to achieve salvation without Divine aid can dispense with the necessity either of Divine Incarnation or of Prophetic Intercession or of Divine Mercy. Unless Divine Grace second the efforts of men (and even dispense with the latter), their final destiny is dark and dismal in the extreme. Hence the Qur'ān had to preach not only submission to the inscrutable will and decree of Allāh but also faith in Divine Justice and hope for Divine Mercy. Thus although there are passages to indicate that Divine Justice can overtake sinning

[245] Sura xix. 96. See ERE. v. 696 :—"The orthodox view is that they (Īmān and Islām) are synonymous, and that a Muslim is a *mu'min*, a believer, By others, Islām is looked upon as a larger term than Īmān. It is said that Islām signifies belief with the heart, confession with the tongue, and good works done by the various parts of the body. Imān refers to the first of these and is, therefore, only a component part of Islām."

[246] Sura liii. 33.

[247] See Sura ix. 114-15.

individuals and nations only at a predestined time,[248] other passages allude to the patience with which Allāh bears their iniquities and the quickness with which He forgives repentant sinners.[249] He is the Patient, the Long-suffering (Aṣ-Ṣabūr), the Clement (Al-Ḥalīm), the Generous (Al-Karīm), the Lenient or Kind (Ar-Ra'ūf), the Forgiver (Al-Ghāfir), the Much Forgiver (Al-Ghafūr), the Forgiver *par métier* (Al-Ghaffār), the Pardoner (Al-'Afuww), the Acceptor of Repentance (At-Tawwāb) and of Prayer (Al-Mujīb). His mercy embraces all things [250] and He never punishes until He has first sent in His mercy an Apostle as a warner,[251] the Qur'ān, for instance, being a mercy unto all creatures.[252] The Lord judges with truth but He is also the God of Mercy.[253] Every sūra in the Qur'ān, with the exception of the ninth, begins with the words, " In the name of God, the Compassionate, the Merciful " (Bismillāh-i'r-Rahmān-i'r-Rahīm).[254] One of the finest verses closes the second sūra of the Qur'ān :[255] " God will not burden any soul beyond its power. It shall enjoy the good which it hath acquired, and shall bear the evil

The test of belief is prayer according to the tradition " Between faith and unbelief lies the neglect of prayer." According to Islamic tradition the seven grave sins are Polytheism, magic, unlawful manslaying, spending the money of orphans, usury, desertion from battle, and slandering chaste but heedless women who are faithful.

" According to the orthodox view polytheism is the only sin which is inconsistent with being a Muslim. A man who is guilty of other sins does not thereby lose this character. Allāh may punish him in Hell, or He may grant him forgiveness even without previous repentance."—See Wensinck, *op cit.*. p. 39 f.; also p. 46; also p. 104 f (the word ' for ever ' of Sura iv. 95 being interpreted as ' for a long time ').

248 Sura xxiii. 45.

249 Sura xl, 1-3; similarly, men are asked to " seek help through patience and prayer : verily God is with the patient " (Sura ii. 148; also Sura iii. 140).

250 Sura vii. 155.

251 Sura xvii. 16.

252 Sura xxi.

253 Sura xxi. 112. The opposite verse is Sura vi. 148 : " Your Lord is of all-embracing mercy : but his severity shall not be turned aside from the wicked."

254 Once only does it occur in the middle of a Sura, *viz.*, in Sura xxvii. 30. For Jewish, Christian and Zoroastrian parallels, see Sale's Preliminary Discourse in his *Comprehensive Commentary on the Qurān*, Vol. I, p. 100 (Sale thinks that the formula was borrowed from the Persian Magi).

255 Sura ii. 286; see also xxiii. 65.

for the acquirement of which it laboured. O our Lord! punish us not if we forget, or fall into sin; O our Lord! and lay not on us a load like that which Thou hast laid on those who have been before us; O our Lord! and lay not on us that for which we have not strength! but blot out our sins and forgive us, and have pity on us. Thou art our protector: help us then against the unbelievers." A prayer like this is farthest removed from belief in unalterable fate and fixed destiny. From a God of this description only good could be expected and the Mu'tazilites drew the inevitable conclusion that, provided men freely acted for it, they were bound to get their reward, for God's wisdom "keeps in view what is salutary (*aṣ-ṣalāḥ*) to His servants "[256] from the religious point of view. They could very well quote Sūra ix. 113: "Those who turn to God in penitence, those who worship, those who pray, who fast, who bow down, who prostrate themselves, who enjoin what is right and forbid what is unlawful, and keep to the bounds of God, shall have their recompense." [257]

There is no doubt that in spite of its pedestinarian teachings the Qur'ān did not consider man's moral struggles as illusory or Divine beneficence as regardless of human justice and prayer. While severe to those who consciously and deliberately flout His laws, God is possessed of an all-embracing mercy [258] that is ever ready to make concession for human weakness, for "He hath imposed mercy on Himself as a law" [259] and none except a disbelieving people need despair of His mercy.[260] "If ye would reckon up the favours of God, ye cannot count them." [261] If men had power over the treasures of the Lord's mercy, they would have assuredly retained them through fear of spending them, for man is

[256] Wensinck, *op. cit.*, p. 62; also pp. 80-82.

[257] See also xxv. 67-9; xvii. 27-8.

[258] Sura ii. 148; see also 1. 31-33.

[259] Sura ii. 12.

[260] Sura xii. 87; also iv. 51; xv. 56.

[261] Suras xiv. 37; xvi. 18.

niggardly;[262] but God's mercy knows no bounds. God is Lord of Grace, merciful and loving, and the least that man can do is to give Him thanks; but man is proud, treacherous, ungrateful and unfaithful and does not understand and appreciate the many mercies with which God has encircled him—the regularity of the seasons and the beauties and bounties of nature.[263] But those who seek God's mercy must approach Him with clean hands; they must not only be not unjust to their fellow-men, mischievous or self-conceited but also be benevolent to the needy and the weak. They must fulfil their social obligations by sharing the bounties of Divine mercy with their less fortunate brethren.[264] The deepest point of this vein of thinking is reached when Allāh is described as the Holy One (Al-Quddūs) (or, as in the Qur'ān, the King, the Holy),[265] the Ever Praiseworthy (Al-Ḥamīd), the One who is to be likened to whatever is loftiest,[266] the Peaceful or the One immune from all lack or defect (As-Salām),[267] the Light (An-Nūr), and the Fact or the Real (Al-Ḥaqq). It has been a matter of conjecture as to what the Qur'ān intended to convey by the words 'Holiness,' 'Peace' and 'Light'[268] and it has also been doubted whether Muhammad could call God 'just'[269] and also whether the Reality of God could leave room for independent finite centres of activity.[270] But if we make no fetish of strict logic but try instead to enter into the spirit of the moral and devotional life of the Muslims, we are bound to admit that these words have exactly the same significance for spiritual life in Islām as in other systems of ethical monotheism and that on the whole the Muslim conception of God, apart from its latent theological contradictions, provides a

262 Sura xvii. 103.
263 Sura lv. The Merciful.
264 Suras lxiv. 17; lxxiii. 20; cvii. 4-7; xx. 84.
265 Suras lix. 23; lxii. 1.
266 Sura xvi. 62.
267 Sura lix. 23.
268 *Enc. Isl.*, I, p. 303.
269 *Enc. Isl.*, I, p. 303.
270 See Macdonald, *Development of Muslim Theology*, p. 203.

striking testimony to the intellectual acumen and ethical insight of its founder even after large deductions have been made from the almost superhuman qualities claimed on behalf of the Prophet by his followers.

Christian writers have sometimes doubted whether the Muslim God is sufficiently personal.[271] The awful majesty of Allāh, His transcendence, the impropriety of conceiving Him after human analogy, the impossibility of fixing His nature definitely in view of the contingent character of all objects, laws and relations, created and decreed by Him—all these are unfavourable factors for personalising Him. But here again we should trust to the belief of the Muslim community rather than to a description of the following type:[272] "But He Himself, sterile in His inaccessible height, neither loving nor enjoying aught save His own and self-measured decree, without son, companion, or counsellor, is no less barren of Himself than for His creatures, and His own barrenness and lone egoism in Himself is the cause and rule of His indifferent and unregarding despotism around." The consideration of Divine names and attributes would be unmeaning except on the supposition that God is personal and deals with the just and the wicked as a personal being would do. Revelation, command, prohibition, threat, encouragement, justice, mercy and love can hardly be predicated of an impersonal Force or Consciousness. It has, however, been more correctly remarked[273] that "with only a little ingenuity in

[271] The following passage from C. J. J. Webb, *Religion and Theism* (1934). p. 47, is instructive in this connection: "It would probably surprise many critics of traditional language to learn what is nevertheless true, that 'the personality of God' is a phrase unknown to Christian theology until well within the last two hundred years; that 'personality' was not reckoned among the divine 'attributes' so-called and was long ascribed to God only in connexion with the 'three persons' worshipped by the Christian Church as one God; and that even the early Socinian divines were not concerned to insist upon ascribing 'personality' to him, but only to contend that, *if* the term were employed in reference to God (which employment they were inclined to deprecate), he would be spoken of as *One* Person, and not as three." (See the same writer's *God and Personality*, Lec. III.)

[272] Hughes, *Dic. Isl.*, p. 147, quoting Palgrave.

[273] *Enc. Isl.*, I, art. ALLAH, p. 306.

onesidedness an absolutely anthropomorphic deity could be put together or a practically pantheistic, or a coldly and aloofly rationalistic" and that "the only impossibility, as the Mu'tazilites found in the end, was a *fainéant* God, a stripped abstract idea." We may close our account by reference to these aspects of Muslim theology.

Although Muslim theologians, in their opposition to idolatry and anthropopathism, took particular care to point out that human qualities predicated of Allāh did not bear the same significance, yet there are passages in the Qur'ān which could be understood only anthropomorphically. The Mu'tazilites were not slow to point out that the qualities of seeing, hearing and speech, when taken separately from knowledge and power, could apply only to a Being possessed of a body and were, therefore, not rightly used of God by the orthodox section of the community. When even spiritual qualities like knowledge, will, mercy, justice, etc., could be only metaphorically used of God or used with a profoundly different connotation, the physical attributes were hardly appropriate as descriptions of Divine nature: so thought the Rationalists of Islām.[274] But, on the other hand, the orthodox felt that some of the descriptions were so realistic that there was obvious danger in taking them as "plastic metaphors"; for once the wit of man was allowed to understand the words of God in its own way, there was no knowing how far allegorical interpretation would extend. Thus, to quote Wensinck,[275] "the Kur'ān speaks of the eyes of Allāh; of His hand in which "is the empire of all things," "in which are plentiful gifts" and which is "over the hands of those who plight fealty to Muhammad." Allāh tells Iblis (Satan) that He had created Adam with His own hands. "Both His hands are outstretched." "The face of Allāh is likewise a representation familiar to the Kur'ān." "All on earth passeth away, but the face of thy Lord abideth." "Finally, the Kur'ān is full of descriptions of

[274] Wensinck, *op. cit.*, p. 68; see also pp. 73 f., 86, 88 f.
[275] Wensinck, *op. cit.*, pp. 66-67.

Heaven and Hell, which are not used in a metaphorical sense. To Heaven belongs the throne of Allāh : He is the Lord of the throne, the noble, large, exalted throne, which is borne by the angels." The faithful of this earth, on entering Paradise, " shall see the angels circling around the throne, uttering the praises of their Lord." Again, Allāh is represented in the Qur'ān, as in the Old Testament, as having spoken with Moses, and the Faithful are assured of seeing Allāh in Paradise just as, according to Muslim tradition, Muhammad had done in the night of the Ascension. He is also described in a tradition as descending every night to the lowest heaven and offering beneficence and forgiveness to all who would ask for them.[276]

While the Mu'tazilites severely criticised the anthropomorphic conceptions of Allāh, preached in popular and traditional literature, and rejected the corporeal vision of God in Paradise and all physical attributes and actions of Allāh, including His occupying a throne supported by eight angels,[277] there were others who were willing to go farther than the orthodox in the direction of anthropomorphism and to invest Allāh with tangible qualities. Thus, " Hishām ibn al-Hakām claimed that that which he worshipped was a body possessing dimensions, height, breadth and thickness, its height being equal to its breadth and to its depth, while its length and breadth are specified only as long and broad. He held, moreover, that its extension upward is no greater than its breadth. In addition, he claimed that the object that he worshipped was a diffusing light, shining as a pure chain of silver, and as a pearl perfectly rounded. This object also possessed, according to him, colour, taste, smell, touch. He also claims that its colour is its taste, its taste its smell, its smell its touch. He does not say that colour and taste are its essence, but he claims that the object itself is colour

276 Wensinck, *op. cit.*, p. 90.

277 *Ibid*, p. 68 f. Thus God's hand and face were taken in the sense of Divine bounty and knowledge.

and taste.''[278] Similarly, Hishām ibn Sālim al-Jawālīki "claimed that the object which he worshipped was in the image of man, but was not flesh and blood, being a diffused white light. He claimed also that he possesses five senses, like the senses of man, and has hands and feet and eyes and ears and nose and mouth, and he hears by a different means from that by which he sees, and the rest of the senses being different in the same way. He goes on to say that the upper half of this being is hollow and the lower is solid." Further, "he claims that his object of worship had black hair, it being a black light, but the rest of the person is white light."[279] Shaibān ibn Salamah al-Khārijī "held the doctrine of the likeness of Allāh to his creatures."[280] These instances must suffice to show that spasmodic attempts to understand God more anthropomorphically were made even in Islām; but it should be added that they were at once stigmatised by the orthodox community as heretical. As a matter of fact, however, orthodoxy fought with equal tenacity both anthropomorphism and allegorisation. Hence the Mu'tazilite attempt to put a spiritual interpretation upon Divine physical acts was equally anathematised. al-Ash'arī voiced the orthodox opinion when he exclaimed, "May Allāh preserve us from a *tanzīh* which would imply negation and *ta'ṭīl*"[281] (*i.e.*, divesting God of what pertains to Him). He was willing to admit that "hand and face are hand as a quality and face as a quality, just as hearing and sight," and so likewise are descending to the lowest Heaven and sitting on the throne qualities of Allāh; but he was against either understanding these in terms of human organs and their activities or regarding them as merely symbolical of spiritual facts.[282] Similarly, in

278 *Moslem Schisms and Sects* (tr. Seelye), p. 67. (See Wensinck, *op. cit.*, p. 67.)

279 *Ibid*, pp. 70-71.

280 *Ibid*, p. 103.

281 Wensinck, *op. cit.*, p. 90.

282 *Ibid*, p. 92 f.

the various formulae of the Muslim creed, the seeing of Allāh by the Faithful in Paradise was accepted as a fact finally settled by tradition on the basis of Quranic texts,[283] although anthropomorphism was sought to be avoided by adding that the beatific vision would be " without description, comparison or modality." [284]

But while the orthodox were speculating how Allāh would reveal Himself to the Faithful in Paradise, a different set of people began to build their philosophy of life and devotion on the more mystical texts of the Qur'ān. While the transcendental aspect of God is predominant in the Qur'ān [285] and orthodoxy tended to accentuate the remoteness of Allāh and the duality of God and the finite spirit, the nearness of God could be equally defended on the Quranic basis. The Sūfis could cite and meditate on certain passages (as they particularly did on the mysterious passages concerning the Night Journey and Ascension) [286] to justify and bring about mystical experience and could also point to Muhammad's habit of retiring into solitude in imitation of Christian ascetics and his ecstatic fit when receiving his inspiration and to that moral and spiritual earnestness of his which could come only to one who had felt the terrible nearness of God.[287] We may quote some of those passages as collected by Nicholson : [288] ' Allāh is the Light of the heavens and the earth ' (xxiv. 35) ; ' He is the first and the last and the outward and the inward ' (lvii. 3) ; ' there is no god but He ; everything is perishing except His Face ' (xxviii. 88) ; [289] ' I

[283] Wensinck, *op. cit.*, pp. 179-80; (see Quranic references there). Wensinck thinks " the meeting with Allāh " possibly means resurrection.

[284] See art. 24 of The Waṣīyat Abī Hanīfa (p. 130) and art. 17 of the Fikh Akbar II (p. 193) and the Fikh Akbar III (p. 266) in Wensinck, *op. cit.* See also pp. 179 and 63 f.

[285] See Archer, *op. cit.*, p. 32 f.; *The Legacy of Islam*, p. 212.

[286] Suras xvii. 1; liii. 1-18; see Nicholson, *The Mystics of Islam*, p. 212.

[287] See Macdonald, *Rel. Att. and Life in Islam*, p. 39.

[288] *The Legacy of Islam*, p. 212.

[289] On this favourite expression of Muhammad (" The Face of Allah "), see Macdonald, *Aspects of Islam*, pp. 186-87, where the different Quranic passages have been quoted.

have breathed into him (man) of My spirit ' (xv. 29); ' Verily, We have created man and We know what his soul suggests to him, for We are nigher unto him than the neck-artery ' (l.15); ' wheresoever ye turn, there is the Face of Allāh ' (ii.109); ' he to whom Allāh giveth not light hath no light at all ' (xxiv.40). It is possible to cite more passages in support of the nearness of God.[290] Allāh ' encompasses all things ' (iv.125) and ' is round about mankind ' (xvii.62); He is ' nigh, ready to answer ' (xi.64) and one need not use a loud voice during prayer to make oneself audible to Him (xvii. 110) for He hears even the whisper of a soul to itself (l.15); He is with every number of men,—the fourth when there are three, the sixth when there are five and so on (lvii.4; lviii.8),[291] and He ' comes in between a man and his own heart ' (viii. 24). The signs of God are in the very selves of men and ' He is His own inner witness in men's hearts.'[292] God is knowable, therefore, not by the senses or the intellect but by illumination, revelation and inspiration.[293] He is high above but He is also in the believer's heart: " God is the Light of the Heavens and of the Earth. His light is like a niche in which is a lamp—the lamp enclosed in glass—the glass, as it were, a glistening star."[294] No wonder, therefore, that, as Macdonald points out, Muhammad should freely admit a certain minor inspiration belonging to the saints (lit. friends) of Allāh and even to every human being in dreams.[295] In fact, a close approximation to the Hindu standpoint can be easily made

290 See Archer, *op. cit.*, p. 36 f.

291 *Cf.* Sura lvi. 84.

292 See Archer, *op. cit.*, p. 38; Suras li. 21; xxxviii. 72; xv. 29; xcvi. 13; lxxxv. 9; liii. 36. See Nicholson, *Mystics of Islam*, pp. 53, 70.

293 Nicholson, *Mystics of Islam*, pp. 69-70. For the relation between the revelation to the Sufis and the Quranic revelation, see Margoliouth, *Ear. Dev. Muh.*, p. 186 f. For dreams as revelations, see Macdonald, *Rel. Att. and Life in Islam*, p 79 f.

294 Sura xxiv. 35. See Nicholson, *Mystics of Islam*, p. 51.

295 Macdonald, *Aspects of Islam*, p. 188; *Rel. Att. and Life in Islam*, Lec. III. The *tariqas* or paths by which they (the Sufis) seek God " are in number as the souls of men."—Nicholson, *Mystics of Islam*, p. 27. (See also p. 87 f. about the equality of all religions.)

out here, for there are passages in the Qur'ān that talk of "an intercourse with God coming to the believer directly, without intermediaries"[296] and the rest, calm and strength that come to man through frequent remembrance of Allāh (*dhikr*).[297] "God truly misleadeth whom He will; and He guideth to Himself him who turneth to Him, those who believe, and whose hearts rest securely on the thought of God."[298] Such religious intuition comes from Allāh Himself[299] and is "opposed to knowledge that comes by human teaching, or by tradition, or through any thinking out by reason."[300] If man has been made in the image of God and He has breathed into man of His spirit, all that is necessary is to polish the mirror of one's own heart in order to know God.[301] Did not a tradition represent God as saying, "My earth cannot contain me, nor my heaven, but the tender and tranquil heart of my believing creature contains me"?[302]

It was reserved for the mystics of Islām to develop the unity, ubiquity and eternity of Allāh in a pantheistic sense among others. Under Christian, Neo-Platonic, Gnostic, Buddhistic and Vedāntic influences[303] the "ascetic-ecstatic life" rapidly grew in prominence,[304] and saints and sūfīs ab-

[296] Macdonald, *Aspects of Islam*, p. 189.

[297] Sura xxxiii. 41. See Nicholson, *Mystics of Islam*, p. 45 f.

[298] Sura xiii. 27-28.

[299] The Sufi doctrine of *istinbāt*, 'mysterious inflow of divinely revealed knowledge into hearts made pure by repentance and filled with the thought of God,' was based on the possibility of direct knowledge from God.—Nicholson, *Mystics of Islam*, p. 23.

[300] Macdonald, *Asp. Isl.*, p. 190. The Sūfis distinguish three organs of spiritual communication: the heart (*qalb*), which knows God; the spirit (*ruh*) which loves Him; and the inmost ground of the soul (*sirr*), which contemplates Him.—Nicholson, *Mystics of Islam*, p. 68.

[301] On al-Ghazālī's interpretation of the function of the heart, see Macdonald, *Rel. Att. and Life in Islam*, Lec. VIII (esp. p. 242); also p. 253. See Nicholson, *Mystics of Islam*, p. 70.

[302] Macdonald, *Rel. Att. and Life in Islam*, pp. 243-44; Nicholson, *Mys. of Isl.*, p. 68; also pp. 8, 53.

[303] See Nicholson, *Mystics of Islam*, p. 10 f., for the origin of Sufism.

[304] Its oldest type is an ascetic revolt against luxury and worldliness; later on the prevailing rationalism and scepticism provoked counter-movements toward intuitive knowledge and emotional faith.—Nicholson, *Mys. of Isl.*, p. 20 (For the equivalents of 'ecstasy,' see p. 59).

sorbed a portion of the reverence paid in orthodox Islām to Allāh alone. Ḥallāj, indeed, had to pay the penalty of his impious presumption with his life, but his *Anā 'l-Ḥaqq* (I am the Real or God) lived on in the theories of *ḥulūl* (fusion of being), *ittiḥād* (identification) and *wuṣūl* (union) and of *fanā* (passing away) and *baqā* (union with the Divine consciousness or life in God).[305] Under the transforming hand of Sūfism the nature and function of Muhammad himself underwent profound alteration. He became more and more assimilated to God and identified with the Divine Spirit and with Universal Reason,[306] and even prayers were offered to him to forgive and annul sins.[307] Man ceased to be regarded as a mere slave of Allāh and the orthodox warning against attempting to think of God in familiar terms—as the Beloved, for instance—was unheeded or ignored.[308] The unity of God was conceived in a way which threatened to take away the reality of the Finite Spirit or else to expand it into, and identify it with, the Infinite. But while in Hinduism the essential identity of the finite (*jīva*) and the infinite (*Brahman*) dominated all religious speculation and belief, in Islām zealous orthodoxy lost no time in denouncing

305 See Nicholson, *The Idea of Personality in Sufism*, p. 14 f; *Mystics of Islam*, p. 148 f.; *Studies in Isl. Mysticism*, p. 125 f.; Macdonald, *Rel. Att. and Life in Islam*, p. 248. Commenting on Sūfi pantheism, Nicholson observes (*Idea of Per. in Sufism*, p. 27): "It would be a mistake to suppose that utterances like the *Subḥāni*, "Glory to me," of Bayazīd, the *Ana'l-Haqq*, "I am God," of Hallaj, and the *Ana Itiya*, "I am She," of Ibnu 'l-Fāriḍ are in themselves evidences of pantheism. So long as transcendence is recognised, the most emphatic assertion of immanence is not pantheism but panentheism—not the doctrine that all is God, but the doctrine that all is *in* God, who is also above all." (See also his *Mystics of Islam*, pp. 18, 58; for the absence of 'self' in a Sufi and its presence in a faqir, see p. 38).

306 See Nicholson, *Idea of Per. in Sufism*, p. 60 f; also *Mys. Isl.*, p. 82, which quotes the tradition "He that hath seen me hath seen Allāh" (an obvious imitation of John 14.9).

307 Nicholson, *Idea of Per. in Sufism*, p. 67.

308 A quotation by Nicholson is instructive: "O my God, I invoke Thee in public as lords are invoked, but in private as loved ones are invoked. Publicly I say, 'O my God!' but privately I say, 'O my Beloved!'" (*Mys. of Isl.*, p. 8). See also p. 73 (quotation from Niffari): "God is the eternal Beauty, and it lies in the nature of beauty to desire love."—*Ibid*, p. 80.

this pantheistic attitude of Sūfī writers and in asserting that Allāh's transcendence could not be questioned and man could not be raised to divine honours or identified with or related to God: *Allāhu akbar*—Allāh is greater than everything that can be said of Him " in any sense of relationship or comparison." [309]

---

[309] Macdonald, *Rel. Att. and Life in Islam*, p. 247. See also Nicholson, *Mystics of Islam*, p. 79 f.

## CHAPTER IX

### God in Zoroastrianism : Gathic

We have now traced at some length the evolution of religious ideas in Hinduism and the living Semitic faiths. From polytheistic and still more primitive beginnings the races of India, Palestine and Arabia have, with more or less frequent lapses, worked their way up to the idea of a single omnipotent, omniscient and moral Deity—beneficent, just, forgiving and loving. In fact, in their eagerness to defend the unity and ubiquity of God, they have very often been tempted to attenuate, and even obliterate, the reality of the finite by their pantheistic and predestinarian doctrines, or at least to detract from the value of the temporal in order to fix men's gaze upon the eternal. The Semitic religions strove to accentuate the creature-consciousness of man, and Hinduism, when it did not fall in line with theism, attempted to equate the Absolute and the Individual ; but the ultimate effect in both cases was to extol the Infinite and to make man feel the littleness of the Finite. All beings were equally involved in the submergence of the finite, so that not only men but also other types of spiritual beings—gods, angels, etc. shared the same fate. These latter types were either roundly declared to be non-existent or suffered to exist as agents and messengers of God, entrusted with the task of assisting in the Divine governance of the world or moulding the moral character of His creatures. Side by side with a growing intellectual appreciation of the nature and function of God has gone on a moral development, and correspondingly the cosmic dealings of God have acquired increasing reference to His ethical dealings with man.

The progressive disappearance of nature-myths and of detached direct dealings of God with the physical and the moral world may be taken as the sign of an enlightened view about the ways of God. No one dares to presume the exact purpose of the Divine creative activity nor to define precisely the degree of reality possessed by each type of existence, material and spiritual. But the almost unanimous conviction of the positive religions that in the last days the physical world would be a matter practically of no concern and only the souls of spiritual beings would be garnered in heaven or hell [1] may be interpreted to mean that the main, if not the only, purpose of creation is to provide a field of moral probation for finite spirits. There is, therefore, much truth in the philosophic position that unless 'creators' or morally responsible persons are created nothing is really created.[2] God is inconceivable as a lonely Robinson Crusoe in a physical world created by himself, nor is the purpose of creation fulfilled by bringing into existence spiritual phantoms, who would view passively the Divine world of ideas from their own limited standpoints, or casual artefacts who would satisfy the Divine longing and love for an other. Religions have always insisted (and to this even Vedāntism and Islām are no exceptions) that the reality of the Finite includes the reality of free choice with all that it implies. Where, as in Vedāntism, the ultimate objective is to transcend both good and evil (and consequently to abjure both heaven and hell), the distinction between God and man disappears also,—whether that does or does not entail the assumption of an impersonal Absolute (*e.g.* Brahman) need not be discussed at present.

We are concerned just now, however, with an opposite problem. Suppose a religion possesses the necessary ethical conditions of a spiritual life: would these suffice for satisfying the religious craving of a community? We have already remarked that in religion, as distinguished from morality, man is in a double relation, namely, in a relation

[1] When bodily resurrection is a part of the religious belief, the raised body is generally supposed not to be physical in the ordinary sense of the term.

[2] Pringle-Pattison, *Idea of God*, p. 285 f; Ward, *Realm of Ends*, p. 271. See Lotze, *Outlines of the Philosophy of Religion* (tr. by Conybeare), p. 93

to something beyond and, through it, in a relation to the things of the world, specially to other spiritual beings of the same order of existence. Some bold spirits have dared to dispense with the first altogether while some others have expressed their belief in the possibility of the second without any reference to the first even though the first is not declared non-existent. It will be found on ultimate analysis that the validity of morality without religion will depend upon the possibility of a sense of oughtness without religious reference. Enlightened self-interest (or prudence) and the conception of an ideal self may both be devoid of a sense of obligation : am I bound to be prudent or to realise my better nature? [3] Is there then an irreducible minimum of religious assumption which no moral action can dispense with? Shall we say that the call of the ideal in agnostic minds serves the same purpose as the demand of religion in devout souls? [4] The fact that, with the decay of faith in traditional religion, passionate pursuit of national, social and other ideals has gained in strength among the most intellectually advanced shows that human sentiments have been diverted from religion to these other channels of expression. The social instinct is thereby reinforced by subsidiary impulses of a semi-religious character: work for self-betterment and service of fellow-men replace worship of God.

But this is essentially a modern phenomenon which has been rendered possible by the development of sociological and scientific theories. Where gaps of ignorance and impotence are large and the laws of mechanical causality and evolution are imperfectly established, a wholesale rejection of Divine operation in the world is absent and impossible. Besides, a life based on mere morality without religious sanction is possible for a few intellectuals and hardly explains that craving for social cohesiveness and concord without which a large community is unthinkable and impossible. Social instincts

[3] Campbell, *Scepticism and Construction*, pp. 218-19, 221.

[4] See Ward, *The Realm of Ends*, p. 134 f.

may bring individuals together; but it is the call of the ideal that regulates conduct and renders the continuance of the group possible. And of all ideals the religious ideal or the sense of religious obligation to be at peace with one's own neighbours and, in fact, with the whole of creation, is the most potent in bringing about the solidarity of the society and the race. We are face to face, in fact, with an essential trait—weakness, if you please—of the finite minds that their welding into a compact mass requires extraneous pressure and cannot be effected by inherent mutual attractions of the components of the social group. Of course, this adventitious condition of social cohesion has not always been supplied by an exalted conception of divinity. A set of common beliefs, rites and practices has often sufficed to keep primitive groups together, and even a tradition of common ancestry or the possession of the same totem has supplied the basis of social understanding and sympathy. As the primitive conceptions of godhead did not include elevated ethicality as a part of the connotation, it would not be true to say that religion is alone responsible for moral relations among mankind; but moral relations, howsoever established, have almost invariably tended to be buttressed by religious bulwark of some kind in a community not uniformly and eminently intellectual in composition.

It would be a mistake to think, however, that religion is a mere offshoot of morality and that the existence of God is, as Kant said, a postulate of moral life. Men have become religious to satisfy some fundamental impulses of life or in reaction to certain constant or recurrent stimuli of the external world. Religion has satisfied a need which morality has never been able to fulfil and it has often persisted where moral aberrations of a most pronounced type have taken place. Much of religious reform is often indeed ethical preaching because very often while an existing faith supplies enough incentive to devotion it fails to provide the necessary basis for higher morality or a more adequate recognition of social obligations: we have illustrated this already from the evolution of the

Jewish religion on the ethical side. But as we travel back to the ancient days we find that very often religious reformation has reference to the needs of the spirit, not on the side of practical morality but on the side of theoretical consistency and emotional satisfaction. The evolution of Hinduism at different stages of its history will afford ample illustration of religious experiments on the side of devotion and intellectual harmony. And when we talk of the needs of devotion we do not mean that they are synonymous with the needs of intellectual consistency; for by the temper, training and intellectual standing of the individual concerned are the needs of devotion determined, whereas intellectual consistency admits of only one standard and develops towards it with culture. Adapting the terminology of Wundt to our purpose, we may say that while intellectual formulations have a tendency to form a unitary whole, devotional needs fall into disparate systems. This is why, belonging to the same institutional religion, individuals tend to develop different personal religions of their own. Sects and heresies represent similar tendencies on a larger scale, and brotherhoods that cut across all communal boundaries (*e.g.* mysticism and theosophy) come into existence to establish contact between kindred spirits owing different religious allegiances, just as philosophical schools are formed on the basis of common intellectual satisfaction irrespective of religious beliefs and geographical positions. We are, however, not unmindful of the fact that religious progress has also taken in the past the form of a double advance—of a deepening of spiritual life and a widening of ethical interest: the reformation of the Arabian religion by Muhammad need alone be mentioned to show what we mean. We may also have cases of religious development on the subjective side where intellectual consistency and moral relation are already guaranteed by the existing conception of God. This will refer to the mode of worship, which we shall discuss at some length in a subsequent chapter. There is hardly any living religion in which visible or invisible changes of one or other of the above types are not going on at every moment. Like the insensible continuous variations in living forms, postulated by Darwin, these changes are slowly modifying the character of some living faiths within the limits of possible variation; of others the character has changed or is changing by rapid strides, much in the fashion of mutations as postulated for biological species by Hugo de Vries. Where the conditions of life remain constant, cultural contact with other creeds is absent or insignificant, and intellectual progress is arrested, there is likely to be a stagnation, just as variation practically ceases among organisms withdrawn from fluctuating conditions of existence. Like living organisms, again, faiths may occasionally be obliged to hibernate or even to retrogress in order to survive and wait for better times to put forth signs of new vitality and growth.

We shall try to illustrate the above propositions by an examination of the development of the idea of God among the remaining independent religions of the cultured world, namely, Zoroastrianism, Buddhism, Jainism, and the three Mongolian religions of Confucianism, Taoism and Shintoism. An examination of these is instructive on one point, namely, how each had to develop or absorb in course of time theistic elements of a certain character in order to provide sufficient materials of devotion to the ordinary laity. Barring Shintoism, each had concentrated more on the ethical side than on the devotional—each was in a sense a strong man's creed, needing the intelligence and the ability to rise above the diversities of phenomenal existence to a conception of the immutable laws of the moral world. Like the earth, religion has its giddy heights; while a few hardy climbers can acclimatise themselves to the rarefied atmosphere of barren abstractions and rigid moral principles, the ordinary toilers have a suffocating sensation and a shortness of breath at that altituds and they take the earliest opportunity to avoid it by descending to lower regions. Some constitutions can stand strong doses of medicine while others can take only diluted measures: the same is the case regarding religion in a heterogeneous population outwardly professing the same cult. Therefore, one of the main tasks of a religious reformer is to raise the level of culture so that the necessary advancement in spiritual understanding and appreciation may follow as a matter of course. Like the microbes in a healthy body, tendencies towards primitive belief are present in every mind, and they gain the upper hand the moment the power of resistance decreases. When even an unrelenting monotheist like Muhammad could, in a moment of weakness, admit the intercessory power of some of the pre-Islāmic pagan gods, we can well understand why people at a lower level of spiritual or intellectual culture should be unable to attain the spiritual heights of their prophet or retain them for long. We have illustrated this in the case of Hinduism where the absolutistic monism of the Upaniṣads could not be popularised and was replaced in popular affection by one or other of the monotheistic cults (some of the later Upaniṣads, like the Śvetāśvatara, themselves developing theistic tendencies) and even by a revived, though refined, polytheism.

A still more instructive example is furnished by Zoroastrianism, the religion of the Parsis of India and of the Gabars of Persia. From all accounts Zarathustra [5] was a remarkable prophet. Once convinced of the futility of his ancestral creed and religious customs, he waged a relentless war against their continuance in any shape or form. He did his work with such systematic thoroughness that it is only by a study of the later developments of his religion under Magian [6] and other influences that we are able to reconstruct, in the light of kindred Vedic beliefs and local survivals in clay tablets and stones, the religion of which his own was a reformation. Few religions have witnessed such remarkable vicissitudes of fortune as the creed he established, and few countries, except perhaps the north-western corner of India, have been

[5] For different spellings and derivations of the name, see C. de Harlez, *Introduction to the Avesta* (tr. P. A. Wadia), pp. 18-19; Jackson, *Zoroaster*, p. 12 f; Moulton, *Early Zoroastrianism*, p. 426; I. J. S. Taraporewala, *The Religion of Zarathushtra*, pp. 23-4.

[6] For the relation of the Magi to Zoroastrianism, see Jackson, *Zoroaster*, p. 6 f, and Moulton, *Ear. Zor.*, Lect. VI. The Magi.

subjected to such alien rule, with religious traditions hostile to the native faith, as unhappy Iran. The religion was born under the most unlucky auspices. The date of the Prophet is still a matter of dispute among Iranian scholars as even the earliest references yield no sure guidance.[7] While the oldest Avesten records, namely, the Gāthās, supposed to have been composed by Zarathustra himself,[8] give sufficient evidence of the prophet's poverty and personal woes and the inhospitable reception of himself and his doctrine, no date of his flight or migration from his home in Western Iran [9] to carry out his religious mission and to seek powerful support marks a new era as in the case of Muhammad,[10] and even no mythical date celebrates his birth as that of Jesus.[11] But he left devoted Apostles and disciples behind [12] and he was fortunate in finding a St. John in his cousin Maidhyoi-māonha and a Constantine in Vishtāspa.[13] We have no means of ascertaining the full extent of his religious reformation, for the five Gāthās are all that are left of the ancient record [14] and even of the later Avestan texts the

7 For discussion about the date of Zoroaster, see Jackson, *Zoroaster*, p. 14 f; Appendix II (p. 150 f); C. de Harlez, *op. cit.*, p. 19 f; Moulton, *The Treasure of the Magi*, p. 13 f.

8 Tiele adduces reasons to show that some of the Gathic verses could not have been composed by Zarathustra himself. See *The Religion of the Iranian People*, I, p. 83 f. (tr. Nariman).

9 For a discussion of Zoroaster's native place and the scene of his ministry, see Jackson, *Zoroaster*, p. 16; Appendix IV (p. 182 f); also Moulton, *Ear. Zor.*, Lect. III. The Prophet and His Reform (p. 80 f); also SBE, IV, Introduction, Chap. III, p. xlvii.

10 See Jackson, *Zoroastrian Studies*, p. 19 f; *Zoroaster*, p. 42 f. An era approximately dating from B.C. 559, observed by a religious sect which immigrated into China in A.D. 600, is noticed by Anquetil du Perron.—See Jackson, *Zoroaster*, p. 165.

11 According to tradition, Zoroaster was born on Khordadsal day which falls on the sixth day of every New Year. The old orthodox New Year's Day was usually the 21st March and therefore the birthday of Zoroaster should fall on the 26th March; but the majority of the Parsees observe their New Year sometime in September and therefore Khordadsal day falls also in September.

12 The succession list comes from the Pahlavi text *Dīnkart*. See Jackson, *Zoroaster*, p. 135 f.

13 *Ibid.*, p. 37. On the identity of Vishtaspa, see E. Herzfeld, *Vishtaspa*, in *Dr. Modi Memorial Volume*, p. 182 f; Jackson, *Zoroaster*, p. 167, 171; Moulton, *Ear. Zor.*, pp. 47, 88.

14 See Haug, *Essays on the Religion of the Parsis*, p. 142 f.

full literature has not been preserved.[15] We find references to the division of the Iranian society into different classes;[16] but we do not know to what class he himself belonged [17] nor exactly whether only the nobility accepted his message.[18] The prophet himself met with a violent death, presumably because he instigated military operations to spread his faith. It is certain that after his death his religion was not permitted to retain its purity for long and that it was not only modified by a priesthood with a different religious outlook and tradition [19] but also contaminated by the resurgence of earlier beliefs either in their crude form or in an altered guise. But even this impure tradition of the later Achaemenian period was broken when Alexander the Great burnt the royal library of Persepolis,[20] and for nearly five hundred years [21] only scattered fragments were all that remained of the Avestan texts. The fragmentary Sassanian collections and the added Pahlavi texts and commentaries were doomed to a similar fate when, after about four centuries of currency, they fell a victim to Arab fanaticism and probably only a fourth of the Avestan texts of the Sassanian

15 See SBE, IV, Intr., Chap. III, p. xxx f., by James Darmesteter Haug, *op. cit.*, p. 93 f, 134 f.

16 SBE, IV, Intr., Chap. III, p. xlviii; Moulton, *Ear. Zor.*, p. 116 f, 355. See Yasna 32.1; 33.3. See Geiger, *Civilisation of the Eastern Iranians in Ancient Times* (tr. Sanjana), II, 64.

17 Ys. 32.1. In the Gāthās the classes are of priests, nobles and husbandmen; in Later Avesta they are of fire-priests, charioteers, nobles, herdsmen and artisans. See Moulton, *Ear. Zor.*, pp. 94, 116-7, 355 n.2; *Treasure of the Magi* p. 14; Söderblom, *The Living God*, pp. 168, 172. Zoroaster is said to belong to the house of Manuschihar, sovereign of Iran.—Jackson, *Zoroaster*, p. 18.

18 This is Moulton's view. See his *Ear. Zor.*, p. 60. See also his *Treasure of the Magi*, p. 14, where he states that Zarathustra probably belonged to the agricultural community. The general belief is that he belonged to the priestly class.

19 Moulton lays the blame of all deviation from the spiritual religion of Zoroaster at the door of the Magi and refers in this connection to Ezekiel 8.16 f, where some pre-Zoroastrian Magian rituals are probably preserved.—See *Dic. Bib.*, IV, p. 989.

20 Moulton doubts the genuineness of this tradition about Alexander's vandalism. See *Treasure of the Magi*, p. 52. But see Haug, *op. cit.*, p. 124.

21 The period would be less if the Parthian king Valkhash is Volagases I (51-78 A.D.) and not Volagases III (148-191 A.D.). See *The Introduction to the Holy Gathas* by Poure Davoud, pp. 32-3; Jackson, *Zor. Stu.*, p. 171; SBE, IV, Intr., Ch. III, p. xxxiii f. See also *Sir J. J. Madressa Jubilee Volume*, p. 10; Huart, *Ancient Persia and Iranian Civilisation*, pp. 110, 112.

period survived.[22] Contingents of the faithful followers of the prophet had to seek an asylum in the hospitable shores of India [23] and their later generations had to watch with despair the rapid dwindling in the number of their co-religionists in their native home.[24] If, then, like the Jews, the followers of the Iranian Prophet have been subjected to so much calamity and oppression and have yet been able to save their religion, it must be due to some inner vitality of the faith they profess. In fact, the distinctiveness of the Zoroastrian message was such that it did not escape the attention of foreign writers, and its solution of the problem of moral and spiritual life was such that Semitic monotheism had no scruple to come under the influence of, or borrow elements from, its later developments.[25]

What religious influences were at work in the cradle of Zoroastrianism it is difficult for us now to reconstruct and it

22 Haug, *op. cit.*, p. 123 f. See, however, Dhalla, *Zoroastrian Theology*, p. 192 f. Almost all of the important Pahlavi works that we possess to-day were written under the Abbasid Caliphs (p. 193). For the list of extant Pahlavi works, see Karaka, *History of the Parsis*, II, pp. 177-8.

23 See Jackson, *Zor. Stu.*, pp. 182-3, for a summary of the history of Parsi emigration to India (also D. F. Karaka, *op. cit.*, I, pp. 23-52).

24 *Ibid.*, p. 179. See ERE, art. GABAR, for a fairly full account; also Karaka, *op. cit.*, I, Ch. II.

25 See Jackson, *Zoroaster*, Appendices V and VI; also Benveniste, *The Persian Religion according to the Chief Greek Texts*. For the relation between Zoroastrianism and Judaism, see Moulton, *Ear. Zor.*, Lect. IX. Zarathushtra and Israel (esp. p. 318 f); Jackson, *Zor. Stu.*, p. 205 f; Mills, *Our Own Religion in Ancient Persia*, p. 26 f (summary of Iranian and Jewish parallels). Mills, while accepting the similarities, repudiates the idea of borrowing from Persian source. " In fact, I would strenuously repeat, and with emphasis, what I wrote in 1894—*viz.*, the principle, that any, or all of the historical, doctrinal, or hortative statements recorded in the Old or the New Testament might, while fervently believed to be inspired by the Divine Power, be yet freely traced, if the facts would allow of it, to other religious systems for their mere mental initiation, —that the historical origin of particular doctrines or ideas which are expressed in the Old or the New Testament does not touch the question of their inspiration, plenary or otherwise " (p. 28). " My claim in argument is, therefore, for a very strong and completely surrounding and enveloping *later* and *supervening* influence of the North Persian One-Godism, Angelology, Immortality, Soteriology, Judgment, Resurrection, Millennium, Heaven, and Recompense, upon the same slightly earlier developments in Israel during the Captivity " (p. 49). It would be curious to know if such wide-spread parallels can be due to mere coincidence, and there is no suggestion that Persia borrowed these from Israel. For the influence of Parsism on Islam, see the paper of Goldziher in Tiele's *Religion of the Iranian People*, I (tr. Nariman), pp. 163-86.

is not possible for us to ascertain when the Iranian and Indian branches bifurcated from a common Aryan stock, whether after the separation there was any interchange of peoples and beliefs between India and Iran, whether an Aryan population conquered an indigenous population in Iran as in India and covered the native faith with an Aryan veneer,[26] and to what extent the religion of Assyria and Babylon influenced the formulation of the pre-Zoroastrian, Zoroastrian and post-Zoroastrian religions.[27] The fact that the later Avestan religion should revive certain elemental deities of the type mentioned by Herodotus in his description of the Persian religion,[28] and that Zarathustra should reserve his denunciations for the daeva-worshippers shows that it was against a Vedic type of belief and practice that he primarily directed his preaching.[29] So it was as an Aryan, deeply moved by the conduct and creed of fellow-Aryans, that Zarathustra spoke with bitterness. It is instructive to note that while Zarathustra thought that the best antidote against the cruel cult of sacrifice was a radical alteration in the conception of God and of the nature of worship, Buddha and Mahāvīra considered it essential to obviate the necessity of God altogether. The effect was that while in Zoroastrianism

26 See Moulton, *Ear. Zor.*, p. 5 f; Jackson, *Zor. Stu.*, p. 206 f; see also A. B. Keith's article on *Mitanni, Iran and India* in *Dr. Modi Memorial Volume*, p. 89, for a similar Aryan element in Mitanni. Tiele suggests a bifurcation of the common East Iranian religion into Indian and Iranian (*op. cit.*, Chs. VI and VII).

27 See Moulton, *Ear. Zor.*, p. 236 f; ERE. iv. 162 (seven zones of the earth). On the different theories of the sources of Zoroastrianism, see Jackson's *Religion of the Achaemenides* (tr. D. Machichan) in *Indo-Iranian Studies* (*Sanjana Commemoration Volume*), pp. 56-7; also his *Zor. Stu.*, p. 206 f. For the Assyrian origin of the Fravashis, see C. de Harlez, *op. cit.*, p. 197. For the Babylonian origin of the Baresman, see Benveniste, *op. cit.*, p. 57. For the alleged influence of Judaism on Parsism (as advocated by Darmesteter), see *Dic. Bib.*, IV, p. 992.

28 Benveniste, *op. cit.*, pp. 11, 23, 26.

29 In view of the fact that both in India and in Iran one set of powers stood for good and another for evil and that for these sets two words Asura and Deva have been used, it has been well said: "The different fortunes of the two names in India and Iran mark no conflict between the two religions, the variance was not in the creed but in the dictionary."—*Faiths of the World*, p. 113. See in this connection, K. C. Chattopadhyaya's paper on *Martin Haug's Theory of Indo-Iranian Religious Schism* in *The Journal of the K. R. Cama Oriental Institute*, No. 31, pp. 209-37.

the law of moral order (*asha* or *arta*) remained subordinate to God, in Buddhism and Jainism the law of Karma practically usurped the place of God, and that while in the former devotion had an assured place, in the latter systems morality and meditation were originally deemed sufficient for salvation.[30]

The genius of Zarathustra can be measured by the fact that while in the localities in which he lived and taught polytheism was rampant and cruel cults and nocturnal orgies passed in the name of religion,[31] he boldly declared the oneness of God and ascribed to Him a spiritual character with which any material form of worship could ill assort. Whence he derived the name of this spiritual God has been a matter of some discussion.[32] It is well-known that in the Gāthās the two separate words Ahura and Mazdāh had not coalesced into the single word Auharmazd of Pahlavi, Auramazdah of the cuneiform inscriptions of the Achaemenian dynasty [33] or Ormazd (or Hormuzd) of later times. They are sometimes used singly, sometimes in an inverted order and always with separate declensions; and sometimes Mazdah Ahura is even used in the plural so as to include the two most prominent personified abstractions of his system—Right (Asha) and

It is interesting to note that " the name Dānava is given both in the Vedas and Zend-Avesta to enemies with whom wars are to be waged. Compare Yt. v. 73 and Atharvaveda IV. 24.2." (Haug, *op. cit.*, p. 279.) (Darmesteter uses the word Dānus in Yasht v. 73 and refers to Yt. xiii. 37-8 where the Turanian Dānus are again mentioned.)

30 For a comparison between Zoroaster and Buddha, see Jackson, *Zoroaster*, p. 2.

31 Ys. 32.10, 14; Ys. 48.10. See Moulton, *Ear. Zor.*, p. 129 (The reference is wrongly printed as Ys. 31.10 there). See also Tiele, *op. cit.*, Ch. VI; Jackson, *Zoroaster*, p. 31.

32 See Benveniste, *op. cit.*, p. 39 f in this connection.

33 See Jackson, *Zoroaster*, p. 171, for an explanation. See also Moulton *Ear. Zor.*, p. 51; also p. 422 where the two exceptions in the Old Persian inscriptions are noted. For the Religion of the Achaemenides, see Jackson's paper in *Sanjana Commemoration Vol.*, p. 31 f; also his *Zor. Stu.*, p. 31; Ch. X. Religion of the Achaemenian Kings (see esp. p. 160); also SBE, IV, Int., Ch. III, p. xiv, lii f.; also Benveniste, *op. cit.*, p. 34 f.; also Casartelli, *The Philosophy of the Mazdayasnian Religion under the Sassanids*, pp. 14-7.

The word Mazdāh has been used without the diacritical mark throughout this volume.

Good Thought (Vohu Manah).[34] It is difficult to say what value should be assigned to Moulton's suggestion that 'for those, among whom Zarathushtra grew up, Ahura Mazdah was the "clan god" of their caste, as superior to the gods of other castes as the Aryan was to the Magus or the Budian, but only "greatest of gods" after all, and that 'it would seem that Zarathushtra's first step was to rise from this higher polytheism to monotheism, from a god who was greatest of gods to a god who stood alone;' [35] but there is much to be said in favour of his supposition that the 'greatest of gods' (*Mathishta bagānām*) [36] of the Behistan inscription of Darius, used of Auramazda, is a distant echo of Zarathustrian reform [37] and that, therefore, the traditional date of the Prophet (660-583 B.C.) is possibly late by three to four hundred years, if not more.[38] The discovery of the use of Mazdaka as a proper name in Media in about 715 B.C. and of the divine name Assara Mazāsh in an Assyrian inscription of the reign of Assur-banipal indicates the existence of a cult of Ahura Mazdah at an unknown antiquity—possibly in the second millennium B.C.;[39] but it would be risky to deduce therefrom any definite date about Zoroaster's advent and his

34 Moulton, *Tr. Mag.*, p. 23; Benveniste, *op. cit.*, p. 48.

35 Moulton, *Ear. Zor.*, pp. 93-4. Söderblom remarks, "Nor is any prohibition of polytheism to be found in the Gathas. But the careful reader of Zarathustra's prayers and poetical sermons will never imagine a Pantheon with many gods. The monotheism of the Gathas is not exclusive like Mosaism. Other gods are not expressly forbidden. But for the Prophet they do not exist. He is entirely occupied with the power and calling of Ahura Mazdah" (*op. cit.*, p. 195). Elsewhere he remarks (p. 187), "The Ahura recognised by the prophet in Mazdah, the All-wise, became by his moral demands and his pure divinity not a god among gods, but God." See ERE. x. 320, art. PRIEST, PRIESTHOOD (Iranian).

36 *Cf.* Ys. 16.1 (mazishtem yazatem); also Ys. 17.16.

37 Moulton, *Ear. Zor.*, pp. 52, 300. For an account of the Old Persian inscriptions, see Weissbach's paper on the subject in *Dr. Modi Memorial Vol.*, p. 673 f.

38 Moulton, *Ear. Zor.*, p. 19; *Tr. Mag.*, p. 13. See also *Zarathustra : His Life and Doctrine* by Prof. C. Bartholomae in *Sanjana Commemoration Vol.*, p. 8. (The date given is about 900 B.C., but a still higher antiquity is hinted at.) See Jackson, *Zoroastrian Studies*, p. 17 (fn. 5); also Söderblom, *op. cit.*, p. 196; Tiele, *op. cit.*, p. 40; *Dr. Modi Memorial Vol.*, p. 543 (quotation from Geldner who suggests 14th century B.C.).

39 Moulton, *Ear. Zor.*, p. 31; also M. R. Pettazzoni, *Ahura Mazda, the Knowing Lord* in *Sanjana Commemoration Vol.*, p. 149; Benveniste, *op. cit.*, p. 41.

exact relation to this religion of Ahura Mazdah. Even at a much later time we find Muhammad fixing upon the well-established name of Allāh for his unitary godhead; we may very well believe that Zarathustra followed the same method.[40] A temporary exaltation of an already well-known god to the supreme position is also met with in the Indian branch of the Aryan race and the Zoroastrian personification of abstract attributes and functions may be similarly matched by Vedic parallels,[41] although not with such monotheistic implications. It is well to remember that God has no name, and provided unworthy associations have not gathered round any particular title, it is distinctly advantageous to utilise a name already familiar to the locality or community in preference to a newly coined word that has no holy association. A modern instance would be Brāhmaism in which the Upaniṣadic term Brahman (occasionally even the Paurāṇic Hari) was chosen in a theistic sense to signify godhead. In the particular case of Zarathustra there was the added advantage that the name chosen was connotative in a spiritual sense—" the Wise (or Knowing) Lord " or " the Lord Wisdom," [42] and its meaning could be spiritually deepened by further suitable associations. We have no means of judging now whether the Indo-Iranians had really two types of gods—the spiritual and moral Asuras-Ahuras and the elemental and ritualistic Devas-Daevas,[43] or whether the name Ahura Mazdah originally signified the sky-

It is significant that seven gods of the sky (*Igigi*) and seven gods of the underworld (*Anunnaki*) follow Assara Mazāsh in the list of Assyrian gods, dated in the middle of the seventh century B.C. (p. 422). But see Moulton, *Ear. Zor.*, p. 99: " Zarathushtra cannot be proved by any valid evidence to have created a Hexad, far less a Heptad, to have given them a collective name and to have depended either on Aryan or Babylonian hints for the invention of abstract ideas strikingly in keeping with his own characteristic thought."

40 Benveniste, *op. cit.*, p. 39 f.

41 For Assyrian parallels, see Moulton, *Ear. Zor.*, p. 31 and p. 422.

42 For wisdom or knowledge as an attribute of God in different religions, see Pettazzoni's paper on *Ahura Mazda, the Knowing Lord*, in *Sanjana Comm. Vol.*, p. 151 f.

43 See Söderblom, *op. cit.*, p. 184; Moulton, *Ear. Zor.*, p. 150; also Haug, *op. cit.*, pp. 267-72, p. 301 (but his remarks are to be modified in the light of subsequent discoveries).

god like the name Dyaus Pitar and its etymological homologues in Indo-European languages.[44] The similarity between Ahura Mazdah and the Amesha Spentas, on the one hand, and Varuṇa and the Ādityas, on the other, has very often been pointed out,[45] and the similarity is enhanced by the fact that, like the Iranian God, Varuṇa, the moral god *par excellence* of the Rigveda, is also called *Asura* and carries very little of elemental association about him. Similarly, the daeva-worshippers against whom Zarathustra spoke so violently—the Kavis and Karapans and the Usijs, led in Iran in Zarathustra's time by Bendva and Grēhma,[46] were not only well-known in Vedic religion but bore practically the same class-names; and if we subscribe to the view that Zarathustra's missionary activity started in Eastern Iran, we may not unreasonably believe that the frontiers of Vedic religion of the time almost abutted on the scenes of Zoroaster's ministry[47] and both opposition and absorption of local ideas are not improbable on Zarathustra's part. Later Iranian literature loved to dwell on the conversion of Hindu sages (*e.g.*, Cangranghācah and Biās) by Zoroaster to his own creed.[48] It is not improbable that Zoroaster was attracted to Eastern Iran by the report of a more advanced culture likely to be more susceptible to the spiritual glamour of his reformed creed. It is not improbable also that Iran was pervaded by

[44] See Jackson, *Zor. Stu.*, p. 40; also Moulton, *Ear. Zor.*, p. 61; also ERE. ix. 568, art. ORMAZD.

[45] Jackson, *Zor. Stu.*, p. 40, 42. See also A. B. Keith, *Mitanni, Iran and India* in *Dr. Modi Memorial Vol.*, pp. 89-91, and also Lommel, *Indo-Iranian Conceptions*, *ibid.*, p. 262; also ERE. ix. 568-9 for a discussion of the relation between Varuṇa and Ahura through Arunas, the Hittite sea-god. See also SBE, IV, Int., Ch. IV, pp. lviii-lxi; also Tiele, *op. cit.*, Ch. VI, for a "conspectus of the religion of the East Iranians, of the yet inseparate Indians and Iranians."

[46] Ys. 44.20; 32. 12-14; 49.1. See Jackson, *Zoroaster*, p. 43 f; Geiger, *op. cit.*, II, 49 f.

[47] See Söderblom, *op. cit.*, p. 229, on the discussion of this subject from the linguistic side. He remarks, "It is noteworthy, however, that among present-day Iranian dialects Afghan is the one which most clearly reveals kinship with the Avesta language." See also Tiele, *op. cit.*, p. 52. From the reference to āsurī metres in the Yajurveda, which are foreign to the Rigveda, Haug infers that the old Gāthā literature (where these metres occur) was well known to the Rishis who compiled the Yajurveda (*op. cit.*, pp. 271-2). See also Geiger, *op. cit.*, II, p. 85 f.

[48] See Jackson, *Zoroaster*, p. 84 f. Śaṅkarācārya and Vyāsa are meant.

an Aryan culture in its topmost classes, and as the Boghaz-Keui inscription, invoking, among others, Indra, Mitra, Varuṇa and the Nāsatyau (the twin Aśvins of the Veda), shows, it was probably a fashion at any rate in that land of composite cult to invoke any god, Vedic or Semitic, suitable for the purpose in question—in this particular case, the purpose of a treaty.[49] There is little doubt, however, that the local worshippers of the daevas were the special objects of Zoroastrian anathema and their temporal and spiritual leaders the targets of his bitter attacks.[50] In the absence of a fuller knowledge, however, of the ebb and flow of the Aryan population between India and Asia Minor in those far-off times the mystery of the extent of Vedic and proto-Aryan polytheism in the land of Zoroaster cannot be satisfactorily solved.

But there can be no doubt about the creed of Zarathustra himself. He was a follower of ancient traditions only in so far as he accepted a familiar name for his God; but he introduced a radical innovation into the Aryan sept in Iran by his belief that a God that comes down by heredity from our ancestors is to be deemed a dead God unless we can be personally introduced into His living presence. He paid homage not to a far-off divinity fabled in ancient scriptures but to a God to whose presence, says the later literature, the Spirit of Good Thought led him in an ecstatic trance in his thirtieth year when he was on the banks of one of the channels of the Dāityā river—the Jordan of the Zoroastrians—in

[49] See Moulton, *Ear. Zor.*, pp. 119 and 396 (quotation from Herodotus) for Persian syncretism. See Moulton, *Ear. Zor.*, pp. 5-7, 26, 115 for a discussion of the Boghaz-keui inscription. See also A. H. Sayce, *The Early Home of Sanskrit*, and A. B. Keith, *Mitanni, Iran and India*, in *Dr. Modi Mem. Vol.* See also Winternitz, *History of Indian Literature* (Eng. Tr.), Vol. I, p. 304 f; also Benveniste, *op. cit.*, p. 38 f.

The habit apparently persisted and the Alexandrian *Sophia* was appropriated in the *Mainyo-i Khard* and appears as Āshno-khart and becomes identified with the Āshno-Khratus of the Avesta. See Casartelli, *op. cit.*, 33 f for similarity between *Mainyo-i Khard* and the Wisdom Literature of the Jews (esp. p. 41). For similar Christian influence on *Dīnkart*, see *ibid.*, p. 42 f (esp. pp. 46-7). Vohūmaṇ is assimilated to God the Son (with some difference).

[50] On the identification of the daeva-worshippers, see Söderblom, *op. cit.*, p. 183 f.

Airyana Vaejah (Adarbaijan).[51] He felt a call to right a double spiritual wrong—a debased religion and a cruel worship, and felt too that with Divine aid he would be able to use effectively his native gift of eloquent speech to convert others.[52] Had he not been ordained for this work 'in the beginning'?[53] Would not the Lord confirm his own conviction by a vision[54] and assure him of the earthly prosperity and blissful immortality of those who, like him, would follow the path of righteousness and piety, and of the earthly discomfiture and never-ending or long-drawn agony in the other world of those who would follow the Lie (Druj or Drauga) in their belief and conduct?[55] Zarathustra sometimes gropes for a right answer to some of the perplexing problems of existence[56] and then it blazes forth through his illuminated intellect and conscience and he closes with the triumphant note of a seer, a *vaedemno* or knower, who can authoritatively declare the nature and will of God as revealed through him to guide individual belief and social conduct.[57] In this way Zarathustra becomes not merely a religious reformer of the ordinary type who removes the cruelties, crudities and contradictions of his ancestral faith by sheer ratiocination or philosophical reflection, but a prophet who claims to have received inspiration for his mission from on High[58] and whose conviction is equalled by his determination to preach the message at all costs.[59] With a zeal more Semitic than Aryan,

51 See Jackson, *Zoroaster*, p. 40 f.

52 Ys. 44.17; also 28.5.

53 Ys. 44.11. See Söderblom, *op. cit.*, p. 193. Mythical predecessors of Zoroaster in this task of receiving revelation are Yima Khshaeta, Hōm Frāshmi and Gaya Maretan.—See *Zarathushtra and Ahuna Vairya Prayer* in *Dr. Modi Mem. Vol.*, p. 608; also Vendidad, 2.2; Yasht 13.87.

54 Ys. 44.16.

55 Ys. 44.18; also Ys. 29.5; 45.7, 9-11; 49. 4-5; 51.9. See also Ys. 33.1 and 48.4 in this connection for the fate of the waverers and the exactly balanced in merit and demerit.

56 See Ys. 44.8-19; 48.8-11; 49.6.

57 Söderblom, *op. cit.*, 197-8.

58 See *Dr. Modi Mem. Vol.*, *The Spenta Mainyu in the Gathas* by S. N. Kanga, p. 236. See also Söderblom, *op. cit.*, p. 202.

59 Ys. 28.4; 43.8.

the Prophet declares relentless war not only against the daevas but also against their worshippers [60] and calls upon temporal potentates to wage wars of aggression against the lands of false beliefs,[61] and himself dies, if tradition speaks the truth, a martyr to his cause when the Hyaonian (or Turanian) Arejat-aspa (Arjāsp), being defied, presumably at Zarathustra's instigation, by Vīshtāspa, storms the latter's capital and, as the champion of the old faith, sacks and destroys the temple of Nūsh-Ādar and quenches the sacred fire in the blood of Zarathustra and his priests.[62] He has no kindly compassion or large-hearted tolerance for those whom he conceived to be in manifest error and whose ignorance of spiritual things was attended with rapacious violence towards and cruel sacrifice of harmless cattle.[63] He studiously avoids

60 Ys. 47.4; 48.7. Casartelli points out (*op. cit.*, p. 144) that "the Eranians had no very clear notion of the spirituality of the dēvs, nor of the essential difference between human nature and that of the dēvs." "Though there are men created by the Evil Spirit, yet men become dēvs by their crimes." Bad men and those who understand neither virtue nor sin are called demi-dēvs. Demi-dēvs are also produced from the intercourse of men and demons. (*Cf.* Muslim belief about the intercourse between men and jinn). Sodomists become demons and apostates serpents (*cf.* Hindu belief in transmigration).

61 Ys. 46. 4, 6; see Moulton, *Ear. Zor.*, p. 373 (fn. 4). See also Ys. 48.6. Moulton suggests that weapons were used in defensive warfare (*Tr. Mag.*, p. 47).

See Jackson, *Zoroaster*, p. 103, for the names of the enemies of Vishtaspa, culled from the Yashts.

Zoroastrianism followed faithfully its prophet's message of intolerance. Speaking of Zoroastrianism under the Sassanids, Casartelli remarks: 'The Mazdayasnian religion was anything but tolerant. It was the only good one among several other religions; all others were bad. The Jewish, Manichaean, and Christian religions were specially condemned. . . . Speaking about the non-Aryan worshippers of demons and about the sectarians and apostates, the *Dīnkart* teaches that any communication with them is a cause of impurity. . . the conversion of an adherent of an evil religion into the good religion is permitted (Alas! this is no longer done.—See Dhalla, *Zor. Th.*, pp. 367-8). . . The government must not be tolerant to apostates but "must deliver up their bodies (to torture) on account of the soul" ' (*op. cit.*, pp. 174-5).

62 See Jackson, *Zoroaster*, p. 118. For other accounts of Zoroaster's death, see Ch. X of the same book. Parsi tradition gives the name of Tūr-ī Brātarvakhsh to the murderer. See Jackson, *Zoroaster*, p. 127 f

63 "Did Zarathushtra eat neat-flesh, as Bartholomae and others imagine, finding support for their view in Yasna 29.7 and 48.5, according to the translation: 'Let the cattle grow fat for our nourishment?' We want to know what the prophet means by the sacrifice which is offered with due service to Ahura and Asha (Yasna 34.3). It agrees best with the whole tenor of the Gathic belief to rule cattle out of the sacrifice of Zarathushtra."—Söderblom, *op. cit.*, p. 180.

mentioning—so great in his hatred towards the cult of his contemporaries—both Haoma (Soma), the intoxicating drink, and Athravan (Atharvan), the priests associated with the fire-rites of the worshippers of the daevas (devayasnians),[64] and although he once calls himself a priest (*Zaotā* = Skt. hotā)[65] and refers to the offering of reverence to the sacred Fire,[66] it was not to the Agni of the Vedic Aryans but to Ātar, the house fire, that adoration was made,[67] the worship was divested of all unworthy material associations and the mind concentrated on Right (Asha),[68] which was regarded as coming to maturity through Fire [69] and Good Thought together.[70] A similar reticence was observed in respect of Mithra [71] whose cult became so wide-spread later on and who, together with Ahura Mazdah and the imported goddess Anāhita, formed the Iranian Trinity from the time of the later Achaemenian kings.[72] This was presumably due to the fact

[64] See Tiele, *op. cit.*, pp. 53-4, 76-7; Söderblom, *op. cit.*, p. 181 f. In the supplement to the Gāthā Haptanghaiti (Ys. 40.4 in Mills's translation in SBE, XXXI, p 291) Haoma and Athravan are mentioned together and fire-priests are said to "come from afar." See Moulton, *Ear. Zor.*, p. 116. See also Geiger, *op. cit.*, II, pp. 48, 61, 80 f.

See Moulton, *Ear. Zor.*, p. 71 f. He remarks, "I am inclined to sugges that the plant used for this purpose failed the people as they migrated westward out of the land where Zarathushtra preached and taught his Gathas. Later substitutes lacked the very element that made Haoma hateful to the Prophet and attractive to the reveller" (p. 73). (The same thing happened in the case of Vedic religion also. See K. C. Chattopadhyaya's paper in the *Journal of the K. R. Cama Oriental Institute*, No. 31, p. 236, for references about substitution of *pūtika* or other creepers for the *soma* creeper.)

[65] Ys. 33.6. See also Geldner, *Zaota*, in *Sanjana Commemoration Vol.*, p. 277 f.

[66] Ys. 43.9.

[67] See Moulton, *Ear. Zor.*, pp. 70, 302. For distinction between Fire in Brahmanism and Fire in Zoroastrianism, see ERE. vi. 29-30, art. FIRE, FIRE-GODS.

[68] See Haug, *op. cit.*, p. 279 f. for parallelism between Brahmanic and Iranian sacrificial rites; see also p. 139.

Strabo gives a fairly full account of the Magian fire worship.—See Moulton, *Ear. Zor.*, pp. 407-9.

[69] See Ys. 46.7.

[70] See Jackson, *Zor. Stu.*, pp. 197-8.

Possibly this fire-association led to Asha Vahishta being called the fairest or the most brilliant Amesha Spenta in Yasht II.7 (also Yt. III. 18 in SBE).

[71] See Moulton, *Ear. Zor.*, pp. 139, 141; Tiele, *op. cit.*, p. 75.

[72] See C. de Harlez, *op. cit.*, p. 163 f. (he thinks that the worship was of Iranian origin though modified by her identification with the Assyrian Mylitta). Artaxerxes

that the Mithra-worship of the time was too intimately associated with plundering hordes and murdered cattle to be safely incorporated within his own religion.[73] When it was revived in Iran after his death, it had lost most of its objectionable features, as an examination of the Mihir Yasht shows,[74] and could be turned to good account because of the ethical functions with which Mithra became invested through association with the all-seeing Sun.

We are now in a position to turn to the positive contribution of Zarathustra to the spiritual conception of God. Of very few prophets of antiquity is there such a chorus of appreciation by persons of alien faiths as of Zoroaster.[75] Even in antiquity his wisdom was far-famed and the Greeks were struck by the fact that although the Persians invoked more than one god they worshipped no images but venerated fire as a sacred symbol and avoided polluting the elements. But Zoroastrianism, as known to the foreigners, was mixed with other elements, with the effect that it was regarded as a typical ditheism with Ormazd and Ahriman dividing the entire realm of existence between them; later Zoroastrian books (like the Vendidad) and the Manichaean heresy are typical, if not logical, developments of the dualistic tendency latent in

Mnemon is the first of the Achaemenian kings to name any god but Mazdah, and he prays to "Auramazda, Anahita, and Mithra."—Moulton, *Ear. Zor.*, p. 239. See also Jackson, *Zor. Stu.*, p. 154. For the relation of these three deities, see Moulton, *Ear. Zor.*, pp. 61-7.

The Vedic parallel is the trinity of Mitra, Varuṇa and Aryaman. The Assyrian triad of Ishtar (or Ramman), Sin and Shamash is supposed by some to be at the root of the Avestan and the Vedic trinity.—See ERE. ix. 569, art. ORMAZD.

Mithra, Rashnu and Sraosha formed also a panel of judges at the Bridge of the Separator for departed souls. They correspond to the Assyrian triad of Shamash, Kettu and Mēsharu.

For Divine Triads, see Clarke, *Ten Great Religions*, II, p. 135 f; Hopkins, *Or. and Ev. of Rel.*, Ch. XVII.

73 See Moulton, *Ear. Zor.*, pp. 138-141.

74 For summary, see Haug, *op. cit.*, p. 202. See also Dhalla, *Zor. Th.*, p. 103 f; C. de Harlez, *op. cit.*, p. 150 f.

For Mithraism, see ERE. viii. 752. It became a very composite cult in later times. See also Moulton, *Ear. Zor.*, p. 139.

75 The curious reader will find a collection of the appreciations of the Zoroastrian religion in a compilation called *Enlightened Non-Zoroastrians on Mazdayasnism* by J. J. Motivala and B. N. Sahiar (1897-99 A.D.).

the Prophet's own teaching.[76] It so happened also that the extent of the Prophet's monotheism was not fully appreciated, and although his claim to have received revelations from Ahura Mazdah was conceded,[77] his personified abstractions were regarded as subordinate gods [78] and they quickly took over the departments of nature from the elemental deities which his teaching had dethroned. The Gāthic language had become obscure and a later literature embodying a new set of beliefs was also ascribed to Zoroaster. The Gāthās were repeated without understanding as the Vedas were in India; but the community lived the life of the later literature with its theoretically dualistic, and even practically polytheistic, scheme of thought. Modern scholarship has partially succeeded in rehabilitating the monotheism of the Prophet, and even Christian writers, who are generally biased when criticising other faiths, have been obliged to admit that the faults of the Iranian Prophet are only those of omission and not of commission as well. They have missed in the message of the Prophet the human love that reaches out to the sinner in order to redeem him [79] and the Divine love that is solicitous of the salvation of the sinning world and bestows grace out of proportion to personal merit.[80] But they have conceded practically without any reserve that his conception of the nature of God, both on the theological and on the moral side, is equalled only by that of the classical Jewish prophets and that he possessed a Semitic zeal in denouncing false gods and spreading an ethical religion. To that conception of God we may now turn.

76 See Söderblom, *op. cit.*, p. 211 f.

77 It appears that Zarathustra had ecstatic visions before the sacred flame. Reference may be made to Ys. 29.3 and 30.1 in Mills's translation (with notes), to Ys. 30.1 in Haug's translation. The difficulty of translating the Gāthās may be gauged when the translations of Spiegel, Haug, Mills and Moulton of these passages are compared.

For other revelations, see Jackson, *Zoroaster*, Ch. IV.

78 Ys. 30.9, where Mazdah and "other Ahuras" are invoked, is likely to create difficulty about Zarathustra's monotheism.

79 Ys. 47.4: "Whether one is lord of little or of much, he is to show love to the righteous, but be ill unto the Liar."

80 See Moulton, *Tr. Mag.*, pp. 201-2.

Zarathustra analysed in his own mind the essential conditions of a religious and ethical life and he discovered that those conditions were : (1) a unitary God, omniscient and moral ; (2) a God who does not so much require material offerings as the devotion of the heart ; (3) a God in whom all untruth, deception, evil and imperfection are totally absent ; (4) a God who guarantees the freedom and the individual responsibility of all finite spirits ; (5) the reality of evil in physical and moral worlds and the possibility and necessity of combating it ; (6) the conviction that good must somehow finally triumph ; (7) faith in the ultimate blessedness of the good and the final doom of the wicked. He felt that the immutable laws of goodness and truth must somehow form part of the nature of God Himself and be intimately associated with the Divine life, and that while there was possibly a justification for the existence of evil in order to make spirits moral and to enable them to rise in perfection, there was no ground for the pessimistic belief that Evil would remain unconquered at the end, which would take away the zest from all strenuous fight on behalf of Good. We need not enter into the details of the later Zoroastrian scheme of world-cycles and the varying fortunes of Good and Evil during each period of three thousand years ;[81] but Zoroaster could read the history of the world not as a progress towards national greatness, as the Jewish prophets generally taught, but as a cosmic progress towards the doom of evil. Again, as God was regarded as the God of the individual and not of this or that particular nation, each individual was directly accountable to Him for his actions and his personal spiritual progress.[82] We shall not tarry to discuss whether

81 Manichaeism took over this Zoroastrian doctrine in its theory of the struggle of Light and Darkness.—See Jackson, *Researches in Manichaeism*, p. 7 f.

82 This raises the important question about the function of the Saoshyant or Universal Saviour in Zoroastrianism. In the oldest texts, as Dr. Pertold points out, salvation is individual. It is only in Pahlavi literature that universal salvation through a saviour becomes an accepted creed.—See Pertold, *The Origin of the Idea of a Universal Saviour*, in *Dr. Modi Memorial Vol.*, p. 470.

Tiele points out that 'Saoshyants,' which means in the later Avesta saviours to come,' bears the sense of 'prophets of an anterior age or of the present' in the older texts. The other titles of the older period are 'zaotar,'

the end of the world is so predestined that only the lapse of the specified time is needed to weaken the forces of evil; for we know that in actual practice each Mazdayasnian is taught that his active endeavour on the side of Good is needed to bring about the downfall of the powers of Evil and that his refusal to range himself on the side of Ahura Mazdah means prolonging the bitter conflict with the Spirit of Evil.[83] As Moulton observes,[84] ' In every other religion, outside Israel, there were demons to be propitiated by any device that terror could conceive. Zarathushtra from the first bade men " resist the devil " ' There were different sorts of evil to be overcome—the demon of Bad Season (Duzyāirya) in the physical world that paralyses the activity, the demon of Anger (Āeshma) that disturbs the emotion, and the demon of falsehood (Druj) that warps the judgment of man. Although, to quote Moulton's opinion again,[85] there were probably many more demons believed in by the people at large—and the later Zoroastrian literature has given a goodly number of them to fear and combat,—the choice of Zarathustra is significant inasmuch as he concentrated men's attention more on the enemies within than on the mischievous supernatural beings of an outside world. Just as the gods of earlier polytheism were ignored, so also its demons;

ratu,' 'mathran' while 'athravan' and 'magian' belong to later times.—Tiele, *op. cit.*, pp. 90-1.

See Moulton, *Ear. Zor.*, p. 242. Moulton remarks, "Saoshyant in the Gathas denoted Zarathushtra and his helpers; but as the Renovation did not come in his time, later thought had to postpone the date but kept up its connection with the Prophet" (*Tr. Mag.* p. 105). *Cf.* A similar Christian belief about the coming of the Kingdom of God (and the Messiah).

See also D. M. Madan, *Discourses on Iranian Literature*, p. 7 f, 29.

83 *Cf.* Hegel: "The consummation of the infinite End consists merely in setting aside the illusion as if the end was not yet accomplished. It is under this illusion that we live, and at the same time it is this illusion alone that stirs us to activity and on which our interest in the world depends." (Quoted by Ward, *The Realm of Ends*, pp. 151-2). See Moulton, *Tr. Mag.*, p. 42, on Ys. 49.10: "The merits of the pious are presented to Mazdah, and when his treasury is full they ensure the coming of the kingdom."

84 Ys. 30.9: "So may we be those that make the world advance!" See Moulton, *Ear. Zor.*, pp. 111, 127; also Ys. 18.7; see also Söderblom, *op. cit.*, pp. 209, 213-4. This is the Avestan *Frasho-kereti*, Forward-making.

85 Moulton, *Ear. Zor.*, p. 130.

and religion was reduced to an affair of the spirit—both on the side of the promptings of man's better nature and on that of the allurements of his baser instincts. And while Indian speculation tended more and more to think that evil was an illusion (*māyā*), to be abolished by spiritual thinking or absolute consciousness, or else a product of the material or bodily aspect (*prakṛti*, *guṇa* or *buddhi*) of the ego, in the system of Zoroaster evil was real and could be abolished only by strenuous moral struggle and the body was a help and a necessity, rather than a hindrance, in the accomplishment of this object. As is to be expected, the Iranian race, like the Jews and the Muhammadans, never put a premium upon asceticism and mortification of the flesh or upon the celibate ideal—which became such distinguishing features of almost all Indian religions, Brāhmaṇic, Buddhistic and Jaina,[86] and Zoroastrianism developed more on the side of practice than on that of speculation, and, in speculation, on the side more of theology than of philosophy, being unlike the Indian religions and comparable most with Judaism in these respects.[87]

Zarathustra did indeed continue the worship of or in the Sacred Fire just as Muhammad continued the adoration of the Sacred Stone at Mecca, but neither the one nor the other was therefore accused of idolatry. In fact, the resemblance proceeds further, for we have the testimony of foreign writers that the Persians had no temples or images or altars.[88] We

[86] Ys. 1.6. See Moulton, *Ear. Zor.*, p. 146 f; Tiele, *op. cit.*, p. 119; Söderblom, *op. cit.*, p. 207; Vendidad 4.47 f.

In the later Avesta many penitentiary exercises were imposed for various offences.—See Moulton, *Ear. Zor.*, p. 152.

Manichaeism, which was so severely repressed by Zoroastrianism as a heresy, emphasised the need of renunciation, ascetic in its rigour, for obtaining perfection and redemption.—See Jackson, *Zor. Stu.*, p. 11; also *Mani's Asceticism from the Zoroastrian point of view* by M. N. Dhalla in *Sir J. J. Madressa Jubilee Volume*, p. 89 f.

In the *Dinkard* the continence of the first human pair (Māshya and Māshyōī) for the first fifty years of their life is attributed to the Evil Spirit.—See Casartelli, *op. cit.*, p. 133.

[87] See ERE. ix. 865, art. PHILOSOPHY (Iranian); Dhalla, *Zor. Th.*, pp. 356-9; *Faiths of the World*, pp. 137-8.

[88] See extract from Herodotus in Moulton, *Ear. Zor.*, p. 67; also p. 391 (with footnote 1); also Söderblom, *op. cit.*, p. 194.

may, therefore, understand the statement of Porphyry that "the body of Oromazdes is like light and his soul like truth"[89] in the sense that the nature of Ahura Mazdah is wholly spiritual but that his most appropriate visible symbol is the sacred fire.[90] The Gāthās, at any rate, do not prescribe any elaborate fire-rites as does the Vedic literature, and the Prophet's reformation was certainly calculated to dethrone the elemental deities of the Aryan religion of his time. It is on the spiritual essence of Ahura Mazdah and not on the practice of adoring Him in fire that Zarathustra concentrated all his attention. He insists not on faultless sacrifice but on good thought, and trusts to the immutable laws of the moral order rather than to the casual boons of a propitiated divinity to win a blessed future for humanity. In our zeal, however, to do justice to the Iranian Prophet's contribution to the fund of spiritual values and verities we need not ignore the fact that in the Vedic religion also a less thorough and systematic attempt to substitute spiritual and ethical concepts for concrete entities was similarly made either in a reforming spirit or more probably by a process of intellectual abstraction. Similar attempts in other religions to think of Divine attributes and functions in terms of personified abstraction are also not unknown. That a consistent religious use, as distinguished from a philosophical speculation, could be made of these was the merit of Zarathustra to discover. This brings us to the puzzling problem of the Amesha Spentas in their relation to Ahura Mazdah. The extant Gāthās present no uniform picture on this subject and what Moulton speaks of the Last Judgment[91] is true of this part of the Zoroastrian theology also, namely, that "it would be

[89] See Moulton, *Ear. Zor.*, p. 67.

[90] We should remember that the *Atash-Niyayish* is not a part of the Gathas and that in spite of the repudiation of fire-worship by enlightened Parsis the prayer to Fire according to the *Atash-Niyayish* is in no way distinguishable from prayer to a god.—See *Parsis and Fire-worship* by M. N. Kuka in *Dr. Modi Mem. Vol.*, p. 211. See Wilson, *Parsi Religion*, p. 235; also A. S. N. Wadia, *The Message of Zoroaster*, p. 45.

[91] Moulton, *Tr. Mag.*, p. 32; see also *Dr. Modi Mem. Vol.*, p. 550, for the nature of the Yazatas in the Gathas in Ervad M. P. Madan's *The Gathas and the Avesta.*

quite impossible to form from his teaching anything like a consistent picture: each image comes in independently to heighten a moral or spiritual conception and is then dropped."

In its original formulation the Zoroastrian theology is surprisingly simple. Ahura Mazdah is prayed to for enlightenment on the problems of creation, preservation, theodicy, final destiny of the righteous and the wicked, the nature of God-vision and the right religion.[92] Let us summarise, in the words of Söderblom, these Gāthic questions.[93] "How will the 'Best World,' 'Best Existence,' *i.e.* paradise and eternal bliss, commence for him who gains it? Who is by creation the Father of the Right (Asha)? Who determines the path of the sun and stars? The waxing and waning of the moon? Who fixed the earth below and the heavens above that they do not fall? Who created water and plants? Who yoked swiftness to winds and clouds?" What artist created light and darkness, sleep and waking, morning, noon and night? "For whom has the pregnant, luck-bringing cow been created?" "Who created together with Dominion, Khshathra, Piety, Armaiti? Who made the son obedient to the father? Then there are questions on the consummation of the world and Daena, religion, the spiritual life, the best religion." Further questions are asked about the opposition between the Lie and Piety, the doom that awaits those that will not receive the Prophet's message, and the genuineness of the Prophet's own inspiration. It is evident that Zoroaster had no doubt that the Omniscient Lord was able to answer all his questions and that He was Himself the creator of the physical world with its laws, the moral world with its dominance over the instincts of men, and the spiritual world with its foundations in the nature of the self, its progress through active effort of man, and its consummation in

92 See, for instance, Ys. 28.5; 29.1; 31.3, 14; 33.7; 34.12; 44.1-20 (the entire Gatha is a series of questions); 48.2, 8-11; 50.1; 51.4, 5, 9.

93 Ys. 44; Söderblom, *op. cit.*, p. 224.

As usual, there is wide divergence in understanding Gathic passages. Compare, for instance, Haug's translation of Ys. 44.7, 8 in his *Essays etc.*, p. 159 (with footnotes).

a separation of the righteous and the vicious in two distinct realms with opposite enjoyments.

The above principles the Prophet has embodied in a series of spiritual abstractions whose exact nature has been a matter of considerable dispute. The scene is laid, for instance, in heaven [94] where before a heavenly synod the oppressed soul of the ox (*Geush urvan*) [95] complains of the violence done to its earthly embodiments by plundering chiefs and sacrificing priests and the Ox-creator (*Geush tashan*) [96] asks Right that protection and provenance should be guaranteed to cattle, whereupon Ahura Mazdah declares that the cattle cannot receive absolute protection, as their meat and milk are meant for men, but that they are entitled to protection from wanton cruelty and for that reason Zarathustra would be sent down to preach the necessary message with his eloquent tongue and to enlist the support of powerful patrons on their behalf. The scene now shifts and we are made to witness the beginning of moral strife when two pri-

94 Ys. 29.

95 Kanga in *Sir J. J. Mad. Jub. Vol.*, p. 21, says that "the Geus Urvan represents the mineral, vegetable and animal kingdoms only, but not the human kingdom also, as is generally supposed." See a comparison of the Gatha and the Bundahishn account there. Geus Urvan becomes a female spirit in Bun Dahesh.—See Casartelli, *op. cit.*, p. 84.

According to the *Mainyo-i Khard*, *Dinkard* and *Bun Dahesh* plants and animals are developed out of the parts of the primeval ox while from Gaymart proceed men and metals.—See Casartelli, *op. cit.*, pp. 113, 118, 129-30.

96 See Tiele, *op. cit.*, p. 112 f. He remarks that Geush Tashan belongs to the primitive folk-lore. Moulton suggests that he is a substitute for Mithra.—See *Ear. Zor.*, p. 347 (f.n.l); also p. 149. Tiele is of the same opinion.—See *op. cit.*, p. 114.

Even Yima, the son of Vivahvant and the first man, became a sinner when he gave people beef to eat to satisfy them and to make them immortal.—See Moulton, *Ear. Zor.*, p. 149, for this as well as for the later Avestan theory that he yielded to lies and lost his kingly glory.

In Ys. 29.5 the Ox-creator is joined by the soul of the pregnant Cow in the prayer to Mazdah to save the right-living and the cattle-tender. Tiele distinguishes between the created steer and the cow which brings good fortune and diffuses blessings. He refers to Ys. 44.20 where watering the kine is regarded as an essential condition of preparation for husbandmen. He, therefore, holds that the luck-bringing cow "is not a kind of the type of cattle but rather a mythical symbolisation of the whole material world, and, as a rule, the earth" (*op. cit.*, p. 114). See Dhalla, *Zor. Th.*, p. 44. Haug also thinks that Gēush urvā means the universal soul of the earth (*op. cit.*, p. 148).

For the place of the cow in Avesta, see Geiger, *op. cit.*, II, p. 119 f.

mal spirits, the Better and the Bad in thought and word and action, stand face to face with each other at the beginning of the world and the holier thus speaks to the enemy: "For us two neither thoughts, nor doctrines, nor wills, nor beliefs, nor words, nor deeds, nor consciences, nor souls agree."[97] The scene changes and we watch the fateful decision made by the wise and the foolish, headed respectively by Ahura Mazdah and the Lie.[98] "Of these twain spirits he that followed the Lie chose doing the worst things; the holiest Spirit chose Right, he that clothes him with the massy heavens as a garment. So likewise they that are fain to please Ahura Mazdah by dutiful actions. Between these twain the demons (*daeva*)[99] also chose not aright, for infatuation came upon them as they took counsel together, so that they chose the Worst Thought. Then they rushed to Violence (Aeshma), that they might enfeeble the world of man." But by their momentous decision each party chose its own future.[100] "And when these twain Spirits came together in the beginning, they established Life and Not-Life; at the last the Worst Existence shall be to the followers of the Lie, but the Best Thought to him that follows Right." The Prophet sees into the future when, through the choice of the wise path, there shall come unto the good man Dominion (Khshathra), Good Thought (Vohu Manah) and Right (Asha), and Piety (Armaiti) shall give continued life to his body and indestructibility, and by the retribution through the molten metal he shall be at the end winner over the evil ones who shall be punished, and the Lie shall be delivered into the hands of Right and at that time the Prophet shall return to act as judge (*ratu*) before Ahura Mazdah the Lord (*ahu*) to whom

[97] Ys. 45.2.

[98] Ys. 30.5, 6. See *The Two Spirits—Spenta and Angra—in the Avesta* by N. D. Khandalavala in *Indo-Iranian Studies in honour of Dastur Darab P. Sanjana* (Sanjana Commemoration Vol.), p. 213.

[99] The Devas are frequently called *mainyava*, spiritual, invisible, in contrast to the human followers of the Devas.—C. de Harlez, *op. cit.*, p. 202. But see Casartelli, *op. cit.*, p. 144.

[100] Ys. 30.4. See Söderblom, *op. cit.*, p. 220; Moulton, *Tr. Mag.*, p. 27.

he will present the good works of the faithful.[101] The famous Parsi creed of Ahuna Vairya (Ahunvar or Honover),[102] to be found not in the Gāthās but in Ys. 27. 13, emphasises the fact that the weal of the individual and the triumph of Ahura are simultaneously achieved by the defeat of evil and that Zarathustra is the Prophet appointed to help and guide the poor and to act as the prophetic adviser to men

[101] See Moulton, *Ear. Zor.*, pp. 106-9.

[102] These are some of the translations of the Ahuna Vairya (Honover) : –

(1) As the Ahū is excellent, so is the Ratu (one who rules) from (his) sanctity, a creator of mental goodness, and of life's actions done for Mazda; and the Kingdom (is) for Ahura, which to the poor may offer a nurturer. (Mills in SBE. A slightly different translation is given by him in ERE. i. 238).

(2) As a heavenly lord is to be chosen, so is an earthly master (spiritual guide), for the sake of righteousness, (to be) the giver of good thoughts, of the actions of life, towards Mazda; and the dominion is for the lord (Ahura) whom he (Mazda) has given as a protector for the poor. (Haug in *Essays on the Religion of the Parsis*, p. 141–f.n. 2; also Geiger, *op. cit.*, I, p. 73).

(3) Even as he (Zarathushtra) is the Lord for us to choose, so is he the Judge, according to the Right, he that bringeth the life-works of Good Thought unto Mazdah, and (so) the Dominion unto Ahura, even he whom they made shepherd for the poor. (Moulton, after Bartholomae, in *Ear. Zor.*, p. 161; also *Tr. Mag.*, p. 89—n. 2, p. 42).

(4) Just-as the Ahu (Zarathushtra) (is) worthy-of-being chosen (as Prophet), so (is Zarathushtra) the Ratu on-account-of (his) righteousness-as-well. He dedicates (the excellence) of-good-mindedness (and) of-the-deeds of-the-human-existence unto Mazda, (and) (volitional) power unto Ahura, (and) whom He (Ahura Mazda) has appointed a regulator or guide for-the-drighus (men of far-reaching Asha-principle, thriving on account of good-mindedness and holiness and leading a righteous life; in other words, men spiritually strong). (K. E. Punegar, *Ahuna Vairya*, in *Dr. Modi Memorial Volume*, p. 15).

(5) As Ahu (Ahura Mazdā or the spiritual Lord) is an independent ruler (because He rules) according to Order (*ashāt*, *i.e.*, according to fixed laws), so should a Ratu (*i.e.*, the temporal Lord) (rule according to fixed laws). The gift of good mind is for the work of the world for (the sake of) Mazda. He who gives (himself up) as the nourisher of the poor (or he who gives nourishment to the poor) gives kingdom to Mazda (*i.e.*, acknowledges him as king). (J. J. Modi in *The Religious Ceremonies and Customs of the Parsis*, p. 348).

(6) The will of the Lord is the law of holiness : the riches of Vohū-Mano shall be given to him who works in this world for Mazda, and wields according to the will of Ahura the power he gave him to relieve the poor. (Darmesteter in SBE, XXIII, 23.)

(7) Just as a Ruler (is) all-powerful (among men), so (too, is) the spiritual Teacher, even by His Asha; the gifts of Good Mind (are) for (those)

on earth [103] and as the advocate and judge after their death. And the Prophet himself offers on his own account the fruits of a spiritual life to Mazdah: "As an offering Zarathushtra brings the life of his own body, the choiceness of good thought, action, and speech, unto Mazdah, unto the Right, Obedience and Dominion."[104] He prays, further, to Ahura Mazdah and Piety and Right and Good Thought and Dominion to be merciful to him when to each man the Recompense will come.[105] The Prophet sums up his message in the stirring words: "Him thou should seek to exalt with prayers of piety, him that is called Mazdah Ahura for ever, for that he hath promised through his own Right and Good Thought that Welfare and Immortality shall be in his Dominion, strength and perpetuity in his house."[106] "By his holy Spirit and by Best Thought, deed and word, in accordance with Right, Mazdah Ahura with Dominion and Piety shall give us Welfare and Immortality."[107] "And this, O Mazdah, will I put in thy care within thy House, the Good Thought and the souls of the Righteous, their worship, their piety and zeal, that thou mayest guard it, O thou of mighty Dominion, with abiding power."[108]

working for the Lord of Life; and the strength of Ahura (is granted) unto (him) who to (his) poor (brothers) giveth help. (I. J. S. Taraporewala in *The Religion of Zarathushtra*, p. 70.)

Parsi orthodoxy would prefer the translations in which reference to Zarathustra is omitted and would not therefore accept Nos. 3 and 4 as correct translations. Without that reference there is nothing to prevent the supposition that the sacred formula is probably pre-Zoroastrian.

103 It was a part of the religious duty of each individual to correct the errors of his fellow-men as Zarathustra did of his contemporaries. In later literature we have a picture of heaven after the Resurrection when all souls would arise and know each other. "The wicked shall upbraid their good friends, saying, 'Why did you not make me know the good part which you yourself chose?' And if one has not done so, he shall sit in heaven ashamed."—*Faiths of the World*, p. 135.

104 Ys. 33.14.

105 Ys. 33.11.

106 Ys. 45.10.

107 Ys. 47.1. See Moulton, *Ear. Zor.*, p. 376, f.n. 5 (also p. 372, f.n. 2). This verse and Ys. 45.10 just quoted contain the names of all the Amesha Spentas (Amshaspands).

108 Ys. 49.10. See Moulton, *Tr. Mag.*, p. 18.

The above will, it is hoped, suffice as a skeleton presentation of Zarathustra's philosophy of religion and conduct. Unfortunately, the Gāthās do not provide sufficient materials for clothing this skeleton with more flesh; and as all key to the historical development of the Prophet's religious consciousness is now lost, we are unable to say if the Gāthās represent a coherent theology or the successive efforts of the Prophet's soul to grapple with the problem of existence and to get a nearer and nearer view of the ultimate principle that pervades the world of matter and spirit. Matters have been complicated by the incorporation within the Prophet's own message of relics of older religious traditions, possibly even of folk-lore and popular myths.[109] An unsympathetic critic would be able to pounce upon contradictions in the theory of creation, in the beginning of evil, in the reality of free will, in the judgment after death, and in the final doom of Evil. Now, as a proper understanding of the nature of God is intimately related to these problems, conflicting solutions of these would affect a coherent theory of God. As a matter of fact, posterity did develop contradictory theories on the Gāthās in addition to reviving some of the older beliefs discarded or allegorised by Zaraṭhustra. Broadly speaking, the philosophically and morally inclined emphasised the dualistic elements either for their own sake or for suggesting a monistic solution while the devotionally inclined accentuated the differences of the moral hypostases within the Divine nature and landed in a practical polytheism. Zoroaster's monotheism thus foundered ultimately on its conception of Angra Mainyu (Ahriman) and the Amesha Spentas (Amshaspands).

Who are the two Spirits that at the beginning stood face to face, divided the allegiance of the entire creation, and created life and non-life respectively? It has been pointed out by Moulton that ' the creative privilege of " the Lie," her independence of Mazdah, the co-eternity in the past of the " Bad Spirit " with the " Holy Spirit," and other crucial notions which later theology developed, cannot be proved from

[109] Moulton, *Ear. Zor.*, p. 148; Tiele, *op. cit.*, p. 113 f.

the Gāthās,' [110] and he suggests that the development of "the Lie" into an independent principle may have been due to a characteristic Magian synthesis of Babylonian, unreformed Aryan, and other beliefs, in which an infernal power has a separate existence.[111] Only once in the Gāthās is the Evil Spirit called Angra,[112] but the stereotyping of the name Angra Mainyu belongs to the later Avesta;[113] and the choice of evil by the Daevas seems to suggest that they elected to abandon their allegiance to Ahura and were originally not the creations of the Evil Spirit, just as darkness no less than light owed its origin to Ahura Mazdah.[114] The "bilateral symmetry" of the Vendidad,[115] where every good creation of Ahura Mazdah is matched by a bad creation of Angra Mainyu, finds no place in the Gāthās except in the form of "Life and Not-life" of Ys. 30. 4; and, in spite of the marked dualism of matter and spirit in the Avesta, there is nowhere any attempt to allocate material existence to Angra Mainyu and to ascribe spiritual existence alone to Spenta Mainyu.[116] The result would have been a neglect or suppression of bodily needs and worldly interests, if not an active mortification of the flesh, from which the religion of Zoroaster is singularly free. But still the Gāthic passages bearing on the two Spirits were sufficiently ambiguous to start divergent speculations. The Prophet was probably averse to ascribing, even indirectly, the introduction of evil into the world to Ahura Mazdah; and yet at the same time he was unwilling to admit the independent existence of an evil principle eternally limiting the beneficent activity of his God, although this became an accepted belief of later times when, like Satan, Ahriman be-

110 Moulton, *Ear. Zor.*, p. 126. Of course, this does not clear up the words "in the beginning" of Ys. 30.4 and "at the first beginning of the world" of Ys. 45.2. See EBE. v. 111, art. DUALISM (Iranian); but also see *Ear. Zor.*, p. 136, in this connection. See Haug, *op. cit.*, p. 301.

111 Moulton, *Ear. Zor.*, p. 128.

112 Ys. 45.2; possibly also 44.12. See Moulton, *Ear. Zor.*, p. 135 (with foot-note), p. 137 (foot-note).

113 Moulton, *Ear. Zor.*, p. 136, also 425; Tiele, *op. cit.*, Ch. VI (esp. p. 136 f).

114 Ys. 44.5. See Moulton, *Ear. Zor.*, p. 291.

115 Fargard I.

116 Moulton, *Ear. Zor.*, p. 147.

came " the opponent of God, the tempter of the Savior, the foe of mankind, the author of lies, a traitor and deceiver, the arch-fiend in command of hosts of demons, and the lord of the infernal regions and of the principalities of hell." [117] Possibly the attractive teaching of the Lie caused infatuation among the demons and they deliberately chose evil. The Prophet could not, however, regard evil as equivalent to man's free submission to the temptations of his own lower nature nor good as his identifying himself with the promptings of his nobler self: [118] good and evil had in the Prophet's eye an objective basis although he did not indicate definitely whether there was a Prince of Darkness in addition to the God of Light.

But whatever be the degree of reality ascribed to the Evil by the Prophet, he had no doubt that it could not be ultimately successful against the Good. It is the optimistic belief in the ultimate victory of Ahura Mazdah that has led Moulton [119] to repudiate the imputation of dualism to Zarathustra's own doctrine of evil although he admits that in Parsism " if we restrict ourselves to the origin of evil and its development during history past and future, we may use the term dualism fairly enough, for until the *Frashokereti* [120] there is a power independent of God which God cannot destroy, sharing his peculiarly divine prerogative of creation." As there is no Ahriman yet, the question of his fate naturally does not arise in the Gāthās; it is not unlikely, however, that the Prophet

117 Jackson, *Zor. Stu.*, p. 79; see also Benveniste, *op. cit.*, p. 17.

118 Parsis who want to put a subjectivistic interpretation on Ahriman refer to the story of the legendary king Takhma Urupi who bridled and rode on Ahriman, who had assumed the form of a horse, for thirty years (Yt. 15.12). For a discussion of this theory in later literature, see Dhalla, *Zor. Th.*, pp. 258-4.

See, however, Jackson, *Zoroastrian Studies*, pp. 73-5. He thinks that in the Gathas there are sufficient indications of a wicked personality who is variously described as the Enemy, the Wicked One, the Evil Teacher, the False Speaker, the Ignorant One, the Evil Spirit, Evil or Worst Thought. See also ERE. v. 111, art. DUALISM (Iranian) and ERE. ix. 866, art. PHILOSOPHY (Iranian).

119 Moulton, *Ear. Zor.*, pp. 125-6; *Tr. Mag.*, p. 27. Jackson calls Zoroastrianism a monotheistic and optimistic dualism (*Zor. Stu.*, p. 35). See, however, Casartelli, *op. cit.*, p. 50 f.

120 Renovation of the World. See Ys. 43.5, 12; Moulton, *Ear. Zor.*, p. 158; Jackson, *Zor. Stu.*, p. 149.

regarded the eternal persistence of Evil in any form or place as a negation of the right of Good to be alone unto eternity and that, therefore, the ultimate purification of the world by molten metal, whereby evil in all forms would be swept out of existence altogether, was a necessary part of the prophetic belief.[121] Immortality belongs to good life alone and the daevas that defraud men of good life make them mortal at the same time in their second life.[122] It is not out of compassion for sinners that Zarathustra does not prescribe an eternal Hell for Evil and its followers : it is only to uphold the dominion of the Good that he denies them eternal existence even in Hell. " The triumph of God is in this respect," says Moore,[123] " more complete than in Christianity, which leaves hell, with the devil and his angels and the wicked in torment for ever, an unconquered realm of evil."

But apart from the question of the final destiny of Evil on which not only the later orthodox theories but also heretical views like Manichaeism were agreed, namely, that the light of goodness would triumph in the end over the darkness of evil, the relation between Ahura Mazdah and Angra Mainyu at the beginning still remains to be discussed. Most, if not all, of the solutions suggested later on have proceeded on the assumption that Reali-

121 See Casartelli, *op. cit.*, p. 64 f, for Sassanian beliefs on this point. " At the end the Evil Spirit will be destroyed in this way that his whole creation will be separated from him, and he will remain alone, motionless, desireless, devoid of memory, a prisoner during the whole eternity. Evil will perish, but not the Evil Spirit " (*ibid.*, p. 68). But others say that the Evil Spirit will also cease to exist (*ibid.*, p. 64). See also *ibid.*, p. 54.

122 Ys. 32.5.

123 G. F. Moore, *His. of Rel.*, I, p. 404.

According to Manichaeism, after the final 1468 years' conflagration has recovered the last vestiges of the lost light of Heaven, " Darkness and Evil will be imprisoned in the dismal abyss to eternity."—See Jackson, *Researches in Manichaeism*, p. 16; *Dr. Modi Mem. Vol.*, p. 102; Casartelli, *op. cit.*, p. 64 f.

In Zamyād Yasht (Yt. 19.96) the evil-being Angra Mainyu is described as fleeing. He is also represented as hiding himself with the demons in the earth. See Dhalla, *Zor. Th.*, p. 183; also ERE. i. 237, art. AHRIMAN; C. de Harlez, *op. cit.*, pp. 201-2. Casartelli points out that in a *Dinkart* passage it is stated that " not only the wicked but also the demons will be saved at the time of the end of the world," but that in another place, although the immortality of Aharman is affirmed, the destruction of the demons is upheld (*op. cit.*, p. 93). See Moulton, *Tr. Mag.*, p. 106.

ity cannot be fundamentally dual in character but that it must somehow be one. If evil is not wholly due to the free will of the finite—and Zarathustra's catalogue of human and animal woes certainly goes beyond the deserts of personal action, it must at least partially be due to objective causes and, in fact, in the last analysis even the weakness and error of the finite will may be due to the operation of an objective cause which tends to make the worse appear the better reason. Now if this objective cause is not an independent principle, it must be somehow dependent on the unitary world-ground. Evil would then be a creation of God who has need of imperfection and opposition in His scheme of the government and history of the world. Now, although Zarathustra admits that suffering as a punishment for evil thought, word and deed is divinely ordained, he is not willing to ascribe all evil to God. What he does, therefore, is to introduce a principle which would have temporary reality (and even coeval existence with God) but should not be co-eternal with God and should therefore be finally non-existent.

To save the monotheism of Zoroaster's teaching it has accordingly been pointed out that the real opposition is not between Ahura Mazdah and Angra Mainyu, but between Spenta Mainyu (Holy Spirit) and Angra Mainyu (Evil Spirit), both being subordinate to Ahura Mazdah.[124] Thus C. de Harlez remarks: [125] "Two passages in the Gāthās, it is true, seem to place them (Ahura Mazda and Aṅro Mainyus)

[124] Jackson, *Zor. Stu.*, p. 70; Ys. 43.16; 19.9. See *The Gathic Doctrine of Dualism* in *Sanjana Comm. Vol.*, p. 166; also Taraporewala, *op. cit.*, Ch. IV. Good and Evil. Paul the Persian in enumerating various philosophical theories mentions one view according to which God possesses contrary qualities—possibly a reference to this particular view (ERE. ix. 867; Casartelli, *op. cit.*, p. 1).

[125] C. de Harlez objects to the identification of Anro Mainyus (meaning the Spirit who overthrows, destroys) with Angra Mainyu, for *anh(as)*, from which Anro is derived, means 'to overthrow' or 'to upset,' whereas *ang*, from which Angra is derived, means 'to restrain' (which being the opposite of Spento has led to the confusion).—See *Introduction to the Avesta* (Eng. Tr.), p. 200. But Casartelli points out (*op. cit.*, p. 55 f) that both the forms are to be found in the Avesta. He points out that in the Bun-Dehesh a positive distinction is drawn between Aharman and Ganāk-mīnoī (or Ganrāk-mīnoī)—a distinction greater than that between Auharmazd and Spenāk-mīnoī (see esp. pp. 56-7).

on the same level (Ys. 30.4; 45.2); and the dualism appears unadulterated in these passages; but everywhere else Ahura Mazda is raised far above his rival. He alone is omniscient and all powerful; Aṅro Mainyus has no insight into the future; he has a knowledge only of what he sees; even the consequences of his own acts are beyond his ken so long as they are not explicitly developed. In the eternal darkness, his original abode, he knew neither Ahura Mazda nor his creations. Ahura Mazda created the entire visible world, Aṅro Mainyus can only produce vices, evils and some malevolent beings. Nowhere does the Avesta attribute to him any other power. He cannot besides take the initiative in the work of creation; he can only imitate or do injury. The power and resources of the evil spirit are exceedingly limited." [126] Geldner puts the relation of Ahura Mazda, Angra Mainyu and Spenta Mainyu thus: "The Wise Lord...is the primeval spiritual being, the All-father, who was existent before ever the world arose....His guiding spirit is the Holy Spirit, which wills the good; yet it is not free, but restricted, in this temporal epoch, by its antagonist and own twin brother, the Evil Spirit......In the Gathas the Good Spirit of Mazdah and the Evil Spirit are the two great opposing forces in the world, and Ormazd himself is to a certain extent placed above them both. Later the Holy Spirit is made directly equivalent to Ormazd." [127] Haug similarly observes that the good mind which produces reality and the evil mind which originates evil are "the two moving causes in the universe, united from the beginning and therefore, called "twins." They are present everywhere; in Ahuramazda as well as in men. These two primeval principles, if supposed to be united in Ahuramazda himself, are not called *vohu-manô* and *akem mano,* but *speñtô mainyush,* "the beneficent spirit," and *angrô mainyush,* 'the hurtful spirit.''......Both are as inseparable as day and night, and though opposed to each

[126] C. de Harlez, *op. cit.*, p. 201. See also Yt. 3.14 17.20; Ys. 29.4 30.3. See in this connection West's Introduction in SBE, V (pp. lxix-lxx).

[127] Enc. Bri., 11th Ed., XXVIII, 1041 (quoted in Moulton, *Ear. Zor.*, p. 135).

other, are indispensable for the preservation of creation." [128] "But in the course of time, this doctrine of the great founder was changed and corrupted, in consequence of misunderstandings and false interpretations. Spentô-mainyush was taken as a name of Ahuramazda himself, and then, of course, Angrô-mainyush, by becoming entirely separated from Ahuramazda, was regarded as the constant adversary of Ahuramazda; thus the dualism of God and Devil arose." [129] It appears, therefore, that it is only in relation to Ahura Mazdah's creative activity that Angra Mainyu is his enemy and rival.[130] To put it in philosophical language, pain and evil are inseparable from the worldly process, or, as Leibniz says, absolute perfection is incompatible with finitude. To quote the apt words of Mills, "If there existed a supreme God whose power could undo the very laws of life, no evil could have been known; but the doctrine denies that there is any such being." [131] Perfection of the world is not an endowment but a conquest; when, however, the conquest is achieved, the world as the field of strife passes away and a new order of everlasting existence is ushered into being. The imperfections of the present world cast no reflection on the goodness of Ahura Mazdah although they may imply an inevitable necessity in the mode of Divine activity.

The Persian solution is not so definitely committed to the absolute limitation of Divine power as some modern conceptions of a "limited God" are, for it maintains only the temporal and phenomenal reality of Evil.[132] But at the same time there is nothing to indicate that Evil was deliberately

[128] Haug, *op. cit.*, pp. 303-4. Haug refers in this connection to Ys. xix.9 and lvii. 2, which, however, have been translated differently by Mills in SBE. Similar objection to Haug's translation of Verse 21 of Hā XIX and Fourth Strophe of Hā XXX is to be found in C. de Harlez, *op. cit.*, p. 129.

[129] Haug, *op. cit.*, p. 305. See also the quotation of Bartholomae's note by Moulton in *Ear. Zor.*, p. 134, f.n.l. See also Casartelli, *op. cit.*, pp. 178; Dhalla, *Zor. Th.*, p. 247 f.

[130] Jackson, *Zor. Stu.*, pp. 69-71; Casartelli, *op. cit.*, p. 17, f.n.2.

[131] SBE, XXI, Int., p. xix.

[132] See Dhalla, *Zor. Th.*, p. 250 f.

created to make the world " a vale of soul-making " [133]—the utmost that the later tradition allowed is that if man had not agreed to fight evil, he would have been condemned to an eternal terror of Ahriman.[134] All that orthodoxy did was to attenuate the positive function of Ahriman—to conceive of him much as Plato conceived of Matter, namely, as a diaphanous principle that mars the good creation of God and has no power to create anything except in an imperfect form.[135] Still Zoroastrianism could not admit that, like the Satan of Jewish and Christian religions, modelled on its own Evil Spirit,[136] Ahriman was created by Ahura Mazdah, that subsequently he rebelled against the latter and fell, and that, though in opposition to the good God, he was unable to create a realm of evil beings.[137] On account of these differences, Casartelli, after giving due weight to the opinions of Moulton and others, is constrained to remark, " There can, we think, be no doubt that all through the Zoroastrian system, from the Avesta down to the Pahlavi theologians, the evil spirit is considered as a real creator, and for this reason, even apart from

[133] It is stated, however, in the *Dīnkart* that " Ormazd allows Ahriman, he father of evil, to commingle with his creation for an allotted period for the experience and training of mankind " (Dhalla, *Zor. Th.*, p. 249).

[134] In the Bundahishn, which is an old Pahlavi work based on the Dāmdat Nask, one of the lost books of the original Avesta, there is directly indicated (in 2.9-11) a choice made by the Fravashis—those pre-existing spiritual counterparts, or guardian geniuses, who were the celestial prototypes of material creations afterward produced—to leave for a time their heavenly state and assume a bodily existence on earth, in order to overcome finally the opposition of Ahriman and ' become perfect and immortal in the future existence, for ever and ever-lasting.'—Jackson, *Zor. Stu.*, p. 227. See C. de Harlez, *op. cit.*, pp. 193-4, and Casartelli, *op. cit.*, p. 84, for the passage in question. See also Söderblom, *op. cit.*, p. 222.

[135] The analogy is not to be pushed too far, for Ahriman was not the naterial cause of the world and materiality was not an evil in Persian religion. At the same time he was the creator of a whole system of evil principles and powers independently of Ahura Mazdah while Platonic Matter is not independently creative although it has the capacity of marring the creation of the Good.

[136] See Moulton, *Ear. Zor.*, pp. 305, 325.

[137] ERE. v. 112. See Jackson, *Zor. Stu.*, p. 231, for the arguments of *Skhand Vimānik Vichār*, a dualistic work. The theory of Ahriman being a reprobate angel who revolted against Ormazd, propounded at a later time, was obviously an imitation of Christian thought. (See Dhalla, *Zor. Th.*, p. 301.)

the question of his origin, the system may justly be termed dualistic." [138]

It is indeed true that at least one Iranian sect, the Gayomarthians, taught that the Evil Spirit proceeded from the Good Spirit by generation or creation—that the Evil Spirit was produced by an evil or doubting thought in the mind of Yazdan the Good Spirit [139] as to the kind of being his rival (if such existed) would be; but they took no trouble to explain how any doubt or evil thought could cross the mind of the Good Spirit at all. Their speculation or fancy would practically involve the assumption of a latent dark aspect in the Divine nature with which some of the post-Kantian thinkers of Germany have familiarised us. The process of the world would commence with the breaking away of the irrational or bad from the rational or good aspect of God and would end with the final overtaking and absorption of the former by the latter. Unlike the speculative dualism sketched above, this theory would not prove evil to be a necessary complement to Divine beneficence in creation, although its theological monotheism would perhaps be assured by its theory of the creation or generation of evil from within the Divine nature. It is doubtful, however, if the necessary positing of Evil in the creation process is a worse solution than an involuntary emission of Evil out of the Divine Mind, and the comparative insignificance of the Gayomarthian sect proves that its solution of the relation of Ahura Mazdah and Ahriman was not much superior to the orthodox dualism in popular estimation.

138 ERE. v. 111. Jackson expresses a similar view: "We may believe that dualism in its characteristic Persian form and especially in its moral and ethical aspects was first taught by Zoroaster himself" (*Zor. Stu.*, p. 30). Haug characterises Zoroaster's theology as monotheism and his speculative philosophy as dualism (*op. cit.*, p. 303; see also Jackson, *Zor. Stu.*, pp. 33, 70).

139 ERE. v. 112; xi. 347; Jackson, *Zor. Stu.*, p. 34; Dhalla, *Zor. Th.*, p. 301; Casartelli, *op. cit.*, p. 52. *Cf.* the origin of Kālī out of Ambikā's anger in *Mārkaṇḍeya-Purāṇa*, Ch. LXXXVII.

The word is derived from *Gayamaretan* (Pahlavi *Gayamart*), the primeval man (the first legendary king in Firdusi's *Shāh-nāmah*), from whom Ahura Mazdah created "the race of all Arian regions, the seed of all Arian lands."—See Geiger. *op. cit.*, I, p. 3; ERE. i.205; xii. 865.

We may very well believe that popular thought divided itself into two opposite camps. There were those who failed to see the utility of drawing any distinction between Ahura Mazdah and Spenta Mainyu and gradually identified the two. It was probably felt that while there was some justification for according some sort of independence to evil there was none whatsoever in the case of the good spirit. Spenta Mainyu had always been distinguished from the Amesha Spentas [140] but its nature was not precisely fixed in the Gāthic literature. Moulton has pointed out how strikingly similar is Spenta Mainyu to the "Spirit of Yahweh" in the Old Testament: "there is the same combination of distinctness and identity, the same stress upon spirituality." [141] Jackson has similarly pointed out the resemblance between Ahura Mazdah and his Holy Spirit, on the one hand, and the Father and the Holy Ghost in the New Testament, on the other: sometimes they are treated as two distinctly separate beings and sometimes as practically identical.[142] We have no means of ascertaining whether the Amesha Spentas were meant to replace the plurality of gods, and Ahura Mazdah and Spenta Mainyu any of the prominent dual divinities in the polytheism of the time (just as the trinity of Ahura Mazdah, Mithra and Anāhita was formed later on probably in imitation of similar Holy Triads). But while Zarathustra had probably no objection against recognising the existence of maleficent demons, the daevas, by the side of Ahura Mazdah, he could not admit the existence of other beneficent gods who might share with Ahura Mazdah the homage of men. We should remember that although the names are to be found in the Gāthās, the Amesha Spentas do not figure as a group of independent archangels before the Gāthā Haptanghaiti, of which the authorship has been ascribed to the followers of the Prophet; [143] and as

140 In Ys. 33.6 Spenta Mainyu replaces Vohu Manah.—See Moulton, *Ear. Zor.*, p. 111.

141 Moulton, *Ear. Zor.*, p. 299.

142 Quoted by Dhalla in *Zor. Th.*, p. 24. See *Dr. Modi Mem. Vol.*, pp. 227, 229.

143 Haug, *op. cit.*, p. 170.

Spenta Mainyu did not attain the status of an archangel in this Gāthā, or even later when the Amshaspands were invested with material domains in addition to spiritual ones, it shows that possibly the tradition of the inseparability of Ahura Mazdah and his holy spirit was too well establisheed to be abandoned or modified. In fact, in many a Gāthic passage, *e.g.*, in Ys. 33.12, 43.2, 44.7, 47 (most of the verses), 51.7, the holy spirit is one of the divine attributes of Ahura Mazdah;[144] and those who saw the illogicality of dissociating a being from its essential attribute naturally refused to continue the distinction between the two and thus ultimately Ahura Mazdah and Spenta Mainyu ceased to be distinguished as different principles. But while this saved an inner disruption of the divine nature, it accentuated the duality of Ahura Mazdah and Angra Mainyu, for there was no longer any shadowy Spenta Mainyu to represent Ahura Mazdah in his struggles with Angra Mainyu. And Angra Mainyu, because of the evil connotation, could not be funded back to Ahura Mazdah as one of his attributes.

Thus the philosophical dualism which was introduced to explain the conflicts of moral life and spiritual conduct hardened into a theological dualism or ditheism under which name the Zoroastrian religion is generally known.[145] The Persian love of symmetry, which was responsible for matching every attribute, attendant, dominion or act of Ahura Mazdah with a similar one of opposite quality belonging to Ahriman, tended in the long run to divide the whole realm of being between the two and to invest them with equal existence and involve them in an eternal conflict.[146] True, the final victory of Ahura Mazdah did not disappear from view; but Ahriman was no longer subordinated to his beneficent rival. This dualism with its bearing upon practical life was fully elaborated by the heretic Mānī early in the third century of the Christian era.[147] The Father God of Light and the Overlord of Darkness at first ruled respectively

[144] See Pour Davoud, *op. cit.*, p. 48.

[145] See Casartelli, *op. cit.*, p. 4 (with the Translator's footnote); p. 50 f.

[146] Moulton, *Ear. Zor.*, p. 220; *Tr. Mag.*, pp. 64, 108.

[147] See Jackson, *Researches in Manichaeism*, pp. 8-16; *Zor. Stu.*, p. 187 f.

over the upper regions of light and the nether regions of darkness and the boundaries of these met at a veritable No-Man's Land, called the Border, the invasion of which by the powers of Darkness started the fateful conflict of the second period of the world's history. The Father of Light, one of whose designations is Zervan or Eternal Time, "evokes" a number of spiritual beings in succession and succeeds in recovering the light, which the Principle of Darkness had imprisoned, with the active co-operation of the faithful after the fourth evocation had ushered in Jesus to awaken Adam from the lethargy which involved sleep and death. When Darkness and Evil will be imprisoned in the dismal abyss to eternity, the Third Time will usher in the eternal dominion of Light with its lost elements completely recovered. But for the fact that Mānī taught the utter badness of matter and regarded family life with unfeigned disfavour, he would not have had to fall a victim to Zoroastrian persecution, for at the time that he preached his doctrines Zoroastrianism itself had become radically dualistic with Ormazd and Ahriman conceived to be in direct opposition to each other from the beginning of time as persons and not as abstractions or hypostases.[148] The murder of Mazdak [149] about 250 years after the martyrdom of Mānī was also for a similar attack upon the family institution in addition to the preaching of socialistic and communistic ideas.[150] But by that time the Sassanian revival had given a new turn to the religious thought of Iran.

The dualistic philosophy and the monotheistic theology in both of which Ormazd could figure were felt to be an incongruity by a sect which had a fairly long history. The interest of the Zervanites was not so much religious as philosophical and, except in the official edict of Mihr Narseh, the prime minister of Yazdigird II, which affirmed that Zervan [151] existed before heaven and earth and begot two sons,

148 See the quotation from Eznig of Goghp in *Indo-Iranian Studies* (*Sanjana Comm. Vol.*), p. 186.

149 See *Two Versions of the History of Mazdak* by Arthur Christensen in *Dr. Modi Mem. Vol.*, p. 321 f.

150 Jackson, *Zor. Stu.*, p. 176.

151 The two other spellings are Zarvan and Zrvan, but, as usual, foreign spellings are different.—See *The Zarvanite System* in *Sanjana Comm. Vol.*, p. 65.

the good and the evil spirit,[152] Zervanism does not seem to have won much popular or state support although Manichaeism was a close imitator.[153] According to this speculation both Ormazd and Ahriman derived their existence from Zervan Akarana, " Boundless Time," who wanted a son who would create heaven and earth and all things therein but whom a doubt assailed, whether such a son would be born, after a thousand years of sacrifice had passed away. They were simultaneously conceived (whence they are " twins ") by their father-mother,—Ormazd, because of the sacrifice, and Ahriman, because of the doubt; but Ahriman was the earlier born, having forestalled Ormazd to whom Zervan wished to give the dominion, and claimed the right of primogeniture promised by Zervan himself. So for the first nine thousand years Ahriman could not be dislodged from the world and it is only at the end of this period that Ormazd recovered the kingdom from him and Ahriman was confined to the dark abyss unto eternity.[154] It is only necessary to add that in Eznik's version the Sun was created by the two spirits to adjudge between their respective rights; apparently, then, Mithra was regarded as the mediator and protector of contracts not only between human parties but also between heavenly combatants, and Mithraism was in this way brought into intimate relation with Zoroastrianism of a sort.[155]

152 *Sanjana Comm. Vol.*, p. 70; Casartelli, *op. cit.*, p. 12 f; ERE. ix. 868.

153 Benveniste, *op. cit.*, pp. 77, 90. See, however, *Sanjana Comm. Vol.*, p. 72: " Zarvanism must have been the form of the Persian religion which came to Armenia." See also Casartelli, *op. cit.*, p. 3; 5 f. Benveniste thinks that Zarvanism was pre-Zoroastrian (*op. cit.*, pp. 114, 116).

154 For the various forms of this speculation or myth, see *The Zarvanite System* in *Sanjana Comm. Vol.*, pp. 61-81 (esp. pp. 70-4 where the quotations from Eznik and ash-Shahrastani are to be found); also Benveniste, *op. cit.*, p. 76 f; Haug. *op. cit.*, p. 13. Eznik's criticism is still the best.—See Wilson, *Parsi Religion*, Appendix D, p. 542 f.

In the *Mainyo-i Khard* one zodiacal sign was placed in charge of each period of 1,000 years.—See Casartelli, *op. cit.*, p. 96.

155 Benveniste, *op. cit.*, pp. 70, 77, 88-90, 92 (Mithra = Srausha); Moulton, *Tr. Mag.*, p. 189; *Sanjana Comm. Vol.*, p. 77. Speaking of Mitro (Mihir) of Sassanian times as a mediator, Casartelli remarks: " It is however certain that the idea of mediation never existed in Mazdaism. The phrase signifies nothing more than ' intervening between,' not as a mediator but as a judge pronouncing the sentence, giving up the sinful to punishment and preserving from the attacks of the demons

It does not appear, however, that the monotheistic solution of Zervanism was very fruitful either from the religious or even from the philosophical point of view. We have no means of ascertaining whether Zarathustra was familiar with the philosophy that left the determination of all things to Time, conceived not merely as a formal principle but also as a principle of causation; his use of the word 'Twins' in respect of Ahura Mazdah and Ahriman in Ys. 30.3 possibly did not have the implication of their being in the same womb of Time as later mythology suggested.[156] But if Zervan can be traced back to the Achaemenian period at least up to the 4th century B.C.—and literary and archaeological remains would probably warrant it,[157] then it is not an improbable suggestion that the concept comes down from a still remoter antiquity and that the Zarathustrian reform, in spite of its partiality for personified abstractions, deliberately set aside the abstract concept of Time as too impersonal and intractable for religious purposes.[158] If, on the other hand, the concept was devised later to overcome the dualism of Zoroastrianism itself, the Zervanite reaction is one of the earliest attempts to overcome the difficulties of a dualistic philosophy. We may in the latter case very well suppose that the mythological account was designed for popular understanding and edification at a time when the other personified abstractions of the Zoroastrian religion were being similarly clothed with flesh and blood in the manner of the pagan deities whom the Zoroastrian reform had superseded.

the righteous who need no mediation to obtain heaven." (*Op. cit.*, p. 79.) See Huart, *Ancient Persia and Iranian Civilisation*, pp. 84-5.

156 Moulton, *Tr. Mag.*, pp. 26, 237. For the Zarvanites, see Dhalla, *Zor. Th.*, p. 203.

157 Damascius (5th century A.D.) quotes from Eudemos of Rhodes (*circa* 300 B.C.) and Plutarch professes to follow Theopompus (*circa* 400 B.C.) in his reference to Zervan. The epitaph of Antiochus I (100 B. C.) also refers to Endless Time.—See *Sanjana Comm. Vol.*, pp. 66, 76; Benveniste, *op. cit.*, p. 78. For other references, see *Sanjana Comm. Vol.*, pp. 61-81; Benveniste, *op. cit.*, pp. 76-94, 100-117.

158 Benveniste, *op. cit.*, p. 114 (Zervanism is pre-Zoroastrian); Casartelli, *op. cit.*, p. 9 (it could not be much posterior to the Mazdayasnian Dualism).

That Time brings into existence all things and in due course destroys them again—that it is both a creator and a devourer, is such an obvious phenomenon that a philosophy based on the omnipotence of time can hardly be expected to be a unique discovery. Both in Greece and in India—in the one in the myth of Kronos devouring his own children and in the other in the theory that Kāla (Time) creates, matures and destroys all things, we have similar religious and philosophical ideas; and the similarity with Greek thought did not escape the notice of some of the foreign writers who came across the Zervanite account.[159] But it seems that there was some difference of opinion about the exact nature of Zervan Akarana. The *Mainyo-i Khard* describes him thus: [160] "He is imperishable and immortal; he is without grief, without hunger, without thirst, without affliction, ever living, sempiternal, whom no one can stay, nor remove his control from his affairs." The religiously inclined would naturally regard Zervan as a personal being:[161] in a later tradition even a wife has been ascribed to him.[162] The impersonal Absolute (Brahman) would naturally be congenial only to the Indian soil where the cognitive aspect was emphasised at the cost of the conative and where practices calculated to bring about the disappearance of the finite body by rigorous asceticism and celibacy and of the finite self by meditational absorption would tend to diminish the importance of personality as an indispensable condition of spirituality. But in Iran, where life was strenuous, the ideal of a householder's life had a strong hold upon the mind of the people and belief in personal immortality (probably in a risen body) was an integral part of life's philosophy, an impersonal God could not prove satisfying. It is only in India, among contemporary Parsi

159 *E.g.*, Moses of Chorene and the pseudo-Agathangelos (both of the 5th century).—See *Sanjana Comm. Vol.*, pp. 69-70.

160 viii. 9 (quoted in ERE. ix. 867); Casartelli, *op. cit.*, p. 7.

161 Moulton, *Tr. Mag.*, p. 190; Dhalla, *Zor. Th.*, p. 365.

162 *Sanjana Comm. Vol.*, pp. 64, 68. In Manichaeism the first evocation by the Father God of Light (Zervan) includes the Mother of Life but not as a wife of Zervan.—See Jackson, *Researches in Manichaeism*, p. 9.

For this habit of ascribing wives to personifications, see ERE. ii. 38, art. ARYAN RELIGION.

58

Theosophists, that Zervan Akarana figures as an impersonal principle in the manner of Brahman and merging in the Universal, as taught in Śaṅkara-Vedānta, has become a part of the creed.[163]

But even the Zervanites of ancient times were not always interested in their First Principle in a religious way. Except in a mythology, Time is difficult to conceive in a personal way, and so what happened was that Zervan became identified with certain impalpable and impersonal principles. Orthodoxy itself drew a distinction between certain independent and uncreate beings and those that are created and contingent. To the former class belonged Time, Space, Light and Destiny,[164] which provided, as it were, the theatre of operation of the two contending Spirits and the law of its consummation. Regarded thus, Time and Space would be principles in which creation takes place. Light and Darkness would constitute eternal abodes and modes of manifestation of Ormazd and Ahriman respectively. Fate or Destiny would be the law that controls the future of Good and Evil. Zervan, we may believe, was latterly conceived not only as resolving the dualism of Ormazd and Ahriman but also as unifying these four impersonal principles. Darmesteter has suggested that these four are phases of the original idea of the sky-god; we find, however, that they were all associated with Zervan by native and foreign writers [165] at some time or other, and thus Space,[166] Destiny and Light as also Time came to be signified by Zervan in Zervanism, Manichaeism and even Zoroastrianism

163 Dhalla, *Zor. Th.*, p. 364. It appears that 18th century Dasturs who assisted Anquetil du Perron in translating the Vendidad thought Zervanism to be orthodox.—See *Sanjana Comm. Vol.*, p. 79; see also West, SBE, V, Int., p. lxx.

164 Jackson, *Zor. Stu.*, p. 34; C. de Harlez, *op. cit.*, pp. 130, 132; Casartelli, *op. cit.*, pp. 10-11.

165 By Damascius and Theodore of Mopsuestia.—See *Sanjana Comm. Vol.*, pp. 66-7. For Iranian references, see *ibid.*, pp. 74-6.

In Vendidad xix. 44 and Sīrōzah 21 Sovereign Heaven and Boundless Time occur together. See ERE. ix. 867; Jackson, *Zor. Stu.*, pp. 32, 34; Benveniste, *op. cit.*, p. 97 (the identity of Ormazd with heaven is transferred from the identity of Zrvan with the starry sky); also Casartelli, *op. cit.*, p. 6.

166 *Thwāsha* (infinite space) as distinguished from *Āsmān* (created heaven).—See Casartelli, *op. cit.*, pp. 10-11.

itself. The development of Zervanism into a kind of Fatalism must have been unpopular with the large body of Mazdayasnians who had been taught by their Prophet to redeem the world and to be the architects of their own fate.[167] This, together with the very vacuous nature of Zervan conceived as Space or Light or Destiny, must have been responsible for the limited religious use of the concept in orthodox literature: [168] in fact, although occasionally Boundless Time is invoked as a spirit, it is sometimes distinguished from Destiny [169] and associated more frequently with heaven.[170] Orthodoxy did not abandon the concept of Boundless Time, for it was Gāthic in origin. What it did in Sassanian times was to regard it as a co-eternal attribute of Ahura Mazdah and neither his creator nor his creature.[171] But though Zervanism was gradually discredited both as a philosophical solution and as a religious system (somewhat pantheistic in its implications) many of its features

[167] It has been pointed out that references to Fate are rare in orthodox Zoroastrianism, the most notable ones being Yt. 8.23, Vd. 5.8 and 21.1.—See *Sanjana Comm. Vol.*, p. 77. For references to later literature, see ERE. v. 792, art. FATE; Dhalla, *Zor. Th.*, pp. 154, 205.

In the Pahlavi *Dinkard* occurs the interesting passage (3 174.2) that "in the rest of the world-creation there are not such lords of their own will as the lord man, except God even alone." See, however, Tansar's letter, quoted in Jackson, *Zor.*, *Stu.*, pp. 242-3: "The wise man should take the middle way between choice and predestination and not be satisfied with one. For the reason that predestination and choice are two bales of a traveler's goods on the back of his animal. . . If the two bales are equal, the traveler will suffer no embarrassment, his animal will be comfortable, and he will arrive at his destination."

For the whole subject, see Jackson, *Zor. Stu.*, Part II. The Zoroastrian Doctrine of the Freedom of the Will; also ERE. v. 792; ix. 869; also Casartelli, *op. cit.*, p. 9.

[168] The *Shāhnāmeh* uses it in the sense of Destiny, this being congenial to the predestinarian belief of its Muhammadan author.—See C. de Harlez, *op. cit.*, p. 130.

[169] C. de Harlez, *op. cit.*, p. 131; ERE. ix. 867 (quoting *Mainog-i-Krat*); Casartelli, *op. cit.*, p. 6.

[170] See Vd. xix. 44; Sirozah I. 21; II. 21; Nyayish I. 8; see also Ys. 72.10. See *Sanjana Comm. Vol.*, p. 65. Casartelli suggests that Zervan might have been understood by some as 'a vast chaos, an infinite pre-existing matter' (ERE. ix. 867; also *op. cit.*, p. 7).

[171] ERE. ix. 867; Casartelli, *op. cit.*, p. 10. In the *Zātsparam*, i. 24, Ahura Mazdah is the creator of Time (see ERE v. 792). See West's Int., SBE, V, p. lxx.

passed over into the orthodoxy of later times.[172] Possibly also it was felt that referring both good and evil to Zervan Akarana did not remove the difficulty of conceiving contradictory functions in the Ultimate Principle while at the same time it reduced Ahura Mazdah to a mere demiurge whose own destruction was necessarily implied in his created nature. Apparently, the strength of mind necessary to declare even Īśvara (God) as temporary, Heaven and Earth as equally destined to pass away, and finite spirits as illusory and impermanent in nature belonged not to theistic Iran but to pantheistic India where polytheism had accustomed men's minds not to feel the want of a Supreme God and theogonic speculations had besides familiarised the idea of transitory gods—of gods that are born and gods that pass away in successive aeons of time.[173]

Paradoxically enough, the future of Zoroastrianism belonged not to the monotheistic but to the polytheistic tendencies of Zarathustra's message. We may very well believe that the Prophet's intolerant utterances[174] were followed with some amount of literalness by royal patrons in power except where, as in the case of the Achaemenian kings, political diplomacy or personal lukewarmness prompted the extension of the pantheon or reverence towards foreign gods.[175] The Prophet had to contend against various inferior types of contemporary belief and practice, the nature of which can be inferred with some amount of certainty not only by studying the Vedic religion but also from the later developments of his own message. Not only were the powers of nature (fire, water, air, etc.) and the shining orbs of heaven worshipped, but departed spirits also received periodic homage from their descendants and the powers of darkness were suitably appeased or exorcised in

172 Casartelli, *op. cit.*, pp. 13-4 : "These Zervanists were anything but a small peculiar sect and they probably formed the most considerable part of the Mazdayasnians for a certain number of centuries."

173 See ERE. i. 201, art. AGES OF THE WORLD (Indian).

174 Ys. 46.18; 48.5, 7.

175 Moulton, *Ear. Zor.*, pp. 30-55 (esp. pp. 53-5); ERE. i. 69 f., art. ACHAEMENIANS; Dhalla, *Zor. Th.*, p. 73.

inferior cults.[176] Personification of certain pervasive principles like Time, Space, etc., and of certain attributes and functions had also possibly taken place among the more philosophically inclined in Iran as in Vedic India; but, as in India again, the efficacy of sacred formulae in driving away evil spirits—possibly also in ensuring the help of benign powers, was believed in. Possibly, as in Vedic India, sacrifices were offered in the open on improvised altars or, as in Canaan, on hill-tops,[177] and special classes specialised in priestly functions. The produce of the flock and the dairy was possibly the main ingredient of worship and it is likely that a certain amount of cruelty and drunkenness attended sacrificial rites.

The Zarathustrian reform was primarily intended to establish the supremacy of One God and that not as a personification but as an ethical personality. Schrader well puts the distinction between the two:[178] "The characteristic mark of a *personal god* is that he is regarded as exercising influence outside of the sphere to which he owes his conceptual origin and his name. *Personification*, however, means, at first, simply the substitution of a human figure for the divine *anima* present in the phenomenon." Ahura Mazdah is not a departmental deity like the Sun, the Moon, the Wind or the Waters; he is the One God who rules over all departments alike, both physical and moral, but who is not responsible for the evils of the world except those perhaps that are meant as punishment for sin.[179] A passage like the following could be quite in the spirit of Zoroaster, even if not

176 We have it from Plutarch that Zoroaster taught the Persians to offer to Horomazes (Ormazd) offerings of vows and thanksgiving and to Areimanious (Ahriman) offerings for averting ill and things of gloom. This would go against all Mazdaean religion, as Benveniste points out (p. 73). This can apply only to Zervanism (p. 76) and Mithraism (p. 74).—See Benveniste, *op. cit.*, p. 69 f.

177 We know that at least in the Achaemenian times there were *āyadanās* (houses of god), for Darius speaks of the places of worship that Gaumata the Magian had destroyed.—See Moulton, *Ear. Zor.*, pp. 52-3; Jackson, *Zor. St.*, pp. 195-6. See Huart, *op. cit.*, pp. 81, 94, 95; also p. 49, f.n.l., where the temples are supposed to belong to peoples conquered by the Persians.

178 ERE. ii. 38, art. ARYAN RELIGION.

179 See ERE. i. 71. Contrast Isaiah 45.7: "I form the light, and create darkness; I make peace, and create evil." But see Ys. 44.5.

actually composed by him: [180] "Here praise we Ahura Mazdah, who created both kine and holiness, and created waters, created both good trees and light, both the earth and all good things." He himself conceives of Ahura Mazdah as the First and the Last, as one who in the beginning filled the blessed worlds with light and created Right as well as men and other things and will at the end judge the actions of life, whether done in the open or in secret.[181] By virtue of his absolute overlordship he will give a perpetuity of communion with Welfare and Immortality and Right with Dominion, with Good Thought, to him that in Spirit and in action is his friend.[182] He is holy, for he has eternally decreed that actions and words shall have their meed—evil for the evil, a good destiny for the good.[183] The Prophet exhorts his hearers to acknowledge their allegiance to Ahura Mazdah by their devotion and practical conduct.[184]

"Him thou shouldst seek to bring to us by praises of worship. "Now have I seen it with mine eye, that which is of the good spirit and of (good) action and word, knowing by Right Mazdah Ahura." May we offer him homage in the House of Song!

"Him thou shouldst seek to propitiate for us together with Good Thought, who at his will maketh us weal and woe. May Mazdah Ahura by his Dominion bring us to work, for prospering our beasts and our men, so that we may through Right have familiarity with Good Thought.

As a specimen of the arguments by means of which Ahura Mazdah's responsibility for the creation of evil is established, we may quote Haug's translation of Ys. 48.4: "He who created, by means of his wisdom, the good and evil mind in thinking, words and deeds, rewards his obedient followers with prosperity. Art Thou (Mazda!) not he, in whom the final cause of both intellects (good and evil) exists?" (*Op. cit.*, p. 167, with n. 2.) Here is Moulton's translation of the same passage: "Whose, O Mazdah, makes his thought now better, now worse, and likewise his self by action and by word, and follows his own inclinations, wishes and choices, he shall in thy purpose be in a separate place at the last" (*Ear. Zor.*, p. 378).

[180] Ys. 37.1. See ERE. i. 71 for similar expressions in the texts of the Achaemenian kings.

[181] Ys. 30.7-9, 11, 13; see also Ys. 44.3-7; 47.1-3.

[182] Ys. 31.21; see also Ys. 33.11, 12.

[183] Ys. 43.5; 51.6.

[184] Ys. 45.8-10.

"Him thou shouldst seek to exalt with prayers of Piety, him that is called Mazdah Ahura for ever, for that he hath promised through his own Right and Good Thought that Welfare and Immortality shall be in his Dominion, strength and perpetuity in his house."

We may very well believe that the Zoroastrian reform was intended not only to draw men's minds away from their many gods but also to emphasise the fact that God is wholly beneficent. Men must thank themselves if by choosing the evil path they separate themselves from righteousness and meet their doom at the Bridge of the Separator. God, whose association with Right or Justice is inseparable, is relentless towards the individual sinner although His Beneficence or Mercy is manifested when at the renovation of the world the realm of suffering souls is also purified by molten metal and He reigns supreme over entire existence. This position curiously resembles the Hindu view that although according to the law of Karma no individual can escape the re-incarnation he has deserved by his sin, yet the merciful Lord periodically dissolves the world at the end of a cycle (*kalpa*) in order to give temporary respite from the round of rebirths to all suffering souls. The Parsi religion did not, however, provide for the return of the sinner to expiate the sins of a previous life nor for intercession on his behalf, immediately after his death or at periodic intervals, to speed his soul on to the realm of Ahura.[185] So far Moulton is probably right, whatever might be the value of his strictures on the inclination of a section of the modern Parsis who follow Hindu beliefs about transmigration instead of the Christian belief in the continuity of the departed soul in another realm under a merciful God who is able and willing to absolve a progressing soul from the bondage of evil by His own grace.[186] But, as has been pointed out so often before, in such matters strict logic can very

[185] See Dhalla, *Zor. Th.*, p. 347.

[186] See Moulton, *Tr. Mag.*, p. 179, 191; Dhalla, *Zor. Th.*, p. 365.

Ward puts the two view-points thus (*Realm of Ends*, p. 401): The one (transmigration or reincarnation) secures a continuity of environment that satisfies the imagination of survivors, but at the sacrifice more or less complete of that

seldom be consistently maintained in any community, and it would not be difficult to show that the pious Zoroastrian also cherishes the belief that Ahura can and does hear prayers and is merciful to the sinning soul that repents,[187] and that other helpers are also available to give warning and to save the unwary soul from false steps and ultimate damnation. The *Mainyo-i Khard* distinguishes, for instance, divine Providence (*bagho-bakht*) and Destiny (*bakht*) as that which i bestowed as the result of prayer and good action and that which is ordained from the very beginning.[188] Divine beneficence would be incomplete without a merciful consideration of the weakness of the human soul and the many temptations by which it is assailed from all directions. God must either strengthen the power of resistance or give fresh opportunities or send timely warning or

personal continuity which we must regard as essential. The other (transfiguration. preserves this, but transfers it to an unseen world difficult o realise."

The Bun-Dehesh pictures the interval between death and Renovation as follows :—

"On the death of a man the soul is separated from the body which is then mingled with the dust. If the souls, as they are in heaven and hell, still possess bodies, they are rather fantastic bodies made expressly for their stay in these places of reward and punishment, because it is only at the time of the *frashkĕrĕto* that the bodies will rise up from the dust. Though the elements of the bodies will be then dispersed by wind and water, yet Auharmazd will gather them up as easily as he has formed them in the womb of the mother."

The Dinkard adds that "if the body will be punished, it will be on account of the sins of the soul."—See Casartelli, *op. cit.*, pp. 136-7 (also p. 29).

187 See Ys. 51.4 : "Where is the recompense for wrong to be found, where pardon for the same?" See also Dhalla, *Zor. Th.*, p. 24 : "Strict are his laws and stern is his judgment. Yet he is not the indiscriminate dispenser of doom to erring humanity. His is the justice tempered with mercy, for mercy and grace abound in his divine kingdom." See Moulton, *Ear. Zor.*, p. 152.

For later beliefs, see Dhalla, *Zor. Th.*, pp. 222, 224, 292-3; also Casartelli, *op. cit.*, p. 200.

188 Casartelli, *op. cit.*, pp. 31-3. ERE. v. 792 quotes Visparad vii. 3 in this connection.

"Pahlavi books depict a treasure-house where works of supererogation were stored for the benefit of those whose credit was inadequate. The idea makes the genuine Hamistakān impossible."—Moulton, *Ear. Zor.*, p. 162. See Pavry, *The Zoroastrian Doctrine of a Future Life*, pp. 101-2. See also Casartelli, *op. cit.*, p. 196 (Translator's footnote). The prayer for all is repeated in the Prefatory liturgy of the Afringan ceremony and is referred to by Herodotus.—See Modi *The Religious Ceremonies and Customs of the Parsis*, p. 382.

annul the consequences of sinful acts or relent after sufficient punishment has been inflicted. Zoroastrianism, like some other religions, has viewed with disfavour the conception of an eternal hell as being incompatible with Divine omnipotence and beneficence alike; but, as Moulton points out, the thought of an eternal "House of the Lie" is not entirely absent in the Gāthās[189] where Divine justice and hatred of wrong are such prominent features.

It is the Zoroastrian conception of the Amesha Spentas (the Immortal Holy Ones), however, that was destined to have a far more interesting history. The term stands for a collection of six divine spirits which appears for the first time as early as the Gāthā Haptanghaiti and could not have been very far from Zarathustra's own thought. These are (1) *Asha* or *Asha Vahishta* (Right, Uprightness, Truth, Order, Harmony) corresponding to the Vedic *Ṛta*; (2) *Vohu Manah* or *Vahishtem Manah* (Good or Best Spirit, Mind or Thought); (3) *Khshathra* or *Khshathra Vairya* (Wished-for Kingdom, Sovereignty, Dominion); (4) *Armaiti* (the Vedic *Aramati*) or *Spentā Ārmaiti* (Devotion or Holy Devotion, Piety); (5) *Haurvatāt* (Welfare, Perfection, Perfect Well-being); and (6) *Ameretāt* (Immortality). As their names imply, they represent certain abstract virtues, certain ethical conceptions, with no naturalistic associations.[190] They do not form inseparable associates in the Gāthās, for they are mentioned not only in lesser or bigger groups but also individually. They do not, again, exhaust the list of Gāthic abstractions, for one at least, *viz.*, *Sraosha* (Obedience to religious lore), is mentioned as often as Haurvatāt,[191] and another, *viz.*, *Ashi* (Recompense, Destiny), is closely associated with Armaiti. In fact, the similarity was so close that

[189] The references are to Ys. 45.7; 48.1; 46.11; 30.11; 31.20; 33.5, 8.—See Moulton, *Ear. Zor.*, p. 174; also p. 157. But see *Dr. Modi Mem. Vol.*, p. 233, for the Parsi belief.

[190] Dhalla, *Zor. Th.*, p. 26; see Moulton, *Tr. Mag.*, p. 22 f.

[191] See Moulton, *Ear. Zor.*, p. 97.

later writers had no scruple in forming a heptad,[192] adding to the list sometimes Ahura Mazdah himself and at other times Sraosha.[193] The only personification having naturalistic association was *Ātar* (Fire) which Zarathustra took over from the ancestral creed and this he converted into a religious symbol: we may even guess that the Zoroastrian belief recorded by Porphyry was both a mnemonic and a pun, namely, that Ahura Mazdah's body is like light or Fire (*ātar*)[194] and his soul like Truth (*arta*[195] = asha). The two other spirits recognised by Zoroaster are Ox-Soul (*Geush urvan*) and Ox-creator (*Geush tashan*); but they were probably created to provide a dramatic setting to the necessity of a new message of kindness to the dumb animals that are useful to man. In consonance with the spiritual interpretation of divine things, Heaven is described with a variety of spiritual epithets. It is indifferently called the region of Endless Light and Best Existence, the House of Song or Praise (Garo demāna = Garothmān = Garonmāna) and the House, Kingdom, Pasture or Glorious Heritage of Good Thought or the Kingdom of Blessings.[196] Quite in keeping with the spirit of the Prophet's teaching, therefore, is the later description of the three heavens as those of Good Thought, Good Word and Good Deed—the three ethical principles of Zarathustra himself—which lead to the

192 Moulton sees Babylonian influence in the raising of the number from six to seven by later writers.—See Moulton, *Ear. Zor.*, pp. 241, 99.

193 Jackson, *Zor. Stu.*, p. 45; C. de Harlez, *op. cit.*, p. 138 (In the post-Avestan Parsi books only six Amesha Spentas are mentioned). For later modifications of this number, see Dhalla, *Zor. Th.*, p. 226. For Jewish and Christian parallels, see Modi, *Religious Ceremonies and Customs of the Parsis*, p. 482; *Anthropological Papers*, p. 173 (where resemblance between Zoroastrianism, on the one hand, and Judaism, Christianity, Neo-Platonism and Gnosticism, on the other, regarding the theory of Seven Spirits, Powers or Archangels is pointed out).

194 It is interesting to note that when later on special worship was paid to the Amesha Spentas, they were regarded as descending to the oblation upon paths of light.—Jackson, *Zor. Stu.*, p. 47. *Cf. Devayāna* in Hinduism.

195 Dhalla says, " The name *asha*, as it is generally now pronounced, must certainly have been pronounced in ancient times as *arta* or *areta*, the latter variant being also found, and it is equivalent to the Vedic *ṛta*." (*Zor. Th.*, p. 30).

196 See Moulton, *Ear. Zor.*, p. 170 f. The materialisation of the heavens and hells belongs to the Pahlavi period.—See Dhalla, *Zor. Th.*, p. 196. Latterly Garothmān was regarded as reserved exclusively for Zoroastrians (*e.g.*, in *Artā Vīrāf Nāmak*).—see D. M. Madan, *op. cit.*, p. 30.

realm of Endless Light.[197] The Prophet dropped entirely the cult of the ancestors which, to judge from Vedic religion and the Gāthā Haptanghaiti,[198] must have been widely practised, and in its place substituted the conception of the man's own spiritual self (daenā) passing on to weal or woe[199]—a conception that was later on elaborated into the theory that the departed soul is greeted on arrival at the Bridge of the Separator by his own conscience and religion in the form of a fair youthful maiden in the case of the righteous[200] and in that of an old hag in the case of the unrighteous. All these go to prove that Zarathustra's reform was systematic and thorough in so far as it related to the spiritual transformation of material concepts. A similar transformation of the principle of Evil and the abode of the unrighteous completes the picture. The Daevas or diabolic spirits—the gods of the older religion worshipped with dark rites, could not be entirely banished; but the other satellites of Angra Mainyu are *Aka* (or *Achishta*) *Manah*, Evil or Worst Mind, *Druj*, Lie or Wickedness, *Aēshma*, Wrath or Violence, and also *Taromaiti*, Heresy. We have no doubts left that nothing short of a complete inwardisation of religion was the Prophet's objective even though he was obliged by circumstances to retain some of the material symbols of spiritual entities and acts.

This would dispose of all descriptions of the **physical** attributes of Ahura[201] and of the ethical personifications symbolised by the Amesha Spentas. Ahura is not surrounded like

197 Yt. 22.15; 3.3. It is interesting to note that Amitābha (Amida) of Japanese Buddhism signifies 'God of Boundless Light.' See Benveniste, *op. cit.*, pp. 96-7. For later belief, see Casartelli, *op. cit.*, p. 186 f.

198 Ys. 37.3.

199 See Moulton, *Ear. Zor.*, p. 264.

200 See Jackson, *The Ethics of Zoroastrianism*, in Sneath (Ed.), *Evolution of Ethics*, p. 148. This is supposed to have been materially conceived as a *houri* in Muhammadanism.—See Casartelli, *op. cit.*, p. 85.

201 No significance attaches to the Sassanian bas-relief at Naksh-i Rustam in which Auharmazd appears mounted on horseback.—See Casartelli, *op. cit.*, p. 27; Jackson, *Zor. Stu.*, p. 47; Söderblom, *op. cit.*, p. 194. See Geiger, *op. cit.*, I, Int., xxvi-xxviii.

There is a good deal of uncertainty about the winged figure of Persepolis before which Darius stands. Casartelli takes it as a representation of Ahura, but

Dyaus (Dyeus) by gods embodying the forces of nature—the sun, the moon, stars, wind, fire, earth, etc., but he is at the head of a number of moral hypostases.[202] The throne on which he is seated is not material or located in any spatial heaven or in the midst of any physical light.[203] The mouth or the tongue with which he speaks, the hands with which he distributes good and evil,[204] the eyes with which he sees all things, secret and open, and the garment (of firmament) which he wears are none of them physically understood; when not poetically regarded, they express some or other spiritual attribute or function of Ahura.[205] Similarly, his fatherhood of Vohu Manah and Armaiti [206] has no physical association about it, just as no sex-difference in the physical sense is intended to be conveyed when Asha Vahishta, Vohu Manah and Khshathra Vairya are later regarded as masculine (actually they are neuter nouns in the Gāthās), Armaiti as feminine, and Haurvatāt and Ameretāt feminine in grammatical declension but masculine as entities.[207]

How then were 'the Holy or Beneficent Immortal Ones,' the archangels or ministering angels of Ahura of later times, conceived by Zarathustra? Moulton remarks,[208] "In the world of thought Zarathushtra lives among qualities and attributes and principles which are as real to him as anything he can see, but never seem to need personification. But the ideal never obscures the real for him, and his communion with shadowy spiritual essences leaves him free to

Moulton considers it to be the Fravashi of Ahura even though the texts of the inscriptions nowhere refer to Fravashis.—See Moulton, *Ear. Zor.*, p. 260; Huart, *op. cit.*, pp. 81, 92. For later beliefs, see Dhalla, *Zor. Th.*, p. 220 f.

202 ERE. ix. 567, art. ORMAZD.

203 In the *Bundahishn* Auharmazd has a fixed residence in eternal or endless light which is a brilliant space; in the *Dinkart* the residence is created and therefore non-eternal.—See Casartelli, *op. cit.*, pp. 26, 27; Moulton, *Ear. Zor.*, p. 172

204 See quotation from *Shāyast lā Shāyast* (SBE, Ch. XV, 2) in Casartelli, *op. cit.*, p. 27 : " I am an intangible spirit," says Auharmazd, " it is not possible to hold me by the hand." See West, SBE, V, p. 372.

205 Dhalla, *Zor. Th.*, p. 20; Moulton, *Ear. Zor.*, p. 95.

206 Dhalla, *Zor. Th.*, p. 21. See C. de Harlez, *op. cit.*, pp. 135-6.

207 Moulton, *Ear. Zor.*, pp. 113-4; C. de Harlez, *op. cit.*, p. 139; Dhalla, *Zor. Th.*, p. 87.

208 Moulton, *Ear. Zor.*, p. 94; *Tr. Mag.*, p. 23; Geiger, *op. cit.*, I, Int., p. xxxiii f.

come down to cows and pastures without any sense of incongruity." But in regard to the Amesha Spentas the converse is almost true, *i.e.*, although only ideally distinguishable from the Wise Lord, they are invested with a semblance of personality sufficient for identification and invocation. To quote Moulton again:[209] "The Ahuras (*i.e.*, the Amesha Spentas and the other spirits mentioned above) are not really separate from Mazdah or subordinate to him: they seem to be essentially part of his own being, attributes of the Divine endowed with a vague measure of separate existence for the purpose of bringing out the truth for which they severally stand." Thus, while, on the one hand, the Prophet replaces Good Thought by 'Thy Thought' in addressing Mazdah, there are, on the other hand, at least two places (Ys. 30.9; 31.4) where Mazdah and the others bearing the title Ahura are invoked together—an association that was exegetically expanded into the Heptad (and even larger groupings) in later literature[210] just as an obscure Vedic passage would be expanded in the Purāṇas. In later times when Dualism had firmly established itself in the Mazdayasnian religion, Angra Mainyu was provided with a similar number of associates with qualities opposite to those of the archangels of Ahura Mazdah, and abstractions passed through personifications into personalities.[211]

The moral hypostases are interesting in so far as they throw light on Zarathustra's conception of the essential conditions of a religious life. The six Amesha Spentas fall into two groups, one representing what Mazdah *is* and the other what he *gives*. Good Thought, Right and Dominion belong

[209] Moulton, *Ear. Zor.*, p. 97; see pp. 100, 293; *Tr. Mag.*, p. 21 f; C. de Harlez, *op. cit.*, p. 137. See *Tr. Mag.*, p. 24: Asha and Vohu Manah are not archangels at all, but Divine attributes within the hypostasis of Deity.

[210] Not even consistently there. See C. de Harlez, *op. cit.*, p. 138. Jackson points out that to the six Amesha Spentas are added at different times Ahura Mazdah, Sraosha, Ātar, Gōshūrvan, Ashi Vañuhi, Airyaman, "Spirit of Wisdom," 24 more (making a total of 30) who preside over the days of the month or 27 more, making a total of 33, which is the number of the lords of the spiritual order (*ratus*) mentioned in Ys. 1.10, and, curiously enough, of the Vedic gods also in some enumerations.—See Haug, *op. cit.*, pp. 275-6; Mills, SBE, XXXI, p. 198, f.n. 7.

[211] The Host of Heaven and the Legions of Hell were finally ranged on opposite sides as follows:—

to the Lord while he bestows on his devotees Devotion, Welfare and Immortality;[212] but we must assume that the gifts are also a part of his beneficent nature and represent the aspects of his holiness which prompt devotion, his interest in the material wealth and welfare of his followers, and his solicitude for the good of his creatures' souls.[213] Zarathustra considered all ethical and spiritual propriety to be summed up in Right or Truth (Asha) and all evil in the Lie (Druj): in the Prophet's eye Asha is probably more important than Vohu Manah (who is however more frequently mentioned in the Gāthās and assumes pre-eminence in later literature) and Lie is far more prominent an adversary than Evil Spirit.[214] The Amesha Spentas represent, in fact, both divine attributes and conditions of human perfection: good mind, uprightness, devotion, conquest over evil, health and prosperity (and obedience to religious prescription) are the necessary elements of that spiritual life which culminates in

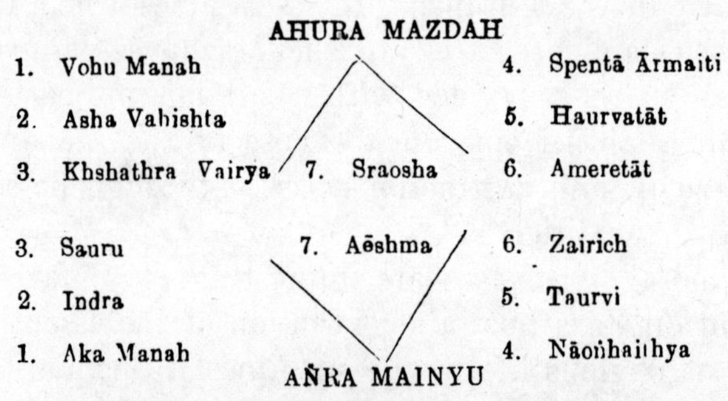


The Spirits with the same number are opposed to each other.—See Jackson, *Zor. Stu.*, p. 46, 85; Moulton, *Ear. Zor.*, p. 113 f. See also Casartelli, *op. cit.*, pp. 75, 89-92; Dhalla, *Zor. Th.*, pp. 257, 264.

212 Ys. 47.1; Vd. xix. 43. See Moulton, *Ear. Zor.*, p. 114. Apparently even the soul had to depend upon Ahura for its immortality. See Kanga, *The Spenta Mainyu in the Gathas*, in *Dr. Modi Mem. Vol.*, p. 229 f: he thinks that Spenta Mainyu is a kind of mediator between God and man and eternal life comes through him alone just as in Christianity it comes through the Divine Spirit and the Son of God.

213 Moulton, *Ear. Zor.*, pp. 293-5. See the comparison between Judaism and Parsism there; see also *Tr. Mag.*, p. 25.

214 C. de Harlez, *op. cit.*, p. 137. See Moulton, *Ear. Zor.*, p. 111: The priority of Asha over Vohumanah in the Gathas is not at all explicit. It may perhaps rest on the idea that Asha is more inclusive, representing Mazdah's action, creation and law, and not only the "Thought" that inspires it. But

human immortality. To him that hath more shall be given: a person striving to possess these essential conditions of religious life is assisted, as it were, by the corresponding ministering angels of Ahura Mazdah in the task. "Piety pleads with the spirit in which there is wavering."[215] The Prophet must have created these ethical entities in order to divert men's minds away from the more prominent lower gods with special domains of their own whom they were wont to worship and to satisfy at one and the same time the craving for plurality within the nature of God and the need of maintaining His unity.[216] The measure of his success is to be judged not by the recrudescence of the suppressed nature-worship as soon as his reforming hand was removed but by the solicitude displayed by his successors to prove that the elements of nature were under the guardianship or leadership of these ethical principles, by the fact that the original functions of many of the revived Indo-Iranian deities were totally forgotten during the period of reformation and these reappeared either as gods with different meanings or as demons possessing hostile qualities,[217] and also by the fact that new deities had to be locally invented or absorbed from foreign cults to fill an

*Vohumanah* is comprehensive enough. He is the Thought of God, and of every good man......He comes very near Mazdah's "Spirit," for once (Ys. 33.6) we actually find "Good Sprit" replacing "Good Thought."' But see *ibid.*, p. 121.

See also *ibid.*, pp. 130-1: 'The supremacy of Truth among the virtues was as conspicuous for the settled agriculturists of Eastern Iran as for Darius and his Persians in the West; and Zarathushtra was following the strongest element in the national character when he concentrated all evil into the figure of Falsehood, *Druj*, the antagonist of Asha, "Truth" or "Right."' See *ibid.*, p. 397, the quotation from Herodotus: "Most disgraceful of all is lying accounted, and next to this to be in debt." See *Tr. Mag.*, p. 21; Jackson, *Zor. Stu.*, pp. 43-5 (the order of frequency is Vohu Manah, Asha Vahishta, Khshathra Vairya, Spentā Ārmaiti, Haurvatāt, Ameretāt). See Taraporewala, *op. cit.*, Ch. III. The Path of Asha, esp. p. 46: "Through the best *Asha*, through the highest *Asha*, may we catch sight of Thee (Ahura), may we approach Thee, may we be in perfect union with Thee!"

215 Ys. 31.12.

216 Moulton, *Tr. Mag.*, p. 24.

217 See Haug, *op. cit.*, pp. 272-9; Moulton, *Tr. Mag.*, p. 88. Further changes took place during the Sassanian revival, *e.g.*, of Mithra.—See Casartelli, *op. cit.*, p. 79. An interesting change is in the meaning of Apām Napāt of the Vedas into the name of a locality in Yt. 5.72; 8.4.—See C. de Harlez, *op. cit.*, p. 166; also Darmesteter, SBE, XXIII, p. 6, n.1.

impoverished pantheon. This probably explains why "mythological synonyms," which are so frequent in the Vedas, are almost absent in the revived pantheon of the Iranian religion—it was expanded just enough to meet pressing needs but the mythology was never so prolific as in India although a few ancient myths and some new ones, with occasional variants, made their appearance. Even these were mostly connected with cosmogony and legendary heroism [218] and not, as in India, devised to embellish the tales of gods and demons in their family histories and their feuds, fancies and friendships. C. de Harlez rightly remarks, "The Avestan mythology is throughout earnest, rigid and ethical in tone. There is here no exuberance of imagination, no erotic adventures nor divine progeny. Everything is linked up with the struggle of life against death, of good against evil." [219]

---

218 See *Indo-Iranian Studies* (*Sanjana Comm. Vol.*), p. 203 f. : *Iran's Primeval Heroes and the Myth of the First Man* by A. J. Carnoy. Wilson in *Parsi Religion*, p. 587 f, gives an abstract of the Historical Legends of Persia (see Appendix I).

219 C. de Harlez, *op. cit.*, p. 145. See also Dhalla, *Zoroastrian Civilisation* Ch. VI.

# CHAPTER X

## God in Zoroastrianism : Post-gathic

The later history of Zoroastrianism shows that the purity of the Iranian Prophet's reform was less lasting than that of the Prophet of Arabia. Possibly this is due to the fact that he had to contend against more formidable difficulties. The Aryan pantheon was much fuller and more spiritually conceived than that of the pre-Islāmic religion of the Arabian desert, and possibly there were schools of traditionalists, poets and priests in Iran who could conserve the ancient beliefs and practices much better than the Arabian poets and the keepers of the Ka'ba and who probably outlived Zoroaster's puny successors in the task of continuing the reform.[1] The environment, again, was more favourable in Arabia than in Iran; for in the latter there was nothing corresponding to the monotheistic communities of the Jews and the Christians of Arabia, and the surrounding nations, Semitic, Aryan and nomadic, were overwhelmingly polytheistic. Then, again, political supremacy favoured a firmer foundation of Muhammadanism, and the political head being also the head of the infant Church, religious persuasion and political coercion could go hand in hand in Islām's career of conquest. An idea of what Zoroastrianism, which was not exactly a tolerant religion,[2] might have been if more powerful state-support than that of the court of Vishtāspa

[1] See Moulton, *Ear. Zor.*, p. 301, where a distinction is drawn between Moses and Zoroaster. The word Irān is a corrupted form of Aryan.

[2] "The *Dinkart* upholds the divine right of kings and states that if the temporal power of the glorious king Jamshid had been blended with the spiritual power of the supreme priest Zoroaster, the Evil Spirit would have lain low long ere this, and the Kingdom of Righteousness would have been established on earth once and for ever."—Dhalla, *Zor. Th.*, p. 192.

It also sanctions the use of force for the conversion of the aliens.—*Ibid.*, p. 198.

The alien faiths were branded as the promptings of the Evil Spirit, and were declared to be teaching a vile law, opposed to the pure law of Mazda.—*Ibid.*, p. 199. (See Ch. XXIII).

had been available at the inception of the reform, can be formed if we refer to what it did become under the Sassanids when Zoroastrianism became the state religion, was purged of some of its excrescences, and put down the schismatic movements of Mānī and Mazdak.[3] What actually happened after Zoroastrian reform, however, was that ancient beliefs and practices were driven underground in localities where the reforming party was in power and the counter-reformation began as soon as circumstances became favourable. Not only did such old beliefs as survived return in their original form or as modified by lapse of memory, absorption of foreign materials,[4] and the Prophet's reform, but, as in Buddhism, Christianity and Muhammadanism, the Prophet himself became the locus of a new cult and distance of time and space only served to magnify his spiritual proportions and miraculous powers.[5] In the absence of any local Aryan scriptures of the type of the Vedas[6] we are unable to reconstruct the religious life of pre-Zoroastrian Iran with absolute certainty and our only guides in this matter are the kindred Vedic literature and such survivals as are recorded in the extant Iranian literary works and inscriptions. It is, therefore, likely that, as Moulton observes,[7] " the Yashts,

Seceders were persecuted and apostasy was made a capital crime by the Zoroastrian Church. See Dhalla, *Zor. Th.*, p. 201. See also Huart, *op. cit.*, pp. 154, 159.

3 Casartelli points out that even then separate tendencies could be distinguished in the classical treatises of the period.—*Op. cit.*, p. 3. For Mani and Mazdak, see Huart, *op. cit.*, pp. 177-84.

4 See Moulton, *Ear. Zor.*, p. 201 (West and South Iranian star-cult), 238-43; Benveniste, *op. cit.*, p. 11.

5 To quote Dhalla's words (*Zor. Th.*, p. 195) : " Zoroaster is a historical personage in the Gathas. In the later Avesta he is surrounded by an aureole, and becomes superhuman; but in the Pahlavi works his personality is enshrouded by miracles, and he is transformed into a myth." See Geiger, *op. cit.*, II, App. I. *Gushtāsp and Zoroaster* by Spiegel (esp. p. 195 f.).

6 We should remember that even the Avestan script has not been recovered—the Avesta we possess is in Pahlavi script written from right to left.—See art. AVESTA in ERE.

7 Moulton, *Ear. Zor.*, p. 182; *Dic. Bib.*, IV, p. 988; Benveniste, *op. cit.*, p. 20 f. Dhalla dissents from this view : " It seems to us that we tread a very delicate path when we set aside as non-Zoroastrian all that does not appear in the Gathas." (*Zor. Th.*, p. 77.)

and kindred parts of the Avesta, represent with tolerable exactness the unreformed Iranian religion " and " they are posterior to Zarathushtra in time but not in matter."

It is evident that the Prophetic reform had overshot its mark—the people at large were not yet ready for the disappearance of so many age-long beliefs and practices. Just as in India the absolutistic Upaniṣadic speculations became theistic towards the end and were then mellowed down further by the infusion of a new polytheism of the monarchical type, so also in Iran the earlier attempts to bring the Prophet's abstractions into relation with the physical world were followed by the re-introduction of much of the older polytheism and demonology. The method adopted originally was probably, as in India, exegetic—the writers professed to do nothing more than systematise the Prophet's utterances and draw out the implications of his teachings; and, as often happens, this probably led to some amount of tampering with the sacred texts to make desirable interpretation and elaboration possible. In this fashion, the Amesha Spentas, the Fravashis, the sacred drink, oblations in the Fire, the Yazatas that rule different realms of being, abstract and concrete, and personifications of the requisites of ritual and magical formulae made their appearance.[8] The distinction between this later Zoroastrianism and Vedicism is noticeable in one important particular, namely, that Ahura Mazdah continued to be the one Lord over all and the lesser spirits were regarded as performing their functions under his supremacy and direction;[9] otherwise people in Iran invoked these archangels (Amesha Spentas or Amshaspands) and angels (Yazatas, Yazads or Izads)[10] for boons with sacrifices, pretty much as the Vedic people invoked the gods in India. As Moulton says,[11] " The monotheistic theology is preserved, but it can hardly be said that monotheistic religion remains."

8 Moulton, *Tr. Mag.*, pp. 88, 90.

9 Subject to rare lapses noticed below. See Moulton, *Tr. Mag.*, pp. 85-7.

10 Casartelli disapproves of the use of the words ' archangel ' and ' angel ' for Ameshospands and Yazatas.—See *Op. cit.* p. 75.

11 Moulton, *Tr. Mag.*, p. 100

And we should add, dualism became more prominent with Ahriman acquiring a more pronounced individuality and independence and spoiling the work of Ormazd by his counter-creations in every realm of being. C. de Harlez correctly describes the development of Zoroastrianism when he says[12] that "the Monotheistic tendencies predominate in the Gāthās, dualism in the Vendidad, naturalism in the Yasna and the revivified cult of the spirits in the Yashts."

Apparently, the return of the nature-gods was mediated by the association established between the ethical attributes of Ahura and certain elements of the physical world with the help of obscure Gāthic passages or of the ordinary laws of cause and effect. Possibly the political conditions were still unfavourable for a direct return to nature-worship and it is not improbable that Zoroastrian intolerance was responsible for the disappearance of the class which could reinstate the suppressed beliefs and practices in their purity and entirety. In every period of religious or social reform the hand of oppression falls most heavily on the priestly class as being the conservers and custodians of ancient wisdom : we may very well suppose that the suppression of the older priestly class by the reformers is responsible for the loss of much of the Aryan tradition in Iran as compared with India where the Upaniṣadic seers did not care much about the type of God the people worshipped (although most of them looked upon the sacrificial cult with disfavour) and were not sufficiently interested in social welfare to seek political aid to enforce their own spiritual views on the people at large. So it happened in Iran that during the period of counter-reformation some of the older Indo-Iranian gods lost their original functions, if not actually degraded into demons, while others —possibly those who had at one time a strong local support and lingered in popular memory—not only recovered their functions but possibly had an extension of their dominion.[13]

12 C. de Harlez, *op. cit.*, p. 122; see Moulton, *Tr. Mag.*, p. 64.
13 See Dhalla, *Zor. Th.*, p. 97.

Later Zoroastrianism remained true to the Prophet's teaching in the sense that it always strove to maintain the supremacy of Ormazd[14] and the superiority (at least in theory, if not always in practice)[15] of the personified abstractions which in the Gāthā Haptanghaiti received the collective name of the Amesha Spentas (Immortal Beneficent Ones). But, by extending the pantheon with the Yazatas (the Adorable Ones) and the Fravashis (the Guardian Angels) and treating them practically as lower gods, it seriously threatened the Prophet's monotheism and in fact tended to view spiritual powers in an anthropomorphic fashion. Thus, while in the Gāthās Ahura Mazdah is most spiritually conceived and the various qualities serve, like so many facets of a single diamond, to indicate his single spiritual nature, in the younger Avestan religion these divine attributes are not only independently, though subordinately, conceived but are assigned distinct elements of nature as their special domains.[16] In this way Vohu Manah, conceived by the Prophet to represent Wisdom and Spiritual Enlightenment as gifts of God,[17]

[14] Except that he is occasionally represented as worshipping some of the Yazatas (see below).

[15] Casartelli, *op. cit.*, p. 76.

[16] Söderblom, *op. cit.*, p. 190. Moulton thinks that the Ameshospands survived Zarathushtra only in name.—*Tr. Mag.*, p. 79. Benveniste thinks that their abstract names are certainly Zoroastrian in origin but that each of them has taken the place of a formerly deified element whose name was abolished (*op. cit.*, p. 83). In Shāyast lā-Shāyast, Ch. XV, 4 (SBE. V, p. 373), it is said that Auharmazd and the Archangels each produced his (or her) own creation.

[17] The first of Ahura Mazda's creation was Vohu Mano, "Good Mind" (both good intelligence and good moral sense), in consultation with whom he produced all his other creatures, just as in the Old Testament (Prov. 8) Wisdom is the first creation of Jehovah, and stood beside him as master-builder when God established the heavens and the earth. What is said of Vohu Mano in the Gathas is sometimes strikingly similar to what Philo says about the Logos. Darmesteter was led by this resemblance, among other things, to think that the Gathas (which he regarded not as the oldest part of the Avesta, but as comparatively recent) were directly influenced by Jewish Alexandrian philosophy.—G. F. Moore, *History of Religions*, I, p. 381. This theory fell practically still-born, and no Iranist of repute accepts it, for notices of the Gathic religion are older than Philo by some centuries. See Moulton, *Ear. Zor.*, p. 9 f.; *Tr. Mag.*, p. 6 Söderblom, *op. cit.*, p 191. For Wisdom and its relation to Divine creation in the *Mainyo-i Khard*, see Casartelli, *op. cit.*, p. 34 f.; for Vohuman, see p. 44 f.

becomes, by virtue of certain stray associations with cattle in the Gāthās,[18] the patron deity of cattle in later literature.[19] Asha Vahishta, who represents Divine Righteousness or the Divine Law of Harmony in individual and social life, becomes, through similar Gāthic association,[20] the lord of fire or light.[21] Khshathra Vairya, Divine Rule and Beneficence, comes to be regarded as the lord of metals,[22] probably through association with the Molten Metal which would finally establish the kingdom of righteousness.[23] Ārmaiti, Holy Skill, Piety or the devotional counterpart of Righteousness,[24] becomes the presiding spirit of earth which provides pasture to cattle[25] and gives continued life and indestructibility to the bodies of the righteous.[26] Haurvatāt, Welfare or Perfection that comes from physical vigour and endurance and a sense of righteous and joyful living,[27] becomes the genius of water,[28] and Ameretāt or Immortality, which

18 Ys. 29.7, 8; 31.10; 47.3.

19 See Dhalla, *Zor. Th.*, p. 29; Jackson, *Zor. Stu.*, p. 49; C. de Harlez, *op. cit.*, p. 140.

20 Ys. 34.4; 43.9; 46.7; 31.3. For other references, see Dhalla, *Zor. Th.*, p. 43 (under ATAR).

21 Dhalla, *Zor. Th.*, p. 35; Jackson, *Zor. Stu.*, p. 49; C. de Harlez, *op. cit.*, p. 141. So also Agni and Ṛta in the Vedas.—See Lommel, *Some Corresponding Conceptions in Old India and Iran* in *Dr. Modi Mem. Vol.*, p. 262.

22 Dhalla, *Zor. Th.*, p. 37; Jackson, *Zor. Stu.*, p. 50; C. de Harlez, *op. cit.*, p. 142; Moulton, *Ear. Zor.*, pp. 111-2.

23 Ys. 30.7; 32.7; 51.9. See Moulton, *Ear. Zor.*, p. 157.

24 Dhalla, *Zor. Th.*, p. 37 f.; Jackson, *Zor. Stu.*, p. 50; C. de Harlez, *op. cit.*, p. 142.

25 Ys. 47.3.

26 Ys. 30.7. See Moulton, *Ear. Zor.*, p. 350, f.n.4. He associates the word with Arā mātā, Earth Mother (*Ear. Zor.*, p. 112). The difficulty is that the Vedas know both Mother Earth and Aramati; the confusion would then be pre-Zoroastrian. " This presumes burial as practised by the Iranians, and notably by the Achaemenian kings."

Söderblom thinks that Zarathushtra saw in the earth a symbol of resignation, piety and devotion (*op. cit.*, p. 201). For resurrection of the body, see Dhalla, *Zor. Th.*, p. 289.

27 Dhalla, *Zor. Th.*, p. 40; Jackson, *op. cit.*, p. 51; C. de Harlez, *op. cit.*, p. 142.

28 Dhalla, *Zor. Th.*, p. 41; Jackson, *Zor Stu.*, p. 52; C. de Harlez, *op. cit.*, p. 143.

stands for the deathlessness and felicific reward of the blessed in Paradise,[29] is set over plants,[30] possibly on the basis of a Gāthic passage which mentions them all together [31] and of another which declares them to be for sustenance (possibly ambrosia and nectar).[32] Thus, out of the Prophet's spiritual message, posterity managed to get the presiding geniuses of earth, water, fire, plants and animals and also of metals. In no time were the other realms also provided with appropriate spirits and in fact duplicates were in some cases also supplied,[33] and even dual divinities.[34] We have it from Herodotus that the Persians worshipped the vault of the Sky, Sun, Moon, Earth, Fire, Water and Winds and also the Assyrian (and Arabian) Mylitta (Anāhita), corresponding to the Greek Aphrodite (Venus), which Herodotus identifies by mistake with Mitra—a true enough picture of the unreformed religion of Iran to which Zoroastrianism almost completely reverted in popular worship.[35]

When once the flood-gates were opened it was difficult to stem the tide of new intrusions into Zarathustra's spiritual monotheism. It seemed as if the abstract and the ethical were in some danger of being swept away by the concrete and the material. The secondary associations also began to encroach upon and replace the primary meanings, and this led to the personification of the ordinary objects and attributes

29 Dhalla, *Zor. Th.*, p. 40; Jackson, *Zor. Stu.*, p. 51; C. de Harlez, *op. cit.*, p. 143.

30 Dhalla, *Zor. Th.*, p. 41; Jackson, *Zor. Stu.*, p. 52; C. de Harlez, *op. cit.*, p. 143.

31 Ys. 51.7.

32 Ys. 34.11. See Dhalla, *Zor. Th.*, p. 40; Moulton, *Ear. Zor.*, p. 363, n.l.

33 Asha Vahishta and Ātar for fire (possibly the one was the transcendent and the other the immanent spirit of fire); Apam Napāt (retained in Ābān Yasht) and Ardvī Sūrā Anāhitā; Armaiti and Zam.

34 " The more prominent of the dual divinities are Ahura-Mithra (corresponding to the Mitra-Varuna of the Vedas), Hvarekhshaeta-Mithra, Mithra-Rashnu, Mithra-Raman, Rashnu-Arshtat, Raman-Vayu, Daena-Chisti, Ashi Vanghuhi-Pārendi and Asman-Zamyat."—Dhalla, *Zor. Th.*, p. 99.

35 See Moulton, *Ear. Zor.*, pp. 391-4, with footnotes; Benveniste, *op. cit.*, p. 26; Ys. 38 and 42.3. For the derivation of Anāhitā, see Moulton, *Ear. Zor.*, p. 238; Benveniste, *op. cit.*, p. 62 f.

of the Gāthās into angelic beings.[36] For contemplation of Divine attributes there was substituted the remembrance of Divine names[37] and, as in India, the magic of manthra (*mantra*) often came to be regarded as more potent than faith in Divine grace and omnipotence.[38] Though higher in the spiritual hierarchy, the Amesha Spentas begin, in fact, to be outshone by the Yazatas, and, as Dhalla remarks,[39] " the angels Anāhita and Tishtrya, Mithra and Verethraghna figure more prominently[40] than the archangels Vohu Manah and Asha Vahishta, Armaiti and Ameretāt," and some of them appropriate the longest rolls of praise. The Fravashis,[41] again, make their appearance in the Avestan religion for the first time, although it is not unlikely that the introduction was facilitated by the Prophet's reference to the soul of the Ox (and of the Kine) laying before the Heavenly throne its woes on earth and to his own self being chosen to succour it in distress.[42]

We have in the worship of the Fravashis the revival of that cult of ancestor-worship which is such a prominent feature of the Hindu religion from Vedic times[43] and which

36 Dhalla, *Zor. Th.*, p. 76. He quotes as illustrations Daena, Chisti, Mithra, Raman, Rata, Manthra, Airyaman, Asha, Hvare, Maonghah, Asman, Ushah, Atar and Zam. See also p. 196.

D. M. Madan in his *Discourses on Iranian Literature* (p. 4 f.) dissociates himself from the view that the Yazads and Amshāspends are personal entities (angels and archangels)—he considers them to be either abstract qualities or material objects personified.

37 See Ormazd Yasht (Yt. 1).

38 Dhalla, *Zor. Th.*, p. 76.

39 *Ibid.*, p. 78.

40 Dhalla makes a guarded statement about their recognition by Zoroaster (*Zor. Th.*, p. 78) while Moulton rejects them *in toto* as objects of Zoroaster's veneration. (*Tr. Mag.*, p. 85 f.).

41 Dr. Modi defines Fravashi as " that power or spiritual essence in a substance which enables it to grow." " Fravashi is a spirit, a guardian spirit, inherent in everything, animate or inanimate, which protects it from decay and enables it to grow, flourish and prosper " (*Religious Ceremonies and Customs of the Parsis*, p. 409).

D. M. Madan thinks that the translation of Fravashi by guardian spirit or guiding spirit is wrong: it ought to mean the individuality that makes the world progress or advance (*op. cit.*, p. 10).

42 Ys. 29.

43 See Barth, *Religions of India*, p. 22 f.; Dhalla, *Zor. Th.*, Ch. XV; Geiger, *op. cit.*, I, p. 112 f.

must have been a feature of Iranian religion also, judging by the early re-appearance of the belief after the Gāthic period was over.[44] If this were so, then, Moulton thinks,[45] the conception of the *daenā* or self, the totality of one's ethical individuality (as distinguished from the *urvan* or soul, the principle of conscious personality), was "Zarathushtra's deliberate substitute for the fravashi" and hence, characteristically enough, the daenā belonged to the righteous and the wicked alike while the fravashi belonged to the righteous alone.[46] It is in their capacity as the souls of ancestors that the fravashis took interest in their living descendants, were invoked and worshipped during the last ten days of the year including the five intercalary days (the *Muktād*), and had the month immediately following (*i.e.*, the first month of the year) and also the 19th day of each month dedicated to them;[47] in return for such acts of filial piety they blessed the house and promoted birth in the family[48]

[44] Ys. 37.3.

[45] Moulton, *Ear. Zor.*, p. 264; *Tr. Mag.*, pp. 36-7.

[46] In Yt. 13.155 the five 'souls' or spiritual elements of a man are the vitality, the self, the perception, the soul and the Fravashi (Moulton, *Ear. Zor.*, p. 256 with fn. 2), or the spirit, conscience, perception, soul and Fravashi (Darmesteter, SBÉ. XXIII, p. 230). See also C. de Harlez, *op. cit.*, 193, for the later grouping from the *Great Bundehesh;* also Jackson, *Zor. Stu.*, p. 123. For the distinction between soul (urvan or Ravān) and guiding spirit (Fravashi), see Modi, *Rel. Cer. and Cus. of the Parsis*, p. 416 f. By the end of the Pahlavi period both of these spiritual faculties, namely, the soul and the Farohar, came to be considered as one and the same.—Dhalla, *Zor. Th.*, p. 245. For the modern reform movement to keep up the distinction and to stop intercessory prayers for the dead, see Dhalla, *Zor. Th.*, pp. 347-8. Söderblom questions Moulton's distinction between the daena and the fravashi as above. See Moulton, *Ear. Zor.*, p. 259; Casartelli, *op. cit.*, p. 85; Geiger, *op. cit.*, I, p. 124 with fn. 2.

[47] Moulton, *Ear. Zor.*, pp. 257, 261; *Tr. Mag.*, pp. 169, 179; ERE. vi. 117; Dhalla, *Zor. Th.*, p. 148; C. de Harlez, *op. cit.*, p. 187; Jackson, *Zor. Stu.*, p. 60; ERE. i. 455; Modi, *Rel. Cer. and Cus. of the Parsis*, pp. 423 f, 466 f.

The period is called Hamaspathmaēdaya, when man was supposed to have been created by God, the order of creation being the heavens, water, earth, vegetable creation, animal creation and man, to each of which a Gāhambār or seasonal festival of five days is dedicated (Modi, *op. cit.*, p. 448). The Fravashis of the dead are offered cakes of meat and flour (*myazda*) in the funeral ceremony called the *āfringān* (homage) and there is a ceremonial partaking of the same by those present and qualified to take them. For the ceremony, see Modi, *op. cit.*, p. 391 f. For the *gāhanbārs*, see ERE. iii. 129.

[48] See Moulton, *Ear. Zor.*, p. 270, for references. Yt. 13.5, 15, 150, 157; Dhalla, *Zor. Th.*, p. 148 (the Fravashis are dreadful when offended).

and also increased the means of their sustenance, namely, plants and waters.[49] But other strands of thought also entered into this fravashi-idea. The fravashis came to be looked upon not only as the beneficent souls of the departed good but also as the guardian angels or protective genii of individuals and societies—an extension of function to be found in the doctrine of saints in Christianity and of *welis* in Islām.[50] But their beneficent activity ranges over wide realms. To quote Moulton:[51] "They are essential for promoting birth: they nourish animals and men, waters and plants; they guard sun, moon and stars: they are constantly present in battle as givers of victory: they watch over the Lake,[52] the stars of the Great Bear, the body of the sleeping Keresāspa,[53] and the seed of Zarathushtra, in preparation for the final Renewal. In time of drought they vie with each other to procure water from Vourukasha, each for his own house, clan or district." Naturally, the Fravashis began to be regarded not merely as the departed souls of dead ancestors but also as the spirits of the glorious dead, of the past heroes of the Iranian world. In the Farvardin Yasht a list of some of the secular and spiritual heroes, who had at any time advanced the cause of the Zoroastrian faith, is to be found.[54]

It is not improbable that the magnitude of the task involved led to a dissociation of the Fravashis into two different groups. The Fravashis as the souls of the departed had to be invested with powers out of all proportion to their

49 Moulton, *Ear. Zor.*, pp. 271, 277-8. See Ys. 44.4.

50 Moulton, *Ear. Zor.*, p. 279; C. de Harlez, *op. cit.*, p. 188. For the order of precedence among the Fravashis, see Yt. 13.17 (see Moulton, *Tr. Mag.*, p. 102).

51 Moulton, *Ear. Zor.*, p. 278: see Dhalla, *Zor. Th.*, pp. 145-7: *Spiegel Memorial Volume*, p. 197 f.

52 Lake Kansaoya in which the seed of Zarathustra is miraculously preserved till the time of Saoshyant's conception. See Moulton, *Ear. Zor.*, p. 89; also Jackson, *Zoroaster*, p. 21.

53 The mythical hero who was not admitted into heaven for being a party to the quenching of fire, but whose body would be raised from the dead by Sraosha and Nairyosangha in order that he might slay Azhi Dahaka on the eve of the final Renovation. See Dhalla, *Zor. Th.*, p. 288; Moulton, *Ear. Zor.*, p. 176; also *The Legend of Keresāspa* in *Spiegel Memorial Volume*, pp. 93-8.

54 C. de Harlez, *op. cit.*, pp. 191-2; Geiger, *op. cit.*, I, p. 116 f.

capacities when embodied on earth as men and they were also required to protect beings and domains with which as men they could not have had any tangible relation. Almost as a matter of necessity, therefore, there was evolved the idea of Fravashis of the elements and of the non-human world of life—of the sky, water, the earth and fire, of plants and cattle, and, in fact, of the entire creation of the good spirit;[55] the innumerable and unnumbered stars that are visible were regarded in some later literature as the fravashis of the terrestrial worlds, for every creature and creation.[56] But once the view was accepted that every creature must have a guardian angel it was difficult to exclude any inmate of the spiritual world from the operation of this fancy. So the theory was propounded that even the Yazatas and the Amesha Spentas—nay, even such abstract entities as Manthra, the community taken as a collective whole, and creation in general had fravashis of their own.[57] And the climax was reached when even Ahura Mazdah himself was furnished with a Fravashi of his own,[58]—the only entity not possessing a

55 C. de Harlez considers them to be only poetic fancies and not as seriously intended (*op. cit.*, p. 191). See Moulton, *Ear. Zor.*, p. 262; Dhalla, *Zor. Th.*, p. 144; Modi, *op. cit.*, p. 411.

According to the Avesta, all natural objects have their Fravashis, but not the objects that have been made from these natural objects. One is reminded in this connection of the Platonic discussion about the types of objects that have Ideas (and also of the 'patterns' of the Bible). See Modi, *op. cit.*, p. 412, 414.

56 All the named stars are ordinary stars; others are Fravashis; moreover the named constellations themselves have Fravashis.—C. de Harlez, *op. cit.*, pp. 194-6; also Casartelli, *op. cit.*, p. 86; Moulton, *Ear. Zor.*, p. 281; Geiger, *op. cit.*, I, p. 119. Casartelli points out (*Op. cit.*, p. 86): "We no longer find in the Pehlevi books the *fravāhars* of Auharmazd and other celestial spirits. On the other hand we still meet with the fravāhars of animals and inanimate objects, as the earth, cattle, trees and waters, and they are mixed up with those of the pious in paradise" (See also C. de Harlez, *op. cit.*, p. 196).

57 Moulton, *Ear. Zor.*, p. 274; ERE. vi. 118 (fravashis of house, family, clan, district); C. de Harlez, *op. cit.*, p. 191. Moulton compares the Fravashi attached to a community with the "princes" of nations in the Book of Daniel and the "angels of the churches" in the Apocalypse (*loc. cit.*). See *Dic. Bib.* IV, p. 991. For comparison with the Roman manes, see Modi, *op. cit.*, p. 426, n. 2. See Ys. 19.18. See also Moulton, *The Teaching of Zarathushtra*, p. 38.

58 See Moulton, *Ear. Zor.*, p. 275; *Tr. Mag.*, p. 103; Yt. 13.80; Ys. 23.2; 26.2. 7. Moulton suggests that the figure in the Persepolis bas-relief is not of Ahura but of his Fravashi (*Ear. Zor.*, p. 260). In this case possibly the Fravashi is not a guardian angel but a double (see Moulton, *Ear. Zor.*, p. 266, for the mean-

fravashi being Spenta Mainyu, presumably because at the time Ahura Mazdah came to possess a fravashi Spenta Mainyu had been identified with him and did not need a separate fravashi for himself.[59]

Reference has already been made to the heavenly synod where the aggrieved soul of the ox was offered consolation by the promise of sending down Zarathustra who was present there, and also to the belief that in due time the saviours of the world would appear to rout the forces of evil. This led to the development of the idea that not only the dead and the living but also the unborn have fravashis; in other words, the souls of beings were invested with pre-existence as well as immortality,[60] and this ante-mundane existence assimilated them still further to the archangels and angels and established their right to the reverence of men. Thus, we are told that not only do they help men as their special protectors all through their lives, admonishing them through their intelligence and their conscience and carrying their prayers to God and His gifts to them, but they return to heaven when life has been well lived and thence continue their protective activity to the succeeding generations also.[61] Now, it is this element of pre-existence that was later expanded into the idea that for the first three thousand years of the world's history the Fravashis had only a spiritual existence in heaven[62] and that it is only when Angra Mainyu invaded the dominion of Ahura Mazdah that they volunteered to fight the Evil Spirit in order to obtain care-free immortality at the Renovation. The informed reader will at once remember the Platonic theory of the souls or essences of things existing in the world

ing of Genius; also Modi, *op. cit.*, pp. 418-9). See Moulton, *The Teaching of Zarathushtra*, p. 95.

59 Dhalla, *Zor. Th.*, p. 85.

60 Modi, *op. cit.*, p. 416 f. See Jackson, *Zoroaster*, p. 23; also *Spiegel Memorial Volume*, pp. 99-106.

61 It should be remembered that a man could invoke the aid of other fravashis also although he was supposed to be under the special protection of one fravashi.—See ERE. vi. 117. As to the ultimate destiny of the fravashis of those who had not lived well it is difficult to get an exact answer. The *Sad-dar Bundahish* (and al-Biruni) consigned them to hell.—See ERE. vi. 117.

62 See ERE. i. 205; vi. 117.

of Ideas before incarnating themselves (and the resemblance becomes closer when we find that both Platonism and later Zoroastrianism placed each soul in his own star); but it is doubtful if Zoroastrianism ever seriously contended for the eternity of the Fravashis since that would take them out of the creative activity of Ahura Mazdah.[63]

But it is easier to multiply entities than to assign to them proper functions. We may very well believe that the puritans of the faith did not take kindly to these innovations and that the more they ignored these creations (or revivals) the more zeal did the counter-reformationists show to prove their reality and power. Judging by parallels from other religions, specially from Hinduism, we may almost take it for granted that the mediating spirits like the Amshaspands and the Fravashis and the departmental deities like the Yazatas served to bring God nearer the hearts and homes of men and to introduce a sense of sanctification of their surroundings much more effectively than the one Ahura Mazdah whom Zarathustra had preached. A God that serves all purposes in all fields equally at all times is as good as one that serves no special purpose of the individual at all. Why, again, should the Lord of all creation personally look to the details of administration when even an earthly king has so many assistants and servants? That the latter is obliged to take help because he is not omnipotent, omniscient and omnipresent, and not because it is beneath his dignity or beyond his desire to do so, is what men with a sense of their own limitations do not understand and appreciate. Wishing unconsciously to get rid of the drudgery and the inconvenience of having to do everything for themselves, they ascribe to God a host of helpers so that He may enjoy the comforts of His sovereign majesty unalloyed by the troubles of personal administration. A solitary God in a lonely heaven, again, is

63 The other point of distinction would be that the Ideas manifested themselves in classes whereas the Fravashis were for individual beings or groups taken as a whole. In Mediaeval speculation in Europe, however, the embodiment of an Idea in a single angel was not unknown.

so repugnant to the human mind that even in strictly monotheistic religions the provision of messengers and agents (in addition to internal distinctions of the Divine nature) has not been felt incongruous with the omnipotent majesty of God. It is not improbable that so long as geographical location and spatial attribute play any part in the conception of heaven and so long as human immortality is conceived in terms of translation to this heavenly residence and persistence of separate individuality, the idea of other denizens of heaven will never disappear. It is in conformity with strict logic, therefore, that the Advaita Vedānta denied at the same time the existence of a spatial heaven and its denizens and the eternal persistence of finite individuals as separate entities.

The introduction of concrete celestial beings by the side of Ahura served not only to jeopardise the monotheism but also to alter the conception of divine nature. Thus, the full effect of occasionally counting Ahura Mazdah himself among the Amesha Spentas was seen when he was considered to be a Yazata himself—a god among gods, and provided, like the other Yazatas, with a Fravashi of his own. Nay more: he is often depicted as sacrificing unto the minor divinities,[64] who are admittedly his own creations, not always to invigorate them by his offerings against their demoniac adversaries (as when he sacrificed to Tishtrya against Apaosha, the demon of drought) but for boons, as when he prays to Ardvi Sūra Anāhita " with the Haoma and meat, with the baresma, with the wisdom of the tongue, with the holy spells, with the words, with the deeds, with the libations and with the rightly-spoken words," to bring Zarathustra to think, speak and act after his law.[65] He does the same to Mithra, the lord of wide pastures, in the shining Garonmāna[66] and to Vayu in the Airyana Vaejah and the latter grants him the boon

[64] See Dhalla, *Zor. Th.*, p. 79 f; Moulton, *Tr. Mag.*, p. 99.

[65] Yt. 5.17-8; see also 8.50-3.

[66] Yt. 10.123; also 92 and 50·1 Hara Berezaiti (Alburz) is the abode of Mithra.

that he (Ahura Mazdah) will smite the creation of Angra Mainyu while nobody would be able to smite the creation of the Good Spirit.[67] We must remember that during the later Avestan period dualism became more pronounced and it was probably felt that Ahura Mazdah needed the assistance of his own creations to undo the work of Angra Mainyu. In fact, not only the Yazatas but also the Fravashis are regarded as coming to his assistance. Ahura Mazdah is made to say that had not the good, powerful and beneficent Fravashis helped him, the wicked Druj would have smitten the good creation and Spenta Mainyu would not have been able to overthrow the kingdom of Angra Mainyu.[68] Thus, the Yazatas and the Fravashis not only assist Ahura Mazdah in the maintenance of creation and the uprooting of evil, but without their boon and help his victory over evil would have been delayed or become uncertain. During the Pahlavi period practically this type of belief persisted,[69] while speculations about the nature of Divine revelation to men introduced a distinction, as in Mosaic revelation, between the visual presentation of God (which was denied) and His symbolic presence in fire or His empirical manifestation through sound (which was affirmed).[70] We are not to suppose, however, that at any time of its history Zoroastrianism was tempted to forsake the spirituality or the pre-eminence of Ahura Mazdah—the exceptions when he is treated on the same footing as his creations are so few that they only serve to prove the general rule.

67 Yt. 15.2-4. See also Yt. 15.44 where Vayu calls himself the All-smiting because he can smite the creations of both the Good Spirit and the Evil Spirit. Darmesteter draws attention to the fact that Zeus is represented as doing the same thing to Thetis, Prometheus and Hecatonchirs (SBE, IV, p. lxi, n.5).

68 See Dhalla, *Zor. Th.*, p. 86, 146. For the functions of the Fravashis, see the opening lines of Yt. 13 (Farvardin Yasht).

69 In Shāyast lā-Shāyast (Ch. IX. 11-3) we are told that the angels and the guardian spirits of the righteous must be invited to a ceremony, for without that invocation it is not possible for them to keep the evil away.—SBE, V, pp. 312-4.

70 Casartelli, *op. cit.*, p. 27; Dhalla, *Zor. Th.*, p. 221: A later text speaks of Ormazd as taking hold of the Prophet's hand and giving him wisdom in the shape of water to swallow.

In later Zoroastrian literature it is the Amesha Spentas that suffered the greatest amount of transformation, for when concrete gods were in demand abstractions and attributes were the least satisfactory from the devotional point of view. Even in the later Avestan literature, as Dhalla points out,[71] "the archangels, who are higher in the spiritual hierarchy have either to content themselves with short laudatory compositions or go entirely without any special dedication" while some of the longest sacrificial hymns are composed in honour of the Yazatas; and "some of the attributes that are the prerogative of Ahura Mazda alone are lavishly applied to the leading angels, but the authors are sparing even to parsimony when they confer honorific epithets on the Amesha Spentas." Even in the Haptān Yasht, supposed to be specially dedicated to the Amesha Spentas, praises of some of the Yazatas and of the Fravashis of the faithful fill nearly half the space. Each is provided with a fravashi like Ahura Mazdah himself, although their old unification through Ahura is retained by means of the supposition that these fravashis of the archangels are all of one thought, one speech and one deed, have the same father and commander, namely, Ahura Mazdah, and see one another's soul.[72] What is more important to note, however, is the tendency to think of them in concrete shapes. They dwell in Garonmāna, the highest heaven, which is less often thought of as the abode of praise than as the region of endless light[73] (just as the Gāthic *Humata*, Good Thought, *Hūkhta*, Good Works, and *Hvarshta*, Good Deeds—the other three heavens in order of excellence, respectively become the realm of the Stars, the Moon and the Sun), and there they occupy golden seats (like Ahura Mazdah).[74] If Geldner's suggestion be correct, it appears that Vohu Manah was worshipped in the form of

[71] Dhalla, *Zor. Th.*, p. 78.

[72] Yt. 13.83-4; 19.16-20.

[73] Similarly the Vedic heaven is *rocana*, the luminous space, and when three heavens are distinguished they are called *trī rocanā*.—Macdonell, *Vedic Mythology*, p. 9.

[74] Vend. 19.31, 32. See also Dhalla, *Zor. Th.*, p. 276; Geiger, *op. cit.*, I, p. 104 with fn. 1; Jackson, *Zor. St.*, p. 147.

an image which, when defiled, could be purified by an appropriate ceremony.[75] It is not improbable, therefore, that the iconic worship of Vohu Manah (Omanus or Omanes), if not of Ameretāt also, in Cappadocia, described by Strabo,[76] was a radical innovation, prompted by the desire to obtain immortality in Garonmāna where Vohu Manah rises from his golden seat to welcome the soul of the faithful led by his beautiful Daena.[77] It has often been pointed out that the Apocalyptic literature of the Bible owes much to Zoroastrianism and it is in Apocalyptic visions that spiritual things tend to assume pictorial form;[78] it is no wonder, therefore, that the Spirit that greets the pious soul should be more materially conceived than the other Amesha Spentas. At a still later age Vohu Manah is represented as supplying the new arrivals in heaven with gold-embroidered robes and golden thrones while material comforts are purveyed by the Fravashis.[79] All the Amesha Spentas are represented as coming down to the oblations in a shining pathway[80] as befitting dwellers of the region of light in whose presence, later writers tell us, Zarathustra fails to see his own shadow.[81]

Further deterioration of the ethical side of the Amesha Spentas takes place during the Pahlavi period although their spiritual character does not disappear altogether. Thus, while their beneficent nature is emphasised by the belief that they form an assembly three times every day in the fire-temple

75 Vend. 19.20-5. See Moulton, *Ear. Zor.*, p. 101. The Pahlavi explanation is different.—See SBE, IV, p. 210, n.6; p. 211, n. 1-4.

76 Moulton, *Ear. Zor.*, pp. 100, 409; *Tr. Mag.*, p. 79. Benveniste (*op. cit.*, p. 63 f) equates Omanes with Verethraghna; see the whole discussion there. See also Jackson, *Zor. Stu.*, pp. 49, 52; Dhalla, *Zor. Th.*, p. 81.

77 Vend. 19.31. In Vend. 7.52 Ahura Mazdah is represented as welcoming him. See Casartelli, *op. cit.*, p. 72, for Sassanian belief.

See Bahman Yasht.

78 See Moulton, *Tr. Mag.*, p. 76 in this connection.

79 See Dhalla, *Zor. Th.*, pp. 179, 277; also Yt. 22.18 where the oil of Zaremaya (spring-butter) is supplied to the soul at the command of Ahura Mazdah.

80 Yt. 13.84; 19.17.

81 See the reference in Dhalla, *Zor. Th.*, p. 226; see also C. de Harlez, *op. cit.*, p. 131.

and "shed good works and righteousness around for the advantage of the devout votaries that frequent the sacred places," it is maintained at the same time that the prayers and offerings must be performed with accuracy[82]—the same emphasis on formality which characterised the Vedic religion during the period of the Brāhmaṇas. They have not only special days dedicated to them but they have their favourite flowers[83] and also their special domains or elements to protect, namely, men, animals, fire, metal, earth, water and plants.[84] Woe unto him who observes the virtues that they represent but fails to take care of the concrete things that are under their special charge! To quote Dhalla:[85] "Vohuman, for instance, as the genius of good mind, did not emphasize the faithful adherence to good thoughts, but contented himself with reminding the prophet to teach mankind to take care of his cattle. Artavahisht, the genius of Righteousness, gave no command to Zaratusht to exhort men to follow the path of Righteousness, but taught him that the best way of propitiating the heavenly spirit was to propitiate his fire." Dhalla refers in this connection to a Pazand penitential prayer of the 4th century A.D. in which the penitent "craves forgiveness for any offence that may have been committed by ill-treating the earthly object over which the genius presides" but no mention is made of the offence against the abstract virtue over which the archangel in question presides. The horror of defiling the elements[86] as also a considerable lapse from spirituality in worship naturally arose out of this attitude of mind. In fact, the material association had a repercussion upon the nature of the Amshaspands themselves, for we are told that they assumed visible forms and came to the

82 See Dhalla, *Zor. Th.*, p. 227.

83 See Modi, *op. cit.*, pp. 396-7. The cock is the favourite bird of Vohuman (see Casartelli, *op. cit.*, p. 74).

84 Dhalla, *Zor. Th.*, p. 227. These are supposed to have been revealed to Zoroaster in separate visions by the archangels.—See Jackson, *Zoroaster*, pp. 46-9. See also p. 50 for conference with Haoma and other angels.

85 Dhalla, *Zor. Th.*, p. 196; see Casartelli, *op. cit.*, p. 75.

86 See Dhalla, *Zor. Th.*, pp. 233, 234.

court of King Gushtāsp (Vīshtāspa) as envoys of Ormazd to certify the divine mission of Zoroaster,[87] just as they had once descended to convey to earth the Fravashi of the Prophet on a stem of the Hom-plant and to his mother his material essence mixed with milk.[88] Nay, when Zoroaster met Vohuman, he could accurately notice his gigantic size, his face, and his dress; even his wide steps did not escape the notice of the Prophet when being led to the council of the Amshaspands.[89] The Farvardin Yasht had told of the fine body of the Fravashi of Ahura Mazdah and of the beautiful and active forms wherewith he clothed the Amesha Spentas:[90] popular imagination took the matter in the way usual to it all the world over—it materialised the conception as thoroughly as circumstances would permit.[91]

It is doubtful, however, if the Amesha Spentas would have been materialised so far had not the conception of the Yazatas been developed in the meantime. Reference has already been made to the fact that the craving for familiar contact with the spiritual powers partially rehabilitated the pre-Zoroastrian polytheism albeit in close alliance with the Prophet's own religion. When spirits rule each department of nature and each spiritual quality, their number must be very large. Although about forty only are mentioned in the Avestan texts, "they are numbered by hundreds and by thousands and by hundreds of thousands, nay even more."[92] Some of them have come down from Indo-Iranian times—Mithra, Airyaman, Haoma, Verethraghna, Pārendi, Rātā(?), Nairyosangha, Apam Napāt, Ushah and Vayu can be easily

87 Dhalla, *Zor. Th.*, pp. 196, 229; Jackson, *Zor. Stu.*, p. 47; *Zoroaster*, pp. 58, 65. Ashavahishto and the Propitious Fire (Būrzhīn-Mitrō) accompany Vohuman.

88 See Jackson, *Zoroaster*, pp. 24-5.

89 Dhalla, *Zor. Th.*, pp. 196, 228; Jackson, *Zoroaster*, p. 41.

90 Yt. 13. 80-1.

91 As an illustration of materialisation may be cited the attribute 'swiftest chargers' given to the Amesha Spentas in the Gathas (Ys. 50. 7) and its transformation in the Persian *Zartūsht Nāmah* into the statement that they rode upon wonderful horses.—See Jackson, *Zor. Stu.*, p. 47.

92 See Dhalla, *Zor. Th.*, p. 96; Jackson, *Zor. Stu.*, p. 55; also Casartelli, *op. cit.*, p. 7f f

identified by their Vedic names[93] and are mostly nature-gods. But there were others of Iranian growth, some spiritual and some natural in origin, of only a few of whom Vedic parallels are known: these are Ātar, Ardvī Sūrā Anāhitā, Hvarekhshaeta, Maonghah, Tishtrya, Drvāspā, Sraosha, Rashnu, Rāman, Daenā, Chisti, Erethe, Rasanstāt, Ashi Vanghuhī, Arshtāt, Asmān, Zamyat, Manthra Spenta, Dāmoish Upamana and Anaghra Raochāo.[94] Very often the personification is thin and the worship lapses from the adoration of the presiding spirits to that of the natural elements themselves;[95] and regarding a few of them details are exceedingly scanty. They are of both sexes, the sex depending generally upon the type of work or virtue represented.[96] Some of them, again, go together on account of functional affinity and form dual Yazatas. To quote Dhalla;[97] "Mithra as the sovereign lord of wide pastures forms a pair with Ahura; as the lord of light, he works in consort with Hvarekhshaeta, the genius of light; as the lord of truth, he works in company with Rashnu; and as the lord of plenty and prosperity, he enters into comradeship with Raman. The more prominent of the dual divinities are Ahura-Mithra, Hvarekhshaeta-Mithra, Mithra-Rashnu, Mithra-Raman, Rashnu-Arshtat, Raman-Vayu, Daena-Chisti, Ashi Vanghuhi-Parendi and Asman-Zamyat." If the last be taken as the Iranian equivalent of the Vedic Dyāvā-pṛthivī and Rashnu-Arshtāt and Daenā-Chisti be excepted, it is interesting to note that in the above list an Iranian and a Vedic god are paired together, possibly to indicate what Iranian Yazata should be taken as equivalent or allied to what pre-Zoroastrian deity, and that Mithra's pre-eminence in popular favour is shown by the fact that at least four Iranian gods are needed to take over his different

93 See Dhalla, *Zor. Th.*, p. 96. Some Vedic gods like Indra, Sarva, Nāsatya, etc., have become demons in Zoroastrianism.

94 Dhalla, *Zor. Th.*, p. 97.

95 *Ibid.*, *loc. cit.*

96 This step falsified the description of Diogenes that the Magi condemn the use of images, and especially the error of those who attribute to the divinities difference of sex.—See Moulton, *Tr. Mag.*, p. 99.

97 Dhalla, *Zor. Th.*, p. 99; also p. 105.

functions, indicating thereby his past glory and presaging his future greatness in the Mithraic cult. It is well known that when Mahāyāna Buddhism was developed, a similar identification of the new Buddhistic deities with the old Hindu gods also took place and that when Mithraism began to spread in the West a similarity between Greek and Iranian deities was established, as of Zeus and Ormazd, Apollo and Mithra, Verethraghna and Herakles.[98]

The whole theory of Yazatas (Izads) was brought into relation with Zoroastrianism in a number of ways. The Yazatas are the creatures of Ahura (some like Ātar being regarded as his children, just as Vohu Manah, Asha and Armaiti were in the Gāthās),[99] and they transmit his will to mankind and assist him in the maintenance of his creation. They are divided into two classes—spiritual and material. Ahura Mazdah is the greatest and the best of the Yazatas and is at the head of the heavenly division, while Zarathustra is the chief of the earthly Yazatas.[100] Then, again, the Amesha Spentas are recognised as higher in the spiritual hierarchy, and in the Persian Calendar the first seven days of the month are dedicated to Ahura Mazdah and the Amshaspands and the last 23 days are dedicated to the Yazatas.[101] The Zoroastrian litanies (Nyaishes) began with a homage to Ahura Mazdah and sometimes to the Amshaspands also. In later times was propounded the theory of *Hamkār*, according to which the Yazatas were supposed to be the collaborators, auxiliaries or fellow-workers of Ormazd and the Amshaspands, the assignment being to Ahura Mazda Dai pa Adar, Dai pa Mihir and Dai pa Din ; to Vohu Manah (Bahman), Maonghah

98 See ERE. iv. 754; Moulton, *Ear. Zor.*, p. 107. Jackson, *Zor. St.*, p. 172. The reference is to the inscription of Antiochus I of Commagene (69-38 B.C.).

99 See Dhalla, *Zor. Th.*, pp. 21, 134. C. de Harlez rightly points out, however, that " often the influence of monotheism is visible only in the addition to the name of a spirit of the epithet Mazda dhāta (created by Mazda), made with a view to subordinate the former to the power of the supreme master " (*Op. cit.*, p. 122). Moulton compares the Roman Catholic and Greek Orthodox systems with the Parsi religion in this respect. (*Tr. Mag.*, p. 100.)

100 Jackson, *Zor. Stu.*, p. 56; Dhalla, *Zor. Th.*, pp. 96-7.

101 Modi, *op. cit.*, pp. 397, 481; ERE. iii. 128 f. For the significance of the various days of the month, see Karaka, *op. cit.*, I, pp. 134-44.

(Māh or Mohor), Geush urvan (Goshūrūn or Gosh) and Rāma Hvāstra (Rām); to Asha Vahishta (Ardibehesht), Ātar (Ādar), Sraosha (Srosh) and Verethraghna (Bahrām);[102] to Khshathra Vairya (Shatravar or Shahrēvar), Hvarekhshaeta (Khurshed), Mithra (Meher or Mihr), Asmān and Anaghra Raochāo (Anērān); to Spenta Ārmaiti (Spandārmad), Apam Napāt (Ābān), Daenā (Dīn), Ashi Vanghuhī (Ashisang or Ard) and Manthra Spenta (Māhraspand or Mārespand); to Haurvatāt (Khordād), Tishtrya (Tīr), the Fravashis (Farvardin or Ardāfarosh) and Vāta (Bād or Guad); and to Ameretāt (Amardād or Murdād), Rashnu Razishta (Rashn), Arshtāt (Āstad) and Zam (Zamyād).[103] But, as has been pointed out above, although in theory pre-eminence belonged to the Amshaspands, in practice the hymns of praise went mostly to the Yazatas. In animal sacrifice during the Pahlavi period, we are told, all the important parts of the slaughtered animal went to the different Īzads (Yazatas) until at last the tail-bone fell to the lot of the august Farohar of Zaratusht and the great archangels had to content themselves merely with

It is interesting to know that every week originally began with Ahura Mazdah. In the present Parsi Calendar the first, second and third weeks begin with him or one of his co-adjutors (see Modi, *op. cit.*, p. 486). As the third and fourth weeks were of 8 days each, the 23rd day is dedicated to another auxiliary of Ahura Mazdah. A further point of interest is that these auxiliaries have been eclipsed by the Yazatas that come next—Ātar, Mithra and Daena, three of the principal Yazatas of Parsism (see SBE. XXIII, p. 6, n. 11) of whom Ātar is the son of Ahura Mazdah, Mithra (also Tishtrya—see Ys. 8.25) is a God invoked by his own name and Daena is the Good Law of the Mazdayasnians (see Sirozah I.9, 16, 24 and Sirozah II.9, 16, 24). Nadershah (quoted in ERE. iii. 129) points out that "this order of the names depends on Ys. 16.3-6 and comprises four groups, containing respectively the Amshaspands, the seven planets, moral objects and religious objects, each headed by the supreme god Ormazd." (See also ERE. iii. 130 for loan from the Persian by other Calendars.) See Jackson, *Zor. Stu.*, p. 126.

102 At the present day Parsis are particularly expected to visit the fire-temple on the first (Hormuzd), third (Ardibehesht), ninth (Adar), seventeenth (Sarosh) and twentieth (Behram) days of each month. With the exception of the first the rest are associated with Asha Vahishta and his auxiliaries.

103 Modi, *op. cit.*, p. 390, n. 2; p. 486. The collaboration was extended to the Yazatas among themselves.—See Jackson, *Zor. Stu.*, p. 63. Although a few are mentioned, the collaborators of the Yazatas are included in many cases. Thus Daena here includes Chisti; Apam Napāt, Ardvī Sūrā Anāhitā; and so on. See Sirozah I and II.

the residue.[104] Nay, as has been noted above, in their enthusiasm to extol the powers of these angels the theological writers of the later Avestan period went to the length of representing Ahura Mazdah as sacrificing unto these Yazatas and asking for their boons. They want, in fact, to be invoked by their own names to command greater reverence among the people at large and the Nyaishes are sung in honour of the four prominent members of their group—the Sun,[105] Moon, Water and Fire.

Reference has already been made to the iconic worship of Anāhita by Artaxerxes Mnemon (B.C. 404-358). Her inclusion within the pantheon did not indeed spread idolatry,[106] but possibly it was of a piece with the belief that some of the Yazatas could assume various shapes in order to carry out their allotted duties. Thus Tishtrya, Verethraghna, Dahmā Āfriti (the Spirit of Divine Blessing) and Dāmoish Upamana (the Spirit of Curse) were pictured as assuming the forms of man, horse, camel, boar, etc.[107] They seem to suffer at the same time from the imperfection which multiplicity involves, for they actively seek praise and sacrifice.[108] They also indicate their preferences, which include not only vegetarian diet but also animal flesh of different kinds, against which cruel practice the Prophet had raised his mighty voice of protest. It appears that, like the *pitṛs* and some of the Vedic gods of India, these Yazatas are maintained in strength by regular offerings, for we are told that it is only when Ahura Mazdah offered to Tishtrya a sacrifice, which men had not done in proper time, that he gained sufficient strength to overthrow Apaosha, the demon of drought.[109] It appears further that although Ahura Mazdah is not jealous when oblations are offer-

104 Dhalla, *Zor. Th.*, p. 238.

105 There are Nyaishes in honour of both Mithra and Khurshed.

Mithra (Mihr) is the angel of light considered independently of the Sun (Khurshed). He precedes the Sun and shows himself on the earth even after sunset.—See C. de Harlez, *op. cit.*, p. 150.

106 Reference has already been made to the image of Vohu Manah.

107 See Dhalla, *Zor. Th.*, pp. 81, 113, 128. Verethraghna had himself assumed ten forms (Dhalla, *Zor. Th.*, p. 114).

108 See Yt. 5. 8; Dhalla, *Zor. Th.*, p. 98.

109 Yt. 8. 24-8; see Dhalla, *Zor. Th.*, p. 130.

ed to the Yazatas, these are jealous of one another for Tishtrya and Mithra complain that men do not sacrifice to them as much as they do to other Yazatas.[110] As in Hinduism, there is also latent the idea that service must be mutual,[111] although it is conceded at the same time that in order to be entitled to the boons of the god worshipped it is enough to please him or her by thought, word and deed and that it is not always necessary to beg expressly for them.[112] During the Pahlavi period a belief in the active beneficence of the Yazatas was widely held and their assistance in knowing God and making moral progress was freely recognised.[113] But probably the Younger Avestan tradition that they and the Fravashis are offended when not sacrificed unto and then they are merciless and difficult to deal with did not completely die out in later belief.[114]

It would be tedious to go through the detailed functions of the Yazatas or of the daevas to whom they are opposed; but we shall attempt a summary of their names with the most important function of each just to show that similarity with Vedic belief was close even to the length of the personification of abstract virtues and the religious veneration paid to scriptures, formulae, symbols and materials. A glance at Yasnas 1 and 70 will show the heterogeneous grouping of the spirits worshipped,[115] which called forth the caricature and condemnation of Christian missionaries.[116] In fact, a whole book, the Visparad, is dedicated to all the *ratus* (*i.e.*, chiefs or lords of the ritual) together, and the various Yashts, though primarily intended to celebrate the glories and sing the praises of individual Yazatas, also adore groups of divinities having affinity with one another, the only relieving feature of much

110 Yt. 8. 24; see Dhalla, *Zor. Th.*, pp. 97, 130.

111 See, for instance, Atash Nyaish, 15-16 (Dhalla, *The Nyaishes*, pp. 179, 181). *Cf.* Ys. 62. 4-6, 9.

112 Yt. 8. 49; see Dhalla, *Zor. Th.*, p. 137.

113 See Dhalla, *Zor. Th.*, pp. 236-8 for Srosh; p. 241 for Khurshed.

114 Dhalla, *Zor. Th.*, p. 79.

115 In the SBE edition.

116 See Wilson, *The Parsi Religion*, pp. 261-7; Moulton, *Tr. Mag.*, pp. 59-62.

of the monotonous recital being a constant reference to the ethical aspects of the divinities concerned and also to the moral aspirations of the worshipper and his determination to stick to the holy Mazdayasnian religion and to abjure the Principle (and Emissaries) of Evil.

First in order of importance are the Spirits of the Physical World—practically the very gods whom Zarathustra sought to supersede and suppress. There was Fire.[117] worshipped by the Indo-Iranians, the earthly symbol of celestial brilliance. Zarathustra had retained the fire-altar in his reformed religion; but it became in his system not the mouth of the gods (Agni) but the purest symbol of Ahura Mazdah (*Ātar*) and a protege of Right (Asha Vahishta).[118] The light of fire was ever kept burning in the fire-altars or fire-temples, and wilful or careless extinction or pollution of the sacred flame became a heinous sin, entailing great misery to the offending soul. *Nairyosangha* (Nēryosangh), probably a personification of the altar-flame like the Vedic Narāśaṃsa, figures as the messenger of Ahura Mazdah; but his history is almost forgotten while Ātar is described in details in the fivefold form[119] in which he exists in the earth (berezisavah or Bahrām), animates human and animal bodies (vohufryāna), keeps up circulation in vegetables (urvāzishta), forms the stuff of the lightning (vāzishta), and constitutes the body of Ormazd (spenishta).[120] On Ātar was fastened the analogue of the Indra-Vṛtra myth of India, for in his lightning form he vanquishes Spenjhaghri, the storm demon, associated with Apaosha, the demon of drought.[121] He is also manifested in

117 See C. de Harlez, *op. cit.*, p. 146 f.; Dhalla, *Zor. Th.*, p. 134 f.

118 See C. de Harlez, *op. cit.*, pp. 333 f., 337 f. (for the distinction between Agni and Ātar). See Söderblom, *op. cit.*, p. 216.

119 See Jackson, *Zoroaster*, p. 99 f., for classification of Fire into those for priests (Ātūr Farnbag), warriors (Ātūr Gūshnasp) and the labouring class (Ātūr Būrzhīn Mitrō). For their location, see Huart, *op. cit.*, p. 153.

120 Ys. 17.11 recounts them all together. See C. de Harlez, *op. cit.*, p. 148; Dhalla, *Zor. Th.*, p. 42; Jackson, *Zor. Stu.*, p. 57.

121 Jackson, *Zor. Stu.*, pp. 96, 119; C. de Harlez, *op. cit.*, p. 162; see Vend. 19.40.

the form of the *hvarenah* which represents the splendour and glory of priests and kings and the departure of which is caused by disobedience to religious prescriptions.[122] Two minor associates are *Airyaman* (Aērmān), the arm of Asha Vahishta, the guardian of fire, and *Shaoka*, the light of wood or oil.[123] The Ātar Nvaish contains the litany of Fire in which boons are asked and expected of the carefully tended fire and the fire-temple is treated to all intents and purposes as a daily rendezvous of the Amesha Spentas who form the highest creation of Ahura Mazdah.[124]

Light primarily belongs to the celestial bodies —the Sun, the Moon and the stars, and also to the heavenly regions.[125] Light as independently conceived is personified as *Mithra*[126] who was wrongly identified at a later time with the Sun for whom the Persians had another name *Hvarekhshaēta* (Khurshed).[127] Mithra is the lord of wide pasturage; as he drives out the daevas from their dark abodes everywhere, he is the strongest, the most valiant, the most victorious and a war-lord of powerful arms, driving along in a high-wheeled chariot drawn by four celestial swiftly-moving white horses.[128] He promotes

122 Jackson, *Zor. Stu.*, p. 57; see esp. C. de Harlez, *op. cit.*, pp. 156-58, and *Sir J. J. Madressa Jubilee Vol.*, pp. 159-66 (Hvareno-Tyche-God-Fortuna-Divine Grace).

Qareno (hvarenah) is shed on the world of Ahura Mazdah from above and invests some of the good spirits with celestial splendour. See ERE. viii. 754. In Yt. 10.16 Mithra rides through all the Karshvars (the seven regions of the world according to the Iranians comparable with the "seven islands" of the Hindu belief), bestowing the *hvareno* (SBE, XXIII, p. 123, n.5). See also Yt. 10.27; 19.34 f.

123 C. de Harlez, *op. cit.*, p. 149

124 Casartelli, *op. cit.*, p. 87.

125 Special reference should be made in this connection to Ys. 36.

126 For Mithra, see Dhalla, *Zor. Th.*, pp. 103-11; 239-40; ERE. viii. 758, art. MITHRAISM; Benveniste, *op. cit.*, p. 53 f; Geiger, *op. cit.*, I, Int., pp. lv-lviii; Huart, *op. cit.*, pp. 112-16; D. M. Madan, *op. cit.*, Lect. III (he takes Mithra as a symbol of love and union and also of justice and moral law).

127 Madan, *op. cit.*, pp. 72, 74. In Pahlavi literature Mithra is the hamkār or associate of the Sun, Hvare Khshaeta. See Madan, *op. cit.*, p. 76.

128 This must be the cause of his popularity with the Roman soldiers who became ardent followers of Mithraism later on. Yt. 10.11 is a typical passage: "Whom the horsemen worship on the back of their horses, begging swiftness for their teams, health for their own bodies, and that they may watch with full success those who hate them, smite down their foes, and destroy at one stroke their

the flow of waters, the growth of plants, the increase of flock and the abundance of joyful life, whence his association with *Rāman Khvāstra* (Hvāstra), the genius of the joy of earthly life.[129] He is at the same time the most glorious of all the spiritual Yazatas and Ahura Mazdah has created him to be as worthy of sacrifice and prayer as himself; for like Ahura Mazdah, Mithra is omniscient, 'a chief in assemblies, pleased with prayer,' and from his elysian abode on Mount Hara Berezaiti, "where neither night nor darkness, nor cold wind nor hot wind, nor sickness, impurity, death and clouds can ever reach," he surveys the doings of men with his thousand senses and ten thousand sleepless eyes[130] and he can never be deceived. He is therefore associated with Ahura (who is sometimes represented as offering him sacrifice) and the boons asked of him are so varied and comprehensive that the small association with the Zoroastrian cult fails to hide the fact that Mithra practically replaces, at least equals, Ahura Mazdah in popular estimation.[131] "Grant us these boons which we beg of thee, O powerful god! in accordance with the words of revelation, namely, riches, strength, and victory, good conscience and bliss, good fame and a good soul; wisdom and the knowledge that gives happi-

adversaries, their enemies, and those who hate them." See also Yt. 10.21, 35 f, 67-8

Modi suggests (*Anthropological Papers*, p. 173 f—esp. p. 179 f) that St. Michael killing the dragon borrowed his features not from Vohu Manah but from Mithra.

129 See SBE, IV, Int., p. lxiv: Rāma Hvāstra, which originally meant "the god of the resting place with good pastures" (meaning the atmospheric air where the clouds rest like a herd of cows), ultimately came to mean through a mistake in language "the god who gives a good flavour to aliments."

130 Yt. 10.7 (*Cf.* RV. iii. 59). In Yt. 20.24 he is described as 'he, of the ten thousand spies, the powerful, all-seeing, undeceivable Mithra.'

The figure 9999 is the Parsi expression for 'innumerable,' *e.g.*, the Fravashis guarding the seed of Zoroaster. Ten thousand is probably a round number for 9999.

'Thousand senses' is replaced by 'thousand ears' in some translations to indicate that no prayer sincerely offered escapes his notice.

Yt. 10.45 refers to the eight spies of Mithra presumably occupying the eight points of the compass (see SBE, XXIII, p. 130, n.3).

131 It is interesting to note that "the fire-temple, where the sacred religious rites are performed, is called the Dar-i-Meher, *i.e.*, the door or the gateway of Meher or Mithra."—Modi, *Anthropological Papers*, p. 189.

ness, the victorious strength given by Ahura, the crushing Ascendant of Asha-Vahishta, and conversation (with God) on the Holy Word. Grant that we, in a good spirit and high spirit, exalted in joy and a good spirit, may smite all our foes, ......all our enemies.......all the malice of Daevas and Men, of the Yātus and Pairikās,[132] of the oppressors, the blind and the deaf (the Kavis and Karapans)."[133] Nay, it is expressly stated in Yasht 10.92 that "the holy Ahura Mazdah confessed that religion and so did Vohu-Mano, so did Asha-Vahishta, so did Khshathra-Vairya, so did Spentā-Ārmaiti, so did Haurvatāt and Ameretāt; and all the Amesha-Spentas longed for and confessed his religion."[134] But, as the god of light, Mithra is not only a witness of men's deeds; he conveys the offered gifts to the House of Praise[135] and comes down when deeds of charity are performed;[136] he is also the protector of truth and, as such, is associated in later theology with *Rashnu*, "the most upright," in the work of assessing the deeds of the departed at the Chinvat Bridge.[137] Woe unto those who lie unto Mithra and break their compact whether with one of the unfaithful or with one who professes the true faith![138] As one who is so beneficent to the living

132 *Yātus* are wizards and black magicians (possibly human) while *Pairikās* (Parsi *Peris*) are supernatural enchantresses with seductive appearance.—Jackson, *Zor. Stu.*, pp. 103-4.

133 Yt. 10.58-9; also 93-4.

134 Yt. 10.92. Immediately after, however, Zoroastrianism asserts itself and we are told 'The kind Mazda conferred upon him the mastership of the world.' See C. de Harlez, *op. cit.*, pp. 150-1.

135 Yt. 10.32.

136 Madan, *op. cit.*, p. 81.

137 In Yt. 10.41 (and 100) Rashnu and Sraosha are associated with Mithra in destroying those who lie unto Mithra and kill faithful men. For the associates of Mithra in routing enemies, see Yt. 10.52, 66, 100, 126, 127. See C. de Harlez, *op. cit.*, p. 155, as to the alleged mediating function of Mithra; also Dhalla, *Zor. Th.*, p. 240; Casartelli, *op. cit.*, p. 79. Madan (*op. cit.*, p. 89) remarks that "whereas the sentiment in the Avestic representation of *Mithra* is that of love, the sentiment underlying *Mithra* as he is depicted in the Pahlavi writings is that of awe and fear."

138 Yt. 10.2. Reference has already been made to Mitra who, with some other Vedic gods, is mentioned in the Boghaz-keui inscription in a formal treaty between the Hittites and the Mitannis. G. F. Moore, remarking on the passage, says, "Perjury is as bad as a hundred heresies—an extraordinary triumph of ethics over orthodoxy." (*His. of Rel.*, I, p. 394.)

and so powerful over the destinies of the dead, Mithra inspired a religious awe and devotion which no other Yazata ever did.

Naturally associated with Mithra, who was latterly identified with him, is *Hvarekhshaēta*, "the brilliant sun," worshipped for his power to drive away darkness, impurity, disease and death.[139] As in the Vedic religion, the Sun could be only imperfectly personified and the poet of the Mihr Yasht often lapses in his adoration from the swift-horsed angel of the Sun to the rolling disc of the visible orb. He is the eye of Ahura Mazdah,[140] possibly also his visible form. To please him is to please Ahura Mazdah and the rest of the good spirits.[141] In Pahlavi speculation Khurshed (Hvarekhshaēta) is represented as delivering to man the morning message of zeal in doing works of merit, the noon-day message of rearing up a family and furthering the Kingdom of Ormazd by social co-operation and service, and the evening message of repentance with a view to obtaining pardon for sin. Like the Sun, the Moon, *Maonghah* or *Māh*,[142] is very imperfectly divinised and his bounties are copied from those of Mithra in a single verse.[143] He is credited with the power of stimulating the growth of plants and preserving the seed of the primeval Bull, the progenitor of the animal world. During his waning period Tishtrya and his three stellar associates fight against Ahriman and during his waxing period they are relieved by him.[144] His ethical side was emphasised during the Pahlavi period when he was regarded as collecting for fifteen days the good deeds of earthly beings and the rewards for their virtue from the heavens and using the next fifteen days in transmitting the former to the heavens and the latter to

139 See Dhalla, *Zor. Th.*, p. 126; C. de Harlez, *op. cit.*, pp. 154, 335 f.

140 Sūrya is similarly compared to the eye of this or that god (Mitra, Varuṇa, Aryaman, Agni). See Macdonell, *Vedic Mythology*, pp. 23, 30, 32; also p. 27 for comparison with Avestan ideas.

141 Yt. 6.4.

142 Dhalla, *Zor. Th.*, p. 127; C. de Harlez, *op. cit.*, p. 155.

143 Yt. 7.5.

144 SBE, XXIII, p. 89, n.5.

the earth.[145] *Ushah* (Vedic *Uṣas*), the goddess of Dawn, is also known to the Iranian priest-poets, and though the delineation is less firm as compared with that of the Vedas, she has a number of auxiliaries, one of whom (Ushahina) has given his name to one of the five parts of the day (*gāhs*).[146]

In order to appreciate the importance and adoration of the stars it is necessary to remember that very early in the history of the human race the position of certain stars indicated the advent of certain changes in nature and that poetic imagination turned these natural phenomena into fables in lands widely separated from one another. This stellar mythology is independent of the theory of stellar influence on human destinies. In Iran the leading role is played by *Tishtrya* (Tīr)[147] who, with *Vanant*, *Satavaēsa* and *Hapto-iringa*,[148] guards the four quarters of the sky against the battalions of Ahriman (including the planets which bear divine names but are really evil) [149] and who rises victorious after defeating Apaosha (Aposh), the demon of drought who seeks to prevent his access to the waters of the celestial sea Vourukasha, and also Duzhyāirya (Dushiyāra), the demon of barrenness and bad year, who seeks to prevent the germination of the seeds that he drops with the released

145 SBE. XXIII. p. 89, n.4.

146 Dhalla, *Zor. Th.*, p. 128; also Gāh Ushahin. The two other auxiliaries are Berejya and Nmānya. See also Geiger, *op. cit.*, I, p. 154 f. for the gāhs and their presiding Spirits.

147 See Moulton, *Ear. Zor.*, pp. 23 f. and 435. He suggests that *Tīra* was distinct from *Tishtrya* and used to represent the planet Mercury. Its identification with Sirius was due to the pre-eminence of this star in the Magian system (p. 402). He also quotes the opinion of Mrs. Maunder that probably by Tishtrya the Sun was meant. He is personally in favour of the view that the Tishtrya myth originated in India and was carried to Iran by an ebb tide of the Aryan emigration to India. Benveniste connects it with Zervanism (*op. cit.*, p. 100).

148 The identification is difficult. While Tishtrya and Hapto-iringa have been identified more or less satisfactorily with Sirius and the Great Bear respectively, Vanant and Satavaesa have been tentatively identified with Vega and Fomalhaut respectively. See Moulton, *Ear. Zor.*, p. 23 f.; Geiger, *op. cit.*, I, p. 141.

149 Casartelli, *op. cit.*, p. 99; Jackson, *Zor. Stu.*, p. 106; see esp. Moulton, *Ear. Zor.*, pp. 211-4. Bousset sees in this a hostility to the Babylonian star-cult—the planets were degraded by the Magi just as the Daevas had been by Zoroaster. See Moulton, *Ear. Zor.*, p. 213, n.1; Geiger, *op. cit.*, I, pp. 135-142.

waters of the celestial sea.[150] Tishtrya complains of the indifference of men to his worship, which was responsible for his initial defeat at the hands of Apaosha, and it is only when Ahura Mazdah himself offers him a sacrifice that he wins the fight. Like Mithra, he too is credited with the power to grant a variety of boons to men. Reference has already been made to the fact that the innumerable unnamed stars were regarded as Fravashis; the named stars were supposed to have fravashis of their own.

The spirits of the air are represented by at least four angels. *Vayu* or personified air,[151] being conceived as permeated by the luminous rays of the celestial bodies, is characterised as shining, with arms, ornaments, garments and chariot all golden. He is approached even by Ahura Mazdah for boons, not to talk of the kings and heroes that approach him for favour. But the personification is thin, and although he is given nearly fifty titles, "almost all of these attributes of Vayu are derived from the function of Vayu as wind, rather than from his activity as the genius of wind."[152] Because of his association with the physical atmosphere where the forces of good and evil contend for mastery (reinforced no doubt by the experience of both the beneficent and the ruinous activity of the element itself), Vayu is regarded as going both through the world which the Good Spirit has made and through the one which the Evil Spirit has made—a conception which was amplified later on by the idea of a neutral void (Vāi) between Ormazd and Ahriman and of Good Fate and Bad Fate (originating in the two spheres of Vayu) struggling for the possession of the soul of the righteous at the Chinvat Bridge.[153] *Vāta* is even less personified than Vayu and represents the lower air touching the

150 Dhalla, *Zor. Th.*, pp. 129, 241; C. de Harlez, *op. cit.*, pp. 155-6. The seeds apparently come from the mythical tree Hvāpī which stands in the midst of Vourukasha. See Jackson, *Zor. Stu.*, pp. 118-9.

151 C. de Harlez, *op. cit.*, p. 158; Dhalla, *Zor. Th.*, p. 132 f.

152 Dhalla, *Zor. Th.*, p. 133.

153 Yt. 15.43. SBE, IV, Intr., pp. lxiv-v; C. de Harlez, *op.cit.*, p. 159; Jackson, *Zor. Stu.*, pp. 61, 95; see also Vend. 5.8, 9.

earth and swifter-moving.[154] Like Vayu he is at once a holy angel and an evil storm-demon.[155] *Rāma Hvāstra*, sometimes distinguished from and sometimes identified with his Hamkār, Vayu,[156] and sometimes also associated with Mithra, is the genius of the enjoyment of earthly life, to whom we owe the savouriness of food. By far the most interesting, however, of the spirits of the air is *Verethraghna*, the Vedic Vṛtrahan with a completely altered function.[157] He is a creature of Ahura Mazdah and is the most courageous in courage, the most victoricus in victory, the most glorious in glory, the most favouring in favour, the best giver of welfare, and the most healing in health-giving[158] therefore, one of the most popular national divinities of Iran in the Sassanian times. He is the god of victory in all fields and is worshipped as such by the civil and the military population alike. He appeared to Zarathustra in ten different forms. In his worship the rules of extreme purity must be observed. The storm-association of the Vedic god has almost entirely disappeared from the Iranian Verethraghna and only faint allusions to the wind and the aspect of fertilisation are to be found in the Bahrām Yasht dedicated to him. In fact, he appears more as the personification of the abstract virtue of victory (including successful defence) than as the victorious angel that releases the waters and makes the soil below fertile.

In a mythology where the release of the celestial waters (on which the growth of plants and the fertility of the soil and indirectly, therefore, the life of the whole human and animal race depend) plays such an important part, it is no wonder that divine honours would be paid to waters.[159] The personification depended upon a double association—their

154 C. de Harlez, *op. cit.*, p. 159. In the Rigveda also " Vāyu is chiefly the god and Vāta the element."—See Macdonell, *Vedic Myth.*, p. 81.

155 Vend. 19.13; 10.14.

156 C. de Harlez, *op.cit.*, pp. 158-9.

157 Dhalla, *Zor. Th.*, p. 112 f.; see esp. C. de Harlez, *op. cit.*, p. 159 f. and Geiger, *op. cit.*, I, Int., li; Jackson, *Zor. Stu.*, p. 60; Macdonell, *Ved. Myth.*, p. 66.

158 Yt. 14.3.

159 See Ys. 68.

origin in the celestial clouds and their manifestation in terrestrial streams, lakes, etc. The close association of water with fertility and growth was responsible for the preponderatingly feminine trait present in the personification of the waters. *Ardvi Sūra Anāhita* was imported from abroad and her cult must have been very popular, judging by the graphic description of her form[160] and the characteristic Iranian conception that even Ahura Mazdah had offered oblations to her.[161] She was supposed to purify the seeds of men and the wombs of women, to make delivery easy, to put milk into the mothers' breasts and, like the other noted Yazatas, to grant a variety of boons, mostly temporal in character.[162] Her closest Vedic parallel would be Sarasvatī;[163] but Anāhita is generally considered to be the heavenly spring or celestial stream that descends to the seven regions of the world and her chariot is regarded as being drawn by four white chargers, which are identified with the wind, the rain, the cloud and the sleet—better still with raining, snowing, hailing and sleeting.[164] She was worshipped by the side of a river or a lake with due regard to the sanctity and purity of the waters, which could not be defiled in any way. Being holy, water was supposed never to kill any one, cases of drowning being ascribed to some evil spirit like Vayu (evil wind or destiny);[165] the faithful were enjoined to remove floating corpses from the waters and thus prevent the defilement with infection, pollution and uncleanliness by the Druj Nasu, the demon of bodily decomposition.[166] It appears, however, that the association with maternity was responsible

160 Yt. 5.126-9. Benveniste (*op. cit.*, p. 62 f) thinks the cult to be of Babylonian origin, the ancient name of the goddess being Ardvi.

161 C. de Harlez, *op. cit.*, p. 163 f; Dhalla, *Zor. Th.*, p. 137 f; SBE, XXIII, p. 53. See Ys. 65 and Yt. 5.

162 C. de Harlez, *op. cit.*, p. 164; Dhalla, *Zor. Th.*, p. 139; Modi, *Anthropological Papers*, p. 153. See also Ys. 65.2 and Yt. 5.2.

163 See the present writer's *Sarasvatī the Goddess of Learning* in *K. B. Pāṭhak Memorial Volume*. Geiger identifies her with the Oxus (*op. cit.*, I, Int., p. xlv; II, p. 95, fn.1).

164 Yt. 5.3-4, 120. Ahura Mazdah brings the river down; see Yt. 5.6 and *Vend.* 5.15-9.

165 Vend. 5.8.

166 Vend. 6. 26-41. See *Shāyast Lā-Shāyast*, Ch. II, 76 f (SBE. V, p. 265 f).

for the identification of Anāhita (Anaitis) with the Assyrian Mylitta, corresponding to the Greek Aphrodite, the Roman Venus and the Syrian Astarte, and this probably led to nocturnal rites of a questionable character which the strict Mazdayasnians sought to prevent by laying down that all offerings made to the goddess after sunset would be unacceptable to her and would go to feed ' six hundred and a thousand Daevas.'[167]

The dominating figure of Anāhita has thrown into the shade two other angels of the waters whose Vedic parallels are known. *Ahurani*,[168] the female Yazata, stands for all the waters and roughly corresponds to the Vedic *Āpas*, regarded as wives or mothers.[169] In the Iranian religion the waters are sometimes regarded as the wives of Ahura and also as mothers;[170] at other times Ahurani is the daughter of Ahura.[171] She represents all the waters—the sea Vourukasha and all waters upon earth, whether standing or running. or waters of the well, or spring-waters which perennially flow, or the drippings of the rains, or the irrigations of canals:[172] but she must be worshipped not only with the usual material and ritualistic ingredients but also with the Zaothras[173] of good thought, word and deed in order that she may confer her varied boons (including, as is to be expected manly offspring). The other spirit is *Apam Napāt*,[174] the male Yazata of the waters, whose name (Apām Napāt) is familiar in the Vedas and has given to the Yasht dedicated to Ardvi Sūra Anāhita the title of Ābān Yasht. He is general-

167 Yt. 5.91, 95.

168 Dhalla, *Zor. Th.*, p. 141; C. de Harlez, *op. cit.*, p. 175.

169 Macdonell, *Ved. Myth.*, p. 85. Darmesteter compares them with gnās, celestial wives (see Macdonell, *ibid.*, pp. 100, 117).

170 Ys. 38. See, however, C. de Harlez, *op. cit.*, p. 176. In view of the fact that Ahura has nowhere a nature spouse, he suggests that Ahurani should mean ' sovereign.

171 Ys. 68.

172 Ys. 68.8. Vourukasha stands either for Lake Aral or for the Caspian Sea according to Geiger (*op. cit.*, II, p. 95, f.n.1).

173 Libations of holy water prepared with certain rites and prayers. See *The word Zaothra used in the Avestan Literature* by A. K. Vasavawala, in *Sir J. J. Madressa Jub. Vol.*, p. 25 f.

174 Dhalla, *Zor. Th.*, p. 141; Jackson, *Zor. Stu.*, p. 56; see esp. C. de Harlez, *op. cit.*, p. 165. See Yt. 19.51-2.

ly located inside the waters (Pahlavi tradition putting him in the region of the Caspian Sea) and has many wives. His Vedic double nature—igneous (celestial fire reddening the clouds) and aqueous (' Son of the waters '), though not totally absent in the Avestan literature, is very faint and he has acquired in addition the meaning of a locality, possibly a hilly region, in the Avesta.[175] He is credited like Anāhita herself with the making of men and furthering the prosperity of the Ahurian lands.

The worship of the firmament and the earth returned also. The sky is not only the garment of Ahura, the battle-field of the powers of god and evil, and the seat of celestial lights, but also a Yazata himself, worshipped under the name of *Asmān* along with Paradise.[176] The Earth was similarly worshipped under the name of *Zām* or *Zamyāt*;[177] and before they came to be looked upon as disfiguring the symmetry of the Ahurian creation and destined to be levelled down at the Renovation, the mountains too received the veneration of men, the two most important ones being Ushi-dhāu Ushi-darena or Oshdāshtār (the giver and keeper of understanding), the seat of holy happiness, and Hara Berezaiti, between two ridges of which was stretched the fateful Bridge of the Separator.[178] It is difficult to understand why in addition to Ārmaiti another spirit of the earth would be needed unless we suppose that the interest was not to provide a guardian spirit but to revive the animistic cult. Exactly for the same

175 C. de Harlez, *op. cit.*, p. 166.

176 Dhalla, *Zor. Th.*, p. 128; see esp. C. de Harlez, *op. cit.*, 174. The sky was regarded as a solid spherical band.

177 Dhalla, *Zor. Th.*, p. 142; C. de Harlez, *op. cit.*, p. 174.

178 See Yt. 19.1 f for an enumeration of the high places known to the later Avesta. The number was fixed at 2244. See SBE. XXIII, p. 289. See also Moulton, *Ear. Zor.*, p. 214; C. de Harlez, *op. cit.*, p. 218; also Casartelli, *op. cit.*, p. 111. Hara Berezaiti stood in the very centre of Airyana Vaeja, the first among the lands created by Mazdā.—See I. J. S. Taraporewala, *The Religion of Zarathushtra*, p. 5. Geiger thinks 'Hara-berzati to have been more than a local name (*i.e.*, not merely the Alburz but high mountains in general) and Aryana-vaija to be only a semi-mythical land and, if real, to be located in Upper Ferghanāh. Ushidhāu Ushidarena (sometimes regarded as one mountain and sometimes as two) has been identified with Kūh-i Khwāja, 'Mountain of the Master,' the table-land of Seistān. (See Jackson, *Zor. St.*, p. 184; Geiger, *op. cit.*, II, pp. 93, 101-07).

reason Ātar was needed in addition to Asha Vahishta and the different gods of the waters in addition to Haurvatāt. Exactly for a similar reason too, Ameretāt failed to satisfy the religious need of a god of the plant-world and Vohu Manah that of a god of the animal world; the people wanted not a guardian but a god. Hence the worship of "growing plants and forest trees" returned during the counter-reformation [179] although the constant epithet 'created by Ahura Mazdah' served to hide the return of the animistic belief. The expanded liturgy demanded veneration for vegetation in connection with three major items—the Baresman, the sacred twig, the Haoma, the sacred drink, and the Draonah (cake or wafer-bread), the consecrated food, just as the Vedic rites demanded Barhis,[180] Soma and Puroḍāśa, and in both it is the sacred drink (Soma = Haoma) that assumed the most important position and became indispensable in certain types of worship (Yajña = Izashne or Yasna).[181]

The later Parsi distinction between the white or celestial *Haoma*,[182] made from the mythical Gaokerena (Gokard) tree belonging to the domain of Ameretāt and, therefore, appropriately enough, regarded as the source of the ambrosia that will confer immortality at the Resurrection, and the yellow or terrestrial Haoma, which is responsible for force, bodily vigour, cure of corporal ailments, and fertility, does not occur in the Avesta. The personification, again, is imperfect and the writers slip unconsciously from the sense of the angel personifying its virtues to that of the physical plant itself

179 See Yt. 71.9. For the oft-quoted panegyric on cultivation which drives away demons, see Vend. 3.23 f. (See G. F. Moore, *His. of Rel.*, I, p. 395). Söderblom is of opinion that Zarathushtra himself refers not to the destruction of crops but to that of pasture (*op. cit.*, p. 226).

180 See Macdonell, *Ved. Myth.*, p. 154.

181 There is this important difference that "the Parsis do not sacrifice to the fire, but the Haoma as well as the consecrated *Darun*-bread are partaken of by the priests present during the ceremony" (see *Zaota* by Prof. K. G. Geldner in *Sanjana Comm. Vol.*, p. 279).

182 See Dhalla, *Zor. Th.*, pp. 119-122; C. de Harlez, *op. cit.*, p. 168; Jackson, *Zor. Stu.*, p. 62; ERE. vi. 506 f; see esp. Casartelli, *op. cit.*, p. 121 f; *Spiegel Memorial Volume*, pp. 1-11, art. *The Homa Tree and the Ten Kar-fish of the Bundahishn*, and pp. 174-180, art. *The Hôm Yasht and "The Bacchae" of Euripides: a contrast.*

Thus, a description of the habitat and physical properties of the earthly plant mingles with that of the supernatural qualities and magical virtues of the celestial plant, and in the same breath its exhilarating effect on the body and its moral influence on the soul are delineated. A story in the Paurāṇic pattern describes how the angel Haoma appeared to Zarathustra in a vision and by narrating the gifts in his power (mostly the gifts of noble sons) persuaded him to introduce his worship in Iran.[183] We have already referred to the myth of the Fravashi of the Prophet being conveyed to earth in a stem of the Haoma plant. As in the Vedas, Haoma's power to improve body, mind, morals and soul is described in extravagant terms, and we are told that 'heaven, health, long life, power to contend against evils, victory against enemies, and forewarnings against coming dangers from thieves, murderers and plunderers' are given by Haoma when properly worshipped but that the sinful and the malicious are cursed by him and not granted their wishes. It is very likely that, as in India in later times, the identity of the plant was lost among migrating tribes and a non-intoxicating substitute was used. As Moulton observes,[184] "In the period of the Yashts, which seems to have been the age of the kings, Haoma reappears in all his glory.......But we gather that the Iranian Bacchus has in the interval signed the pledge. There is no suggestion of alcohol, and Haoma is a magical, mystical drink which to all appearance is harmless enough, whether it bestowed immortality or no." There must have been a good deal of 'secondary elaboration' in Iran after the Aryan tradition was partially lost because we find that the word Haoma began to be used in a variety of senses, including that of a prophetic precursor of Zarathustra in Mazdayasnian religion.[185]

Apparently also, for the cattle the guardianship of Vohu Manah did not suffice; nor even *Geush Tashan* and *Geush*

183 Ys. 9.

184 Moulton, *Ear. Zor.*, pp. 72-3.

185 See ERE. vi. 506, art. HAOMA; Modi, *Rel. Cer. and Cus. of the Parsis*, p 300 f; *Anthropological Papers*, p. 225.

*Urvan*,[186] either because the former was too closely identified with Ahura Mazdah and the latter too helpless himself to be a helper or because the animistic cult required a veneration of the animals themselves. So *Drvāspā* [187] becomes the personified animal creation and has a Yasht dedicated to her. She looks after the health of the flocks and thereby maintains the people in comfort (whence she is called the maintainer). But as cattle constituted wealth in those days, she was credited with giving the same boons as the genius of Plenty (Ashi Vanghuhī).[188] Still, the older figures did not disappear altogether and sacrifices to Geush Urvan were enjoined.[189] Reference has already been made to the extensive cult of *the Fravashis* [190] which had apparently its origin in the deification of ancestors and which was subsequently expanded and sublimated and ceased to be the worship of the spirits of men. Though Iran had many a legend about heroes it does not appear that she paid any divine honours to them, with the exception of Zoroaster who received a kind of deification in later times [191] and was accordingly worshipped as the head of the earthly Yazatas and whose seeds were supposed to be preserved miraculously in the Kansaoya Lake till the three millennial prophets would be born successively in the wombs of three maidens.[192] It may be added that Space and Time, that play not an inconsiderable part in the cosmic drama, were also personified, but because of their abstract nature they were not officially included within the class of angels. *Zervan Akarana* (Eternity or Boundless Time) and *Zervan Daregho-Khvadhāta* (Sovereign Time of Long Dura-

186 Dhalla, *Zor. Th.*, p. 125.

187 Dhalla, *Zor. Th.*, p. 125; Jackson, *Zor. Stu.*, p. 58; C. de Harlez, *op. cit.*, p. 198.

188 See Dhalla, *Zor. Th.*, p. 125.

189 *Ibid.*, p. 126.

190 See Jackson, *Zor. St.*, p. 59.

191 See Söderblom, *op. cit.*, p. 229.

192 For the advent of the millennial prophets, see West's *Introduction* in SBE, V, p. lvf; also Ch. XXX of the *Bundahish* (p. 120 f.); Jackson, *Zor. St.*, p. 285.

tion) as also *Thwāsha Khvadhāta* (Sovereign Space) are invoked along with the Yazatas.[193]

Thus we see that nature-religion had its full vengeance on the Zoroastrian reform inasmuch as the worship of the departmental deities, which is such a familiar feature of the Vedic religion, returned with its rituals and its festivals, not as an allegory or a mere figure of speech but as an earnest cult.[194] To quote C. de Harlez :[195] "As the Mazdaean theories postulate that the struggle between the good and the evil principle is not only a struggle in the world of morality but is also a struggle relatively traceable in things nonmoral and physical, it follows that the duty of the Mazdaean is to pay honour to the whole creation of Ahura Mazda and to work for its development and its triumph, by making of it a cult. Consequently the prayers of the Avesta, the homage of the faithful, are frequently addressed to human souls in the first place, and then to the souls of animals, to the vegetable kingdom, to the springs, to the waters, to rivers, to the earth and mountains and fields, to the wind, to the visible sky, to the stars, to the invisible heavens and all its parts." The whole thing was given a Zoroastrian veneer by ascribing the origin of the revived polytheism to Zoroaster himself or by the conceit that the departmental deities were the sons or daughters or wives or creatures of Ahura Mazdah (although that was partially nullified by picturing Ahura Mazdah as worshipping at least some of them) or the auxiliaries of the various Amesha Spentas or by investing these spirits with ethical qualities in keeping with the main tenets of Zoroastrianism. In its various transformations the Iranian religion never for a moment let go its sheet-anchor that the gods were moral as well as beneficent and that their aid could not be expected in the execution of wicked intentions by maleficent minds, human or supernatural. The long list of evil

193 Dhalla, *Zor. Th.*, p. 150; Jackson, *Zor. Stu.*, pp. 64, 111 (it is in the phenomenal time of the long period that the world's history of 12,000 years takes place); C. de Harlez, *op. cit.*, pp. 220, 132. See esp. Casartelli, *op. cit.*, pp. 10-1.

194 See C. de Harlez, *op. cit.*, p. 177.

195 *Ibid.*, p. 173.

spirits [196] and the similarity of some of the names with Vedic titles prove that popular superstitions about the invisible physical and moral enemies of man were not forgotten during the counter-reformation; but the people always treated them as evils to be fought and conquered and never as powers to be propitiated or bought off by apotropaic rites.

But Iran did not surrender completely to the temptation of worshipping the powers of nature. Side by side with the development of nature-worship there went on a deepening of the consciousness of certain spiritual conditions of religion and favourable future destiny, and this led to the personification of certain abstract virtues after the model of the Amesha Spentas. To begin with the most worldly. *Pārendi*,[197] in her rapidly moving chariot and personifying bodily activity and mental alertness, became traditionally associated, like the Vedic Puraṃdhi, with buried treasure and was therefore rightly made a companion of Mithra, the lord of wide pastures, on the one hand, and of Ashi Vanghuhī, the spirit of plenty, on the other. Adoration is also paid to *Shavo* and *Saokā*,[198] the angels of utility and welfare, to *Air-Yaman*,[199] the genius of health, and to *Rāma Hvāstra*, the genius of the joys of life,[200] and practically every important Yazata is credited with the gift of temporal blessing in addition to spiritual advancement. *Ashi Vanghuhī*,[201] the guardian of earthly riches, is by far the most important angel belonging to this group and takes the place of Lakṣmī, the Hindu goddess of wealth, in Parsi eyes; but in the Gāthās she represents sanctity and this association is not lost in later literature. She represents in essence "the happiness which is the reward of virtue, of obedience to the law," *i.e.*, spiritual riches and intellectual gifts. So she is at once the

196 See Jackson, *Zor. Stu.*, Ch. VI. The Legions of Hell, p. 67 f.; C. de Harlez, *op. cit.*, p. 199 f; Dhalla, *Zor. Th.*, Chs. XVIII, XXX.

197 C. de Harlez, *op. cit.*, p. 167; Dhalla, *Zor. Th.*, p. 124.

198 C. de Harlez, *op. cit.*, pp. 182, 187; Jackson, *Zor. Stu.*. p. 63; Sirozah I.3; Yt. 12.4; 13.42.

199 Dhalla, *Zor. Th.*, p. 119.

200 *Ibid.*, p. 114.

201 C. de Harlez, *op. cit.*, p. 183; Dhalla, *Zor. Th.*, pp. 43, 122; Yt. 17

angel of plenty and the angel of piety, and Daēnā, the spirit of religion, is her sister.[202] She is rich in all sorts of desirable things, but her gifts are reserved for a household where the youths and maidens marry in time and the sanctity of the obligations of married life is scrupulously maintained.[203] She comes with all sorts of flocks, with all victory, with all intelligence, with all glory and with virtuous offspring; but she expects her temporal gifts to be shared with the deserving and the needy—"let Ashi, with fulness of welfare, follow the man who gladdens the faithful with his gifts."[204] Her picture is powerfully drawn and the prayer to her is fervent and lifted above all sordid selfishness by associating her with all orders of spiritual beings from Ahura Mazdah downwards. We see, therefore, that all lawful gain was encouraged and people were taught to welcome and appreciate the good things of the world provided by God.

It was a good idea to associate Spentā Ārmaiti with Ashi Vanghuhī, on the one hand, and with *Rātā*, on the other.[205] Poverty is responsible for so much evil not only in personal lives but also in social relations that the faithful are enjoined to adore Rātā, the genius of charity, " with the eyes of love," so that miserliness and selfish greed may not take possession of their soul. Any good that is within one's power to give should be given with grace. Thus, " if one of the faith approaches another, seeking goods, or a wife, or knowledge, the man of means should help him with goods, he should arrange for the marriage of this poor co-religionist, he should pay for his instruction in religious matters." [206] And the whole world knows how faithfully the Parsis have kept this prescription of their religion.

202 Dhalla, *Zor. Th.*, p. 101.

203 In later Persian literature (*e.g.*, *Sad Dar*) the importance of leaving a son, natural or adopted, was as much emphasised as in Hindu Dharma Śāstras. (See Pavry, *The Zoroastrian Doctrine of a Future Life*, pp. 109-10. He refers to Ys. 62.5; Yt. 13.134.)

204 Yt. 18.4-5.

205 Yt. 17.16. Sirozah I.5; II.5; Dhalla, *Zor. Th.*, p. 114; Moulton, *Tr. Mag.*, p. 115.

206 Dhalla, *Zor. Th.*, p. 115.

The national trait so early noted by Herodotus, *viz.*, regard for truth,[207] had a number of angels corresponding to its various nuances of meaning. Reference has already been made to *Mithra*, the presiding genius of contracts, compacts and truthful dealings between individuals and also between nations : a violator of agreements was a *Mithro-druj*, deceiver of Mithra. Naturally associated with him is *Rashnu*,[208] called ' the most just ' (razishta), as the presiding genius of justice, for the violation of undertakings is the flouting of justice also. His vision encompasses all objects, celestial and terrestrial, and he is always present in ordeals, when invoked, to see that strict justice is done to a suspect. Thieves and disturbers of peace have most to dread from him. During the Pahlavi period, when eschatological interest increased in importance, Rashnu (Rashn) as the genius of justice was depicted as holding the golden scales in which the good and evil deeds of souls are weighed.[209] As the genius of truth, Rashnu has a female associate with the same function, namely, *Arshtāt* [210] who personifies rectitude and is the guide of celestial and terrestrial beings. A variant of that name is *Rasanstāt* who is invited along with *Erethe*, another minor female angel of rectitude.[211] Closely related to Mithra as the god of war is *Ākhshti*, the spirit of peace. Appropriately enough,

[207] See Yt. 11.3; " The word of truth is the fighter that is the best of all fiend-smiters."

[208] Dhalla, *Zor. Th.*, pp. 111, 240; C. de Harlez, *op. cit.*, p. 181.

[209] See Pavry, *op. cit.*, pp. 67, 82, 89; Casartelli, *op. cit.*, p. 79. In *Dātastān-i-Dēnik* there are four takers of account—(1) Vohuman takes account of deeds thrice every day; (2) Mihr takes account of all promises kept or broken; (3) Rashnu (and Srosh) reckons the deeds of the departed; (4) Oharmazd takes account of all things by his omniscience at the time of the Resurrection (see Pavry, *op. cit.*, pp. 89-90).

It is interesting to note that "some of the Rabbis even taught that righteousness and wickedness were determined by the excess of good over evil actions. A balance of one good deed, they held, was sufficient to make a man righteous." See Lindsay Dewar, *Imagination and Religion*, p. 66.

[210] Dhalla, *Zor. Th.*, p. 112; C. de Harlez, *op. cit.*, p. 182; Jackson, *Zor. Stu.*, p. 61. Dhalla makes Arshtāt out to be a female angel while C. de Harlez (Eng. Tr.) uses the term as masculine. Arshtāt is one of Rashnu's company at the Chinvat Bridge in Pahlavi literature. See Pavry, *op. cit.*, p. 85; Dhalla, *Zor. Th.*, p. 177.

[211] Dhalla, *Zor. Th.*, p. 112; C. de Harlez, *op. cit.*, p. 182.

she is associated also with Vohu Manah, good mind, and *Khratu*, worldly wisdom (or Chisti, religious wisdom),[212] for peace can come only out of a peaceful attitude of mind and an intelligent (and religious) conviction about the futility of strife and discord.

The remaining personifications are connected with the Mazdayasnian religion itself in its twofold aspect of faith and practice. *Sraosha* (Srosh)[213] as a personified abstraction comes down from Gāthic times and is, as Dhalla remarks, " one of the few angels whose prominence increases with the lapse of time " He is Ahura's own, the personification of obedience to the Mazdayasnian law—" the priest-divinity who acts as an embodiment of the divine service " and prompts men to pay heed to the message of goodness. He is the Gabriel of the Zoroastrian religion and communicates to man Divine wishes and orders. His later development into an assessor of the deeds of men along with Mithra and Rashnu is foreshadowed in the Gāthās [214] and becomes complete in the Pahlavi period when he becomes the escort of the individual soul across the Chinvat Bridge. Special ceremonies [215] are performed in his honour during the first three days and nights after death, when the departed soul is to take the three fateful steps towards heaven or hell,[216] in order to secure his help at that time in warding off the demons and also later on at the seat of Judgment—in fact, a man may have the ceremonies in honour of Sraosha performed in his life-time (the Zindeh-

212 Dhalla, *Zor. Th.*, p. 115; Jackson, *Zor. Stu.*, p. 63.

213 Dhalla, *Zor. Th.*, pp. 41, 101, 238; Modi, *Rel. Cer. and Cus. of the Parsis*, p. 434 f; also pp. 77-8; Pavry, *op. cit.*, p. 58; C. de Harlez, *op. cit.*, p. 179; Ys. 57; Yt. 11; Casartelli, *op. cit.*, p. 80. See esp. Madan, *op. cit.*, p. 34 f and esp. p. 54 (he thinks that Sraosha stands not for obedience but for knowledge or inspiration).

214 Carnoy, in ERE. ix. 569, points out the resemblance between the Assyrian god Shamash, accompanied in his capacity as the god of law by two divinised abstractions—Kettu, 'justice,' and Mēsharu, 'rectitude,' and the Zoroastrian Mithra, accompanied by Rashnu, 'justice,' and Sraosha, 'discipline,' 'rectitude,' and also Auramazda of the Behistan inscription proceeding with justice and equity.

215 See Modi, *Rel. Cer. and Cus. of the Parsis*, p. 436, for the Sraosh ceremonies; also Pavry, *op. cit.*, pp. 10, 103-04.

216 See Pavry, *op. cit.*, p. 15.

ravān ceremony) lest they should not be duly performed for some reason or other after his death.[217] Sraosha has not enjoyed sleep since the time when the two Spirits made the world, namely, the good Spirit and the evil One,[218] and with spells which form his very body (*tanumanthra*) and his weapons he fights the fiendish Druj and guards the world after sunset, against Aēshma who is iniquity incarnate (*peshotanus*) and other emissaries of evil who prevent men from performing their religious duties, by coming down thrice during the day and thrice during the night. But inasmuch as religion does not thrive on obedience alone, a second Yazata, *Chisti* (or Chistā),[219] personifies religious wisdom. She wears the white garment of purity or holiness and is invoked to bestow clearest vision. She is a companion of Rasanstāt, the angel of equity, presumably because profession of religion and upright dealing must go hand in hand; and also of *Daenā*, the genius of the Holy Mazdayasnian Law,[220] possibly because faith gives rise to knowledge, as the Bhagavadgītā and St. Augustine have also affirmed. Daenā represents, however, not only the objective system of beliefs but also the religion as lived—the good or bad religious conscience or the reflection of the inner being of a departed soul.[221] It is this second meaning that becomes prominent in connection with eschatological speculations and Daenā is conceived as coming to greet a soul (either before or after the Judgment)[222] in the form of a lovely maiden in the case of a good man and in that of a hideous hag in the case of a wicked one.

Religion as a system of formulae and incantations gave rise to another set of personifications, the most important of

217 Modi, *Rel. Cer. and Cus. of the Parsis*, p. 444 f; Pavry, *op. cit.*, p. 18.

218 Yt. 11.2; Ys. 57.17.

219 Dhalla, *Zor. Th.*, p. 101.

220 Dhalla, *Zor. Th.*, p. 101; C. de Harlez, *op. cit.*, p. 186; Casartelli, *op. cit.*, p. 82; Jackson, *Zor. St.*, p. 146, f.n. 8.

221 Ys. 46.11. See Pavry, *op. cit.*, Chs. IV-VI, esp. p. 28.

222 There is a difference of opinion about the exact time when the Daena meets the soul.—See Pavry, *op. cit.*, pp. 37, 39, 44. The most wicked acts are burning the dead, idol-worship, causing oppression and cutting down trees. See Hadhokht Nask, 13, quoted by Pavry in *op. cit.*, p. 35 (with footnotes).

which was *Manthra* (or *Māthra*) *Spenta* (Māhraspand)[223] who was invoked with the Law of Zarathustra, the good Law of the worshippers of Mazdah, and the long-traditional Teaching and Wisdom, both spiritual and secular. He is the lord of Holy Spells and specially prevails against the demons, whence he is the most potent help of a Mazdaean in distress. Did not Zarathustra himself smite Angra Mainyu with the *Ahuna Vairya*, "as strong a weapon as a stone big as a house?"[224] Is not a correct recitation of it with proper intonation worth the chanting of a hundred Gāthās?[225] The soul of Ahura Mazdah is the Māthra Spenta which was pronounced by him before anything else was, and given to the Prophet in boundless time.[226] There are other spells too,[227] the most potent of them being the *Airyaman Ishya* (which smites all manners of disease and death, being associated with Airyaman who heals with holy spells),[228] the *Ashem Vohu* (which is associated with Asha and is so efficacious when uttered at the time of death)[229] and the *Yenghē Hātam* prayer.[230] The praises bes-

223 Dhalla, *Zor. Th.*, p. 115; C. de Harlez, *op. cit.*, p. 184.

224 Yt. 17.20 describes Asha Vahishta (Ashem Vohu) as behaving like melting brass; Vend. 19.9 (the other weapons are the sacred mortar, the sacred cup and the Haoma). See also Bund. 1.8, about the progressive effect of the Honover on Angra Mainyu (SBE. V, p. 8). See also Modi, *Rel. Cer. and Cus. of the Parsis*, p. 341 f; Moulton, *Tr. Mag.*, p. 77; Dhalla, *Zor. Th.*, p. 173.

225 Ys. 19.5. The 21 books (*nasks*) of the ancient Avestan literature are said to have corresponded to the 21 words of the Ahunavar.

226 Ys. 19.3, 4; Vend. 19.9.

227 For the holy prayers, see Visparad, 1. See SBE. IV, p. lxxviii; Haug, *op. cit.*, p. 141.

228 Dhalla, *Zor. Th.*, p. 119. The prayer has been translated thus: "May the vow-fulfilling Airyaman come here, for the men and women of Zarathushtra to rejoice, for Vohumano to rejoice; with the desirable reward that Religion deserves. I solicit for holiness that boon that is vouchsafed by Ahura."—Darmesteter, quoted by Moulton in *Tr. Mag.*, p. 91, n.1. For Mills' translation, see SBE, XXXI, Ys. LIV, p. 293. See Yt. 3.5.

229 Ys. 27.14. Modi, *Rel. Cer. and Cus. of the Parsis*, p. 348. The prayer has been translated thus: "Holiness is the best of all good. Well is it for it, well is it for that holiness which is perfection of holiness" (Moulton, *Tr. Mag.*, p. 91, n.2), or, "Piety is the best good and happiness. Happiness to him who is pious for the best piety" (Modi, *op. cit.*, p. 349).

230 Ys. 4.26 (SBE, XXXI, p. 218). The prayer has been translated thus: "Ahura Mazda knows (lit., is the knower of), who among the living is the best in prayer through righteousness (*i.e.*, says his prayer in the best way possible by observing *asha*, *i.e.*, righteousness). We praise them (those recognised as above

towed on the different prayers and the recital of benefits to be derived from repeating them on different occasions and in different quantities[231] show that the Iranian religion ran dangerously near the view that magical efficacies pertain to the repetition of sacred texts; and even if it did not go to the length of the Brāhmaṇa position that the gods could be coerced into beneficence by suitable incantations, it did not fall far below the conception of automatic reward of sacred recitals and of the coercion of demons by magical formulae.[232] Apparently, it was felt difficult to limit personification to the sacred manthras alone, for in due time the different parts of the Avesta were offered sacrifices, especially the five Gāthās which came to be set over the five divisions of the day.[233] It does not appear that the system of "disciplinary and judicial injunctions" (*Dātem*) was personified;[234] but sacrifices were nevertheless offered to almost everything connected with the ritual order.[235] Thus, Benediction upon the righteous becomes the yazata *Dahmā Āfriti* (Dahmān Afrīṇ)[236] and Malediction upon the unrighteous takes the form of the angel *Dāmoish Upamana*,[237] and, appropriately enough, the one comes in the shape of a camel while her counterpart takes the form of a ferocious boar.[238] Zoroastrianism included within its creed uncompromising hostility towards the wicked, the infidel and the apostate; hence "the redoubted and swift Curse of the wise" was a part of the Mazdayasnian religion.

by Ahura Mazda) whether male or female" (Modi, *Rel. Cer. and Cus. of the Parsis*, p. 349). See also Moulton, *Tr. Mag.*, p. 91, n.2; SBE. XXXI, p. 218 (Ys. 7.27).

231 Modi, *Rel. Cer. and Cus. of the Parsis*, p. 340 f.

232 G. F. Moore, *His. of Rel.*, I, pp. 390, 393.

233 SBE, XXXI, p. 379 f (esp. p. 382—Gāh II.5). See Moulton, *Tr. Mag.*, p. 60. It has been suggested that the five Muslim daily prayers were taken over from the Persian practice of prayers at the five Gāhs.

234 Dātem is often invoked but does not seem to be personified. See C. de Harlez, *op. cit.*, p. 185.

235 Gāh III.5.

236 Dhalla, *Zor. Th.*, p. 118. For the various Āfrins, see Modi, *Rel. Cer. and Cus. of the Parsis*, p. 387 f.

237 Dhalla, *Zor. Th.*, p. 118.

238 Vis, I.7; Dhalla, *Zor. Th.*, p. 118.

The later literature gives us not only an extended pantheon but also an extensive description of 'the legions of hell '[239] which it was the duty of the faithful to beware of and resist. Many of these are similar to Vedic malevolent spirits, but some Vedic gods also figure as demons in Iranian religion. Some of these evil spirits were genuine revivals from ancient superstitions and represented a class of objective beings—' malevolent powers and evil personages,' as Jackson calls them.[240] Some again were mythical monsters or impersonations of witchcraft or of the evil forces of nature that destroy the fruits of human labour or endanger human life and property. The Rivāyats give us some idea of the popular formulae of spell to withstand the hostile forces that threaten man's life and happiness from outside.[241] But the spiritual character of the Zoroastrian religion can be indirectly brought out by enumerating the evil spirits that were supposed to sap the foundations of religion in the inner being of the faithful themselves.[242] The most formidable demons belong to human nature itself. They are *Aka Manah*, vile thoughts, *Indra* (or *Andra*), apostasy, *Sauru* or Saurva (the Brāhmanic Sarva), misgovernment, anarchy and drunkenness, *Nāonghaithya* (Vedic Nāsatya),[243] later identified with *Taromaiti*, pride, presumption, disobedience, insubordination, contempt, heresy, and *Aēshma*, wrath, fury, rapine and outrage (specially in relation to cattle); also the falsely spoken word (*Draoga Mithaokhta*), malice, envy, jealousy (*Araska*), lust (*Vareno*), untimely sleep, lethargy, (*Bushyanstā*), stinginess, miserliness and hoarding (*Arāiti, Pūsh*), luxury (*Ari*), greed (*Āzi*), incredulity (*Ereshi*), lying, deceit, untruth (*Druj, Arāst, Daiwi Daeva*), slander and gossip (*Spazga*), revenge, spite

239 Jackson, *Zor. Stu.*, Ch. VI; Dhalla, *Zor. Th.*, Chs. VI, XVIII, XXX; C. de Harlez, *op. cit.*, p. 199 f; Casartelli, *op. cit.*, p. 88 f.

240 Jackson, *Zor. Stu.*, p. 103.

241 See Dhalla, *Zor. Th.*, p. 309.

242 See Jackson, *Zor. Stu.*, p. 85 f.

243 The other two arch-demons are Tauru (or Taurvi) and Zairicha, who represent hunger and thirst (or demons that generate and apply poison to kill plants and animals)—the two potent bodily causes of religious inattention.

(*Kasvi Daeva*), beggary, poverty (*Driwi Daeva*), debauchery (*Jahi*), drunkenness (*Kunda*), murder (*Khru, Khrvighni*). discord (*Anākhshti*), disobedience (*Asrushti*), and idolatry (*Khnanthaiti*). As Jackson remarks,[244] "Only the hosts of angels and the watchfulness of man hold in check the hordes of Ahriman, his demons and fiends. Any lapse from the path of righteousness, any act of wrongdoing or carelessness, any neglect of goodness or lack of attention to the prescribed mode of living places man in the power of some demon or of some other evil force which constantly lurks ready to take possession of him and to destroy his body and his soul." "This conception of life as a war with the demons," rightly observes G. F. Moore,[245] "gives its peculiar colour to the religion, morals and customs. In many particulars these resemble the lower religions in which self-defence against evil spirits is the principal feature; but the central theistic and ethical ideas give them a different significance." Much of the penitential and purificatory literature, however, owes its origin to the dread of being the victim of this or that demon.

Plutarch, in his list of Persian gods, mentions Ahura Mazdah, Mithra, the six gods (Amesha Spentas) originally created by Ahura Mazdah, Sirius (Tishtrya) and other stars, as also twenty-four other gods created subsequently by Ahura Mazdah—an enumeration which gives thirty-three gods,[246] a number familiar to us in Vedic literature. The method of invoking the several spirits bordered closely upon polytheism as the Amesha Spentas, the Yazatas and the Fravashis were directly approached for boons within their own jurisdiction. What, then, was the distinction between Vedic polytheism and Persian polytheism? We have already seen that, excepting a few rare lapses on the part of Indra, the Vedic gods always act together and the jealousy.

244 Jackson, *Zor. Stu.*, p. 108. See Dhalla, *Zor. Th.*, p. 309, for the virtues ascribed to the incantations of Pazand and Persian *nirangs* (formulae of spell).

245 G. F. Moore, *His. of Rel.*, I, p. 387.

246 Omitting the other stars. For the quotation from Plutarch, see Haug, *Essays on the Religion of the Parsis*, p. 9 (Mithra is not specifically mentioned but Ahura Mazdah is supposed to have sprung out of the purest light). But see Yasna 1, where the thirty-three *ratus* or chiefs are mentioned (see Haug, *op. cit.*, p. 276).

rivalry and conflict of the gods are generally unknown in India till we come down to the time of the sectarian religions. The same was the case in Persian religion, for barring a casual complaint by this or that spirit that men are partial to other angels in the frequency of their worship, we do not hear of gods squabbling or fighting among themselves. There is, however, one important distinction between Hinduism and Parsism: Hinduism never succeeded in establishing a single supreme god like Ahura Mazdah and hence different sects claimed different gods as supreme. Zervan Akarana is the only Being who ever contested seriously with Mazdah for the headship of the Iranian pantheon, but it does not appear that he ever became for long a living force to the people at large.[247] The Yazatas whom Ahura Mazdah is represented in the Yashts as worshipping were never meant to be regarded as occupying a position superior or even equal to that of Ahura Mazdah, and none except Mithra, the god of the older Aryan solar cult, ever attained any important position even outside the Iranian church or set up a rival sect to that of Ahura Mazdah. The writers had always the consciousness that in the last resort the angels and archangels were subordinate to and even creatures of Ahura Mazdah, and in the same piece of composition would occur the expressions that Mazdah (sometimes himself regarded as a Yazata) worships a particular Yazata and that he is the latter's creator or father; or that he is one of the Amesha Spentas and that he is their creator.[248] Brāhmanic India did evolve the idea of a unitary principle of existence, namely, Brahman, but this was conceived not in theistic but in pantheistic terms: and while India chose to be philosophical, not only in her Brāhmanism but also in her Jainism and Buddhism, Persia preferred to be religious. Being practically free, even in its later forms, from idolatry, Zoroastrianism did not turn the revived departmental deities into local gods of this or that city as was done by Egypt, Babylon

[247] See Casartelli, *op. cit.*, p. 12 f.

[248] See C. de Harlez, *op. cit.*, pp. 133-6, 138, 147.

or even Greece. While probably local emphasis upon this or that aspect could not be entirely avoided, the religion was common to the whole population and there was a single body of scriptures, binding upon the entire religious community. It is only in *Dabistān*, a 17th century work composed in India, that we have as many as fourteen Zoroastrian sects mentioned;[249] but orthodox Parsis disavow the genuineness of their differences as also any distinction drawn by that work between exoteric and esoteric religion (the latter being really a mixture of Greek metaphysics through its Arabic version, Hindu Yoga and Persian Sūfism).[250]

What, in spite of the revival of nature worship, the religion of the later Avesta was, can be made out if we consult the catalogue of divine names which the pious Zoroastrian was taught to recite and meditate upon. In the Ormuzd Yasht occur two such lists, probably compiled at different times and then put together in one place, which prove that the multiplication of good spirits was never intended to detract from the majesty of Ahura Mazdah.[251] The first list gives the following twenty names :—the One to be questioned, Herd-giver, the Strong One, Perfect Holiness (Asha Vahishta), All Mazdah-made Asha-born Good, Understanding, the Understanding One, Intelligence, the Intelligent One, Holiness (Weal or Beneficence), the Holy One,[252] the Lord (Ahura), Mightiest, Beyond reach of enmity (He in whom there is no harm), the Unconquerable One, Mindful of desert, the All-seeing One, the Healer, the Creator, the Wise One (Mazdah). The second list is longer and the reader will at once notice how, as in the names of Allāh, a quality is reinforced by the use of stronger language. The names given are—Protector, Creator, Maintainer, Knower, Holiest Spirit (Beneficent

[249] Dhalla, *Zor. Th.*, p. 312.

[250] *Ibid.*, p. 316.

[251] See Moulton, *Tr. Mag.*, p. 95; also Casartelli, *op. cit.*, p. 21 f. *Cf.* Yasna 1.1. See Geiger, *op. cit.*, I, Int., xxv f.

[252] These three pairs declare that Holiness and Intelligence are not only the qualities but also the essence of God—the nearest approximation to the Vedāntic idea that Brahman is consciousness (qualified by the theistic idea of Zoroastrianism that God is also personal).

Spirit), Best Healer, Priest, Best Priest, the Lord (Ahura), Wise (Mazdah), Righteous (Holy), Most Righteous (Most Holy), Glorious, Most Glorious, Wide-seeing, Widest-seeing, Far-seeing, Farthest-seeing, Watcher (Keeper), Tracker (Well-wisher), Creator, Protector, Maintainer, Knower, Best Knower, Prosperity-producer (Cattle-owner), Word of Prosperity (Word of the Cattle-owner), Desiring Dominion (King who rules at his will), Most Desiring Dominion (King who rules most at his will), Mild of Dominion (Liberal King), Most Mild of Dominion (Most Liberal King), Who cannot deceive, Free from deceit (Who cannot be deceived), Keeper, Destroyer of malice, Conqueror at one stroke, All-conqueror, All-Creator (Shaper of everything), All-blessing (All-weal), Wide-blessing (Full Weal), Blessed (Master of Weal), Of mighty benefits (Who can benefit at his wish), Of mighty beneficence (Who can best benefit at his wish),[253] Powerful (Energetic), Most Powerful,[254] Holiness (Asha), the Great one (High), Dominant (Good Sovereign), Most Dominant (Best of Sovereigns), Of good insight (the Wise one), Of best insight (the Wisest of the wise), He who does good for a long time (Who sees afar). These names are declared to be the most fiend-smiting; even if we leave aside the magical aspect of their recitation, there can be no doubt that they sum up the most essential attributes of the Divine nature and will compare very favourably with the conception of God in any other advanced ethical monotheism, especially if we include under blessing and beneficence the active love of God for his own creation. The tradition lived on, for in the *Dīnkart* Ahura Mazdah is described in an antithetical way in the following manner:[255]—" Sovereign, and not servant; father, and not child; prior, and not dependent; master, and not obedient; chief, and not having a chief; lord, and not subject to a master; protector, and not protected; immutable, and without

253 'Beneficent' and 'Most Beneficent' are repeated here.

254 Moulton uses this in lieu of 'Most Beneficent.'

255 Casartelli, *op. cit.*, p. 24. He misses in the list any attribute of immensity or infinity. In the *Bun-Dehesh* the infinity of God is expressly *excluded* (*Ibid.*, p. 25).

desires; possessing in himself living knowledge, and not by any medium; disposing, and not disposed; distributing, but not receiving anything; illuminating, and not illuminated; co-operating but not receiving co-operation;[256] co-acting and not subject to any co-action; directing, and not directed." His creative activity is unconditionally affirmed: "He has created through his own essential power and knowledge six supreme Ameshospands and numerous Yazds, the most excellent paradise and the Gārôtmān, the vault of the sky, the burning sun, the shining moon and the stars of numerous germs, the wind and the atmosphere, the fire and the water, the earth and the plants, the animals, metals and man." [257] Nor is his moral government of the world forgotten. He protects and sustains his creation. He makes his existence and nature known to man through his visible creation as also through scriptural revelations. He and his angels assist the good creation and out of the evil introduced by Ahriman he can draw out good. He rewards virtue and punishes wickedness.[258] He harms no creature for he is beneficent by nature; but Ahriman and his brood will have no mercy from him, and even if the Evil Spirit cannot be annihilated, his creation will be taken away from him and the Renovation will leave Ormazd in sole charge of all existing things.[259] The faithful are enjoined never to injure a righteous man: "Since the righteous man is a counterpart of Auharmazd the lord and when the righteous man acts it is caused by him who is Auharmazd, whoever propitiates the righteous man, his fame and welfare exist a long time in the world, and the splendour of Auharmazd and pleasure and joy become his own in heaven (vahisht)." [260]

256 This attribute is striking in view of the later Avestan passages describing the help that the Yazatas and Fravashis render to Ahura Mazdah.

257 Casartelli, *op. cit.*, p. 30; see his summary on pp. 30-1.

258 *Ibid.*, *loc. cit.*

259 Casartelli, *op. cit.*, p. 64 f. The *Bun-Dehesh* contemplates the final non-existence of Ahriman while the *Dīnkart* believes in the immortality of Ahriman and thinks that though the demons would be destroyed and the wicked in hell purified and saved by the fire, Ahriman will continue to live, albeit totally powerless to harm the world of Ahura Mazdah any more.

260 *Shāyast Lā-Shāyast*, Ch. XV. 8 (SBE. V, p. 374).

Here our story of Zoroastrianism must abruptly end. Since the tragedy of exile from the father-land the Parsis have only preserved the mutilated wisdom of their saints and sages but have contributed practically nothing to the philosophical or theological development of their own faith or to the quickening of other faiths. They have also ceased now to convert aliens. The Iranian religion possesses literature in diverse tongues; but it does not appear that the attempts of Neryosangh Dhaval and others to establish a sacred Sanskrit literature for the exiles in India succeeded in evoking any considerable response.[261] The Parsis adopted Gujrati as their language and could not escape the influence of Hindu social customs and popular religious ideas altogether;[262] but their own influence on the contiguous Hindu religion has been surprisingly small. This phenomenon may be due either to the growing ignorance of the immigrants of their own religious literature—a literature which has become known with some degree of fulness only during the last 200 years, or it may be due to a kind of Jewish exclusiveness which the community has observed since its appearance on the Indian arena, or it may be due to the great religious and philosophical revival in India as a result of the active preaching of Vedānta doctrines by Śaṅkara (and later by Rāmānuja), or it may be due to the lack of that speculative thinking through which alone Hindu thought could be influenced. Not being at any time in political power and never attempting to thrust their language and belief upon the Hindus, the Parsis failed to quicken the religious thought of their neighbours as the Muslims did at a later time. But, although some of its religious practices are very similar to those of the Vedic form of religion, Parsism has succeeded in maintaining its integrity intact and resisted absorption by the more powerful and ex-

261 The extant Parsi literature produced in this tongue comprises the translation into Sanskrit of the greater part of the Avestan Yasna, Khordah Avesta, and Aogemadaecha, based on their Pahlavi versions; also a Sanskrit translation of the Pahlavi works Menuk-i Khrat, Shikand Gumanik Vijar, and Arda Viraf Namah, and the Sanskrit version of the Pazand Ashirvad.—Dhalla, *Zor. Th.*, p. 306.

262 Dhalla, *Zor. Th.*, p. 343.

tensive Hindu cult. Possibly, the tradition of hostility to the Daevas, the concentration of the entire population within a narrow area of India, and the prevention of a large influx of people of alien faiths into the community are responsible for the maintenance of the Parsi tradition; and the consciousness of possessing a revealed book in the communities concerned must also be taken into account when explaining why Hinduism, which had engulfed so many other religious and communities in the past, failed to absorb Parsism, Islām and Christianity. The appeal of Hindu pantheism, asceticism and occultism to Parsism has, however, not gone in vain; and it is only in recent years that a more intimate knowledge of the Avestan literature has prompted a reform movement pledged to weed out unsuitable accretions to the Zoroastrian faith.[263] The religion of the Prophet is now being interpreted on strictly monotheistic lines and allegorical interpretation is being put on inconvenient passages bearing on belief and conduct. A religion with a great past, a religion from which even Judaism [264] (and through it Christianity) and Islām [265] did not disdain to borrow materials, can have greater vitality infused into it if its adherents would only learn that a good religion, like light, is meant to be diffused and also that there is no virtue in clinging fast to cults and superstitions that go radically against the spiritual words which the Prophet claimed to have heard from God Himself.[266]

---

263 Dhalla, *Zor. Th.*, p. 336.

264 There is a tendency among Christian writers to deny this in spite of inconvenient parallels. See *Dic. Bib.*, IV, p. 988 f, art. ZOROASTRIANISM (by Moulton). The influences are on compositions (like the Book of Tobit, the Book of Esther and the Wisdom Literature), the relation between star and fravashi (Mt.2), resurrection, eschatology, apocalyptic, angelology (including the theory of the genii), demonology, the practices of the Essenes, etc.

265 For the influence of Parsism on Islām, see Goldziher's paper on the subject and the translator's note thereon in G. K. Nariman's *Persia and Parsis*, Part I, pp. 39-74 (also in Tiele, *op. cit.*, pp. 163-186).

266 For justification of this persistence, see Madan, *op. cit.*, p. 21.

# INDEX


Aaron 78, 282
Abaser, the (Al-Khāfid) 388
Âbhīras 205
Abiding laws of truth and morality 93
Abiding love 87
Abihu 282
Abject submission 389
Abnegation of the temporal 138
Abraham 76-77, 132, 135, 256, 263-66, 277, 283, 296, 350, 353
Absence of effusiveness and passion 116
Absence of black magic 182
Absolute 179, 181, 286
Absolute Inane 101
Absolutistic monism 203
Absorption of indigenous culture 200
Abstaining from backbiting 107
Abstention from creative activity 226
Abstention from self-determination 95
Abusers of themselves 344
Accepter of prayer (Al-Mujīb) 401
Access to supernatural planes 47
Accommodativeness 158
Achaemenian period 456
Active Charity 332
Adad (or Hadad) 258
Adam 132, 286, 405, 454
Adaptation 19
Adequate comprehension of the nature of god beyond man's capacity 371
Aditi 168, 196-97, 199, 238
Āditya 224, 236
Ādityas 168, 196, 427
Admission into the realm of everlasting life 345
Adoration of sexual restraint 226
Adṛṣṭa 94, 183, 185
Adulterers 344
Adultery 127
Advaita Vedānta 180, 486
Advaitism 231
Advent of the Messiah 123
Aegean 36
Aēshma 467, 470, 516
Affective needs of the heart 180
Aggression always the best defence 29
Aghora 230
Agni 155, 165, 175, 179, 189-90, 194, 431
----, kindling of 183
----, origin of 176
Agnosticism 109, 164
Agnostics 146
Agriculture unknown to Zarathustra 138
Ahab 287
Ahalyā 42
Ahaz 57, 258
Ahi Budhnya 167
Ahijah 53
Ahriman 445, 450, 453-54, 456, 458, 476, 492, 501-503
Ahuna Vairya 517
Ahura 427, 437, 441, 444, 464, 467-69, 492, 500
Ahura Mazdah 78, 94, 139, 140, 141-42, 206, 426-27, 431, 433, 435, 438-40, 442, 446, 448-50, 452-53, 456, 459-62, 466, 469-71, 477, 483-88, 493, 495, 497-500, 503-505, 508, 511, 513, 517, 520-22
Ahura Mazdah, final victory of 453
----as the 'clan god' 425
----described in an antithetical way 523
Ahura Mithra 492
Ahurani 506
Airyaman 491, 498, 512, 517
Airyana Vaejah 486
Aiśvarya (power) 218
Aja Ekapād 167
Ajātaśatru 214
Aka (or Achista) 467, 470
Aka Manah 519
Akriyāvādins (Philosophers of non-action) 94

Al-Ash'arī 407
Alexander the Great 421
Al-Ghazālī 396, 398
Alone in his attributes (Al-Ahad) 379
Altar of Abraham 260
Altar of Jacob 260
Altar or stone-pillar of Isaac 260
Alvars 66
All-compelling, the (Al-Jabbār) 379
All-comprehending, the (Al-Wāsi) 384
'All are Brahman' 73
All equally insignificant before God 390
All-Father 177, 190
Allāh 66
----, army of 136
----, as the name of God 350
----, glorious (or auspicious) and the terrible aspects of 377
----, names of 378-79
----, omnipotence of 388
Allāh absolutely incomprehensible and unknowable 372
Allāh absolutely indefinite and described only negatively 372
Āllāh's transcendence 412
'Allāh' the personal name of the Muslim God 376
Allāh truly is the Hearing (As-Sāmī) 384
Allāhu Akbar 412
Allegorical interpretation 8, 29, 405
Allegories 162-63
Allegorisation 407
Allegory of the mutual yearning 211
Âlvārs 209
Ameretāt 465, 470, 478, 480, 489, 500, 508
Amesha Spentas (Immortal Beneficent Ones) 199, 427, 437, 443, 452, 465, 467, 469, 477, 479, 483, 486, 488-89, 491, 493, 498, 511-12, 520-21
Amida 44, 99
Amon-Rā 167
Amorous life of Kṛṣṇa 163
Amos 57, 59, 70, 76
Amshapands 453, 485, 490, 493-94
Amulets and Charms 164
Anaghra Raochāo 492
Anāhita (Anaitis) 431, 480, 505-506
Anākhshti 520
Ancestor worship 260, 262, 480
Angelolatry 44
Angels 47, 83
Angels and other spirits as His messengers 133
Aṅgirases 189
Angra 444
Angra Mainyu 41, 302, 443-44, 446-47, 469-70, 477, 484, 487, 517
Angrô-mainyush 449
Anher 167
Animal Sacrifice 494
Animism 36, 169, 178, 253
Animistic belief 154
Annunciation of Virgin Mary 83
Aṅro Mainyus 448
Anthropomorphic Conceptions of Allāh 406
Anthropomorphic functions of Yahweh 283
Anthropomorphism 165, 194, 196, 279, 408
Anthropopathism 288, 405
Anthropopathy 285
Anti-Gentilic feeling 298
Anti-Gentilic passages, disappearance of from the New Testament 315
Anumati 155
Apām Napāt 167-68, 491, 506
Apaosha (Aposh), the demon of drought 486, 495, 502
Āpas 166, 506
Aphrodite 506
Apocalyptic literature 123
Apocalyptic vision 48
Apocrypha 305
Apollo and Mithra 493
Apostasy 134
Apostates 104
Apostle of the Gentiles 158
Apostles 76
Apostleship of Muhammad 397
Apostolic Age 335
Apotheosis 40, 131
Apotheosising the prophet 75
Appeal to the spiritual nature 103
Apūrva 94, 183
Arab bigotry 89
Arab fanaticism 421

Arab soothsayers 350
Arabinda Ghosh 247
Arāiti 519
Aramati 155
Arāst 559
Archangels and angels 484
Ardhanārīśvara images 226
Ardvī Sūra Anāhitā 486, 492, 505
Arejat-aspa 430
Arhat in Buddhism 5
Ari 519
Aristotle 107
Arjuna 205, 219
Ark, the 284
Ark of Noah 259
Ārmaiti (the Vedic Aramati) 465, 468, 478, 480, 493, 507
Arshtāt 492, 514
Artavahisht 490
Arul Nandi 240
Ārya Samāj as reviver of Vedicism 246
Ārya Samājism 29
Ārya Samājists 16
Aryaman 168, 197, 199, 236
Aryan religion 36
Aśani (Bhīma) 224, 230
Ascension 408
Ascetic and mortificatory practices 101
Asceticism 436
Asceticism condemned 138
Ascetic organisation 111
Ascription of eternal qualities to God 373
Asha 493, 517
Asha Vahishta 465, 468, 470, 478, 497-98, 500, 508
Ashem Vohu 517
Asherah 228, 272-73, 284
Ashi (Recompense, Destiny) 465
Ashi Vanghuhī 492, 512-13
Ashi Vanghuhi-Parendi 492
Ashtaroth with Tammuz (Adonis) 241
Ashtoreth 55
Asmān 492, 507
Asman-Zamyat 492
Asrushti 520
Assara Mazāsh 425
Assur-banipal 425
Assyria 58
Assyrians 13, 36
Astartes 269-70, 506
Astrology 48
Asura 427
Aśvapati Kaikeya 214
Aśvins 169, 189
Ātar (Fire) 431, 466, 492, 508
Ataraxy 109
Atavistic reversion 157
Aten 167
Atharva-Veda 167, 173
Atheism 68, 154, 164, 248
Athravan (Atharvan) 431
Atmospheric gods 167
Atmu 167
Atonement of man's sins 322
Attainment of the eternal 138
Attainment of the superhuman powers 183
Attis 12
Attis and Osiris 313
Attitude in worship 213
Attributes separate or different from essence 382
Attributists 382
Auharmazd 424
Authorities of heaven 187
Authority of the Vedas slackened by admission of non-Vedic authority 232
Avatāra 73, 231
Avesta 141
Awe of dead ancestors 154
Āzi 519

Baal 55, 266, 269-70, 272
Baalim 258, 266
Baals and astartes 271
Baal-Zebub, the god of Ekon 269, 273
Bab 45
Babylon 58
Babylonian 13, 36
Babylonian Catastrophe 61
Babylonian Exile 310
Back-sliding 153
Bad Fate 503
Balarāma 73, 75, 206, 211
Banishment from native soil 122
Baqā (Union with the Divine Consciousness or life in God) 411

Baresman 508
Barhis 155, 508
Barrenness, a curse among the Hebrews 257
Battle of Badr 359
Beatitudes 125
Beauty and adaptation of the physical world 148
Behistun inscription 78
Being 175
Belief in angels 85
Belief in destiny beyond the grave 352
Belief in future life 348
Belief in magic 197
Bendva 427
Benign aspects (of Rudra) 224
Benignity 98
Benignity of God 98
Benjamin Kidd 106
Berezisavah or Bahrām 497
Bergson 160, 162
Bertrand Russell 123
Best Existence 466
Bestower, the (Al-Wahhāb) 378
Beth-el or "abode of deity" 261
Bethshemesh 266
Bhaga 168
Bhagavadgītā 15, 69, 96, 318, 516
Bhagavat 205
Bhāgavata Purāṇa 73
Bhakti 147, 232
Bhakti Cult 15, 142, 212
Bhava 224, 230
Bhīma 230
Bhūtas 224
Bigotry 22
Bilvamaṅgala 79
Bismillah-i'r-Rahmān-i'r-Rahīm 401
Black art 93
Black Stone of the Ka'ba 132, 276, 351
Bloomfield 166, 168
Boar, the 203
Bodhisattvas 6, 99-100, 117
Bodily Resurrection 321
Boon-giving capacity of the Vedic gods 94
Boundless Time 459
Bradley 286
Brahmā 6, 72-73, 172, 191-92, 202, 218, 231, 241
Brahmā flying in his swan vehicle 228
Brahmā has no avatāras 231
Brāhmaism 246, 426
Brāhma Samāj 29, 246
Brahma Sūtra of Bādarāyaṇa 66
Brahmā treated as subject to dissolution 187
Brahmā, viṣṇu and Śiva as a trinity 193, 245
Brahman 111, 178-79, 186, 192, 233, 238, 248, 286, 300, 380, 457-58, 521
Brāhmaṇas 490
Brahmaṇaspati 179, 202
Brahmanic ascendancy 214
Brahmanic gods 43
Brahmanism 15, 37-38, 73, 184
Brahmarṣideśa 26
Brāhmas 16
Brahmāvarta 26
Brahmavihārabhāvanā 108
Brazen Serpent 268, 272, 275, 284
Breach of the moral law 96
Break with tradition 18
Bṛhadāraṇyaka Upaniṣad 76
Bṛhaspati 189
Bridge of the separator 467, 507
Brotherhood of man 87, 248, 251, 334
Buddha 41, 44, 70, 73-74, 87, 94, 103, 114, 117, 124, 130, 147, 159, 187
Buddha as an incarnation of Viṣṇu 45
Buddha compares morality to a raft 108
Buddhi 436
Buddhism 15, 21, 37-38, 100, 106, 116, 131, 177, 184, 424
Buddhism and Jainism 181, 251
Buddhism contaminated by the Bon religion 157
Buddhists, absorption of 69
Bull-image of Dan and Bethel 284
Burāq 359
Burial customs 120
Bushyanstā 519

Caitanya 67, 70, 147, 246
Caitanya as incarnation of Kṛṣṇa and Rādhā 73
Caitanya School 217
Call of Social obligation 101

Campā 232
Cāmundā 239
Candī 239
Canaanite gods (baals) 263
Canaanites 269, 287
Cannibalism 102
Cappadocia 489
Carlyle 40
Carpenter 207
Caste-distinctions 65, 215
Caste-organisation 87, 208
Caste prejudice 64
Caste System 66, 69
Catalogue of divine names 522
Catholicism 100
Causes leading to suffering 87
Celestial gods 167
Celibacy 136, 457
Celibate ideal 436
Centralization of all worship 292
Ceremonial observances 63
Ceremonial slaughter of criminals and enemies 276
Ceremonialism 307
Ceremonialists 146
Ceremoniousness 116
Chāndogya Upaniṣad 76, 175
Character of all degenerate faiths 20
Charan Das 67
Charity 108
Charms 275
Cheats 224
Chemosh 54, 269
Cherubim 262
Chinnamastā 239
Chinvat Bridge 503, 515
Chisti (or Chistā) 492, 515-16
Chosen race 284
Christ 6, 44, 46, 70, 75, 82, 87, 127, 322, 353, 357
Christ, conception of 315
Christ as the second person of the Trinity 147
Christian apologists 163
Christian doctrine of incarnation 307
Christian doctrine of messiah 323
Christian doctrine of trinity 305, 319
Christianity 13, 37, 74-75, 90, 131, 157, 161, 246, 277, 446
Christian missionaries 496
Christian morality 119
Christian revelation 123
Christians 151
Christological Speculation 346
Christology 319
Christ's death 68
Christ's manifestations 71
Churning of the Ocean 219, 268
Circumcision 62, 256, 258, 316, 334, 350
Civil power 52
Clement, the (Al-Halīm) 401
Clohim 277
Code of morals 103
Codes of social and individual ethics 197
Coenobite 102
Coenobium 102
Cognition 309
Cold speculative unity of Brahman 203
Collective responsibility 61
Commandment of love 125
Compassionate intermediaries 100
Complementary character of the major deities 216
Complete inwardisation of religion 467
Complete nudity 225
Composite animals with human faces 170
Composite temple-religion of the Israelites 268
Comte 109
Concept of Satan 63
Conception of a unitary Solar deity 236
Confession of sin 199, 345
Conformity to social organisation 68
Confucianism 38, 90, 115, 117-18, 157
Confucianists 99
Confucius 30, 44, 112-16
Confusion of the varṇas 69
Congregational worship 243
Conqueror of death (Mṛtyuñjaya) 220
Conquest over sexual passion 226
Conscious make-believe 24
Contagion of faith 69
Contemplation 108
Continence and austerity 175
Continuous inspiration 80
Contradictory qualities assigned to

Allāh 381
Contraction of His realm 302
Costly sacrifice 67
Conversion 69, 246, 250
Conversion of Cangranghācah and Bīās 427
Converts 104, 247
----to Mohammadanism and Christianity 28
Conveying warning to an erring nation (a function of the Prophet) 50
Correct procedure an an accurate pronunciation essential (in religious rites) 181
Correct uttering of the mantras essential (in sacrifice) 172
Corruption 26
Cosmic functions of creation, preservation and destruction 245
Cosmodicy 94
Cosmological and teleological arguments 277
Counter formation 512
Counter reformists 485
Covetous, the 344
Cow as aghnyā 170
Craving for tangible vehicles of supernatural power 153
Creation 375, 443
Creation of evil 302
Creation of second creators 390
Creator of souls (Al-Khāliq) 378
Creative-consciousness of man 413
Creed of Ahuna Vairya 441
Crucifixation of Jesus 135
Crude semitic myths 77
Crude superstition 164
Cruel cults 424
Cruel custom 137
Cruelty and drunkenness 461
Cult of compassion and non-injury 99, 217
----of dead 301
----of dead ancestor 262
----of grace 97
----of heavenly bodies 267
----of Manasā 268
----of the Manes 260
----of Śakti 200
----of Shamash 266
----of Śiva 221
----of Stoical atarxia 181
----of tomb stones 260
Cultural conquest 250
Customary morality 126
Cybele with Attis 241

Dabbling in foretelling 48
Dādu 67
Daenā 140, 481, 489, 492, 513, 516
Daena-Chisti 492
Daevas 141, 430, 444, 446, 452, 496, 498, 500, 506
Daevas or diabolic Spirits 467
Daeva-worshippers 423, 427
Daevayasnians 141
Dagon 54, 269
Dahmā Āfriti (Dahmān Afrin) 495, 518
Daiwi Daeva 519
Dakṣa 223
Dakṣiṇā 155
Dāmoish Upamana 492, 495, 518
Dancing 92
Dante 97
Darkness 454, 458
Daśabhūmiśāstra 101
David 56, 59, 126
David's blunder 291
Daun 188, 197
Day of Atonement 330
----of Judgement 323, 356, 368, 398
Dayananda Saraswati 17
Dead religion 36
Death of all the first-born of Egypt 291
----of Christ on the cross 316
Debaser the (Al-Mudhil) 389
Decalogue 105
Decline of spiritual vision and moral uprightness 72
Deep-rooted religious convictions 67
Defilement 344
Degeneration into Pantheism 309
----of the spiritual element in religion 346
Deification 45, 324
----of certain objects and implements 172

----of Christ 130
----of the proletariat 105
----of prophets 147
Deified and immortalised men (Ṛbhus) 170
----forces of nature 169
Deifying the prophets 112
Deities of the field (Kṣetrasyapati) 170
----of the household (Vāstoṣpati) 170
----of spirits of air (Gandharvas) 170
----of water (Apsarases) 170
Deliverance through right contemplation 99
Deliverer of His people 390
Delusion 87
Demand for regularity 95
Demand of conscience 148
Democratic ideal of Islām 389
Demon of Anger (Āeshma) 435
----of Bad Season (Duzyāirya) 435
----of eclipse 41
----of falsehood (Druj) 435
Demons 171, 186, 253
Demon-slayers 189
Denying the authority of the Vedas 109
Departed ancestors (Pitaraḥ) 170, 253
Departmental deities 511, 521
Dependent Origination (Pratītya-Samutpāda) 94
Despotism 390
Destiny (Bakht) 458-59, 464-65
Destroyer, the (Al-Muzil) 379
Detachment 162
Details of social organisation 152
Destruction and the God of destruction 227
Destruction of the Temple of Jerusalem 285
Deutero-Isaiah 59, 63, 293
Deuteronomic prohibition 55
Deuteronomy 61, 78, 281, 284
Devakī 205
Devatā 110
Devendra Nath Tagore 246
Device of cunning priests, religion as a 24
Devotion 65, 116, 165, 173, 244, 246, 424, 465, 470
Devotion to God 232
Devotional revelations 147
Devotionalism 30
Devotion as the only sure way of Knowing Him 209
Director, the (Ar-Rashīd) 378
Dharma (law of morality) 218
Dhātṛ (Supporter) 155, 191
Dhruva 70
Dictation of the Mahābhārata by Vyāsa 238
Dictum of Sir Henry Maine 105
Differences between Islam and Judaism 134
Differences in equipment 77
Differences of opinion 317
Digambara 225
Dignity of women 243
Dīkṣā 243
Disappearance of the Ark 285
Discarded gods of polytheism 83
Disinterested love of God 209
----service 213-14
----Spectator 82
Dispensing with the necessity of circumcision 316
Dissension 249
Dissolution of cosmic cycle 187
----of the world 184
Distinction between a higher and a lower religion 151
----between religion and magic 182
----between Vedic polytheism and Persian polytheism 520
Distresser, the (Aḍ-Ḍārr) 389
Ditheism 164, 432, 453
Divination 48, 64, 76, 91
----and prophecy 275
Divine Beneficence 402
----caprice 95
----command 74
----communication 70, 79
----decree 392
----dispensation 117
----favour 81
----forgiveness 294
----function of instruction 72
----governance of the world 244,

413
----grace 150, 208, 344, 400
----grace as producing faith in believers 395
----guardianship 47
----guidance 398
----honours 68
----incarnation 45, 85, 400
----injunction 74
----inspiration, exclusiveness of 80
----Judgement 322
----Justice 399
----Kingdom 330
----Law of Harmony 478
----mercy 51, 399
----messengers and agents 83
----Power 172
----Providence (bagho-bakht) 345, 464
----revelations 162
----righteousness 478
----ruler and judge 319
----sonship of Jesus 357
----spirit 305
----trinities 45, 315
----volition in relation to human destiny 398
----will as prompting unbelief in infidels 395
Divinity of Christ 346
Docetic doctrines 320
Docetism 45
Doctrine of abrogation 385
----of Karma 110
----of Light of Muhammad 369
----of Original sin 290
----of prophet's omniscience 34
----of sacrifice (Karman) 145
----of saints 481
----of supererogation 100
----of the Mean 115
----of transmigration 117
Doctrines of Saṃsāra 170
----of tanzīh (removal) and mukhālafa (difference) 372
Dogma 8, 152
Dogmatic Christianity 27
Dominant, the (Al-Qahhār) 379
Dominion (Khshathra) 440, 465, 469
Dominion of the Good 446
Doors leading to the sacrificial field 172
Double negation 381
Draoga Mithaokhta 519
Dream 79, 91
Drinking 132
Driwi Daeva 520
Druj 139, 467, 487, 516, 519
Druj Nasu, the demon of bodily decomposition 505
Drunkards 344
Drvāspā 492, 510
Dual divinities 492
Dualism 445, 456, 469, 476
----of God and Devil 449
----of matter and spirit 444
Dualistic philosophy 454
Duality 146
Durgā 239, 243
Duties of one's status and station 208
Dutiness 116
Duzhyāirya (Dushiyāra), the demon of barrenness and bad year 502
Dwarf, the 73, 203
Dyaus (Dyeus) 155, 189, 468
Dyaus Pitar 188, 427
Dyāvā-pṛthivī 492

Earth 197
Earthly gods comprehensively called Vasus 189
Eating of the tree of Knowledge 82
Ebionites 45, 316
Ecstasies 107
Ecstasy 4, 80, 81, 91
Ecstatic fits 92
----trance 30
----visions 162
Edict of Mihr Narseh 454
Educated persons 29
Effect of speculation on faith 165
Effeminate 344
Egg theory repudiated 193
Egyptian religion 20
Egyptians 36, 287
Eighteenth century deists 148
Elaborate system of sacrifice 171
El Elyon (God Most High) 254
Elijah 42, 53, 64, 76, 273, 325
Elisah 53

Elisha 42
Elohim (Deity) 254, 301, 303, 323
El Shaddai (almighty God) 254
Emerson 87
Emotional frenzy 30
Empiric faith 148
Empty formalities of faith 88
Ender of everything, the (al-Mu'akhkhir) 378
Endless Light 466, 467
Enemies within 435
Enlightened mind 151
----self-interest 415
Enoch 42
Enricher, the (Al-Mughnī) 389
Entry into paradise 380
Ephod, the 284
Epicurus 82, 109
Equal right of women with men 142
Ereshi 519
Erethe 492, 514
Eschatological message of Zarathustra 141
Esotericism 158
Esoteric religion 522
----Society 24
Esperanto 103
Eternal, the (Aṣ-Ṣamad, Al-Azalī) 379
Eternal and uncreate truths 143
Eternal Arabic Qur'ān 385
----Dominion of light 454
----hell 465
----hell-fire 133
----laws of morality 114
----laws of righteousness 116
----moral order 111
----order (ṛta) 195
----persistence of evil 446
Eternity of the Qur'ān 385
----of the Fravashis 484
Ethical Idealism 339
----needs 103
----monotheism 140, 158, 160, 403
----non-ritualistic monotheism 246
Ethics of the Gospel 119
Evangelisation 79
Eve 302
Ever great, the (Al-Kabīr) 379
Ever maintainer, the (Al-Muqīt) 378
Ever praiseworthy, the (Al-Ḥamīd) 403
Evidence for inspiration 91
Evident, the (Az-Zāhir) 384
Evil 443, 449, 497
Evil, a creation of God 447
Evil or worst mind 467
Evil Spirit 444, 448, 450, 451, 461, 481
Evil was an illusion 436
Evolution of man's consciousness of the supernatural 123
----of the Śakti cult 242
Exaltation to heaven 183
Exalted, the (Al-Alī, Al-Aāla) 379
Exalter, the (Ar-Rāfi) 389
Excessive drinking of Soma 176
----veneration for the law 135
Exclusive alliance of Yahweh with Israel 297
Exclusiveness of different religions organisations 89
Exile 77
----of the leading Jews 14
Existence of God 148
Expiatory death of Christ 129
Explanation of Vedic texts by Dayānanda Sarasvati 163
Extension of Yahweh's jurisdiction 302
External conformity 250
External inspiration (Waḥyl Zāhir) 386
----observance of formalities 344
Extortioners 344
Extraordinary things 114
Extreme rationalism 164
Ezekiel 59, 62, 306
Ezekiel's visions of God 283
Ezra 62-63, 135

Faith 3, 128, 173, 332, 344
----, primitive forms of 3
----and morality 104
----in collective wisdom 151
Faithful enjoined not to shout during devotional exercises 385
Fallibility of man 74
Fall of Adam 302
----of Jerusalem 47, 58
False and pagan prophets 48
----faith 137
----guides 11

Falsehood and evil 88
----and wickedness 88
False sense of security 125
Familiarity that breeds contempt 81
Family life 454
Fanā (passing away) 411
Fanaticism 22, 289
Far Eastern Hindu colonies 232
Far-off God 304
Farvardin Yasht 491
Fashioner of the image in the womb (Al-Muṣawwir) 378
Fasting 92
Fatalists 146
Fates 157
Father 127
Father God of light 453
Fatherhood of God 87, 248, 300, 310, 331, 334, 371
----of the Lord 216
Father in Heaven 104
Father of Light 454
Fear of off ending the social group 151
----of the Lord 97
----of the unknown 24
Feast of Tabernacles or of Ingathering 257
Feats of strength 114
Female consorts 272
----deities (Baalath) 269
Fetishes 169
Fetishism 136, 169
Fidelity 116
Fifth head of Prajāpati 220
Final doom of evil 443
----of the wicked 434
Finder, the (Al-Wājid) 384
Fire as a sacred symbol 432
Firm, the (Al-Matīn) 379
First, the (Al-Awwal) 379
First Commandment 126
----missionary 10
----person of the trinity 172
Firstlings sacrificed to Yahweh 257
Fish, the 72, 203
Fitful monotheism of the Vedas 200
Fits of unconsciousness 162
Five Constants 115
Five-faced god 228
Five gods (Pañcadevatā) 234
----human relationships 115
----M's 243
----sectarian gods 229
----(or ten) Śīlas 108
Food taboos 217
Forbearance 116
Forbidden speculations 161
Forced conversion 163
Forcible entry into the Vedic pantheon 223
Forerunner, the (Al-Muquddim) 379
Foretelling 64
----of a future prophet 48
----the future 47
Forgiver, the (Al-Ghāfir) 401
Forgiver par métier, the (Al-Ghaffār) 401
Formal expiation 54
Formality, emphasis on 490
Formation of man's body and mind 375
Formulae for blessings and curses 350
Fornicators 344
Foundation-sacrifices 57
Fourteen Zoroastrian Sects 522
Fravashi (the Guardian Angels) 100, 477, 480-85, 488-89, 491, 503, 520
----of Ahura Mazdah 491
Frashokereti 445
Frazer 154
Free Will 392, 443
Freedom and the individual responsibility of all finite spirits 434
----from ritualistic complications 164
----of the will 398
Freethinkers 37, 175
Freud 154, 168
Freudian principle 42
Friends of God 162
Fruit of the Tree of Knowledge 286
Fuller recognition of the unity and ubiquity of God 251
Fundamental principles 107
Futility of polytheism and idolatry 350

Gabriel 84-85, 133, 371, 386-87, 515
Gad 269

Gambling 132
Gaṇas 224
Gāndhī 247-48
Gaṇeśa 220-21, 234, 237, 245
----supremacy of 237
----as a giver of success (siddhi) in all undertakings 237
Gaokerena 508
Garden of Eden 302
Garodemāna 140
Garonmāna 486, 488
Gāthās 420
Gatherer, the (Al-Jāmi) 378
Gaurī 243
Gautama 6
Gāyatrī 235
Gayomarthians 451
General dissolution of world 72
Generous, the (Al-Karīm) 401
Genial protection of households 238
Gentile Christians 298
----conversion 68
Gentiles 298, 300-301, 314-15
Geush Urvan 510
Ghora Âṅgirasa 205
Ghṛta 155
Gideon 282
Gifted individuals 76
Gifts to the temple 334
Giver, the (Al-Mu'ṭi) 389
Glad tidings 96
Glorification of Israel 296
Glorious, the (Al-Majīd) 379
Glory 78
Gnosis 145
Gnosticism 158
God 109, 286
----, surrender and dedication of self to 208
----above the law of Karma 232
----as a father 390
----as father (of Jesus) 125
----as a postulate of moral life 416
----as an hypothesis 165
----as mother 240
----as power 190
----as understood in the Semitic religions 185
----as wholly inaccessible 81
----in relation to man 85
----in the form of a prophet 75
----Incarnate 67
----is a person 309
----man 74, 87
----of Abraham 320
----of Israel 56
----of Light 445
----of love 219
----of mercy and love 123
----of power and wrath 123
----significantly defined as the first preceptor 72
----the father 125, 128, 332, 338
----'the most merciful' yet he tortures children according the Qur'ān 374
----the Son 332, 338
----the unmoved mover 86
Goddess Asherah 268
Godlessness 186
Gods 253
Gods as "fathers" of different human groups 254
Gods in conflict with one another 188
God's Kingdom 344
Gods needed self-Knowledge 187
Gods of Song 189
Gods to have been originally mortal 175
God's ways are mysterious 80
Gods would have to be reborn as men to get their salvation 187
Golden age 31
Golden mean 107
Golden rule 115, 118
Good 446
Good and Evil 458
Good Deed 466
Good faith 115
Good fate 503
Good Spirit 448
Good Thought (Vohu Manah) 425, 440, 466, 469
Good Word 466
Gopīs 69
Gospel of compassion 99
Gospel of Divine participation 308
Gospels 312
Governor, the (Al-Wahī) 379
Grace 96
Grace of god 232

Gracious 390
Grand, the (Al-Aẓim) 379
Grant Allen 228
Grāvan 155
Great, the (Al-Mutakabbir) 379
Great Beginner, the (Al-Mubdi) 378
Greatest of gods (Mathishta Bagānām) 425
Greek 36
Gregariousness 118
Grēhma 427
Griswold 166, 195
Guardian, the (Al-Wakīl) 378
Guardian angels 481
----of the moral order (ṛtasya gopā) 196
----over all 390
----spirit 47
Guide, the (Al-Hādī) 384
Guṇa 436
Gurus 100

Hadad 269
Haggai 62
Hallāj 411
Hamkār 504
Hanifs 132, 349
Haoma (Soma) 431, 491, 508-509
Haptān Yasht 488
Haptoiringa 502
Hara Berezaiti 507
Harappa 221
Hari 18, 70
Harihara, the composite divinity 216
Harmony 465
Haurvatāt 470, 478, 500, 508
He (Hoo) 379
He has no form 134
He is the Ever-Hearer of Prayers (Al-Mujīb) 385
Heading remedies 222
Heaven 49, 138, 197
Heaven, grades of 49
Heaven and Hell 406
Heavenly book 83
Heavenly court 126
Heavenly dancers 186
Heavenly father 123
Heavenly gods (Ādityas) 189
Heavenly lawgiver 127
Heavenly residence not indispensable (for finite souls) 187
Hebrew prophets 16, 68, 121
Hebrew religion 62, 251
Hebrews 61, 121, 314
Hegel 1
Heliodara 209
Hell 49, 141
Hellenism 319
Hell-fire theology 98
Henotheism 195
Henotheistic attitude 196
Hersy 467
Heretics 146
Herodotus 139, 423, 514
Hero-worship 40
Hezekiah 58, 267, 301
Hezekiah's reform 268
Hidden, the (Al-Bāṭin) 384
Hierarchy of heavenly beings 83
Hieratic religion 173
High Priest 63
Higher righteousness 125
Highly trained priesthood 171
Hīnayāna Buddhism 99
Hindu Missions 247
Hinduism 16, 38, 72, 82, 90, 100, 143, 252, 277, 279, 284, 300, 485
Hinduism and Judaism 157
Hindus 153
Hiraṇyagarbha 191
His (i.e. god's) beloved son 127
Hishām ibn al-Hakām 406
Hishām ibn Sālim al-Jawālīki 407
Hobal 132
Holy Ghost 336-37, 452
Holy One (Al-Quddūs) 403
Holy One of Israel, the 295
Holy Spirit 305, 307, 309, 322, 329, 335, 338-39, 448, 452
Holy Triads 452
Homeric tales 20
Honourer, the (Al-Mu'izz) 389
Hope 98
Hopkins 155, 182
Horned altars of Yahweh 266
Hosea 59, 303
Hostility to the Daevas 526
House of lie 465
House of Song or Praise 138, 466
Household gods (Teraphim) 275
Householder's life always praised 138

Hu-t'u (Empress Earth) 111
Hugo de Vries 418
Huitzilopochtli 104
Hūkhta (Good Works) 488
Hulūl (fusion of being) 411
Human offerings to Rudra 223
Human sacrifice as a foundation-rite 269, 271
Human sacrifices to Yahweh 55
Humata (Good Thought) 488
Humility 108
Hvarekhshaēta (Khurshed) 492, 498, 501
Hvarekhshaeta-Mithra 492
Hvarenah 498
Hymns more powerful than the gods 183
Hymns of the Ṛig-Veda 166
Hymns offered to Śiva, as to Viṣṇu, purest expressions of monotheistic Mahākāla 233
Hypnotism 79

Iblis (Satan) 405
Ionic worship of Anāhita by Artaxerxes Mnemon 495
Idea of God, as a string of negotiations 372
Idea of the supernatural 154
Idea of transitory gods 460
Ideas 485
Identification of Ātman (the self) with Brahman 194
Identification of Deity with the world 309
Identification of God and man 308
Identifying Śiva and Viṣṇu 216
Identity of essence 321
Identity of the finite (Jīva) and the infinite (Brahman) 411
Idolators 344
Idolatry 30, 55-56, 66, 112, 130, 133, 140, 164, 247, 275, 284-85, 405, 436, 495, 521
Idolatry banished from the Jewish religion 301
Idolatry discouraged 113
Idolisation 40
Ignorance 87
Ikṣvāku 72
Ilhām 9
Il-Haqq 411
Illumination 101
Illusoriness of free choice 395
Images of the combined deities 216
Imitation 118
Imitativeness 150
Immaculate conception 83, 301, 336
Immanence of God 329
Immensity and immeasurability of the Infinite 145
Immortality 109, 446, 465, 470, 484
Immortality in Garonmāna 489
Immutable laws of the moral order 437
Impending calamity 49
Imperfect representations of Yahweh 285
Imperfectly humanised forces of nature 174
Imperial oppression 67
Impersonal Absolute 146, 186, 246, 414
Impersonal Brahman 96, 177
Impersonal Moral Order 186, 197
Impersonalistic spiritualism 96
Impossibility of better revelations 161
Inadequacy of the merely moral 112
Incarnation 96, 72, 131, 147, 171
----, theory of 204
Incarnation of Viṣṇu 170
Incest 132, 192
Inclusion of non-Hindus within the fold of Hinduism 301
Incomparable, the (Al-Badi) 379
Incubatio 92
Independent or Self-sufficient, the (Al-Ghanī) 379
Indian Archipelago 232
Indian saints 67
Indifference of gods 109
Individuality 87
Individual responsibility 61, 122
Indra 76, 167, 169-70, 174, 188-89, 224, 428, 470
Indra (or Andra) 519
Indra-Virocana episode 76, 191
Indra-Vṛtra myth 497
Indulgences 244
Industry 116
Inexorability of law 94
Inexorable law of causality 94

Inexorableness 309
Infallibility of the scriptures 161
Infanticide 132
Infantile regression 157
Infidels 104
Influx of divinity 92
Influx of inspiration 80
Inheritor, the (Al-Wārith) 379
Injustice 396
Innate conservation 24
Innate idea of His (i.e. creator's own existence 154
Innate sympathy 118
Inscrutable nature of the Absolute 180
Inscrutable nature of God 160
Inscrutable will of God 96
Insensitiveness to suffering 3
Insight 309
Inspiration 79, 91
Instinct 22, 155
Intellectual consistency 417
Intellectual discipline 107
Intellectual Insight 87
Intellectualistic monism 180
Intellectualistic revelations 147
Intelligence 70
Intensification of the ascetic ideal of life 112
Intercession 367-68
Intercessory power of the Prophet 367
Interested action (Kāmātmatā) 213
Intermediaries 83
Intermediate beings and angels 283
Intermittent inspirations 80
Intermixture of castes 69
Interpolations 162-63
Interpreters of the Law 61
Interpreting the divine will (as a function of the prophet) 50
In the image of God 283
Intoxicants 92
Introduction of Semitic monotheism in India 246
Intuition 70, 149
Investiture with the Holy Spirit of Christ 135
Inviolable world order 199
Invisible powers 253
Iranian trinity 431
Isaac 77, 266
Isaiah 59, 61, 96, 263, 306
Īśāna 230
Ishmael 76, 349
Isis 12
Isis with Horus 241
Islām 37, 161, 163, 246, 277
'Islām' i.e, 'resignation to the will of God' 389
Israel as God's Son 295
Israel as God's chosen race 296
Īśvara 95
Ittiḥād (identification) 411

Jabrites 392
Jacob 77, 266, 282-83
Jacobites 132
Jahi 520
Jahweh 261
Jainism 15, 37, 74, 100, 177, 184, 187, 215, 424
Jairus's daughter 42
James 4
Janaka 214
Jehovah 279
Jeremiah 59, 61, 65, 76, 326, 331
Jeroboam 54
Jerusalem 27, 41, 300
Jesus 4, 41, 64, 68, 76, 80, 83, 96, 124-26, 136, 159, 318, 336, 341, 359, 420, 454
Jesus, advent of 14
----as mere conglomeration of ideas 124
Jesus' descent into Hell 369
Jesus transubstantiates water into wine and multiplies leaves and fishes 42
Jewish angels 43
----Christians 298
----conception of the revealed God 122
----Decalogue 108
----exclusiveness 296
----History 52
----God a tangible and visible being 78
----ideal of a householder's life 136
----laws 264
----Messiah 341

Jews 153, 298, 315
Jews afraid of uttering god's name 303
Jibril 83
Jinn 187
Jīva 95
Jīvanmuktas 80
Jñāna 147, 218
Jñānamārga 185
Job 287
John Marshall 170, 228
John the Baptist 14, 325, 327, 340, 344, 352
Joseph 266
Joshua 46, 288
Josiah 13, 61, 267, 270
J.S. Mill 165
Judah 274
Judaism 16, 37, 67-68, 83, 117, 120, 147, 319
Judaism as influenced by Cananite culture 157
Judaism influenced by Platonism, Gnosticism, Mithraism and Zoroastrianism 310
Judgement after death 302, 443
Judgement Day 50, 133
Jung 18, 35
Jupiter in the Roman religion 188
Jurisdiction of Yahweh over the dead 302
Justice 309
Justification for the existence of evil 434
Ka'ba 351
Kabir 65, 67, 246
Kaivalya 242
Kāla 457
Kālamukha 230
Kālī 104, 239, 247
Kālī, cult of 247
Kalīmu'llāh, Converser with God 384
Kāma (Cupid) 226
Kāmboja 232
Kamma-niyama 108
Kansaoya Lake 510
Kant 109
Kāpāla 230
Kapila 73
Karaites 281
Karapans 142, 427, 500
Karma 147, 184
Karmasannyāsa (renunciation of the fruits of action) 213
Karuṇā 108
Kasvi Daeva 520
Kaṭha Upaniṣad 96, 149
Kavis 142, 427, 500
Kebla 135
Keith 174
Keshab Chandra Sen, introducer of many Christian conceptions (in Hinduism) 246
Khārijite view 380
Khepera 167
Khnanthaiti 520
Khratu 515
Khṛvighni 520
Khshathra 465
Khshathra-Vairyu 465, 468, 470, 478, 500
Khurshed (Hvarekh-Shaēta) 501
Killer, the (Al-Mumīt) 378
Kindliness 116
Kindness 115
King, the (Al-Malik) 379
Kingdom of blessings 466
Kingdom of god 125-28, 323, 340-43
Kingdom of heaven 50, 325-26
Kingdom on earth 330
King Gushtāsp 491
King of all Kingdoms (Māliku'l-mulk) 379
Kirāta 219, 224
Knower, the (Al-Alīm) 384
Knower of Brahman himself becomes Brahman 82
Knower of subtleties (Al-Latīf) 384
Knowledge (Ilm) 381
Koran 84
Kṛṣṇa 18, 75, 124, 205, 210-11, 247, 332
Kṛṣṇa, many previous births of 231
Kṛṣṇa and Rādhā 211
Kṛṣṇa Devakīputtra 205, 213
Kṛṣṇaism 212
Kṛṣṇa multiplied Draupadī's vegetable-shred 42
Kṛṣṇa's flute 69
Kṣatriyas 214
Kunda 520
Kusumāñjali 72

Kwannon 99

Lack of individual judgement 151
Laissez Faire 54, 146
Lakṣmī 512
Lakṣmī and Nārāyaṇa 211
Lao-tse 95
Lapse in insight 80
Lapses into idolatry and polytheism 371
Large tolerance of the Hindu mind 145
Last, the (Al-Ākhir) 379
Last judgement 352
Last Prophet, the 336
Law 94
Law giver 94
Law of Holiness 63
Law of Karma 13, 103, 424, 463
Law of Moral Justice 96
Law of Moral Order (asha or arta) 424
Law of Moses 316
Law of Righteousness 88
Law of Transmigration 244
Laws of Babylon 264
Laws of Hammurabi 264
Laws of morality 117
Lazarus 42
Left-handed Śāktaism 212
Legalism 307
Legalistic sage 62
Legend of Moses and Zipporah 258
Leibniz 449
Lenient or Kind, the (Ar-Ra'ūf) 401
Lenin 106
Levites 62, 292
Liberation to be attained by personal endeavour 111
Lie 440, 445, 467
Life (hayāh) 381
Life beyond the reach of death 128
Life-giver or Quickener, the (Al-Muḥyī) 378
Life of a pasture-keeper and a cattle-tender 138
Light 458-59
Light, the (An-Nūr) 403
Light of the Heavens 409
Limited God 449
Limited polytheism 245
Liṅga 226-27
Liṅga, shedding of 226
Liṅga in a reliquary hung round the neck 230
Liṅga-worship 221
Lingāyats 229
Litany of Fire 498
Living, the (A-Haiy) 379
Loaves and fishes, multiplication of 42
Local saints, deification of 247
Logical thinking 162
Logos 74, 130, 321, 335
Long-suffering (Aṣ-Ṣabūr) 401
Loose association of functions and attributes with the gods 189
Lord Kṛṣṇa 213
Lord of Grace 403
Lord of Hosts 123, 267
Lord of internal regions 445
Lord of Majesty and Liberality (Dhu'ljalāli Wa'l-ikrān) 379
Lord of prayer 172
Lords of malevolent spirits 237
Lot 76
Love 81, 309
Love of god 61
Love thy neighbour as thyself 87, 127
Love toward God 128
Loving devotion 200
Lower deities (shen) 113
Lower form of the ultimate principle 286
Luke 317
Lust of power and persecution 136

Maccabean 14
Macdonell 174, 183, 188, 194, 199
Madhva 209
Madonna 18
Magic 35, 42, 253
Magic effect of name 215
Magical belief 183
Magical efficacy of Vedic rites 96
Magical feats 92
Magical practice 244
Magis 140
Mahābhārata 16
Mahā Kāla 233, 239
Mahān-deva (or Mahādeva) 224, 230
Mahānirvāṇa Tantra 241

Mahāvīra 41, 74, 110-11, 147, 187, 423
Mahāyāna Buddhism 99, 232, 493
Mahāyāna School 44
Mahiṣamardinī 239
Mahratta mystics 65
Maidhyoi-Māonha 420
Maitri 108
Majestic, the (Al-Jalīl) 379
Majority verdict of Indian philosophers 185
Maker of bodies (Al-Bāri) 378
Malachi 62
Malevolent spirits 171
Manasā, the goddess of snakes 239
Manasseh 57, 258
Man ceased to be regarded as a mere slave of Allāh 411
Mānī 453-54
Mānī, martyrdom of 454
Manichaeism 158, 446, 455, 458
Manikkavasagar 79
Man is the author of his acts 161
Man-lion 12
Man wholly responsible for moral evil 399
Manoah and his wife 282
Manthra 480, 483
Manthram (or Māthra) Spenta (Māhraspand) 492, 517
Mantras 181
Mantras and the rites more important than gods 184
Mantras have an efficacy 183
Manu 72, 160, 193, 203, 236
Many Christian Conceptions (introduced by Keshab Chandra Sen) in the relation of God to man 246
Maonghah 492
Māra 41, 106
Marriage of Widows 243
Maruts 167, 188-89
Marvellous power and wisdom discernible in the government of this Universe 375
Marx 106
Mary 337
Mass Conversion 30
Maṣṣebah 284
Masses 100
Mass movement 67
Master, the (Al-Mālik) 379
Mātariśvan 167, 190
Materialists 146, 185
Materials and mantras 65
Matter 450, 454
Mathew 317
Matrimonial alliances 163
Max Müller's theory of Vedic henotheism 194
Māyā 179, 210, 227, 238
Mazda 44
Mazdāh 424
Mazdayasnian 141, 435
Mazdayasnian religion 497
Mecca 27
Mediator 129
Medicine man 2, 35
Medieval Saints of India 64
Meditational absorption 457
Mediterranean religions 163
Megalomania 296
Memorial of Joshua 260
Memra 309
Men are Viṣṇus 73
Merciful 390
Mercy 309
Message for the mass 103
Message of Ahiṃsā 215
Message of Christianity 68
Message of hope 97, 99
Message of morality and compassion 131
Message of redemption 98
Messages regarded as coming from god 70
Messengers and agents 486
Messengers of God 76
Messiah 129, 322, 346
Messianic intermediary 315
Messianic Salvation 63
Method of Divine manifestation 306
Micah 62
Middle path 375
Midarsh 305
Mighty, the (Al-Aziz) 379
Milcom/Milkon 55, 269
Mildness 116
Milkah 265
Mīmāṃsakas 185
Minor prophets 76
Miracle 42, 91-92, 96, 327

Miracle of the Qur'ān 358
Miracles as signs and credentials of spiritual greatness 46
Mīriam 78
Mithra 12, 431-32, 455, 479-80, 491-92, 496, 498-99, 501, 503-504, 512, 514-15, 520
Mithra druj 514
Mithraism 37, 158, 236, 313, 455, 493
Mithra is only witness of men's deeds 500
Mithra-Raman 492
Mithra-Rashnu 492
Mithras-worship, 314, 432
Mitra 155, 166, 168, 197, 236, 428
Mitra simply the replica of Varuṇa 199
Mixed marriages 53
Moderation 116
Modesty 116
Mohenjo Daro 170, 221
Molech 55
Monadism 323
Monasticism 136
Mongolian religion 36
Monism 190
Monolaters 253
Monolatry 65, 123, 196, 253
Monoliths 266
Monotheism 65, 123, 136, 139, 163, 189, 190, 195-96, 203, 244, 253, 433, 443, 451
Monotheism, germs of 177
Monotheism of the West 246
Monotheistic interpretation to the Vedic religion 246
Monotheistic theology 454
Moral consciousness 196
Moral corruption 55
Moral earnestness 87
Morality 108
Moralisation 30
Moralistic revelations 147
Morality without religions 111
Moral lapses 198
Moral law 96, 115, 186, 198
Moral probation 414
Moral responsibility 111
Moral self-discipline 107
Moral struggle 402, 436
Mortification of the flesh 107, 436, 444
Mosaic law 331
Mosaic revelation 487
Mosaic stories 78
Moses 46, 66, 76-78, 81, 102, 120, 134-35, 147, 159, 254-55, 261, 263, 276-77, 281-82, 287, 296-97, 306, 353, 384, 406
Moses' contribution 256
Moslem asceticism 395
Mother and Child 315
Mother-cult 239
Mother Goddess 100
Mother Kālī 79
Motive involved in the deification of Christ 320
Motives 295
Mouth of the gods 181
Mount Kailāsa 231
Mount Sinai 134, 255, 263, 278
Much forgiver, the (Al-Ghafūr) 401
Muditā 108
Muhammad 15, 41, 66, 76, 83-85, 102, 133, 135, 147, 159, 163, 389, 420, 426
Muhammadanism 15, 85, 90-100, 117, 157, 366, 473
Muhammadan Oppression 69
Muhammad as a living intercessor at the throne of God 368
Muhammad as a warner 352
Muhammad as the last prophet 356
Muhammad multiplying food and drink 46
Mukhaliṅga images 228
Mūlādhāra 243
Multiplicity of gods 177
Multiplicity of heavens 49
Multiplicity reduced to a unity 195
Murder of Mazdak 454
Muji'itism 380
Musalmans 153
Music 92, 132
Muslim domination of European countries 85
Mutations 418
Mu'tazilities 381, 395, 398-99, 402, 405-407
Mu'tazilites felt justified in rejecting the doctrine of intercession 367

Mu'tazilites, free thinkers of Islām 161
Mutual dependence of the deities 190
Mylitta 506
Mysteries of spiritual and intellectual insight 87
Mystery religions 12, 158, 313
Mystic/Mystics 4, 87, 146, 162
Mystic contemplation 180
Mystic core of religion 22
Mystic fear of novel experiments 150
Mystic speculation 89
Mystic way of life 100-101
Mystical discipline 107
Mysticism 102-103, 116, 161, 417
Myth, dogma and ritual 7
Myth of Kronos 457
Myths of Kōjiki 21

Nāanhaithya 470
Nabi 77
Nadab 282
Nahor 265
Nairyosangha 491, 497
Nāmadeva 246
Name greater than the God 67
Nānak 65, 67, 246
Nāon-ghaithya 519
Nārada 73
Narāśaṃsa 497
Nārāyaṇa 18, 192, 204-205
Nārāyaṇa section of the Mahābhārata 204-205
Nārāyaṇa, Vāsudeva and viṣṇu as three phases of the same God 206
Nāsatyau 428
Nathan 53
Nation of meat-eaters 217
National festivals 271
National purity 61
Natural moral order 94
Natural religion 148
Natural religionists 154
Nature of revelation 150
Nature-gods 492
Nature-religion 511
Nature-worship 142, 262, 512
Nazirites 257, 271
Necessity of intermediaries in God's government 310
Necessity of training in Mysticism 159
Needs of devotion 153
Needs of doctrinal consistency 153
Negative attitude towards the world 101
Neighbourliness 116
Neo-platonism 158
Neo-Vedāntic movement 248
Nepal 232
Nereids 157
Nestorians 132
Neti neti 180
Netṛ 155
New awakening 90
New converts 69
New messiah 68
New rituals 69
New Testament 33, 313, 315, 318
Night Journey from Mecca to Jerusalem 359, 408
Night of Ascension 406
Nimbārka 209
Nirṛti 155
Nirvāṇa 107, 117
Niṣādas 224
Noah 62, 76
Noble eightfold path 107-108
Nocturnal orgiastic sacrifices 138
Nocturnal orgies 424
Nomadic habit 142
Nomadic races 61
Nomistic fatalism 96
Non-action (akriyāvāda) 213
Non-being 175
Non-brahmin reformers 65
Non-difference of Hari (Viṣṇu) and Hara (Śiva) 245
Non-observance 344
Non-injury 247
North Indian saints 66
Nothing 175
Nothingness (Śūnya) 108
Nourisher, (Ar-Rabb) 378
Nūsh Ādar 430
Nyaishes 493, 495

Obedience 128
Obedience to the law 123, 345
Object of prayer 123
Obligatory works 393

Obscene figures 211
Obscurantism 25, 157
Observance of the national feasts 334
Observers of order 199
Obsessional neurosis 23
Occasional lapses 232
Occult powers 190
Offerings 171
Offerings of animals 292
Old Testament 27, 63, 85, 252, 256, 305
Old Wives' tales 42
Omens 91
Omnipotence of God 390
One, the (Al-Wāḥid) 190, 379
One above all others, the (Al Muta'ālī) 379
One God as an ethical personality 461
One important distinction between Hinduism and Parsism 521
One unborn, the 190
One unknown, the 190
Oppression 163
Oracles 48, 93, 350
Order 465
Order and design 374
Orderliness 110
Orgiastic rites 212, 225, 229
Original Buddhism 109
Original non-Aryan population of India 221
Origin of religion 155
Ormazd 88, 424, 432, 448, 454, 458, 476, 485, 501, 503
Ormazd, supremacy of 477
Orphic cult 37
Osiris 12
Otto 154
Overlord of Darkness 453
Ox-creator (Geush tashan)
Ox-soul (Geush Urvan) 466

Pagan rites and festivals 8
Paganism 64, 314
Pain and evil inseparable 449
Parikās 500
Palastine, the land of Yahweh 272
Pan-Babylonist school of Winckler 253
Pan-Islamism 90
Pañca-makāra 243
Pāñcarātra 206
Pāñcāyatana Pūjā 229
Pantheism 143, 154, 178
Pantheism, germs of 177
Pantheistic attitude of Sūfī writers 412
Pantheistic India 460
Pantheon 472
Pantheon of Buddhas and Bodhisattvas 44
Paradise of Amitābha 117
Paraśurāma 73, 75
Pardoner, the (Al-Afuww) 401
Pārendi 491, 512
Parjanya 166, 189, 224
Pārśvanātha 110
Partiality for the traditional 153
Pārvatī 82, 243
Passions of the flesh 101
Passive contemplation 162
Passover 257, 271
Paśupati 224, 230
Paśupati, a single god 230
Paternity of the gods 188
Path of illumination 107
Patience 116
Paul 68, 129
Pauliene Gospels 315
Peace 247, 344
Peculiarities about the Judaic revelation 121
Pedestinarian teachings 402
Penitence 402
Penitent, the 294
Pentacost of the Feast of weeks 257
Pentateuch 252
Perfect well-being 465
Perfection 465
Perfection, the way of 116
Performance of miracles 358
Periodical incarnation 75
Persecution 118
Persecution delusion 296
Persian Sufis 180
Personal gods of later Hinduism 200
Personal holiness 61
Personal immortality 497
Personal penance and divine grace 150
Personal purity and social morality without a moral law-giver 111

Personal regligion 123
Personal salvation 67
Personal weakness 67
Personality of reformer 67
Personification 172, 284, 461
Personification of abstract virtues 496
Pervasiveness 384
Peshotanus 516
Pessimism 98, 117
Peter 4, 68
Phallic cult 225, 228
Phallism 170, 229
Pharaoh's personal guilt 291
Pharisees 14, 129
Phenomenal apearances of Yahweh 309
Philistines 287
Philosopher to enlighten by articulated thinking 159
Philosophers 146
Philosophical dualism 453
Philosophy 21
Philosophy and Religion more intimately associated in India 233
Physical presence of God 80
Physical proximity of God 81
Physician gods 189
Piety (Armaiti) 173, 440, 465
Pilgrimage to Mecca 135, 351
Pitṛs 495
Plato 32, 450
Platonic theory of the souls or essences of things 484
Platonism 484
Plato's philosopher 6
Plurality of gods 173
Plurality of humanised gods 174
Plurality of personal gods 111
Plurality of power 164
Politeness 116
Political circumstances 67
Political domination 250
Polydaemonism 254, 270
Polygamy 132
Polytheism 44, 55, 66, 133, 140, 143, 154, 165, 254, 263, 270, 424, 443, 452, 460, 475
Polytheism an unpardonable sin in Islam 379
Polytheism, germs of 177
Polytheistic belief 164
Polytheistic religions 174
Popular cults, superstitions and beliefs 173
Porphyry 437, 466
Possessed spirit 42
Possession 80
Possession by demons 254
Possession by the spirit of God 23
Post-exilic Judaism 89
Power (Qudra) 194, 309, 381, 387
Power and faculties of the soul infinitely exalted 70
Powerful, the (Al- Qādir) 379
Pradyumna 206
Prahiāda 70
Prajāpati 76, 179, 191-92, 203, 224
Prakṛti 236, 436
Prārthanā Samāj 246
Pratītya Samutpāda 103
Prayer 114, 308, 334, 344
Prayer for the forgiveness of guilt 199
Prayer for the remission of penalty 199
Prayer for worldly goods 199
Prayers 171, 185
Prayers for blessings 222
Pre-Aryan religion 170
Pre-exilic Judaism 116
Pre-existence 484
Pre-Islamic Polytheism of Arabia 15
Pre-Mosaic Hebrew beliefs 253
Pre-Mosaic monotheism 253
Pre-Vedic gods 169
Pre-Zoroastrian polytheism 491
Preacher 5, 6, 7
Precepts of love 126
Predestinarian belief 395
Predestinarian position 393
Predestination 392
Predestination and free will 393
Preman 204
Prescriptions 171
Presence 306
Preserver, the (Al-Hāfiẓ) 378
Press-stone 172
Presuppositions of morality 109
Prevailing, the (Al-Muqtadir) 379
Priest 2
Primal Unitary Being 175
Primeval Bull 501

Primeval Puruṣa 192
Primeval waters 175
Primitive beliefs 275
Primitive magic 164
Primitive religions 104
Primitive thinking 163
Prince of Darkness 445
Principle of Darkness 454
Principle of reciprocal service 197
Problem of adjusting Divine justice to Divine decree 397
Profiter, the (An-Nāfi) 389
Progenitor of the human race 193
Progress towards the doom of evil 434
Progression of Śiva towards ultimate supremacy 224
Prohibiting the casting of lots 48
Prohibitions 171
Proofs of the existence of God 148
Prophet 2, 8, 12, 40, 87, 149
Prophet as a divine incarnation 75
Prophet as a medium of communication 79
Prophet as a warner 48
Prophet seeks to ennoble by integral visions 159
Prophet worship 44
Prophetic inspiration, four classes of 70
Prophetic intercession 400
Prophetic knowledge of the future 48
Prophetic message 80
Prophetic oracles 91
Prophetic religions 157
Prophetic revelation 149
Prophetic warnings 51
Prophets are born and not made 86
Proselytism 132
Prospetic converts 85
Protection against the anger of an evil from other gods 222
Protection from wanton cruelty 439
Protective and functional deities 54
Protector, the (Al-Muhaimin) 379
Protestants 27-28, 33
Proto-Aryan polytheism 428
Provider, the (Ar-Razzāq) 378
Provider of daily bread 390
Pṛthivī Mātar 188
Prudence 415
Psychical phenomena 79
Pulindas 224
Puraṃḍhi 169, 512
Purāṇa 69
Purāṇa suitable śāstra in Dvāpara 232
Purgation 101
Purification of human lives 110
Purity (of thought, speech and action) 139
Puroḍāśa 508
Puruṣa 178, 238
Puruṣa Sūkta 178
Pūṣan 155, 166, 236
Pūsh 519
Puṣkara 233

Qadarite free cuiltists 392
Qadarites 392, 398
Quarrel (peoples) about the greatness of their prophets 46
Quarrels, jealousies and pettinesses of contending gods 174
Quietistic and the activistic attitude 6
Quran 85
Quran, generally more opposed to anthropomorphism 281
Quran is not eternal 161
Quran is to prevent the assimilation of God to worldly things 371

Ra 167
Rabbinic Judaism 304
Rabbis 303
Rabindranath Tagore 106, 248
Rādhā 332
Radhakrishnan 145
Rain-giving gods 189
Raising the dead 50
Rāma 18, 42
Rāma and Sītā 211
Rāma Hvāstra 504
Rāmacandda 73
Rāmakṛṣṇa Paramahaṃsa 45, 79, 245, 247
Rāman 492
Rāman Khvāstra (Hvāstra) 499, 512
Raman Vayu 492
Rāmānanda 67, 246
Rāmānuja 209
Rāmānuja is Śeṣa reborn 73
Rammohan Roy 17, 246, 333

Ram Prasad Sen 247
Ranade 150
Rasanstāt 499, 514
Rashdall 148
Rashnu (Rashn) 492, 500, 514-15
Rashnu-Arshtat 492
Rātā 491, 513
Rationalisation 30
Rationalism 161
Rationalists and free thinkers 161
Rational religion 11
Ready bestowal of boons 219
Real, the (Al- Haqq) 403
Realisation in one's own life 160
Reality of evil 434
Reality of free choice 414
Reason 162
Reasoning 160
Rebellious disorder 114
Rechabites 271
Reckoner, the (Al-Hasīb) 384
Recluse 5, 6
Recompense 465
Reconciliation between Divine Justice and Divine Mercy 334
Recorder, the (Al-Muḥṣt) 384
Redemption 290
Redemption through the logos 302
Redemption without merit 96
Re-establishing the true religion 147
Reference to the past 28
Reformed religion 31
Reformer 17, 26, 29, 31
Reforming movement 33
Reform movement 65, 246
Reform movement in Hinduism 69
Reform movements of Mahavira and Buddha 213
Reform of Josiah 55
Refusing to discuss the necessity and the nature of God 109
Regal conception of Yahweh 310
Regard for truth, 514
Regeneration of the masses 67
Regularity 95, 143
Reincarnation 463
Re-introduction of Polytheism and demonology 475
Relation between law of Karman and God 184
Relativity of revelation 75
Relaxation of caste-rules 244
Release of the soul 185
Religion and neurosis 156
Religion entirely free from two types of dangers 163
Religion of humanity 110
Religion of love 217
Religion of the prophets 62
Religion relegated mostly to the state 113
Religion, the obsessional neurosis of humanity 154
Religious aristocracy 52
Religious beggarliness 208
Religious beliefs of the conquerors 250
Religious formality 64
Religious genius 8
Religious instinct 153
Religious nondescripts 37
Religious persecution 120
Religious quarrels have no meaning 146
Religious reformer 419
Relilgious revivals 247
Religious revolution 34
Religious suicide 98
Religious symbols 17
Religious teachers as gods reborn 73
Religious wars and persecutions 146
Remmarriage of widows 257
Remnants of the sacrifice 172
Renan 253
Renovation 484, 507, 524
Renunciation 247
Repentance 125, 232
Repentant sinners 401
Representation of God 134
Repulsive features 225
Resemblance between Hinduism and Judaism 307
Resignation 390
Restoring the moral balance of the world 147
Restrainer, the (Al-Qābid) 388
Resurrection 133, 302, 508
Resurrection of the Dead 307
Retirement to a lonely place 158
Return-movement 33
Return of nature-gods 476
Return of past greatness to Israel 50

Return of nature-worship 476
Revealed religion 148
Revealed religion is necessary 374
Revealing an Arabic Qur'ān for the Arabs 135
Revealation 96, 387
Reverence 115 ·
Reverence of ancestors 150
Revilers 344
Reviver of His people 390
Reward and retribution in the life hereafter 88
Reward to merit 117
Rhea with the young Zens 241
Rhys Davids 94
Right (Asha) 309, 424, 431, 440, 465, 469-70
Right absorption 107
Right belief 107
Right conduct 107
Right effort 107
Righteous living 334
Righteousness 344
Righteousness is serving Allah 399
Right means of subsistence 107
Right of naturalisation 126
Right reflection 107
Right resolution 107
Right speech 107
Rigorous asceticism 457
Rig-veda 167, 221
Ring of truth and authority 79
Rise of Buddhism 67
Ṛita-asha 94
Ritualistic practices 65
Ritualistic worship 334
Rituals 152, 171
Rivāyat 27
Robbers 224
Rogues 224
Roman Catholicism 27, 46, 100
Romans 20, 33, 36
Rousseau 106
Ṛta 93, 143, 465
Rudra 167, 189, 23-24, 230, 239
Rudra's similarity to some non-Aryan divinity 225

Śabaras 224
Sabbath 14, 62, 308
Sabbath-keeping 334
Sacred book 353
Sacred fire 436
Sacred Prostitution 55, 258, 271
Sacred stone at Mecca 436
Sacred tree 262
Sacrifice 173
Sacrifice, first aim of 183
Sacrifice, second aim of 183
Sacrifice of the first born 258
Sacrifices 92
Sacrifice to departed spirits 114
Sacrifice to one's own ancestors 113
Sacrificial butter 172
Sacrificial cruelty 120, 215
Sacrificial grass 172
Sacrificial ladles 172
Sacrificial post 172
Sacrificial rite 142, 461
Sacrificial waters 172
Saducees 14
Sadyojāta 230
Sahasrāra 243
Saint Anselm 74
Saint Augustine 74, 79, 516
Saint John 420
Saint Paul 26, 77, 290, 298, 316, 317, 319, 333
Saint Peter 325
Saints 100
Saint Theresa 101
Śaiva Agamas non-Vedic and non-Aryan in Origin 232
Śaivism 79, 99,216,218, 220-21, 225, 249, 268
Śaivites 231
Śaktāism 211
Śakti 73, 221, 234, 240, 245
Śakti identified with Brahman 241
Śaktimat 240
Śáktism 170, 243
Salagrāma 228
Sālokyo-mukti 242
Salvation 63, 180, 424
Salvation through prophetic mediation 99
Samādhi 185
Sāmīpya-Mukti 242
Sāṃkhya 99, 185
Sāṃkhya Prakṛti 227
Samson 266
Samuel 53

Śaṅkara 180, 186, 209, 286, 380, 525
Śaṅkara identified with Śiva 73
Śaṅkara-Vedānta 458
Saṅkarṣaṇa 206
Saṅkīrtana 30, 67
Saptarṣi 171
Sarah 265
Sarasvatī 166, 172, 242, 505
Sārṣṭi-mukti 242
Śarva 224, 230
Sassanian revival 454
Satan 41, 287, 302, 319, 396, 450
Śatarūpā 193
Satavaēsa 502
Satī or immolation of women 243
Sātvata tribe 205
Satya 93
Saul 53
Sauru 470
Sauru or Saurva 519
Savitar 166
Savitṛ 155, 175, 191, 197, 236
Sāyujya-mukti 242
Scandinavian 36
Sceptical schools 15
Scepticism 8, 175-76, 248
Sceptics 185
Schismatic sects 17
Schools of families of seers 142
Scribe of the gods 238
Scribes 14
Scriptural texts 162
Scriptures 160
Sea of Galilee 41
Secondary elaboration 168
Second person of the Trinity 173
Secret cult 24
Secret of prophetic success 69
Sectarianism 66, 200
Sectarian jealousy 66
Sects and schisms 18
Seeing (baṣar) 381
Seer, the (Al-Baṣīr) 384
Seers and preachers 7
Seizing the property of other gods 223
Self-analysis 112
Self-betterment 415
Self-control 116
Self-discipline 99, 116
Self-emptying 108
Self-knowledge 99, 116, 178
Self-subsisting, the (Al-Quaiyūm) 379
Self-sufficiency of the moral law 183-84
Semites 253
Semitic monotheism 163, 422
Semitic religion 36
Semitic types 146
Sense of obligation 415
Sense of oughtness 415
Sense of sin and suffering 98
Sense of numinous 154
Sensuality 87
Sensuous presence of Yahweh 306
Seraphim 262
Sermon at the Deer Park 107
Sermon on the Mount 317, 327
Serpent-worship 268
Servant of the God 319
Servants of Allah 389
Service of fellowmen 415
Service to man 232
Servitude 389-90
Settled life 138
Seven Attributes assigned to Allāh 381
Seventy-three Muslim sects 17
Sexual cult 259
Sexual restraint 230
Sexual virility 212
Shahada 366
Shaman 2, 35
Shang Tí (Supreme Ruler) 112-14
Shaoka 498
Shavo and Saoka 512
Sheehinah 309
Shemaiah 53
Shemesh 269
Shin sect 99
Shintoism 38, 90, 418
Shintoists 99
Shrinkage of the ego 101
Shrūti a suitable shāstra in Satyayuga 232
Sibylline books 33
Siddhas 110
Signs 91
Signs of a merciful Providence 376
Signs of a unitary God 376
Sikhism 29, 38, 67, 89
Sikhs 16

Silence over theological questions 109
Similarity of belief 104
Simpler forms of worship 244
Sin and death 302
Sin and ignorance 86
Sinfulness of man 302
Sinful works 393
Single heavenly family 143
Sin of Adam 290
Sin-offering 62
Śiśnadevas (devotees of the Phallic cult) 221
Śītalā, the goddess of smallpox 239
Śiva 72-73, 82, 187, 200, 218, 231, 234, 241, 243
Śiva and Rudra 223
Śiva and Śakti 240
Śiva as the third person of the Hindu Trinity 227
Śiva as the ultimate principle of existence 220
Śiva-Liṅga, once fixed, should on no account be removed 227
Śivaloka 231
Śiva-nāme-bodham 79
Śiva-Śakti cult 226-27
Śiva, Viṣṇu and Brahmā as children of Śakti 241
Six divine attributes 206
Six divine spirits 465
Six Pāramitās 108
Skanda 218
Sky as a Yazata 507
Sky-god 458
Slaughter of animals 291
Snenishta 497
Social concord 251
Social government 137
Sociality 151
Social harmony 116
Social morality 118
Social quickening 250
Social relations, five 115
Social service 65, 251
Socrates 317
Söderblom 159
Solar cult as survival of Vedic worship 235
Solar cult in Indian assimilated into the cult of the Trinity 236
Solar worship 13
Solitude 101
Soloman 54, 56, 263, 273
Solution of Cosmic problems 88
Solution of the riddles of suffering 87
Soma 166, 175, 191, 194, 508
Soma plant 181
Son of God 319, 322, 334, 337
Son of Man 340
Sonship 129
Sonship of man 128, 366
Sons of God 83
Sons of Terah 265
Soothsaying 48
Sorcery 35, 76
Soul as only a transient aggregation of five factors 106
Sovereignty 465
Space 458-59, 461
Spazga 519
Spectacular ascent to heaven 50
Speculative monism 244
Speculative movement 181
Speech (Kalām) 381, 385
Spells 182
Spencer 154
Spenjhaghri 497
Spenta Ārmaiti 465, 470, 500, 513
Spenta Mainyu (Holy Spirit) 206, 447-48, 452-53, 484, 487
Spentó-mainyush 449
Sphoṭavāda 183
Spirits 305
Spirit of detachment 208
Spirit of God 306
Spirits 253
Spirits of departed ancestors 113
Spirits of the air 503
Spirits of the glorious dead 481
Spirits of the physical world 497
Spiritual Enlightenment 108
Spiritual insight as a gift of god 76
Spiritual meaning of Maithuna or coition 244
Spiritual monotheism 479
Spiritual needs of man 91
Spiritual selfishness 101
Splitting of the moon 359
Spread of Vaiṣṇavism in India 164
Śraddhā 155, 204
Śrāddhas 100
Sraosha (obedience to religious lore)

83, 140, 465-66, 470, 492, 515-16
Śrīcakra 243
Stagnation of religion 7
Statutory methods of salvation 145
Sthānakvāsi 17
Sthāṇu 227
Stone circle (Cromlech) 260
Stone heap (Cairn) 260
Stone of phallic shape 259
Stone-table (dolman) 260
Stories of Muhammad's achievements 359
Stories of miracles 67
Strength 309
Strenuosity 108
Strong, the (Al-Qawi) 379
Struggle against evil and imperfection 138
Struggle and suffering 88
Studiousness 116
Sublimating the lower instincts 243
Submergence of the finite 413
Submission 390
Submission to authority 157
Subordination of law of Karma to Divine grace 244
Śuddhi (purification) movement 69
Śūdras 232
Suffering 447
Suffering to demerit 117
Sufis 8, 21, 162
Sufism 411
Sufistic experiment 89
Suggestibility 151
Suggestion 118
Sumerian 36
Sun 197, 432
Sun in Egyptian religion 167
Sunnah 26
Supererogatory works 393
Superiority of the personified abstractions 477
Superiority to the faces of evil 128
Supernatural intensifying the natural 70
Supernatural power 46
Supernatural powers 3
Superstition 146, 244
Supremacy of Gaṇeśa 237
Supreme God 177
Supreme power 112
Survivals of primitive faith 157
Survivor or Enduring, the (Al-Bāqī) 379
Sūrya 155, 166, 190, 245
Sūrya, a Vedic god 235
Svayambhū (self-born) 192
Svayambhū Liṅga 228
Śvetāśvatara 96
Swan 204
Synagogue 62, 294
Synagogue prayer 331
Syncretism and toleration 245
Synergism 95
Synonyms of Allāh 377
Synoptic gospels 125, 315, 317

Tablets of stone 78
Taboos 276
Talisman 275
Talmud 305
Talmudic tradition 28
Tamil saints 65-66
Tampering of the Mosaic revelations 121
Tanit with her son 241
Tantra suitable shāstra in Kaliyuga 232
Tantric intiation 243
Tao 95, 195
Taoism 38, 90, 110
Tapas 93
Taromaiti 467
Tatpuruṣa 230
Taurvi 470
Teacher of teachers 72
Temperamental differences in methods of aproach 213
Temple-cult 293
Temple sacrifice 331
Temples in Orissa 211
Temple of Jeruṣalem 14, 268
Ten agencies 309
Ten Commandments 53, 78, 126
Ten sefirot of the Kabhalists 310
Ten words 259, 261
Teraphim 135, 260, 284-85
Terrestrial gods 167
Teutonic 36
Teutons 13
Thanksgiving festivals 271

Theism 137, 154, 200
Theistic bent of the human mind 244
Theistic neo-brāhamaṇism 213
Theodicy 94
Theological dualism 453
Theologumena 283
Theophany 329
Theories of incarnation and visible presence 81
Theory of an Arabic Qur'ān in heaven 85
Theory of a finite God 165
Theory of a perfect revelation of God's nature 34
Theory of Hamkār 493
Theory of Last Revelation 335
Theory of Pre-Jahwistic Hebrew monotheism 253
Theosophy 38, 47
Theriolatry 20, 163
Theriomorphism 258, 269
Thieves 344
Things are in their own nature good or evil 161
Third Isaiah 62
Thirty-nine articles of faith 23
Three Heavens 466
Three stages in the development of the Jewish conception of God 62
Three strides 202
Throne of Allāh 406
Throne supported by eight angels 406
Thwāsha Khvadhāta (Sovereign Space) 511
Tí 112
T'ien (Heaven) 112-13, 115
T'ien Yeh 113
Tilak 247
Time 458, 461
Time as a principle of causation 456
Time as creator and devourer 457
Tīrthaṅkaras 100, 110
Tiruvāśagam 79
Tishtrya 480, 486, 492, 495-96, 501-503
Toleration 247
Tortoise 72, 203
Totemism 169, 269
Tower of Babel 286
Traditional morality 98
Trailana 167
Transcending both good and evil 414
Transformed local deities 43
Transmigration 463
Trayastriṃśat 41
Trayī 182
Tree of religion 35
Tree-faced god 170
Tree-goddesses 170
Triadic rhythm of devotion, hypocrisy and doubt 12
Trials by ordeal 275
Tribal custom 98
Tribal faith 123
Tribal God 62
Tribal monolatry 186
Tribal paranoia 296
Tribal polytheism 348
Trimūrti 216
Trinity 130, 177
Trinity of Ahura Mazdah, Mithra and Anahita 454
Trinity of Brahmā, Viṣṇu and Śiva 216, 245
Trita 167
Trita Āptya 167-68, 189
Tritheism 357
Tritheistic tendency 43
Triumph of God 446
Triumph of good over evil 88
Triumph of spiritual over the material 41
Trust in a higher power 112
Truth (Asha) 465, 470
Truth about the self to be learnt first from scriptures 160
Truth and morality 72
Truth to be understood with the help of argument favourable to the sacred literature 160
Tulasīdāsa 246
Tum 167
Tutelary deities 174
Tvaṣṭr 191
Twelve Apostles 124
Twenty-four Tīrthaṅkaras 74
Two seemingly contradictory views of God appear in the Qur'ān 371
Two typical opinions about Koran 84

Ugra 224, 230

Ultimate blessedness of the good 434
Ultimate identity of all finite spirits 248
Ultimate victory of Ahura Mazdah 445
Umā Haimavatī 242-43
Uncompromising fatalism 393
Uncompromising monotheism 347
Unconscious attachment to one's own ancestral faith 29
Undue veneration 17
Unethical polytheism 163
Unification 101
Union with Absolute 111
Union with Brahman 109
Unitary God 434
Unity of Allah, a fundamental article of belief 380, 397
Unity of God 378
Universal Church 90
Universal compassion 217
Universal disinclination to tamper with a sacred text 249
Universalism 131
Unmeaning ceremonies 157
Unmerited suffering of Jesus 290
Unseen universe 117
Upādhi 145
Upaniṣadic Brahman 15
Upaniṣadic seers 159
Upaniṣadic speculations 475
Upaniṣads 89, 177, 233
Upekṣā 108
Upright stones (meṣṣebah) 259
Uprightness 116, 465
Ūrdhva-Liṅga 230
Ūrdhva-retas 230
Urvan 481
Urvāzishta 497
Uṣas 166
Useless formalities 17
Ushah 491
Ushah, goddess of Dawn 502
Ushahina 502
Ushi-darena or Oshdāshtār 507
Ushi-dhāv 507
Usijs 142, 427
Using equivocal language in spiritual matters 244
Uthmān 249
Uzzah 61
Vairāgya (Dispassion or Detachment) 218
Vaiṣṇava 17
Vaiṣṇava monotheism 246
Vaiṣṇava religions 212
Vaiṣṇavism 75, 99, 181, 200, 205, 215-17, 247-48, 268, 377
Vaiṣṇavism, rise of 202
Vaiṣṇavism and Śaivism two opposite types of religious appeal 231
Vaiṣṇavite names 66
Vaiṣṇavite poets 65
Validity of the moral law 116
Vallabhācārya 209
Vāmadeva 82, 230
Vanant 502
Vareno 519
Variety of nature's happenings 143
Varuṇa 93-94, 111, 142, 169, 186, 189-90, 196-99, 218, 427-28
Varuṇa, downfall of 197
Varuṇa, fetters of 200
Varuṇa has a benign as well as a terrible aspect 198
Varuṇa, the "Indian Yahweh" 196
Varvaras 224
Vaśiṣṭhas 186
Vāstoṣpati 192
Vāsudeva 73, 205-206
Vāsudeva Kṛṣṇa 205, 212, 216
Vāta 155, 189, 503
Vāyu 224, 486, 491, 503
Vāzishta 497
Vedānta 99, 233, 248
Vedānta Sutra 50
Vedāntic Absolute 233
Vedāntic Māyā 227
Vedāntic monism 245
Vedic Aryans 217
Vedic gods 175, 495
Vedic invocation to the Sun 25
Vedic Polytheism 15, 244, 428
Vedic Puruṣa 204
Vedic religion 165, 490
Vedic religion, mixed up with the indigenous cults of India 157
Vedic revelations, as laboured compositions of sophisticated poets 143
Vedic revelations, as lyrical outbursts

of primitive minds 142
Vedic revelations, as songs of shepherds and peasants 142
Vedic seers 72, 178
Vedic worship 178
Vengeance for a transgression 294
Venus 506
Verethraghna 480, 491, 495, 504
Verethraghna and Herakles 493
Vidhātṛ (Disposer) 191
Vināyakas 237
Violence (Aeshma) 440, 467
Virgin birth of Christ 135
Virgin Mary 18
Virocana 76
Virtue of repentance 294
Vishtāspa 420, 430
Visible presence to Moses 281
Visible symbols 78
Vision 79-80
Visions of the future 48
Visits to the tombs of saints 164
Viṣṇu 18, 72, 75, 155, 166-67, 172, 189, 200, 202-203, 218, 234, 236, 241
----as a boar 228
----as the moral governor 203
Viṣṇu identified with Puruṣa Nārāyaṇa 203
Viṣṇu-Nārāyaṇa-Kṛṣṇa 207
Viśvakarman (All-creating) 155, 179, 191
Viśvedevāḥ 179, 189
Vivasvān 71
Vivasvant 155, 167
Vivasvat 168, 236
Vivekānanda 106, 248
Vohu Manah 140, 468, 470, 477, 488-89, 493, 508-509, 515
Vohu Manah or Vahishtem Manah (God or best Spirit) 465
Vohu Mano 83, 500
Vohufryāna 497
Vohuman 490
Voice of conscience 105
Voice of god 69
Voice of the tribe 105
Voltaire 106
Vourukasha 481, 502
Vrātyas 69, 104
Vṛtrahan 504
Vyāsa 73, 238
Vyūhas, theory of 206

Wahhabi movement 17
Waḥy 9
Walis 100
Want of human freedom 395
War-lord of the Israelites 288-89
Watcher, the (Ar-Raqīb) 384
Water into wine, transubstantiation of 42
Waters 189
Welfare 465, 470
Welfare for men and beasts 222
Welis 481
Whitaker 91
Wickedness 467
Wickedness of Sodom 286
Widow's son 42
Will (Irādā) 381, 387
Will of god 91, 133
Will to believe 234
Wiliam James 87
Wind-god 193
Wisdom 115, 309
Wisdom of god 305
Wise, the (Al-Hakīm) 384
Wise Lord 469
Wished-for Kingdom 465
Witchcraft 35
Withholder, the (Al-Māni) 389
Witness, the (Ash-Shahīd) 384
Wives of Ahura 506
Wives of gods 171
Wives of Vedic gods 238
Wooden posts (asherah) 259
Word 309
Wordy battles 146
World-catastrophy 49
World ruled by regularity and law 191
Worship 173
----of ancestors 260
----of God 415
----of heavenly King 310
----of moon-god sin 265
----of nature-gods 179
----of Trinity 227
----of unitary god 252
----on tablets 100
Worshippers of the daevas (devayasnians) 428, 431

Worshipping trees, springs, rivers, caves and mountains 253
Wrath 467
Wresting boons from the invigorated and gratified deities 183
Wuṣūl (Union) 411

Yahweh 53-54, 56-63, 66, 70, 76, 78, 96, 102, 104, 116, 112, 140, 254-55, 256, 259, 263, 267-73, 275-76, 281, 284, 289, 291, 294, 297, 300-01, 303, 305, 330, 335, 371
----, angel of 283
----, concept of 275
----, glory of 283
----, holiness of 302
----, name of 283
---- as a bull of gold in Dan and Bethel 258
---- as a truly natural god of the Israelites 272
----a young bull 258
----as the heavenly father 295
----as the lord of fertility and population 257
----as the storm-god 262
----, his association with sacred stones 258
----his marital temper 287
----, his partiality towards Israel 287
Yahweh not really invisible 282
Yahweh represented quite anthropomorphically 77
Yahweh's form 282
Yajña-Izashne or Yasna 508
Yajña-puruṣa 184
Yajurveda 236
Yama 190, 236
Yama the progenitor of the race in which Rama was born 236
Yashts 496
Yāska 167
Yātus 500
Yazdan 451
Yazatas 100, 477, 480, 483, 485-86, 488, 495-96, 499, 520-21
----, theory of 493
Yenghē Hātam 517
Yoganidrā 187
Yoga system 180
Yogins 162
Yūpa 155

Zairich 470
Zām of Zamyāt 492, 507
Zaothras 506
Zarathustra 6, 15, 30, 41, 44, 78, 8, 137-38, 140, 141, 147, 419, 423-24, 426-27, 429, 434-35, 437, 439, 441-42, 446-47, 452, 456, 466, 468, 470, 484, 485
----, positive contribution of 432
---- as the chief of the earthly Yazatas 493
Zechariah 62
Zen 99
Zervan or Eternal time 454, 459
Zervan Akarana (Eternity of Boundless Time) 455, 457-58, 460, 510, 521
Zervan Daregho-Khvadhāta (Sovereign Time of Long Duration) 510
Zervanism 455-56, 458-59
Zervanites 454, 458
Zeus 194
Zeus and Ormazd 493
Zeus Pater in the Greek religion 187
Zodokites 62
Zoolatry 170
Zoroastr 434, 510-11
Zoroastrian reform 511
Zoroastrian reformation 146
Zoroastrian system of angels 310
Zoroastrian theology 438
Zoroastrianism 83, 88, 89, 100, 141, 147, 157, 206, 458, 473-74, 477, 484
----infected by later Magian beliefs 157
Zoroastrians of India 37